T0185009

Lecture Notes in Computer Science   11723

More information about this series at http://www.springer.com/series/7410

Zhiqiang Lin · Charalampos Papamanthou ·
Michalis Polychronakis (Eds.)

Information Security

22nd International Conference, ISC 2019
New York City, NY, USA, September 16–18, 2019
Proceedings

 Springer

Editors
Zhiqiang Lin
The Ohio State University
Columbus, OH, USA

Charalampos Papamanthou
University of Maryland
College Park, MD, USA

Michalis Polychronakis
Stony Brook University
Stony Brook, NY, USA

ISSN 0302-9743 ISSN 1611-3349 (electronic)
Lecture Notes in Computer Science
ISBN 978-3-030-30214-6 ISBN 978-3-030-30215-3 (eBook)
https://doi.org/10.1007/978-3-030-30215-3

LNCS Sublibrary: SL4 – Security and Cryptology

This Springer imprint is published by the registered company Springer Nature Switzerland AG
The registered company address is: Gewerbestrasse 11, 6330 Cham, Switzerland

Preface

On behalf of the Program Committee, it is our pleasure to present the proceedings of the 22nd Information Security Conference (ISC 2019), which took place in New York City, USA, during September 16–18, 2019. ISC is an annual international conference covering research in theory and applications of information security. Both academic research with high relevance to real-world problems, as well as developments in industrial and technical frontiers fall within the scope of the conference.

The 22nd edition of ISC was organized by Stony Brook University and was held at the SUNY Global Center in Manhattan. Professor Michalis Polychronakis (Stony Brook University) served as the general chair, and Professors Zhiqiang Lin (Ohio State University) and Charalampos Papamanthou (University of Maryland) served as the program co-chairs. The Program Committee comprised 41 members from top institutions around the world. Out of 86 submissions, the Program Committee eventually selected 23 papers (8 of which were accepted after a shepherding process) for presentation in the conference and publication in the proceedings, resulting in an acceptance rate of 26.7%. The submission process was double-blind, and the review process was organized and managed through the HotCRP online reviewing system, with all papers receiving at least three reviews. The final program was quite balanced in terms of topics, containing both theoretical/cryptography papers, as well as more practical/systems security papers. Beyond the research papers, the conference program also included two insightful keynote talks by Professors Engin Kirda (Northeastern University) and Elaine Shi (Cornell), on advanced malware and consensus protocols, respectively.

A successful conference is the result of the joint effort of many people. We would like to express our appreciation to the Program Committee members and external reviewers for the time spent reviewing papers, participating in the online discussion, and shepherding some of the papers to ensure the highest quality possible. We also deeply thank the members of the Organizing Committee for their hard work in making ISC 2019 such a successful event, and our invited speakers for their willingness to participate in the conference. We are wholeheartedly thankful to our sponsors, Facebook and Springer, for generously supporting ISC 2019. We also thank Springer for publishing these proceedings as part of their LNCS series, and the ISC Steering Committee for their continuous support and assistance.

Finally, ISC 2019 would not have been possible without the authors who submitted their work and presented their contributions, as well as the attendees who came to the conference. We would like to thank them all, and we look forward to their future contributions to ISC.

July 2019

Zhiqiang Lin
Charalampos Papamanthou
Michalis Polychronakis

Organization

General Chair

Michalis Polychronakis   Stony Brook University, USA

Program Chairs

Zhiqiang Lin   Ohio State University, USA
Charalampos (Babis)   University of Maryland, USA
    Papamanthou

Publicity Chair

Cheng Huang   Sichuan University, China

Organizing Committee

Kathy Germana   Stony Brook University, USA
Andrew Solar-Greco   Stony Brook University, USA

Steering Committee

Ed Dawson   Queensland University of Technology, Australia
Javier Lopez   University of Malaga, Spain
Masahiro Mambo   Kanazawa University, Japan
Mark Manulis   University of Surrey, UK
Eiji Okamoto   University of Tsukuba, Japan
Michalis Polychronakis   Stony Brook University, USA
Susanne Wetzel   Stevens Institute of Technology, USA
Yuliang Zheng   University of Alabama at Birmingham, USA
Jianying Zhou   Singapore University of Technology and Design,
    Singapore

Program Committee

Elias Athanasopoulos   University of Cyprus, Cyprus
Foteini Baldimtsi   George Mason University, USA
Alex Chepurnoy   IOHK, USA, and Ergo Platform, Russia
Sherman Chow   Chinese University of Hong Kong, SAR China
Dana Dachman-Soled   University of Maryland, USA
Lucas Davi   University of Duisburg-Essen, Germany
Brendan Dolan-Gavitt   New York University, USA

Sanjam Garg	UC Berkeley, USA
André Grégio	Federal University of Parana, Brazil
Esha Ghosh	Microsoft Research, USA
Alexandros Kapravelos	NC State University, USA
Vasileios Kemerlis	Brown University, USA
Evgenios Kornaropoulos	Brown University, USA
Alp Kupcu	Koc University, Turkey
Andrea Lanzi	University of Milan, Italy
Juanru Li	Shanghai Jiaotong University, China
Xiapu Luo	Hong Kong Polytechnic University, SAR China
Alex Malozemoff	Galois Inc., USA
Masahiro Mambo	Kanazawa University, Japan
Mark Manulis	University of Surrey, UK
Daniel Masny	Visa Research, USA
Kartik Nayak	VMware Research, USA
Nick Nikiforakis	Stony Brook University, USA
Dimitris Papadopoulos	HKUST, SAR China
Giancarlo Pellegrino	Stanford University, USA, and CISPA, Germany
Mike Reiter	University of North Carolina at Chapel Hill, USA
Brendan Saltaformaggio	Georgia Tech, USA
Roberto Tamassia	Brown University, USA
Nikos Triandopoulos	Stevens Institute of Technology, USA
Cong Wang	City University of Hong Kong, SAR China
Ding Wang	Peking University, China
Ruoyu (Fish) Wang	Arizona State University, USA
Xiao Wang	MIT and Boston University, USA
Xinyu Xing	Penn State University, USA
Arkady Yerukhimovich	George Washington University, USA
Yu Yu	Shanghai Jiaotong University, China
Moti Yung	Columbia University, USA
Yupeng Zhang	UC Berkeley, USA
Yajin Zhou	Zhejiang University, China
Jianying Zhou	Singapore University of Technology and Design, Singapore
Vassilis Zikas	University of Edinburgh, UK

Sponsors

Facebook
Stony Brook University

Contents

Crypto III: Signatures and Authentication

Attacks and Cryptanalysis

IBWH: An Intermittent Block Withholding Attack with Optimal Mining Reward Rate

Junming Ke[1], Pawel Szalachowski[2], Jianying Zhou[2], Qiuliang Xu[3(✉)], and Zheng Yang[2]

[1] School of Computer Science and Technology, Shandong University, Jinan, China
junmingke1994@gmail.com
[2] Singapore University of Technology and Design, Singapore, Singapore
{pawel,jianying_zhou,zheng_yang}@sutd.edu.sg
[3] School of Software, Shandong University, Jinan, China
xql@sdu.edu.cn

Abstract. A trend in clustering mining power into mining pools in proof-of-work (PoW) blockchain systems raises severe concerns on the stability and security of these systems. Such pools can misbehave by strategically withhold found solutions (i.e., blocks). It has been shown that the reward of a large malicious mining pool can be significantly increased by deviating from the honest mining strategy. Moreover, a malicious pool can launch the block withholding (BWH) attack making the target's pool reward system unfair by letting malicious participants receive unearned shares while pretending to contribute work. Although these attacks are well-known, they are usually investigated in a simplified static reward model.

This paper gives a detailed analysis of the dynamic reward of the BWH attacker while considering a more realistic model with the computing power changing incessantly. We propose a novel attack called the intermittent block withholding (IBWH) attack and we prove that this attack is optimal in our model. IBWH is a strategy where an attacker influences the reward period time, consequently enlarging the reward rate. Furthermore, in our model, we include the dynamics of the Bitcoin network's computing power, and even with the changing attacker's reward rates, we show that the IBWH's reward rate remains optimal. We consider both the selfish mining attack and the fork after withholding (FAW) attack, and we show that these attacks do not outperform IBWH.

Keywords: Blockchain security · Block withholding attack · Reward rate

1 Introduction

Since the dawn of Bitcoin, a popular cryptocurrency proposed by Nakamoto [19] in 2008, this system has attracted more and more attention. The Bitcoin system is a peer-to-peer network and a transaction system introducing a native cryptocurrency. Bitcoin is permissionless and uses a proof-of-work (PoW) scheme to limit the number of votes per entity and thus renders decentralization, where every active entity, called a miner,

© Springer Nature Switzerland AG 2019
Z. Lin et al. (Eds.): ISC 2019, LNCS 11723, pp. 3–24, 2019.
https://doi.org/10.1007/978-3-030-30215-3_1

has the right (proportional to the miner's computing power) to write transactions to the globally distributed ledger called a blockchain. Bitcoin miners collect transactions, validate them, and keep trying to find new valid blocks including those transactions. A block is found, announced to the network, and becomes part of the blockchain when one of the miners finds a nonce value that solves a computational-heavy PoW puzzle [6, 13]. The miner who found the new block is awarded by the system with bitcoins (native cryptocurrency tokens).

In the Bitcoin network, multiple miners join hands in order to form mining pools that sum up their computing power creating huge computational consortia [16]. Pooled mining effectively reduces the variance of the block generation rewards, spreading it out more smoothly over time. Usually, in such a mining pool every miner needs to regularly submit a PoW to the pool manager to demonstrate their work towards solving the PoW associated with a Bitcoin block [15, 18]. If a mining pool finds a new block, it splits the reward to the miners, proportionally to the amount of work they contributed to the probability of finding a block. Finding a valid solution leading to a new block depends only on computation power, therefore, the pool manager distributes sub-puzzles to each miner. A miner engages in the sub-puzzle to generate partial proof-of-work (PPoW) and submits corresponding solutions to the sub-puzzle. These PPoWs provide evidence that the miners try to find a full proof-of-work (FPoW). The difficulty of sub-puzzles is lower than the block puzzle. Therefore, the more PPoWs miners submit, the higher possibility FPoWs yields with. Once again, only FPoWs give a pool block rewards, while PPoWs are used only for internal in-pool accounting.

Each blockchain's block contains a hash pointer to the previous block forming a chain. A Bitcoin miner can maliciously or accidentally "fork" the current chain [20], thereby starting a new concurrent chain of blocks. Other miners who agree with this new chain can start appending their new blocks to this chain as well. Eventually, if the new chain extends the old chain, the forks will be resolved by the longest chain principle which advises miners to work on the top of the longest chain they have. The longest chain principle ensures that the network will recognize the chain with the most work as the main chain. (In practice, the rule prefers stronger chains over longer chains, but the chain with the most work is typically, but not always, the longest of the forks).

The amount of PoW required to create a new block is determined through the dynamic target value. For the reasons of stability and reasonable waiting times for transaction validation, the target value is adjusted every 2016 blocks. It is then re-calculated to meet the verification rate of approximately one block every 10 min. Thus, on average, every two weeks (= 2016 * 10 min) the target is recalculated. The new target T is calculated as $T = T_{prev} \frac{t_{actual}}{2016*10\,min}$. Where T_{prev} is the previous target value and t_{actual} the time span it actually took to generate the last 2016 blocks. If 2016 blocks were generated during a time span shorter than two weeks, this indicates that the overall computing power has increased, so that the PoW difficulty should also be increased.

There has been increasing attention to the issue of stability and security of the Bitcoin consensus scheme [1, 5, 10–12, 17]. However, the limitation of the previous work is due to the simplified system model assumed, where rewards and mining power of Bitcoin miners are static. Such a model does not capture fundamental complexity and dynamics of Bitcoin.

Contribution. The main contribution of this work is the first analysis of the dynamic reward of the BWH attack with or without the changing difficulty. In order to propose a more realistic model, this paper gives a comprehensive analysis with the changing Bitcoin mining power.

Second, we propose a novel adversarial strategy for reward rate named the intermittent block withholding attack (IBWH). It is based on the observation that although some withholding attacks are profitable for adversaries they slow down the Bitcoin network and finally reduce the mining difficulty.

Finally, we extend our analysis to other scenarios. In particular, we introduce some other attacks accompanying with its dynamic rewards, such as the selfish mining attack [1,2,12] and the fork after withholding attack [22]. We show that in these cases the adversary's dynamic reward changes a lot compared with the static reward.

2   Related Work

Rosenfeld [16] first proposed the BWH attack. An attacker joins a victim pool and pretends to contribute to the victim pool and gets paid, the victim pool suffers a loss. Courtois et al. [21] generalized the formal concept of the BWH attack, considering an attacker who mines both solo and in pools. In 2015, Eyal [11] first proposed a game between two block withholding attacking pools and discovered the miner's dilemma, which is analogous to the prisoner's dilemma: when two pools attack each other because it creates a mutual loss, both will take a loss in equilibrium. This attack was carried out against the "Eligius" mining pool in 2014, with the pool losing 300 bitcoin. In 2015, Luu et al. [14] found the optimal BWH attack strategy against one pool and multiple pools by defining the power splitting game.

Kwon [22] proposed a novel attack, the fork after withholding (FAW) attack, combining selfish mining see below and a BWH attack. When the attacker finds an FPoW as an infiltration miner in FAW attack, she does not immediately propagate it to the pool manager, waiting instead for an external honest miner to publish theirs, at which point she propagates the FPoW to the manager hoping to cause a fork. This work significantly improves the total reward of the attacker and gives a detailed analysis of the FAW attack.

Selfish mining has been proposed by Eyal [12]. A selfish miner does not propagate a valid solution to the rest of the network when she finds one. Instead, the selfish miner continues to mine the next block and aims at maintaining its lead. Once the rest of the network is about to catch up with the selfish miner, then she releases her solved blocks into the network, thus replaces the currently known longest chain and gets the reward. Sapirshtein et al. [2] has considered selfish mining in a formal model and proposed an optimal strategy of selfish mining. Gervais et al. [1] have introduced a novel quantitative framework to analyze the security and performance implications of various consensus and network parameters of PoW blockchains. Based on the framework, they devised optimal adversarial strategies for double spending and selfish mining while taking into account the real world constraints.

Garay et al. [8] give a convenient assumption on the "hashing power" of the adversary relative to network synchronicity, which introduces hardness related to difficulty.

Motivated by his research, in this paper we are looking for the relationship between the difficulty and hash power in the BWH attack. Another motivation is mentioned in Luu et al. [14], where they claim that it is not always the case that the rate of reward is strictly better. In fact, the attacker most likely gains profit by carrying out the attack in a long period of time, but that may not hold in the short term.

3   Preliminaries

In this section, we give a description of the block withholding attack (BWH) model and notation utilized in the rest of the paper. Due to the complexity of the analysis, we only consider that one attacker targets one open pool, we leave the analysis of multiple target pools as the future work.

3.1   Block Withholding Attack

We assume that there exists an attacker pool a, the victim pool b, where:

1. α: Computational power of the attacker;
2. β: Computational power of the victim pool;
3. τ: the infiltration mining power as a proportion of the attacker α.

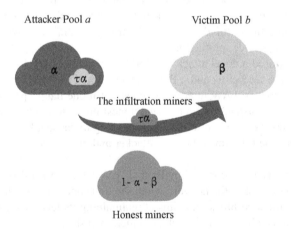

Fig. 1. The withholding attack model. The attacker splits her computing power α as innocent mining $\alpha - \tau\alpha$ and infiltration mining $\tau\alpha$, aiming at a victim pool β, the rest computing power is $1 - \alpha - \beta$.

Figure 1 illustrates the outline of the BWH attack [11,14,22]. The attacker pool with α computational power splits its mining power into "innocent" miner with power $\alpha - \tau\alpha$ and infiltration miner with power $\tau\alpha$, aiming at a victim pool β. More specifically, the infiltration miner $\tau\alpha$ joins the victim pool β and within the pool submits only

PPoWs, but not FPoWs. Once the infiltration miner finds FPoW, the infiltration miner withholds this FPoW. Due to the PPoWs, the infiltration miner gets its share from the victim pool, but the pool never benefits from miner's found FPoWs.

Therefore the following proportions are derived:

1. $\tau\alpha$: The infiltration mining power,
2. $\alpha - \tau\alpha$: The attacker innocent mining power,
3. $\beta + \tau\alpha$: The whole victim pool computational power including the infiltration mining power.
4. $1 - \alpha - \beta$: The honest mining power.

With the BWH attacker, the Bitcoin network has only $1 - \tau\alpha$ "effective" computation power, thus the expected reward in one block of each party can be represented as follows:

1. An attacker a with α computational power can earn $\frac{(1-\tau)\alpha}{1-\tau\alpha}$ with its innocent miner and $(\frac{\beta}{1-\tau\alpha})\frac{\tau\alpha}{\beta+\tau\alpha}$ with its infiltration miner's share from the victim pool, and we use $R_a(\tau)$ to represent the expected reward in one block of the attacker: $R_a(\tau) = \frac{(1-\tau)\alpha}{1-\tau\alpha} + (\frac{\beta}{1-\tau\alpha})\frac{\tau\alpha}{\beta+\tau\alpha}$.
2. The victim pool b with β computational power can earn its own share from its own mining rewards, and we use $R_b(\tau)$ to represent the expected reward in one block of the victim pool: $R_b(\tau) = (\frac{\beta}{1-\tau\alpha})\frac{\beta}{\beta+\tau\alpha}$.
3. We use $R_{remain}(\tau)$ to represent the expected reward in one block of the honest miners: $R_{remain}(\tau) = \frac{1-\alpha-\beta}{1-\tau\alpha}$.

For the attacker, her only motivation is to maximize $R_a(\tau)$.

Theorem 1. *When the honest miners have mining power larger than 0, i.e., $\alpha + \beta < 1$, we can obtain $R_a(\tau) \geq \alpha$ when $0 \leq \tau \leq \frac{\beta}{1-\alpha}$ in the BWH attack, which means that the attacker can get more rewards than her proportional mining power α.*

Proof. We have $0 \leq \tau \leq 1$ from the definition, then we prove $R_a(\tau) \geq \alpha$ when $0 \leq \tau \leq \frac{\beta}{1-\alpha}$ holds.

$$\frac{(1-\tau)\alpha}{1-\tau\alpha} + (\frac{\beta}{1-\tau\alpha})\frac{\tau\alpha}{\beta+\tau\alpha} \geq \alpha \Leftrightarrow \frac{1-\tau}{1-\tau\alpha} + (\frac{\beta}{1-\tau\alpha})\frac{\tau}{\beta+\tau\alpha} \geq 1 \Leftrightarrow$$
$$(1-\tau)(\beta+\tau\alpha) + \tau\beta \geq (1-\tau\alpha)(\beta+\tau\alpha) \Leftrightarrow$$
$$\beta + \tau\alpha - \tau\beta - \tau^2\alpha + \tau\beta \geq \beta + \tau\alpha - \tau\alpha\beta - \tau^2\alpha^2 \Leftrightarrow \tau \leq \frac{\beta}{1-\alpha} \qquad \square$$

3.2 Notations for the Reward Rate

As we stated before, for the reasons of stability and waiting times for transaction blocks, the target value is adjusted every 2016 blocks in Bitcoin. We define mining those 2016 blocks as an epoch, and the epoch 1 represents the first 2016 blocks, then the epoch 2 represents second 2016 blocks, that is, from the 2017th block to the 4032nd block. Without loss of generality, an epoch sustains b blocks, and epoch k is from the $(b * k + 1)$th to the $(b * (k + 1))$th block.

We use hash/s as a unit of the computation power, representing how many hashes could be calculated in one second. In epoch k, the Bitcoin mining power is n hash/s, the hardness (as defined in [7]) is p, that means, the expected number of finding a valid PoW is $\frac{1}{p}$ hash calculations, i.e., after $\frac{1}{p}$ hashes has been calculated, a valid PoW is expected to be found by a miner. We can get the duration of an epoch by converting b into the real-time period t. We use Δt to represent the time cost of mining one block. In Bitcoin, the expected time to mine a block is about 10 min and the difficulty will change every 2016 blocks (i.e, $b = 2016$) to maintain the time of mining one block as $\Delta t = 600$ s. In this case, t is $\Delta t \times b = 600 \times 2016$ s.

4   The Reward Rate of Block Withholding Attack Under Static Mining Power

We assume every party is mining honestly in epoch k, which implies the attacker has not started the attack yet. The hash power in epoch k is n hash/s and the attacker's computing power is αn hash/s. At this point we assume the computing power is static – we will discuss the changing computing power in Sect. 6. The expected time of mining a block in epoch k is about Δt seconds, thus the epoch k will be Δtb seconds.

We assume that the attacker adopts the honest mining strategy before the attacker launches the BWH attack in epoch k, so the attacker's reward in epoch $k - 1$ is αb blocks and the attacker's reward rate is $\frac{\alpha b}{\Delta tb} = \frac{\alpha}{\Delta t}$ in epoch $k - 1$.

In such a setting, the entire Bitcoin network have calculated Δtbn hashes and received b block rewards, and the hardness p equals to the block number b divided by the total hash times Δtbn, i.e., $p = \frac{b}{\Delta tbn}$.

In epoch $k + 1$, the attacker launches the BWH attack by splitting $\tau\alpha$ computing power as an infiltration miner into a victim pool, and keeps submitting only PPoWs, but not FPoWs. In other words, $\tau\alpha$ computing power will make no effect on the Bitcoin network, thus the whole Bitcoin network's computing power will drop to $(1 - \tau\alpha)n$ hash/s. In that time period, the Bitcoin network's difficulty remains the same as in the previous epoch because the previous computing power was constant. In epoch $k + 1$, the Bitcoin network computes Δtbn hash and get b blocks, this epoch will last $\frac{\Delta tbn}{(1-\tau\alpha)n} = \frac{\Delta tb}{1-\tau\alpha}$ seconds.

The attacker's total reward in epoch $k + 1$ can be divided into two cases.

1. The attacker's earnings from block rewards through mining honestly: $\frac{\alpha-\tau\alpha}{1-\tau\alpha}b$.
2. When the victim pool finds a valid block and broadcasts it to the Bitcoin network: $\frac{\beta}{1-\tau\alpha}b$ and the infiltration miner gets her dividends: $\frac{\beta}{1-\tau\alpha}b \times \frac{\tau\alpha}{\beta+\tau\alpha}$.

So in epoch $k + 1$, the BWH attacker can earn $(\frac{\alpha-\tau\alpha}{1-\tau\alpha} + \frac{\beta}{1-\tau\alpha} \times \frac{\tau\alpha}{\beta+\tau\alpha})b$ block rewards in total.

The attacker's reward rate is the attacker's expected reward $(\frac{\alpha-\tau\alpha}{1-\tau\alpha} + \frac{\beta}{1-\tau\alpha} \times \frac{\tau\alpha}{\beta+\tau\alpha})b$ divided by the duration $\frac{\Delta tb}{1-\tau\alpha}$: $\frac{(\frac{\alpha-\tau\alpha}{1-\tau\alpha} + \frac{\beta}{1-\tau\alpha} \times \frac{\tau\alpha}{\beta+\tau\alpha})b}{\frac{\Delta tb}{1-\tau\alpha}} = \frac{\alpha-\tau\alpha}{\Delta t} + \frac{\beta\tau\alpha}{(\beta+\tau\alpha)\Delta t}$.

In epoch $k+2$, the difficulty of the Bitcoin network will change to maintain the expected time of mining a block to about Δt seconds. The Bitcoin network evaluates the computing power according to the time that the last period lasts in the previous epoch. In the previous epoch, the whole Bitcoin network's computing power was $(1-\tau\alpha)n$ hash/s, so the whole Bitcoin network calculates $\Delta tb(1-\tau\alpha)n$ hashes and gets b blocks while the hardness p equals to the total hash $\Delta tb(1-\tau\alpha)n$ divided by the number of blocks $= b$, where, $p = \frac{b}{\Delta tb(1-\tau\alpha)n}$.

In epoch $k+2$, the attacker's reward is also divided into two cases analogical like in the epoch $k+1$: $(\frac{\alpha-\tau\alpha}{1-\tau\alpha} + \frac{\beta}{1-\tau\alpha} \times \frac{\tau\alpha}{\beta+\tau\alpha})b$.

If the Bitcoin network's computing power would not change, due to the difficulty adjustment, epoch $k+2$ will last for Δtb seconds. The attacker's reward rate is the attacker's expected reward divided by the epoch duration: $\frac{\frac{\alpha-\tau\alpha}{1-\tau\alpha} + \frac{\beta}{1-\tau\alpha}\frac{\tau\alpha}{\beta+\tau\alpha}}{\Delta t}$.

Because $\frac{\alpha-\tau\alpha}{1-\tau\alpha} + \frac{\beta}{1-\tau\alpha}\frac{\tau\alpha}{\beta+\tau\alpha} > \alpha$ [11], we have: $\frac{\frac{\alpha-\tau\alpha}{1-\tau\alpha} + \frac{\beta}{1-\tau\alpha}\frac{\tau\alpha}{\beta+\tau\alpha}}{\Delta t} > \frac{\alpha}{\Delta t}$.

The above inequality indicates that after the attacker launches the BWH attack, firstly, her reward rate will decrease, is less than the reward rate if the attacker mines honestly. After that epoch time period, due to difficulty changes, her reward rate will increase and will be greater than the reward rate if the attacker mines honestly (see Fig. 2).

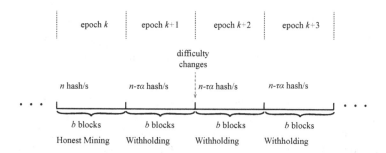

Fig. 2. Dynamic withholding attack. Each epoch includes b blocks. In epoch k, assuming that every party is mining honestly, the attacker launches the withholding attack in epoch $k+1$, the Bitcoin's computing power changes in epoch $k+1$, the Bitcoin would change its difficulty in epoch $k+2$ to maintain the block validation rate.

Because the Bitcoin network's computing power does not change in the following epochs $k+3, k+4...$, the attacker's reward will equal the attacker's earnings from the epoch $k+2$, maintaining a stable state.

5 Intermittent Withholding Attack

In this section, we introduce and analyze our attack strategy.

5.1 Reward Rate

As in the epoch $k+2$ the difficulty changes, the Bitcoin network only needs to calculate $\Delta tb(1-\tau\alpha)n$ hashes to get b blocks and end up this epoch. For a BWH attacker, she could control the infiltration miner τ and she could change the proportion $\tau\alpha$ as $\tau'\alpha$.

In epoch $k+2$, if the proportion of the infiltration miner is $\tau'\alpha$, then the proportion of the attacker's innocent mining power is $\alpha - \tau'\alpha$. The epoch $k+2$ will end in $\frac{\Delta tb(1-\tau\alpha)n}{(1-\tau'\alpha)n} = \frac{\Delta tb(1-\tau\alpha)}{(1-\tau'\alpha)}$ seconds. The attacker's reward can be represented as $(\frac{\alpha-\tau'\alpha}{1-\tau'\alpha} + \frac{\beta}{1-\tau'\alpha}\frac{\tau'\alpha}{\beta+\tau'\alpha})b$, therefore, the attacker's reward rate is the attacker's reward divided by the epoch $k+2$'s real-time: $\dfrac{\frac{\alpha-\tau'\alpha}{1-\tau'\alpha} + \frac{\beta}{1-\tau'\alpha}\frac{\tau'\alpha}{\beta+\tau'\alpha}b}{\frac{\Delta tb(1-\tau\alpha)}{(1-\tau'\alpha)}} = \dfrac{\alpha + \frac{-\tau'^2\alpha^2}{\beta+\tau'\alpha}}{(1-\tau\alpha)\Delta t}$.

Theorem 2. *In the epoch $k+2$, as $\tau'(0 \le \tau' \le 1)$ increases, the attacker's reward rate $\dfrac{\alpha + \frac{-\tau'^2\alpha^2}{\beta+\tau'\alpha}}{(1-\tau\alpha)\Delta t}$ will decrease. When $\tau' = 0$, the maximum reward rate is $\dfrac{\alpha}{(1-\tau\alpha)\Delta t}$.*

Proof. We use a derivative method to prove that the attacker's reward rate $\dfrac{\alpha + \frac{-\tau'^2\alpha^2}{\beta+\tau'\alpha}}{(1-\tau\alpha)\Delta t}$ will decrease with the $\tau'(0 \le \tau' \le 1)$ increases.

We set $f(\tau')$ to represent the attacker's reward rate: $f(\tau') = \dfrac{\alpha + \frac{-\tau'^2\alpha^2}{\beta+\tau'\alpha}}{(1-\tau\alpha)\Delta t}$.

We can get the derivative of $f(\tau')$ is: $f'(\tau') = -\dfrac{2\tau'\alpha^2\beta + \tau'^2\alpha^3}{(1-\tau\alpha)\Delta t(\beta+\tau'\alpha)^2}$, where for any $0 \le \tau' \le 1$, $f'(\tau') < 0$ always holds. Thus, the attacker's reward rate $f(\tau')$ will decrease as τ' increases. □

Then we propose a novel withholding attack (see Fig. 3). If an attacker launches the withholding attack, the whole Bitcoin network's computing power decreases, so consequently, the difficulty for the whole Bitcoin network will decrease. The attacker who mines honestly for Δtb seconds in epoch k gets the reward as $\frac{\alpha}{\Delta t}$. However, in the epoch $k+2$, if the attacker adopts the honest mining strategy, due to the difficulty changes, epoch $k+2$ will end up in $\Delta tb(1-\tau\alpha)$ seconds, thus the attacker's reward is $\frac{\alpha}{(1-\tau\alpha)\Delta t}$.

By combining the above rewards, we can distinguish the following four kinds of rewards rates:

1. The reward rate of the attacker mining honestly: $\frac{\alpha}{\Delta t}$
2. The attacker launches the withholding attack, at the first epoch, thus the attacker's reward rate is: $\frac{\alpha-\tau\alpha}{\Delta t} + \frac{\beta\tau\alpha}{(\beta+\tau\alpha)\Delta t}$
3. The attacker launches the withholding attack, after the first epoch, thus the attacker's reward rate is: $\dfrac{\frac{\alpha-\tau\alpha}{1-\tau\alpha} + \frac{\beta}{1-\tau\alpha}\frac{\tau\alpha}{\beta+\tau\alpha}}{\Delta t}$

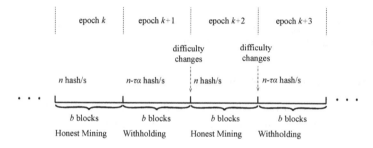

Fig. 3. The dynamic intermittent withholding attack. Each epoch includes b blocks. In epoch k, assuming that every party is mining honestly, the attacker launches the withholding attack in epoch $k+1$, the Bitcoin's computing power changes in epoch $k+1$ and the Bitcoin would decrease its difficulty in epoch $k+2$ to maintain the block validation rate. If the attacker adopts the honest mining strategy in epoch $k+2$, the attacker will get a better reward rate. After that, the attacker could launch withholding attack in epoch $k+3$ again.

4. After the attacker launches the withholding attack, the attacker adopts the honest mining strategy in the next epoch, thus the attacker's reward rate is $\frac{\alpha}{(1-\tau\alpha)\Delta t}$

Theorem 3. *The relationships among the above four kinds of reward rates satisfy that*

$$\frac{\alpha}{(1-\tau\alpha)\Delta t} > \frac{\frac{\alpha-\tau\alpha}{1-\tau\alpha} + \frac{\beta}{1-\tau\alpha}\frac{\tau\alpha}{\beta+\tau\alpha}}{\Delta t} > \frac{\alpha}{\Delta t} > \frac{\alpha-\tau\alpha}{\Delta t} + \frac{\beta\tau\alpha}{(\beta+\tau\alpha)\Delta t}.$$

Proof. It is sufficient to prove that the following inequality holds:

$\frac{\alpha}{(1-\tau\alpha)\Delta t} > \frac{\frac{\alpha-\tau\alpha}{1-\tau\alpha} + \frac{\beta}{1-\tau\alpha}\frac{\tau\alpha}{\beta+\tau\alpha}}{\Delta t}$. Namely, we have that

$$\frac{\alpha}{(1-\tau\alpha)\Delta t} > \frac{\frac{\alpha-\tau\alpha}{1-\tau\alpha} + \frac{\beta}{1-\tau\alpha}\frac{\tau\alpha}{\beta+\tau\alpha}}{\Delta t} \Leftrightarrow \alpha > \alpha - \tau\alpha + \frac{\beta\tau\alpha}{\beta+\tau\alpha} \Leftrightarrow \tau\alpha > \frac{\beta\tau\alpha}{\beta+\tau\alpha} \Leftrightarrow \tau\alpha > 0,$$

where $\tau > 0$ and $\alpha > 0$, the above inequality always holds. $\square$

When an attacker launches the BWH attack in epoch k, her reward rate will decrease even though the total reward is increased. In short, because the attacker reduces the Bitcoin network's computing power, the same amount of blocks needed more time to be mined, thus the attacker will earn less reward per time unit.

After an attacker adopts the withholding strategy over a long time period, for example, in the epoch $k+k_1$, where k_1 indicates after k_1 epochs. if the attacker still adopts BWH attack, the attacker will get $\frac{\frac{\alpha-\tau\alpha}{1-\tau\alpha} + \frac{\beta}{1-\tau\alpha}\frac{\tau\alpha}{\beta+\tau\alpha}}{\Delta t}$ as the reward rate, which is similar to the one in the epoch $k+2$.

In the epoch $k+k_1$, the Bitcoin mining power is static. The Bitcoin network, including the attacker's mining power, only needs to calculate $\Delta tb(1-\tau\alpha)n$ hashes to get b blocks and end up this epoch. The attacker owns α computing power and only $\alpha - \tau\alpha$ is in operation. If the attacker adopts the honest mining strategy with all of the α computing power, epoch $k+k_1$ will end up in $\Delta tb(1-\tau\alpha)$ seconds, and the attacker's reward is $\frac{\alpha}{(1-\tau\alpha)\Delta t}$.

Hence, due to $\frac{\alpha}{(1-\tau\alpha)\Delta t} > \frac{\frac{\alpha-\tau\alpha}{1-\tau\alpha} + \frac{\beta}{1-\tau\alpha}\frac{\tau\alpha}{\beta+\tau\alpha}}{\Delta t}$, at any time the attacker will get a better reward rate if she adopts the honest mining strategy.

5.2   The Intermittent Block WithHolding (IBWH) Attack

Now we describe the intermittent block withholding attack (IBWH), which is a novel attack modifying the BWH attack to make the reward rate optimal.

Attack Model. Our attack model is similar to previous attacks of this class. Firstly, in our attack, an attacker can be a miner or a mining pool with appropriate mining power. Second, the attacker could split her mining power as many individual miners, such like Sybil attacks [3], the attacker controls the individual miners, i.e., the attacker could generate different identities as many as they could, all of the identities could join other open pools. Third, the attacker can instantly and reliably control its created identities. In particular, we assume that the attacker has the ability to let the identity to stop the attack, i.e., change the attack strategy to mining honestly strategy. Finally, the attacker's computation power is finite, that means, the Bitcoin network should have other honest miners. In general, the attacker's computing power is not larger than 50%.

Attack Strategy. The attack is conducted as follows: The attacker with computation power α splits her computing power as innocent mining with computation power $\alpha - \tau\alpha$ and infiltration mining power with computation power $\tau\alpha$. The infiltration miner $\tau\alpha$ joins the victim pool with computation power β and submits only PPoWs, but not FPoWs (as in the previous attack). Once the infiltration miner finds FPoW, the infiltration miner withholds this FPoW. Due to the PPoWs, the infiltration miner gets its share from the victim pool in the case the victim pool shares a reward. Once the attacker realizes the attack will end within one epoch, she turns all of her computing power α into mining honestly until the attack ends. Thanks to this step, the attacker will benefit from a better reward rate.

Reward Rate. The reward rate of the attacker can be divided into four parts:

1. The attacker earns $\frac{\alpha}{\Delta t}$ as a reward rate through innocent mining.
2. The attacker earns $\frac{\alpha-\tau\alpha}{\Delta t} + \frac{\beta\tau\alpha}{(\beta+\tau\alpha)\Delta t}$ as reward rate through the infiltration mining in the first epoch.
3. The attacker earns $\frac{\alpha}{(1-\tau\alpha)\Delta t}$ as a reward rate through the infiltration mining in the last epoch.
4. The attacker earns $\frac{\frac{\alpha-\tau\alpha}{1-\tau\alpha} + \frac{\beta}{1-\tau\alpha}\frac{\tau\alpha}{\beta+\tau\alpha}}{\Delta t}$ as a reward rate through the infiltration mining in other epochs.

It has been proved as Theorem 2 that the attacker's reward rate remains optimal when adopting the IBWH strategy, we also prove (see Theorem 4) that the attacker's reward rate remains optimal under dynamic mining power.

5.3 Discussion

In the first place, we want to explain the reason why the attacker knows the attack will end within one epoch (i.e, the epoch $k+7$ in Fig. 7). For example, the attacker would like to upgrade its computing equipment at some point and will be offline for a while; the Bitcoin or its network encounters some critical problem and will not be accessible a period of time [9]. More formally, Bonneau [4] shows how an attacker might purchase mining power for a short duration via a bribery, therefore, they could also rent mining power for the BWH attack and return it at some point. Also as mentioned in [18], the honest party could hire a BWH attacker to attack target pools, which means, the purchaser will no longer hire the attacker at some time. In these situations, the attacker should adopt the honest mining strategy in the final epoch before she has to stop the attack.

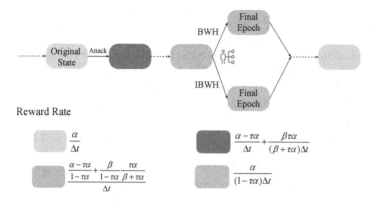

Fig. 4. States of the BWH and IBWH attacks. At first, the original state indicates that every party is mining honestly. When an attacker launches BWH, it would cause a new state, and the reward rate of the attacker would decrease. After an epoch, due to the difficulty adjustment, the reward rate of the attacker would increase and maintain a stable state. After that, once the attacker needs to finish the attack, the attacker could adopt IBWH because it will give the attacker a better reward rate.

IBWH could be deployed with multiple variants of the BWH attack, for example, the fork after withholding attack (we will discuss it in Sect. 8) and a variant has been proposed [18], where the authors treated the attacker as a mercenary, and some other honest pools would like to employ them to attack other pools, the reason why the honest miner wants to hire the attacker is that an attacker attacking a victim pool will make the third party's (i.e., the remaining computing power mining honestly) reward increasing as we stated in Sect. 3.

Though IBWH can allow an attacker to earn a higher reward rate in one epoch than that in the BWH attack, it is ineffective in the following epochs, thus it is rational if she terminates the attack within one epoch. Because when the attacker mines honestly in the next epoch, the Bitcoin's difficulty will increase according to the computing power in the Bitcoin network, so the attacker is not longer benefiting from honest mining. And if the attacker launches a BWH attack again, it will fall back to its original state, as shown in Fig. 4.

6   The Reward Rate of BWH and IBWH Under Dynamic Mining Power

In the above analysis, the Bitcoin network's computation power only changes when the attacker launches the BWH attack. However, in reality, the computing power is dynamic and changes frequently. Therefore, we consider a scenario where the mining power changes, and we evaluate the IBWH strategy in this setting.

In the epoch k, every party is mining honestly and the hash power is n hash/s. The attacker's computing power is αn hash/s, and the attacker would earn αb blocks in epoch k. With stable computing power, the expected time of mine a block is about Δt seconds, thus the epoch k will continue $\Delta t b$ seconds, and the attacker's reward rate is the attacker's expected reward divided by the duration: $\frac{\alpha}{\Delta t}$.

In epoch k, assuming the Bitcoin network's computation power changes by n_* hash/s (i.e., increases by n_* hash/s or decreases by n_* hash/s – for negative n_*), the Bitcoin network's computation power is $(n+n_*)$ hash/s. The Bitcoin network's difficulty remains at the same level as in the previous epoch, that is, $\Delta t b n$ hashes renders b blocks, therefore this epoch will last $\frac{\Delta t b n}{n+n_*}$ seconds. The attacker is mining honestly with computation power αn, therefore, the attacker could earn $\frac{\alpha n b}{n+n_*}$ blocks in epoch k. The attacker's reward rate is the attacker's expected reward divided by the duration: $\frac{\frac{\alpha n b}{n+n_*}}{\frac{\Delta t b n}{n+n_*}} = \frac{\alpha}{\Delta t}$. The attacker's reward rate would not change within one epoch even if the computation power changes (this is the same when considering the following epochs). We do not repeat the computation power changes within one epoch and now we analyze the computation power changes across the epochs.

At first, the difficulty is influenced by the computation power, moreover, the difficulty is not influenced by each moment's computation power, but the average computation power over 2016 blocks. When the Bitcoin network's computation power changes, the difficulty does not change immediately. At the end of the epoch, according to the block mining rate, the difficulty changes and it will influence the next epoch. The block mining rate is related to the average mining computation power, therefore, the difficulty is related to the average computation power.

In epoch $k + 1$, assuming the Bitcoin network's computation power changes by n_1^* hash/s (i.e., increases n_1^* hash/s, and negative n_1^* means the computation power decreases), thus, the Bitcoin network's computation power is $(n + n_1^*)$ hash/s. The attacker launches the BWH attack with the infiltration miner $\tau \alpha$, therefore, the Bitcoin network's computation power changes to $(n + n_1^* - \tau \alpha n)$ hash/s. The Bitcoin network's difficulty remain the same as in the previous epoch, that is, computing $\Delta t b n$ hashes renders b blocks, and this epoch will last $\frac{\Delta t b n}{(1-\tau\alpha)n+n_1^*}$ seconds.

The attacker's total reward in the epoch $k + 1$ can be divided into two cases:

1. The first is the attacker earns a reward through innocent mining: $\frac{(\alpha-\tau\alpha)n}{(1-\tau\alpha)n+n_1^*}b$.

2. The second is the victim pool submits a valid block to the Bitcoin network: $\frac{\beta n}{(1-\tau\alpha)n+n_1^*}b$ and the infiltration miner can get her dividends: $\frac{\beta n}{(1-\tau\alpha)n+n_1^*}b \times \frac{\tau\alpha}{\beta+\tau\alpha}$.

So in the epoch $k+1$, the withholding attacker can earn $(\frac{(\alpha-\tau\alpha)n}{(1-\tau\alpha)n+n_1^*} + \frac{\beta n}{(1-\tau\alpha)n+n_1^*} \times \frac{\tau\alpha}{\beta+\tau\alpha})b$ blocks.

The attacker's reward rate is the attacker's expected reward divided by the duration:

$$\frac{(\frac{(\alpha-\tau\alpha)n}{(1-\tau\alpha)n+n_1^*} + \frac{\beta n}{(1-\tau\alpha)n+n_1^*} \times \frac{\tau\alpha}{\beta+\tau\alpha})b}{\frac{\Delta tbn}{(1-\tau\alpha)n+n_1^*}} = \frac{\alpha-\tau\alpha}{\Delta t} - \frac{\beta\tau\alpha}{(\beta+\tau\alpha)\Delta t}.$$

This is similar to the reward rate when the computation power does not change. Which means, even though the external computation power is changing, the reward rate of the attacker will not change in the first epoch.

In the epoch $k+2$, due to the computation power change in the epoch $k+1$, the hardness p will change to $p = \frac{b}{\Delta tb((1-\tau\alpha)n+n_1^*)}$, the computation power increases to $(1-\tau\alpha)n+n_1^*+n_2^*$, and the epoch $k+2$ lasts $\frac{\Delta tb((1-\tau\alpha)n+n_1^*)}{(1-\tau\alpha)n+n_1^*+n_2^*}$ seconds.

The attacker's reward equals $(\frac{(\alpha-\tau\alpha)n}{(1-\tau\alpha)n+n_1^*+n_2^*} + \frac{\beta n}{(1-\tau\alpha)n+n_1^*+n_2^*} \times \frac{\tau\alpha}{\beta+\tau\alpha})b$, which is the expected number of blocks that attacker can mine in the epoch $k+1$. In the epoch $k+2$, the attacker's reward rate is $\frac{(\frac{(\alpha-\tau\alpha)n}{(1-\tau\alpha)n+n_1^*+n_2^*} + \frac{\beta n}{(1-\tau\alpha)n+n_1^*+n_2^*} \times \frac{\tau\alpha}{\beta+\tau\alpha})b}{\frac{\Delta tb((1-\tau\alpha)n+n_1^*)}{(1-\tau\alpha)n+n_1^*+n_2^*}} = \frac{(\alpha-\tau\alpha)n}{((1-\tau\alpha)n+n_1^*)\Delta t} +$

$\frac{\beta n}{((1-\tau\alpha)n+n_1^*+n_2^*)\Delta t} \times \frac{\tau\alpha}{\beta+\tau\alpha}$.

This above attacker's reward rate is related to the computation changes, that is, under the influence of the parameter n_1^*. It is not difficult to deduce the reward representation in the epoch $k+h$: $\frac{(\alpha-\tau\alpha)n}{((1-\tau\alpha)n+\sum_{u=1}^{h-1}n_u^*)\Delta t} + \frac{\beta n}{((1-\tau\alpha)n+\sum_{u=1}^{h-1}n_u^*)\Delta t} \times \frac{\tau\alpha}{\beta+\tau\alpha}$.

For a BWH attacker, she could control the infiltration miner τ and she could change the proportion $\tau\alpha$ as $\tau'\alpha$ in the epoch $k+2$.

In the epoch $k+2$, the hardness is $p = \frac{b}{\Delta tb((1-\tau\alpha)n+n_1^*)}$, the attacker changes the proportion $\tau\alpha$ as $\tau'\alpha$, so the Bitcoin network's computation power is $(n+n_1^*+n_2^* - \tau'\alpha)$, the epoch $(k+2)$ lasts $\frac{\Delta tb((1-\tau\alpha)n+n_1^*)}{n+n_1^*+n_2^*-\tau'\alpha}$ seconds, and the attacker's reward is equal to $(\frac{(\alpha-\tau'\alpha)n}{(1-\tau'\alpha)n++n_1^*+n_2^*} + \frac{\beta n}{(1-\tau'\alpha)n++n_1^*+n_2^*} \times \frac{\tau'\alpha}{\beta+\tau'\alpha})b$.

Therefore, the attacker's total reward rate is: $\frac{(\frac{(\alpha-\tau'\alpha)n}{(1-\tau'\alpha)n++n_1^*+n_2^*} + \frac{\beta n}{(1-\tau'\alpha)n++n_1^*+n_2^*} \times \frac{\tau'\alpha}{\beta+\tau'\alpha})b}{\frac{\Delta tb((1-\tau\alpha)n+n_1^*)}{n+n_1^*+n_2^*-\tau'\alpha}} =$

$\frac{(\alpha-\tau'\alpha)n+\beta n \times \frac{\tau'\alpha}{\beta+\tau'\alpha}}{\Delta t((1-\tau\alpha)n+n_1^*)}$.

Theorem 4. *In the epoch $k+2$, as $\tau'(0 \le \tau' \le 1)$ increases, the attacker's reward rate $\frac{(\alpha-\tau'\alpha)n+\beta n \times \frac{\tau'\alpha}{\beta+\tau'\alpha}}{\Delta t((1-\tau\alpha)n+n_1^*)}$ will decrease. When $\tau' = 0$, the maximum reward rate is $\frac{\alpha n}{\Delta t((1-\tau\alpha)n+n_1^*)}$.*

Proof. We use a derivative method to prove the attacker's reward rate $\frac{(\alpha-\tau'\alpha)n+\beta n \times \frac{\tau'\alpha}{\beta+\tau'\alpha}}{\Delta t((1-\tau\alpha)n+n_1^*)}$ will decrease with the $\tau'(0 \le \tau' \le 1)$ increases.

We set $f(\tau')$ to represent the attacker's reward rate: $f(\tau') = \dfrac{(\alpha-\tau'\alpha)n+\beta n\times\frac{\tau'\alpha}{\beta+\tau'\alpha}}{\Delta t((1-\tau\alpha)n+n_1^*)}$.

We can get the derivative of $f(\tau')$ is: $f'(\tau') = -\dfrac{\tau'^2\alpha^3 n}{\Delta t((1-\tau\alpha)n+n_1^*)(\beta+\tau'\alpha)^2}$, where for any $0\le\tau'\le 1$, $f'(\tau')<0$ always holds. Thus, the attacker's reward rate $f(\tau')$ will decrease as τ' increases.   □

When $\tau'=0$, the attacker adopts honest mining strategy in the epoch $k+2$. In the epoch $k+2$, the hardness is $p=\dfrac{b}{\Delta tb((1-\tau\alpha)n+n_1^*)}$, the attacker mines honestly, so the Bitcoin network's computation power is $(n+n_1^*+n_2^*)$, and the epoch $k+2$ lasts $\dfrac{\Delta tb((1-\tau\alpha)n+n_1^*)}{n+n_1^*+n_2^*}$ seconds.

The attacker's reward is $\dfrac{\alpha n}{n+n_1^*+n_2^*}b$ in the epoch $k+2$, so the attacker's reward rate is: $\dfrac{\frac{\alpha n}{n+n_1^*+n_2^*}b}{\frac{\Delta tb((1-\tau\alpha)n+n_1^*)}{n+n_1^*+n_2^*}} = \dfrac{\alpha n}{\Delta t((1-\tau\alpha)n+n_1^*)}$.

The reward rate in the epoch $k+h$ is $\dfrac{\alpha n}{\Delta t((1-\tau\alpha)n+\sum_{u=1}^{h-1}n_u^*)}$.

Therefore, from the above statements, we can have:

$$\frac{\alpha n}{\Delta t((1-\tau\alpha)n+\sum_{u=1}^{h-1}n_u^*)} > \frac{(\alpha-\tau\alpha)n}{((1-\tau\alpha)n+\sum_{u=1}^{h-1}n_u^*)\Delta t} + \frac{\beta n}{((1-\tau\alpha)n+\sum_{u=1}^{h-1}n_u^*)\Delta t}\times\frac{\tau\alpha}{\beta+\tau\alpha}.$$

Thus, even the Bitcoin mining power changes, for any epoch $k+h(h\ge 1)$, the reward rate obtained via the IBWH attack is greater than the reward rate of the BWH attack.

7   Evaluation

In this section we consider a specific case: an attacker with computational power $\alpha = 0.2, 0.3, 0.4$, who launches the BWH attack and the IBWH attack against the Bitcoin network.

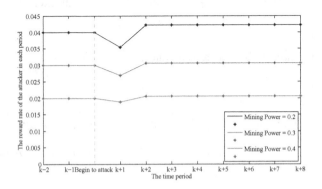

Fig. 5. Dynamic BWH attack reward rate when $\alpha = 0.2, 0.3, 0.4$. The attacker begins to attack at the end of the epoch k, the attacker's reward rate decreases firstly and then increases, the reward rate after going up is greater than the reward rate of mining honestly.

To begin with, we evaluate the BWH attacker's dynamic reward rate in a specific situation.

In the Bitcoin network, we assume the attacker's computing power $\alpha = 0.2, 0.3, 0.4$, the Bitcoin computing power is $n = 10000$ hash/s, the victim pool's computing power $\beta = 0.4$ and the infiltration miner's computing power is $\tau\alpha = 0.08, 0.12, 0.16$, i.e., $\tau = 0.4$. Each epoch contains $b = 10000$ blocks, we split the first epoch as 10 days, hence, before epoch $k + 1$, each party is mining honestly, $\Delta t = 10$ days. In epoch $k + 1$, the attacker begins to attack, the attacker's reward rate shown in Fig. 5.

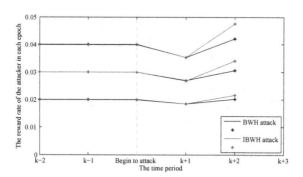

Fig. 6. Dynamic BWH attack and IBWH attack reward rate when $\alpha = 0.2, 0.3, 0.4$ (IBWH is launched after one epoch). The IBWH attacker's reward rate would be greater than the BWH attacker's reward rate in epoch $k + 2$.

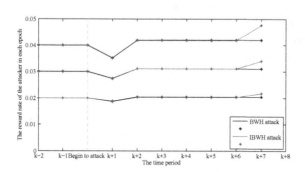

Fig. 7. Dynamic BWH attack and IBWH attack reward rate when $\alpha = 0.2, 0.3, 0.4$ (Launches IBWH after five epochs). The IBWH attacker's reward rate would be greater than the BWH attacker's reward rate in epoch $k + 7$.

For an arbitrary attacker with $\alpha = 0.2, 0.3, 0.4$ computing power, once the attacker launches the BWH attacker, its reward rate would decrease in the first epoch and then would increase to a stable level. The first epoch's reward rate is less than the attacker deserved before the epoch k since the attacker drops its computing power which extends this epoch's period. After the first epoch, the attacker's reward rate is increased to a stable level, the reward rate of this level is greater than the reward rate of mining honestly, the reason why this case is the Bitcoin's difficulty adjustment which makes the attacker reward more than before but the epoch real-time is same. Here the higher the attacker's computing power is, the more obvious the reward rate rises (the epoch $k+2$ as shown in Fig. 5).

Then we apply the IBWH attack in order to compare BWH with IBWH, where the BWH's parameter is the same as before. Here we evaluate two cases: (i) the attacker launches the BWH attack after one epoch; (ii) the attacker launches the IBWH strategy after one epoch (see Fig. 6) and after five epochs (see Fig. 7).

In the first scenario, the attacker launches IBWH after one epoch in Fig. 6, the black line indicates the BWH attacker's reward rate, the red line indicates the IBWH attacker's reward rate. Before the epoch $k+2$, the reward of both BWH attacker and IBWH attacker are the same, in the epoch $k+2$, the IBWH attacker's reward rate would be greater than the BWH attacker's reward rate, the reason why this case is that, if the attacker computing power appeals, the epoch $k+2$ would end earlier than expected. Because the reward rate is influenced by the time period, the time period decreases, thus the reward rate increases.

Table 1. Comparison between BWH and IBWH, when $\alpha = 0.2, 0.3, 0.4$ (Launches IBWH after five epochs).

			Epoch							
			k	k+1	k+2	k+3	k+4	k+5	k+6	k+7
$\alpha = 0.4$	BWH	Reward rate	0.04	0.0357	0.0425	0.0425	0.0425	0.0425	0.0425	0.0425
		Time period (day)	10.0	11.9048	10.0	10.0	10.0	10.0	10.0	10.0
		Total reward	0.4	0.4253	0.4253	0.4253	0.4253	0.4253	0.4253	0.4253
	IBWH	**Reward rate**	0.04	0.0357	0.0425	0.0425	0.0425	0.0425	0.0425	**0.0476**
		Time period (day)	10.0	11.9048	10.0	10.0	10.0	10.0	10.0	**8.4**
		Total reward	0.4	0.4253	0.4253	0.4253	0.4253	0.4253	0.4253	0.4
$\alpha = 0.3$	BWH	Reward rate	0.03	0.02650	0.0301	0.0301	0.0301	0.0301	0.0301	0.0301
		Time period (day)	10.0	11.3636	10.0	10.0	10.0	10.0	10.0	10.0
		Total reward	0.3	0.3011	0.3011	0.3011	0.3011	0.3011	0.3011	0.3011
	IBWH	**Reward rate**	0.03	0.02650	0.0301	0.0301	0.0301	0.0301	0.0301	**0.0341**
		Time period (day)	10.0	11.3636	10.0	10.0	10.0	10.0	10.0	**8.8**
		Total reward	0.3	0.3011	0.3011	0.3011	0.3011	0.3011	0.3011	0.3
$\alpha = 0.2$	BWH	Reward rate	0.02	0.0191	0.0208	0.0208	0.0208	0.0208	0.0208	0.0208
		Time period (day)	10.0	10.8696	10.0	10.0	10.0	10.0	10.0	10.0
		Total reward	0.2	0.2076	0.2076	0.2076	0.2076	0.2076	0.2076	0.2076
	IBWH	**Reward rate**	0.02	0.0191	0.0208	0.0208	0.0208	0.0208	0.0208	**0.0217**
		Time period (day)	10.0	10.8696	10.0	10.0	10.0	10.0	10.0	**9.2**
		Total reward	0.2	0.2076	0.2076	0.2076	0.2076	0.2076	0.2076	0.2

In the second scenario, the attacker launches IBWH after five epochs in Fig. 6, the black line indicates the BWH attacker's reward rate, the red line indicates the IBWH attacker's reward rate. Analogously, before the epoch $k+7$, the reward of both BWH attacker and IBWH attacker are the same; in the epoch $k+7$, the IBWH attacker's reward rate is greater than that of the BWH attacker. Here is the evaluation data in Table 1, the reward rate equals to the total reward divided by the time period in both BWH and IBWH (Fig. 8).

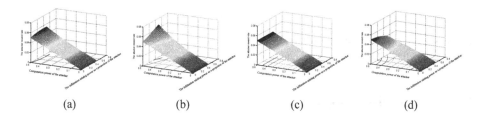

(a)   (b)   (c)   (d)

Fig. 8. The reward rate in each state. (a) The reward rate of the attacker launches a BWH attack. (b) The reward rate of the attacker launches IBWH attack. (c) The reward rate when the attacker adopts honest mining strategy. (d) The reward of the attacker firstly launches BWH attack in one epoch.

For example, where $\alpha = 0.4$, in epoch $k+7$, the total reward of the BWH attacker is 0.4253 due to the attack, which is greater than mining honestly. If the attacker adopts honest mining strategy in epoch $k+7$, the total reward is only 0.4, which is equal to the reward of mining honestly. However, the epoch $k+7$ will end earlier than expected, where the exact time period is 8.4 days. Therefore, the IBWH attacker's reward rate in epoch $k+7$ is 0.0476, which is larger than the BWH attacker's reward rate in epoch $k+7$, which is 0.0425. And worth noted is epoch $k+1$, the epoch will be ended later than expected due to the attack, though the total reward of the attacker increases, actually the reward rate of the attacker decreases.

We then compared the reward rate in each state as mentioned in Fig. 4 with varying infiltration miner and the attacker, that is, τ and α.

The illustration reveals that for any $0 < \tau < 0.5$ and $0 < \alpha < 0.5$, the reward rate of the attacker satisfied: (b) > (a) > (c) > (d). This indicate for any attacker, the reward rate of the attacker will be greater in the IBWH attack than in the BWH attack.

We also evaluate the reward rate of the BWH and IBWH under dynamic mining power in epoch $k+2$, we use $n = 10^6$ and $n^* = 10^5$ to represent the Bitcoin network computation power is 10^6 hash/s in epoch k, and the Bitcoin network computation power increases 10^5 hash/s across the epochs. The Fig. 9 indicates that the IBWH attacker's reward rate is greater than BWH attacker's reward rate for every τ and α, i.e., the computation power of the infiltration miners and the computation power of the attacker.

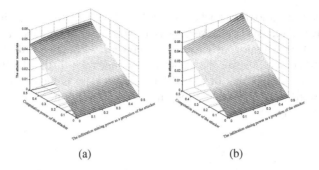

Fig. 9. The reward rate of BWH and IBWH under dynamic mining power. (a) The reward rate of BWH in epoch $k+2$. (b) The reward rate of IBWH in epoch $k+2$.

8   Further Discussions

So far we have presented the analysis of the reward rate of the BWH attack and the IBWH attack combing with difficulty changes. Similarly, other attacks aiming at Bitcoin could also be analyzed through this methodology. Here we consider the fork after withholding [22] and the selfish mining [12] attack strategies.

8.1   The Reward Rate of Fork After Withholding

The core idea of the FAW attack [22] is that an attacker can split his computing power into innocent mining and infiltration mining respectively, such as the BWH attack. In a FAW attack, the attacker does not immediately submit the FPoW to the pool manager when she finds a valid solution through infiltration miner, waiting instead for an external honest miner to publish theirs, at which point she propagates the FPoW to the manager hoping to cause a fork.

For a FAW attacker, she makes a similar effect on the Bitcoin computing power as the BWH attacker. Namely, the FAW attacker only submits PPoWs. Once the FAW attacker finds a block as the infiltration miners, she will observe the external circumstance, after an honest third party propagates a valid block, the FAW attacker submits its PPoW and hopes to cause a fork. Note that the infiltration miners do not make any contribution to the Bitcoin computing power, i.e., the infiltration miner's work does not affect the block rate, the worker from the infiltration miners only works on replacing some blocks of the longest chain. Therefore, the attacker will not affect the Bitcoin's difficulty. In other words, the attacker is actually duplicating the honest third party's work, using the same amount blocks swap the honest third party's block.

However, after the FAW attacker causes a fork through the infiltration miner, it actually influences the Bitcoin's computing power. Due to the fork, the Bitcoin network will make some useless work on the one fork which will not be the longest chain, that could have been avoided if the infiltration miners never submit an FPoW. Then, the Bitcoin network's computing power will decrease due to the influences of the infiltration miners, consequently, the Bitcoin's difficulty will decrease in the next epoch.

After the FAW attacker launches attack for a long time, the whole Bitcoin network's computing power is at most $(1 - \tau\alpha)n$ hash/s. The whole Bitcoin network calculates $\Delta tb(1 - \tau\alpha)n$ hashes and gets b blocks in one epoch. The hardness p equals to the total hash $\Delta tb(1 - \tau\alpha)n$ divide the number of blocks b, where, $p = \frac{b}{\Delta tb(1-\tau\alpha)n}$.

In that epoch, the FAW attacker's reward is divided into three cases:

1. The attacker finds a block as innocent miner with the probability $\frac{\alpha-\tau\alpha}{1-\tau\alpha}$;
2. The victim pool finds a block and gives the infiltration miner its share $\frac{\tau\alpha\beta}{(1-\tau\alpha)(\beta+\tau\alpha)}$, like the BWH attack; and the third party finds a block;
3. The infiltration miner submits a FPoW to the victim pool which becomes the final longest chain's block, the victim pool gives the attacker its share $c\tau\alpha\frac{1-\alpha-\beta}{1-\tau\alpha}\frac{\tau\alpha}{\beta+\tau\alpha}$, where c is probability that an attacker's FPoW through infiltration mining will be selected as the main chain, thus, $c < 1$.

Due to the stable state, this epoch will end in Δtb seconds.

Therefore, the FAW attacker's reward rate is $\frac{\frac{\alpha-\tau\alpha}{1-\tau\alpha}+(\frac{\beta}{1-\tau\alpha}+c\tau\alpha\frac{1-\alpha-\beta}{1-\tau\alpha})\frac{\tau\alpha}{\beta+\tau\alpha}}{\Delta t}$.

If the attacker adopts the honest mining strategy at the end epoch of the attack, the attacker's reward rate will be at least $\frac{\alpha}{(1-\alpha)\Delta t}$, since the infiltration miner lets the Bitcoin's difficulty decrease.

We have found that IBWH is also applicable to the FAW attack, because $\frac{\alpha}{(1-\tau\alpha)\Delta t} > \frac{\frac{\alpha-\tau\alpha}{1-\tau\alpha}+(\frac{\beta}{1-\tau\alpha}+c\tau\alpha\frac{1-\alpha-\beta}{1-\tau\alpha})\frac{\tau\alpha}{\beta+\tau\alpha}}{\Delta t}$ for any $c < \frac{1}{1-\alpha-\beta}$. When FAW will end within one epoch, the attacker could adopt honest mining strategy to make the reward rate optimism. However, the above analysis is only estimated, meanwhile, the infiltration miner would cause many forks if she adopts FAW strategy for a long time, we are not clear whether this would increase the possibility of revealing the identity of an attacker.

8.2 The Reward Rate of Selfish Mining

Selfish mining [12] is a method for mining pools to increase their returns by playing unfairly. For a selfish miner, she does not propagate the valid block to the rest of the network when she finds a valid one. she continues to mine the next block. When the rest of the network is about to catch up with the selfish miner, she releases solved blocks into the Bitcoin's network. The result is that their chain is longer, so the rest of the network accepts their block solutions and they claim the block rewards [1,23].

For a selfish miner α, we roughly estimate the effect it makes on the Bitcoin computing power. The selfish miner is similar to the FAW attacker. When the selfish miner publishes a block or more blocks, it aims at replacing the existing unstable blocks in the Bitcoin network, therefore, the selfish miner makes no effect or negligible effect to the Bitcoin block validation rate. After the selfish miner publishes blocks, the rest of the network would choose one chain to mine which finally partial will be the invalid work, so the appearance of the selfish miner would decrease the Bitcoin's difficulty.

In the epoch k, each party is mining honestly, and the hash power in the epoch is n hash/s. The attacker's computing power is αn hash/s. The expected time to mine a block in the epoch k is about Δt seconds, thus the epoch will last for Δtb seconds, where b indicates the epoch k contains b blocks.

In the epoch $k+1$, the selfish miner adopts selfish mining strategy, the selfish miner mines the block offline, it indicates the Bitcoin computing power will drop to $(1-\alpha)n$ hash/s, the epoch k will end in $\frac{\Delta tnb}{(1-\alpha)n} = \frac{\Delta tb}{(1-\alpha)}$ seconds. In the offline, the selfish miner will continue mining until the epoch ends, each block costs $n\Delta t$ hashes, so the selfish miner would get $\frac{\alpha b}{1-\alpha}$ blocks in the epoch $k+1$. However, all of these blocks are not visible to others, once the selfish miner propagates these blocks, some of these blocks could be the longest chain (i.e., the selfish miner publishes a longer chain than the visible chain.), some could not (i.e., the selfish miner publishes one block and competes with the visible chain.), that is to say, the selfish miner total reward in epoch $k+1$ may be less than $\frac{\alpha b}{1-\alpha}$, concomitantly, the reward rate is less than $\frac{\alpha}{\Delta t}$, which is the reward rate of the selfish miner mines honestly deserved.

In the epoch $k+2$, due to the difficulty adjustment, the epoch $k+2$ will end in Δtb seconds, thus the b blocks will only need $b\Delta t(1-\alpha)n$ hashes. In the offline, the selfish miner would get $\frac{\alpha b}{1-\alpha}$ blocks, like it was in epoch $k+1$, the reward rate is $\frac{\alpha}{(1-\alpha)\Delta t}$. Like we pointed out, the reward rate will be lower due to the fork.

However, if the selfish miner starts mining honestly, the epoch $k+2$ will end in $(1-\alpha)\Delta tb$ seconds, the miner's reward is αb blocks, hence, the selfish miner's reward rate is $\frac{\alpha}{(1-\alpha)\Delta t}$.

Comparing the above two situations, the selfish miner's reward rate is less than $\frac{\alpha}{(1-\alpha)\Delta t}$, if the selfish miner adopts honest mining strategy, the reward rate is $\frac{\alpha}{(1-\alpha)\Delta t}$. Hence, the underlying concept is similar to the IBWH attack.

Unfortunately, there are a few challenges and limitations. For example, the above analysis is limited as we do not take the specific changes in the fork possibility into account. We have said that the selfish miner makes a negligible effect on the Bitcoin block validation rate. Actually in the state machine of the selfish mining [2], once the selfish miner exceeds the online main chain, because the selfish miner wants to avoid a fork, she will propagate one more block in the next time, that will influence the Bitcoin's difficulty.

Our analysis raises an interesting question. For any type of dropping computation power's attack, is it always profitable for the attack's reward rate to adopt the honest mining strategy at the end epoch of the attack? We leave these considerations as an open problem.

9   Conclusion

This paper gives a detailed analysis of the dynamic reward of the BWH attacker while considering the difficulty changing, which opens up a more realistic analysis of the attacks' reward rate of this class. We present a novel attack strategy named the intermittent block withholding attack that yields the optimal attacker's revenue.

In order to get closer to the real-world scenario, this work gives a comprehensive analysis of the attacks' reward rate while the Bitcoin mining power changes, i.e., increases or decreases. Our analysis has also uncovered a more subtle analysis of other attacks related to the computing power, such as the selfish mining attack and the fork after withholding attack, the adversary's dynamic reward is also better compared to the static reward, and we leave the detailed exploration of this aspect as future work.

Finally, we have given an overall evaluation of the dynamic reward rate in each scenario, which confirmed our analytical analysis. The figures show the reward rate of each attack and a comparison among them.

Miner's strategy and reward in Bitcoin mining process are currently studied intensively, however, because of the variability of the Bitcoin, it is necessary to discuss the dynamic adjusted strategy and reward in Bitcoin. This research offers some initial guidelines for analyzing the dynamic periodic reward, however, there is still a substantial number of future work to be undertaken.

Acknowledgments. The first author's work was done during his internship in SUTD supported by the SUTD start-up research grant SRG-ISTD-2017-124. This work was supported by an MOE AcRF Tier 2 grant (MOE2018-T2-1-111), the National Natural Science Foundation of China under Grant No. 61872051, 61572294 and 61632020. The authors would like to thank the anonymous reviewers for their detailed reviews and helpful comments.

References

1. Gervais, A., Karame, G.O., Wüst, K., Glykantzis, V., Ritzdorf, H., Capkun, S.: On the security and performance of proof of work blockchains. In: ACM CCS (2016)
2. Sapirshtein, A., Sompolinsky, Y., Zohar, A.: Optimal selfish mining strategies in bitcoin. In: Grossklags, J., Preneel, B. (eds.) FC 2016. LNCS, vol. 9603, pp. 515–532. Springer, Heidelberg (2017). https://doi.org/10.1007/978-3-662-54970-4_30
3. Babaioff, M., Dobzinski, S., Oren, S., Zohar, A.: On bitcoin and red balloons. In: ACM Conference on Electronic Commerce, pp. 56–73. ACM (2012)
4. Bonneau, J.: Why buy when you can rent? In: Clark, J., Meiklejohn, S., Ryan, P.Y.A., Wallach, D., Brenner, M., Rohloff, K. (eds.) FC 2016. LNCS, vol. 9604, pp. 19–26. Springer, Heidelberg (2016). https://doi.org/10.1007/978-3-662-53357-4_2
5. Carlsten, M., Kalodner, H., Weinberg, S.M., Narayanan, A.: On the instability of bitcoin without the block reward. In: ACM CCS (2016)
6. Tschorsch, F., Scheuermann, B.: Bitcoin and beyond: a technical survey on decentralized digitalcurrencies. IEEE Commun. Surv. Tutor. **18**, 2084–2123 (2016)
7. Garay, J., Kiayias, A., Leonardos, N.: The bitcoin backbone protocol: analysis and applications. In: Oswald, E., Fischlin, M. (eds.) EUROCRYPT 2015. LNCS, vol. 9057, pp. 281–310. Springer, Heidelberg (2015). https://doi.org/10.1007/978-3-662-46803-6_10
8. Garay, J., Kiayias, A., Leonardos, N.: The bitcoin backbone protocol with chains of variable difficulty. In: Katz, J., Shacham, H. (eds.) CRYPTO 2017. LNCS, vol. 10401, pp. 291–323. Springer, Cham (2017). https://doi.org/10.1007/978-3-319-63688-7_10
9. Giechaskiel, I., Cremers, C., Rasmussen, K.B.: On bitcoin security in the presence of broken crypto primitives. In: ESORICS (2016)
10. Heilman, E., Kendler, A., Zohar, A., Goldberg, S.: Eclipse attacks on bitcoin's peer-to-peer network. In: USENIX Security Symposium (2015)
11. Eyal, I.: The miner's dilemma. In: S&P (2015)
12. Eyal, I., Sirer, E.G.: Majority is not enough: bitcoin mining is vulnerable. Commun. ACM **61**(7), 95–102 (2018)
13. Bonneau, J., Miller, A., Clark, J., Narayanan, A., Kroll, J.A., Felten, E.W.: SoK: research perspectives and challenges for bitcoin and cryptocurrencies. In: S&P (2015)

14. Luu, L., Saha, R., Parameshwaran, I., Saxena, P., Hobor, A.: On power splitting games in distributed computation: the case of bitcoin pooled mining. In: IEEE CSF (2015)
15. Luu, L., Velner, Y., Teutsch, J., Saxena, P.: Smart pool: practical decentralized pooled mining. In: USENIX Security Symposium (2017)
16. Rosenfeld, M.: Analysis of bitcoin pooled mining reward systems. arXiv (2011)
17. Nayak, K., Kumar, S., Miller, A., Shi, E.: Stubborn mining: generalizing selfish mining and combining with an eclipse attack. In: IEEE EuroS&P (2016)
18. Bag, S., Ruj, S., Sakurai, K.: Bitcoin block withholding attack: analysis and mitigation. IEEE TIFS **12**, 1967–1978 (2017)
19. Nakamoto, S.: Bitcoin: a peer-to-peer electronic cash system (2008)
20. Dexter, S.: Longest chain - how are blockchain forks resolved?. https://www.mangoresearch.co/blockchain-forks-explained/. Accessed 19 June 2018
21. Courtois, N.T., Bahack, L.: On subversive miner strategies and block withholding attack in bitcoin digital currency. arXiv preprint arXiv:1402.1718 (2014)
22. Kwon, Y., Kim, D., Son, Y., Vasserman, E., Kim, Y.: Be selfish and avoid dilemmas: fork after withholding (FAW) attacks on bitcoin. In: ACM CCS (2017)
23. Zhang, R., Preneel, B.: Publish or perish: a backward-compatible defense against selfish mining in bitcoin. In: Handschuh, H. (ed.) CT-RSA 2017. LNCS, vol. 10159, pp. 277–292. Springer, Cham (2017). https://doi.org/10.1007/978-3-319-52153-4_16

Full Database Reconstruction with Access and Search Pattern Leakage

Evangelia Anna Markatou$^{(\boxtimes)}$ and Roberto Tamassia

Brown University, Providence, RI 02912, USA
markatou@brown.edu, rt@cs.brown.edu

Abstract. The widespread use of cloud computing has enabled several database providers to store their data on servers in the cloud and answer queries from those servers. In order to protect the confidentiality of data in the cloud, a database can be stored in encrypted form and all queries can be executed on the encrypted database. Recent research results suggest that a curious cloud provider may be able to decrypt some of the items in the database after seeing a large number of queries and their (encrypted) results. In this paper, we focus on one-dimensional databases that support range queries and develop an attack that can achieve full database reconstruction, inferring the exact value of every element in the database. We consider an encrypted database whose records have values from a given universe of N consecutive integers. Our attack assumes access pattern and search pattern leakage. It succeeds after the attacker has seen each of the possible query results at least once, independent of their distribution. If we assume that the client issues queries uniformly at random, we can decrypt *the entire* database with high probability after observing $O(N^2 \log N)$ queries.

1 Introduction

During the past decade, an increasing number of organizations have started to outsource their computing infrastructure to cloud providers. This usually means that they store their data in the cloud and run most of their applications, including databases, in the cloud as well. Outsourcing data storage and computation to the cloud has several advantages, including reliability, availability, and economies of scale.

Unfortunately, outsourcing the IT infrastructure to the cloud has its drawbacks as well. For example, an organization's data may contain confidential information that should not be leaked to unauthorized third parties. Storing this information outside the organization's premises may be challenging, and in some cases unfeasible, due to a multitude of business and regulatory constraints.

One way to deal with these restrictions and risks is to store data in the cloud in *encrypted* form. Indeed, data leaks are no threat to encrypted data as decryption is unfeasible without possession of the key. Besides malicious attacks, encryption also protects data from "curious" eyes, including the cloud provider itself.

© Springer Nature Switzerland AG 2019
Z. Lin et al. (Eds.): ISC 2019, LNCS 11723, pp. 25–43, 2019.
https://doi.org/10.1007/978-3-030-30215-3_2

Unfortunately, even encrypted data is not safe from curious eyes when searched upon. Indeed, previous work has demonstrated that an attacker who monitors query results might be able to gain information about the data—even when stored and transmitted in encrypted form. In particular, *range queries* (queries that return database records with attribute values in a given interval) are particularly susceptible, as they have the potential to leak information about the data they access. Such information may include the *order* of the (encrypted) records (i.e., which has larger and which has smaller value) as well as the actual values of the (encrypted) records. This latter information essentially implies that the database can be practically decrypted.

In this paper, we focus on encrypted one-dimensional databases that support range queries on encrypted data. We assume an *honest but curious* attacker who is able to monitor all (encrypted) queries and their (encrypted) results. We develop an attack that can fully reconstruct the database after seeing enough queries. The attack first reconstructs the order of all the (encrypted) database elements and then reconstructs their values.

Our attack utilizes two common types of leakage, *access pattern leakage* and *search pattern leakage*. Previous algorithms on the full database reconstruction problem depend on access pattern leakage and on a client issuing *queries from a known distribution* [8,14], or only work on dense databases [18]. Also, some of the previous work considers additional assumptions on the database, such as the existence of points in particular intervals and/or a minimum distance between such points [8]. However, it is unlikely that a client issues queries uniformly at random in practical applications. Also, not all databases are dense. Finally, special assumptions on nonempty intervals and minimum distance between points may not hold.

We have developed a *general* attack on encrypted databases that achieves full database reconstruction, recovering the exact values of all elements, after seeing all possible query results.

1.1 Organization of the Paper

This paper presents an attack on encrypted databases that support range queries. We assume that the attacker has observed all possible queries at least once. We exploit access pattern leakage to achieve *full ordering reconstruction* (*FOR*), that is, reconstruct the order of the database elements induced by their values (but not the values themselves). Next, we exploit both access pattern leakage and search pattern leakage to achieve *full database reconstruction* (*FDR*), that is, we are able to reconstruct the exact value of all elements in the database.

After defining our model (Sect. 2) and reviewing related work (Sect. 3), we present our algorithm for full ordering reconstruction in Sect. 4 and our algorithm for full database reconstruction in Sect. 5. Finally, Sect. 6 concludes the paper outlining directions for future work.

1.2   Contributions

Previous attacks that achieve full database reconstruction (FDR) use access pattern leakage and a client that issues queries according to a known distribution. Our attack makes a different assumption. We do not assume that the client issues queries in any particular distribution, but we do assume that the searchable encryption scheme leaks the search pattern. Notably, typical searchable encryption schemes do leak the search pattern.

We provide in Table 1 a comparison of our work with selected papers [6,8,14,18] on full database reconstruction (FDR) and full ordering reconstruction (FOR) from range queries on one-dimensional encrypted databases. For each approach, the table shows the assumptions on the leakage observed by the attacker and knowledge of the query distribution by the attacker. Also, for the scenario of a client that issues queries uniformly at random (a standard scenario in the literature), the table shows the query complexity of FDR and FOR attacks on various types of databases. As shown in the table, our method improves or matches the query complexity reported in previous work, albeit under different assumptions.

Table 1. Comparison of approaches to full database reconstruction (FDR) and full ordering reconstruction (FOR) from range queries on one-dimensional encrypted databases. We compare our work with three relevant papers in the area by showing the assumptions on the attacker's capabilities and the query complexity of the attack for the case of a client that issues queries uniformly at random, highlighting the best asymptotic bounds. The query complexity is expressed in terms of the size of the universe of database elements, N. The following types of databases are considered: "Any" refers to an arbitrary database, "Dense" refers to a dense database, which has at least one record for each possible value, and "Any*" refers to the assumption introduced in [6,8] that requires the existence of values in particular intervals and/or forces a minimum distance between such points.

	Previous Work			This Paper
	Kellaris et al. [14]	Lacharité et al. [18]	Grubbs et al. [6, 8]	
Assumptions				
Access Pattern Leakage	✓	✓	✓	✓
Search Pattern Leakage				✓ (only FDR)
Known Distribution	✓ (only FDR)		✓ (only FDR)	
Database / Problem				
Dense / FDR	$O(N^2 \log N)$	$N \log N + O(N)$	$O(N \log N)$	$O(N \log N)$
Any / FOR	$O(N^2 \log N)$			$O(N^2 \log N)$
Any* / FOR	$O(N^2 \log N)$		$O(N \log N)$	$O(N \log N)$
Any / FDR	$O(N^4 \log N)$		$O(N^4 \log N)$	$O(N^2 \log N)$
Any* / FDR	$O(N^4 \log N)$		$O(N^2 \log N)$	$O(N^2 \log N)$

The main contributions of this paper are summarized as follows, where N denotes the size of the universe of database elements:

1. We show that we can achieve FOR after $O(N^2 \log N)$ uniformly-at-random queries with high probability $(1 - 1/N^2)$ (Theorem 1).
2. We show that we can achieve FOR in a dense database after $O(N \log N)$ uniformly-at-random queries with high probability $(1 - 3/N^3)$ (Theorem 2).
3. For datasets that have two data points in $[N/4, \, 3N/4]$ and their distance is larger than $N/3$, we show that we can achieve FOR after $O(N \log N)$ uniformly-at-random queries with high probability $(1 - 3/N^3)$ (Theorem 3).
4. We show that we can achieve FDR after $O(N^2 \log N)$ distinct queries with high probability $(1 - 1/N^2)$ (Theorem 4).

Kellaris et al. [14] have shown that there exist datasets which cannot be distinguished by attackers that observe significantly fewer than $O(N^4)$ queries chosen uniformly at random. However this lower bound works for attacks that use access pattern or communication volume leakage. We use an additional type of leakage, search pattern leakage, which allows us to achieve faster attacks.

2   Model and Problem Statement

We consider a client that stores information on an encrypted database hosted by a server. The client issues range queries to the server using tokens, and the server returns responses to the queries.

We define a *database* as a collection of n records, where each record (r, x) comprises a unique *identifier*, r, from some set R, and a *value* $x = val(r)$ from an interval of integers $X = [1, ..., N]$, which is the universe of database values. A database is called *dense* if for all $x \in X$, the database contains some record (r, x) such that $val(r) = x$. Note that there may be multiple records with the same value. A *range query* $[a, b]$, where $a \le b$ are integers, returns the set of identifiers $M = \{r \in R : val(r) \in [a, b]\}$.

The adversarial model we consider is a persistent passive adversary who is able to observe communication between the client and the server. The adversary aims to recover value $val(r)$ for each identifier, r, in the database. Note that the adversary is not able to *decrypt* any observed encrypted data. The information learnt by the adversary depends on some scheme-dependent leakage.

We examine two types of common leakage:

- *Access Pattern Leakage:* If whenever the server responds to a query, the adversary observes the set of all matching identifiers, M, we say that the scheme allows for *access pattern leakage*. We assume that the identifier r reveals no information on $val(r)$.
- *Search Pattern Leakage:* If the adversary can observe search tokens and determine whether two tokens, t_1 and t_2, correspond to the same range query, we say that the scheme allows for *search pattern leakage*. Note that we do not assume that a token reveals the query the client issues. That is, the token

does not indicate the range $[a, b]$. We just assume that the adversary can distinguish whether two query ranges are the same or different by observing the corresponding tokens.

In this paper, we consider the following two problems and present efficient algorithms for them.

Problem 1 (Full Database Reconstruction). (*FDR*) Given a one-dimensional encrypted database that allows range queries, reconstruct the exact value of all elements.

Problem 2 (Full Ordering Reconstruction). (*FOR*) Given a one-dimensional encrypted database that allows range queries, reconstruct the order of all elements' values.

Our algorithms assume that the adversary knows the size of the universe of database values, N. Our FOR algorithm, presented in Sect. 4, assumes access pattern leakage while our FDR algorithm, presented in Sect. 5, assumes both access pattern leakage and search pattern leakage.

3   Related Work

3.1   Context

In this line of research we assume an *honest but curious* adversary. For example, this can be the cloud server. The server can easily observe all incoming and outgoing traffic and may possibly be able to draw conclusions about the values that exist in the database. We assume that the adversary is honest: she will not try to change the protocol, alter data, inject faulty information, collude with malicious users, etc. The adversary just monitors (encrypted) data.

Given that data are stored in an encrypted form, one might be tempted to think that it is not possible to decrypt them unless the decryption key can be found. Unfortunately, this is not the case. If the database supports range queries, an adversary who monitors the traffic is able to find *some* information about the records observed. For example, one piece of information that can be easily found is that *all the results of a range query belong in the same range* (by definition) and are, in one way or another, "close" to each other. By observing queries for a very long time, one might be able to infer which records are likely to be in proximity of each other (e.g., those that frequently occur together in query results) and which records are likely to be more distant from each other (e.g., those which do not frequently occur together in query results).

Despite the availability of this approximate proximity information, the reader will notice that all these records (whether nearby to or far-away from each other) are still encrypted. Thus, the adversary might be able to know that $encrypted(2)$ is close to $encrypted(3)$, but she can not know that the values observed are actually 2 and 3 as the adversary only sees $encrypted(2)$ and $encrypted(3)$. To be able to "break" the encryption, most of the literature makes some extra assumptions, which usually relate to the query distribution. One frequent such assumption made by several papers is that all range queries are issued uniformly at random by the client. That is, there are $N(N + 1)/2$ possible queries $([1, 1], ..., [1, N], [2, 2], ..., [2, N], ..., [N - 1, N], [N, N])$, and each one of them is issued with probability $\frac{2}{N(N+1)}$. Note that even though all queries are issued with the same probability, some elements are queried more than others. Specifically, elements close to the middle of the database are queried more than elements towards the endpoints.

Our approach does not depend on the query distribution. Instead, we exploit search pattern leakage, a common leakage of searchable encryption schemes. This leakage allows us determine whether two search tokens correspond to the same query. For example, suppose there are 100 distinct queries that all return $\{a\}$, and 4 distinct queries that all return $\{b\}$. We can tell that the unoccupied space surrounding a is larger than the unoccupied space surrounding b.

3.2   Previous Results

In the following review of previous work in the area, we denote with N is the size of the universe (interval) of database values.

A seminal paper by Kellaris, Kollios, Nissim, and O'Neill [14] is the first systematic study of the problems of full ordering reconstruction and full database reconstruction from range queries. They prove that full database ordering can be done with $O(N^2 \log N)$ queries. This attack assumes that the adversary observes the answers to all possible queries. Thus, based on the coupon collector problem, the assumption holds with high probability after $O(N^2 \log N)$ queries. They also show that full database reconstruction can be done with high probability after observing $O(N^4 \log N)$ queries. Our work differs from [14] in the use of data structures, Namely, we maintain the partial order of observed identifiers in a PQ tree [1]. As we observe more queries, we gain more information about the ordering of the identifiers, which is efficiently maintained in the PQ-tree. Eventually, once we observe all queries, we have a fully ordered set (up to reflection). With respect to query complexity, for full database ordering, we match the $O(N^2 \log N)$ bound of [14]. Also, we achieve full reconstruction after seeing $O(N^2 \log N)$ queries, while the approach by [14] needs $\Omega(N^4 \log N)$ queries. We obtain this improvement thanks to our assumption of search pattern leakage, which allows us to count the distinct queries that have been issued, while the method of [14] is based on the statistical properties of the query distribution.

Lacharité, Minaud and Paterson [18] focus on the reconstruction of a dense database, i.e., a database for which there exists at least one record for each possible value in the universe of values, $[1, N]$. Using this density assumption, they achieve an impressive speedup in the query complexity of the attack. Indeed, they achieve full database reconstruction from access pattern leakage after observing $O(N \log N)$ uniformly at random queries. We are able to match this bound by using a datastructure called a PQ tree [1]. Note that neither their method nor ours assumes knowledge of the query distribution by the adversary.

The recent work by Grubbs, Lacharité, Minaud and Paterson [6,8] presents a comprehensive approach to database reconstruction. They generalize the problem by introducing a new approximate way of reconstruction, called ϵ-approximate database reconstruction (ϵ-ADR). In this model, ϵ is the error the attack is allowed to have in the reconstruction. That is, for each original value x, the reconstructed value is in the interval $[x - \epsilon N, x + \epsilon N]$. Note that full database reconstruction (FDR) is the special case of ϵ-ADR achieved by setting $\epsilon = 1/N$. Regarding data structures, our use of PQ-trees is similar to theirs. To compare our FDR attack to theirs, we set the approximation parameter ϵ in their ϵ-ADR model equal to $1/N$ and consider the standard scenario of queries issued uniformly at random. They achieve FDR on an arbitrary database with $O(N^4 \log N)$ queries using access pattern leakage. Instead, we obtain FDR with $O(N^2 \log N)$ queries using both access pattern leakage and search pattern leakage. They further achieve FDR with $O(N^2 \log N)$ queries under the additional assumption that the database has a record with value in the interval $[0.2N, 0.3N]$.

Regarding ordering reconstruction, they are able to achieve FOR with $O(N \log N)$ queries under the following additional assumption on the database values: there are two values in range $[N/4,\ 3N/4]$ and their distance is larger than $N/3$. Note that this implies that FDR can also be achieved in dense databases with $O(N \log N)$ queries.

Note that Grubbs et al. [6,8] as well as Lacharité et al. [18] are also able to achieve approximate database reconstruction assuming access to an auxiliary distribution for the database values. Our work focuses on exact database reconstruction, not approximate, and thus this result is less relevant.

There have been plenty of attacks on different types of leakage as well. Kornaropoulos, Papamanthou and Tamassia [15] developed an approximate reconstruction attack utilizing leakage from k-nearest neighborhood queries. Grubbs, Lacharité, Minaud, and Paterson [7] utilize volume leakage from responses to range queries to achieve full database reconstruction. Grubbs, Ristenpart, and Shmatikov [10] present a snapshot attack that can break the claimed security guarantees of encrypted databases. While most of the above attack papers assume that the client issues queries uniformly at random, in recent work, Kornaropoulos, Papamanthou and Tamassia [16,17] develop distribution-agnostic reconstruction attacks from range and k-nearest neighbor (k-NN) queries using search pattern leakage.

There are also attacks on property-revealing-encryption schemes (which reveal more information than we assume) and attacks that assume a more active adversary [2,5,9,11,19,20].

4   Full Ordering Reconstruction

In this section, we present our algorithm for full ordering reconstruction, which infers the order of the database records by value. The algorithm uses access pattern leakage, but not search pattern leakage.

4.1 Approach

The ordering reconstruction algorithm is based on the following observation. Suppose we have two query responses, M_1 and M_2, each consisting of the set of identifiers of a query response. Let $B = M_1 \cap M_2$, $A = M_1 - B$, and $C = M_2 - B$. We have $M_1 = A \cup B$ and $M_2 = B \cup C$, where A and C are disjoint, as shown in Fig. 1.

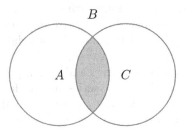

Fig. 1. Intersection and differences between two range query responses, M_1 and M_2, where $B = M_1 \cap M_2$, $A = M_1 - B$, and $C = M_2 - B$.

Then, there can be only two correct (partial) orderings of the elements in M_1 and M_2 by value: (i) A, followed by B, followed by C or (ii) C, followed by B, followed by A, as illustrated in Fig. 2.

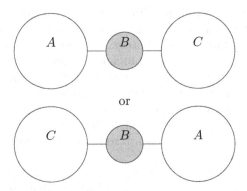

Fig. 2. The two possible ordering of the elements in the query responses $M_1 = A \cup B$ and $M_2 = B \cup C$ from Fig. 1.

The above observation serves as a building block of our algorithm for ordering the elements of the database. That is, every time we see two query results that have a non-empty intersection, we know that there are two ordering possibilities: the one reflection of the other. Suppose now that we see a query result $M_3 = B \cup A_1$ and that $A_1 \cup A_2 = A$. Then, we refine the ordering as follows: A_1

followed by A_2, followed by B, followed by C, or C followed by B, followed by A_1, followed by $A2$. It seems that most query results we see have the potential to refine this partial ordering, possibly until the point where all elements will have been ordered.

Although keeping and maintaining this partial ordering may seem complicated, fortunately, Booth and Lueker [1] designed a data structure that does just that: maintains a partial ordering of a set of elements. The data structure is called a PQ tree.

PQ Trees. A PQ tree is a data structure that can efficiently store all permissible permutations of a set of elements.

A PQ tree is built from three types of nodes, P nodes, Q nodes, and leaf nodes:

1. *Leaf node.* A leaf node stores a single element and has no children.
2. *P node.* The children of a P node can assume any ordering. (Similar to a set.)
3. *Q node.* The children of a Q node can assume only the ordering they are in, or the reverse order. (Similar to an ordered list.)

To use a PQ tree, one first creates a root P node that contains all elements as children leaf nodes. Then, the PQ tree can consume sets of elements that need to be contiguous and modify itself to represent these requirements, by reorganizing the leaf nodes in P and Q nodes as appropriate. The order is fully reconstructed if the PQ tree contains one Q node, whose children are all leaves.

Each range response is essentially a set of identifiers that are all contiguous. The PQ tree can consume these range responses to identify all permissible permutations of the ordering of the identifiers.

4.2   Algorithm

We show in Algorithm 1 our method for full ordering reconstruction. Similarly to [3] and [8], we use PQ trees [1] to store the partial ordering of the set of database elements. The adversary initializes a PQ tree. Then, it feeds it sets of identifiers as answers to queries are observed. For each answer set, M, the PQ tree updates the partial order of the identifiers seen so far in time proportional to the size of M by means of operation update(M) The details of operation update can be found in [1].

Note that in this work, much like all previous papers, we are not concerned with the *computational complexity* of the algorithms we use (as long as it is within reasonable polynomial bounds), but with the *number of queries* needed to achieve the database order/value reconstruction necessary. At every point the adversary has access to all allowable permutations of the identifiers using the PQ-tree.

Algorithm 1. Full Ordering Reconstruction

1: Initialize an empty PQ-tree, T
2: **while** a new answer set M is observed **do**
3:　　T.update(M)

4.3　Query Complexity Analysis

The query complexity of our FOR algorithm is summarized in the following theorem.

Theorem 1. *Using access pattern leakage, Algorithm 1 reconstructs the order of the database identifiers with respect to their values after observing $2.1N^2 \log N$ uniformly at random issued queries, with probability greater than $1 - 1/N^2$, where N is the size of the universe of database values.*

Proof. There are $N(N+1)/2$ possible queries. Given that queries come uniformly at random, the probability that a given query is not issued after $2.1N^2 \log N$ queries is

$$\left(1 - \frac{2}{N(N+1)}\right)^{2.1N^2 \log N} \leq \frac{1}{e^{4 \log N}} \leq \frac{1}{N^4}.$$

By Union Bound, the probability that at least one query is not issued after $2.1N^2 \log N$ queries is at most

$$\sum_{i=1}^{N(N+1)/2} \frac{1}{N^4} \leq \frac{N(N+1)}{2N^4} \leq \frac{1}{N^2}.$$

Thus, after $2.1N^2 \log N$ queries, all queries will have been issued with probability greater than $1 - \frac{1}{N^2}$.

□

Note that Algorithm 1 works with any query distribution—not just with uniform ones. In the theorem above, we have made the assumption that the client issues queries uniformly at random so as to be able to compare our results with the results previously reported in the literature which make this assumption.

4.4　Lower Bound

Lemma 1. *Let A be an adversary that can reconstruct the order of the records with only access to access pattern leakage. If the client queries ranges uniformly at random, then adversary A needs to observe $\Omega(N^2)$ queries before successfully completing the reconstruction in expectation.*

Proof. We are going to base our proof on a database that is difficult to reconstruct. Suppose we have the following database:

$$
\begin{array}{ccc}
K & L & M \quad N \\
\end{array}
$$

$$
\begin{array}{ccc}
1 & 2 & N-1 \quad N \\
\end{array}
$$

The only element values in it are 1,2, $N-1$ and N. That is we have one small cluster at 1,2 and one small cluster at $N-1$, and N.

Given that adversary A only has access to access pattern leakage, the possible sets A can observe are:

$$\{K\}, \{L\}, \{M\}, \{N\}$$
$$\{K,L\}, \{L,M\}, \{M,N\}$$
$$\{K,L,M\}, \{L,M,N\}$$
$$\{K,L,M,N\}$$

Given that the queries come uniformly at random, A will be able to tell that K and L are clustered together and that M and N are also clustered together relatively quickly. What drives this lower bound is that one of $\{L,M\}$, $\{K,L,M\}$, and $\{L,M,N\}$ is necessary in order to glue the two clusters together.

Note that there are $O(N^2)$ possible queries. The only query that returns $\{L,M\}$ is $[2, N-1]$, the only query that returns $\{K,L,M\}$ is $[1, N-1]$, and the query that returns $\{L,M,N\}$ is $[2, N]$.

The probability that a random query is either one of those is $\frac{3}{O(N^2)} = \frac{1}{O(N^2)}$. Thus, Adversary A has to observe at least $\Omega(N^2)$ queries to access one of the necessary results in expectation.

$\square$

4.5 Dense Databases

For dense databases, reconstructing the ordering of the elements corresponds to a full reconstruction of the database (up to reflection). In this setting, Algorithm 1 matches the best previously known complexity for dense full database reconstruction [6,8,18].

Theorem 2. *Suppose an attacker uses Algorithm 1 to reconstruct a dense database. Then, the attacker can reconstruct the database after the client issues $8.2N \log N + 4 \log N$ uniformly at random queries with probability greater than $1 - \frac{3}{N^3}$, where N is the size of the database.*

Proof. First, let's split the database in two equal parts, A and B.

$$
\begin{array}{ccc}
& A & B \\
\end{array}
$$

$$
\begin{array}{ccc}
0 & N/2 & N \\
\end{array}
$$

By Lemma 2, after $4.1N \log N$ uniformly at random queries, for each value $a \in A$, the client issues a query $[a, b]$, for some $b \in B$ with high probability.

Let's look at the first 2 records in A, r_{A_1} and r_{A_2}. By Lemma 2, the attacker will see some response that contains $\{r_{A_1}, r_{A_2}, ...\}$, and a response that contains $\{r_{A_2}, ...\}$. Note that $\{r_{A_1}, r_{A_2}, ...\}$ contains all records in A, and $\{r_{A_2}, ...\}$ contains all elements in A besides r_{A_1}.

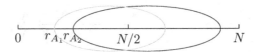

Given the two responses the PQ tree will be able to at least tell that r_{A_1} is to the left (or to the right) of r_{A_2} and all the other elements in A.

Similarly, given some r_{A_k}, and $r_{A_{k+1}}$, the attacker sees responses $\{r_{A_k}, r_{A_{k+1}}, ...\}$, and a response that contains $\{r_{A_{k+1}}, ...\}$. When she updates the PQ tree with the responses, the PQ tree will again be able to tell that r_{A_k} is to the left (or to the right) of $r_{A_{k+1}}$ and all the other elements in A higher than $r_{A_{k+1}}$.

In this way, the attacker can order all elements in A, and get

$$r_{A_1} - r_{A_2} - .... - r_{A_{max}}.$$

The attacker knows this order, but doesn't know if r_{A_1} or $r_{A_{max}}$ is the smallest element. Using a similar argument, accompanied by Lemma 3, the attacker can order all elements in B.

$$r_{B_1} - r_{B_2} - .... - r_{B_{max}}.$$

With only the above information, the PQ tree will be equivalent to one whose root will have two children P nodes. The first P node will contain the elements in A and the second P node will contain the elements in B.

It remains to show that the PQ tree can connect the two together. According to Lemma 4, the client will issue some query $[a, b]$, which is not of the form $[N/2 - i, N/2 + i + 1]$, and starts in $A - \{1\}$ and ends in $B - \{N\}$. As the database is dense, this query will result to a set S that contains some records from A and some records from B. Importantly, this query doesn't query 1 or N, and breaks the symmetry if all other queries were of the form $[N/2-i, N/2+i+1]$. Because the query returns only a subset of A and a subset of B, the PQ tree is able to deduce that $r_{A_{max}}$ and r_{B_1} are contained in S, and thus must be next to each other. Thus, the PQ tree will return the following order:

$$r_{A_1} - r_{A_2} - .... - r_{A_{max}} - r_{B_1} - r_{B_2} - .... - r_{B_{max}}.$$

Thus, we conclude by Union Bound, that after $8.2N \log N + 4 \log N$ queries the attacker can reconstruct the dense database with probability greater than $1 - \frac{3}{N^3}$.

□

Below, we prove the Lemmas used above.

Lemma 2. *After $4.1N \log N$ uniformly at random queries, for each value $a \in A$, the client issues a query $[a, b]$, for some $b \in B$ with probability greater than $1 - \frac{1}{N^3}$.*

Proof. Let's look at one value $a \in A$. There are $N/2$ values $b \in B$. The probability that a single query issued is of the form $[a, b]$ is

$$\frac{N/2}{N(N+1)/2} = \frac{1}{N+1}.$$

After $4.1N \log N$ queries, the probability that no query is of the desired form is

$$\left(1 - \frac{1}{N+1}\right)^{4.1N \log N} \leq \frac{1}{e^{4 \log N}} \leq \frac{1}{N^4}.$$

Now, let's look at every $a \in A$. After $4.1N \log N$ queries, by Union Bound the probability that for at least one a the client doesn't issue a query of the form $[a, b]$ is less than

$$N \cdot \frac{1}{N^4} \leq \frac{1}{N^3}.$$

$\square$

Lemma 3. *After $4.1N \log N$ uniformly at random queries, for each value $b \in B$, the client issues a query $[a, b]$, for some $a \in A$ with probability greater than $1 - \frac{1}{N^3}$.*

The proof follows similarly to Lemma 2.

Lemma 4. *After $4 \log N$ uniformly at random queries, the client issues a query $[a, b]$ that is not of the form $[N/2 - i, N/2 + i + 1]$, for some $a \in A - \{1\}$, $b \in B - \{N\}$, and $i \in [1, N/2)$, with probability greater than $1 - \frac{1}{N^3}$.*

Proof. There are $N/2 - 1$ desirable queries that start on each $a \in A - \{1\}$, as one of them is not of the desired form. Thus, there are $(\frac{N}{2} - 1)(\frac{N}{2} - 1)$ queries of desired form.

Thus, the probability that a query issued is not of the form $[N/2 - i, N/2 + i + 1]$ is

$$\frac{(\frac{N}{2} - 1)(\frac{N}{2} - 1)}{\frac{N(N+1)}{2}} \leq \frac{1}{4},$$

for $N > 8$. Thus, the probability that after $3 \log N$ issued queries the client only issued undesirable queries is less than

$$\left(\frac{1}{4}\right)^{4 \log N} \leq \frac{1}{N^3}.$$

$\square$

4.6 Databases with Special Properties

Grubbs et al. [8] assume that the database contains two records $a, b \in [N/4, 3N/4]$, such that $b - a \geq N/3$, and there are at least three records in the database, at least 1 apart.

Theorem 3 shows that Algorithm 1 matches Grubbs et al. [8] query complexity.

Theorem 3. *Suppose an attacker uses Algorithm 1 to reconstruct a database similar to the one in* [8]. *Then, the attacker can reconstruct the database after the client issues* $14.4N \log N$ *uniformly at random queries with probability greater than* $1 - \frac{3}{N^3}$, *where N is the size of the database.*

Proof. Similarly to the proof of Theorem 2, the attacker will be able to reconstruct the order of the two halves in the database after $8.2N \log N$ queries. It remains to show that she can combine them together successfully.

Like [8], we assume that the database contains two records $a, b \in [N/4, 3N/4]$, such that $b - a \geq N/3$. Thus, $a \in A$ and $b \in B$.

Like [8], we also assume that there is at least one more point in the database. This point c can be in one of three intervals, in $[0, val(a)]$, $[val(a), val(b)]$, or in $[val(b), N]$.

1. $c \in [0, val(a)]$

In this case, the attacker knows that a and c are in A, and b is in B. To resolve the ordering, the attacker needs to observe set $\{a, b\}$, in order to determine that c is not between a and b.
Note that even if a and c were right next to each other there are at least $N/4$ possible queries that return $\{a, b\}$.

2. $c \in [val(a), val(b)]$

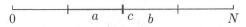

Without loss of generality, let's assume that the attacker knows that c is in B. In order to resolve this, the attacker has to observe some query that returns $\{a, c\}$. No matter how close a and c are, there are at least $N/4$ queries that return $\{a, c\}$. They are of the form $[x, val(c)]$, where $x \in [0, val(a)]$.

3. $c \in [val(b), N]$

This is similar to the first item. There are at least $N/4$ queries that return a query whose result is $\{a, b\}$.

In all cases above, there are at least $N/4$ queries that can resolve the ordering. The probability that none of the queries issued after $6.2N \log N$ queries is of the desired form is

$$\left(1 - \frac{N/4}{N(N+1)/2}\right)^{6.2N \log N} = \left(1 - \frac{1}{2(N+1)}\right)^{6.2N \log N}$$

$$\leq \frac{1}{e^{3.1 \log N}}$$

$$\leq \frac{1}{N^3}$$

Thus, after $14.4N \log N$ queries the adversary will successfully reconstruct the order of the database with probability greater than $1 - \frac{3}{N^3}$.   □

5   Full Database Reconstruction

In this section, we present our algorithm for full database reconstruction, which infers the values of the database records. The algorithm uses both access pattern leakage and search pattern leakage. It assumes that Algorithm 1 for full ordering reconstruction has been already executed, hence the attacker knows the ordering of the n database records by value, $r_1, r_2, \cdots, r_n$. By using search pattern leakage, the attacker counts the number of distinct queries observed until this count reaches $N(N+1)/2$, where N is the size of the universe of database elements. This occurs when the attacker has seen all possible queries.

5.1   Example

Suppose the server is hosting a database with records r_1, r_2, r_3, and r_4, as shown in Fig. 3.

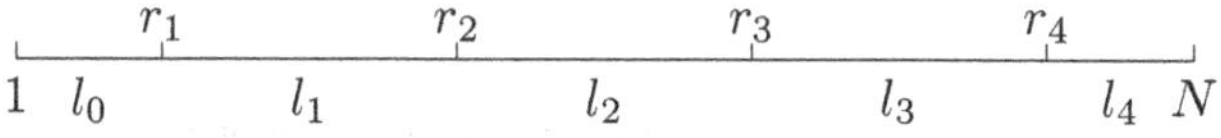

Fig. 3. Example of a database with four records with values in the interal $[1, N]$.

At this stage we assume that the attacker has already found the order of the records (up to reflection) and now is trying to determine the distances between consecutive records, denoted

l_0 (distance between 1 and r_1),
l_1 (distance between r_1 and r_2),
l_2 (distance between r_2 and r_3),
l_3 (distance between r_3 and r_4), and
l_4 (distance between r_4 and N).

To determine l_0 and l_1 we focus on all the possible range queries that return (only) r_1 as a response. These queries are as follows:

$$[1, l_0], [1, l_0 + 1], \ldots, [1, l_0 + l_1 - 1]$$
$$[2, l_0], [2, l_0 + 1], \ldots, [2, l_0 + l_1 - 1]$$
$$\cdots$$
$$[l_0, l_0], [l_0, l_0 + 1], \ldots, [l_0, l_0 + l_1 - 1]$$

The number of the above queries is $l_0 \cdot l_1$. In other words, there exist exactly $l_0 \cdot l_1$ distinct queries that all return r_1 as a response. Similarly, we can show that there exist exactly $l_1 \cdot l_2$ distinct queries that return r_2 as a response, and so on.

The above result can be generalized for query answers comprising two records. For example, there exist exactly $l_0 \cdot l_2$ distinct queries that return the pair $\{r_1, r_2\}$ as a response.

Once all queries have been seen, the attacker can count how many queries return each possible response. For example, let us assume that the attacker has seen exactly q_1 different queries which have returned as a result only r_1. Let us also assume that the attacker has seen exactly q_2 different queries which have returned as a result only r_2. Finally, let us also assume that the attacker has seen exactly q_{12} different queries which have returned as a result a set containing both r_1 and r_2.

This implies that the following equations hold:

$$l_0 \cdot l_1 = q_1$$
$$l_1 \cdot l_2 = q_2$$
$$l_0 \cdot l_2 = q_{12}$$

By solving the above set of three equations, the attacker can find the values of distances l_0, l_1 and l_2. Once these three have been determined, the attacker can easily compute the remaining distances l_3 and l_4 in a similar way, thus achieving full reconstruction of the database values.

Note that search pattern leakage is instrumental for this algorithm. The attacker has to calculate the query counts (i.e., the q_i constant terms in the system of equations) precisely and can do so only by determining whether two tokens correspond to the same query.

5.2   Algorithm

The above example generalizes to any number of database records as follows. Let us assume that the attacker has determined the full ordering of the records of a database of size n, denoted $r_1, r_2, \ldots, r_n$. Let us also assume that the number of distinct queries which return as a result only record r_i is q_i and the the number of distinct queries which return as a result only the pair or records $\{r_1, r_2\}$ is q_{12}.

The attacker builds the following system of $n + 1$ equations over variables l_i, $i = 0, \ldots, n$.

$$l_0 \cdot l_1 = q_1$$
$$l_1 \cdot l_2 = q_2$$
$$\ldots \tag{1}$$
$$l_{n-1} \cdot l_n = q_n$$
$$\text{and}$$
$$l_0 \cdot l_2 = q_{12}$$

In the above system, the meaning of the variables is as follows:

- l_0 denotes the distance between 1 and r_1;
- for $i = 1, \ldots, n - 1$, l_i denotes the distance between records r_i and r_{i+1}; and
- l_n denotes the distance between r_n and N.

One way to solve this system of equations is to first solve the subsystem

$$l_0 \cdot l_1 = q_1, l_1 \cdot l_2 = q_2, \text{ and } l_0 \cdot l_2 = q_{12}$$

for l_0, l_1 and l_2. Then, since the remaining equations are of the form $l_i \cdot l_{i+1} = q_{i+1}$, for $i \geq 2$, one can just solve for l_{i+1} one by one using the recovered values, starting with $i = 2$.

The resulting method for full database reconstruction is shown in Algorithm 2.

5.3   Analysis

Theorem 4. *After receiving $2.1N^2 \log N$ queries issued uniformly at random, Algorithm 2 will succeed in a full reconstruction of the database with probability greater than $1 - 1/N^2$, where N is the size of the universe of database values.*

Proof. Similarly to the proof of Theorem 1 we can show that after $2.1N^2 \log N$ uniformly at random issued queries with probability greater than $1 - 1/N^2$, the attacker will observe all queries at least once.

Then, the attacker can solve the system of Eq. (1) to determine the distances between all record values and thus fully reconstruct the database.   □

Algorithm 2. Full Reconstruction

1: Run Algorithm 1 until the answers to all possible distinct queries have been observed
2: Let *order* be the ordered list of records returned by Algorithm 1
3:
4: **for** i in range $[1, n]$ **do**
5:    $r = order[i]$
6:    Let q_i be the number of distinct queries that returned response $\{r\}$
7:    Create equation $l_{i-1} \cdot l_i = q_i$
8:
9: Let q_{12} be the number of distinct queries that returned response $\{order[1], order[2]\}$
10: Create equation $l_0 \cdot l_2 = q_{12}$
11:
12: Solve the resulting system of equations
13: Return l_i, $i \in [0, n]$

---

6 Conclusions

In this paper, we have presented an attack that reconstructs the values of an encrypted database from access pattern leakage and search pattern leakage. As in previous constructions, complete exact reconstruction requires observing a large number of queries and bounds on the query complexity of the attack are proved for a uniform query distribution. Recently, a reconstruction method has been presented whose efficiency does not rely on assumptions about the query distribution [17], which opens an interesting research direction. Also, in response to attack papers on searchable encryption, there is an interesting body of work that focuses on leakage reduction (e.g., [4,12,13]). Another promising avenue for future work is developing methods to attack the above improved schemes.

Acknowledgments. We would like to thank Thibaut Bagory, Paul Grubbs, Marie-Sarah Lacharité, Brice Minaud, and Kenneth G. Paterson and for their helpful comments and suggestions on a previous version of this paper.

References

1. Booth, K.S., Lueker, G.S.: Testing for the consecutive ones property, interval graphs, and graph planarity using PQ-tree algorithms. J. Comput. Syst. Sci. **13**(3), 335–379 (1976)
2. Cash, D., Grubbs, P., Perry, J., Ristenpart, T.: Leakage-abuse attacks against searchable encryption. In: Proceedings of the ACM Conference on Computer and Communications Security, CCS (2015)
3. Dautrich Jr., J.L., Ravishankar, C.V.: Compromising privacy in precise query protocols. In: Proceedings of the International Conference on Extending Database Technology, EDBT (2013)

4. Demertzis, I., Papadopoulos, S., Papapetrou, O., Deligiannakis, A., Garofalakis, M.: Practical private range search revisited. In: Proceedings of the ACM International Conference on Management of Data, SIGMOD (2016)
5. Durak, F.B., DuBuisson, T.M., Cash, D.: What else is revealed by order-revealing encryption? In: Proceedings of the ACM Conference on Computer and Communications Security, CCS (2016)
6. Grubbs, P., Lacharité, M., Minaud, B., Paterson, K.G.: Learning to reconstruct: statistical learning theory and encrypted database attacks. In: IEEE Symposium on Security and Privacy, pp. 513–529 (2019)
7. Grubbs, P., Lacharité, M.S., Minaud, B., Paterson, K.G.: Pump up the volume: practical database reconstruction from volume leakage on range queries. In: Proceedings of the ACM Conference on Computer and Communications Security, CCS (2018)
8. Grubbs, P., Lacharité, M.S., Minaud, B., Paterson, K.G.: Learning to reconstruct: statistical learning theory and encrypted database attacks. Cryptology ePrint Archive, Report 2019/011 (2019). https://eprint.iacr.org/2019/011
9. Grubbs, P., McPherson, R., Naveed, M., Ristenpart, T., Shmatikov, V.: Breaking web applications built on top of encrypted data. In: Proceedings of the ACM Conference on Computer and Communications Security, CCS (2016)
10. Grubbs, P., Ristenpart, T., Shmatikov, V.: Why your encrypted database is not secure. In: Proceedings of the Workshop on Hot Topics in Operating Systems, HotOS (2017)
11. Grubbs, P., Sekniqi, K., Bindschaedler, V., Naveed, M., Ristenpart, T.: Leakage-abuse attacks against order-revealing encryption. In: 2017 IEEE Symposium on Security and Privacy, SP (2017)
12. Kamara, S., Moataz, T.: Computationally volume-hiding structured encryption. In: Ishai, Y., Rijmen, V. (eds.) EUROCRYPT 2019. LNCS, vol. 11477, pp. 183–213. Springer, Cham (2019). https://doi.org/10.1007/978-3-030-17656-3_7
13. Kamara, S., Moataz, T., Ohrimenko, O.: Structured encryption and leakage suppression. In: Shacham, H., Boldyreva, A. (eds.) CRYPTO 2018. LNCS, vol. 10991, pp. 339–370. Springer, Cham (2018). https://doi.org/10.1007/978-3-319-96884-1_12
14. Kellaris, G., Kollios, G., Nissim, K., O'Neill, A.: Generic attacks on secure outsourced databases. In: Proceedings of the ACM Conference on Computer and Communications Security. ACM (2016)
15. Kornaropoulos, E.M., Papamanthou, C., Tamassia, R.: Data recovery on encrypted databases with k-nearest neighbor query leakage. In: Proceedings of the IEEE Symposium on Security and Privacy, SP, pp. 245–262 (2019)
16. Kornaropoulos, E.M., Papamanthou, C., Tamassia, R.: The state of the uniform: attacks on encrypted databases beyond the uniform query distribution. Cryptology ePrint Archive, Report 2019/441 (2019). https://eprint.iacr.org/2019/441
17. Kornaropoulos, E.M., Papamanthou, C., Tamassia, R.: The state of the uniform: attacks on encrypted databases beyond the uniform query distribution. In: Proceedings of the IEEE Symposium on Security and Privacy, SP (2020, to appear)
18. Lacharité, M.S., Minaud, B., Paterson, K.G.: Improved reconstruction attacks on encrypted data using range query leakage. In: Proceedings of the IEEE Symposium on Security and Privacy, SP (2018)
19. Pouliot, D., Wright, C.V.: The shadow nemesis: inference attacks on efficiently deployable, efficiently searchable encryption. In: Proceedings of the ACM Conference on Computer and Communications Security, CCS (2016)
20. Zhang, Y., Katz, J., Papamanthou, C.: All your queries are belong to us: the power of file-injection attacks on searchable encryption. In: Proceedings of the USENIX Security Symposium (2016)

Cube Cryptanalysis of Round-Reduced ACORN

Jingchun Yang[1,2], Meicheng Liu[1,2], and Dongdai Lin[1,2(✉)]

[1] State Key Laboratory of Information Security,
Institute of Information Engineering,
Chinese Academy of Sciences, Beijing, China
{yangjingchun,liumeicheng,ddlin}@iie.ac.cn
[2] School of Cyber Security, University of Chinese Academy of Sciences,
Beijing, China

Abstract. The cube attack is one of the most powerful techniques in cryptanalysis of symmetric cryptographic primitives. The basic idea of cube attack is to determine the value of a polynomial in key bits by summing over a cube (a subset of public variables, *e.g.*, plaintext bits or IV bits). If the degree of the polynomial is relatively low, then we can obtain a low-degree equation in key bits, thus may contribute to reducing the complexity of key recovery.

In this paper, we use cube cryptanalysis to analyze the authenticated stream cipher ACORN (one of the 6 algorithms in the final portfolio of the CAESAR competition), and give some new results in both distinguishing attacks and key recovery attacks. Firstly, we give a new method of finding cube testers, which is based on the greedy algorithm of finding cubes, and the numeric mapping method for estimating the algebraic degree of NFSR-based cryptosystems. We apply it to ACORN, and obtain the best practical distinguishing attacks for its 690-round variant using a cube of size 38, and its 706-round variant using a cube of size 46. Then we theoretically analyze the security bound of ACORN via the division property based cube attack. By exploiting the embedded property, we find some new distinguishers for ACORN, so the zero-sum property of the output of its 775-round variant can be observed with a complexity of 2^{127}. Finally, we propose a key recovery attack on ACORN reduced to 772 rounds. The time complexity to recover the linear superpoly of the 123-dimensional cube is $2^{127.46}$. As far as we know, this is the best key recovery attack on round-reduced ACORN. It is also worth noting that this work does not threaten the security of ACORN.

Keywords: Cube cryptanalysis · ACORN · Distinguishing attack ·
Key recovery · Numeric mapping · Division property based cube attack

This work was supported by the National Natural Science Foundation of China (Grant No. 61872359 and No. 61672516) and Youth Innovation Promotion Association CAS.

Z. Lin et al. (Eds.): ISC 2019, LNCS 11723, pp. 44–64, 2019.
https://doi.org/10.1007/978-3-030-30215-3_3

1   Introduction

In modern cryptographic primitives, nonlinear feedback shift register (NFSR) plays an important role in the applications with constrained environments, like the radio-frequency identification devices (RFID) and sensor networks. Based on the structure of NFSR, many symmetric ciphers have been proposed, such as the stream ciphers TRIVIUM [6] and Grain [12], the authenticated stream cipher ACORN [25], the lightweight block cipher family KATAN/KTANTAN [7], and the hash function family QUARK [3–5]. All these algorithms possess an efficient hardware implementation and a high level security at the same time.

Cube attack was first proposed by Dinur and Shamir [8] at EUROCRYPT 2009. This attack views a cryptosystem as a black-box polynomial f. The basic idea of this attack is that the symbolic sum of all the derived polynomials obtained from the function f by assigning all the possible values to the cube variables (a subset of public variables) is exactly the superpoly (the coefficient) of the term with maximum degree over the cube. Cube attacks work by finding a number of linear superpolys in secret variables and then recovering the secret information by solving the system of linear equations. At FSE 2009, Aumasson et al. [2] proposed the notion of cube testers. The main idea of cube testers is similar to cube attacks, however, it aims to find some superpolys which have the distinguishable properties (e.g., the superpoly is equal to a zero constant, which is most commonly used).

For cube attacks and cube testers, the key to success is to search good cubes and their superpolys. Traditional approaches [1,9,13,15,17] of finding cube testers are experimental and very limited to the current computing power. For a given cube c, to verify the balance property of this cube, we need to compute the cubesum on this cube for a number of random keys, and the complexity of this process is $r \cdot 2^{|c|}$, where r is the amount of keys. When $|c|$ is large (e.g., $|c| > 50$), it is difficult to verify the cube since the complexity is exponential to $|c|$.

However, this headache has been solved gradually in recent years. At CRYPTO 2017, Liu [14] proposed a new technique, called *numeric mapping*, to iteratively estimate the upper bound on the algebraic degree of the internal states of an NFSR-based cryptosystem. For TRIVIUM-like ciphers, some cube testers of sizes greater than 50 were presented for the first time. Simultaneously, at CRYPTO 2017, Todo et al. [20] proposed the *division property based cube attack* to analyze the ANF of the superpoly. Based on the propagation of the bit-based division property [19,22] of stream ciphers, they gave a proposition to decide which key bits do not exist in the superpoly. This technique led to the possible key recovery attack of 704-round ACORN. Later at CRYPTO 2018, Wang et al. [23,24] proposed some new techniques (flag technique, degree evaluation, and term enumeration) to improve the division property based cube attack. In the end, they presented a new possible key recovery attack on 750-round ACORN with a cube of size 101, which is also the best known key recovery attack on round-reduced ACORN.

1.1   Our Contributions

In this paper, we evaluate the security of authenticated stream cipher ACORN [25] (one of the 6 algorithms in the final portfolio of the CAESAR competition) from the aspect of cube cryptanalysis, and propose some new distinguishing attacks and a new possible key recovery attack. All of our attacks are currently the best attacks in terms of the number of attacked rounds or the feasibility of attack.

Firstly, we give a new method of finding cube testers with a much shorter time. Our method is based on the greedy algorithm of finding cubes [13,17], and the numeric mapping method for estimating the algebraic degree of NFSR-based cryptosystems [14]. With this new method, we can efficiently search cube testers in a much larger space. We apply it to ACORN, and obtain the best practical distinguishing attacks for its 690-round variant using a cube of size 38, and its 706-round variant using a cube of size 46.

Then we theoretically analyze the security bound of ACORN via the division property based cube attack. We demonstrate that the embedded property [18] proposed at ASIACRYPT 2017 can also be applied to the search of zero-sum cube testers. Based on the embedded property for cube tester, we propose several algorithms to find the zero-sum cube testers efficiently. This leads us to find some distinguishers for ACORN, so the zero-sum property of the output of its 775-round variant can be observed with a complexity of 2^{127}.

We also propose an algorithm to find suitable cubes for key recovery attacks. The basic idea is that a cube which leads to an r-round cube tester might lead to an $(r + 1)$-round cube attack as well. In the process of cube searching, we try to maximize the number of attacked arounds. Meanwhile, we keep the cube dimension and the complexity to recover the superpoly be reasonable. Finally, we find a key recovery attack on ACORN reduced to 772 rounds. The time complexity to recover the linear superpoly of the 123-dimensional cube is $2^{127.46}$. As far as we know, this is the best key recovery attack on round-reduced ACORN.

Our results for ACORN are summarized in Table 1, and the comparisions with previous attacks on ACORN are also included.

Organization. The rest of the paper is organized as follows. In Sect. 2 we introduce some basic definitions and theories. In Sect. 3 we briefly describe the ACORN cipher. Section 4 shows our new method to search good cube testers, and its applications to ACORN. In Sect. 5, we propose several algorithms to search zero-sum cube testers and suitable cubes for key recovery attacks in the division property based cube attack. Then we use these algorithms to analyze the security of ACORN. Section 6 concludes the paper.

2   Preliminaries

2.1   Cube Attacks and Cube Testers

Almost any cryptosystem can be described as a Boolean function $f(x_1, \cdots, x_n)$. Given a term t_I containing variables from an index subset $I \subsetneq \{1, \cdots, n\}$ that

Table 1. Summary of the distinguishing attacks and key recovery attacks on ACORN.

Attack types	#Rounds	Cube size	Complexity†	Ref.
Distinguishing attacks	676	-	$\approx 2^{40.6}$	[10]
	690	**38**	2^{38}	Section 4.3
	706	**46**	2^{46}	Section 4.3
	715	**54**	2^{54}	Section 4.3
	775	**127**	2^{127}	Section 5.3
Key recovery attacks	503	5	Practical	[16]
	704	64	2^{122}‡	[20, 21]
	750	101	$2^{120.92}$‡	[23, 24]
	772	**123**	$2^{127.46}$‡	Section 5.3

† For distinguishing attacks, it refers to the data complexity. For key recovery attacks, it refers to the complexity to recover one superpoly.
‡ All these three attacks are derived by the division property based cube attack, and the real superpolys can not be obtained due to the impractical complexity, so we can recover at most 1 bit key information respectively.

are multiplied together, the function can be written as the sum of terms which are supersets of I and terms that miss at least one variable from I,

$$f(x_1, \cdots, x_n) = p_S(I) \cdot t_I + q(x_1, \cdots, x_n),$$

where $p_S(I)$ is called the superpoly of I in f. The basic idea of cube attacks [8] is that the symbolic sum of all the derived polynomials obtained from the function f by assigning all the possible values to the subset of variables in the term t_I is exactly $p_S(I)$. Cube attacks work by finding a number of linear superpolys in secret variables and then recovering the secret information by solving the system of linear equations. While cube testers [2] work by evaluating superpolys of carefully selected terms t_I's, and trying to distinguish them from a random function. Especially, the superpoly $p_S(I)$ is equal to a zero constant, if the algebraic degree of f in the variables from I is smaller than the size of I.

2.2   Numeric Mapping

Let $f(x) = \bigoplus_{u=(u_1, \cdots, u_m) \in \mathbb{F}_2^m} a_u^f \prod_{i=1}^m x_i^{u_i}$ be a Boolean function on m variables. Denote by $\mathbb{B}_m$ the set of all m-variable Boolean functions. The *numeric mapping* [14], denoted by DEG, is defined as

$$\text{DEG} : \mathbb{B}_m \times \mathbb{Z}^m \to \mathbb{Z},$$

$$(f, D) \mapsto \max_{a_u^f \neq 0} \left\{ \sum_{i=1}^m u_i d_i \right\},$$

where $D = (d_1, d_2, \cdots, d_m)$ and a_u^f's are coefficients of the ANF of f. Let g_i $(1 \leq i \leq m)$ be Boolean functions on n variables, and denote $\deg(G) =$

$(\deg(g_1), \deg(g_2), \cdots, \deg(g_m))$ for $G = (g_1, g_2, \cdots, g_m)$. The numeric degree of the composite function $h = f \circ G$ is defined as $\mathtt{DEG}(f, \deg(G))$, denoted by $\mathtt{DEG}(h)$ for short. We call $\mathtt{DEG}(f, D)$ a super numeric degree of h if $d_i \geq \deg(g_i)$ for all $1 \leq i \leq m$, where $D = (d_1, d_2, \cdots, d_m)$. We can check that the algebraic degree of h is always less than or equal to the numeric degree of h, $i.e.$,

$$\deg(h) = \deg(f(g_1, g_2, \cdots, g_m)) \leq \mathtt{DEG}(h) = \max_{a_u^f \neq 0} \{ \sum_{i=1}^{m} u_i \deg(g_i) \}.$$

Based on numeric mapping, Liu [14] developed an algorithm for estimating the algebraic degree of NFSR-based cryptosystems. We refer to [14] for more details.

2.3   Mixed Integer Linear Programming

Mixed Integer Linear Programming (MILP) is an optimization or feasibility program. A MILP model $\mathcal{M}$ takes an objective function $\mathcal{M}.obj$ and a system of linear constraints $\mathcal{M}.con$ where variables $\mathcal{M}.var$ are restricted to integers. A MILP solver aims to search for an optimal solution which not only satisfies all the constraints but also minimizes/maximizes the objective function. Moreover, if there is no objective function, the MILP solver only returns whether the model is feasible or not. In this paper, we use Gurobi Optimizer [11] for our experiments.

2.4   Bit-Based Division Property and MILP Representation

The division property, proposed at EUROCRYPT 2015 [19], is a generalization of the integral property for the detection of better integral characteristics for word-oriented cryptographic primitives. Later, the bit-based division property was proposed in [22] to describe the propagation of integral characteristics more precisely. The bit-based division property is defined as follows.

Definition 1 ((Bit-Based) Division Property [22]). *Let $\mathbb{X}$ be a multiset whose elements take a value of $\mathbb{F}_2^n$. Let $\mathbb{K}$ be a set whose elements take an n-dimensional bit vector. When the multiset $\mathbb{X}$ has the division property $\mathcal{D}_{\mathbb{K}}^{1^n}$, it fulfills the following conditions:*

$$\bigoplus_{\boldsymbol{x} \in \mathbb{X}} \boldsymbol{x}^{\boldsymbol{u}} = \begin{cases} unknown & \textit{if there exist } \boldsymbol{k} \in \mathbb{K} \textit{ s.t. } \boldsymbol{u} \succeq \boldsymbol{k}, \\ 0 & \textit{otherwise}, \end{cases}$$

where $\boldsymbol{u} \succeq \boldsymbol{k}$ if $u_i \geq k_i$ for all i, and $\boldsymbol{x}^{\boldsymbol{u}} = \prod_{i=1}^{n} x_i^{u_i}$.

In [19,22], the propagation rules copy, xor, and are provided when the bitwise operations COPY, XOR, AND are applied to the elements in $\mathbb{X}$.

Represent the Propagation of Division Property Using MILP. At ASI-ACRYPT 2016, Xiang *et al.* [26] first introduced a new concept *division trail* to describe the propagation of the division property, and showed that the basic propagation rules copy, xor, and of the division property can be translated as some variables and constraints of an MILP model. With this method, all possible division trails can be covered with an MILP model $\mathcal{M}$ and the division property of some output bit can be known according to the solutions of $\mathcal{M}$.

2.5 Bit-Based Division Property and Cube Attack

In cube attack, we want to recover the superpoly $p_S(I)$ for a cube I. Let $x_0, x_1, \ldots, x_{n-1}$ be all key bits. If the initialization is not enough for thorough diffusion, the superpoly may only be related to a part of key bits $J \subsetneq \{0, 1, \cdots, n-1\}$. At CRYPTO 2017, Todo *et al.* [20] proposed an algorithm for determining such a set J by using the bit-based division property. This algorithm is based on the following proposition.

Proposition 1 (Determining the involved key bits in the superpoly [20]). *Let $f(\boldsymbol{x}, \boldsymbol{v})$ be a polynomial, where $\boldsymbol{x}$ and $\boldsymbol{v}$ denote the secret and public variables, respectively. For a set of indices $I = \{i_1, i_2, \ldots, i_{|I|}\} \subset \{0, 1, \ldots, m - 1\}$, let C_I be a set of $2^{|I|}$ values where the variables in $\{v_{i_1}, v_{i_2}, \ldots, v_{i_{|I|}}\}$ are taking all possible combinations of values. Let $\boldsymbol{k}_I$ be an m-dimensional bit vector such that $\boldsymbol{v}^{\boldsymbol{k}_I} = t_I = v_{i_1} v_{i_2} \ldots v_{i_{|I|}}$, i.e. $k_i = 1$ if $i \in I$ and $k_i = 0$ otherwise. Assuming there is no division trail such that $(\boldsymbol{e}_\lambda, \boldsymbol{k}_I) \xrightarrow{f} 1$, x_λ is not involved in the superpoly of the cube C_I.*

Later at CRYPTO 2018, Wang *et al.* [23,24] proposed some techniques to improve the division property based cube attack. The main contribution of [23] can be summarized as follows.

Flag Technique. In previous MILP modeling of the basic bitwise operations (COPY, XOR, AND), each intermediate state bit b is assigned a binary value $b.val$ to represent its bit-based division property value. In [23], Wang *et al.* added a 'flag' value for each state bit. The flag value $b.F$ can be $0_c, 1_c$ or δ to indicate whether the state bit is constant 0, constant 1 or variable. This change mainly affects the MILP model for AND. If the flag value $b.F$ of state bit b is 0_c, then we add a constraint $b.val = 0$, thus may improve the accuracy of MILP model description of the division property propagation.

Degree Evaluation and Term Enumeration. To recover the superpoly more efficiently, Wang *et al.* [23] proposed another two algorithms to compute the algebraic degree and enumerate all possible terms of the superpoly, respectively. The two algorithms are based on the following proposition, which is actually a generalization of Proposition 1.

Proposition 2 (Degree evaluation and term enumeration of the super-poly [23]). *Let $f(\boldsymbol{x}, \boldsymbol{v})$ be a polynomial, where $\boldsymbol{x}$ and $\boldsymbol{v}$ denote the secret and public variables, respectively. For a set of indices $I = \{i_1, i_2, \ldots, i_{|I|}\} \subset \{0, 1, \ldots, m-1\}$, let C_I be a set of $2^{|I|}$ values where the variables in $\{v_{i_1}, v_{i_2}, \ldots, v_{i_{|I|}}\}$ are taking all possible combinations of values. Let $\boldsymbol{k}_I$ be an m-dimensional bit vector such that $\boldsymbol{v}^{\boldsymbol{k}_I} = t_I = v_{i_1} v_{i_2} \ldots v_{i_{|I|}}$. Let $\boldsymbol{k}_\Lambda$ be an n-dimensional bit vector. Assuming there is no division trail such that $(\boldsymbol{k}_\Lambda \| \boldsymbol{k}_I) \xrightarrow{f} 1$, the term $x^{\boldsymbol{k}_\Lambda}$ is not involved in the superpoly of the cube C_I.*

For convenience, in the rest of this paper, we denote the algorithm [23] of the degree evaluation of the superpoly, and the term enumeration of the superpoly by Algorithm A, and Algorithm B respectively.

3 A Brief Description of ACORN

ACORN [25] is an authenticated encryption stream cipher, and it has been selected as one of the 6 algorithms in the final portfolio of the CAESAR competition. ACORN has a 128-bit key and a 128-bit initialization vector. As an authenticated encryption scheme, ACORN has 4 procedures: initialization, processing the associated data, encryption, and finalization. In this paper, we only focus on the process of initialization, because the number of rounds we can attack is smaller than the 1792 initialization rounds. For more details about ACORN, we refer to [25].

Denote the internal state (at step t) of ACORN by $S_t = (s_t, s_{t+1}, \ldots, s_{t+292})$, where $t \in \{0, \ldots, 1791\}$. The initial state $S_0 = (s_0, s_1, \ldots, s_{292})$ is set to $(0, \ldots, 0)$. Denote the key and initialization vector by K and IV respectively. Let

$$m_t = \begin{cases} K_t & \text{for t = 0 to 127,} \\ IV_{t-128} & \text{for t = 128 to 255,} \\ K_0 \oplus 1 & \text{for t = 256,} \\ K_{t \bmod 128} & \text{for t = 257 to 1791.} \end{cases}$$

At each step t, where $t \in \{0, \ldots, 1791\}$, the state is updated as follows.

1. update using six LFSRs.
   $s_{t+289} = s_{t+289} \oplus s_{t+235} \oplus s_{t+230};$
   $s_{t+230} = s_{t+230} \oplus s_{t+196} \oplus s_{t+193};$
   $s_{t+193} = s_{t+193} \oplus s_{t+160} \oplus s_{t+154};$
   $s_{t+154} = s_{t+154} \oplus s_{t+111} \oplus s_{t+107};$
   $s_{t+107} = s_{t+107} \oplus s_{t+66} \oplus s_{t+61};$
   $s_{t+61} = s_{t+61} \oplus s_{t+23} \oplus s_t;$
2. generate the keystream bit.
   $ks_t = s_{t+12} \oplus s_{t+154} \oplus s_{t+235} s_{t+61} \oplus s_{t+235} s_{t+193} \oplus s_{t+61} s_{t+193} \oplus s_{t+230} s_{t+111} \oplus s_{t+230} s_{t+66} \oplus s_{t+66};$

3. generate the nonlinear feedback bit.

$f_t = s_t \oplus s_{t+107} \oplus 1 \oplus s_{t+244}s_{t+23} \oplus s_{t+244}s_{t+160} \oplus s_{t+23}s_{t+160} \oplus s_{t+196} \oplus ks_t;$

4. update with the feedback bit f_t.

$s_{t+293} = f_t \oplus m_t;$

4 A New Method to Search Good Cube Testers

During the process of cube attack, searching good cubes is the most important and time-consuming part. In this section, we will give a new method to find good cube testers more efficiently. The search algorithm is inspired by the work of Stankovski [17] and Karlsson et al. [13]. We first introduce the greedy algorithm of finding cube testers, then we give our new method to accelerate the process of searching, finally we apply this method to ACORN.

4.1 Greedy Algorithm for Finding Cube Testers

In 2010, Stankovski [17] utilized the greedy algorithm for finding a practical (e.g., the size of the bitset is no more than 40) bitset S as a cube which leads to a distinguisher or nonrandomness detector. The main procedure of this algorithm can be described as follows:

1. Choose an optimal starting bitset of a small size s_0 (which can be zero).
2. Add n bits into the bitset and select the best bitset of size $s_1 = s_0 + n$ which leads to a distinguisher or a nonrandomness detector with the largest number of rounds.
3. Repeat step 2, until a cube of expected size $s_i = s_0 + in$ is derived.

In 2017, Karlsson et al. [13] improved the greedy nonrandomness detectors with a more general solution. Their main idea is to extend the naive greedy algorithm by examining more possible paths. The main procedure is described as follows:

1. Consider a set of candidates from a previous iteration, or from an optimal starting set.
2. For each candidate in the list, add the k_i best bitsets (each bitset has n_i new bits) and store them in a new list. Now, we have one such new list for each candidate in the original list.
3. Merge all lists, sorting by the number of distinguishable rounds. This gives a list of $k_i \prod_{t=0}^{i-1} k_t \alpha_t$ items.
4. Finally, reduce the size of this list with the factor $\alpha_i (0 < \alpha_i \leq 1.0)$, limiting the size of the combined list to $\prod_{t=0}^{i} k_t \alpha_t$ items.
5. Repeat steps $1 \sim 4$, until a bitset of the expected size has been found.

4.2   Accelerating the Greedy Algorithm via Numeric Mapping

From the previous subsection, the greedy algorithm can surely find a good cube of a practical size, however, when the size increases, this searching process becomes extremely time-consuming. While using the numeric mapping method [14], one can estimate the algebraic degree of the output bit of NFSR-based cryptosystems. Regardless of the size of the cube, this estimation can give an upper bound of real algebraic degree of the output bit in a linear time complexity. If the estimated degree of the output bit is smaller than the size of cube, then we obtain a zero-sum distinguisher.

We give the accelerated greedy algorithm in Algorithms 1 and 2. When we compute the number of distinguishable rounds of a cube, we do not need to compute the cubesum on this cube and repeat this calculation on enough random keys to observe the bias of the cubesum. Instead, we use the degree estimation method to compute the lower bound of the maximum number of distinguishable rounds of this cube. The degree estimation algorithm usually costs a complexity of about $\mathcal{O}(N)$, where N is the number of initialization rounds. While the traditional approach needs a complexity of $\mathcal{O}(r \cdot 2^{|c|})$, where r is the number of random keys, and $|c|$ is the size of the cube.

Algorithm 1. Accelerated Greedy Algorithm

Input : Key K, IV V, bit space B, the number of iterations: m, vector $\boldsymbol{k}$, vector $\boldsymbol{n}$, vector $\boldsymbol{\alpha}$.

Output: Bitset S_m.

1: $S_0 = \{\emptyset\}$;
   /* The set S_0 contains a single empty bitset */
2: **for** each $i \in \{0, \ldots, m-1\}$ **do**
3:    **for** each $c \in S_i$ **do**
4:       $L_c = $ **FastFindBest** (K, V, B, c, k_i, n_i);
5:    **end for**
6:    $S_{i+1} = $ concatenate (all L_c from above);
7:    sort S_{i+1};
8:    reduce the number of elements in S_{i+1} by a factor α_i;
9: **end for**
10: **return** S_m;

4.3   Applications to ACORN

We apply our new method to ACORN cipher. Based on our observations on the updated functions of ACORN, we first construct a linear-time algorithm for determining the upper bound on the algebraic degree of the cipher. Then, we apply our accelerated greedy algorithm to finding good cube testers of ACORN.

Algorithm 2. FastFindBest

Input : Key K, IV V, bit space B, current bitset c, the number of best
           bitsets to retain: k, the number of bits to add: n.
Output: k bitsets each of size $|c| + n$.

```
/* let comb(S, k) denote the set of all k-combinations of a set S */
```
1: $S = \emptyset$;
2: **for each** n-tuple $\{b_1, \ldots, b_n\} \in \text{comb}(B \setminus c, n)$ **do**
3:    **using numeric mapping method, compute the lower bound z of the**
      maximum number of distinguishable rounds for the bitset
      $c \cup \{b_1, \ldots, b_n\}$;
4:    **if** z is among the k highest values **then**
5:       add $c \cup \{b_1, \ldots, b_n\}$ to S;
6:       reduce S to k elements by removing element with lowest z;
7:    **end if**
8: **end for**
9: **return** S;

The Algorithm of Degree Estimation of ACORN. We present an algorithm for ACORN to compute the upper bound of the algebraic degree of the output for a given cube. The algorithm is depicted in Algorithm 3.

In this algorithm, $d^{(t)}$ (where $t \in \{0, \ldots, N + 292\}$) are global variables. Each $d^{(t)}$ gives the estimated (real when $t \leq 292$) algebraic degree of the internal state bit s_t. We first initialize the degree of s_t (where $t \in \{0, \ldots, 292\}$) by $-\infty$, since the initial state is set to $\{0, \ldots, 0\}$. At each step, we need to compute the estimated degrees of six updated bits and the keystream bit. Two subfunctions $\text{KSG128}(t)$ and $\text{FBK128}(t)$ (see Appendix A) are used to compute the estimated degree of the keystream bit and the feedback bit separately. In lines $7 \sim 14$, $d^{(t+293)}$ is updated by the feedback function $s_{t+293} = f_t \oplus m_t$. The algebraic degrees of cube variables are equal to 1. We set other non-cube IV variables to 0, so their degrees are $-\infty$. The degrees of key bits are equal to 0, since they are constants with respect to cube variables in X. Lines $16 \sim 21$ are justified by the rule of update using six LFSRs. Finally, the algorithm returns $ks^{(N)}$ as the estimated degree of the first keystream bit after N initialization rounds.

Theorem 1. *Algorithm 3 gives an upper bound on the algebraic degree of the first keystream bit of N-round ACORN cipher with X as cube variables.*

We give our proof of Theorem 1 in Appendix B. Both $\text{KSG128}(t)$ and $\text{FBK128}(t)$ can be executed in constant time, thus Algorithm 3 has a time complexity of $\mathcal{O}(N)$. It requires a memory of $\mathcal{O}(N)$.

Experimental Results. In Algorithm 1, we need to specify the number of iterations m, vector $\boldsymbol{k}$, vector $\boldsymbol{n}$, and vector $\boldsymbol{\alpha}$. We set the maximum size of cube to 66. The number of iterations m is 16. At each iteration, we retain 100 best cubes of the current size. At the first iteration, we exhaust all possible cubes of size 6. After that, we add 4 new bits at each iteration.

Algorithm 3. Degree Estimation of ACORN Cipher

Require: Given the initialization rounds N, and the set X of cube variables.

1: **for** t from 0 to 292 **do**
2:    $d^{(t)} \leftarrow -\infty$;
3: **end for**
4: **for** t from 0 to $N-1$ **do**
5:    $ks^{(t)} \leftarrow \text{KSG128}(t)$;
6:    $f^{(t)} \leftarrow \text{FBK128}(t)$;
7:    **if** $128 \leq t \leq 255$ **then**
8:       **if** $IV_{t-128} \in X$ **then**
9:          $d^{(t+293)} \leftarrow \max\{f^{(t)},\ 1\}$;
10:      **else**
11:         $d^{(t+293)} \leftarrow f^{(t)}$;
12:      **end if**
13:   **else**
14:      $d^{(t+293)} \leftarrow \max\{f^{(t)},\ 0\}$;
15:   **end if**
16:   $d^{(t+289)} \leftarrow \max\{d^{(t+289)},\ d^{(t+235)},\ d^{(t+230)}\}$;
17:   $d^{(t+230)} \leftarrow \max\{d^{(t+230)},\ d^{(t+196)},\ d^{(t+193)}\}$;
18:   $d^{(t+193)} \leftarrow \max\{d^{(t+193)},\ d^{(t+160)},\ d^{(t+154)}\}$;
19:   $d^{(t+154)} \leftarrow \max\{d^{(t+154)},\ d^{(t+111)},\ d^{(t+107)}\}$;
20:   $d^{(t+107)} \leftarrow \max\{d^{(t+107)},\ d^{(t+66)},\ d^{(t+61)}\}$;
21:   $d^{(t+61)} \leftarrow \max\{d^{(t+61)},\ d^{(t+23)},\ d^{(t)}\}$;
22: **end for**
23: $ks^{(N)} \leftarrow \text{KSG128}(N)$;
24: **return** $ks^{(N)}$;

We list part of output of our program in Table 2 in Appendix C. Our experiments show that, with the new method of finding cubes, we can surely obtain better cryptanalytic results with a much shorter time. For example, we have found a cube tester when the cube size increases to 54, and the number of rounds we can attack is 715.

Moreover, we have also obtained a cube of a practical size 38, which can lead to a 690-round zero-sum distinguisher. We randomly select 64 different keys, and then compute the 64 different cubesums of the first 64 keystream bits produced by 690-round ACORN. The results show that the cubesums of the first keystream bit are always equal to zero. The cubesums of other keystream bits are all non-zero. This result further justifies the 690-round zero-sum cube tester.

5   Searching Cubes in Division Property Based Cube Attack

In this section, we propose a method to find zero-sum cube testers for an iterated cipher via the division property based cube attack. We apply this method to ACORN, and obtain the best distinguishing attack for 775-round ACORN. Based on the embedded property for cube tester, we also propose an algorithm to find suitable cubes for key recovery attacks. In the end, we find the best key recovery attack for 772-round ACORN.

5.1   Finding Cube Testers via Division Property Based Cube Attack

In [18], Sun *et al.* proposed the algorithms to find optimal integral distinguishers for ARX ciphers by exploiting the embedded property (see Appendix D). Next, we will show that, the embedded property can apply to the search of cube testers as well. We first introduce the following lemma which was proposed in [23].

Lemma 1 ([23]). *If $\boldsymbol{k} \succeq \boldsymbol{k}'$ and there is division trail $\boldsymbol{k} \xrightarrow{f} \boldsymbol{l}$, then there is also division trail $\boldsymbol{k}' \xrightarrow{f} \boldsymbol{l}'$ s.t. $\boldsymbol{l} \succeq \boldsymbol{l}'$.*

Based on this lemma, we propose the following proposition.

Proposition 3. *Let $f(\boldsymbol{x}, \boldsymbol{v})$ be a polynomial, where $\boldsymbol{x}$ and $\boldsymbol{v}$ denote the secret and public variables, respectively. For a set of indices $I = \{i_1, i_2, \ldots, i_{|I|}\} \subset \{0, 1, \ldots, m-1\}$, let $\boldsymbol{k}_I$ be an m-dimensional bit vector such that $\boldsymbol{v}^{\boldsymbol{k}_I} = t_I = v_{i_1} v_{i_2} \ldots v_{i_{|I|}}$. Let $\boldsymbol{k}_\Lambda$ be an n-dimensional bit vector. For a given set of indices $I_S \subsetneq I$, if there is no division trail such that $(\boldsymbol{k}_\Lambda \| \boldsymbol{k}_{I_S}) \xrightarrow{f} 1$ for any $\boldsymbol{k}_\Lambda \in \mathbb{F}_2^n$, then there is also no division trail such that $(\boldsymbol{k}_\Lambda \| \boldsymbol{k}_I) \xrightarrow{f} 1$ for any $\boldsymbol{k}_\Lambda \in \mathbb{F}_2^n$.*

Proof. From Lemma 1, if $\boldsymbol{k} \succeq \boldsymbol{k}'$ and there is division trail $\boldsymbol{k} \xrightarrow{f} 1$, then there is also division trail $\boldsymbol{k}' \xrightarrow{f} 1$. Suppose there is a division trail such that $(\boldsymbol{k}_\Lambda^* \| \boldsymbol{k}_I) \xrightarrow{f} 1$ for a fixed $\boldsymbol{k}_\Lambda^* \in \mathbb{F}_2^n$, then there is also a division trail such that $(\boldsymbol{k}_\Lambda^* \| \boldsymbol{k}_{I_S}) \xrightarrow{f} 1$ (since $(\boldsymbol{k}_\Lambda^* \| \boldsymbol{k}_I) \succeq (\boldsymbol{k}_\Lambda^* \| \boldsymbol{k}_{I_S})$), which leads to a contradiction.   □

Denote the superpoly of cube I by $p_S(I)$. From the above Proposition and Proposition 2 in Sect. 2, we know that,

Proposition 4 (Embedded Property for Cube Tester). *For an r-round iterated cipher, if I_S is a subset of cube I, and there is no monomials in $p_S(I_S)$ (i.e., $\deg(p_S(I_S)) = 0$), then there is also no monomials in $p_S(I)$ (i.e., $\deg(p_S(I)) = 0$). Likewise, if $\deg(p_S(I)) \neq 0$, then $\deg(p_S(I_S)) \neq 0$.*

This simple property helps to search cube testers efficiently in the division property based cube attack scenario. In the following, we propose Algorithms 4, 5, and 6 to efficiently reduce the complexity of searching. Algorithm 4 is used to determine the maximum number of distinguishable rounds r_m for a given cube indices

I. Algorithm 4 can be seen as a subfunction of Algorithm 5. In Algorithm 5, we determine the maximum number of distinguishable rounds for a specific cipher, and restrict the search scope. In Algorithm 6, we use the output of Algorithm 5 as input, and returns a set of zero-sum cube testers.

Algorithm 4. Determining the Maximum Number of Distinguishable Rounds for a Given Cube

---

    Input   : Iterated cipher f with R initialzation rounds, cube indices I.
    Output: The maximum number of distinguishable rounds r_m for cube I.

1: $r_h = R$, $r_l = 0$, $r_m = 0$, $r = 0$, $flag = 0$;
2: **while** $r_h - r_l > 1$ **do**
3:    $r = \lfloor (r_h + r_l)/2 \rfloor$
4:    use Algorithm A to evaluate the degree d of the superpoly of cube I for f
       reduced to r rounds;
5:    **if** $d == 0$ **then**
6:       $r_l = r$, $flag = 0$;
7:    **else**
8:       $r_h = r$, $flag = 1$;
9:    **end if**
10: **end while**
11: **if** $flag == 0$ **then**
12:    $r_m = r$;
13: **else**
14:    $r_m = r - 1$;
15: **end if**
16: **return** r_m;

The basic idea of Algorithm 4 is binary search, which can reduce the complexity of searching. In Algorithm 4, we set two variables r_h and r_l to indicate the upper bound and lower bound of the maximum number of distinguishable rounds r_m for a specific cipher. For a cipher f with R initialzation rounds, we first use Algorithm A to evaluate the degree d of the superpoly of cube I for f reduced to $\lfloor (r_h + r_l)/2 \rfloor = \lfloor R/2 \rfloor$ rounds. If $d == 0$, then r_m is at least $\lfloor R/2 \rfloor$, so we set $r_l = r$. Otherwise, we set $r_h = r$. We iteratively repeat this process, so the distance between r_h and r_l can be reduced quickly. In the end, we can determine the value of r_m with at most $\lceil \log_2 R \rceil$ iterations.

In Algorithm 5, we first check all cubes of dimension $m - 1$, where m is the number of public variables. For each $(m - 1)$-dimensional cube I, we use Algorithm 4 to compute its maximum number of distinguishable rounds as cube testers. Among all m cubes, we select those cubes which can lead to the longest (r_{max}-round) cube tester, and store their missing index i of public variables in $\mathbb{S}$. We claim that the elements in the complementary set $\bar{\mathbb{S}} = \{0, 1, \ldots, m-1\} \backslash \mathbb{S}$ of $\mathbb{S}$ are 'necessary' bit indices to obtain an r_{max}-round cube tester. By Proposition 4, if any index which belongs to $\bar{\mathbb{S}}$ is not in cube indices I, then this cube will not lead to an r_{max}-round cube tester. In the following, we call $\bar{\mathbb{S}}$ the *necessary set*,

Algorithm 5. Determining the Maximum Number of Distinguishable Rounds & Restricting the Search Scope

---

Input : Iterated cipher f with m public variables $(v_0, \ldots, v_{m-1})$.
Output: The maximum number of distinguishable rounds r_{max} of cube testers, and the index set $\mathbb{S}$.

1: $r_{max} = 0$, $\mathbb{S} = \emptyset$;
2: **for** $i = 0$; $i < m$ **do**
3:    let cube indices $I_i = \{0, 1, \ldots, m - 1\} \setminus \{i\}$;
4:    use Algorithm 4 to compute the maximum number of distinguishable rounds r_i for cube I_i, and store (I_i, r_i);
5:    **if** $r_{max} < r_i$ **then**
6:       $r_{max} = r_i$;
7:    **end if**
8: **end for**
9: **for** $i = 0$; $i < m$ **do**
10:    **if** $r_i == r_{max}$ **then**
11:       $\mathbb{S} = \mathbb{S} \cup \{i\}$;
12:    **end if**
13: **end for**
14: **return** $r_{max}, \mathbb{S}$;

---

whose elements must be in the cube indices, while $\mathbb{S}$ is called the *sufficient set*, and the elements in $\mathbb{S}$ are called *sufficient indices*.

In Algorithm 6, we first test whether the cube $I = \{0, 1, \ldots, m - 1\} \setminus \mathbb{S}$ will lead to the r_{max}-round cube tester. If not, we gradually increase the dimension of cubes by reducing the value of t where we pick t indices from $\mathbb{S}$, and check whether the cube tester exists or not. After t is fixed (Line 14 in Algorithm 6), there exists at least one cube which will lead to the r_{max}-round cube tester, so Algorithm 6 returns a set of zero-sum cube testers.

5.2   Finding Cubes for Key Recovery Attacks

In this subsection, we give an algorithm (see Algorithm 7) to search a suitable cube which might lead to a key recovery attack for an iterated cipher f reduced to r-rounds.

The basic idea of Algorithm 7 is that a cube which leads to an r-round cube tester might lead to an $(r + 1)$-round cube attack as well, as long as the cube dimension and the complexity to recover the superpoly is reasonable. The complexity to recover the superpoly is $2^{|I|} \times (1 + \sum_{t=1}^{d} |J_t|)$ [23], where I is the cube indices, d is the algebraic degree of the superpoly, and J_t is all possible terms of degree t. Suppose the length of key is n bits. To recover secret information, the superpoly should contain at least 1 key bit. To make the attack meaningful, we also have $2^{|I|} \times (1 + \sum_{t=1}^{d} |J_t|) < 2^n$. Thus we need to restrict $|I| + 1 < n$. In other words, the dimension of cube can not exceed $n - 2$.

Suppose there are m public variables. In Algorithm 7, we first find the sufficient set $\mathbb{S}$ for $(r - 1)$-round cube tester. Then we gradually test cubes of

Algorithm 6. Finding the Zero-Sum Cube Testers

Input : Iterated cipher f with m public variables $(v_0, \ldots, v_{m-1})$, the maximum number of distinguishable rounds r_{max} of cube testers, and the sufficient set $\mathbb{S}$.

Output: A set Res containing the zero-sum cube testers.

1: $Res = \emptyset, \ flag = 0$;
2: $t = |\mathbb{S}|$;
3: **while** $flag == 0$ **do**
4:     **for** every t-tuple $(i_0, i_1, \ldots, i_{t-1})$ of $\mathbb{S}$ **do**
5:         let cube indices $I = \{0, 1, \ldots, m-1\} \setminus \{i_0, i_1, \ldots, i_{t-1}\}$;
6:         use Algorithm A to evaluate the degree d of the superpoly of cube I for f reduced to r_{max} rounds;
7:         **if** $d == 0$ **then**
8:           $flag = 1$;
9:           **break**;
10:        **end if**
11:     **end for**
12:     $t = t - 1$;
13: **end while**
14: $t = t + 1$;
15: **for** every t-tuple $(i_0, i_1, \ldots, i_{t-1})$ of $\mathbb{S}$ **do**
16:     let cube indices $I = \{0, 1, \ldots, m-1\} \setminus \{i_0, i_1, \ldots, i_{t-1}\}$;
17:     use Algorithm A to evaluate the degree d of the superpoly of cube I for f reduced to r_{max} rounds;
18:     **if** $d == 0$ **then**
19:         $Res = Res \cup \{I\}$;
20:     **end if**
21: **end for**
22: **return** Res;

---

dimensions range from $m - 2$ to $m - |\mathbb{S}|$. For $(m-k)$-dimensional cube, there are $\binom{|\mathbb{S}|}{k}$ different choices. If a cube I can lead to the $(r-1)$-round cube tester, then we test whether this cube would lead to the key recovery attack of the r-round cipher. For all tested cubes of dimension $(m-k+1)$, if none of them can lead to the $(r-1)$-round cube tester, then by the embedded property for cube tester, we do not need to test cubes of dimension $(m-k)$, we just quit the while loop and return an emptyset.

5.3 Applications to ACORN

In this part, we apply our methods of finding cubes for cube testers and key recovery attacks to ACORN. Our experiments are based on the MILP model of division property for ACORN, Algorithm A, and Algorithm B given in [23]. We use Gurobi Optimizer [11] with Python interface to solve the MILP problems.

Algorithm 7. Finding Cube for Key Recovery Attack

Input : Iterated cipher f reduced to r-rounds, with m public variables
$\quad\quad\quad (v_0, \ldots, v_{m-1})$ and n secret variables $(x_0, \ldots, x_{n-1})$.
Output: Cube indices I for key recovery attack of f reduced to r-rounds.

1: $r_D = r - 1$, $flag = 1$;
2: similar to Algorithm 5, find the sufficient set $\mathbb{S}$ for f reduced to r_D rounds;
3: **if** $|\mathbb{S}| \leq 1$ **then**
4: $\quad$ **return** $\emptyset$;
5: **end if**
6: $t = 2$;
7: **while** $flag == 1$ **do**
8: $\quad flag = 0$;
9: $\quad$ **for** every t-tuple $(i_0, i_1, \ldots, i_{t-1})$ of $\mathbb{S}$ **do**
10: $\quad\quad$ let cube indices $I = \{0, 1, \ldots, m-1\} \setminus \{i_0, i_1, \ldots, i_{t-1}\}$;
11: $\quad\quad$ use Algorithm A to compute the degree d_D of the superpoly of cube I for f
$\quad\quad\quad$ reduced to r_D rounds;
12: $\quad\quad$ **if** $d_D == 0$ **then**
13: $\quad\quad\quad flag = 1$;
14: $\quad\quad\quad$ use Algorithm A and Algorithm B to compute the degree d and the involved
$\quad\quad\quad\quad$ monomials $J_1, \ldots, J_d$ of the superpoly of cube I for f reduced to
$\quad\quad\quad\quad r$ rounds, where J_k is all possible terms of degree k;
15: $\quad\quad\quad$ **if** $2^{|I|} \times (1 + \sum_{k=1}^{d} |J_k|) < 2^n$ **then**
16: $\quad\quad\quad\quad$ **return** I;
17: $\quad\quad\quad$ **end if**
18: $\quad\quad$ **end if**
19: $\quad$ **end for**
20: $\quad$ **if** $t == |\mathbb{S}|$ **then**
21: $\quad\quad$ **break**;
22: $\quad$ **end if**
23: $\quad t = t + 1$;
24: **end while**
25: **return** $\emptyset$;

Cube Testers of 775-round ACORN. Using Algorithm 6, we find 6 cubes of dimension 127, all of which can lead to the cube tester for 775-round ACORN. The cube indices are as follows.

$$I_1 = \{0, 1, \ldots, 127\} \setminus \{1\}, \quad I_2 = \{0, 1, \ldots, 127\} \setminus \{2\}, \quad I_3 = \{0, 1, \ldots, 127\} \setminus \{11\},$$
$$I_4 = \{0, 1, \ldots, 127\} \setminus \{18\}, I_5 = \{0, 1, \ldots, 127\} \setminus \{26\}, I_6 = \{0, 1, \ldots, 127\} \setminus \{27\}.$$

A Key Recovery Attack of 772-round ACORN. Using Algorithm 7, we find a cube of dimension 123 which can lead to a key recovery attack for 772-round ACORN. The cube indices is as follows,

$$I = \{0, 1, \ldots, 127\} \setminus \{1, 2, 11, 26, 27\}.$$

By running Algorithm A, we know the degree of the superpoly of this cube is 1. Using Algorithm B, we know only the following 21 key bits might exist in the superpoly, key indices := $\{0, 1, 2, 4, 5, 6, 7, 8, 10, 11, 12, 19, 24, 31, 33, 35, 39, 41, 44, 45, 78\}$.

Thus, the complexity to recover the linear superpoly is $2^{123} \times (1 + 21) \approx 2^{127.46}$. In online phase, we can sum over this cube with a complexity of 2^{123}, then we obtain one bit secret information, and the remaining 127 bits can be recovered by brute force.

6   Conclusions

In this paper, we analyzed the security of the authenticated stream cipher ACORN with cube cryptanalysis. Firstly, we gave a new method of finding cube testers. We applied it to ACORN, and obtained the best practical distinguishing attacks. Then we proposed several algorithms to search zero-sum cube testers and suitable cubes for key recovery in the division property based cube attack. We found some new distinguishers for 775-round ACORN. We also found a key recovery attack on ACORN reduced to 772 rounds.

Acknowledgements. We are grateful to the anonymous reviewers of ISC 2019.

A   KSG128(t) and FBK128(t)

Algorithm 8. KSG128(t)

1: $d_1 \leftarrow \max\{d^{(t+12)}, d^{(t+154)}, d^{(t+111)}\}$;
2: $d_2 \leftarrow \max\{d^{(t+61)}, d^{(t+23)}, d^{(t)}\}$;
3: $d_3 \leftarrow \max\{d^{(t+193)}, d^{(t+160)}, d^{(t+154)}\}$;
4: $d_4 \leftarrow \max\{d^{(t+230)}, d^{(t+196)}, d^{(t+193)}\}$;
5: $d \leftarrow \max\{d_1, d^{(t+107)}, d^{(t+235)} + \max\{d_2, d_3\},$
   $d_2 + d_3, \max\{d^{(t+111)}, d^{(t+66)}\} + d_4, d^{(t+66)}\}$;
6: **return** d;

Algorithm 9. FBK128(t)

1: $d_1 \leftarrow \max\{d^{(t+12)}, d^{(t+154)}, d^{(t+111)}\}$;
2: $d_2 \leftarrow \max\{d^{(t+61)}, d^{(t+23)}, d^{(t)}\}$;
3: $d_3 \leftarrow \max\{d^{(t+193)}, d^{(t+160)}, d^{(t+154)}\}$;
4: $d_4 \leftarrow \max\{d^{(t+230)}, d^{(t+196)}, d^{(t+193)}\}$;
5: $d \leftarrow \max\{d^{(t)}, d^{(t+61)}, 0, d^{(t+244)} + \max\{d^{(t+23)}, d^{(t+160)}\}, d^{(t+196)}, d_1,$
   $d^{(t+235)} + \max\{d_2, d_3\}, d^{(t+61)} + d_3, \max\{d^{(t+193)}, d^{(t+154)}\} + d^{(t+23)},$
   $d^{(t)} + d_3, \max\{d^{(t+111)}, d^{(t+66)}\} + d_4\}$;
6: **return** d;

B   Proof of Theorem 1

Proof. It is sufficient to justify Algorithms 8 and 9. By the rule of state update of ACORN, we have

$$
\begin{aligned}
ks_t &= s_{t+12} \oplus (s_{t+154} \oplus s_{t+111} \oplus s_{t+107}) \oplus s_{t+235}(s_{t+61} \oplus s_{t+23} \oplus s_t) \oplus s_{t+235} \\
&\quad (s_{t+193} \oplus s_{t+160} \oplus s_{t+154}) \oplus (s_{t+61} \oplus s_{t+23} \oplus s_t)(s_{t+193} \oplus s_{t+160} \oplus s_{t+154}) \\
&\quad \oplus (s_{t+230} \oplus s_{t+196} \oplus s_{t+193})(s_{t+111} \oplus s_{t+66}) \oplus s_{t+66} \\
&= \underline{(s_{t+12} \oplus s_{t+154} \oplus s_{t+111})} \oplus \underline{s_{t+107}} \oplus \underline{s_{t+235}((s_{t+61} \oplus s_{t+23} \oplus s_t) \oplus (s_{t+193}} \\
&\quad \underline{\oplus s_{t+160} \oplus s_{t+154}))} \oplus \underline{(s_{t+61} \oplus s_{t+23} \oplus s_t)(s_{t+193} \oplus s_{t+160} \oplus s_{t+154})} \\
&\quad \oplus \underline{(s_{t+230} \oplus s_{t+196} \oplus s_{t+193})(s_{t+111} \oplus s_{t+66})} \oplus \underline{s_{t+66}},
\end{aligned}
$$

and

$$
\begin{aligned}
f_t &= s_t \oplus (s_{t+107} \oplus s_{t+66} \oplus s_{t+61}) \oplus 1 \oplus s_{t+244}s_{t+23} \oplus s_{t+244}s_{t+160} \oplus s_{t+23}s_{t+160} \\
&\quad \oplus s_{t+196} \oplus s_{t+12} \oplus (s_{t+154} \oplus s_{t+111} \oplus s_{t+107}) \oplus s_{t+235}(s_{t+61} \oplus s_{t+23} \oplus s_t) \oplus \\
&\quad s_{t+235}(s_{t+193} \oplus s_{t+160} \oplus s_{t+154}) \oplus (s_{t+61} \oplus s_{t+23} \oplus s_t)(s_{t+193} \oplus s_{t+160} \oplus \\
&\quad s_{t+154}) \oplus (s_{t+230} \oplus s_{t+196} \oplus s_{t+193})(s_{t+111} \oplus s_{t+66}) \oplus s_{t+66} \\
&= \underline{s_t} \oplus \underline{s_{t+61}} \oplus \underline{1} \oplus \underline{s_{t+244}(s_{t+23} \oplus s_{t+160})} \oplus \underline{s_{t+196}} \oplus \underline{(s_{t+12} \oplus s_{t+154} \oplus s_{t+111})} \\
&\quad \oplus \underline{s_{t+235}((s_{t+61} \oplus s_{t+23} \oplus s_t) \oplus (s_{t+193} \oplus s_{t+160} \oplus s_{t+154}))} \oplus \underline{s_{t+61}(s_{t+193} \oplus} \\
&\quad \underline{s_{t+160} \oplus s_{t+154})} \oplus \underline{s_{t+23}(s_{t+193} \oplus s_{t+154})} \oplus \underline{s_t(s_{t+193} \oplus s_{t+160} \oplus s_{t+154})} \oplus \\
&\quad \underline{(s_{t+230} \oplus s_{t+196} \oplus s_{t+193})(s_{t+111} \oplus s_{t+66})}.
\end{aligned}
$$

In the above expressions, each underlined term corresponds to an estimated algebraic degree. For example, we have

$$
\begin{aligned}
\deg(s_{t+244}(s_{t+23} \oplus s_{t+160})) &\leq \deg(s_{t+244}) + \max\{\deg(s_{t+23}), \deg(s_{t+160})\} \\
&\leq d^{(t+244)} + \max\{d^{(t+23)}, d^{(t+160)}\}.
\end{aligned}
$$

Hence, the super numeric degree of $s_{t+244}(s_{t+23} \oplus s_{t+160})$ is $d^{(t+244)} + \max\{d^{(t+23)}, d^{(t+160)}\}$, which can be found at line 5 in Algorithm 9. One can check that the degrees of all underlined terms are evaluated. Thus, our algorithms of degree estimation of ACORN are correct.   □

C   Cube Testers of Different Dimensions

Table 2. Some cubes found by the accelerated greedy algorithm. The sizes of these cubes range from 38 to 54.

Cube Size	#Rounds	Cube indexes
38	690	52, 53, 58, 62, 63, 77, 82, 84, 86, 87, 88, 91, 92, 93, 96, 97, 101, 102, 106, 107, 109, 110, 111, 112, 114, 115, 116, 117, 118, 119, 120, 121, 122, 123, 124, 125, 126, 127
42	697	52, 53, 58, 60, 63, 77, 82, 84, 85, 86, 87, 89, 90, 91, 92, 93, 96, 97, 101, 102, 103, 106, 107, 108, 109, 110, 111, 112, 114, 115, 116, 117, 118, 119, 120, 121, 122, 123, 124, 125, 126, 127
46	706	52, 53, 57, 58, 60, 62, 63, 69, 77, 78, 82, 84, 85, 86, 87, 89, 90, 91, 92, 93, 96, 97, 101, 102, 103, 106, 107, 108, 109, 110, 111, 112, 114, 115, 116, 117, 118, 119, 120, 121, 122, 123, 124, 125, 126, 127
50	706	44, 48, 49, 52, 53, 58, 60, 61, 63, 69, 77, 81, 82, 83, 84, 85, 86, 87, 89, 91, 92, 93, 96, 97, 99, 100, 101, 102, 103, 106, 107, 108, 109, 110, 111, 112, 114, 115, 116, 117, 118, 119, 120, 121, 122, 123, 124, 125, 126, 127
54	715	48, 52, 53, 58, 60, 62, 63, 67, 69, 70, 77, 78, 81, 82, 83, 84, 85, 86, 87, 88, 89, 91, 92, 93, 95, 96, 97, 99, 100, 101, 102, 103, 104, 106, 107, 108, 109, 110, 111, 112, 114, 115, 116, 117, 118, 119, 120, 121, 122, 123, 124, 125, 126, 127

D   Embedded Property

The embedded property [18] says that, for different initial division properties k_0 and k_1 s.t. $k_0 \succeq k_1$, there is no need to test k_1, if the output multi-set under k_0 does not have integral property, likewise, it is not necessary to test k_0, if the output multi-set under k_1 has integral property.

References

1. Aumasson, J.P., Dinur, I., Henzen, L., Meier, W., Shamir, A.: Efficient FPGA implementations of high-dimensional cube testers on the stream cipher Grain-128. In: Special-Purpose Hardware for Attacking Cryptographic Systems, SHARCS 2009, p. 147 (2009)
2. Aumasson, J.-P., Dinur, I., Meier, W., Shamir, A.: Cube testers and key recovery attacks on reduced-round MD6 and trivium. In: Dunkelman, O. (ed.) FSE 2009. LNCS, vol. 5665, pp. 1–22. Springer, Heidelberg (2009). https://doi.org/10.1007/978-3-642-03317-9_1
3. Aumasson, J.-P., Henzen, L., Meier, W., Naya-Plasencia, M.: QUARK: a lightweight hash. In: Mangard, S., Standaert, F.-X. (eds.) CHES 2010. LNCS, vol. 6225, pp. 1–15. Springer, Heidelberg (2010). https://doi.org/10.1007/978-3-642-15031-9_1

4. Aumasson, J.P., Henzen, L., Meier, W., Naya-Plasencia, M.: Quark: a lightweight hash. J. Cryptol. **26**(2), 313–339 (2013)
5. Aumasson, J.P., Knellwolf, S., Meier, W.: Heavy quark for secure AEAD. DIAC-Directions in Authenticated Ciphers (2012)
6. Cannière, C.: TRIVIUM: a stream cipher construction inspired by block cipher design principles. In: Katsikas, S.K., López, J., Backes, M., Gritzalis, S., Preneel, B. (eds.) ISC 2006. LNCS, vol. 4176, pp. 171–186. Springer, Heidelberg (2006). https://doi.org/10.1007/11836810_13
7. De Cannière, C., Dunkelman, O., Knežević, M.: KATAN and KTANTAN—a family of small and efficient hardware-oriented block ciphers. In: Clavier, C., Gaj, K. (eds.) CHES 2009. LNCS, vol. 5747, pp. 272–288. Springer, Heidelberg (2009). https://doi.org/10.1007/978-3-642-04138-9_20
8. Dinur, I., Shamir, A.: Cube attacks on tweakable black box polynomials. In: Joux, A. (ed.) EUROCRYPT 2009. LNCS, vol. 5479, pp. 278–299. Springer, Heidelberg (2009). https://doi.org/10.1007/978-3-642-01001-9_16
9. Fouque, P.-A., Vannet, T.: Improving key recovery to 784 and 799 rounds of trivium using optimized cube attacks. In: Moriai, S. (ed.) FSE 2013. LNCS, vol. 8424, pp. 502–517. Springer, Heidelberg (2014). https://doi.org/10.1007/978-3-662-43933-3_26
10. Ghafari, V.A., Hu, H.: A new chosen IV statistical distinguishing framework to attack symmetric ciphers, and its application to ACORN-v3 and Grain-128a. J. Ambient Intell. Hum. Comput. **10**, 1–8 (2018)
11. Gurobi: Gurobi Optimizer. http://www.gurobi.com/
12. Hell, M., Johansson, T., Maximov, A., Meier, W.: The grain family of stream ciphers. In: Robshaw, M., Billet, O. (eds.) New Stream Cipher Designs. LNCS, vol. 4986, pp. 179–190. Springer, Heidelberg (2008). https://doi.org/10.1007/978-3-540-68351-3_14
13. Karlsson, L., Hell, M., Stankovski, P.: Improved greedy nonrandomness detectors for stream ciphers. In: ICISSP, pp. 225–232 (2017)
14. Liu, M.: Degree evaluation of NFSR-based cryptosystems. In: Katz, J., Shacham, H. (eds.) CRYPTO 2017. LNCS, vol. 10403, pp. 227–249. Springer, Cham (2017). https://doi.org/10.1007/978-3-319-63697-9_8
15. Liu, M., Lin, D., Wang, W.: Searching cubes for testing Boolean functions and its application to Trivium. In: ISIT, pp. 496–500. IEEE (2015)
16. Salam, M.I., Bartlett, H., Dawson, E., Pieprzyk, J., Simpson, L., Wong, K.K.-H.: Investigating cube attacks on the authenticated encryption stream cipher ACORN. In: Batten, L., Li, G. (eds.) ATIS 2016. CCIS, vol. 651, pp. 15–26. Springer, Singapore (2016). https://doi.org/10.1007/978-981-10-2741-3_2
17. Stankovski, P.: Greedy distinguishers and nonrandomness detectors. In: Gong, G., Gupta, K.C. (eds.) INDOCRYPT 2010. LNCS, vol. 6498, pp. 210–226. Springer, Heidelberg (2010). https://doi.org/10.1007/978-3-642-17401-8_16
18. Sun, L., Wang, W., Wang, M.: Automatic search of bit-based division property for ARX ciphers and word-based division property. In: Takagi, T., Peyrin, T. (eds.) ASIACRYPT 2017. LNCS, vol. 10624, pp. 128–157. Springer, Cham (2017). https://doi.org/10.1007/978-3-319-70694-8_5
19. Todo, Y.: Structural evaluation by generalized integral property. In: Oswald, E., Fischlin, M. (eds.) EUROCRYPT 2015. LNCS, vol. 9056, pp. 287–314. Springer, Heidelberg (2015). https://doi.org/10.1007/978-3-662-46800-5_12

20. Todo, Y., Isobe, T., Hao, Y., Meier, W.: Cube attacks on non-blackbox polynomials based on division property. In: Katz, J., Shacham, H. (eds.) CRYPTO 2017. LNCS, vol. 10403, pp. 250–279. Springer, Cham (2017). https://doi.org/10.1007/978-3-319-63697-9_9

21. Todo, Y., Isobe, T., Hao, Y., Meier, W.: Cube attacks on non-blackbox polynomials based on division property. IACR Cryptology ePrint Archive 2017, 306 (2017). http://eprint.iacr.org/2017/306

22. Todo, Y., Morii, M.: Bit-based division property and application to SIMON family. In: Peyrin, T. (ed.) FSE 2016. LNCS, vol. 9783, pp. 357–377. Springer, Heidelberg (2016). https://doi.org/10.1007/978-3-662-52993-5_18

23. Wang, Q., Hao, Y., Todo, Y., Li, C., Isobe, T., Meier, W.: Improved division property based cube attacks exploiting algebraic properties of superpoly. IACR Cryptology ePrint Archive 2017, 1063 (2017). http://eprint.iacr.org/2017/1063

24. Wang, Q., Hao, Y., Todo, Y., Li, C., Isobe, T., Meier, W.: Improved division property based cube attacks exploiting algebraic properties of superpoly. In: Shacham, H., Boldyreva, A. (eds.) CRYPTO 2018. LNCS, vol. 10991, pp. 275–305. Springer, Cham (2018). https://doi.org/10.1007/978-3-319-96884-1_10

25. Wu, H.: ACORN: a lightweight authenticated cipher (V3). Candidate for the CAESAR Competition (2016). https://competitions.cr.yp.to/round3/acornv3.pdf

26. Xiang, Z., Zhang, W., Bao, Z., Lin, D.: Applying MILP method to searching integral distinguishers based on division property for 6 lightweight block ciphers. In: Cheon, J.H., Takagi, T. (eds.) ASIACRYPT 2016. LNCS, vol. 10031, pp. 648–678. Springer, Heidelberg (2016). https://doi.org/10.1007/978-3-662-53887-6_24

Crypto I: Secure Computation and Storage

Auditable Compressed Storage

Iraklis Leontiadis[1,2(✉)] and Reza Curtmola[3]

[1] Inpher, New York, USA
iraklis@inpher.io
[2] Inpher, Ecublens, Switzerland
[3] New Jersey Institute of Technology, Newark, NJ, USA
reza.curtmola@njit.edu

Abstract. Outsourcing data to the cloud for personal use is becoming an everyday trend rather than an extreme scenario. The frequent outsourcing of data increases the possible attack window because users do not fully control their personal files. Typically, once there are established secure channels between two endpoints, communication is considered secure. However, in the cloud model the receiver–the cloud–cannot be fully trusted, either because it has been under adversarial control, or because it acts maliciously to increase its revenue by deleting infrequent accessed file blocks. One approach used by current literature to address the aforementioned security concerns is via Remote Data Integrity Checking (RDIC) protocols, whereby a data owner can challenge an untrusted cloud service provider (CSP) to prove faithful storage of its data.

Current RDIC protocols assume that the original data format remains unchanged. However, users may wish to compress their data in order to enjoy less charges. In that case, current RDIC protocols become impractical because, each time compression happens on a file, the user has to run a new RDIC protocol. In this work we initiate the study for *Auditable Compressed Storage* (ACS). After defining the new model we instantiate two protocols for different widely used compression techniques: run length encoding and Huffman encoding. In contrast with conventional RDIC, our protocols allow a user to delegate the compression to the cloud in a provably secure way: The client can verify correctness of compression without having to download the entire uncompressed file and check it against the compressed one.

1 Introduction

The proliferation of information available to individuals, companies and institutions in conjunction with the adoption of the cloud as the *de facto* outsourcing service, drives the delegation of data storage to third party cloud services. As the cloud may misbehave by not storing data at their entire form or tampering with it, new mechanisms for remote data integrity checking (RDIC) are vital. It is almost a decade since the first protocols for RDIC paved the way for secure outsourced storage: *Provable Data Possession* (PDP) [1,2] and *Proofs of Retrievability* (POR) [9,11].

© Springer Nature Switzerland AG 2019
Z. Lin et al. (Eds.): ISC 2019, LNCS 11723, pp. 67–86, 2019.
https://doi.org/10.1007/978-3-030-30215-3_4

Despite the remarkable scientific literature impact of remote data integrity checking protocols (Google Scholar reports $\approx 6,300$ citations for PDP [1,2] and POR [9,11] at the time of this writing), there is a common restrictive setting under which current RDIC protocols operate: A cloud service provider (CSP) can only provide proofs of data possession for the original data file format that was initially uploaded. This model can abstract the procedure of outsourcing storage of archival data in general. However, specific use case scenarios require the transformation of raw data to a different format at the cloud, e.g: *compressing* the original data. As the current RDIC protocols do not allow for such versatility, neither the CSP can take advantage of current *compression* techniques to reduce its storage space, nor the user can demand compression of the original data without skyrocketing egress costs: The need to download the uncompressed file, compress it and upload both the new compressed file and the verification metadata for the RDIC protocol increases the communication cost and the charges subsequently.

Motivating Scenario: We consider an online storage service equipped with backup functionality. At first, the user uploads data with the corresponding verification metadata. The user engages with the CSP in a challenge-response protocol part of the RDIC scheme, in order to attest intact storage of its data. Periodically, at the end of fixed time slots, the CSP compresses the original files into backup files. The purpose is to allow the user retrieve old versions of its data and provide also reliability in case of a catastrophic attack of the current file. The user needs to attest integrity of the compressed file as well, but this is now impossible based on the current verification metadata which is computed over the original uncompressed data.

In this paper, we seek to design and analyze protocols for *Accountable Compressed Storage* (ACS). Such protocols will allow an honest user who uploads its data to an economically motivated CSP—with adversarial behavior—to attest faithful and intact storage of the compressed version of the data. The CSP is motivated to proceed with a wrong compression in order to maximize its profit. For example, the CSP does not compress the data optimally in order to charge for more storage; or, it stores an incorrect (*i.e.*, smaller) compressed version of the data, in order to save on storage. One way to overcome this adversarial behavior is to transfer the task of compression to the user, who then engages in a new RDIC protocol with the CSP based on the compressed data. However, this results in increased communication costs and, ultimately, higher charges for the user: The user has to download the uncompressed file and upload the compressed version thereof. Thus, to accomplish our goal, we need to address two challenges:

Challenge 1: *Reduce communication overhead during compression*: As the original uncompressed data is deleted locally at the user side and rests (ostensibly) at the cloud side, whenever data needs to be compressed, the user can retrieve this data, verify its integrity, compress the data and compute the new verification metadata, and upload the compressed data with the corresponding metadata to the CSP. This solution incurs high communication costs, as the user has to download the entire uncompressed data.

Challenge 2: *Enable tag versatility according to compression without sacrificing security.* To avoid the increased communication costs, a solution could be to delegate the compression to the cloud service provider. However, as the CSP holds only verification metadata for the uncompressed data, the user would not be able to verify the integrity of the compressed data. The CSP could forward the compressed data to the user, who can then compute the new verification metadata, but the user does not hold the original data to check the correctness of compression. Retrieving the original uncompressed data to verify compression correctness would also incur increased communication costs.

For the aforementioned reasons, delegating the compression of the data and the computation of the new verification metadata to the CSP without violating the security goals, renders the design of an *Accountable Compressed Storage* protocol challenging.

Contributions. In this work, we make the following contributions. We first introduce the framework of *Auditable Compressed Storage* (ACS). ACS allows the user to delegate the compression of presumably stored data to an untrusted CSP. The CSP, however, may not store the correctly compressed data in order to maximize its profits. In contrast with previous work on RDIC protocols, ACS expands the model with **(1)** an extra challenge-response protocol whereby the CSP proves to the user not only that it faithfully stores the compressed version of the original data, but also that the compression is correct, and **(2)** a tag transformation procedure, which allows the untrusted CSP to compute the new verification metadata for the compressed data without holding secret key information. Second, we design two protocols for *Auditable Compressed Storage*: ACS-RLE for run-length-encoding compression and ACS-HUFF for Huffman encoding. We analyze their security in a provable way following the novel security model for ACS schemes and we make a thorough efficiency analysis thereof.

2   Background

2.1   Compression Algorithms

Compression reduces the original size of a transmitted file in order to save storage when saving it and also reduces time and costs when transmitting it. Below we elaborate on two popular compression techniques: Run Length Encoding and Dictionary-based Encoding with Huffman Prefix trees.

2.1.1   Run Length Encoding (RLE)

RLE compresses a stream of data F composed of symbols b from some alphabet $b \in S$ with a compact representation thereof. The compact representation consists of tuples of the form $(b : frq)$: where frq is the frequency of each symbol b in file F. RLE exploits the redundancy that occurs over the symbols of the stream in order to compactly encode the stream in a format that can decompress in a lossless manner the compressed stream. Obviously the higher the redundancy of the stream the higher the compression ratio. Redundancy is considered as a consecutive subset of equal symbols inside the original

stream F. As an example, F = "*AAAAAAGGGGTTTTTTTCCCCCEF*" then
F' = $(A : 6, G : 4, T : 7, C : 5, E : 1, F : 1)$.

2.1.2   Dictionary-Based Encoding (DBE)

With DBE, variable length frequent patterns of symbols are replaced with
shorter codewords c from a code alphabet $c \in \varPhi$. The mapping is implemented
using a dictionary $D := (b, \mathsf{frq}, c)$ where c corresponds to a binary codeword for
symbol $b \in S$ and frq is the frequency of b in F. Hereafter, we write D_i to refer
to the ith row and $D_i[b], D_i[\mathsf{frq}], D_i[c]$ to refer to the ith symbol, frequency or
code, correspondingly. With $D_i[b]_k$, in case of a block with multiple symbols we
refer to the k symbol of block b in row i. For the implementation of the dictionary the invariant is: the more frequent symbols or patterns are assigned to
shorter codes. Huffman tree prefix encoding avoids the ambiguity of codewords
which share common prefixes for different symbols by building a prefix binary
tree. Leaves of the tree correspond to the symbols/patterns, left path nodes are
assigned the 0 value and right side nodes the 1 value. To ensure the invariant of
DBE, less frequent items are placed at the lowest level of the tree. The order of
elements in a level does not matter for the correctness of the prefix tree encoding.
Huffman [8] proposed a bottom-up approach to recursively build the tree. The
algorithm starts by picking the two less frequent symbols b_1, b_2. Assign them to
left-0 and right-1 leaf and put them under the parent of the meta symbol $b_1 || b_2$.
Remove from the original data stream b_1, b_2, add $b_1 || b_2$ and recompute the fre-
quencies. The process is repeated until $|F| = 2$, where the algorithm returns the
left and the right subtree of the root node. The codeword of each symbol is the
path to its leaf. The DBE outputs the dictionary D and the encoded stream F'
according to D. For the stream F = "*AAAAAAGGGGTTTTTTTCCCCCEF*"
the Huffman Prefix Tree T is shown in Fig. 1. The encoding dictionary
D is shown in Table 1 and the compressed stream (in binary) is F' =
101010101010011011011011111111111111111000000000001000101. The size of the
compressed stream is $6 \cdot 2 + 4 \cdot 3 + 2 \cdot 7 + 2 \cdot 5 + 2 \cdot 4 = 56$ bits, while the uncompressed stream has size $24 \cdot 8 = 192$ bits, assuming symbols are 8 bits long. Thus
compression ratio equals $3.42 : 1$.

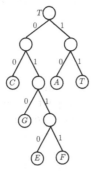

Fig. 1. Huffman Encoding Prefix Tree.

Table 1. Dictionary Huffman encoding

Symbol	Frequency	Codeword
T	7	11
A	6	10
C	5	00
G	4	011
E	1	0100
F	1	0101

2.2   Related Work

2.2.1   Remote Data Integrity

Remote Data Integrity Checking (RDIC) [2,9,11], allows data owners to efficiently audit the integrity of their outsourced data stored at an untrusted CSP. During a Setup phase, the user preprocesses its file F and computes verification metadata σ using some secret key information. User $\mathcal{U}$ then uploads F and σ to the CSP and deletes them from her local storage. $\mathcal{U}$ keeps in storage a small, constant, amount of information related to her secret key. At a later point in time, the data owner challenges the CSP to prove possession of a randomly chosen subset of file blocks. The CSP can only compute a valid proof as long as it stores the challenged file blocks with the corresponding verification metadata. Finally, the owner checks the correctness of the proof and is convinced about the faithful storage of the file F by the CSP when the proof is successfully verified.

2.2.2   Dynamic Remote Data Integrity

RDIC was initially designed to handle static datasets. To handle dynamic data that changes over time (*i.e.*, data blocks are altered, new blocks are inserted and existing blocks are deleted), dynamic RDIC protocols have been proposed.

Dynamic PDP. Ateniese *et al.* [3] introduced the notion of scalable provable data possession. Their solution allows deletions, changes and appends of new data blocks but not insertions. Erway *et al.* [5] addressed the dynamicity of existing PDP schemes with an authenticated skip list, which keeps track of ranking information. The proposed solution enables insertions of blocks as well without the need to recompute the tags of the existing blocks. Wang *et al.* [14] gave a solution for dynamic PDP based on Merkle trees. Other solutions with extra properties (replication and transparency [7], variable block size [6], multiple access to shared data [15]) have been presented in the literature.

Dynamic POR. Stefanov *et al.* [13] proposed *Iris*, a PoR scheme for authentic outsourced storage, which supports dynamic datasets. The client has to locally store erasure-code data to allow edits on the uploaded file. Shi *et al.* [12] used a combination of erasure encoded log buffers with authenticated data structures to achieve dynamicity of data for a proof of retrievability protocol. In contrast with previous solutions Cast *et al.* [4] employed an oblivious RAM scheme to support dynamic data and Etemad *et al.* [10] presented generic constructions for DPoR schemes.

In contrast with all dynamic RDIC protocols, whereby some blocks of data are inserted, deleted, or changed, our *auditable compressed storage* framework requires a different approach. The compressed file is treated as a completely new file consisting of different blocks. Thus, employing a dynamic RDIC scheme is not suitable, because the blocks of the compressed file are different compared to those in the original file.

3   Model and Security Guarantees

In this section, we describe the model for an *Auditable Compressed Storage* (ACS) system. First, we set up the environmental setting with the functional requirements of an ACS. Next, we analyze the adversarial model and we present the sufficient security guarantees for an ACS scheme.

3.1   System Model

A user $\mathcal{U}$ uploads a file F to an untrusted cloud service provider CSP. The file F consists of n blocks. Each file block consists of 8-bit ω symbols, and is thus $w = 8 \cdot \omega$ bits long. As the CSP may act maliciously, in order to guarantee storage integrity for the file F, $\mathcal{U}$ uploads verification metadata for each block, computed with a secret key. This metadata allows $\mathcal{U}$ to get guarantees about faithful storage by running an RDIC protocol such as PDP [2], POR [9,11].

At a later point in time, the CSP compresses F into F' using a compression algorithm $(, = \mathsf{Encode}, \mathsf{Decode})$. $\mathcal{U}$ needs to check the integrity of the compressed file F' and to get assurances that **(1)** $\mathsf{Decode}(\mathsf{Encode}(\mathsf{F}')) = \mathsf{F}$, where F' is the correct compression encoding of the original uploaded file F, and **(2)** the compressed file F' is faithfully stored. ACS introduces a Compress phase whereby the CSP compresses F to F' and transforms the tags of the uncompressed data blocks to correspond to the compressed blocks. $\mathcal{U}$ is also exposed to the traditional RDIC algorithms: $\mathsf{TagFile}, \mathsf{Challenge}_\mathsf{F}, \mathsf{Prove}, \mathsf{Verify}$, whereby $\mathcal{U}$ computes authentication tags on top of each file block $b_1, \ldots, b_n$ and later on during a challenge response protocol, $\mathcal{U}$ challenges the CSP on a random subset of blocks. The CSP as long as it faithfully stored the blocks of F proves to $\mathcal{U}$ that it stores F and $\mathcal{U}$ verifies the proof. In contrast with a traditional RDIC protocol, in ACS during the $\mathsf{Challenge}_{\mathsf{F}'}$ phase the CSP demonstrates that **(1)** F' is the correct compression encoding version of F and **(2)** it faithfully stores F' in its entire form. We can describe an ACS system in 4 phases (also illustrated in Fig. 2):

- Setup: The system parameters params are initialized and user $\mathcal{U}$ chooses secret key information sk. $\mathcal{U}$ according to params splits the file in n blocks: $\mathsf{F} = b_1, b_2, b_3, \ldots, b_n$ and computes auxiliary information aux related to the compression of the file. Some of aux may be stored at the user (aux_U), whereas some of it may be sent to the CSP (aux_C). For each block b_i, it calls TagFile, which computes an authentication tag σ_i. Finally, $\mathcal{U}$ uploads F, $\{\sigma_i\}_{i=1}^n$, and aux_C to the CSP.
- Compress: The CSP compresses F to F' using the Encode algorithm. Note that F' has n' blocks, where n' may normally be different than n. The CSP then transforms the tags $\sigma_1, \ldots, \sigma_n$ of the uncompressed file blocks into the ones for the compressed version of the file, $S_1, \ldots, S_{n'}$.
- $\mathsf{Challenge}_{\mathsf{F}'}$: The user engages in a challenge-response protocol to verify that F' is a correct compression of F and to attest the faithful storage of F' at the CSP.
- $\mathsf{Challenge}_\mathsf{F}$: The user engages in a challenge-response protocol to attest the faithful storage of F at the CSP.

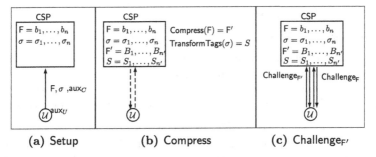

(a) Setup   (b) Compress   (c) Challenge$_{F'}$

Fig. 2. ACS model. Interrupted lines during the Compress phase denote that the user may not need to interact with the CSP.

3.2 Adversarial Model

We assume an adversary $\mathcal{A}$ controlling the CSP to be a rational player in the protocol. That is, it will deviate from the protocol as long as it has some economic incentive to proceed in a malicious behavior. An ACS adversary $\mathcal{A}$ can misbehave as follows:

AM1 (Incorrect compression): The CSP may claim storage of a file F'', which does not correspond to the compressed version F' of F. The CSP acting rationally has the economical motivation to compute and store F'' such that the size of F'' is either smaller (to save on storage costs) or larger (to charge the user for more storage) than the size of F'. A rational CSP can potentially misbehave in the following two ways when compressing or transforming the tags: **(AT1)** reduce the frequency of a block (cf. Fig. 3), or **(AT2)** increase the frequency of a block (cf. Fig. 4).

AM2 (Compression Integrity): As in traditional RDIC protocols, the CSP may discard rarely accessed blocks of the compressed file F' or it may try to hide data loss incidents to maintain its reputation.

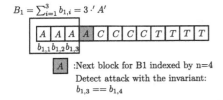

Fig. 3. Remove block attack.

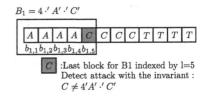

Fig. 4. Add block attack.

3.3   Security Guarantees

We seek to design an ACS system with the following security guarantees:

SG1 (Proof of correct compression): Through an interactive proof the user can check the correctness of the compression F'.

SG2 (Remote compressed data integrity): The user can detect with high probability if the CSP stores a large fraction of blocks of the compressed file F'.

As ACS extends the current RDIC protocols with the compression functionality, we extend the standard RDIC security game in order to capture the proof of correct compression property. We model the security of an ACS scheme through the $\mathbf{G}_{\mathcal{A}}^{ACS}$ game (cf. Fig. 5), in which a challenger $\mathcal{C}$ interacts with the adversary $\mathcal{A}$ with the following interface:

- Setup: $\mathcal{C}$ first runs the $\mathcal{O}^{Setup}$ which forwards the public parameters to $\mathcal{A}$.
- TagFile: $\mathcal{A}$ asks for tags of its choice based on file blocks and gets the correct authentication tags from the $\mathcal{O}^{TagFile}$ oracle. It gets the tags $\sigma_1, \ldots, \sigma_n$ for file blocks $b_1, \ldots, b_n$. Finally, it stores $b_1, \ldots, b_n$ and tags $\sigma_1, \ldots, \sigma_n$.
- Compress: After $\mathcal{A}$ having asked for the tags of all file blocks, $\mathcal{C}$ asks $\mathcal{A}$ to compress the file F. $\mathcal{C}$ also transforms the old tags to new ones $S_1 \ldots S_{n'}$ corresponding to the compressed file. That is an interactive process as in the real protocol the CSP interacts with $\mathcal{U}$ to transform the tags in case of the dictionary based encoding, while in the run-length-encoding protocol there is no interaction. At the end of the interaction $\mathcal{C}$ outputs a bit $b = 0, 1$. It sets the bit to 0 if $\mathcal{A}$ did not compute the correct compression metadata and 1 otherwise.
- Challenge$_{F'}$: $\mathcal{C}$ generates a challenge Q' for the compressed file F' and asks $\mathcal{A}$ to provide a proof for the possession of blocks in the challenge.
- Challenge$_F$: $\mathcal{C}$ generates a challenge Q for the uncompressed file F and asks $\mathcal{A}$ to provide a proof for the possession of blocks in the challenge.

$\mathbf{G}_{\mathcal{A}}^{ACS}$:

$pub = F, n \leftarrow_\$ \mathcal{A}^{\mathcal{O}^{Setup}()}$

$\sigma_i \leftarrow_\$ \mathcal{A}^{\mathcal{O}^{TagFile}(b_i)}$

$F' = (B_1, \ldots, B_{n'}), (S_1 \ldots S'_n) \leftarrow_\$ \mathcal{A}^{\mathcal{O}^{Compress}(F)} \leftrightarrow \mathcal{C}$

$\beta_1 = 0/1 \leftarrow \mathcal{C}$

$\beta_2 = 0/1 \leftarrow \text{Challenge}_F(CSP : [F, \sigma_1, \ldots, \sigma_n], \mathcal{C} : [sk, a])$

$\beta_3 = 0/1 \leftarrow \text{Challenge}_{F'}(CSP : [F', S_1, \ldots, S_n], \mathcal{C} : [sk, a])$

if $\beta_1 == 1 \wedge \beta_2 == 1 \wedge \beta_3 == 1$ **return 1 else return 0**

Fig. 5. $\mathbf{G}_{\mathcal{A}}^{ACS}$ game

We say that $\mathcal{A}$ wins the $\mathbf{G}_{\mathcal{A}}^{ACS}$ game if $\mathbf{G}_{\mathcal{A}}^{ACS}$ outputs 1: $\mathbf{G}_{\mathcal{A}}^{ACS} \Rightarrow 1$. The advantage of $\mathcal{A}$ in winning the game is: $\mathbf{Adv}_{ACS}(\mathcal{A}) = \Pr[\mathbf{G}_{\mathcal{A}}^{ACS} \Rightarrow 1]$.

Definition 1. *A scheme* S = (ACS.Setup, ACS.Compress, ACS.Challenge$_{F'}$, ACS.Challenge$_F$) *securely instantiates* ACS *if whenever* $\mathcal{A}$ *wins the* $\mathbf{G}_{\mathcal{A}}^{ACS}$ *game with high probability, then an extractor* $\mathcal{E}$ *can interact with* $\mathcal{A}$ *during the* Challenge$_F$ *and* Challenge$_{F'}$ *algorithms to construct the uncompressed and compressed file respectively.*

Intuitively our security definition demonstrates the concept of knowledge extractor as it has already been presented in the RDIC literature [2,9,11], whereby whenever $\mathcal{A}$ succeeds in the game, then $\mathcal{E}$ can extract the files F, F' or putting another way: $\mathcal{A}$ succeeds in the game $\mathbf{G}_{\mathcal{A}}^{ACS}$ whenever it successfully stores F, compresses it and stores the compressed version F'. The difference with the previous games for remote data integrity protocols is the proof for possession of both the uncompressed and compressed files F, F' (check bits β_2 and β_3 in the $\mathbf{G}_{\mathcal{A}}^{ACS}$ game) and also the proof of correct compression, which is embed in the game through the interaction with the challenger $\mathcal{C}$ (check bit β_1), which represents a user $\mathcal{U}$ in the system.

4   Auditable Compressed Storage

In this section, we present our two core contributions. A protocol for auditable compressed storage for run-length encoding dubbed ACS-RLE, and second a protocol for auditable compressed storage tailored for dictionary-based Huffman encoding: ACS-HUFF. Before delving into the details of the two protocols, we highlight the challenges and sketch a first attempt with its shortcomings.

Strawman Solution 1. During the Compress phase, the user downloads the uncompressed file, compresses it, computes the authentication tags on the compressed files and finally uploads the tags and the compressed data blocks to the CSP. Despite its simplicity, this approach is fraught with increased costs. The user is burdened with increased communication costs as it has to download the uncompressed file and then upload the compressed one with the new tags. Moreover, the compression of the file and the computation of the tags on the compressed blocks is performed entirely by the user, thus amplifying its computation costs.

Strawman Solution 2. The user may try to reduce its computation costs by delegating to the CSP the compression of the file. The CSP then sends the compressed file to the user and the user computes the new tags. However, this approach raises two concerns:

1. The user still has to download compressed file data blocks, but now the total communication overhead will be less than downloading the entire uncompressed file.
2. Most importantly the user has no mean of verifying the correctness of compression as it has deleted the uncompressed file. To circumvent that, the user has to store some metadata in order to check correctness of compression e.g: sign or tag with an authentication mechanism the original file and keep the signatures/tags to verify it when it uncompresses the compressed file. However, that approach incurs extra computation and storage costs.

$(a, \mathsf{sk}, b_1, \ldots, b_n, \sigma_1, \ldots, \sigma_n, \mathsf{aux}) \leftarrow \mathsf{RLE.Setup}(1^\lambda)$:

1 :   User runs $\mathsf{sk} \leftarrow \mathsf{KeyGen}(1^\lambda)$ to generate uniformly random key sk.

2 :   User runs $((\sigma_1, \ldots, \sigma_n), a) \leftarrow \mathsf{RLE.TagFile}(\mathsf{sk}, \mathsf{F})$

3 :   User runs $\mathsf{RLE.Aux}$ to generate the aux auxiliary data.

4 :   User uploads $b_1, \ldots, b_n$ and $\sigma_1, \ldots, \sigma_n$, to the CSP and stores $a, \mathsf{sk}, \mathsf{aux}$.

5 :   **return** $(a, \mathsf{sk}, b_1, \ldots, b_n, \sigma_1, \ldots, \sigma_n, \mathsf{aux})$

$(\mathsf{F}', S_1, \ldots, S_{n'}) \leftarrow \mathsf{RLE.Compress}(\mathsf{F})$:

1 :   CSP runs $\mathsf{F}' \leftarrow \mathsf{RLE}(\mathsf{F})$ to generate the compressed version
$\mathsf{F}' = B_1, \ldots, B_{n'}$ of F.

2 :   CSP transforms $\sigma_1, \ldots, \sigma_n$ to $S_1, \ldots, S_{n'}$, for the compressed blocks
$B_1, \ldots, B_{n'}$ by running $S_1, \ldots, S_{n'} \leftarrow \mathsf{RLE.TransformTags}(B_1, \ldots, B_{n'}, \sigma_1, \ldots, \sigma_n)$.

3 :   CSP stores $B_1, \ldots, B_{n'}, S_1, \ldots, S_{n'}$

4 :   **return** $(\mathsf{F}', S_1, \ldots, S_{n'})$

$(1, 0) \leftarrow \mathsf{RLE.Challenge}_{\mathsf{F}'}(\mathsf{CSP} : [\mathsf{F}', S_1, \ldots, S_{n'}, \sigma_1, \ldots, \sigma_n], \mathcal{U} : [\mathsf{sk}, a])$:

1 :   User generates the challenge $Q = (i, r_i)$ where $i \in [n']$ and $r_i \in \mathbb{Z}_p$

2 :   CSP runs $\mathsf{RLE.Prove}(\mathsf{F}', S_1, \ldots, S_{n'}, \sigma_1, \ldots, \sigma_n, Q)$ to generate the
proof $= (\{\mu_i\}_{i \in Q}, S, \mathsf{pcc})$.

3 :   User runs $\mathsf{RLE.Verify}(\mathsf{proof}, \mathsf{sk}, Q, a)$ to verify correct compression
of the compressed blocks.

4 :   **if** $\mathsf{RLE.Verify}(\mathsf{proof}, \mathsf{sk}, Q, a) == 1$ **return** 1 **else return** 0

$(1, 0) \leftarrow \mathsf{RLE.Challenge}_{\mathsf{F}}(\mathsf{CSP} : [\mathsf{F}, \sigma_1, \ldots, \sigma_n], \mathcal{U} : [\mathsf{sk}, a])$:

1 :   User generates the challenge $Q = (i, r_i)$ where $i \in [n]$ and $r_i \in \mathbb{Z}_p$

2 :   CSP runs $\mathsf{CPOR.Prove}(\mathsf{F}, \sigma_1, \ldots, \sigma_n, Q)$ to generate the
proof $= (\{\mu_i\}_{i \in Q}, S, \mathsf{pcc})$

3 :   User runs $\mathsf{CPOR.Verify}(\mathsf{proof}, \mathsf{sk}, Q, a)$ to verify correct data possession
of the compressed blocks

4 :   **if** $\mathsf{CPOR.Verify}(\mathsf{proof}, \mathsf{sk}, Q, a) == 1$ **return** 1 **else return** 0

Fig. 6. ACS-RLE scheme.

4.1   ACS-RLE Scheme

We assume f is a secure pseudorandom function (PRF), indexed by a key $\mathsf{sk} \xleftarrow{\$} \mathcal{K}$.
Let $f : \{0, 1\}^* \times \mathcal{K} \rightarrow \mathbb{Z}_p$, where p is a prime. All operations are computed
modulo p, unless otherwise noted. The ACS-RLE scheme is described in Fig. 6,

supported by algorithms in Figs. 7 and 8. In the RLE.Challenge$_F$ phase, we use the CPOR.Prove and CPOR.Verify algorithms from [11].

$sk \leftarrow \mathsf{KeyGen}(1^\lambda)$:

1 :　　$sk \xleftarrow{\$} \{0,1\}^\lambda$

2 :　　**return** sk

$\mathsf{FRQ} \leftarrow \mathsf{RLE.Aux}(b_1, \ldots, b_n)$:

1 :　　Compute the frequencies $\mathsf{FRQ} = \{e_i - s_i + 1 = \mathsf{frq}_i\}$ of consecutive blocks

2 :　　**return** $MI_i = (s_i, e_i), 1 \leq i \leq n' = \sum \mathsf{frq}_i$

$(\{\sigma_i\}_{i=1}^n, a) \leftarrow \mathsf{RLE.TagFile}(sk, F)$:

1 :　　Initialize ω, n, w.

2 :　　User selects uniformly at random $a \in \mathbb{Z}_p$.

3 :　　User splits F in n blocks $b_1, \ldots b_n$ of size $w = 8 \cdot \omega$　bits each.

4 :　　**for** $(i = 1, i \leq n, i++)$ **do**

5 :　　　$\sigma_i = f_{sk}(i) + \sum_{k=1}^{\omega} ab_{ik}$ // Compute the verification tag

6 :　　**return** $\{\sigma_i\}_{i=1}^n, a$

$(S_1, \ldots, S_{n'}) \leftarrow \mathsf{RLE.TransformTags}(B_1, \ldots, B_{n'}, \sigma_1, \ldots, \sigma_n)$:

　　Compute the new tags $S_1, \ldots, S_{n'}$ by aggregating identical σ_i.

1 :　　**for** $(i = 1, i \leq n', i++)$ **do**

2 :　　　**parse** $B_i = \mathsf{frq}_i \cdot' b_i'$

3 :　　　$S_i = \sum_{j=i}^{\mathsf{frq}_i + i} \sigma_j$

4 :　　**return** $(S_1, \ldots, S_{n'})$

Fig. 7. ACS-RLE algorithms.

Intuitively, we mitigate (**AT1**) by requiring the CSP to provide extra information about the next uncompressed block after the currently challenged one during the challenge response phase of RLE.Challenge$_{F'}$. Namely, the user $\mathcal{U}$ can extract from the tag S_i', which encodes identical blocks, the encoded block and check whether it equals the extracted block from the next indexed uncompressed tag (lines 3–5, algorithm RLE.Verify, Fig. 8). If the check is correct, $\mathcal{U}$ infers that the CSP conducted an **AT1** type of attack. For instance, in Fig. 3, a malicious CSP during RLE.Compress(F), computed a wrong block $B_1 = \sum_{i=1}^3 b_{1,i} = 3 \cdot A$. It transforms the tags that correspond to $b_{1,1}, b_{1,2}, b_{1,3}$ into a singleton tag

$(\{\mu_i\}_{i\in Q}, S, \mathsf{pcc}) \leftarrow \mathsf{RLE.Prove}(F', S_1, \ldots, S_{n'}, \sigma_1, \ldots, \sigma_n, B_i, \ldots, B'_n, Q)$:

1 : **foreach** $(i, r_i) \in Q$ **do** $\mu_i = \sum_{j=1}^{w} r_i B_{ij}$

2 : $S = \sum_{(i,r_i)\in Q} r_i S_i$

Add the checkpoints for each $(i, r_i) \in Q$:

3 : **foreach** $i \in Q$ **do**

map i to i', i' is the starting position of the compressed block in the file

4 : $i' \in [1 \ldots n] \leftarrow \mathsf{FindRange}(i \in [1 \ldots n'])$

// E.g: F=$'$rrrrree$'$, then $6 \leftarrow \mathsf{FindRange}(2)$

5 : $\mathsf{pcc}{+} = \sigma_{i'+\mathsf{frq}_i - 1}, \sigma_{i'+\mathsf{frq}_i}, i', \mathsf{frq}_i$

6 : **return** proof $= (\{\mu_i\}_{i\in Q}, S, \mathsf{pcc})$

$(0, 1) \leftarrow \mathsf{RLE.Verify}(\text{proof}, \mathsf{sk}, Q, a)$:

1 : **parse** pcc as $(\sigma_l, \sigma_n, i', \mathsf{frq}_i), l = i' + \mathsf{frq}_i - 1, w = i' + \mathsf{frq}_i \forall i \in Q$

Check whether the CSP accumulated the correct range for each symbol:

2 : **foreach** $(i, r_i) \in Q$ **do**

Check whether the CSP reduced the frequency:

3 : $s = (\sigma_w - f_{\mathsf{sk}}(w))/\sum_{j=1}^{w} a$ // Extract the block from the uncompressed

block tag

4 : $s' = \mu_{i+1}/\mathsf{frq}_i r_i \sum_{j=1}^{w} a$ // Extract the block from the compressed block tag

5 :   **if** $s == s'$ **then return** 0

Check whether the CSP increased the frequency:

6 : $s = (\sigma_l - f_{\mathsf{sk}}(l))/\sum_{j=1}^{w} a$ // Extract the block from the uncompressed

block tag

7 : $s' = \mu_i/\mathsf{frq}_i r_i \sum_{j=1}^{w} a$ // Extract the block from the compressed block tag

8 :   **if** $s! = s'$ **then return** 0

Check correctness of mapping ranges to indexes using the MI dictionary

9 : **foreach** $i \in Q$ **if** $MI_i \neq (i', \mathsf{frq}_i - i = 1)$**return** 0

Check correctness of data possession proof on the compressed blocks:

10 : **if** $S \neq \sum_{i, r_i \in Q} (r_i f_{\mathsf{sk}}(i) + \sum_{j=1}^{w} a\mu_i)$ **then return** 0

11 : **return** 1

Fig. 8. ACS-RLE algorithms for the challenge protocol of the compressed blocks.

$S = \sigma_1 + \sigma_2 + \sigma_3$, excluding the block $b_{1,4}$, which should have been included in the transformation. However, the user during the challenge response protocol can detect the malicious behavior of the CSP by demanding the tag σ_4 and checking whether the encoded symbol 'A' equals the symbol of the tag returned by the CSP for the compressed block B_1. Notice that the tags σ_i for the uncompressed blocks are unforgeable and incorporate the block index. To mitigate **(AT2)**, a similar detection mechanism is adopted: By obtaining next block tag, $\mathcal{U}$ can check whether the last symbol of the block does not match with the block of the challenged block (lines 6–8, algorithm RLE.Verify, Fig. 8). In the case of a mismatch, $\mathcal{U}$ detects a malicious behavior by the CSP. Those two invariant checks are incorporated in the RLE.Challenge$_{F'}$ phase which follows a challenge-response approach of probabilistically checking intact storage of the compressed file F'.

4.2 ACS-HUFF Scheme

Our ACS-HUFF scheme is based on Huffman encoding to create a dictionary, which assigns shorter codes to blocks. As the mapping translates symbols-blocks of the uncompressed file to the new ones with different codes, the aggregate technique of uncompressed tags to compute the new tags will be inconsistent with the new codes of the blocks-symbols. A naive approach would be the user to compute the new tags on the compressed blocks based on the compressed file and the dictionary the cloud provides to her. However, that increases the communication costs of the protocol overall. In our approach, the user stores a small state during the Setup phase, which allows her to validate the correctness of the Huffman dictionary. The user then computes some auxiliary information for each new tag which is used by the CSP to convert the tags of uncompressed file to the compressed ones.

The details of the ACS-HUFF scheme are given in Figs. 9 and 10. We use the same conventions with the ACS-RLE scheme regarding the PRF f and the encoding of each block to a number in $\mathbb{Z}_p$. All operations are performed modulo p. For the DBE.Challenge$_F$ and DBE.Challenge$_{F'}$ phases, we use the CPOR.Prove and CPOR.Verify algorithms from [11].

4.3 Differences Between ACS-RLE and ACS-HUFF

Notice that ACS-RLE and ACS-HUFF have a different algorithmic design, which nonetheless follows our unified model for ACS as presented in Sect. 3. Namely, due to the nature of the RLE compression technique and the transformation of the tags by the CSP, the Compress algorithm is non-interactive and does not demonstrate any proof of compression correctness. The proof of compression correctness is embedded in the Challenge$_{F'}$ phase, whereby $\mathcal{U}$ is convinced not only about the faithful storage of F', but also about the valid compression of F'. This is possible because RLE encoding does not change the codes of the new compressed blocks. We changed the challenge-response protocol of CPOR in order to establish the following: correct proof of faithful storage of F' demonstrates

---

$(a, \mathsf{sk}, b_1, \ldots, b_n, \sigma_1, \ldots, \sigma_n, \mathsf{aux}) \leftarrow \mathsf{DBE.Setup}(1^\lambda)$:

1 :   User runs $\mathsf{sk} \leftarrow \mathsf{KeyGen}(1^\lambda)$ to generate uniformly random key sk.

2 :   User runs $((\sigma_1, \ldots, \sigma_n), a) \leftarrow \mathsf{DBE.TagFile}(\mathsf{sk}, \mathsf{F})$

3 :   User runs $\mathsf{DBE.Aux}$ to generate the aux auxiliary data

4 :   User uploads data $b_1, \ldots, b_n$ and authentication tags $\sigma_1, \ldots, \sigma_n$, to the CSP

and stores $a, \mathsf{sk}, \mathsf{aux}$.

5 :   **return** $(a, \mathsf{sk}, b_1, \ldots, b_n, \sigma_1, \ldots, \sigma_n, \mathsf{aux})$

$(\mathsf{F}', S_1, \ldots, S_n) \leftarrow \mathsf{DBE.Compress}(\mathsf{F})$:

1 :   CSP runs $D \leftarrow \mathsf{HuffmanTree}(\mathsf{F})$ and sends D to $\mathcal{U}$

2 : $\mathcal{U}$ verifies if D is correct by calling $\mathsf{Check}(\mathsf{aux}, D)$

3 :   **if** $\mathsf{Check}(\mathsf{aux}, D) == 0$ **then return** ;

4 :   **else** $\mathcal{U}$ runs $T \leftarrow \mathsf{DBE.Metatag}(D)$

5 :   CSP runs $\mathsf{F}' \leftarrow \mathsf{DBE}(\mathsf{F}, D)$ to generate the compressed version
$\mathsf{F}' = B_1, \ldots, B_n$

6 :   CSP transforms $\sigma_1, \ldots, \sigma_n$ to $S_1, \ldots, S_n$, for the compressed blocks
$B_1, \ldots, B_n$ by running $S_1, \ldots, S_n \leftarrow \mathsf{TransformTags}(\sigma_1, \ldots, \sigma_n, T)$.

7 :   CSP stores $B_1, \ldots, B_n, S_1, \ldots, S_n$

$(1, 0) \leftarrow \mathsf{DBE.Challenge}_{\mathsf{F}'}(\mathsf{CSP} : [\mathsf{F}', S_1, \ldots, S_{n'}], \mathcal{U} : [\mathsf{sk}, a])$:

1 :   User generates the challenge $Q = (i, r_i)$ where $i \in [n], r_i \xleftarrow{\$} \mathbb{Z}_p, |Q| = m \leq n$.

2 :   CSP runs $\mathsf{CPOR.Prove}(\mathsf{F}', S_1, \ldots, S_n, Q)$ to generate the $\mathsf{proof} = (\{\mu_i\}_{i \in Q}, S)$.

3 :   User runs $\mathsf{CPOR.Verify}(\mathsf{proof}, \mathsf{sk}, Q, a)$ to verify correct compression

---

$(1, 0) \leftarrow \mathsf{DBE.Challenge}_{\mathsf{F}}(\mathsf{CSP} : [\mathsf{F}, \sigma_1, \ldots, \sigma_n], \mathcal{U} : [\mathsf{sk}, a])$:

1 :   User generates the challenge $Q = (i, r_i)$ where $i \in [n], r_i \xleftarrow{\$} \mathbb{Z}_p, |Q| = m \leq n$.

2 :   CSP runs $\mathsf{CPOR.Prove}(\mathsf{F}, \sigma_1, \ldots, \sigma_n, Q)$ to generate the $\mathsf{proof} = (\{\mu_i\}_{i \in Q}, S)$.

3 :   User runs $\mathsf{CPOR.Verify}(\mathsf{proof}, \mathsf{sk}, Q, a)$ to verify data possession

Fig. 9. ACS-HUFF scheme.

correctness during compression. With the ACS-HUFF this is not doable and a different treatment was needed. Basically, the ACS-HUFF.Compress is interactive and deviates from ACS-RLE.Compress because (1) $\mathcal{U}$ checks the correctness of intermediate compression information: the Huffman dictionary and (2) $\mathcal{U}$ provides the metatags to CSP in order the latter to compute the new tags on F'. Moreover since the proof of correct compression is established at this step, in the ACS-HUFF.Challenge$_{\mathsf{F}'}$ phase there is no need to demonstrate a proof of correct compression and a standard CPOR challenge-response protocol is called for the proof of intact storage of F'.

$\{\sigma_i\}_{i=1}^n \leftarrow$ DBE.TagFile(sk, F):

1 :   Initialize ω, n, w.

2 :   User selects uniformly at random $a = \{a_k\}, k \in [1 \dots \omega] \in \mathbb{Z}_p$.

3 :   User splits F in n blocks $b_1, \dots b_n$ of size $w = 8 \cdot \omega$ bits each.

4 :   **for** $(i = 1, i \leq n, i++)$ **do**

5 : $\sigma_i = f_{\mathsf{sk}}(i) + \sum_{k=1}^{\omega} a_k b_{ik}$ // Compute the verification tag

6 :   **return** $\{\sigma_i\}_{i=1}^n, a$

FRQ $\leftarrow$ DBE.Aux$(b_1, \dots, b_n)$:

1 :   Compute the frequencies FRQ $= \{\mathsf{frq}_i\} \forall s_i \in$ F

2 :   **return** FRQ

$(1, 0) \leftarrow$ DBE.Check(aux, D):

1 :   **parse** aux as FRQ$_i$

2 :   **for** $i = \{1, \dots, |D|\}$

3 :   if $D_i[\mathsf{frq}] \stackrel{?}{=}$ FRQ$_i$

$(T) \leftarrow$ DBE.Metatag(D):

1 : $\mathcal{U}$ selects uniformly at random $a' \in \mathbb{Z}_p$.

2 : $\mathcal{U}$ **for** $i = \{1, \dots, |D|\}$ computes $t_i = \sum_{k=1}^{\omega} a' D_i[b]_k - \sum_{k=1}^{\omega} a D_i[s]_k$

and sends $T = \{t_i\}_{i=1}^{|D|}$

3 :   **return** T

$(S_1, \dots, S_n) \leftarrow$ DBE.TransformTags$(\sigma_1, \dots, \sigma_n, T)$:

1 :   **parse** $T = \{t_i\}_{i=1}^{|D|}$

2 :   **for** $(i = 1, i \leq n, i++)$ **do**

3 :   CSP computes $S_i = \sigma_i + t_i$

4 :   **return** $(S_1, \dots, S_{n'})$

Fig. 10. ACS-HUFF algorithms.

5   Analysis

In this section we analyze both ACS-RLE and ACS-HUFF protocols. We start with the security analysis before exploring the efficiency.

5.1 Security

Theorem 1. ACS-RLE *is a secure accountable compressed storage system according to Definition 1 against a PPT adversary $\mathcal{A}$ and a polynomial extractor $\mathcal{E}$, as long as f is a secure* PRF.

Proof. Throughout, n' is the number of blocks of the compressed file F', m is the size of the challenge Q, and s is the number of blocks $\mathcal{A}$ stores. $\mathsf{Adv}_f(\mathcal{B})$ is a negligible quantity on the success probability of probabilistic polynomial time adversary $\mathcal{B}$ against the security of the underlying PRF f: fixed on a key, the output of the PRF should be indistinguishable from a truly random function.

Learning phase Adversary $\mathcal{A}$ plays the $\mathbf{G}_{\mathcal{A}}^{\mathsf{ACS}}$ game with a challenger $\mathcal{C}$. $\mathcal{C}$ first calls the $\mathcal{O}^{\mathsf{Setup}}$ oracle which returns $\mathsf{pk} = n, \omega, w$ and sk. $\mathcal{C}$ forwards the public key information pk to $\mathcal{A}$. $\mathcal{A}$ chooses a file F and asks the tags σ_i for each block b_i from $\mathcal{C}$. $\mathcal{A}$ forwards tuples (i, b_i) to $\mathcal{C}$, who calls $\mathcal{O}^{\mathsf{TagFile}}(b_i)$ and forwards the tags to $\mathcal{A}$. There are no restrictions here at the side of $\mathcal{A}$. From those tags it can extract a and forge the tags. When $\mathcal{A}$ finishes with queries on tags, then it stores all tags σ_i and blocks b_i.

Compress phase $\mathcal{C}$ asks $\mathcal{A}$ to compress the file F. $\mathcal{A}$ runs RLE.Compress(F) to compress file F to F' and $S_1, \ldots, S_{n'} \leftarrow$ RLE.TransformTags($B_1, \ldots, B_{n'}$, $\sigma_1, \ldots, \sigma_n$) to transform tags $\sigma_1, \ldots, \sigma_n$ to $S_1, \ldots, S_{n'}$.

Challenge phase $\mathcal{C}$ creates a random challenge $Q = (i, r_i), i \in [1 \ldots n']$ and sends it to $\mathcal{A}$. $\mathcal{A}$ constructs the $\mathsf{proof} = (\{\mu_i\}_{i \in Q}, S, \mathsf{pcc})$ calling the RLE.Prove($F', S_1, \ldots, S_{n'}, \sigma_1, \ldots, \sigma_n, Q$) algorithm and returns it to $\mathcal{C}$.

We consider two events bad_1 and bad_2. $\mathsf{bad}_1 = 1$ happens whenever $\mathcal{A}$ convinces $\mathcal{C}$ during the challenge protocol without holding the required challenged blocks and $\mathsf{bad}_2 = 1$ when $\mathcal{A}$ does not transform correctly the blocks for the compressed blocks or does not store them at all. We categorize bad_2 event with two possible cases: bad_{21} considers the *remove block attack* event and bad_{21} the event when *add block attack* occurs. The success probability of $\mathcal{A}$ in winning the $\mathbf{G}_{\mathcal{A}}^{\mathsf{ACS}}$ game without storing the requested blocks or compressing and transforming the tags without being detected by a benign verifier ($\mathcal{C}$, or user in the real protocol) is bounded by:

$$\Pr[\mathsf{bad}_1 = 1] + \Pr[\mathsf{bad}_{21} = 1] + \Pr[\mathsf{bad}_{22} = 1] \tag{1}$$

$$= 2 \cdot \sum_{i=0}^{m} \frac{i}{m} \cdot \mathsf{Adv}_f(\mathcal{B}) + 1 - \frac{n' - s}{m} \tag{2}$$

$$= 2 \cdot \frac{m(m-1)}{2m} \cdot \mathsf{Adv}_f(\mathcal{B}) + 1 - \frac{n' - s}{m} \tag{3}$$

$$= (m-1) \cdot \mathsf{Adv}_f(\mathcal{B}) + 1 - \frac{n' - s}{m} \tag{4}$$

Thus the success probability of an extractor $\mathcal{E}$ to extract the file equals:

$$\Pr[\mathcal{E} \Rightarrow 1] = 1 - (\Pr[\mathbf{G}_{\mathcal{A}}^{\mathsf{ACS}} \Rightarrow 1] \wedge (\Pr[\mathcal{A} \text{ not store } \mathsf{F}']$$
$$\vee \Pr[\mathcal{A} \text{ not compress correctly}]))$$
$$= 1 - (\Pr[\mathrm{bad}_1 = 1] + \Pr[\mathrm{bad}_{21} = 1] + \Pr[\mathrm{bad}_{22} = 1])$$
$$= 1 - (m-1) \cdot \mathsf{Adv}_f(\mathcal{B}) + 1 - \frac{n'-s}{m}$$
$$\leq 1 - \mathsf{negl}(\lambda)$$

Theorem 2. ACS-HUFF *is a secure accountable compressed storage system according to Definition 1 against a PPT adversary $\mathcal{A}$ and a polynomial extractor $\mathcal{E}$, as long as f is a secure* PRF.

Proof. Similarly with the ACS-RLE proof, we analyze the success probabilities of an extractor to extract the correct file or providing proofs of compression.

$$\Pr[\mathcal{E} \Rightarrow 1] = 1 - (\Pr[\mathbf{G}_{\mathcal{A}}^{\mathsf{ACS}} \Rightarrow 1] \wedge (\Pr[\mathcal{A} \text{ not store } \mathsf{F}'] \vee$$
$$\Pr[\mathcal{A} \text{ not compress correctly}]))$$
$$= 1 - (\Pr[\mathrm{bad}_1 = 1] + \Pr[\mathrm{bad}_2 = 1])$$
$$= 1 - (\sum_{i=0}^{m} \frac{i}{m} \cdot \mathsf{Adv}_f(\mathcal{B}) + 1 - \frac{n'-s}{m})$$
$$= 1 - (\frac{(m-1)}{2} \cdot \mathsf{Adv}_f(\mathcal{B}) + 1 - \frac{n'-s}{m})$$
$$\leq 1 - \mathsf{negl}(\lambda)$$

5.2 Performance

We perform a theoretical performance analysis of ACS-RLE and ACS-HUFF, two vanilla protocols V1 and V2 as baseline. V1 consists of a straightforward approach in which the user $\mathcal{U}$ whenever seeks to compress its already outsourced data file F, downloads the entire file F, compresses it to F', computes the new tags $\{S\}_{i=1}^{n}$ and finally uploads both F' and $\{S\}_{i=1}^{n}$ to the CSP. In V2, the user asks the CSP to compress the file F', downloads it to check correctness of compression, computes the new tags $\{S\}_{i=1}^{n}$ and uploads them to the CSP.

Tables 2 and 3 show the comparison. We take into account the following factors in order to compare the protocols: The **PreComputation** time for the user during the Setup phase. The **Storage** overhead after the Setup $\mathcal{U}$ needs to allocate. The computation time for the Compress algorithm for $\mathcal{U}$ and the CSP, denoted as **Compress** in the table. The communication overhead (**Compress.C**) that is required for compression. And finally, the running time overhead during the challenge response protocol Challenge$_{\mathsf{F}'}$ for the computation of the **Challenge**, the **Prove** and the verification (**Verify**).

Table 2. Comparison table. **PreComputation** depicts the computation time for the user $\mathcal{U}$ for the Setup phase. **Storage** is the space overhead for $\mathcal{U}$ after uploading file F and tags. **Compress** shows computation time for $\mathcal{U}$ and CSP, and the communication overhead (C) needed for the compression at the CSP.

Protocol	PreComputation	Storage	Compress $[\mathcal{U}|$CSP$|C]$		
V1	$\mathcal{O}(n)$	$\mathcal{O}(1)$	$\mathcal{O}(n+n')$	0	$\mathcal{O}(n+2n')$
V2	$\mathcal{O}(n)$	$\mathcal{O}(1)$	$\mathcal{O}(n')$	$\mathcal{O}(n)$	$\mathcal{O}(2n')$
ACS-RLE	$\mathcal{O}(n)$	$\mathcal{O}(n')$	0	$\mathcal{O}(n+n')$	0
ACS-HUFF	$\mathcal{O}(n)$	$\mathcal{O}(|D|)$	$\mathcal{O}(|D|)$	$\mathcal{O}(n+|D|)$	$\mathcal{O}(|D|)$

Table 3. Comparison table. **Challenge**, **Prove** and **Verify** present the computation overhead to compute the Challenge, the proof time of the CSP and the time $\mathcal{U}$ spends to verify the proof respectively. n is the number of blocks in the uncompressed file F, n' is the number of the compressed blocks, m is the size of the challenge and $|D|$ is the size of entries for the dictionary of Huffman encoding for ACS-HUFF scheme.

Protocol	Challenge	Prove	Verify
V1	$\mathcal{O}(1)$	$\mathcal{O}(m)$	$\mathcal{O}(1)$
V2	$\mathcal{O}(1)$	$\mathcal{O}(m)$	$\mathcal{O}(1)$
ACS-RLE	$\mathcal{O}(1)$	$\mathcal{O}(m)$	$\mathcal{O}(m)$
ACS-HUFF	$\mathcal{O}(1)$	$\mathcal{O}(m)$	$\mathcal{O}(1)$

PreComputation is the same $\mathcal{O}(n)$ for all protocols as it consists of splitting the file F in n blocks and computing n tags with the same mechanism (CPOR tags). The **Storage** in both vanilla protocols is $\mathcal{O}(1)$. In ACS-RLE, the user storage cost is increased to $\mathcal{O}(n')$ due to the auxiliary table MI, which stores ranges of symbols. In ACS-HUFF, $\mathcal{U}$ has to store the frequencies of all symbols of the file F in order to check for the correctness of compression during the ACS-HUFF.Compress phase. This results in a storage complexity of $\mathcal{O}(|D|)$. Notice that $|D|$ is considerably smaller than n and depends only on the vocabulary of the file F and the block size w of each block. The latter is due to the heuristic that the bigger the w the less unique patterns, thus entries, in D.

The advantages of our two auditable compressed storage protocols ACS-RLE and ACS-HUFF are obvious during the Compress algorithm which is assessed in the **Compress** column of Table 2. As in both ACS-RLE and ACS-HUFF the compression is delegated to the CSP, $\mathcal{U}$'s computation time complexity is minimal: 0 for ACS-RLE and $\mathcal{O}(|D|)$ for ACS-HUFF. V1 requires $\mathcal{O}(n+n')$ computation time for $\mathcal{U}$ as the user compresses the file and computes the new tags. It also results in $\mathcal{O}(n+2n')$ total communication complexity. V2 splits the computation overhead for compression in $\mathcal{O}(n')$ for $\mathcal{U}$ and $\mathcal{O}(n)$ for the CSP. Recall that in V2 the user computes the new tags for the compressed file and the CSP compresses. In contrast with the vanilla protocols, ACS-RLE and ACS-RLE demand constant communication complexity for compression. ACS-RLE communication complexity is reduced to 0, whereas in ACS-HUFF the complexity is slightly increased to $\mathcal{O}(|D|)$ due to the extra check $\mathcal{U}$ has to perform to check the correctness of Huffman based compression. Finally, during the $\mathsf{Challenge}_{F'}$ phase the verification time for the ACS-RLE protocol is increased from $\mathcal{O}(1)$ to $\mathcal{O}(m)$ due to the extra checks for compression correctness. Note that m refers to the size of the challenge Q on the compressed file F'. ACS-RLE verification time is the same as with the vanilla protocols, as it is a conventional CPOR verification [11]. We let as future work the design of an auditable compress storage protocol which will enjoy the low Compress complexity user running time and communication overhead as with ACS-RLE, with the constant verification time of ACS-HUFF.

Another baseline method could use an existing RDIC scheme for the uncompressed file and one for the compressed one. The asymptotic performance of such a scheme would be optimal in terms of compression costs compared with all the aforementioned ones. However, there is a metric which is not included in that case. The Cloud has to store $2n$ tags instead of n tags, which asymptotically is equivalent with the existing baselines but for large files it might be a prohibitive solution for the CSP.

Notice also that for high entropy files both ACS-RLE and ACS-HUFF require the client to store up to $O(n)$ information. That however imposes that the compression ratio would be very small due to high entropy; so the client would not have any incentive a-priori to use any compression techniques.

6   Conclusion

We initiated the study of *Auditable Compressed Storage*, whereby the original data changes format during its lifetime, when outsourced to a cloud infrastructure. This setting poses new threats and challenges in secure outsourcing storage as the task of compressing the data is delegated to the cloud, who is in charge of transforming the authentication tags of the original data to tags corresponding to the compressed data. As the Cloud Service Provider is economically motivated to cheat by not applying a correct compression to the original data, we demonstrate how to extend existing Remote Data Integrity Check protocols to encompass a proof of correct compression in conjunction with proofs of faithful storage. We designed and analyzed two protocols: ACS-RLE for Run Length Encoding compression and ACS-HUFF for Huffman Dictionary-based encoding. Our protocols fulfill the security guarantees for correct compression and faithful storage.

Acknowledgments. This research was supported by the US National Science Foundation under Grants No. CNS 1801430, CNS 1054754, and DGE 1565478.

References

1. Ateniese, G., et al.: Remote data checking using provable data possession. ACM Trans. Inf. Syst. Secur. **14**, 12:1–12:34 (2011)
2. Ateniese, G., et al.: Provable data possession at untrusted stores. In: Proceedings of the 14th ACM CCS, pp. 598–609 (2007)
3. Ateniese, G., Di Pietro, R., Mancini, L.V., Tsudik, G.: Scalable and efficient provable data possession. In: Proceedings of the 4th SecureComm, pp. 9:1–9:10 (2008)
4. Cash, D., Küpçü, A., Wichs, D.: Dynamic proofs of retrievability via oblivious RAM. J. Cryptol. **30**(1), 22–57 (2017)
5. Erway, C., Küpçü, A., Papamanthou, C., Tamassia, R.: Dynamic provable data possession. In: Proceedings of the 16th ACM CCS, pp. 213–222 (2009)
6. Esiner, E., Kachkeev, A., Braunfeld, S., Küpçü, A., Özkasap, O.: FlexDPDP: flexlist-based optimized dynamic provable data possession. Trans. Storage **12**(4), 23:1–23:44 (2016)
7. Etemad, M., Küpçü, A.: Transparent, distributed, and replicated dynamic provable data possession. In: Proceedings of the 11th ACNS, pp. 1–18 (2013)
8. Huffman, D.A.: A method for the construction of minimum-redundancy codes. Proc. Inst. Radio Eng. **40**(9), 1098–1101 (1952)
9. Juels, A., Kaliski Jr., B.S.: PORs: proofs of retrievability for large files. In: Proceedings of the 14th ACM CCS, pp. 584–597 (2007)
10. Mohammad Etemad, M., Küpçü, A.: Generic efficient dynamic proofs of retrievability. In: Proceedings of the ACM CCSW, pp. 85–96 (2016)
11. Shacham, H., Waters, B.: Compact proofs of retrievability. In: Pieprzyk, J. (ed.) ASIACRYPT 2008. LNCS, vol. 5350, pp. 90–107. Springer, Heidelberg (2008). https://doi.org/10.1007/978-3-540-89255-7_7
12. Shi, E., Stefanov, E., Papamanthou, C.: Practical dynamic proofs of retrievability. In: Proceedings of the 2013 ACM CCS, pp. 325–336 (2013)
13. Stefanov, E., van Dijk, M., Juels, A., Oprea, A.: Iris: a scalable cloud file system with efficient integrity checks. In: Proceedings of the 28th ACSAC, pp. 229–238 (2012)
14. Wang, Q., Wang, C., Li, J., Ren, K., Lou, W.: Enabling public verifiability and data dynamics for storage security in cloud computing. In: Backes, M., Ning, P. (eds.) ESORICS 2009. LNCS, vol. 5789, pp. 355–370. Springer, Heidelberg (2009). https://doi.org/10.1007/978-3-642-04444-1_22
15. Zhang, Y., Blanton, M.: Efficient dynamic provable possession of remote data via update trees. Trans. Storage **12**(2), 9:1–9:45 (2016)

Decentralized Evaluation of Quadratic Polynomials on Encrypted Data

Chloé Hébant[1,2], Duong Hieu Phan[3], and David Pointcheval[1,2(✉)]

[1] DIENS, École normale supérieure, CNRS, PSL University, Paris, France
`David.Pointcheval@ens.fr`
[2] Inria, Paris, France
[3] Université de Limoges, Limoges, France

Abstract. Since the seminal paper on Fully Homomorphic Encryption (FHE) by Gentry in 2009, a lot of work and improvements have been proposed, with an amazing number of possible applications. It allows outsourcing any kind of computations on encrypted data, and thus without leaking any information to the provider who performs the computations. This is quite useful for many sensitive data (finance, medical, etc.).

Unfortunately, FHE fails at providing some computation on private inputs to a third party, in cleartext: the user that can decrypt the result is able to decrypt the inputs. A classical approach to allow limited decryption power is distributed decryption. But none of the actual FHE schemes allows distributed decryption, at least with an efficient protocol.

In this paper, we revisit the Boneh-Goh-Nissim (BGN) cryptosystem, and the Freeman's variant, that allow evaluation of quadratic polynomials, or any 2-DNF formula. Whereas the BGN scheme relies on integer factoring for the trapdoor in the composite-order group, and thus possesses one public/secret key only, the Freeman's scheme can handle multiple users with one general setup that just needs to define a pairing-based algebraic structure. We show that it can be efficiently decentralized, with an efficient distributed key generation algorithm, without any trusted dealer, but also efficient distributed decryption and distributed re-encryption, in a threshold setting. We then provide some applications of computations on encrypted data, without central authority.

Keywords: Decentralization · Fully Homomorphic Encryption · 2-DNF

1 Introduction

Decentralized Cryptography is one of the main directions of research in cryptography, especially in a concurrent environment of multi-user applications, where there is no way to trust any authority. Recently, the rise of blockchain's applications also witnessed the importance of decentralized applications. However, the blockchain mainly addresses the decentralized validation of transactions,

© Springer Nature Switzerland AG 2019
Z. Lin et al. (Eds.): ISC 2019, LNCS 11723, pp. 87–106, 2019.
https://doi.org/10.1007/978-3-030-30215-3_5

but it does not help in decentralizing computations. For the computational purpose, though general solutions can be achieved via multi-party computation, reasonably efficient solutions only exist for a limited number of protocols, as decentralization usually adds constraints to the design of protocols: in broadcast encryption [13], the decentralized protocol in [26] is much less efficient than the underlying original protocol [25]; in attribute-based encryption [27], the decentralized scheme [8] implies some constraints on the access control policy, that are removed in [24], but at the cost of the use of bilinear groups of composite order with 3 prime factors; etc.

Decentralized Computing over Encrypted Data. In the last decade, the most active research direction carries on computing over encrypted data, with the seminal papers on Fully Homomorphic Encryption (FHE) [18] and on Functional Encryption (FE) [6,16,21]. FE was generalized to the case of multi-user setting via the notion of multi-input/multi-client FE [19,20,22]. It is of practical interest to consider the decentralization for FHE and FE without need of trust in any authority. In FE, the question in the multi-client setting was recently addressed by Chotard *et al.* [9] for the inner product function and then improved in [1,10], where all the clients agree and contribute to generate the functional decryption keys, there is no need of central authority anymore. Note that, in FE, there are efficient solutions for quadratic functions [3,17] but actually, only linear function evaluations can be decentralized as none of the methods to decentralize linear schemes seems to apply, and no new method has been proposed so far. We consider, in this paper, the practical case of decentralizing FHE in multi-user setting. However, the general solution for FHE is still not yet practical, as FHE decryption requires rounding operations that are hard to efficiently distribute. Thus we only consider decentralized evaluation of quadratic polynomials. Moreover, as only decentralized linear computation was possible before, this paper can improve the efficiency of multi-party computation scheme by allowing quadratic steps and thus, improve the number of interactions needed. To motivate our work, we focus on some real-life applications in the last section which only require evaluations of quadratic polynomials so that specific target users can get the result in clear, by running re-encryption in a distributed manner under the keys of the target users.

1.1 Technical Contribution

We design an efficient distributed evaluation for quadratic polynomials, with decentralized generation of the keys. Boneh-Goh-Nissim [5] proposed a nice solution for quadratic polynomials evaluation. However, their solution relies on a composite-order elliptic curve and thus on the hardness of the integer factoring. This possibly leads to a distributed solution, but that is highly inefficient. Indeed, no efficient multi-party generation of distributed RSA modulus is known, except for 2 parties. But even the recent construction [14], the most efficient up to now, is still quite inefficient as it relies on oblivious transfer in the semi-honest setting, and on an IND-CPA encryption scheme, coin-tossing, zero-knowledge and secure two-party computation protocols in the malicious setting. Catalano and Fiore [7] introduced an efficient technique to transform a linearly-homomorphic encryption into a scheme able to evaluate quadratic operations on ciphertexts. They are able to support decryption of a large plaintext space after the multiplication. However, as in Kawai *et al.* [23] which used this technique to perform proxy re-encryption, they only consider a subclass of degree-2 polynomials where the number of additions of degree-2 terms is bounded by a constant. This is not enough for most of the applications and we do not try to decentralize these limited protocols.

Our Approach. Freeman [15] proposed a conversion from composite-order groups to prime-order groups for the purpose of improving the efficiency. Interestingly, Freeman's conversion allows multi-user setting, since a common setup can handle several keys. But we additionally show it is well-suited for distributed evaluation of 2-DNF formulae. Actually, working in prime-order groups, we can avoid the bottleneck of a distributed generation of RSA moduli. However, it is not enough to have an efficient distributed setup. One also needs to distribute any use of the private keys in the construction: for decryption and re-encryption (see Sect. A.2). Unfortunately, the Freeman's generic description with projection matrices does not directly allow the design of a decentralized scheme, *i.e.*, with efficient distributed (threshold) decryption without any trusted dealer. We thus specify particular projections, with well-chosen private and public keys. This leads to an efficient decentralized version with distributed private computations. Our main contribution is to prove that using particular projection matrices does not weaken the global construction.

Related Work. In a previous and independent work, Attrapadung *et al.* [2] proposed an efficient two-level homomorphic encryption in prime-order groups. They put forward a new approach that avoids the Freeman's transformation from BGN encryption. Interestingly, our work shows this scheme falls into the Freeman's framework because their construction is similar to the simplified non-decentralized version of our scheme which is obtained from BGN via a Freeman transformation with a particular choice of projections. The concrete implementations in [2] show that such a scheme is quite efficient, which applies to our construction, and even to the distributed construction as each server, for a partial decryption, essentially has to perform a decryption with its share. In another unpublished work [11], Culnane *et al.* considered a universally verifiable MPC protocol in which one of the two steps is to distribute the key generation in somewhat homomorphic cryptosystems. However, as we mentioned above, the Freeman's generic description with projection matrices, as considered in [11], does not lead to an efficient distributed decryption. In short, our result bridges the gap between the objective of decentralization as in [11] and the efficiency goal as in [2].

1.2 Applications

Boneh, Goh, and Nissim proposed two main applications to secure evaluation of quadratic polynomials: private information retrieval schemes (PIR) and electronic voting protocols. However, the use of our decentralized scheme for electronic voting is much more preferable than the BGN scheme, as there is no way to trust any dealer in such a use-case. We propose two more applications that are related to the group testing and the consistency model in machine learning. Our applications are particularly useful in practice in a decentralized setting, as they deal with sensitive data. Interestingly, the use of distributed evaluation for quadratic polynomials in these applications is highly non-trivial and will be explained in the last section.

2 Preliminaries

2.1 Notations

We denote by $x \xleftarrow{\$} X$ the process of selecting x uniformly at random in the set X. Let $\mathbb{Z}_p = \mathbb{Z}/p\mathbb{Z}$ be the ring of integers *modulo* p. For any group $\mathbb{G}$, we denote by $\langle g \rangle$ the space generated by $g \in \mathbb{G}$.

2.2 Bilinear Group Setting

A *bilinear group generator* $\mathcal{G}$ is an algorithm that takes as input a security parameter λ and outputs a tuple $(\mathbb{G}_1, \mathbb{G}_2, \mathbb{G}_T, p, g_1, g_2, e)$ such that $\mathbb{G}_1 = \langle g_1 \rangle$ and $\mathbb{G}_2 = \langle g_2 \rangle$ are cyclic groups of prime order p (a λ-bit prime integer), and $e : \mathbb{G}_1 \times \mathbb{G}_2 \to \mathbb{G}_T$ is an *admissible pairing*:

- e is bilinear: for all $a, b \in \mathbb{Z}_p, e(g_1^a, g_2^b) = e(g_1, g_2)^{ab}$;
- e is efficiently computable (in polynomial-time in λ);
- e is non-degenerate: $e(g_1, g_2) \neq 1$.

Furthermore, the bilinear setting $(\mathbb{G}_1, \mathbb{G}_2, \mathbb{G}_T, p, g_1, g_2, e)$ is said *asymmetric* when $\mathbb{G}_1 \neq \mathbb{G}_2$. This will be our setting, while the BGN encryption scheme uses a symmetric setting, with composite-order groups.

2.3 Computational Assumption

Our security results rely on the Decisional Diffie-Hellman assumption:

Definition 1. *Let $\mathbb{G} = \langle g \rangle$ be a cyclic group of prime order p. The advantage $\mathrm{Adv}_{\mathbb{G}}^{\mathsf{ddh}}(\mathcal{A})$ of an adversary $\mathcal{A}$ against the Decisional Diffie-Hellman (DDH) problem in $\mathbb{G}$ is defined by:*

$$\Pr\left[\mathcal{A}(g, g^x, g^y, g^{xy}) = 1 | x, y \xleftarrow{\$} \mathbb{Z}_p\right] - \Pr\left[\mathcal{A}(g, g^x, g^y, g^z) = 1 | x, y, z \xleftarrow{\$} \mathbb{Z}_p\right].$$

We say that the DDH *problem in $\mathbb{G}$ is (t, ε)-hard if for any advantage $\mathcal{A}$ running within time t, its advantage $\mathrm{Adv}_{\mathbb{G}}^{\mathsf{ddh}}(\mathcal{A})$ is bounded by ε.*

We denote by $\mathrm{Adv}_{\mathbb{G}}^{\mathsf{ddh}}(t)$ the best advantage any adversary can get within time t.

$$\mathrm{Exp}_{\mathcal{E}}^{\mathsf{ind\text{-}cpa\text{-}}b}(\mathcal{A}): \quad \mathsf{param} \leftarrow \mathsf{Setup}(\lambda); (\mathsf{sk}, \mathsf{pk}) \leftarrow \mathsf{Keygen}(\mathsf{param}); (s, m_0, m_1) \leftarrow \mathcal{A}(\mathsf{pk})$$
$$C \leftarrow \mathsf{Encrypt}(\mathsf{pk}, m_b); b' \leftarrow \mathcal{A}(s, C); \mathbf{return}\ b'$$

Fig. 1. Experiment of IND-CPA

2.4 Security Notions

Let us now recall the semantic security, *a.k.a.* indistinguishability (or IND-CPA), for a public-key encryption scheme, according to the experiment presented in Fig. 1, where the attack is in two steps, and so the adversary outputs a state s to resume the process in the second step.

Definition 2. *Let $\mathcal{E}$ = (Setup, Keygen, Encrypt, Decrypt) be an encryption scheme. Let us denote $\mathrm{Exp}_{\mathcal{E}}^{\mathsf{ind\text{-}cpa\text{-}}b}(\mathcal{A})$ the experiment defined in Fig. 1. The advantage $\mathrm{Adv}_{\mathcal{E}}^{\mathsf{ind\text{-}cpa}}(\mathcal{A})$ of an adversary $\mathcal{A}$ against* indistinguishability under chosen plaintext attacks *(IND-CPA) is $\Pr[\mathrm{Exp}_{\mathcal{E}}^{\mathsf{ind\text{-}cpa\text{-}1}}(\mathcal{A}) = 1] - \Pr[\mathrm{Exp}_{\mathcal{E}}^{\mathsf{ind\text{-}cpa\text{-}0}}(\mathcal{A}) = 1]$. We say that an encryption scheme $\mathcal{E}$ is $(t, \varepsilon) - \mathrm{IND\text{-}CPA}$ if for any adversary $\mathcal{A}$ running within time t, its advantage $\mathrm{Adv}_{\mathcal{E}}^{\mathsf{ind\text{-}cpa}}(\mathcal{A})$ is bounded by ε.*

We denote by $\mathrm{Adv}_{\mathcal{E}}^{\mathsf{ind\text{-}cpa}}(t)$ the best advantage any adversary $\mathcal{A}$ can get within time t.

3 Encryption for Quadratic Polynomial Evaluation

To evaluate 2-DNF formulae on encrypted data, Boneh-Goh-Nissim described a cryptosystem [5] that supports additions, one multiplication layer, and additions. They used a bilinear map on a composite-order group and the secret key is the factorization of the order of the group. Unfortunately, composite-order groups require huge orders, since the factorization must be difficult, with costly pairing evaluations.

3.1 Freeman's Framework

In order to improve on the efficiency, Freeman in [15, Section 5] proposed a system on prime-order groups, using a similar property of noise that can be removed, with the general definition of subgroup decision problem. Let us recall the Freeman's cryptosystem:

Keygen(λ): Given a security parameter λ, it generates a description of three Abelian groups G, H, G_T and a pairing $e : G \times H \to G_T$. It also generates a description of two subgroups $G_1 \subset G, H_1 \subset H$ and two homomorphisms π_1, π_2 such that G_1, H_1 are contained in the kernels of π_1, π_2 respectively. It picks $g \xleftarrow{\$} G$ and $h \xleftarrow{\$} H$, and outputs the public key $\mathsf{pk} = (G, H, g, h, G_1, H_1)$ and the private key $\mathsf{sk} = (\pi_1, \pi_2)$.

Encrypt(pk, m): To encrypt a message m using public key pk, one picks $g_1 \xleftarrow{\$} G_1$
and $h_1 \xleftarrow{\$} H_1$, and outputs the ciphertext $(C_A, C_B) = (g^m \cdot g_1, h^m \cdot h_1) \in G \times H$.

Decrypt(sk, C): Given $C = (C_A, C_B)$, output $m \leftarrow \log_{\pi_1(g)}(\pi_1(C_A))$ (which
should be the same as $\log_{\pi_2(h)}(\pi_2(C_B))$).

The Freeman's scheme is also additively homomorphic. Moroever, if an homo-
morphism π_T exists such that, for all $g \in G, h \in H$, $e(\pi_1(g), \pi_2(h)) = \pi_T(e(g, h))$, we can get, as above, a ciphertext in G_T of the product of the two
plaintexts, when multiplying the ciphertexts in G and H. The new encryption
scheme in G_T is still additively homomorphic, and allows evaluations of 2-DNF
formulae.

Remark 3. We note that in the Freeman's cryptosystem, ciphertexts contain
encryptions of m in both G and H to allow any kind of additions and multiplication. But one could focus on just one ciphertext when one knows the formula
to be evaluated.

3.2   Optimized Version

In the Appendix A, we present the translation of the Freeman's approach with
projection matrices. This indeed leads to a public-key encryption scheme that
can evaluate quadratic polynomials in $\mathbb{Z}_p$, under the DDH assumption. However,
because of the secret key that must be a projection matrix, the distributed generation, while possible (see Appendix A.2), is not as efficient as one can expect.
We thus now propose a particular instantiation of projections, which allows very
compact keys and ciphertexts. In addition, this will allow to generate keys in a
distributed manner, without any trusted dealer. While in the generic transformation of Freeman, the secret key belongs to the whole projection matrix space,
our particular instantiation of projections means that the secret key will belong
to a proper sub-space of the projection matrix space.

Indeed, it is possible to reduce by a factor two the size of the keys: for
$s \in \{1, 2\}$, the secret key is just one scalar and the public key one group element
in $\mathbb{G}_s$. For the keys, we will consider orthogonal projections on $\langle (1, x) \rangle$, for any
$x \in \mathbb{Z}_p$. Thus, sk_s can simply be described by $x \in \mathbb{Z}_p$, which is enough to define
the projection. The public key pk_s can simply be described by $g_s^{-x} \in \mathbb{G}_s$, which
is enough to define (g_s^{-x}, g_s), as $(-x, 1)$ is a vector in the kernel of the projection,
to add noise that the secret key will be able to remove.

More precisely, we can describe our optimized encryption schemes, for $s \in \{1, 2, T\}$, as $\mathcal{E}_s$: (Setup, Keygen$_s$, Encrypt$_s$, Decrypt$_s$) with a common Setup:

Setup(λ): Given a security parameter λ, run and output

$$\mathsf{param} = (\mathbb{G}_1, \mathbb{G}_2, \mathbb{G}_T, p, g_1, g_2, e) \leftarrow \mathcal{G}(\lambda).$$

Keygen$_s$(param): For $s \in \{1, 2\}$. Choose $x_s \xleftarrow{\$} \mathbb{Z}_p$ and output the public key
$\mathsf{pk}_s = g_s^{-x_s}$ and the private key $\mathsf{sk}_s = x_s$. From $(\mathsf{pk}_1, \mathsf{sk}_1) \leftarrow \mathsf{Keygen}_1(\mathsf{param})$

and $(\mathsf{pk}_2, \mathsf{sk}_2) \leftarrow \mathsf{Keygen}_2(\mathsf{param})$, one can consider $\mathsf{pk}_T = (\mathsf{pk}_1, \mathsf{pk}_2)$ and $\mathsf{sk}_T = (\mathsf{sk}_1, \mathsf{sk}_2)$, which are associated public and private keys in $\mathbb{G}_T$.

$\mathsf{Encrypt}_s(\mathsf{pk}_s, m)$: For $s \in \{1, 2\}$, to encrypt a message $m \in \mathbb{Z}_p$ using public key pk_s, choose $r \xleftarrow{\$} \mathbb{Z}_p$ and output the ciphertext

$$C_s = (c_{s,1} = g_s^m \cdot \mathsf{pk}_s^r, c_{s,2} = g_s^r) \in \mathbb{G}_s^2.$$

For $s = T$, to encrypt a message $m \in \mathbb{Z}_p$ using public key $\mathsf{pk}_T = (\mathsf{pk}_1, \mathsf{pk}_2)$, choose $r_{11}, r_{12}, r_{21}, r_{22} \xleftarrow{\$} \mathbb{Z}_p^4$ and output the ciphertext

$$C_T = \begin{pmatrix} c_{T,1} = e(g_1, g_2)^m \cdot e(g_1, \mathsf{pk}_2)^{r_{11}} \cdot e(\mathsf{pk}_1, g_2)^{r_{21}}, \\ c_{T,2} = e(g_1, g_2)^{r_{11}} \cdot e(\mathsf{pk}_1, g_2)^{r_{22}}, \\ c_{T,3} = e(g_1, \mathsf{pk}_2)^{r_{12}} \cdot e(g_1, g_2)^{r_{21}}, \\ c_{T,4} = e(g_1, g_2)^{r_{12}+r_{22}} \end{pmatrix} \in \mathbb{G}_T^4$$

$\mathsf{Decrypt}_s(\mathsf{sk}_s, C_s)$: For $s \in \{1, 2\}$, given $C_s = (c_{s,1}, c_{s,2})$ and the private key sk_s, compute $d = c_{s,1} \cdot c_{s,2}^{\mathsf{sk}_s}$ and output the logarithm of d in basis g_s. For $s = T$, given $C_T = (c_{T,1}, c_{T,2}, c_{T,3}, c_{T,4})$ and $\mathsf{sk}_T = (\mathsf{sk}_1, \mathsf{sk}_2)$, compute $d = c_{T,1} \cdot c_{T,2}^{\mathsf{sk}_2} \cdot c_{T,3}^{\mathsf{sk}_1} \cdot c_{T,4}^{\mathsf{sk}_1 \cdot \mathsf{sk}_2}$ and output the logarithm of d in basis $e(g_1, g_2)$.

In $\mathbb{G}_1$ and $\mathbb{G}_2$, this is actually the classical ElGamal encryption. We essentially extend it to $\mathbb{G}_T$, to handle quadratic operations:

$\mathsf{Add}(C_s, C_s')$ just consists of the component-wise product in $\mathbb{G}_s$;
$\mathsf{Multiply}(C_1, C_2)$ for $C_1 = (c_{1,1} = g_1^{m_1} \cdot \mathsf{pk}_1^{r_1}, c_{1,2} = g_1^{r_1}) \in \mathbb{G}_1^2$ and $C_2 = (c_{2,1} = g_2^{m_2} \cdot \mathsf{pk}_2^{r_2}, c_{2,2} = g_2^{r_2}) \in \mathbb{G}_2^2$, consists of the tensor product:

$$C_T = (e(c_{1,1}, c_{2,1}), e(c_{1,1}, c_{2,2}), e(c_{1,2}, c_{2,1}), e(c_{1,2}, c_{2,2})) \in \mathbb{G}_T^4$$

$\mathsf{Randomize}_s(\mathsf{pk}_s, C_s)$ is, as usual, the addition of a random ciphertext of 0 in the same group $\mathbb{G}_s$. For $s \in \{1, 2\}$: Given a ciphertext $C_s = (c_{s,1}, c_{s,2})$ with its public key pk_s, it chooses $r \xleftarrow{\$} \mathbb{Z}_p$ and outputs $(c_{s,1} \cdot \mathsf{pk}_s^r, c_{s,2} \cdot g_s^r)$; while for $s = T$, a public key pk_T and a ciphertext $(c_{T,1}, c_{T,2}, c_{T,3}, c_{T,4})$, it chooses $r_{11}', r_{12}', r_{21}', r_{22}' \xleftarrow{\$} \mathbb{Z}_p$ and outputs $(c_{T,1} \cdot e(g_1, \mathsf{pk}_2)^{r_{11}'} \cdot e(\mathsf{pk}_1, g_2)^{r_{21}'}, c_{T,2} \cdot e(g_1, g_2)^{r_{11}'} \cdot e(\mathsf{pk}_1, g_2)^{r_{22}'}, c_{T,3} \cdot e(g_1, \mathsf{pk}_2)^{r_{12}'} \cdot e(g_1, g_2)^{r_{21}'}, c_{T,4} \cdot e(g_1, g_2)^{r_{12}'+r_{22}'})$.

3.3 Security Properties

Whereas the correctness directly comes from the correctness of the Freeman's construction, presented in the Appendix A, and verification is straightforward, the semantic security comes from the classical ElGamal encryption security, under the DDH assumptions, for the basic schemes in $\mathbb{G}_1$ and $\mathbb{G}_2$:

Theorem 4. *For $s \in \{1, 2\}$, $\mathcal{E}_s$ is* IND-CPA *under the DDH assumption in $\mathbb{G}_s$: for any adversary $\mathcal{A}$ running within time t,* $\mathsf{Adv}_{\mathcal{E}_s}^{\mathsf{ind\text{-}cpa}}(\mathcal{A}) \leq 2 \times \mathsf{Adv}_{\mathbb{G}_s}^{\mathsf{ddh}}(t)$.

Corollary 5. *$\mathcal{E}_T$ is* IND-CPA *under the DDH assumptions in $\mathbb{G}_1$ or $\mathbb{G}_2$.*

Proof. The semantic security for ciphertexts in $\mathbb{G}_T$ comes from the fact that:

$$\mathsf{Encrypt}_T(\mathsf{pk}_T, m) = \mathsf{Multiply}(\mathsf{Encrypt}_1(\mathsf{pk}_1, m), \mathsf{Encrypt}_2(\mathsf{pk}_2, 1))$$
$$= \mathsf{Multiply}(\mathsf{Encrypt}_1(\mathsf{pk}_1, 1), \mathsf{Encrypt}_2(\mathsf{pk}_2, m))$$

Indeed, with this relation, each ciphertext in $\mathbb{G}_1$ can be transformed into a ciphertext in $\mathbb{G}_T$ (idem with a ciphertext in $\mathbb{G}_2$). Let $\mathcal{A}$ be an adversary against IND-CPA of $\mathcal{E}_T$, in $\mathbb{G}_T$.

Game $\mathbf{G}_0$: In the first game, the simulator plays the role of the challenger in the experiment $\mathsf{Exp}_{\mathcal{E}_T}^{\mathsf{ind\text{-}cpa\text{-}0}}(\mathcal{A})$, where $b = 0$:
- param $= (\mathbb{G}_1, \mathbb{G}_2, \mathbb{G}_T, p, g_1, g_2, e) \leftarrow \mathsf{Setup}(\lambda)$
- $(\mathsf{sk}_1, \mathsf{pk}_1) \leftarrow \mathsf{Keygen}_1(\mathsf{param}),(\mathsf{sk}_2, \mathsf{pk}_2) \leftarrow \mathsf{Keygen}_2(\mathsf{param})$
- $m_0, m_1 \leftarrow \mathcal{A}(\mathsf{param}, (\mathsf{pk}_1, \mathsf{pk}_2)); C_T = \mathsf{Encrypt}_T((\mathsf{pk}_1, \mathsf{pk}_2), m_0)$
- $\beta \leftarrow \mathcal{A}(\mathsf{param}, (\mathsf{pk}_1, \mathsf{pk}_2), C_T)$

We are interested in the event E: $b' = 1$. By definition,

$$\Pr_{\mathbf{G}_0}[E] = \Pr\left[\mathsf{Exp}_{\mathcal{E}_T}^{\mathsf{ind\text{-}cpa\text{-}0}}(\mathcal{A}) = 1\right].$$

Game $\mathbf{G}_1$: The simulator interacts with a challenger in $\mathsf{Exp}_{\mathcal{E}_1}^{\mathsf{ind\text{-}cpa\text{-}0}}(\mathcal{A})$, where $b = 0$. It thus first receives $\mathsf{param}, \mathsf{pk}_1$ from that challenger, generates pk_2 by himself to provide ($\mathsf{pk}_T = (\mathsf{pk}_1, \mathsf{pk}_2)$) to the adversary. The latter sends back (m_0, m_1) the simulators forwards to the challenger. It gets back $C_1 = \mathsf{Encrypt}_1(\mathsf{pk}_1, m_0)$. It can compute $C_T = \mathsf{Multiply}(C_1, \mathsf{Encrypt}_2(\mathsf{pk}_2, 1))$, to be sent to the adversary. This game is perfectly indistinguishable from the previous one: $\Pr_{\mathbf{G}_1}[E] = \Pr_{\mathbf{G}_0}[E]$.

Game $\mathbf{G}_2$: The simulator interacts with a challenger in $\mathsf{Exp}_{\mathcal{E}_1}^{\mathsf{ind\text{-}cpa\text{-}1}}(\mathcal{A})$, where $b = 1$:

$$\Pr_{\mathbf{G}_2}[E] - \Pr_{\mathbf{G}_1}[E] \leq \mathsf{Adv}_{\mathcal{E}_1}^{\mathsf{ind\text{-}cpa}}(t + 4 \cdot t_p + 4 \cdot t_e),$$

where t_p is the time for one pairing and t_e the time for one exponentiation.

Game $\mathbf{G}_3$: In this final game, the simulator plays the role of the challenger in $\mathsf{Exp}_{\mathcal{E}_T}^{\mathsf{ind\text{-}cpa\text{-}1}}(\mathcal{A})$, where $b = 1$. This game is perfectly indistinguishable from the previous one: $\Pr_{\mathbf{G}_3}[E] = \Pr_{\mathbf{G}_2}[E]$.

One can note, that in this last game, $\Pr_{\mathbf{G}_3}[E] = \Pr\left[\mathsf{Exp}_{\mathcal{E}_T}^{\mathsf{ind\text{-}cpa\text{-}1}}(\mathcal{A}) = 1\right]$, hence

$$\mathsf{Adv}_{\mathcal{E}_T}^{\mathsf{ind\text{-}cpa}}(\mathcal{A}) \leq \mathsf{Adv}_{\mathcal{E}_1}^{\mathsf{ind\text{-}cpa}}(t + 4 \cdot t_p + 4 \cdot t_e),$$

which concludes the proof, since it works exactly the same way for $\mathbb{G}_2$. $\square$
We stress that the security of $\mathcal{E}_T$ only requires the DDH assumption in one of the two groups, and not the SXDH assumption (which means that the DDH assumption holds in both $\mathbb{G}_1$ and $\mathbb{G}_2$).

4   Decentralized Homomorphic Encryption

Our main motivation was a decentralized key generation and a distributed decryption in order to be able to compute on encrypted data so that nobody can decrypt intermediate values but the result can be provided in clear to a target user. We now show that our optimized construction allows both decentralized key generation without a trusted dealer and distributed decryption. They are both quite efficient. When a result should be available to a unique user, a classical technique called proxy re-encryption [4] is to re-encrypt to this target user: this is a virtual decryption followed by encryption under the new key. We also show this is possible to do it in a distributed way, without any leakage of information.

4.1   Decentralized Key Generation

In fact, a classical decentralized t-out-of-n threshold secret sharing allows to generate the shares of a random element and it seems hard (if one expects efficiency) to use it to generate the shares of a structured matrix, such as projections required in the generic construction, because its elements are not independently random. In our specific construction, the secret keys in $\mathbb{G}_1$ and $\mathbb{G}_2$ are now one scalar and one can perform a classical t-out-of-n threshold secret sharing: each player i generates a random polynomial P_i of degree $t-1$ in $\mathbb{Z}_p[X]$, privately sends $x_{i,j} = P_i(j)$ to player j, and publishes $g_s^{-P_i(0)}$; each player i then aggregates the values into $\mathsf{sk}_i = \sum_j x_{j,i} = P(i)$, for $P = \sum_j P_j$, which leads to a share of $x = P(0)$, and the public key is the product of all the public values.

4.2   Distributed Decryption

In order to decrypt $C_s = (c_{s,1}, c_{s,2})$ in $\mathbb{G}_1$ or $\mathbb{G}_2$, each player in a sub-set of t players sends its contribution $c_{s,2}^{\mathsf{sk}_i}$, that can be multiplied with Lagrange coefficients as exponents to obtain the mask $c_{s,2}^{\mathsf{sk}} = \mathsf{pk}_s^{-r}$. To decrypt $C_T = (c_{T,1}, c_{T,2}, c_{T,3}, c_{T,4})$ in $\mathbb{G}_T$, one can first use the shares of sk_1 to compute $c_{T,3}^{\mathsf{sk}_1}$ and $c_{T,4}^{\mathsf{sk}_1}$, and then the shares of sk_2 to compute $c_{T,2}^{\mathsf{sk}_2}$ and $c_{T,4}^{\mathsf{sk}_1 \cdot \mathsf{sk}_2}$. Under the DDH assumptions in $\mathbb{G}_1$, $\mathbb{G}_2$ and $\mathbb{G}_T$, one can show that the intermediate values $c_{s,2}^{\mathsf{sk}_i}$, or $c_{T,3}^{\mathsf{sk}_1}$, $c_{T,4}^{\mathsf{sk}_1}$, $c_{T,2}^{\mathsf{sk}_2}$, and $c_{T,4}^{\mathsf{sk}_1 \cdot \mathsf{sk}_2}$ do not leak more than the decryption itself. Of course, classical verifiable secret sharing techniques can be used, for both the decentralized generation and the distributed decryption. This can allow, with simple Schnorr-like proofs of Diffie-Hellman tuples, universal verifiability.

4.3   Distributed Re-encryption

Besides a distributed decryption, when outsourcing some computations on private information, a distributed authority may want to re-encrypt the encrypted result to a specific user, so that the latter can get the result in clear, and nobody else. More precisely, we assume the input data were encrypted under the keys

pk_1, pk_2, and $\mathsf{pk}_T = (\mathsf{pk}_1, \mathsf{pk}_2)$, which leads, after quadratic evaluations, to a resulting ciphertext under the key pk_T, for which the distributed authorities, knowing a t-out-of-n additive secret sharing $(\mathsf{sk}_{1,i}, \mathsf{sk}_{2,i})_i$ of $(\mathsf{sk}_1, \mathsf{sk}_2)$, will re-encrypt under $\mathsf{PK}_T = (\mathsf{PK}_1, \mathsf{PK}_2)$ for the target user.

Of course, such a re-encryption can be performed using multi-party computation, but we will show an efficient way to do it. And we start with the re-encryption of $c_s = (c_{s,1} = g_s^m \cdot \mathsf{pk}_s^r, c_{s,2} = g_s^r)$: player i chooses $r_i' \xleftarrow{\$} \mathbb{Z}_p$, computes $\alpha_i = c_{s,2}^{\mathsf{sk}_{s,i}} \cdot \mathsf{PK}_s^{r_i'}$ and $\beta_i = g_s^{r_i'}$, and outputs (α_i, β_i). Then, anybody can compute, for the appropriate Lagrange coefficients λ_i's,

$$C_s = (C_{s,1} = c_{s,1} \times \prod \alpha_i^{\lambda_i} = g_s^m \mathsf{pk}_s^r g_s^{r \cdot \mathsf{sk}_s} \cdot \mathsf{PK}_s^{r'} = g_s^m \cdot \mathsf{PK}_s^{r'}, C_{s,2} = \prod \beta_i^{\lambda_i} = g_s^{r'})$$

with $r' = \sum \lambda_i r_i'$, where the sum is on the t members available.

For $s = T$, given a ciphertext $c_T = (c_{T,1}, c_{T,2}, c_{T,3}, c_{T,4})$, player i chooses $u_i \xleftarrow{\$} \mathbb{Z}_p$, and first computes and sends $\alpha_{3,i} = c_{T,4}^{\mathsf{sk}_{1,i}} \cdot e(g_1, g_2)^{-u_i}$. With a linear combination for the appropriate Lagrange coefficients λ_i's, anybody can compute, $\alpha_3 = \prod \alpha_{3,i}^{\lambda_i} = c_{T,4}^{\mathsf{sk}_1} \cdot e(g_1, g_2)^{-u}$, with implicit $u = \sum \lambda_i u_i$. Then each player i chooses $r_{11,i}', r_{12,i}', r_{21,i}', r_{22,i}', v_i \xleftarrow{\$} \mathbb{Z}_p$ and computes

$$\alpha_{1,i} = c_{T,2}^{\mathsf{sk}_{2,i}} \cdot e(\mathsf{PK}_1, g_2)^{r_{21,i}'} \qquad \beta_i = e(g_1, g_2)^{r_{11,i}' + u_i} \cdot e(\mathsf{PK}_1, g_2)^{r_{22,i}'}$$

$$\alpha_{2,i} = c_{T,3}^{\mathsf{sk}_{1,i}} \cdot e(g_1, \mathsf{PK}_2)^{r_{11,i}'} \qquad \gamma_i = e(g_1, \mathsf{PK}_2)^{r_{12,i}'} \cdot e(g_1, g_2)^{r_{21,i}' + v_i}$$

$$\alpha_{4,i} = \alpha_3^{\mathsf{sk}_{2,i}} \cdot e(\mathsf{PK}_1, g_2)^{v_i} \qquad \delta_i = e(g_1, g_2)^{r_{12,i}' + r_{22,i}'}$$

Again, with linear combinations for the appropriate Lagrange coefficients λ_i's, anybody can compute, with $r_{jk}' = \sum \lambda_i r_{jk,i}'$, for $j, k \in \{1, 2\}$, and $v = \sum \lambda_i v_i$:

$$\alpha_1 = c_{T,2}^{\mathsf{sk}_2} \cdot e(\mathsf{PK}_1, g_2)^{r_{21}'} \qquad C_{T,2} = e(g_1, g_2)^{r_{11}' + u} \cdot e(\mathsf{PK}_1, g_2)^{r_{22}'}$$

$$\alpha_2 = c_{T,3}^{\mathsf{sk}_1} \cdot e(g_1, \mathsf{PK}_2)^{r_{11}'} \qquad C_{T,3} = e(g_1, \mathsf{PK}_2)^{r_{12}'} \cdot e(g_1, g_2)^{r_{21}' + v}$$

$$\alpha_4 = c_{T,4}^{\mathsf{sk}_1 \mathsf{sk}_2} \cdot e(g_1, \mathsf{PK}_2)^u \cdot e(\mathsf{PK}_1, g_2)^v \quad C_{T,4} = e(g_1, g_2)^{r_{12}' + r_{22}'}$$

Then, $C_{T,1} = c_{T,1} \times \alpha_1 \alpha_2 \alpha_4 = e(g_1, g_2)^m \cdot e(g_1, \mathsf{PK}_2)^{r_{11}' + u} \cdot e(\mathsf{PK}_1, g_2)^{r_{21}' + v}$, so that $C_T = (C_{T,1}, C_{T,2}, C_{T,3}, C_{T,4})$ is a re-encryption of c_T under PK_T.

For random scalars, the re-encryption algorithms (which is just a one-round protocol in $\mathbb{G}_1$ and $\mathbb{G}^2$, but 2-round in $\mathbb{G}_T$) generate new ciphertexts under appropriate keys that look perfectly fresh. In addition, one can claim:

Theorem 6. *The above distributed protocols for re-encryption do not leak additional information than the outputs of the non-distributed algorithms.*

Proof. The goal of this proof is to show that the distributed protocol to re-encrypt a ciphertext under PK_s does not leak more information than a direct encryption under PK_s. For $s \in \{1, 2\}$, one is given $c_s = \mathsf{Encrypt}_s(m, \mathsf{pk}_s; r) = (c_{s,1}, c_{s,2})$ and $C_s = \mathsf{Encrypt}_s(m, \mathsf{PK}_s; R) = (C_{s,1}, C_{s,2})$, two ciphertexts of the same message m under pk_s and PK_s respectively. One can then note that $C_{s,1}/c_{s,1} = \mathsf{PK}_s^R/\mathsf{pk}_s^r = c_{s,2}^{\mathsf{sk}_s}/C_{s,2}^{\mathsf{SK}_s}$.

The Re-Encryption in $\mathbb{G}_s$, *for* $s \in \{1, 2\}$.

Game G_0: In the first game, the simulator just receives $c_s = (c_{s,1}, c_{s,2})$, and plays the real protocol using the t-out-of-n distributed keys $(\mathsf{sk}_{s,i})_i$ to provide the keys to the corrupted users and to generate the values $\alpha_i = c_{s,2}^{\mathsf{sk}_{s,i}} \cdot \mathsf{PK}_s^{r_i}$ and $\beta_i = g_s^{r_i}$, on behalf of the non-corrupted players. We assume that among t players, ℓ are honest and $t - \ell$ are corrupted. The latter are assumed to receive the secret keys $\mathsf{sk}_{s,i}$ and to generate their own outputs (α_i, β_i). The view of the attacker consists of the set of all the honest (α_i, β_i).

Game G_1: The simulator is now given $c_s = (c_{s,1}, c_{s,2})$ and $C_s = (C_{s,1}, C_{s,2})$ that encrypt the same message. We want, for the appropriate Lagrange coefficients λ_i

$$C_{s,1} = c_{s,1} \cdot \prod_i \alpha_i^{\lambda_i} \qquad C_{s,2} = \prod_i \beta_i^{\lambda_i}.$$

Hence, the simulator can take, for all the honest players except the last one, $r_i' \xleftarrow{\$} \mathbb{Z}_p$ to compute $\alpha_i = c_{s,2}^{\mathsf{sk}_{s,i}} \cdot \mathsf{PK}_s^{r_i'}$ and $\beta_i = g_s^{r_i'}$. For the last honest player, from all the honest-user shares and corrupted-user shares, one sets

$$\alpha_\ell = (C_{s,1}/c_{s,1} \cdot \prod_{i \neq \ell} \alpha_i^{-\lambda_i})^{1/\lambda_\ell} \quad \beta_\ell = (C_{s,2} \cdot \prod_{i \neq \ell} \beta_i^{-\lambda_i})^{1/\lambda_\ell}.$$

Then, for the t players: $\prod \alpha_i^{\lambda_i} = c_s^{\mathsf{sk}_s} \cdot \mathsf{PK}_s^{r'}$ and $\prod \beta_i^{\lambda_i} = g_s^{r'}$, for $r' = \sum \lambda_i r_i'$ and with the implicit $r_\ell' = (R - \sum_{i \neq \ell} \lambda_i r_i')/\lambda_\ell$. So $r' = R$. The view of the attacker remains exactly the same.

Game G_2: In this game, the simulator also takes as input a Diffie-Hellman tuple $(A = g^r, B = \mathsf{PK}_s^r)$ with (g_s, PK_s): it first derives enough independent pairs $(A_i, B_i) = (g_s^{x_i} \cdot A^{y_i}, \mathsf{PK}_s^{x_i} \cdot B^{y_i})$, for random x_i, y_i, for all the non-corrupted players (excepted the last one), and computes $\alpha_i = c_{s,2}^{\mathsf{sk}_{s,i}} \cdot B_i, \beta_i = A_i$. Since $(g_s, \mathsf{PK}_s, A, B)$ is a Diffie-Hellman tuple, the view is perfectly indistinguishable from the previous one.

Game G_3: In this game, the simulator now receives a random tuple (A, B), which makes all the (A_i, B_i) independent random pairs, the rest is unchanged: under the DDH assumption in $\mathbb{G}_s$, the view is computationally indistinguishable.

Game G_4: This is the final simulation, where all the honest shares (α_i, β_i) are chosen at random, except the last ones $(\alpha_\ell, \beta_\ell)$ that are still computed as above to complete the values using c_s and C_s: the view is perfectly indistinguishable from the previous one and does not leak information.

As a consequence, we have proven that there is a simulator (defined in the last game) that produces a view indistinguishable from the real view, with just the input-output pairs. This proves that nothing else leaks. $\square$

The Re-Encryption in $\mathbb{G}_T$. The proof follows the same path as in the previous proof: one is given two ciphertexts $c_T = \mathsf{Encrypt}_T(m, (\mathsf{pk}_1, \mathsf{pk}_2); r_{11}, r_{12}, r_{21}, r_{22})$ and $C_T = \mathsf{Encrypt}_T(m, (\mathsf{PK}_1, \mathsf{PK}_2); R_{11}, R_{12}, R_{21}, R_{22})$ of the same message m under pk_T and PK_T respectively. One needs to simulate all the

$\alpha_{1,i}, \alpha_{2,i}, \alpha_{3,i}, \alpha_{4,i}, \beta_i, \gamma_i, \delta_i$ for all the non-corrupted players. Since c_T and C_T encrypt the same message, and we want

$$C_{T,1} = c_{T,1} \cdot \prod \alpha_{1,i}^{\lambda_i} \cdot \alpha_{2,i}^{\lambda_i} \cdot \alpha_{4,i}^{\lambda_i} \quad C_{T,2} = \prod \beta_i^{\lambda_i} \quad C_{T,3} = \prod \gamma_i^{\lambda_i} \quad C_{T,4} = \prod \delta_i^{\lambda_i}$$

the simulator can take, for all the honest players except the last one, $r'_{11,i}, r'_{12,i}, r'_{21,i}, r'_{22,i}, u_i, v_i \xleftarrow{\$} \mathbb{Z}_p$ to compute, in the first round:

$$\alpha_{3,i} = c_{T,4}^{\mathsf{sk}_{1,i}} \cdot e(g_1, g_2)^{-u_i} \qquad \alpha_{3,\ell} \xleftarrow{\$} \mathbb{G}_T \qquad \alpha_3 = \prod \alpha_{3,i}^{\lambda_i}$$

and in the second round, for all but the last honest player

$$\alpha_{1,i} = c_{T,2}^{\mathsf{sk}_{2,i}} \cdot e(\mathsf{PK}_1, g_2)^{r'_{21,i}} \qquad \beta_i = e(g_1, g_2)^{r'_{11,i}+u_i} \cdot e(\mathsf{PK}_1, g_2)^{r'_{22,i}}$$

$$\alpha_{2,i} = c_{T,3}^{\mathsf{sk}_{1,i}} \cdot e(g_1, \mathsf{PK}_2)^{r'_{11,i}} \qquad \gamma_i = e(g_1, \mathsf{PK}_2)^{r'_{12,i}} \cdot e(g_1, g_2)^{r'_{21,i}+v_i}$$

$$\alpha_{4,i} = \alpha_3^{\mathsf{sk}_{2,i}} \cdot e(\mathsf{PK}_1, g_2)^{v_i} \qquad \delta_i = e(g_1, g_2)^{r'_{12,i}+r'_{22,i}}$$

and for the last honest player:

$$\alpha_{2,\ell} \xleftarrow{\$} \mathbb{G}_T \qquad\qquad \beta_\ell = (C_{T,2} \times \prod_{i \neq \ell} \beta_i^{-\lambda_i})^{1/\lambda_\ell}$$

$$\alpha_{4,\ell} \xleftarrow{\$} \mathbb{G}_T \qquad\qquad \gamma_\ell = (C_{T,3} \times \prod_{i \neq \ell} \gamma_i^{-\lambda_i})^{1/\lambda_\ell}$$

$$\delta_\ell = (C_{T,4} \times \prod_{i \neq \ell} \delta_i^{-\lambda_i})^{1/\lambda_\ell}$$

which implies implicit values for $r'_{11,\ell}, r'_{12,\ell}, r'_{21,\ell}, r'_{22,\ell}, u_\ell, v_\ell$ because the above system is invertible, where X, Y, and Z are the constant values introduced by $c_{T,i}^{\mathsf{sk}_j}$, for some i, j:

$$\lambda_\ell \times \begin{pmatrix} \log \beta_\ell \\ \log \gamma_\ell \\ \log \delta_\ell \\ \log \alpha_{4,\ell} \\ \log \alpha_{3,\ell} \\ \log \alpha_{2,\ell} \end{pmatrix} = \begin{pmatrix} 0 \\ 0 \\ 0 \\ X \\ Y \\ Z \end{pmatrix} + \begin{pmatrix} 1 & 0 & 0 & -\mathsf{sk}_1 & 1 & 0 \\ 0 & \mathsf{sk}_2 & 1 & 0 & 0 & -1 \\ 0 & 1 & 0 & 1 & 0 & 0 \\ 0 & 0 & 0 & 0 & \mathsf{sk}_{2,\ell} & -1 \\ 0 & 0 & 0 & 0 & 1 & 0 \\ 1 & 0 & 0 & 0 & 0 & 0 \end{pmatrix} \begin{pmatrix} r'_{11,\ell} \\ r'_{12,\ell} \\ r'_{21,\ell} \\ r'_{22,\ell} \\ u_\ell \\ v_\ell \end{pmatrix}$$

Then it is possible to set: $\alpha_{1,\ell} = (C_{T,1}/(c_{T,1} \cdot \alpha_2 \alpha_4) \times \prod_{i \neq \ell} \alpha_{1,i}^{-\lambda_i})^{1/\lambda_\ell}$.

First, this is clear that the $\alpha_{3,i}$'s do not leak anything as they contain random masks $e(g_1, g_2)^{-u_i}$. Then, to prove that all the $\alpha_{1,i}, \alpha_{2,i}, \alpha_{4,i}, \beta_i, \gamma_i, \delta_i$ do not leak information, one can perform a similar proof as above for $\mathbb{G}_s$, by using the DDH assumption in both $\mathbb{G}_1$ and $\mathbb{G}_2$. Indeed, each element is masked using a pair either (g_2^r, PK_2^r) or (g_1^r, PK_1^r), for some random r. If one wants to have an indistinguishability under the SXDH assumption (and thus only one DDH assumption in one group), one could add more masks. But this does not make sense to have one key compromised and not the other one, for the same user. Hence, we tried to make the re-encryption as efficient as possible.   □

We stress that for the re-encryption in $\mathbb{G}_1$ or $\mathbb{G}_2$, one just needs the DDH assumption in this group $\mathbb{G}_s$. But for the re-encryption in $\mathbb{G}_T$, one needs the DDH assumption in both $\mathbb{G}_1$ and $\mathbb{G}_2$ (the so-called SXDH assumption). We could rely on only one of the two, by adding masking factors, but this does not really make sense for a user to have his private key sk_1 being compromised without sk_2 (or the opposite).

In addition, zero-knowledge proofs can be provided to guarantee the re-encryption is honestly applied: they just consist in proofs of representations, when $g_s^{\mathsf{sk}_{s,i}}$ are all made public, for $s \in \{1, 2\}$ and all indices i.

4.4   Efficiency

In the concrete case where we have n servers able to perform a distributed protocol as described above, each of them has two scalars corresponding to a secret key for the encryption in $\mathbb{G}_1$ and a secret key for the encryption in $\mathbb{G}_2$. We recall that a ciphertext, in $\mathbb{G}_1$ or $\mathbb{G}_2$, is composed of two group elements, and a ciphertext in $\mathbb{G}_T$ is composed of four group elements. A recipient, that wants the result of either a decryption or a re-encryption with the help of t servers, has to perform a few exponentiations. The table below details the number of exponentiations for each player involved in the distributed protocols.

	Per server	Recipient
Distributed decryption in $\mathbb{G}_1/\mathbb{G}_2$	1	t
in $\mathbb{G}_T$	4	$4t$
Distributed re-encryption in $\mathbb{G}_1/\mathbb{G}_2$	3	t
in $\mathbb{G}_T$	13	$7t$

5   Applications

5.1   Encryption for Boolean Formulae

In this part, we detail the specific case of the evaluation of 2-DNF.

First, as explained in [5], a way to guarantee the ciphertexts are encryption of inputs in $\{0, 1\}$, the verification can be done with our scheme (or the one of BGN or Freeman) with the additional term $\mathsf{Add}_j(\mathsf{Multiply}(C_{x_j}, \mathsf{Add}(C_{x_j}, C_{-1})))$, multiplied by a random constant, so that it adds zero if inputs are correct, or it adds a random value otherwise. This introduces a quadratic term, just for the verification. This is at no extra cost if the Boolean formula is already quadratic, which will be the case of our applications.

Every Boolean formula can be expressed as a disjunction of conjunctive clauses (an OR of ANDs). This form is called disjunctive normal form (DNF) and, more precisely, k-DNF when each clause contains at most k literals. Thus, a 2-DNF formula over the variables $x_1, \ldots, x_n \in \{0, 1\}$ is of the form

$$\bigvee_{i=1}^{m} (\ell_{i,1} \wedge \ell_{i,2}) \text{ with } \ell_{i,1}, \ell_{i,2} \in \{x_1, \overline{x_1}, \ldots, x_n, \overline{x_n}\}.$$

The conversion of 2-DNF formulae into multivariate polynomials of total degree 2 is simple: given $\Phi(x_1, \ldots, x_n) = \bigvee_{i=1}^{m} (\ell_{i,1} \wedge \ell_{i,2})$ a 2-DNF formula, define $\phi(x_1, \ldots, x_n) = \sum_{i=1}^{m} (y_{i,1} \times y_{i,2})$ where $y_{i,j} = \ell_{i,j}$ if $\ell_{i,j} \in \{x_1, \ldots, x_n\}$ or $y_{i,j} = (1 - \ell_{i,j})$ otherwise. In this conversion, a true literal is replaced by 1, and a false literal by 0. Then, an OR is converted into an addition, and an AND is converted into a multiplication. A NOT is just $(1 - x)$ when $x \in \{0, 1\}$. $\phi(x_1, \ldots, x_n)$ is the multivariate polynomial of degree 2 corresponding to $\Phi(x_1, \ldots, x_n)$. As just said, this conversion works if for the inputs, we consider $1 \in \mathbb{Z}_p$ as true and $0 \in \mathbb{Z}_p$ as false, but for the output, $0 \in \mathbb{Z}_p$ is still considered as false whereas any other non-zero value is considered as true.

To evaluate the 2-DNF in an encrypted manner, we propose to encrypt the data and to calculate the quadratic polynomial corresponding to the 2-DNF as seen above by performing Adds and Multiplys. Because the result of the 2-DNF is a Boolean, when a decryption is performed, if the result is equal to 0, one can consider it corresponds to the 0-bit (false) and else, it corresponds to the 1-bit (true).

Hence, when encrypting bits, we propose two different encodings before encryption, depending on the situation: either the 0-bit (false) is encoded by $0 \in \mathbb{Z}_p$ and the 1-bit (true) is encoded by any non-zero integer of $\mathbb{Z}_p^*$; or the 0-bit (false) is encoded by $0 \in \mathbb{Z}_p$ and the 1-bit (true) is encoded by $1 \in \mathbb{Z}_p$. With this second solution, it offers the possibility to perform one NOT on the data before Adds and Multiplys by the operation $1 - x$. However, one has to be aware of making Randomize before decryption to mask the operations but also the input data in some situations: for example, if an Add is performed between three 1s, the result 3 leaks information and needs to be randomized.

Because one just wants to know whether the result is equal to 0 or the result is different from 0, we do not need to compute the logarithm: we can decrypt by just checking whether $c_{s,1} \cdot c_{s,2}^{\mathsf{sk}_s} = 1_s$ or not (for $s = T$, if $c_{T,1} \cdot c_{T,2}^{\mathsf{sk}_2} \cdot c_{T,3}^{\mathsf{sk}_1} \cdot c_{T,4}^{\mathsf{sk}_1 \cdot \mathsf{sk}_2} = 1_T$).

5.2   Group Testing on Encrypted Data

In this application we assume that a hospital collects some blood samples and wants to check which samples are positive or negative to a specific test. Group testing [12] is an efficient technique to detect positive samples with fewer tests in the case the proportion of positive cases is small. The technique consists in mixing some samples, and to perform tests on fewer mixes. More precisely, we denote $\mathbf{X} = (x_{ij})$ the matrix of the mixes: $x_{ij} = 1$ if the i-th sample is in the

j-th mix, otherwise $x_{ij} = 0$. The hospital then sends the (blood) mixes to a laboratory for testing them: we denote y_j the result of the test on the j-th mix.

If a patient (its sample) is in a mix with a negative result, he is negative (not infected). If a patient (its sample) is in a mix with a positive result, we cannot say anything. However, for well-chosen parameters, if a patient is not declared negative, he is likely positive. Thus, for a patient i, the formula that we want to evaluate is $\neg F_i(\mathbf{X}, \mathbf{y})$, which means the patient's test is positive (infected) or not, for $F_i(\mathbf{X}, \mathbf{y}) = \bigvee_j (x_{ij} \wedge \neg y_j)$. The latter is indeed true if there is a mix containing a i-th sample for which the test is negative, and this should claim patient i negative (false). The matrix $\mathbf{X}$ of the samples needs to be encrypted since the patient does not want the laboratory to know his result. Because of the sensitiveness of the data, the result of the tests needs to be encrypted too. But the patient will need access to his own result.

In this scenario, the hospital computes for all i, j, $C_{x_{ij}} \in \mathbb{G}_1^2$, the encryption of x_{ij}, and the laboratory computes for all j, $C_{\overline{y_j}} \in \mathbb{G}_2^2$, the encryption of $\overline{y_j}$. Then, they both send the ciphertexts to an external database. With our homomorphic encryption scheme, to compute $\neg F_i$, we can publicly evaluate the following formula: $C_i = \mathsf{Randomize}(\mathsf{Add}_j(\mathsf{Multiply}(C_{x_{ij}}, C_{\overline{y_j}})))$. Anybody can publicly verify the computations and if it is correct, a pool of controllers perform a distributed re-encryption of the result of patient i under his key PK_i. In this way, the patient cannot decrypt the database or the result of the tests directly, but only with the help of a pool of controller. The goal of the controllers is to limit access to the specific users only. Under an assumption about the collusions among the controllers, nobody excepted the users will have access to their own results.

5.3 Consistency Model on Encrypted Data

Another famous application is machine learning, where we have some trainers that fill a database and users who want to know a function of their inputs and the database. For privacy reasons, trainers do not want the users to learn the training set, and users do not want the trainers to learn their inputs. As in the previous case, we will involve a pool of distributed controllers to limit decryptions, but the controllers should not learn anything either.

Suppose a very large network of nodes in which some combinations should be avoided as they would result to failures. When a failure happens, the combination is stored in a database. And before applying a given combination, one can check whether it will likely lead to a failure, and then change. For example, the network can be a group of people where each of them can receive data. But, for some specific reasons, if a subgroup A of people is knowing a file a, the subgroup B must not have the knowledge of a file b. This case of application can be viewed as a consistency model [28] which can be formally described as: the input is a vector of states (each being either true or false), and if in the database all the j-th states are true a new input needs to have its j-th state to be true; if all the j-th states in the database are false, the new input needs to have its j-th state to be false; otherwise the j-th state can be either true or false. As a consequence, if we denote the i-th element of the database as a vector $\mathbf{x}_i = (x_{ij})_j$ and the user's vector by $\mathbf{y} = (y_j)$, that vector $\mathbf{y}$ is said consistent with the database if the following predicate is true:

$$\bigwedge_j \left(((\wedge_i x_{ij} \wedge y_j) \vee (\wedge_i \overline{x_{ij}} \wedge \overline{y}_j) \vee (\vee_i x_{ij} \wedge \vee_i \overline{x_{ij}}) \right).$$

Let $X_j = \wedge_i x_{ij}$, $Y_j = \wedge_i \overline{x_{ij}}$, and $Z_j = \vee_i x_{ij} \wedge \vee_i \overline{x_{ij}}$. We define $\mathsf{F}(\mathbf{x}_1, \ldots, \mathbf{x}_m, \mathbf{y})$ the formula we want to compute on the encrypted inputs:

$$\mathsf{F}(\mathbf{x}_1, \ldots, \mathbf{x}_m, \mathbf{y}) = \bigwedge_j \left((X_j \wedge y_j) \vee (Y_j \wedge \overline{y}_j) \vee Z_j \right).$$

By definition, X_j, Y_j, and Z_j are exclusive, as X_j means the literals are all true, Y_j means the literals are all false, and Z_j means there are both true and false literals. So we have: $X_j \vee Z_j = \overline{Y_j}$ and $Y_j \vee Z_j = \overline{X_j}$. Thus, we have

$$\neg\mathsf{F}(\mathbf{x}_1, \ldots, \mathbf{x}_m, \mathbf{y}) = \bigvee_j \left((Y_j \vee \overline{y_j}) \wedge (X_j \vee y_j) \right).$$

Now, we see how the encryption and the decryption is performed to obtain the result of an evaluation. First, we explain how the trainers can update the database, when adding a vector $\mathbf{x}_m$. The values X_j are updated into X_j' as

$$X_j' = \bigwedge_{i=1}^{m} x_{ij} = \bigwedge_{i=1}^{m-1} x_{ij} \wedge x_{mj} = \begin{cases} X_j = \wedge_{i=1}^{m-1} x_{ij} & \text{if } x_{mj} = \text{true} \\ \text{false} & \text{otherwise} \end{cases}$$

which is easy to compute for the trainer, since it knows $\mathbf{x}_m$ in clear, even if X_j is encrypted: the trainer can dynamically compute C_{X_j} the encryption of X_j, when adding a new line in the database, by just making a Randomize if x_{mj} is true (to keep the value X_j unchanged), or by replacing the value by a fresh encryption of 0 otherwise. Similarly, the trainer can update C_{Y_j}, the encryption of Y_j. On the user-side, he can compute C_{y_j} and $C_{\overline{y_j}}$ the encryptions of his inputs y_j and $\overline{y_j}$ respectively. Then, everyone and thus the controllers can compute:

$$C_j = \mathsf{Randomize}\left(\mathsf{Add}_j \left(\mathsf{Multiply}(\mathsf{Add}(C_{Y_j}, C_{\overline{y_j}}), \mathsf{Add}(C_{X_j}, C_{y_j})) \right) \right).$$

Because of the Multiply, C_{Y_j} and $C_{\overline{y_j}}$ must be ciphertexts in $\mathbb{G}_1$, while C_{X_j} and C_{y_j} must be ciphertexts in $\mathbb{G}_2$. To allow a control of the final decryption, a pool of controllers re-encrypt for the user in a distributed way.

Acknowledgments. This work was supported in part by the European Community's Seventh Framework Programme (FP7/2007-2013 Grant Agreement no. 339563 – CryptoCloud) and the French ANR ALAMBIC Project (ANR16-CE39-0006).

A   Freeman's Approach

A.1   Description

For the Freeman's construction, we will use the brackets notation, also extended to vectors and matrices, as explained in Fig. 2.

- For $x \in \mathbb{Z}_p, \mathbf{A} \in \mathcal{M}_{m,n}(\mathbb{Z}_p)$: $[x] = g^x$, $[\mathbf{A}] = g^{\mathbf{A}} = (g^{a_{ij}})_{ij}$

- For $x \in \mathbb{Z}_p, \mathbf{A}, \mathbf{B} \in \mathcal{M}_{m,n}(\mathbb{Z}_p), \mathbf{X} \in \mathcal{M}_{n,n'}(\mathbb{Z}_p), \mathbf{Y} \in \mathcal{M}_{m',m}(\mathbb{Z}_p)$:

$$x \cdot [\mathbf{A}] = g^{x\mathbf{A}} \qquad [\mathbf{A}] \cdot \mathbf{X} = g^{\mathbf{AX}} \qquad \mathbf{Y} \cdot [\mathbf{A}] = g^{\mathbf{YA}} \qquad [\mathbf{A}] + [\mathbf{B}] = [\mathbf{A} + \mathbf{B}]$$

- For $\mathbf{A} \in \mathcal{M}_{m,n}(\mathbb{Z}_p), \mathbf{B} \in \mathcal{M}_{m',n'}(\mathbb{Z}_p)$: $[\mathbf{A}]_1 \bullet [\mathbf{B}]_2 = [\mathbf{A} \otimes \mathbf{B}]_T$

Fig. 2. Bracket notations

The main goal of Freeman's approach was to generalize the BGN cryptosystem to any hard-subgroup problems. We instantiate a variant of the Freeman's cryptosystem allowing multiple users, without the twin ciphertexts (in G and H). Since we will work in groups $\mathbb{G}_1$, $\mathbb{G}_2$, and $\mathbb{G}_T$, the algorithms Keygen, Encrypt and Decrypt will take a sub-script s to precise the group $\mathbb{G}_s$ in which they operate, but the Setup is common.

Setup(λ): Given a security parameter λ, run and output param $= (\mathbb{G}_1, \mathbb{G}_2, \mathbb{G}_T, p, g_1, g_2, e) \leftarrow \mathcal{G}(\lambda)$.

Keygen$_s$(param): For $s \in \{1,2\}$, choose $\mathbf{B}_s \xleftarrow{\$} GL_2(\mathbb{Z}_p)$, let $\mathbf{P}_s = \mathbf{B}_s^{-1}\mathbf{U}_2\mathbf{B}_s$ (where $\mathbf{U}_2$ is the canonical matrix for projection on the first coordinate, in dimension 2) and $\mathbf{p}_s \in \ker(\mathbf{P}_s) \setminus \{\mathbf{0}\}$, and output the public key $\mathsf{pk}_s = [\mathbf{p}_s]_s$ and the private key $\mathsf{sk}_s = \mathbf{P}_s$. In the following, we always implicitly assume that the public keys contain the public parameters param, and the private keys contain the public keys. From $(\mathsf{pk}_1, \mathsf{sk}_1) \leftarrow$ Keygen$_1$(param) and $(\mathsf{pk}_2, \mathsf{sk}_2) \leftarrow$ Keygen$_2$(param), one can consider $\mathsf{pk}_T = (\mathsf{pk}_1, \mathsf{pk}_2)$ and $\mathsf{sk}_T = (\mathsf{sk}_1, \mathsf{sk}_2)$.

Encrypt$_s$(pk_s, m, A_s): For $s \in \{1,2\}$, to encrypt a message $m \in \mathbb{Z}_p$ using public key pk_s and $A_s = [\mathbf{a}]_s \in \mathbb{G}_s^2$, choose $r \xleftarrow{\$} \mathbb{Z}_p$ and output the ciphertext $C_s = (m \cdot [\mathbf{a}]_s + r \cdot [\mathbf{p}_s]_s, [\mathbf{a}]_s) \in \mathbb{G}_s^2 \times \mathbb{G}_s^2$. For $s = T$, with $A_s = ([\mathbf{a}_1]_1, [\mathbf{a}_2]_2)$, set $[\mathbf{a}]_T = [\mathbf{a}_1]_1 \bullet [\mathbf{a}_2]_2 \in \mathbb{G}_T^4$, choose $[\mathbf{r}_1]_1 \xleftarrow{\$} \mathbb{G}_1^2, [\mathbf{r}_2]_2 \xleftarrow{\$} \mathbb{G}_2^2$, and output $C_T = (m \cdot [\mathbf{a}]_T + [\mathbf{p}_1]_1 \bullet [\mathbf{r}_2]_2 + [\mathbf{r}_1]_1 \bullet [\mathbf{p}_2]_2, [\mathbf{a}]_T) \in \mathbb{G}_T^4 \times \mathbb{G}_T^4$.

Decrypt$_s$(sk_s, C_s): For $s \in \{1,2\}$, given $C_s = ([\mathbf{c}_{s,1}]_s, [\mathbf{c}_{s,2}]_s)$ and $\mathsf{sk}_s = \mathbf{P}_s$, let $C_s' = ([\mathbf{c}_{s,1}]_s \cdot \mathbf{P}_s, [\mathbf{c}_{s,2}]_s \cdot \mathbf{P}_s)$. For $s = T$, compute $C_T' = ([\mathbf{c}_{T,1}]_T \cdot (\mathbf{P}_1 \otimes \mathbf{P}_2), [\mathbf{c}_{T,2}]_T \cdot (\mathbf{P}_1 \otimes \mathbf{P}_2))$.
In both cases, output the logarithm of the first component of $\mathbf{c}_{s,1}'$ in base the first component of $\mathbf{c}_{s,2}'$.

One can note that matrices $\mathbf{B}_1$ and $\mathbf{B}_2$ are drawn independently, so the keys in $\mathbb{G}_1$ and $\mathbb{G}_2$ are independent. For any pair $(\mathsf{pk}_1 = [\mathbf{p}_1]_1, \mathsf{pk}_2 = [\mathbf{p}_2]_2)$, one can implicitly define a public key for the target group. To decrypt in the target group, both private keys $\mathsf{sk}_1 = \mathbf{P}_1$ and $\mathsf{sk}_2 = \mathbf{P}_2$ are needed. Actually, one just needs $\mathbf{P}_1 \otimes \mathbf{P}_2$ to decrypt: $C_T' = ([\mathbf{c}_{T,1}]_T \cdot (\mathbf{P}_1 \otimes \mathbf{P}_2), [\mathbf{c}_{T,2}]_T \cdot (\mathbf{P}_1 \otimes \mathbf{P}_2))$, but $\mathbf{P}_1 \otimes \mathbf{P}_2$ and $(\mathbf{P}_1, \mathbf{P}_2)$ contain the same information and the latter is more compact.

A.2   Distributed Decryption

When a third-party performs the decryption, it is important to be able to prove the correct decryption, which consists of classical zero-knowledge proofs. But this is even better if the decryption process can be distributed among several servers, under the assumption that only a small fraction of them can be corrupted or under the control of an adversary.

To decrypt a ciphertext in $\mathbb{G}_s$ with $s \in \{1, 2\}$, one needs to compute $([\mathbf{c}_{s,1}]_s \cdot \mathsf{sk}_s, [\mathbf{c}_{s,2}]_s \cdot \mathsf{sk}_s)$. In a Shamir's like manner [29], one can perform a t-out-of-n threshold secret sharing by distributing sk_s such that $\mathsf{sk}_s = \sum_{i \in I} \lambda_{I,i} \mathsf{sk}_{s,i}$ with $I \subset \{1, \ldots, n\}$ a subset of t users, and for all $i \in I$, $\lambda_{I,i} \in \mathbb{Z}_p$ and $\mathsf{sk}_{s,i}$ is the secret key of the party P_i. For $s = T$ and with just the distribution of sk_1 and sk_2, it is also possible to perform a distributed decryption, using the relation $\mathsf{sk}_1 \otimes \mathsf{sk}_2 = (\mathsf{sk}_1 \otimes 1) \times (1 \otimes \mathsf{sk}_2)$. One can thus make a two-round decryption, first in $\mathbb{G}_1$ and then in $\mathbb{G}_2$.

However, in this scheme, the secret key must be a projection matrix, which is not easy to generate at random: for this key generation algorithm, a trusted dealer is required, which is not ideal when nobody is trusted.

References

1. Abdalla, M., Benhamouda, F., Kolhweiss, M., Waldner, H.: Decentralizing inner-product functional encryption. Cryptology ePrint Archive, Report 2019/020 (2019). https://eprint.iacr.org/2019/020
2. Attrapadung, N., Hanaoka, G., Mitsunari, S., Sakai, Y., Shimizu, K., Teruya, T.: Efficient two-level homomorphic encryption in prime-order bilinear groups and a fast implementation in WebAssembly. In: Kim, J., Ahn, G.J., Kim, S., Kim, Y., López, J., Kim, T. (eds.) ASIACCS 2018, pp. 685–697. ACM Press (2018)
3. Baltico, C.E.Z., Catalano, D., Fiore, D., Gay, R.: Practical functional encryption for quadratic functions with applications to predicate encryption. In: Katz, J., Shacham, H. (eds.) CRYPTO 2017. LNCS, vol. 10401, pp. 67–98. Springer, Cham (2017). https://doi.org/10.1007/978-3-319-63688-7_3
4. Blaze, M., Bleumer, G., Strauss, M.: Divertible protocols and atomic proxy cryptography. In: Nyberg, K. (ed.) EUROCRYPT 1998. LNCS, vol. 1403, pp. 127–144. Springer, Heidelberg (1998). https://doi.org/10.1007/BFb0054122
5. Boneh, D., Goh, E.-J., Nissim, K.: Evaluating 2-DNF formulas on ciphertexts. In: Kilian, J. (ed.) TCC 2005. LNCS, vol. 3378, pp. 325–341. Springer, Heidelberg (2005). https://doi.org/10.1007/978-3-540-30576-7_18
6. Boneh, D., Sahai, A., Waters, B.: Functional encryption: definitions and challenges. In: Ishai, Y. (ed.) TCC 2011. LNCS, vol. 6597, pp. 253–273. Springer, Heidelberg (2011). https://doi.org/10.1007/978-3-642-19571-6_16
7. Catalano, D., Fiore, D.: Using linearly-homomorphic encryption to evaluate degree-2 functions on encrypted data. In: Ray, I., Li, N., Kruegel, C. (eds.) ACM CCS 2015, pp. 1518–1529. ACM Press, October 2015
8. Chase, M., Chow, S.S.M.: Improving privacy and security in multi-authority attribute-based encryption. In: Al-Shaer, E., Jha, S., Keromytis, A.D. (eds.) ACM CCS 2009, pp. 121–130. ACM Press, November 2009

9. Chotard, J., Dufour Sans, E., Gay, R., Phan, D.H., Pointcheval, D.: Decentralized multi-client functional encryption for inner product. In: Peyrin, T., Galbraith, S. (eds.) ASIACRYPT 2018. LNCS, vol. 11273, pp. 703–732. Springer, Cham (2018). https://doi.org/10.1007/978-3-030-03329-3_24

10. Chotard, J., Sans, E.D., Gay, R., Phan, D.H., Pointcheval, D.: Multi-client functional encryption with repetition for inner product. Cryptology ePrint Archive, Report 2018/1021 (2018). https://eprint.iacr.org/2018/1021

11. Culnane, C., Pereira, O., Ramchen, K., Teague, V.: Universally verifiable MPC with applications to IRV ballot counting. Cryptology ePrint Archive, Report 2018/246 (2018). https://eprint.iacr.org/2018/246

12. Dorfman, R.: The detection of defective members of large populations. Ann. Math. Stat. **14**(4), 436–440 (1943)

13. Fiat, A., Naor, M.: Broadcast encryption. In: Stinson, D.R. (ed.) CRYPTO 1993. LNCS, vol. 773, pp. 480–491. Springer, Heidelberg (1994). https://doi.org/10.1007/3-540-48329-2_40

14. Frederiksen, T.K., Lindell, Y., Osheter, V., Pinkas, B.: Fast distributed RSA key generation for semi-honest and malicious adversaries. In: Shacham, H., Boldyreva, A. (eds.) CRYPTO 2018. LNCS, vol. 10992, pp. 331–361. Springer, Cham (2018). https://doi.org/10.1007/978-3-319-96881-0_12

15. Freeman, D.M.: Converting pairing-based cryptosystems from composite-order groups to prime-order groups. In: Gilbert, H. (ed.) EUROCRYPT 2010. LNCS, vol. 6110, pp. 44–61. Springer, Heidelberg (2010). https://doi.org/10.1007/978-3-642-13190-5_3

16. Garg, S., Gentry, C., Halevi, S., Raykova, M., Sahai, A., Waters, B.: Candidate indistinguishability obfuscation and functional encryption for all circuits. In: 54th FOCS, pp. 40–49. IEEE Computer Society Press, October 2013

17. Gay, R.: Functional encryption for quadratic functions, and applications to predicate encryption. Cryptology ePrint Archive, Report 2016/1106 (2016). http://eprint.iacr.org/2016/1106

18. Gentry, C.: Fully homomorphic encryption using ideal lattices. In: Mitzenmacher, M. (ed.) 41st ACM STOC, pp. 169–178. ACM Press, May/June 2009

19. Goldwasser, S., et al.: Multi-input functional encryption. In: Nguyen, P.Q., Oswald, E. (eds.) EUROCRYPT 2014. LNCS, vol. 8441, pp. 578–602. Springer, Heidelberg (2014). https://doi.org/10.1007/978-3-642-55220-5_32

20. Goldwasser, S., Goyal, V., Jain, A., Sahai, A.: Multi-input functional encryption. Cryptology ePrint Archive, Report 2013/727 (2013). http://eprint.iacr.org/2013/727

21. Goldwasser, S., Kalai, Y.T., Popa, R.A., Vaikuntanathan, V., Zeldovich, N.: Reusable garbled circuits and succinct functional encryption. In: Boneh, D., Roughgarden, T., Feigenbaum, J. (eds.) 45th ACM STOC, pp. 555–564. ACM Press, June 2013

22. Gordon, S.D., Katz, J., Liu, F.H., Shi, E., Zhou, H.S.: Multi-input functional encryption. Cryptology ePrint Archive, Report 2013/774 (2013). http://eprint.iacr.org/2013/774

23. Kawai, Y., Matsuda, T., Hirano, T., Koseki, Y., Hanaoka, G.: Proxy re-encryption that supports homomorphic operations for re-encrypted ciphertexts. IEICE Trans. Fundam. Electron. Commun. Comput. Sci. **E102.A**, 81–98 (2019)

24. Lewko, A., Waters, B.: Decentralizing attribute-based encryption. In: Paterson, K.G. (ed.) EUROCRYPT 2011. LNCS, vol. 6632, pp. 568–588. Springer, Heidelberg (2011). https://doi.org/10.1007/978-3-642-20465-4_31

25. Naor, D., Naor, M., Lotspiech, J.: Revocation and tracing schemes for stateless receivers. In: Kilian, J. (ed.) CRYPTO 2001. LNCS, vol. 2139, pp. 41–62. Springer, Heidelberg (2001). https://doi.org/10.1007/3-540-44647-8_3
26. Phan, D.H., Pointcheval, D., Strefler, M.: Decentralized dynamic broadcast encryption. In: Visconti, I., De Prisco, R. (eds.) SCN 2012. LNCS, vol. 7485, pp. 166–183. Springer, Heidelberg (2012). https://doi.org/10.1007/978-3-642-32928-9_10
27. Sahai, A., Waters, B.: Fuzzy identity-based encryption. In: Cramer, R. (ed.) EURO-CRYPT 2005. LNCS, vol. 3494, pp. 457–473. Springer, Heidelberg (2005). https://doi.org/10.1007/11426639_27
28. Schapire, R.: Computer science 511 - theoretical machine learning (2014). http://www.cs.princeton.edu/courses/archive/spring14/cos511/
29. Shamir, A.: How to share a secret. Commun. Assoc. Comput. Mach. **22**(11), 612–613 (1979)

Robust Distributed Pseudorandom Functions for mNP Access Structures

Bei Liang$^{(\boxtimes)}$ and Aikaterini Mitrokotsa

Chalmers University of Technology, Gothenburg, Sweden
{lbei,aikmitr}@chalmers.se

Abstract. *Distributed pseudorandom functions* (DPRFs) formally defined by Naor *et al.* (EUROCRYPT'99) provide the properties of regular PRFs as well as the ability to distribute the evaluation of the PRF function; rendering them useful against single point of failures in multiple settings (*e.g.*, key distribution centres). To avoid the corruption of the partial PRF values computed by distributed servers, Naor *et al.* proposed the notion of *robust distributed PRFs*, which not only allows the evaluation of the PRF value by a set of distributed servers, but also allows to verify if the partial evaluation values are computed correctly.

In this paper, we investigate different approaches to build non-interactive robust distributed PRFs for a general class of access structures, going beyond the existing threshold and monotone span programs (MSP). More precisely, our contributions are two fold: *(i)* we first adapt the notion of single round robust distributed PRFs for threshold access structures to one for any mNP access structure (monotone functions in NP), and *(ii)* we provide a provably secure general construction of robust distributed PRFs by employing puncturable PRFs, a non-interactive witness indistinguishable proof (NIWI) and indistinguishable obfuscation. We compare our robust DPRF with existing DPRFs in terms of security guarantees, underlying assumptions and required primitives.

Keywords: Robust distributed PRFs · Threshold access structures · Monotone functions · Puncturable PRFs

1 Introduction

Distributed pseudorandom functions (DPRFs), defined by Naor *et al.* [26], provide the properties of regular PRFs (*i.e.*, indistinguishability from random functions) and the capability to evaluate the function f (approximate of a random function) among a set of distributed servers. More precisely, Naor *et al.* [26] considered the setting where the PRF secret key is split among N servers and at least t servers are needed to evaluate the PRF. The user who wishes to get the PRF value on input x, sends x to each server, and receives partial function values from at least t out of N servers. It then combines the t partial values into a PRF value on x. There is no other interaction in the system, namely the servers do not need to communicate during the protocol. Non-interactive distributed PRFs

© Springer Nature Switzerland AG 2019
Z. Lin et al. (Eds.): ISC 2019, LNCS 11723, pp. 107–126, 2019.
https://doi.org/10.1007/978-3-030-30215-3_6

in this setting are known as *distributed PRFs* for threshold access structures. The main feature of distributed PRFs is that in order to evaluate the PRF, it is not required to reconstruct the key at a single location (*e.g.*, client).

Distributed PRFs provide strong guarantees against single point of failures and can be employed in key distribution centres [26] as well as to provide reliable byzantine agreement protocols [27]. However, standard distributed PRFs do not provide a guarantee about the correct computation of the pseudorandom function value, which is rather important in secure multi-party settings. For instance, corrupted servers controlled by adversaries could send to a client incorrect partial evaluations of the PRF, thus, preventing the user (client) from computing the correct (combined) PRF value. To avoid such cases, Naor *et al.* [26] proposed the *robustness* property for the distributed PRFs, which requires an additional procedure to verify that the partial values received from the servers on some input are computed correctly.

Although robust distributed PRFs have received some attention all existing solutions [4,5,23,26] require either threshold structures or monotone access programs (MSP). In this paper, we address the following question: *Is it possible to build non-interactive robust distributed PRFs for a general class of access mechanisms (e.g., that can be described by an access predicate) going beyond existing threshold and monotone span programs (MSP) access structures?* More precisely, we investigate whether it is possible to transform a PRF into a *robust distributed PRF* for an even more general class of access structures.

The answer is affirmative and our contributions are two-fold: *(i)* we adapt the notion of single round robust distributed PRFs for threshold access structures to one for any mNP access structure (monotone functions in NP), and *(ii)* we provide a provably secure general construction of robust distributed PRFs by employing puncturable PRFs, a non-interactive witness indistinguishable proof (NIWI) and indistinguishable obfuscation.

An immediate application of distributed PRFs is to construct a distributed key distribution centre (DKDC), where the task of generating a key is distributed among N servers, such that any t of them together can obtain the key (which corresponds to the PRF value). With our proposed robust distributed PRF for mNP access structures, it is feasible to construct a DKDC in such a way that only properly authorized servers – *i.e.*, who satisfy an access predicate (*e.g.*, the servers are within some predetermined distance) – can learn the key. Furthermore, our proposed robust DPRF is secure against malicious servers and can detect corrupted servers that broadcast incorrect values by using a proof to verify that the servers' partial computations are carried out correctly. For example as shown in Fig. 1, imagine the scenario, where many users in a conference (associated with a public value H_C) need a key to get access to the online resources of this conference. There are N servers that can be accessed and distributed around the whole conference centre. When a user asks for the key, he contacts the servers that are located within a distance δ away from the user's electronic device, and sends them H_C as the input for the distributed PRF evaluation. Then, each server within distance δ, sends the partial value y_i

and the corresponding proof π_i of correctness for the evaluation of y_i on H_C. Once having received the response from the contacted servers, the user checks the proofs of correctness π_i of the partial values y_i. If the proofs received in the previous phase are verified, by employing the Combine algorithm, the user can compute the PRF value y on the input H_C, where y is the key to access the online resources. Note that all users in the conference learn the same PRF value y from different subsets of servers on the same input H_C, even though the servers located around different users (who sit in different areas within distance δ) usually are not the same.

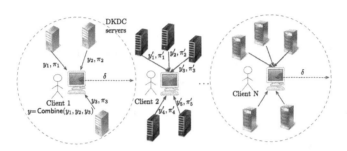

Fig. 1. An application of robust distributed PRFs for mNP to DKDC

In Table 1, we provide a comparison of our robust distributed PRF for mNP access structures to existing distributed PRFs. We compare them in terms of used access structure classes, the assumptions and building blocks they are based on, as well as the security that they can achieve. It is important to note that existing robust DPRFs do not provide the flexibility of general access structures that ours does and thus, could not be employed in the example described above, where the distance of the servers from the user (client) is used as an access predicate.

Naor *et al.* [26] pointed out that the robustness property can be achieved either via error-correcting properties of Reed-Solomon codes [24] w.r.t. their threshold construction of an ℓ-wise independent function, or via a zero-knowledge variant of Schnorr's proof for the value of the Diffie-Hellman function [30] w.r.t. their DDH-based distributed PRF scheme. Such proof techniques, however, require interaction[1], are tailored to the DDH-type of PRF schemes, and none of them is known to be compatible with existing PRFs based on other types of assumptions (such as one-way functions). Libert *et al.* [23] recently showed how to use fully homomorphic signatures [14] that are context-hiding to generally compile distributed PRFs (more precisely, Libert *et al.* [23] construct key-homomorphic PRFs) into robust distributed PRFs against malicious servers. Boneh, Lewi, Montgomery and Raghunathan [5] proposed a generic construction of threshold distributed PRFs from key-homomorphic PRFs, which is

---

[1] Except of the case where a non-interactive proof is computed in the random oracle model.

instantiated for the first time in the standard model under the LWE assumption. Boneh *et al.* [4] suggested another generic robust distributed PRF construction from a general "universal thresholdizer" tool, which is a natural generalization of a threshold fully homomorphic encryption scheme with robustness. Boneh *et al.* [4] also showed that the robustness of a universal thresholdizer can be enforced either by using NIZK with pre-processing, which can be constructed from one-way functions [10], or homomorphic signatures [14]. However, contrary to our proposed distributed PRF none of the existing ones can be employed for general access structures *e.g.*, structures that satisfy an access predicate (for instance being within some predetermined distance as described in the example above).

Table 1. Comparison of existing distributed PRF schemes.

Distributed PRF	Access structure	Robustness	Pseudorandomness	Tool	Assumption
Naor *et al.* [26]	Threshold & monotone span programs	✓*	Message-adaptive & selective-corruption	Reed-Solomon codes & Schnorr's proof	ℓ-wise independence or DDH
Libert *et al.* [23]	Threshold	✓	Message-adaptive & adaptive-corruption	Homomorphic signatures	LWE
Boneh *et al.* [5]	Threshold	No	Message-adaptive & selective-corruption	Key-homomorphic PRFs	LWE
Boneh *et al.* [4]	Monotone boolean formulas	✓	Message-adaptive & selective-corruption	Universal thresholdizer	LWE
Ours	mNP	✓	Message-selective & adaptive-corruption	NIWI & Commitment & $i\mathcal{O}$	$i\mathcal{O}$ & one-way permutation[†]

* Naor *et al.* [26] mentioned that their constructions can be amended to be robust based either on error-correcting mechanisms or on proof techniques, but no concrete construction is given.
† In order not to bring in more assumptions, here we use the NIWI construction given by Bitansky and Paneth [2] assuming the existence of $i\mathcal{O}$ and one-way permutations. NIWI proofs also can be constructed based on the decisional linear assumption [17]. The commitment scheme used in our robust DPRF is a perfectly binding non-interactive commitment, without trusted setup, which can be constructed from certifiably injective one way functions. Goyal *et al.* [15] also proposed alternative constructions of perfectly binding non-interactive commitment (without trusted setup) under the learning parity with low noise (LPLN) assumption and the learning with errors (LWE) assumption.

Our Contributions. In this work, we consider single round robust DPRFs for monotone functions in NP, also known as mNP that was initially studied by Komargodski *et al.* [20]. We also show that robust DPRFs for an mNP access structure can be constructed generally from the ingredients of puncturable PRFs [6,9,19], a non-interactive witness indistinguishable proof (NIWI) and indistinguishable obfuscation [11].

Specifically, a single round robust DPRF for an mNP access structure is defined as follows: given an access structure, the setup algorithm outputs a public parameter PP and a secret key msk which defines a PRF. On input the PRF key msk, there is an algorithm that "splits" it into different pieces (shares) sk_i and then distributes the shares of the key to a collection of servers. Each server, using its own secret share sk_i, is allowed to compute a partial function value y_i and its proof π_i on input x. Using the proof π_i, anyone can locally verify the correctness of the computation for the partial function value y_i on point x with a local verification algorithm. For the "qualified" subsets, there is a witness attesting to this fact and given the witness along with the (correct) partial values y_i of these "qualified" servers, it should be possible to reconstruct the evaluation of the PRF on an input x. On the other hand, for the "unqualified" subsets there is no witness, and so it should be impossible to reconstruct the PRF on the input x. Let us consider the application scenario described in Fig. 1 as an example. For client 1, the "qualified" set of servers refers to a subset of N servers that consists of all the servers whose distance from client 1 is not bigger than δ. Let us denote them as S_1, S_2 and S_3. The witness corresponding to such a qualified set $T = \{S_1, S_2, S_3\}$ is the set of distances of S_1, S_2 and S_3 to client 1, i.e., $(\delta_1, \delta_2, \delta_3)$. The set $T' = \{S_1, S_2, S_4, S_5\}$ can be recognized as an "unqualified" set, since it includes the servers S_4 and S_5, whose distance from client 1 is beyond δ as depicted in Fig. 2. Furthermore, except of the correctness, verifiability, and pseudorandomness properties, robust DPRFs should satisfy the *robustness* property, which requires that it should be infeasible for a corrupted server holding the secret share sk_j to come up with an incorrect partial value y_j, for some input x', that can be still verified.

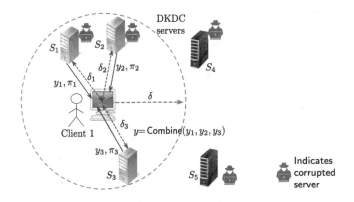

Fig. 2. An example of qualified/unqualified servers in DKDC

The main challenge is how to provide a non-interactive proof for the correct computation of the partial evaluation, while allowing the reconstruction for the final function value. To address this problem, Libert *et al.* [23] proposed one solution that employs homomorphic signatures in a black-box manner so that each server can produce a valid signature for the partial evaluation of the PRF on any input x using its own share sk_i and the corresponding signature. The robustness guarantee is provided by the unforgeability property of the homomorphic signatures. However, Libert et $al.$'s approach requires homomorphic signatures that are simultaneously context-hiding and adaptively unforgeable, which, to the best of our knowledge, are not known to be instantiated yet.

In this work, we employ Goyal et $al.$'s verifiable random function (VRF) scheme [15] to provide the NIWI proof for the partial evaluation, which is computed from a new independent PRF with the secret key sk_i on an input x. The robustness is guaranteed by the uniqueness of Goyal et $al.$'s VRF [15], which in turn relies on the soundness of the NIWI proof system. In order to reconstruct the final PRF value from the totally independent (partial) PRF values, we use program obfuscation which outputs the correct final PRF value if each partial PRF value is verified by the specific NIWI proof system.

Overview of Our Techniques. We now give a high level overview of our technical approach. Our basic scheme is rather easy to describe. Let $\mathbb{A} \in \mathsf{mNP}$ be an access structure on N servers $S_1, \ldots, S_N$. Given the verification procedure $V_{\mathbb{A}}$ for an mNP access structure $\mathbb{A}$, a trusted third party samples the PRF key K as well as N independent PRF keys $K_1, \ldots, K_N$. Each server receives a key K_i for $i \in \{1, \ldots, N\}$. For an input x, each server computes the partial evaluation $y_i = \mathsf{PRF}(K_i, x)$ and the corresponding proof π_i for certifying that the server's output y_i is the evaluation of $\mathsf{PRF}(K_i, x)$. We employ the basic idea of Goyal et $al.$'s VRF [15] scheme, which is to create a NIWI proof π_i for the statement that at least two out of three commitments (c_{i1}, c_{i2}, c_{i3}) (in the verification key) open to keys K_{i1}, K_{i2} such that $y_i = \mathsf{PRF}(K_{ij}, x) = \mathsf{PRF}(K_{ij'}, x)$ where $j, j' \in \{1, 2, 3\}$ and $j \neq j'$, using $(j = i1, j' = i2, K_i, K_i, r_{i1}, r_{i2})$ as witness. In order to reconstruct the function value on input x from a set of shares of qualified servers Γ, with witness w, the client runs the public obfuscated program $i\mathcal{O}(\mathsf{Prog})$, which is setup as part of the public parameters. The program Prog is hardwired with a PRF key K, the verification $V_{\mathbb{A}}$ and three independent commitments (c_{i1}, c_{i2}, c_{i3}) for each server's key K_i. Prog takes as input the valid witness w of the set of qualified servers $\Gamma \subseteq S_1, \ldots, S_N, \{y_i, \pi_i\}_{i \in \Gamma}$ and x and checks if the condition $V_{\mathbb{A}}(\Gamma, w) = 1$ and (x, y_i, π_i) is verified by the NIWI verification procedure for every $i \in \Gamma$. If the condition holds, the program Prog outputs $\mathsf{PRF}(K, x)$; otherwise it outputs $\bot$. We show that the robustness property is implied by the soundness of the NIWI proof system. We also show that the resulting robust DPRF remains selectively pseudorandom even when a set of unqualified servers $T \subseteq \{S_1, \ldots, S_N\}$, namely $T \notin \mathbb{A}$, are corrupted and the adversary is given the share of the servers that are uncorrupted on the inputs of its choice. For instance in our application scenario described above, we show that the pseudorandomness of our DPRF (on some input that has never been queried) is still maintained even if the adversary corrupts a subset of qualified and a subset of unqualified servers, $e.g.$, if the servers S_1, S_2, S_4 and S_5 are corrupted by the adversary as depicted in Fig. 2.

Related Work. Function secret sharing is closely related to distributed PRFs. The notion of function secret sharing (FSS) was introduced by Boyle et $al.$ [7] as a natural generalization of distributed point functions (DPF). More precisely, a *function secret sharing* scheme for a class $\mathcal{F}$, which is a class of efficiently computable and succinctly described functions $f : \{0,1\}^n \to \mathbb{G}$, allows to split an arbitrary $f \in \mathcal{F}$ into p functions $f_1, \ldots, f_p$ such that: (1) $f(x) = \Sigma_{i=1}^p f_i(x)$ (on every input x), (2) each f_i is described by a short key k_i that enables its efficient evaluation, yet (3) any strict subset of the keys completely hides f.

Boyle *et al.* [7] have also initiated a study of FSS for general polynomial-time computable functions that can be obtained either from *virtual black-box* (VBB) obfuscation or from *probabilistic iO* (*piO*). Indeed, function secret sharing for pseudorandom functions is a special case of our distributed PRFs for any mNP access structure, where the access structure $\mathbb{A}$ is set to be the N-out-of-N threshold access structure.

Following the work of FSS [7], Boyle *et al.* [8] introduced the notion of verifiable FSS, where on the one hand, a function f can be split into functions $f_1, \ldots, f_m$, described by the corresponding keys $k_1, \ldots, k_m$, such that for any input x we have that $f(x) = f_1(x) + \ldots + f_m(x)$ and every strict subset of the keys hides f; on the other hand, there is an additional m-parties interactive protocol Ver for verifying that the keys $(k_1^*, \ldots, k_m^*)$, generated by a potentially malicious client, are consistent with some f. We should note that Boyle *et al.*'s VFSS can be employed to verify the validity of the function shared by the authority. For instance, the key shares could be generated by a potentially untrusted authority, but the evaluation algorithm should be performed by semi-honest servers. However, our robust DPRF can be employed even if the servers are malicious and can be used to verify that the partial values that a user receives from the servers on some input are computed correctly.

Boneh *et al.* [4,18] proposed an alternative method to build non-interactive robust distributed PRFs for any threshold access structure, using a universal thresholdizer (UT), which is a natural generalization of a threshold fully homomorphic encryption (TFHE) scheme with robustness. Boneh *et al.* [4] also showed that the robustness of a universal thresholdizer can be enforced either by using NIZK with pre-processing, which can be constructed from one-way functions [10], or homomorphic signatures [14]. Using their approach, it is possible to construct distributed PRFs that support arbitrary access structures such as monotone boolean formulas assuming a secure TFHE scheme exists for the access structures. Boneh *et al.* [4] also gave an FSS construction for any access structure from a universal thresholdizer, which relies on homomorphic signatures and allows the verification of the correctness of the servers' computations.

Another primitive related to distributed PRFs is the one-round t-out-of-N threshold signatures. One-round (t, N) threshold signatures are digital signatures that allow to share a signing key among N servers and any subset of t servers out of N are able to generate a valid signature, but that disallows the generation of a valid signature if fewer than t servers participate in the combination algorithm. The one-round threshold signature requires that for a user who wishes to sign a message m, he sends m to all N servers, and receives replies from t of them. The user then combines the t replies, and obtains the final signature on m. There is no other interaction between them. In particular, the servers may not communicate with one another, or interact further with the user. The unforgeability property must hold even if the adversary is allowed to corrupt any subset of less than t servers. Many threshold signature schemes have been proposed, such as the threshold variations based on RSA signatures [13,31], Schnorr signatures [32], (EC)DSA signatures [12], BLS signatures [3].

The robust distributed PRF bears resemblance with one-round threshold signatures on the sharing phase of the secret key and the combination of partial values to produce the PRF value (correspondingly signature) on some input (correspondingly message). However, their difference lies on how the verification procedure works. That is, robust distributed PRFs verify the proof of correctness of the partial evaluation, while in threshold signatures there is no partial verification for partial signatures, instead there is a single verification algorithm to check whether the combined signature generated from the t servers' replies is a valid signature or not.

In this paper, we explore new methods in order to achieve robustness for distributed PRFs and establish the connection of robust DPRFs with other non-interactive witness indistinguishable proofs (NIWI) and indistinguishable obfuscation primitives; going beyond the existing DPRFs based on universal thresholdizers and homomorphic signatures. Contrary to existing work [4,18] our robust distributed PRFs can be employed for general access structures (*e.g.,* structures that satisfy a general access predicate), away from existing threshold access structures and monotone span programs.

Organization. The paper is organised as follows. In Sect. 2, we provide the definitions and building blocks used throughout the paper. In Sect. 3, we present the syntax and security notion of robust distributed pseudorandom functions (DPRFs) for any mNP access structure. In Sect. 4, we provide our construction of robust distributed PRFs and its security proof. Finally, Sect. 5 concludes the paper.

2   Preliminaries

2.1   Monotone-NP and Access Structures

We recall the essential background knowledge of access structures and monotone-NP (mNP) as defined by Komargodski, Naor and Yogev in [20] as well as by Komargodski and Zhandry in [21]. The definitions below are taken from [20,21].

A function $f : 2^{[n]} \to \{0,1\}$ is said to be monotone if for every $\Gamma \subseteq [n]$, such that $f(\Gamma) = 1$, it also holds that $\forall \Gamma' \subseteq [n]$ such that $\Gamma \subseteq \Gamma'$, then it holds that $f(\Gamma') = 1$. A monotone boolean circuit is a boolean circuit with AND and OR gates (without negations). A non-deterministic circuit is a Boolean circuit whose inputs are divided into two parts: standard inputs and non-deterministic inputs. A non-deterministic circuit accepts a standard input if and only if there is some setting of the non-deterministic input that causes the circuit to evaluate to 1. A monotone non-deterministic circuit is a non-deterministic circuit, where the monotonicity requirement applies only to the standard inputs, that is, every path from a standard input wire to the output wire does not have a negation gate.

Definition 1 ([16,20,21]). *We say that a function L is in mNP if there exists a uniform family of polynomial-size monotone non-deterministic circuit that computes L.*

Lemma 1 ([16,20,21]). mNP $=$ NP $\cap$ mono, *where* mono *is the set of all monotone functions.*

Definition 2 (Access structure [20,21]). *A monotone access structure $\mathbb{A}$ on $\mathcal{S}$ is a monotone set of subsets of $\mathcal{S}$. That is, for all $\Gamma \in \mathbb{A}$ it holds that $\Gamma \subseteq \mathcal{S}$ and for all $\Gamma \in \mathbb{A}$ and Γ' such that $\Gamma \subseteq \Gamma' \subseteq \mathcal{S}$ it holds that $\Gamma' \in \mathbb{A}$.*

Following the idea of Komargodski, Naor and Yogev [20] in defining access structures in secret sharing schemes, here we consider an access structure $\mathbb{A}$ as a characteristic function $\mathbb{A} : 2^{\mathcal{P}} \to \{0,1\}$ that outputs 1 given as input $\Gamma \subseteq \mathcal{S}$ if and only if Γ is in the access structure, namely $\Gamma \in \mathbb{A}$. We assume $\mathbb{A} : 2^{\overline{\mathcal{P}}} \to \{0,1\}$ to be an access structure corresponding to a language $L \in$ mNP that can be recognized by a polynomial-sized verification circuit $V_{\mathbb{A}}$.

2.2   Non-interactive Witness Indistinguishable Proofs

Definition 3 (NIWI). *A pair of PPT algorithms $(\mathcal{P}, \mathcal{V})$ is a NIWI for a language $\mathcal{L} \in$ NP with witness relation $\mathcal{R}$, if it satisfies the following conditions:*

- *(Perfect Completeness) For all (x, w) such that $\mathcal{R}(x, w) = 1$,*

$$Pr[\mathcal{V}(x, \pi) = 1 : \pi \leftarrow \mathcal{P}(x, w)] = 1.$$

- *(Statistical Soundness) For every $x \notin \mathcal{L}$ and $\pi \in \{0,1\}^*$,*

$$\mathbf{Pr}[\mathcal{V}(x, \pi) = 1] \leq 2^{-\Omega(|x|)}.$$

- *(Witness Indistinguishability) For any sequence $\mathcal{I} = \{(x, w_1, w_2) : \mathcal{R}(x, w_1) = 1 \wedge \mathcal{R}(x, w_2) = 1\}$, it holds:*

$$\{\pi_1 : \pi_1 \leftarrow \mathcal{P}(x, w_1)\}_{(x,w_1,w_2)\in\mathcal{I}} \approx_c \{\pi_2 : \pi_2 \leftarrow \mathcal{P}(x, w_2)\}_{(x,w_1,w_2)\in\mathcal{I}}.$$

Barak, Ong, and Vadhan [1] provided constructions for NIWIs based on Nisan-Wigderson type pseudorandom generators [28] and ZAPs (two-message public-coin witness indistinguishable proofs). Groth, Ostrovsky, and Sahai [17] then provided the first NIWI construction based on standard assumptions on bilinear maps such as the Decision Linear Assumption, the Symmetric External Diffie Hellman assumption, or the Subgroup Decision Assumption. Bitansky and Paneth [2] have recently provided NIWI proofs based on iO indistinguishability obfuscation and one-way permutations.

2.3   Perfectly Binding Commitments (with No Setup Assumptions)

A commitment scheme with message space $\{\mathcal{M}_\lambda\}_\lambda$, randomness space $\{\mathcal{R}_\lambda\}_\lambda$ and commitment space $\{\mathcal{C}_\lambda\}_\lambda$ consists of a pair of polynomial time algorithms (Commit, Verify) with the following syntax:

- Commit($1^\lambda, m \in \mathcal{M}_\lambda; r \in \mathcal{R}_\lambda$) : The commit algorithm is a randomized algorithm that takes as input the security parameter λ, message m to be committed and random coins r. It outputs a commitment/opening pair (c, d).
- Verify($m \in \mathcal{M}_\lambda, c \in \mathcal{C}_\lambda, d \in \mathcal{R}_\lambda$) : The verification algorithm takes as input the message m, commitment c and an opening d. It outputs either 0 or 1.

Definition 4. [15] *A pair of polynomial time algorithms (Commit, Verify) is a perfectly binding computationally hiding commitment scheme if it satisfies the following conditions:*

- *(Perfect Correctness) For all security parameters $\lambda \in \mathbb{N}$, message $m \in \mathcal{M}_\lambda$ and randomness $r \in \mathcal{R}_\lambda$, if $(c, r) \leftarrow$ Commit($1^\lambda, m; r$), then Verify(m, c, r) = 1.*
- *(Perfect Binding) For every (c, m_1, r_1, m_2, r_2) such that $m_1 \neq m_2$, the following holds for at least one $i \in \{1, 2\}$:*

$$\mathbf{Pr}[\text{Verify}(m_i, c_i, r_i) = 1] = 0.$$

- *(Computationally Hiding) For all security parameters $\lambda \in \mathbb{N}$, two messages $m_1, m_2 \in \mathcal{M}_\lambda$, it holds*

$$\{c_1 : (c_1, r_1) \leftarrow \text{Commit}(1^\lambda, m_1; r_1); r_1 \leftarrow \mathcal{R}_\lambda\} \approx_c$$
$$\{c_2 : (c_2, r_2) \leftarrow \text{Commit}(1^\lambda, m_2; r_2); r_2 \leftarrow \mathcal{R}_\lambda\}.$$

Perfectly binding commitments (without trusted setup) can be constructed from certifiably injective one way functions. Goyal *et al.* [15] proposed alternative constructions of perfectly binding non-interactive commitment (without trusted setup) under the learning parity with low noise (LPLN) assumption and learning with errors (LWE) assumption.

In the rest of the paper, we also employ the notions of indistinguishability obfuscation (iO) [11] and puncturable PRFs [29]. Due to space constraints, we provide these definitions in the Appendix A.1.

3   Robust Distributed Pseudorandom Functions for mNP

In this section, we formally define the syntax and security notion of robust distributed pseudorandom functions (DPRFs) for any mNP access structure $\mathbb{A}$ on N servers. On the one hand, it is a natural generalization of the definition of robust DPRFs for threshold access structures, which was initially proposed by Naor, Pinkas and Reingold [26] and formally defined by Libert, Stehlé, and Radu

Titiu [23]. On the other hand, it can be seen as a robustness augmentation of the DPRFs for any mNP access structure proposed by Liang and Mitrokotsa [22].

Recall that a PRF [25] is a function $F : \mathcal{K} \times \mathcal{X} \rightarrow \mathcal{Y}$ that can be computed by a deterministic polynomial time algorithm, where $\mathcal{K}$ is a secret key space, $\mathcal{X}$ is a domain, and $\mathcal{Y}$ is a range (and these sets may be parameterized by the security parameter λ). We define a robust distributed PRF for any mNP access structure $\mathbb{A}$ over N servers $\mathcal{S} = \mathcal{S}_N = \{S_1, \ldots, S_N\}$, and each server S_i can be identified with its index i.

For $N \in \mathbb{N}$, let $\mathbb{A}$ be an mNP access structure on N servers $S_1, \ldots, S_N$. A robust distributed PRF for $\mathbb{A}$ is a tuple of polynomial time algorithms $\Pi = (\mathsf{Setup}, \mathsf{GEval}, \mathsf{Share}, \mathsf{PEval}, \mathsf{PVerify}, \mathsf{Comb})$ with the following syntax:

- $\mathsf{Setup}(1^\lambda, N, V_{\mathbb{A}})$: On input the security parameter λ, the number N of servers and the verification procedure $V_{\mathbb{A}}$ for an mNP access structure $\mathbb{A}$ on N servers, the setup algorithm outputs the public parameters PP and a master secret key α.
- $\mathsf{GEval}(\alpha, x)$: On input the master secret key α and an input $x \in \mathcal{X}$, the global function evaluation algorithm executes as in an ordinary PRF and outputs a function value $y \in \mathcal{Y}$.
- $\mathsf{Share}(\alpha)$: On input the master secret key α, the key sharing algorithm outputs a tuple of N shares, $(\alpha_1, \ldots, \alpha_N)$.
- $\mathsf{PEval}(i, \alpha_i, x)$: On input a server index i, a key share α_i and input $x \in \mathcal{X}$, the partial evaluation algorithm outputs a tuple (x, y_i, π_i), where $y_i \in \mathcal{Z}_i$ is the server S_i's share of the function value $\mathsf{GEval}(\alpha, x)$ and π_i is the corresponding proof for the correct computation of y_i.
- $\mathsf{PVerify}(\mathsf{PP}, i, x, y_i, \pi_i)$: On input the public parameters PP, the index $i \in [N]$, an input x and a partial evaluation y_i on behalf of the server S_i, together with a corresponding proof π_i, the verification algorithm outputs a bit; 1 if (x, y_i, π_i) is deemed valid and 0 if it does not.
- $\mathsf{Comb}\big(\mathsf{PP}, V_{\mathbb{A}}, w, x, \{(y_i, \pi_i)\}_{i \in \Gamma}\big)$: On input the public parameters PP, the verification procedure $V_{\mathbb{A}}$ for an mNP language $\mathbb{A}$, a witness w, and a set of shares $\{y_i\}_{i \in \Gamma}$ for a set of servers $\Gamma \subseteq \{S_1, \ldots, S_N\}$ (where we recall that we identify a server S_i with its index i), the combining algorithm outputs a value $y \in \mathcal{Y} \cup \bot$;

and satisfying the following requirements:

Verifiability: For any $(\mathsf{PP}, \alpha) \leftarrow \mathsf{Setup}(1^\lambda, N, V_{\mathbb{A}}), (\alpha_1, \ldots, \alpha_N) \leftarrow \mathsf{Share}(\alpha)$, any index $i \in [N]$, any input $x \in \mathcal{X}$, and any $(x, y_i, \pi_i) \leftarrow \mathsf{PEval}(i, \alpha_i, x)$, we have $\mathsf{PVerify}(\mathsf{PP}, i, x, y_i, \pi_i) = 1$.

Robustness: Informally, the robustness property guarantees that it should be impossible for any corrupted server S_j holding the secret share α_j to generate an incorrect partial evaluation y_j, for some input x, that can be successfully verified, namely, $\mathsf{PVerify}(\mathsf{PP}, j, x, y_j, \pi_j) = 1$. More precisely, for any $j \in [N]$ and any PPT adversary $\mathcal{A}$, there exists a negligible function $negl(\lambda)$ such that:

$$\Pr\left[\begin{array}{c|c} y_j'' \neq y_j' \wedge & (\text{PP}, \alpha) \leftarrow \text{Setup}(1^\lambda, N, V_{\mathbb{A}}), \\ \text{PVerify}(\text{PP}, j, x', y_j'', \pi_j'') = 1 & \begin{array}{l} (\alpha_1, \ldots, \alpha_N) \leftarrow \text{Share}(\alpha), \\ (x', y_j'', \pi_j'') \leftarrow \mathcal{A}(\text{PP}, j, \alpha_j), \\ (y_j', \pi_j') \leftarrow \text{PEval}(j, \alpha_j, x'), \end{array} \end{array}\right] \leq negl(\lambda)$$

where the probability is taken over the random choices of Setup, Share and PEval, and the coin tosses of $\mathcal{A}$.

Correctness: If for all $\lambda, N, t \in \mathbb{N}$, any mNP access structure $\mathbb{A}$, any $x \in \mathcal{X}$, and any set of qualified servers $\Gamma = \{i_1, \ldots, i_t\} \subseteq \{S_1, \ldots, S_N\}$ with valid witness w (i.e., $V_{\mathbb{A}}(\Gamma, w) = 1$), it holds that:

$$\Pr\left[\begin{array}{c|c} \text{Comb}(\text{PP}, V_{\mathbb{A}}, w, x, \{(y_{i_j}, \pi_{i_j})\}_{j \in [t]}) & (\text{PP}, \alpha) \leftarrow \text{Setup}(1^\lambda, N, V_{\mathbb{A}}), \\ = \text{GEval}(\alpha, x) & \begin{array}{l} (\alpha_1, \ldots, \alpha_N) \leftarrow \text{Share}(\alpha), \\ (x, y_{i_j}, \pi_{i_j}) \leftarrow \text{PEval}(i_j, \alpha_{i_j}, x) \text{ for } \forall j \in [t], \end{array} \end{array}\right] = 1$$

Selective Pseudorandomness: Consider the following indistinguishability challenge experiment for corrupted servers $T \subseteq [N]$:

1. On input the security parameter 1^λ and number N, the adversary $\mathcal{A}$ outputs the challenge input x^*, an access structure $\mathbb{A} \in \text{mNP}$ and an unqualified set $T \subseteq [N]$ (that is, $T \notin \mathbb{A}$).
2. The challenger runs $(\text{PP}, \alpha) \leftarrow \text{Setup}(1^\lambda, N, V_{\mathbb{A}})$ and $(\alpha_1, \ldots, \alpha_N) \leftarrow \text{Share}(\alpha)$, and publishes the public parameters PP to the adversary $\mathcal{A}$.
3. The challenger sends the corresponding keys $\{\alpha_i\}_{i \in T}$ to $\mathcal{A}$.
4. The adversary (adaptively) sends queries $x_1, \ldots, x_Q \in \mathcal{X}$ to the challenger such that $x^* \notin \{x_1, \ldots, x_Q\}$, and for each query x_j the challenger responds with $\text{PEval}(i, \alpha_i, x_j)$ for all $i \in [N] \backslash T$.
5. The challenger chooses a random bit $b \leftarrow \{0, 1\}$. If $b = 0$, the challenger returns a uniformly random $y^* \in \mathcal{Y}$ to the adversary. If $b = 1$, the challenger responds with $y^* = \text{GEval}(\alpha, x^*)$.
6. The adversary $\mathcal{A}$ outputs a bit $b' \in \{0, 1\}$.

Let us denote by $\text{Adv}_{\Pi, \mathcal{A}}^{\text{pseudo}} := \Pr[b' = b] - 1/2$ the advantage of the adversary $\mathcal{A}$ in guessing b in the above experiment, where the probability is taken over the randomness of the challenger and of $\mathcal{A}$. We say the robust DPRFs Π for an mNP access structure $\mathbb{A}$ is selectively pseudorandom if there exists a negligible function $negl(\lambda)$ such that for all non-uniform PPT adversaries $\mathcal{A}$, it holds that $\text{Adv}_{\Pi, \mathcal{A}}^{\text{pseudo}} \leq negl(\lambda)$.

4   General Construction of Robust Distributed PRFs for mNP

In this section, we describe our construction of robust distributed PRFs in details. We present a general construction of robust DPRFs from perfectly binding commitments, NIWIs, puncturable PRFs and indistinguishability obfuscation $i\mathcal{O}$. We also prove that it satisfies the verifiability, robustness, correctness and pseudorandomness properties (as described in Sect. 3).

Let $(\mathcal{P}, \mathcal{V})$ be a NIWI proof system for a language $\mathcal{L}$ (which will be defined later), (CS.Commit, CS.Verify) be a perfectly binding commitment scheme with $\{\mathcal{M}_\lambda\}_\lambda$, $\{\mathcal{R}_\lambda\}_\lambda$ and $\{\mathcal{C}_\lambda\}_\lambda$ as the message, randomness and commitment space, and PRF $=$ (PRF.Setup, PRF.Puncture, PRF.Eval) be a puncturable PRF with $\{\mathcal{X}_\lambda\}_\lambda$, $\{\mathcal{Y}_\lambda\}_\lambda$, $\{\mathcal{K}_\lambda\}_\lambda$ and $\{\mathcal{K}_\lambda^p\}_\lambda$, as its domain, range, key and punctured key spaces. Here we assume that $\mathcal{K}_\lambda \cup \mathcal{K}_\lambda^p \subseteq \mathcal{M}_\lambda$, which means that all the PRF master keys and punctured keys lie in the message space of the commitment scheme CS.

Define the language $\mathcal{L}$, which contains instances of the form $(c_1, c_2, c_3, x, y) \in \mathcal{C}_\lambda^3 \times \mathcal{X}_\lambda \times \mathcal{Y}_\lambda$ with the following witness relation:

$$\exists \imath, \jmath \in \{1, 2, 3\}, K, K' \in \mathcal{K}_\lambda \cup \mathcal{K}_\lambda^p, r, r' \in \mathcal{R}_\lambda \text{ such that}$$
$$\imath \neq \jmath \wedge \text{CS.Verify}(K, c_\imath, r) = 1 \wedge \text{CS.Verify}(K', c_\jmath, r') = 1$$
$$\wedge \text{PRF}(K, x) = \text{PRF}(K', x) = y.$$

It is obvious that the above language is in NP as it can be verified in polynomial time.

Next we describe our construction for selectively-secure robust DPRFs with message space $\{\mathcal{X}_\lambda\}_\lambda$ and range space $\{\mathcal{Y}_\lambda\}_\lambda$.

Setup$(1^\lambda, N, V_\mathbb{A})$: On input 1^λ, the number N and the verification procedure $V_\mathbb{A}$ for an mNP access structure $\mathbb{A}$, it does as following:
  - Sample $N + 1$ PRF keys for punctured PRF as $K \leftarrow$ PRF.Setup(1^λ) and $K_i \leftarrow$ PRF.Setup(1^λ) for $i \in [N]$, and for each $i \in [N]$ generate three independent commitments to the key K_i as $c_{i1} \leftarrow$ CS.Commit$(1^\lambda, K_i, r_{i1})$, $c_{i2} \leftarrow$ CS.Commit$(1^\lambda, K_i, r_{i2})$ and $c_{i3} \leftarrow$ CS.Commit$(1^\lambda, K_i, r_{i3})$ where r_{i1}, r_{i2}, r_{i3} are sampled randomly in $\mathcal{R}_\lambda$.
  - Create an obfuscation for the program Recon defined below as described in Fig. 3.
  - Set PP $= (\{c_{i1}, c_{i2}, c_{i3}\}_{i \in [N]}, i\mathcal{O}(\text{Recon}))$ and msk $= (K, \{(K_i, r_{i1}, r_{i2}, r_{i3})\}_{i \in [N]})$.
GEval(msk, x): It parses msk $= (K, \{(K_i, r_{i1}, r_{i2}, r_{i3})\}_{i \in [N]})$. On input $x \in \mathcal{X}$, it computes $y =$ PRF.Eval(K, x).
Share(msk): It parses msk $= (K, \{(K_i, r_{i1}, r_{i2}, r_{i3})\}_{i \in [N]})$, and then sets sk$_i = (K_i, r_{i1}, r_{i2}, r_{i3})$ for all $i \in [N]$.
PEval(i, sk_i, x): It parses sk$_i = ((K_i, r_{i1}, r_{i2}, r_{i3})$ and runs the PRF evaluation algorithm on x as $y_i =$ PRF.Eval(K_i, x). It also computes a NIWI proof π_i for the statement $(c_{i1}, c_{i2}, c_{i3}, x, y_i) \in \mathcal{L}$ using the NIWI prover algorithm $\mathcal{P}$ with $(\imath = i1, \jmath = i2, K_i, K_i, r_{i1}, r_{i2})$ as witness, and outputs (y_i, π_i) as the partial evaluation and corresponding proof for the server S_i on input x.
PVerify$(\text{PP}, i, x, y_i, \pi_i)$: It runs the NIWI verifier to check the proof π_i as $\mathcal{V}((c_{i1}, c_{i2}, c_{i3}, x, y_i), \pi_i)$ and accepts the proof (outputs 1) iff $\mathcal{V}$ outputs 1.
Comb$(\text{PP}, V_\mathbb{A}, w, \{(x, y_i, \pi_i)\}_{i \in \Gamma})$: The client is expected to derive the function value from a set of qualified servers' partial evaluations and proofs. It executes the obfuscated program $i\mathcal{O}(\text{Recon})$ on inputs w, PP and $\{(x, y_i, \pi_i)\}_{i \in \Gamma}$ to obtain y.

Recon

Hardwired into the circuit: V_A, K, $\{c_{i1}, c_{i2}, c_{i3}\}_{i \in [N]}$.

Input to the circuit: x, w, $\{(y_i, \pi_i)\}_{i \in \Gamma}$.

Algorithm:
1. Execute the following tests:
   (a) For all $i \in \Gamma$ verify that $V(c_{i1}, c_{i2}, c_{i3}, x, y_i, \pi_i) = 1$;
   (b) Verify that $V_A(\Gamma, w) = 1$;
2. If any of the above tests fails, output $\bot$;
   otherwise, compute $y = \mathsf{PRF}(K, x)$ and output y.

Fig. 3. The description of the program Recon.

Theorem 1. *If $i\mathcal{O}$ is a secure indistinguishability obfuscator, $(\mathcal{P}, \mathcal{V})$ is a secure NIWI proof system for a language $\mathcal{L}$, (CS.Commit, CS.Verify) is a secure perfectly binding commitment scheme, and PRF is a secure puncturable PRF, then the above construction is a selectively-secure robust distributed PRF satisfying verifiability, robustness, correctness and selective pseudorandomness properties as described in Sect. 3.*

Verifiability. For the honestly generated keys $(\mathsf{PP}, \mathsf{msk}) \leftarrow \mathsf{Setup}(1^\lambda, N, V_A)$ and $\{\mathsf{sk}_i\}_{i \in [N]} \leftarrow \mathsf{Share}(\mathsf{msk})$ where $\mathsf{sk}_i = (K_i, r_{i1}, r_{i2}, r_{i3})$ and $\mathsf{PP} = (\{c_{i1}, c_{i2}, c_{i3}\}_{i \in [N]}, i\mathcal{O}(\mathsf{Recon}))$, we know that for every $i \in [N]$ both c_{i1} and c_{i2} are commitments to the PRF key K with r_{i1} and r_{i2} as the corresponding openings. Therefore, by the perfect correctness of the puncturable PRF and the NIWI proof system, we can conclude that $\mathsf{PVerify}(\mathsf{PP}, x, y_i, \pi_i) = 1$ for all $i \in [N]$.

Correctness. The *correctness* property can be verified in a straightforward manner from the proof of the verifiability property. Since on the one hand, we have shown that for every honestly generated keys $\mathsf{PP}, \mathsf{sk}_i$, by the perfect correctness of the puncturable PRF and NIWI proof system, for any set of qualified servers Γ with valid witness w (i.e., $V_A(\Gamma, w) = 1$), we can conclude that $\mathsf{PartVerify}(\mathsf{pk}_i, x, (y_i, \sigma_i)) = 1$ for all $i \in \Gamma$. On the other hand, from the correctness property of $i\mathcal{O}$ we have $\mathsf{Comb}(\mathsf{PP}, V_A, w, x, \{(y_i, \pi_i)\}_{i \in \Gamma}) = \mathsf{PRF}(K, x) = y$.

Robustness. We prove this by contradiction. Assume that for the corrupted server S_{j^*} holding the secret share K_{j^*} there exists (x', y_j'', π_j'') such that $y_j'' \neq y_j' \wedge \mathsf{PVerify}(\mathsf{PP}, j, x', y_j'', \pi_j'') = 1$ where $(y_j', \pi_j') \leftarrow \mathsf{PEval}(j, K_j, x')$. From the construction, it is implied that there exists $(x', (y_j'', \pi_j''), (y_j', \pi_j'))$ such that $y_j'' \neq y_j'$ and $\mathcal{V}(c_{ji}, c_{j2}, c_{j3}, x', y_j', \pi_j') = \mathcal{V}(c_{j1}, c_{j2}, c_{j3}, x', y_j'', \pi_j'') = 1$. However, this is not possible.

– Since the commitment scheme is perfectly binding, then for each $t \in \{1, 2, 3\}$ there exists at most one key K_j^t such that there exists an r_j^t, which is a valid opening for c_{jt}, i.e., $\mathsf{CS.Verify}(K_j^t, c_{jt}, r_j^t) = 1$.

– Suppose c_{jt} is a commitment to the key K_j^t for $t \in \{1, 2, 3\}$, and $\mathsf{PRF}(K_j^1, x') = \mathsf{PRF}(K_j^2, x') = y_j'$. Now since $y_j'' \neq y_j'$, thus even when $\mathsf{PRF}(K_j^3, x') = y_j''$ holds, we know that $(c_{j1}, c_{j2}, c_{j3}, x', y_j'') \notin \mathcal{L}$ because there are no two keys out of K_j^1, K_j^2, K_j^3 such that their function values equal to y_j'' on input x'. Therefore, π_j'' is a proof for an incorrect statement. Thus, it contradicts the statistical soundness of the NIWI proof system.

Pseudorandomness. To show that the *pseudorandomness* property holds, we prove it through a sequence of hybrid games. Let $\mathcal{A}$ be a PPT adversary that wins in the pseudorandomness game (described in Sect. 3) for the above construction of robust DPRFs with non-negligible probability. Let $Q = Q(\lambda)$ be a polynomial upper bound on the number of queries made by $\mathcal{A}$ to the partial evaluation oracles w.r.t. the uncorrupted servers. We argue that such an adversary must break the security of at least one of the underlying primitives.

To formally prove our theorem, we describe the following sequence of games, where the first game models the real pseudorandomness security game. Let $\mathsf{Adv}_{\mathcal{A},i}$ denote the advantage of an adversary $\mathcal{A}$ in the Game$_i$ of guessing the bit b. We then show via a sequence of lemmas that if $\mathcal{A}$'s advantage is non-negligible in Game$_i$, then it has non-negligible advantage in Game$_{i+1}$ as well. Note that in each successive hybrid, we only provide the steps that differ.

Game$_0$ this game is defined as the original selective pseudorandomness security game described in Sect. 3, instantiated by our construction of robust DPRFs.

1. $\mathcal{A}$ first chooses a challenge input x^* and an access structure $\mathbb{A} \in \mathsf{mNP}$, and outputs an unqualified set $T \subseteq [N]$ (that is, $T \notin \mathbb{A}$).
2. The challenger samples PRF keys $K, K_1, \ldots, K_N$, and for each $i \in [N]$, $t \in \{1, 2, 3\}$ generates three independent commitments to the key K_i as $c_{it} \leftarrow \mathsf{CS.Commit}(1^\lambda, K_i, r_{it})$, where r_{it} is sampled randomly in $\mathcal{R}_\lambda$. It creates an obfuscation for the program Recon defined in Fig. 3. The challenger sets $\mathsf{PP} = (\{c_{i1}, c_{i2}, c_{i3}\}_{i \in [N]}, i\mathcal{O}(\mathsf{Recon}))$, and sends PP to the adversary $\mathcal{A}$.
3. Queries to the oracle $\mathsf{O}_{\mathsf{PEval}}$: $\mathcal{A}$ sends the query (i, x) to $\mathsf{O}_{\mathsf{PEval}}$ where $i \in [N] \setminus T$ and $x \neq x^*$, the challenger computes $y_i = \mathsf{PRF}(K_i, x)$ and a NIWI proof π_i for the statement $(c_{i1}, c_{i2}, c_{i3}, x, y_i) \in \mathcal{L}$ using the NIWI prover algorithm $\mathcal{P}$ with $(i1, i2, K_i, K_i, r_{i1}, r_{i2})$ as the witness.
4. The challenger chooses a random bit $b \leftarrow \{0, 1\}$. If $b = 1$, the challenger computes $y^* = \mathsf{PRF}(K, x^*)$, else it samples $y^* \in \mathcal{Y}$, and sends y^* to $\mathcal{A}$.
5. $\mathcal{A}$ outputs a bit $b' \in \{0, 1\}$. $\mathcal{A}$ wins if $b' = b$.

For each $i \in [N] \setminus T$, we define the following intermediate hybrid experiments, which are the hybrid games that are performed iteratively.

Game$_{1,i,1}$ the challenger uses $(i2, i3, K_i, K_i, r_{i2}, r_{i3})$ as the witness instead of $(i1, i2, K_i, K_i, r_{i1}, r_{i2})$ for generating the NIWI proof for the server S_i.
Game$_{1,i,2}$ the challenger generates c_{i1} as $c_{i1} \leftarrow \mathsf{Com}(K_i^*; r_{i1})$ instead of using a commitment to $c_{i1} \leftarrow \mathsf{Com}(K_i; r_{i1})$.
Game$_{1,i,3}$ the challenger uses $(i1, i3, K_i^*, K_i, r_{i1}, r_{i3})$ as the witness instead of $(i2, i3, K_i, K_i, r_{i2}, r_{i3})$ for generating the NIWI proof for server S_i.

Game$_{1,i,4}$ the challenger generates c_{i2} as $c_{i2} \leftarrow \mathsf{Com}(K_i^*; r_{i2})$ instead of using a commitment to $c_{i2} \leftarrow \mathsf{Com}(K_i; r_{i2})$.

Game$_{1,i,5}$ the challenger uses $(i1, i2, K_i^*, K_i^*, r_{i1}, r_{i2})$ as the witness instead of $(i1, i3, K_i^*, K_i, r_{i1}, r_{i3})$ for generating the NIWI proof for the server S_i.

Game$_2$ after the previous polynomial intermediate hybrid experiments, for each $i \in [N] \backslash T$ the commitments c_{i1}, c_{i2}, c_{i3} are generated as the commitments to the same punctured key K_i^* with different randomness. In this game, we replace the obfuscation of the program Recon which is defined in Fig. 3 with the obfuscation of the program Recon^1 defined in Fig. 4. Namely, the challenger computes $\hat{y} = \mathsf{PRF}(K, x^*)$ and creates an obfuscation for the program Recon^1 defined in Fig. 4, which is hardwired with $K^*, x^*, \hat{y}, \{c_{i1}, c_{i2}, c_{i3}\}_{i \in [N]}$, instead of being hardwired only with K. Namely,

1. $\mathcal{A}$ first chooses a challenge input x^* and an access structure $\mathbb{A} \in \mathsf{mNP}$, and outputs an unqualified set $T \subseteq [N]$ (that is, $T \notin \mathbb{A}$).
2. The challenger generates the PRF keys $K, K_1, \ldots, K_N$ and computes the punctured key $K^* \leftarrow \mathsf{PRF.Punctured}(K, x^*)$.
3. For each $i \in T$, the challenger generates independent commitments to the key K_i as $c_{it} \leftarrow \mathsf{CS.Commit}(1^\lambda, K_i, r_{it})$ for each $t \in \{1, 2, 3\}$, where $K_i \leftarrow \mathsf{PRF.Setup}(1^\lambda)$ and $r_{it} \leftarrow \mathcal{R}_\lambda$. For each $i \in [N] \backslash T$, the challenger generates independent commitments to the key K_i^* as $c_{it} \leftarrow \mathsf{CS.Commit}(1^\lambda, K_i^*, r_{it})$ for each $t \in \{1, 2, 3\}$, where $K_i^* \leftarrow \mathsf{PRF.Punctured}(K_i, x^*)$ and $r_{it} \leftarrow \mathcal{R}_\lambda$. The challenger computes $\hat{y} = \mathsf{PRF}(K, x^*)$ and creates an obfuscation for the program Recon^1 defined in Fig. 4. The challenger sets $\mathsf{PP} = (\{c_{i1}, c_{i2}, c_{i3}\}_{i \in [N]}, i\mathcal{O}(\mathsf{Recon}^1))$, and sends PP to the adversary $\mathcal{A}$.
4. Queries to the oracle $\mathsf{O_{PEval}}$: $\mathcal{A}$ sends the query (i, x) to $\mathsf{O_{PEval}}$ where $i \in [N] \backslash T$ and $x \neq x^*$, the challenger computes $y_i = \mathsf{PRF}(K_i^*, x)$ and a NIWI proof π_i for the statement $(c_{i1}, c_{i2}, c_{i3}, x, y_i) \in \mathcal{L}$ using the NIWI prover algorithm $\mathcal{P}$ with $(i1, i2, K_i^*, K_i^*, r_{i1}, r_{i2})$ as the witness.
5. The challenger chooses a random bit $b \leftarrow \{0, 1\}$. If $b = 1$, the challenger computes $y^* = [\mathsf{PRF}(K, x^*)]_1$, else it samples $y^* \in \{0, 1\}$, and sends y^* to $\mathcal{A}$.
6. $\mathcal{A}$ outputs a bit $b' \in \{0, 1\}$. $\mathcal{A}$ wins if $b' = b$.

The security of $i\mathcal{O}$ implies that this game is indistinguishable from Game$_{1,i,5}$.

Game$_3$ the challenger randomly chooses $\hat{y} \in \mathcal{Y}$ instead of computing from $\hat{y} = \mathsf{PRF}(K, x^*)$.

Game$_4$ the challenger replaces the obfuscation of the program Recon^1 with the obfuscation of the program Recon.

Game$_5$ the challenger replaces back the key to K_i from K_i^* committed in the (c_{i1}, c_{i2}, c_{i3}) for each $i \in [N] \backslash T$.

Due to space constraints, we will not present the proofs of the indistinguishability between each adjacent game in details. The complete proof is provided in the full version of this article.

Recon[1]

Hardwired into the circuit: V_A, $\{c_{i1}, c_{i2}, c_{i3}\}_{i \in T}$, $\{c_{i1}, c_{i2}, c_{i3}\}_{i \in [N] \setminus T}$, Punctured key K^*, x^*, $\hat{y}_,$.

Input to the circuit: x, w, $\{(y_i, \pi_i)\}_{i \in \Gamma}$.

Algorithm:
  1. If $x \neq x^*$, execute the following tests:
     (a) For all $i \in \Gamma$ verify that $\mathcal{V}(c_{i1}, c_{i2}, c_{i3}, x, y_i, \pi_i) = 1$;
     (b) Verify that $V_A(\Gamma, w) = 1$;
     If any of the above tests fails, output $\perp$;
     otherwise, compute $y = \mathsf{PRF}(K^*, x)$ and output y.
  2. Else if $x = x^*$, execute (a) and (b);
     If both of the tests verify, output $\hat{y}$. Otherwise, output $\perp$;

Fig. 4. The description of the program Recon[1].

5 Conclusions

Distributed PRFs is a very useful cryptographic primitive that can be employed in multiple settings in order to avoid single point of failures (*e.g.*, distributed key distribution centres, byzantine agreement protocols, consensus protocols). However, in many cases when a PRF value is computed in a distributed way, guarantees are needed for the correctness of the distributed partial evaluations of the PRF value. Robust distributed PRFs (DPRFs) can provide a proof of correctness π_i that a partial evaluation y_i is computed correctly. Existing robust DPRFs are suitable only for threshold access structures or monotone span programs, restricting thus, the application scenarios of robust DPRFs. In this paper, we investigated whether it is possible to construct robust distributed PRFs for a very general class of structures (mNP) rendering them appropriate for any access predicate (*i.e.*, a predicate satisfied by the distributed parties *e.g.*, all parties within a predefined distance) and thus, allowing a wider spectrum of applications. More precisely, we investigate whether it is possible to transform a PRF into a *robust distributed PRF* for monotone functions in NP, also known as mNP [20]. The answer is affirmative and we show that robust DPRFs for an mNP access structure can be constructed generally from the ingredients of puncturable PRFs [6,9,19], a non-interactive witness indistinguishable proof (NIWI) and indistinguishable obfuscation [11]. We believe that our robust DPRFs can have important impact in a broad range of application scenarios that require the distributed computation of a pseudorandom value.

Acknowledgements. This work was partially supported by the Swedish Research Council (Vetenskapsrådet) through the grant PRECIS (621-2014-4845).

A   Appendix

A.1   Preliminaries

Definition 5 (Indistinguishability obfuscation [11]**).** *A probabilistic polynomial time (PPT) algorithm* $i\mathcal{O}$ *is said to be an indistinguishability obfuscator for a circuit class* $\{\mathcal{C}_\lambda\}$, *if the following conditions are satisfied:*

– *For all security parameters* $\lambda \in \mathbb{N}$, *for all* $C \in \mathcal{C}_\lambda$, *for all inputs* x, *we have that*

$$\Pr[C'(x) = C(x) : C' \leftarrow i\mathcal{O}(\lambda, C)] = 1.$$

– *For any (not necessarily uniform) PPT adversaries* (Samp, D), *there exists a negligible function* $negl(\cdot)$ *such that the following holds: if* $\Pr[\forall x, C_0(x) = C_1(x) : (C_0, C_1, \sigma) \leftarrow \mathsf{Samp}(1^\lambda)] > 1 - negl(\lambda)$, *then we have:*

$$\big|\Pr[D(\sigma, i\mathcal{O}(\lambda, C_0)) = 1 : (C_0, C_1, \sigma) \leftarrow \mathsf{Samp}(1^\lambda)]$$
$$- \Pr[D(\sigma, i\mathcal{O}(\lambda, C_1)) = 1 : (C_0, C_1, \sigma) \leftarrow \mathsf{Samp}(1^\lambda)]\big| \le negl(\lambda).$$

Definition 6 (Puncturable PRFs [29]**).** *A puncturable family of PRFs* F *mapping is given by a triple of Turing Machines* $(\mathsf{Setup}_F, \mathsf{Puncture}_F, and \mathsf{Eval}_F)$, *and a pair of computable functions* $\tau_1(\cdot)$ *and* $\tau_2(\cdot)$, *satisfying the following conditions:*

– **(Functionality preserved under puncturing)** *For every PPT adversary* $\mathcal{A}$ *such that* $\mathcal{A}(1^\lambda)$ *outputs a set* $S \subseteq \{0,1\}^{\tau_1(\lambda)}$, *then for all* $x \in \{0,1\}^{\tau_1(\lambda)}$ *where* $x \notin S$, *we have that:*

$$\Pr[\mathsf{Eval}_F(K, x) = \mathsf{Eval}_F(K_S, x) : K \leftarrow \mathsf{Setup}_F(1^\lambda),$$
$$K_S = \mathsf{Puncture}_F(K, S)] = 1.$$

– **(Pseudorandom at punctured points)** *For every PPT adversary* $(\mathcal{A}_1, \mathcal{A}_2)$ *such that* $\mathcal{A}_1(1^\lambda)$ *outputs a set* $S \subseteq \{0,1\}^{\tau_1(\lambda)}$ *and state* σ, *consider an experiment where* $K \leftarrow \mathsf{Setup}_F(1^\lambda)$ *and* $K_S = \mathsf{Puncture}_F(K, S)$. *Then, we have:*

$$\big|\Pr[\mathcal{A}_2(\sigma, K_S, S, \mathsf{Eval}_F(K, S)) = 1]$$
$$- \Pr[\mathcal{A}_2(\sigma, K_S, S, U_{\tau_2(\lambda) \cdot |S|}) = 1]\big| = negl(\lambda),$$

where $\mathsf{Eval}_F(K, S)$ *denotes the concatenation of* $\mathsf{Eval}_F(K, x_1), \ldots, \mathsf{Eval}_F(K, x_k)$ *where* $S = \{x_1, \ldots, x_k\}$ *is the enumeration of the elements of* S *in lexicographic order,* $negl(\cdot)$ *is a negligible function, and* $U_{\tau_2(\lambda) \cdot |S|}$ *denotes the uniform distribution over* $\tau_2(\lambda) \cdot |S|$ *bits.*

Theorem 2. [29] *If one-way functions exist, then for all efficiently computable functions* $\tau_1(\lambda)$ *and* $\tau_2(\lambda)$, *there exists a family of puncturable PRFs that maps* $\tau_1(\lambda)$ *bits to* $\tau_2(\lambda)$ *bits.*

References

1. Barak, B., Ong, S.J., Vadhan, S.: Derandomization in cryptography. SIAM J. Comput. **37**(2), 380–400 (2007)
2. Bitansky, N., Paneth, O.: ZAPs and non-interactive witness indistinguishability from indistinguishability obfuscation. In: Dodis, Y., Nielsen, J.B. (eds.) TCC 2015. LNCS, vol. 9015, pp. 401–427. Springer, Heidelberg (2015). https://doi.org/10.1007/978-3-662-46497-7_16
3. Boldyreva, A.: Threshold signatures, multisignatures and blind signatures based on the gap-Diffie-Hellman-group signature scheme. In: Desmedt, Y.G. (ed.) PKC 2003. LNCS, vol. 2567, pp. 31–46. Springer, Heidelberg (2003). https://doi.org/10.1007/3-540-36288-6_3
4. Boneh, D., et al.: Threshold cryptosystems from threshold fully homomorphic encryption. In: Shacham, H., Boldyreva, A. (eds.) CRYPTO 2018. LNCS, vol. 10991, pp. 565–596. Springer, Cham (2018). https://doi.org/10.1007/978-3-319-96884-1_19
5. Boneh, D., Lewi, K., Montgomery, H., Raghunathan, A.: Key homomorphic PRFs and their applications. In: Canetti, R., Garay, J.A. (eds.) CRYPTO 2013. LNCS, vol. 8042, pp. 410–428. Springer, Heidelberg (2013). https://doi.org/10.1007/978-3-642-40041-4_23
6. Boneh, D., Waters, B.: Constrained pseudorandom functions and their applications. In: Sako, K., Sarkar, P. (eds.) ASIACRYPT 2013. LNCS, vol. 8270, pp. 280–300. Springer, Heidelberg (2013). https://doi.org/10.1007/978-3-642-42045-0_15
7. Boyle, E., Gilboa, N., Ishai, Y.: Function secret sharing. In: Oswald, E., Fischlin, M. (eds.) EUROCRYPT 2015. LNCS, vol. 9057, pp. 337–367. Springer, Heidelberg (2015). https://doi.org/10.1007/978-3-662-46803-6_12
8. Boyle, E., Gilboa, N., Ishai, Y.: Function secret sharing: improvements and extensions. In: Proceedings of the 2016 ACM SIGSAC Conference on Computer and Communications Security, CCS 2016, pp. 1292–1303. ACM (2016)
9. Boyle, E., Goldwasser, S., Ivan, I.: Functional signatures and pseudorandom functions. In: Krawczyk, H. (ed.) PKC 2014. LNCS, vol. 8383, pp. 501–519. Springer, Heidelberg (2014). https://doi.org/10.1007/978-3-642-54631-0_29
10. De Santis, A., Micali, S., Persiano, G.: Non-interactive zero-knowledge with preprocessing. In: Goldwasser, S. (ed.) CRYPTO 1988. LNCS, vol. 403, pp. 269–282. Springer, New York (1990). https://doi.org/10.1007/0-387-34799-2_21
11. Garg, S., Gentry, C., Halevi, S., Raykova, M., Sahai, A., Waters, B.: Candidate indistinguishability obfuscation and functional encryption for all circuits. In: Proceedings of FOCS 2013, pp. 40–49. IEEE Computer Society, Washington (2013)
12. Gennaro, R., Goldfeder, S., Narayanan, A.: Threshold-optimal DSA/ECDSA signatures and an application to bitcoin wallet security. In: Manulis, M., Sadeghi, A.-R., Schneider, S. (eds.) ACNS 2016. LNCS, vol. 9696, pp. 156–174. Springer, Cham (2016). https://doi.org/10.1007/978-3-319-39555-5_9
13. Gennaro, R., Jarecki, S., Krawczyk, H., Rabin, T.: Robust and efficient sharing of RSA functions. In: Koblitz, N. (ed.) CRYPTO 1996. LNCS, vol. 1109, pp. 157–172. Springer, Heidelberg (1996). https://doi.org/10.1007/3-540-68697-5_13
14. Gorbunov, S., Vaikuntanathan, V., Wichs, D.: Leveled fully homomorphic signatures from standard lattices. In: Proceedings of STOC 2015, pp. 469–477. ACM, New York (2015)

15. Goyal, R., Hohenberger, S., Koppula, V., Waters, B.: A generic approach to constructing and proving verifiable random functions. Technical report, IACR Cryptology ePrint Archive (2017)
16. Grigni, M., Sipser, M.: Monotone complexity (1990)
17. Groth, J., Ostrovsky, R., Sahai, A.: New techniques for noninteractive zero-knowledge. J. ACM (JACM) **59**(3), 11 (2012)
18. Jain, A., Rasmussen, P.M., Sahai, A.: Threshold fully homomorphic encryption. IACR Cryptology ePrint Archive, 2017:257 (2017). https://eprint.iacr.org/2017/257
19. Kiayias, A., Papadopoulos, S., Triandopoulos, N., Zacharias, T.: Delegatable pseudorandom functions and applications. In: Proceedings of the 2013 ACM SIGSAC Conference on Computer and Communications Security, CCS 2013, pp. 669–684. ACM, New York (2013)
20. Komargodski, I., Naor, M., Yogev, E.: Secret-sharing for NP. J. Cryptol. **30**(2), 444–469 (2017)
21. Komargodski, I., Zhandry, M.: Cutting-edge cryptography through the lens of secret sharing. In: Kushilevitz, E., Malkin, T. (eds.) TCC 2016. LNCS, vol. 9563, pp. 449–479. Springer, Heidelberg (2016). https://doi.org/10.1007/978-3-662-49099-0_17
22. Liang, B., Mitrokotsa, A.: Distributed pseudorandom functions for general access structures in NP. In: Qing, S., Mitchell, C., Chen, L., Liu, D. (eds.) ICICS 2017. LNCS, vol. 10631, pp. 81–87. Springer, Cham (2018). https://doi.org/10.1007/978-3-319-89500-0_7
23. Libert, B., Stehlé, D., Titiu, R.: Adaptively secure distributed PRFs from LWE. IACR Cryptology ePrint Archive, 2018:927 (2018). https://eprint.iacr.org/2018/927
24. McEliece, R.J., Sarwate, D.V.: On sharing secrets and reed-solomon codes. Commun. ACM **24**(9), 583–584 (1981)
25. Micali, S., Rabin, M.O., Vadhan, S.P.: Verifiable random functions. In: Proceedings of FOCS 1999, pp. 120–130 (1999)
26. Naor, M., Pinkas, B., Reingold, O.: Distributed pseudo-random functions and KDCs. In: Stern, J. (ed.) EUROCRYPT 1999. LNCS, vol. 1592, pp. 327–346. Springer, Heidelberg (1999). https://doi.org/10.1007/3-540-48910-X_23
27. Nielsen, J.B.: A threshold pseudorandom function construction and its applications. In: Yung, M. (ed.) CRYPTO 2002. LNCS, vol. 2442, pp. 401–416. Springer, Heidelberg (2002). https://doi.org/10.1007/3-540-45708-9_26
28. Nisan, N., Wigderson, A.: Hardness vs randomness. J. Comput. Syst. Sci. **49**(2), 149–167 (1994)
29. Sahai, A., Waters, B.: How to use indistinguishability obfuscation: deniable encryption, and more. In: Proceedings of STOC 2014, pp. 475–484. ACM (2014)
30. Schnorr, C.P.: Efficient identification and signatures for smart cards. In: Brassard, G. (ed.) CRYPTO 1989. LNCS, vol. 435, pp. 239–252. Springer, New York (1990). https://doi.org/10.1007/0-387-34805-0_22
31. Shoup, V.: Practical threshold signatures. In: Preneel, B. (ed.) EUROCRYPT 2000. LNCS, vol. 1807, pp. 207–220. Springer, Heidelberg (2000). https://doi.org/10.1007/3-540-45539-6_15
32. Stinson, D.R., Strobl, R.: Provably secure distributed schnorr signatures and a (t, n) threshold scheme for implicit certificates. In: Varadharajan, V., Mu, Y. (eds.) ACISP 2001. LNCS, vol. 2119, pp. 417–434. Springer, Heidelberg (2001). https://doi.org/10.1007/3-540-47719-5_33

Machine Learning and Security

Can Today's Machine Learning Pass Image-Based Turing Tests?

Apostolis Zarras[1]([⊠]), Ilias Gerostathopoulos[2], and Daniel Méndez Fernández[2]

[1] Maastricht University, Maastricht, The Netherlands
apostolis.zarras@maastrichtuniversity.nl
[2] Technical University of Munich, Munich, Germany

Abstract. Artificial Intelligence (AI) in general and Machine Learning (ML) in particular, have received much attention in recent years also thanks to current advancements in computational infrastructures. One prominent example application of ML is given by image recognition services that allow to recognize characteristics in images and classify them accordingly. One question that arises, also in light of current debates that are fueled with emotions rather than evidence, is to which extent such ML services can already pass image-based Turing Tests. In other words, can ML services imitate human (cognitive and creative) tasks to an extent that their behavior remains indistinguishable from human behavior? If so, what does this mean from a security perspective? In this paper, we evaluate a number of publicly available ML services for the degree to which they can be used to pass image-based Turing Tests. We do so by applying selected ML services to 10,500 randomly collected CAPTCHAs including approximately 100,000 images. We further investigate the degree to which CAPTCHA solving can become an automated procedure. Our results strengthen our confidence in that today's available and ready-to-use ML services can indeed be used to pass image-based Turing Tests, rising new questions on the security of systems that rely on this image-based technology as a security measure.

1 Introduction

Artificial Intelligence (AI) has been coined by pioneers like Alan Turing in the 1950's [35] and deals ever since with the fundamental effort *"to automate intellectual tasks normally performed by humans"* [6]. One core area of AI is Machine Learning (ML) where—in contrast to rather classical instruction-based programming in which machines process given datasets based on predefined rules—machines are *trained* with large datasets to recognize representation patterns in the data and produce the processing rules, thus, they "learn" how to recognize and classify given phenomena [6].

Thanks to recent advancements in computational infrastructures and the availability of large datasets that are fundamental to ML, artificial intelligence has been making long and decisive strides forward from the 1990's on. These

© Springer Nature Switzerland AG 2019
Z. Lin et al. (Eds.): ISC 2019, LNCS 11723, pp. 129–148, 2019.
https://doi.org/10.1007/978-3-030-30215-3_7

advancements are made along two main paths: (i) the research in introducing new and improving existing ML techniques and methods (e.g., deep learning, convolutional neural networks, Gaussian processes) and (ii) the widespread adoption of ML techniques and methods in both research and practice. As for the latter, there exist nowadays many "ML-as-a-service" offerings, which simplify the access to and the use of powerful ML-enabled functionalities.

A representative example of one such type of offering is given by image recognition services. A number of providers, from large companies such as Amazon, IBM, Google, and Microsoft, to startups such as Clarify and Cloudsight, offer paid services allowing other companies or individuals to add advanced image recognition capabilities to their systems. Such capabilities include, inter alia, classifying/labeling an arbitrary image with a number of tags at certain confidence levels, determining whether an image contains a given element (object/person), or finding similar images in a collection.

Fueled by, at least from an application perspective, major advancements in machine learning, we can witness very optimistic marketing slogans accompanying available services ("build apps that see the world like you do" [7]). Needless to say, also negative future scenarios on threats potentially imposed by ML are heavily spread in the public sphere [29]. In fact, today's public debates are too often comparable to a hype full of emotions and conventional wisdom rather than rational debates on basis of concrete evidence on the state of the practice and reasonable implications this has on security issues. Without any prejudice and expectations on future applications of AI, one interesting and important question yet remains: How far we have actually come as of today with current technologies? In other words, could current ML advancements pass the Turing Test, i.e., could they imitate human (cognitive and creative) tasks to an extent that their behavior remains indistinguishable from human behavior?

To the best of our knowledge, there exists little evidence about the extent to which Machine Learning currently can pass Turing Tests and the implications this has on topics like security. Indeed, there has been so far no systematic attempt to validate and compare the effectiveness and applicability of ML techniques in controlled settings.

With this paper, we contribute a curiosity-driven study with the aim to provide a first step in closing the knowledge gap on the state of ML with respect to (image-based) Turing Tests. In essence, our goal is to critically evaluate a number of ML services by the degree to which they can be used to pass Turing Tests. This shall allow to critically reflect upon the security implications that current advancements in AI and in ML have.

Turing Tests are embodied in the latest versions of widely used CAPTCHA services (e.g., Google's reCAPTCHA). Image-based CAPTCHAs rely on the assumption that a specific task, in this case that of image recognition, is presumingly difficult for AI but easy for humans based on their cognitive abilities and experiences. If the capabilities of currently available cloud-based ML services suffice to solve such problems, creating an automatic solver for image-based CAPTCHAs by relying on these services would be technically feasible and even economically viable. A consequent question therefore is for us: To which extent do image-based CAPTCHAs still pose a reliable Turing Test and what are the security implications?

The reason behind choosing image-based CAPTCHAs as our benchmark is manifold. First, they provide a neutral ground for comparing the different image recognition services, as none of these services is tailored to breaking CAPTCHAs, i.e., to pass the Turing Test based on image recognition. A further reason is of pragmatic nature: CAPTCHAs are, same as ML services, largely available to the public facilitating studies, replications, and the public discourse. Finally, we consider it important that the demonstration facilitates a discussion on a larger scale since it shall put forward important security considerations for the future of ML in general, but also of CAPTCHAs in particular. We consider a re-evaluation of mechanisms such as ones incorporated in the de-facto standard CAPTCHAs to be important, because of their criticality to the security of many of today's systems.

In summary, we make the following main contributions:

- We investigate the effectiveness of in total *six* image recognition ML services.
- We design a system capable of accurately solving CAPTCHAs by leveraging the aforementioned services.
- We discuss the impact and implications on the security of systems relying on CAPTCHAs.

2 Fundamentals

In the following, we discuss the fundamentals to the extent necessary in context of our study. More precisely, we first provide information regarding the advances in ML and how these can be used for image recognition. Next, we briefly introduce how these image recognition algorithms are embodied in cloud-based services. Finally, we provide details of the current state of CAPTCHAs.

2.1 Image Recognition via Machine Learning

The ML technology empowering almost all of the image recognition tasks is deep learning, i.e., learning using information processing architectures with several layers [12]. One particular architecture, widely-known as convolutional neural networks (CNNs) [26], has proven very effective in image classification and object detection [12]. Its application relies on the existence of large amounts of annotated image data, from which a classifier is trained by iteratively learning higher-level features from lower-level ones. CNNs consist of multiple layers of convolution and pooling. While convolutional layer extracts features from data samples by moving the convolution filter in a predefined window, pooling layer takes the results of a convolutional layer as input and extracts the most important features. The convolutional filter is used in recognizing distinct objects in an image, almost invariant of their position. Research in image recognition with CNNs is fueled by the ImageNet annual competition [31]. Apart from image recognition, deep learning has been successfully applied in other fields such as speech and audio recognition, natural language processing, machine translation, and even malware detection [10,17,23,24].

Although image recognition via the latest machine learning techniques mentioned above can produce excellent results, it requires (i) considerable expertise in the ML algorithms, (ii) the availability of large datasets for training, and (iii) the operation of the necessary (typically GPU-enabled) infrastructures. The use of image recognition services lifts these assumptions.

2.2   ML Image Recognition Services

To provide a quick start in using image recognition for several business needs (e.g., social media photo tagging, digital asset management, or identification of common problems in health images), several image recognition as-a-service offerings have emerged. These are cloud-hosted services that require an image and provide one or more of the following functionalities: (i) Annotating the image with a set of labels, according to detected objects, living beings, scenes, and actions; (ii) Searching for similar images in a repository or in the Web; (iii) Categorizing the image according to a predefined taxonomy; (iv) Detecting and analyzing faces (including identifying age, gender, and/or emotional state) in the image; (v) Detecting celebrities, landmarks, logos, and/or inappropriate (violent, adult) content in the image; (vi) Detecting and extracting text in the image via Optical Character Recognition.

Since 2015, there has been a growth in the number and quality of publicly-accessible commercial image recognition services [16]. Such services are provided by large companies such as Amazon [1], IBM [19], Google [14], and Microsoft [28], but also smaller ones such as Clarifai [7], Cloudsight [9], Imagga [21], scale [33], Crimson Hexagon [20], Saltlab World [32], Jastec [22], and Cliq Orange [8].

Apart from using their pre-trained ML classifiers in providing the functionalities listed above, some providers allow the creation of custom classifiers or "models", upon provision of labeled datasets. This way, more specific business needs can be met, for instance, related to the analysis of a particular type of images. There are also companies that focus exclusively on such custom image recognition classifiers and APIs, most notably hive.ai [18] and Vize.ai [36].

2.3   CAPTCHA

The idea of discriminating humans from computers by letting them apply sensory and cognitive skills to solve simple problems, which have proven to be extremely hard for computer software, goes back to 1997 [30]. The term CAPTCHA (i.e., *Completely Automated Public Turing Test To Tell Computers and Humans Apart*) was first introduced by von Ahn et al. in an attempt to create automated tests that humans could pass and computer programs could not [37]. The main application of CAPTCHAs has been the detection of bots that perform malevolent activities such as generating large amounts of emails or accounts, participating in online polls, or posting messages in popular services.

There exist different types of CAPTCHA challenges, each requiring a human end-user to perform a specific cognitive task. The most common type requires the user to identify the characters of a distorted text box (text-based CAPTCHAs).

Other common options include transcribing speech (audio-based CAPTCHAs) and identifying images that belong to a particular category (image-based CAPTCHAs). In any case, CAPTCHAs rely on a hard underlying AI problem, in particular, that of text, speech, or image recognition. As a result, apart from security reasons, CAPTCHAs are being used also as benchmarks for AI technologies.

There have been several attempts to create automatic solvers of CAPTCHAs from security researchers. So far, both text-based and audio-based CAPTCHAs have proven vulnerable to different attacks [3,4]. That is why popular and widely-used CAPTCHA implementations, such as Google's reCAPTCHA, are shifting towards image-based CAPTCHAs. In our work, we focus on solving image-based CAPTCHAs using publicly available ML image recognition services.

3   Study Design

Our overall objective is to better understand the extent to which image-based CAPTCHAs still pose a reliable Turing test and what are the implications on security. To this end, we formulate the set of research questions described below before introducing the data collection and analysis procedures.

3.1   Research Questions

To achieve our overall objective, we first need to understand what the potential of ML is with respect to image-based CAPTCHAs and accordingly design our study along three research questions:

RQ1: What is the precision and recall of ML services?
RQ2: What is the absolute accuracy of ML services when considering breaking CAPTCHAs?
RQ3: What is the sufficient accuracy of ML services when considering breaking CAPTCHAs?

First, we want to understand what is the precision and recall of given ML services to recognize the images included in the CAPTCHAs (*RQ1*). This allows us to obtain a basic understanding on the general potential of the services. As the images strongly differ in the content they represent (e.g., a river versus a car), we want to further understand whether there are differences with respect to the particularities of the images themselves and what they represent respectively. Once we understand the general potential of the ML services, we want to analyze the extent to which they can be used to "break" CAPTCHAs, i.e., how well available services can be trained to bypass the today's widespread image-based Turing tests.

We do so in two steps (*RQ2* and *RQ3*): First, by analyzing the *absolute accuracy* of the services in terms of their potential to correctly classify all images of single CAPTCHAs into correct answers to that CAPTCHA or not. Second, image-based CAPTCHAs, if used in context of security mechanisms such as login mechanisms, usually allow for a specific failure tolerance (e.g., by allowing to classify one image wrongly). To lay the ground for our second contribution discussing the impact on security issues, we want to know what the *sufficient accuracy* of the services is in breaking CAPTCHAs. Given that this discussion is based, in parts, on analytical work, we also provide a brief discussion of the security impact analysis procedure to the extent necessary to reproduce our work (Sect. 5).

3.2   Data Collection and Analysis

In the following, we introduce the data collection and the analysis procedures used in this study.

Data Collection: The raw dataset of our study consists of the images contained in 10,500 image CAPTCHAs. For our study, we use six image-recognition services (i.e., *Google's Cloud Vision, IBM's Watson Visual Recognition, Amazon's Rekognition, Microsoft's Computer Vision, Clarify's Visual Search,* and *Cloudsight*). The selection of these services is made based on their popularity. To conduct our study where we compare these image-recognition services, we have to first prepare the data by establishing an oracle (i.e., ground truth) which we use to train a meta-classifier for each ML service-CAPTCHA category pair. Next, we employ the services and analyze the results with respect to our research questions.

In brief, to prepare the dataset for our study, we (*i*) retrieve the images contained in 10,500 CAPTCHAs (99,108 images), (*ii*) manually solve the CAPTCHAs in the sense of annotating TRUE/FALSE labels to the embedded images, and finally (*iii*) submit each image to each of the image recognition services, retrieve, and store the results. In the following, we provide further details for each of the aforementioned steps.

First, we leverage Google's reCAPTCHA service [13] to create our corpus of image CAPTCHAs. For ethical reasons and to not interfere with the traffic of a legitimate website, we set up a reCAPTCHA challenge on a website created for the sole purpose of this study. Next, we scrap the contents of the reCAPTCHA challenges to retrieve the embedded images; we repeat the process 10,500 times. To automate the process, we utilize *Selenium*, a software-testing framework for web applications that has the ability to programatically control a real web browser, in our case Google Chrome. During each challenge, we store in a MongoDB database all the information regarding the category of the challenge, (e.g., "Select all images with street numbers") and the individual images. Since reCAPTCHA returns a single image file and the image grid (e.g., "3 × 3"), we crop the larger image according to the grid to obtain the individual images. Such an exemplary cropped image can be seen in Fig. 1.

Second, we go through the collected 10,500 challenges and manually solve them by marking the images that are correct answers to each challenge with a TRUE flag. It is worth mentioning here that not all the images have an unambiguous semantics (e.g., a building can have also a store). Sometimes is equally difficult for a human to solve a CAPTCHA as it is for an automated system. Hence, in cases where the actual semantics of an image are not completely clear, a majority vote determines the final solution.

Fig. 1. An exemplary image that was marked as correct answer to the challenge of category "Select all images with cars."

Third, we apply the image-recognition services to automatically label each of the collected images with metadata describing this image. As such, we leverage the image labeling APIs of the six different image recognition services we evaluate. Each API requires a jpeg-encoded file as input and provides a JSON-encoded response with metadata in the form of labels, concepts, classes, tags, or captions. For the remainder of the paper, we refer to these as *keywords*. With the exception of Cloudsight, all services provide a numeric value capturing the confidence value or score of each keyword, to which we refer from now on as *confidence*. We access all services and save the obtained raw results directly in the database for later analysis.

Finally, in context of the data collection, we issue 99,108 requests per service. As this exceeded the evaluation quota per service, we opt, where necessary and possible, for specific (academic) licenses.

Testing and Training Data: To obtain the results described in Sect. 4, we split the collected data, i.e., our corpus of 10,500 CAPTCHAs, into two disjunct sets: a training and a testing set. While the training set is used to create the meta-classifiers, the testing set is used for evaluating the ML services in the context of solving CAPTCHA challenges (*RQ1–RQ3*). We perform 10-fold cross-validation by randomly splitting the collected data into 10 subsamples with data equally distributed along the different categories. Out of the 10 subsamples, always one constitutes the testing data (10%) and the rest nine constitute the training data (90%). We made 10 passes in which we considered the first subsample as testing data, then the second subsample, then the third, etc. The results reported and discussed in Sect. 4 are the average of the results for each pass.

Data Analysis: To answer *RQ1*, we calculate the precision and recall based on the manually classified images, as a reference to the ground truth. On the other hand, to answer *RQ2* and *RQ3*, we need to calculate the accuracy of the ML services with respect to breaking the CAPTCHAs. Thus, we devise a method to compare the results of each service with the ground truth of previously manually labeled images. One key challenge is to build a meta-classifier that predicts, based on the results of a service, whether each individual image is a correct answer to its encompassing challenge or not. We build such a meta-classifier for each service S and for each challenge category C. We implement each meta-classifier for $[S, C]$ following three main steps: (i) Collect all keywords K retrieved from S for images belonging to the challenges of C; (ii) For each keyword, find the confidence threshold T that yields the highest accuracy in predicting a correct (TRUE/FALSE) flag for an image; (iii) Find the best combination of $[K, T]$ pairs with the highest accuracy in predicting an accurate answer for a challenge.

At first, we collect all the keywords that are retrieved from S for all the images that belong to a challenge of category C. This is straightforward in all the services except for Microsoft's, whose response contains both a text with a confidence and a number of tags. Therefore, we have to select a different strategy for Microsoft's service. As such, we chose to extract the keywords for this service by tokenizing the text and omitting the tags.

Next, for each keyword K, we assume a confidence threshold T. We go through all images of C and corresponding responses from S and mark as true positive the cases where the image is manually labeled as correct answer to the challenge and (i) K is found by case-insensitive String matching in the response of S and (ii) the retrieved confidence is equal to or higher than T. Accordingly, we calculate the number of true negatives, false positives, and false negatives. We also calculate the per-case *accuracy* by diving the sum of true positives and true

Table 1. Excerpt from generated dataset for the keyword "automobile" for the AWS service and for the "Select all images with cars" challenge category.

Threshold	Confusion matrix				Accuracy (%)
	TP	TN	FP	FN	
48	465	1627	3	677	75.46
49	465	1627	3	677	75.46
50	**465**	**1627**	**3**	**677**	**75.46**
51	462	1627	3	680	75.36
52	457	1627	3	685	75.18
53	451	1627	3	691	74.96

negatives to the total number of images. Technically, we start with a threshold value of 0 and increase it with a step of 1 up to 100. We apply the above process for each K in the $[S, C]$ pair. An example of the produced dataset is depicted in Table 1. As it can be seen, with increasing confidence thresholds values, accuracies decrease since the comparison becomes stricter. Having this dataset in place for each K, selecting the "best" confidence threshold is simply a matter of picking the one with the highest accuracy. In case two or more thresholds have the same accuracy (e.g., 48–50 in Table 1), we select the one with the highest value to avoid potential false positives. Finally, we create a list of all the keywords along with their best confidence thresholds and the accuracies that correspond to these thresholds; we sort the list by the accuracies.

As the aforementioned example shows, trying to find the keyword "automobile", accompanied by a confidence threshold greater than or equal to 50%, in the response of the AWS service to an image of a "cars" challenge is a promising way of getting an accurate prediction on whether to select this image as an answer or not. However, will the prediction improve if we include more $[K, T]$ pairs? If so, what is the optimal number of pairs that should be included?

To investigate these questions, we calculate the number of challenges that would be accurately solved (without any mistake) when considering only the head of list. Specifically, we mark as TRUE the images whose responses from S (i) contain the keyword of the head of the list and (ii) the accompanying confidence is greater or equal to the confidence threshold of the head of the list. In our example, this case is when the response of the AWS service for images belonging to the "cars" category contains the keyword "automobile" with a confidence greater or equal to 50%. We then compare the marked images to the manually labeled ones—a match indicated an accurate solution of the challenge.

We repeat the above process by considering this time the first two items in the list, then the first three items, and so on. In the end, we are able to determine the $[K, T]$ pairs that yield the most accurate predictions—we call these pairs "optimal keywords" for the $[S, C]$ pair.

4   Evaluation

In this section, we present the results of our study and structure them according to the three research questions. In detail, for each question, we first report on the results and then provide a preliminary (subjective) interpretation. Prior to that, we give an overview of the datasets and services we used in our study.

4.1   Datasets and Services Used

Our corpus consists of 10,500 CAPTCHAs belonging to seven different categories. Each category corresponds to the original prompt of the challenge such as "Select all images with house/-store front/street number". The distribution of CAPTCHAs per categories is depicted in Fig. 2. As can be seen, the two most popular categories are *Store Front* and *Street Number*, which occupy 40% and 34% of the study data, respectively. The smallest category, *Road*, amounts to 2% of the

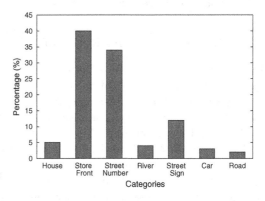

Fig. 2. Distribution (in percentage) of collected CAPTCHAs in categories.

study data, in particular to 192 CAPTCHAs. Each CAPTCHA contains 8, 9, or 16 images (CAPTCHA *size*) arranged in a grid of 2 × 4, 3 × 3 and 4 × 4, respectively. CAPTCHAs of different sizes are not uniformly distributed in the categories. Instead, 16-sized CAPTCHAs belong exclusively to the *Street Sign* category, 8-sized ones belong exclusively to the *Store Front* category, and 9-sized ones belong exclusively to the one of the other five categories. We discuss how the different per-category sizes may have influenced the results of our study in

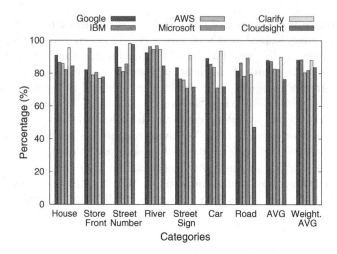

Fig. 3. Precision of ML services in classifying an image as a correct answer to the encompassing CAPTCHA challenge.

the next sections. It is worth to be mentioned that we could have normalized the results by artificially enforcing size 8 for all categories, however we chose to preserve the original CAPTCHA sizes in order to be able to draw valid conclusions on the ability to break the original CAPTCHAs. The total number of images we collected and processed was 99,108 (on average 9.44 images per CAPTCHA).

4.2   RQ1: Precision and Recall of ML Services

To investigate the differences between the performance of ML services in the different categories, we calculate the precision and recall of each meta-classifier that corresponds to a service-category pair across all images contained in all CAPTCHAs of the category. The results are illustrated in Figs. 3 and 4.

A first observation from Fig. 3 is that, with a single exception that of Cloudsight in *Road*, all services yield a precision higher than 70% in all categories, while the best precision in all categories is higher than 90%. On average, the best precision (irrespective of the service providing it) is 94%.

Looking at the results of the services across all categories (two rightmost groups in the Fig. 3), *average* is the mean value of calculated per-category precisions, while *weighted average* is the precision calculated on the total number of images, irrespective of the category of their encompassing CAPTCHAs. Since some categories contain more CAPTCHAs, these two values are different for each service, with the weighted average "boosting" the services which score higher in the popular categories of *Store Front* and *Street Number*. Yet, both statistics yield values between 76% and 89%, with small variations among the services.

Figure 4 depicts the recalls of our meta-classifiers corresponding to each service-category pair. The best recall per category (irrespective of the service

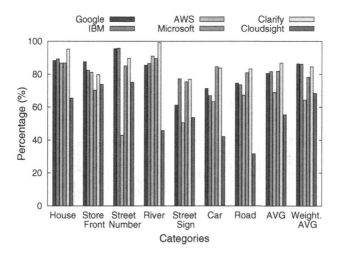

Fig. 4. Recall of ML services in classifying an image as a correct answer to the encompassing CAPTCHA challenge.

providing it) ranges from 77% to 99% with an average value of 89%. The categories with the highest recalls are *House*, *Street Number*, and *River*, while the one with the lowest recalls is *Street Sign*. With respect to the services, Cloudsight scores consistently low in all categories (an average of 55%). The rest of the services score consistently high (more than 80% on average), with the exception of AWS which scores a mere 43% in *Street Number* and 50% in *Street Sign* (and obtains an average recall of 69%).

Interpretation: Our meta-classifiers yield a consistently high precision. As for the recall, the low values of *Street Sign* can be attributed to the following reason. Images of street signs, contrary to images of other categories such as cars, are usually fragmented across several individual images. Human cognition should be able to easily identify fragments of street signs by imagining the missing parts; it seems that this is challenging for ML algorithms, which miss a number of correct responses (an increase in false negatives).

4.3   RQ2: Absolute Accuracy of ML Services

Absolute accuracy is the case in which we try to solve CAPTCHAs without tolerating a single mistake in the binary classification (*selected* or *not selected*) of the images included in each CAPTCHA. Figure 5 depicts the results for this case.

Similar to the precision and recall case, the second group from the right, *average*, is the mean value of calculated per-category accuracies. The rightmost group, *weighted average*, is the accuracy calculated on the total number of CAPTCHAs, irrespective of their category.

The results indicate that for each category there is at least one service that scores higher than 35%, with *House*, *Street Number* and *River*, having services

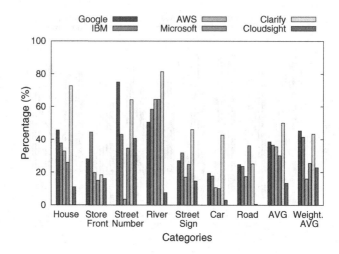

Fig. 5. Absolute accuracy (in percentage) of ML services: solving CAPTCHAs without any mistake tolerance.

that score up to 72%, 75%, and 81%, respectively. Overall, the services score lower in *Store Front*, *Street Sign*, *Car*, and *Road* and higher in *River*. There are also many differences in the performance of the services in different categories. For example, Microsoft and Google provide the most accurate services for *Road* and *Street number*, respectively, while Clarifai is the most accurate in *House*, *River*, *Street Sign*, and *Car*. AWS scores comparatively high in *House* and *River*, but extremely low (3%) in *Street Number*. At any rate, on average, Clarifai and Google, closely followed by IBM and AWS, are the most accurate services, with an average accuracy of close to 40%.

Interpretation: With the exception of Clarifai and Cloudsight, which are scoring consistently high and low respectively, the high variation in the results of the other services can be attributed to the difference in the datasets used in the training of their internal ML classifiers. The reason why some categories yield lower accuracy could be as follows. A street number, although blurry, is entirely contained in an image, while a river can be recognized by its characteristic shape and color. A street sign, however, does not have any characteristic color and, as explained also in the case of recall, its characteristic shape is often not identifiable as it is typically not entirely contained in an image. Further, the low accuracy in the *Street Sign* category should also be attributed to the larger CAPTCHA size (16 images per CAPTCHA).

Finally, although the average accuracy of services is not high, note that the absolute accuracy test is also challenging for humans. That might be also the reason why CAPTCHA services such as reCAPTCHA typically allow for one mistake per challenge. In the following, we report our results for this very case.

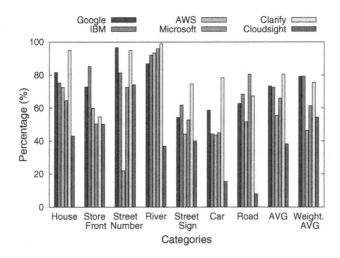

Fig. 6. Sufficient accuracy (in percentage) of ML services: solving CAPTCHAs by tolerating one mistake.

4.4   RQ3: Sufficient Accuracy of ML Services

Sufficient accuracy describes the case in which we try to solve CAPTCHAs by tolerating one mistake in the binary classification of images included in each CAPTCHA. Figure 6 shows the results for this case.

A first observation is that for each category there is at least one service with a sufficient accuracy of 75% or more; for three categories, the best accuracy is even 95% or more (River, Street Number, Road). On average, the best accuracy (irrespective of the service providing it) is 87%. Similarly to the analysis of the absolute accuracy, *Street Sign* and *Car* are the worst performing categories. We can also observe sharp differences in the performance of services in some categories: AWS scores a mere 22% in *Street Number*, where all other services score more than 70%. In the categories *House* and *Store Front*, the services of Clarifai and of Microsoft stand out as far better than the other services scoring accuracies of 95% and 85%, respectively.

The two rightmost groups have been calculated as it was the case for the absolute accuracy. It seems clear that, on average, the three most accurate services are the ones offered by IBM, Clarifai, and Google with a weighted average accuracy 79%, 79%, and 75% respectively. Microsoft scores a weighted average accuracy of 61%, while Cloudsight and AWS score 54% and 46%, respectively.

Finally, comparing the results of the sufficient accuracy case with the absolute accuracy, we can observe that in most categories the relative difference between the services accuracies is preserved, while the absolute values have strongly increased. When looking at the best performing services per category, their accuracy across the two cases is increased on average by 30% units, with a minimum increase of 17 units (Clarify for *River*) and a maximum of 44 units (Microsoft for *Road*).

Interpretation: Similarly to the absolute accuracy case, the sharp variations in the performance of services across different categories can be explained by different datasets used in the training of the internal ML classifiers, while differences between categories can be attributed to both the object containment case as well as the CAPTCHA size.

5   Security Impact and Implications

The main question that still remains is: Assuming that CAPTCHA systems are widely used to tell humans from computers apart, are these systems vulnerable to attacks that utilize modern image recognition services?

5.1   Automated CAPTCHA Solver

To investigate the above question, we implemented an automated program (bot) which visits websites that contain CAPTCHAs and attempts to automatically break them, without any human interaction. To do so, the bot performs the following steps:

Step 1: Visit a website, find and retrieve the `iframe` which contains the checkbox CAPTCHA, and automatically click it.

Step 2: Extract the individual images contained in the CAPTCHA challenge. If we have low confidence for this challenge category or if this is a completely new category for which we do not have any information, press the reload button at the bottom left of the challenge and retrieve a new challenge (presumably of different category). If such a case occurs, we additionally store the new images for further advancing our prediction model.

Step 3: Submit the extracted images to the image recognition service with the most promising results for the particular challenge category and retrieve the results (keywords and confidence).

Step 4: Predict whether each image is a correct answer to the challenge using our meta-classifier for the service-category pair. In particular, check whether at least one keyword from the service is included in the optimal keywords of the meta-classifier and the confidence of the included keyword is higher than the optimal threshold.

Step 5: Use the predictions from the meta-classifier and based on that click accordingly.

Step 6: Press the `VERIFY` button on the bottom right corner. In case the challenge is correctly solved, the bot retrieves an *"I'm not a robot"* response.

We implemented the above process with Selenium, a browser automation framework, which is able to render the DOM of a web page, execute JavaScript, and handle keyboard and mouse events. We implemented the bot in Python; it consists of less than 200 lines of code. In the rest, we elaborate on the selection of the optimal service per category as well as the economic viability of our solver.

Optimal Service for Category: Based on our study results, there is not a single service to rule them all. However, for each CAPTCHA category, there exists a service that yields the most promising results, measured by the accuracy of its meta-classifier described above. In particular, based on the sufficient accuracy results reported in Sect. 4.4, we created a mapping between categories and services. When this metric had the same value for more than one services (*Clarifai* and *Microsoft* in *river*), we looked into the absolute accuracy results to determine the optimal service (in this case, *Clarifai*). Table 2 provides an overview of the optimal service per CAPTCHA category. When considering the optimal categories, our prototype bot implementation yielded fruitful results in the sense of breaking the CAPTCHAs with the sufficient accuracies described above.

Table 2. Service selection per CAPTCHA category.

Challenge	Service
House	Clarifai
Store front	IBM
Street number	Google
River	Clarifai
Street sign	Clarifai
Car	Clarifai
Road	Microsoft

Economic Feasibility: Since CAPTCHA solving is offered as a paid service in the underground economy, it is worthwhile briefly assessing also the economic feasibility of our approach when using an automated solver. All services employ a pay-as-you-go model and most of them charge a similar amount of money per request (i.e., for the labeling of a single image). The time this work took place, the services considered in our study, except Cloudsight, charge from $1 to $2 per 1000 requests. Cloudsight charges a higher amount, about $50 per 1000 requests. One reason behind this might be that Cloudsight relies not only on ML algorithms, but also on human labor for image labeling as part of crowd-sourcing. Nevertheless, since Cloudsight does not appear in the optimal services group shown in the section before, the operational cost of our CAPTCHA solver, assuming an average of 10 images per CAPTCHA, would be $0.01 to $0.02.

5.2 What Does This Mean for the Future of CAPTCHAs?

There exist currently millions of websites leveraging CAPTCHAs as protection mechanism against web spam, online attacks, and automated scripts. The most resilient type of CAPTCHAs has, so far, been image-based CAPTCHAs. At the same time, the most widely used implementation of image-based CAPTCHAs is embodied in Google's reCAPTCHA service.

Our work shows that it is possible to create an automated solver for reCAPTCHA, notably *without being a machine learning expert, without having access to a large corpus of images, or setting up and operating any ML infrastructures.* In fact, invoking publicly available services following a pay-as-you-go model would even be feasible from an economic (underground) perspective as shown above.

Our approach relies on a small upfront effort in manually solving a sufficient number of challenges from each CAPTCHA category. As an indicator for the necessary effort, the smallest training set we used (for *Road* category) contained only 172 CAPTCHAs and provided already an average sufficient accuracy of 56% across all services. It is reasonable to expect that this will only increase by increasing the number of samples for this category. Since reCAPTCHA contains only a limited number of categories (during our study, we encountered 16 categories, out of which we selected the first seven w.r.t number of samples for inclusion), the manual effort required for keeping the solver up-to-date is not high. After manually solving a number of challenges per category, the operation of the solver is fully automated. Importantly, *its expected accuracy is as high as 88%* (average of best sufficient accuracies per category from Sect. 4.4).

From the security perspective, the creation of the automated CAPTCHA solver signifies a successful generic ML-based attack. Since our attack is based on Cloud services that are expected to continue to be available, appropriate countermeasures should be taken to prevent similar attacks in the future. One possibility lies in distorting the images so that the ML cannot recognize the objects anymore with high confidence. The limitation here is, of course, that the images have to still be recognizable by humans; unfortunately, there is not much room for further blurring or distorting the reCAPTCHA images for humans. Another possibility lies in increasing the semantic information necessary to solve the challenge. Consider, for instance, requesting the user to identify a combination of specific items or actions, e.g., groups of two to three persons drinking beer. Finally, CAPTCHAs could rely more on fragmented views of a scene, such as the *Street Sign* CAPTCHAs in our study; we observed that these pose a challenge to ML (low accuracies) but not at all to humans.

In any case, and given the current state of using image-based CAPTCHAs as a security measure, we conclude that they are insufficient to be kept as the de-facto standard to prevent automated security attacks.

6 Threats to Validity

The presented study is a curiosity-driven study with many manual and automated tasks. Inherent to such tasks are a number of threats to validity out of which we now discuss those that appear to be major ones from our own perspective. One major threat to validity concerns the trustworthiness of the used oracle (ground truth) to train and test the ML services. This ground truth was defined manually by solving all images and, thus, it affects the internal validity of the whole study. We tried to minimize the threat by defining the ground truth dataset in pairs of researchers. Still, we cannot guarantee that we did not wrongly classify some of the images even though we postulate that it would negatively affect the accuracy of all the ML services probably in the same way.

Another threat to validity arises from the fact that we do not know the extent to which the source of the images matter. We took all images from Google to train all ML services, but argue that the choice of images seems to have a lower impact as (*i*) they resemble regular photos of real-life situations and (*ii*) the results do not indicate to perpetually better scores by Google's ML service. To the best of our knowledge, we see no clear indicator that the choice of images for the training and testing dataset has influenced the outcome of the study.

Finally, another threat to validity concerns the external validity and eventually the conclusion validity. Are we able to draw conclusions that go beyond the image-recognition services? For instance, can we draw conclusions on the general field of machine learning? Please note that, again, our study was a curiosity-driven one and we deliberately (and also opportunistically) chose the services described in the paper. Although our intention was not to draw any conclusions beyond the selected services, we can still argue that the effects observed in the setting described in this paper could be observed in different settings.

7 Related Work

Since the concept of CAPTCHA was first introduced, a lot of research has been done in this area to create CAPTCHAS that are easy for humans to solve, yet extremely difficult for machines. The most popular category, since recently, was the text-based CAPTCHAS. However, modern *Optical Character Recognition* (OCR) algorithms were able to solve the presented challenges with pretty high accuracy [5,39,40]. The suitability of CAPTCHAS as a means to implement Turing Tests in a usable manner has since then been discussed for some years now. In particular, Bursztein et al. [3] introduced a novel approach to solving CAPTCHAS in a single step that uses machine learning to attack the segmentation and the recognition problems simultaneously. Baecher et al. [2] analyzed three recent generations of reCAPTCHA and presented an algorithm that is capable of solving at least 5% of the challenges generated by these versions. Cruz-Perez et al. [11] presented a novel approach for automatic segmentation and recognition of reCAPTCHA in websites which is based on CAPTCHA image preprocessing with character alignment, morphological segmentation with three-color bar character encoding, and heuristic recognition.

Therefore, alternatives to text-based CAPTCHAS were considered a necessity. Goswami et al. [15] presented FaceDCAPTCHA, a face detection-based CAPTCHA, in which four to six distorted face/non-face images are embedded in a complex background and a user has to correctly mark the center of all the face images within a defined tolerance. Another alternative is the video-based CAPTCHA challenges such as NuCAPTCHA. However, Xu et al. [38] presented flaws in the design of video-based CAPTCHAS by implementing automated attacks based on computer vision techniques as a proof of concept.

Another category of CAPTCHAS discussed in literature is based on audio. Nevertheless, researchers, once again, were able to break these challenges. For instance, Kopp et al. [25], pointed out flaws and weak spots of frequently used solutions and concluded with consequent security risks. Meutzner et al. [27] suggested to use speech recognition rather than generic classification methods for better analyzing the security of audio-based reCAPTCHAS. They showed that their attack, based on an automatic speech recognition system, can defeat reCAPTCHA with a significantly higher success rate than reported in previous studies.

The closest work to our study is the one from Sivakorn et al. [34]. The authors propose an attack that uses deep learning technologies to annotate images. They focus, on trying to automatically break reCAPTCHA challenges and succeed in roughly 70% of the cases. In particular, they also used Clarifai as their main service to break a CAPTCHA. However, as we have shown in our work, Clarifai did not perform equally good in all of the reCAPTCHA challenges. In fact, although the scope of their work differs in the sense of providing an (also technical) analysis of CAPTCHAs, their work inspired some technicalities in our own study design which aims at providing a broader analysis of the suitability of publicly available ML services to break CAPTCHAs and the security implications this has.

Compared to previous works that attempt to break CAPTCHAs by implementing a specific approach or algorithm, we took a different path. The motivating question is to understand the extent to which publicly available ML services can pass image-based Turing Tests and the security implications this has. We are, thus, leveraging working solutions, which are offered in the form of online image recognition services, and apply them for CAPTCHA infiltration. Another key difference with the previous works is that the sole goal of our study is not to break the CAPTCHA mechanism, but to compare existing services and evaluate their ability to extract valuable and accurate knowledge from an image. We only use the CAPTCHA mechanism as benchmark for our comparison. Yet, we also saw that the overall image recognition technology has advanced to the point that can be used for malicious purposes as well. To the best of our knowledge, we are the first to perform such a comparison among different image recognition services.

8 Conclusion

In this study, we wanted to understand the extent to which today's publicly available ML services can be used to pass image-based Turing Tests. Thus, we employed six ML services to a broad set of available CAPTCHAs. Our results strengthened our confidence in the suitability of available ML services to break CAPTCHAs and pose a security threat if used automatically. Interestingly, it was possible to create an automated solver for reCAPTCHAs, notably without prior expertise in machine learning, without having build up an own large corpus of images, and without setting up and operating specific ML infrastructures on our own. This manifests the idea that today's available and ready-to-use ML services can indeed be used to pass image-based Turing Tests and rises new questions to the security of systems that rely on this technology as a security measure.

Acknowledgments. This work was supported by the European Union's Horizon 2020 research and innovation programme under grant agreement No. 833115 (PREVISION).

References

1. Amazon Rekognition. Deep Learning-Based Image Recognition—Search, Verify, and Organize Millions of Images. https://aws.amazon.com/rekognition/
2. Baecher, P., Büscher, N., Fischlin, M., Milde, B.: Breaking reCAPTCHA: a holistic approach via shape recognition. In Future Challenges in Security and Privacy for Academia and Industry (2011)
3. Bursztein, E., Aigrain, J., Moscicki, A., Mitchell, J.C.: The end is nigh: generic solving of text-based CAPTCHAs. In USENIX Workshop on Offensive Technologies (WOOT) (2014)
4. Bursztein, E., Beauxis, R., Paskov, H., Perito, D., Fabry, C., Mitchell, J.: The failure of noise-based non-continuous audio captchas. In: IEEE Symposium on Security and Privacy (2011)
5. Chellapilla, K., Simard, P.Y.: Using machine learning to break visual human interaction proofs (HIPs). In: Advances in Neural Information Processing Systems (2005)
6. Chollet, F.: Deep Learning With Python. Manning, Shelter Island (2017)
7. Clarifai. Artificial Intelligence With a Vision. https://clarifai.com/
8. Cliq Orange. https://www.cliqorange.com/
9. Cloudsight. Visual Cognition—High Quality Understanding of Images Within Seconds. https://cloudsight.ai/
10. Collobert, R., Weston, J.: A unified architecture for natural language processing: deep neural networks with multitask learning. In: International Conference on Machine Learning (2008)
11. Cruz-Perez, C., Starostenko, O., Uceda-Ponga, F., Alarcon-Aquino, V., Reyes-Cabrera, L.: Breaking reCAPTCHAs with unpredictable collapse: heuristic character segmentation and recognition. In: Carrasco-Ochoa, J.A., Martínez-Trinidad, J.F., Olvera López, J.A., Boyer, K.L. (eds.) MCPR 2012. LNCS, vol. 7329, pp. 155–165. Springer, Heidelberg (2012). https://doi.org/10.1007/978-3-642-31149-9_16
12. Deng, L., Yu, D.: Deep learning: methods and applications. Found. Trends Sig. Process. **7**(3–4), 197–387 (2014)
13. Google. reCAPTCHA: Protect Your Site From Spam and Abuse. https://developers.google.com/recaptcha/
14. Google Cloud Vision. Derive Insight From Images With Our Powerful Cloud Vision API (2017). https://cloud.google.com/vision/
15. Goswami, G., Powell, B.M., Vatsa, M., Singh, R., Noore, A.: FaceDCAPTCHA: face detection based color image CAPTCHA. Future Gener. Comput. Syst. **31**, 59–68 (2014)
16. de Gyor, H.: Keywording Now: Practical Advice on Using Image Recognition and Keywording Services. Another DAM Consultancy (2017)
17. Hinton, G., et al.: Deep neural networks for acoustic modeling in speech recognition. IEEE Sig. Process. Mag. **29**, 82–97 (2012)
18. Hive.AI. Powering Artificial Intelligence. https://thehive.ai/
19. IBM. Watson Visual Recognition (2017). https://www.ibm.com/watson/services/visual-recognition/
20. ICrimson Hexagon. https://www.crimsonhexagon.com/
21. Imagga. Build Your Apps on Top of an Advanced Image Tagging Technology. https://imagga.com/
22. JASTEC: A Pioneer of Image Recognition. http://www.jastec.fr/

23. Kolosnjaji, B., Eraisha, G., Webster, G., Zarras, A., Eckert, C.: Empowering convolutional networks for malware classification and analysis. In: International Joint Conference on Neural Networks (IJCNN), pp. 3838–3845. IEEE (2017)

24. Kolosnjaji, B., Zarras, A., Webster, G., Eckert, C.: Deep learning for classification of malware system call sequences. In: Kang, B.H., Bai, Q. (eds.) AI 2016. LNCS (LNAI), vol. 9992, pp. 137–149. Springer, Cham (2016). https://doi.org/10.1007/978-3-319-50127-7_11

25. Kopp, M., Pistora, M., Holena, M.: How to mimic humans, guide for computers. In: ITAT (2016)

26. Lecun, Y., Bottou, L., Bengio, Y., Haffner, P.: Gradient-based learning applied to document recognition. Proc. IEEE **86**(11), 2278–2324 (1998)

27. Meutzner, H., Nguyen, V.-H., Holz, T., Kolossa, D.: Using automatic speech recognition for attacking acoustic CAPTCHAs: the trade-off between usability and security. In: Annual Computer Security Applications Conference (ACSAC) (2014)

28. Microsoft. Computer Vision API. https://azure.microsoft.com/en-us/services/cognitive-services/computer-vision/

29. NY Times. Please Prove You're Not a Robot. https://www.nytimes.com/2017/07/15/opinion/sunday/please-prove-youre-not-a-robot.html

30. Reshef, E., Raanan, G., Solan, E.: Method and system for discriminating a human action from a computerized action (2004)

31. Russakovsky, O., et al.: ImageNet large scale visual recognition challenge. Int. J. Comput. Vis. **115**(3), 211–252 (2015)

32. Saltlab World. Image & Object Recognition System & API. http://saltlabworld.com/

33. Scale. Image Annotation API. https://www.scaleapi.com/image-annotation

34. Sivakorn, S., Polakis, I., Keromytis, A.D.: I am robot: (deep) learning to break semantic image CAPTCHAs. In: IEEE European Symposium on Security and Privacy, EuroS&P (2016)

35. Turing, A.M.: Computing machinery and intelligence. Mind **59**(236), 433–460 (1950)

36. Vize.ai. Custom Image Recognition API. https://vize.ai/

37. von Ahn, L., Blum, M., Hopper, N.J., Langford, J.: CAPTCHA: using hard AI problems for security. In: Biham, E. (ed.) EUROCRYPT 2003. LNCS, vol. 2656, pp. 294–311. Springer, Heidelberg (2003). https://doi.org/10.1007/3-540-39200-9_18

38. Xu, Y., Reynaga, G., Chiasson, S., Frahm, J.-M., Monrose, F., van Oorschot, P.C.: Security and usability challenges of moving-object CAPTCHAs: decoding codewords in motion. In: USENIX Security Symposium (2012)

39. Yan, J., El Ahmad, A.S.: Breaking visual captchas with Naive pattern recognition algorithms. In: Annual Computer Security Applications Conference (ACSAC) (2007)

40. Yan, J., El Ahmad, A.S.: A low-cost attack on a microsoft CAPTCHA. In: ACM Conference on Computer and Communications Security (CCS) (2008)

PD-ML-Lite: Private Distributed Machine Learning from Lightweight Cryptography

Maksim Tsikhanovich[1,4]($\boxtimes$), Malik Magdon-Ismail[2,4], Muhammad Ishaq[3,4], and Vassilis Zikas[3,4]

[1] Amazon.com, Inc., Seattle, USA
maksimtsikhanovich@gmail.com
[2] Computer Science Department, Rensselaer Polytechnic Institute, Troy, USA
magdon@gmail.com
[3] School of Informatics, University of Edinburgh, Edinburgh, UK
m.ishaq@inf.ed.ac.uk
[4] School of Informatics, University of Edinburgh & IOHK, Edinburgh, UK
vzikas@inf.ed.ac.uk

Abstract. Privacy arises to a major issue in distributed learning. Current approaches that do not use a trusted external authority either reduce the accuracy of the learning algorithm (e.g., by adding noise), or incur a high performance penalty. We propose a methodology for *private distributed ML from light-weight cryptography* (in short, PD-ML-Lite). We apply our methodology to two major ML algorithms, namely non-negative matrix factorization (NMF) and singular value decomposition (SVD). Our protocols are communication optimal, achieve the same accuracy as their non-private counterparts, and satisfy a notion of privacy—which we define—that is both intuitive and measurable. We use light cryptographic tools (multi-party secure sum and normed secure sum) to build learning algorithms rather than wrap complex learning algorithms in a heavy multi-party computation (MPC) framework.

The full version of this work is available at [TMIZ19].

M. Tsikhanovich and M. Ishaq—Work done in part while the author was at Rensselaer Polytechnic Institute.

V. Zikas—This work was done in part while the author was at Rensselaer Polytechnic Institute and UCLA and supported in part by DARPA and SPAWAR under contract N66001-15-C-4065 and by the Office of the Director of National Intelligence (ODNI), Intelligence Advanced Research Projects Activity (IARPA), via 2019-1902070008. The views and conclusions contained herein are those of the authors and should not be interpreted as necessarily representing the official policies, either expressed or implied, of ODNI, IARPA, or the U.S. Government. The U.S. Government is authorized to reproduce and distribute reprints for governmental purposes notwithstanding any copyright annotation therein.

Electronic supplementary material The online version of this chapter (https://doi.org/10.1007/978-3-030-30215-3_8) contains supplementary material, which is available to authorized users.

© Springer Nature Switzerland AG 2019
Z. Lin et al. (Eds.): ISC 2019, LNCS 11723, pp. 149–167, 2019.
https://doi.org/10.1007/978-3-030-30215-3_8

We showcase our algorithms' utility and privacy for NMF on topic modeling and recommender systems, and for SVD on principal component regression, and low rank approximation.

1 Introduction

More data is better for all forms of learning. When the data is distributed among several parties, the best learning outcome requires data sharing. However, sharing raw data can be uneconomic and/or subject to policies or legislation. Consider these (distributed) ML scenarios:

Private Distributed Topic Modeling. Agencies with protected data (FBI, CIA, ...) must to build a peer-to-peer information retrieval system using a topic model over all their data [TXD03, YA09].

Private Distributed Recommender Systems. Businesses with proprietary consumer data want recommender systems that leverage data across all the businesses without compromising the privacy of any party's data [LSS10].

We focus on two fundamental tools for computing compact representations of data: non-negative matrix factorization (NMF) and singular value decomposition (SVD). NMF is NP-hard [Vav09], while SVD can be solved in cubic time [GVL12]. For both tasks, there are families of algorithms with acceptable performance in practice, e.g., for NMF [Lin07, CZA07, Ho08] and for SVD [GVL12]. Many of these NMF heuristics can be performed efficiently even when the data is distributed [GNHS11, DLCL14, BMPS03], and there is significant interest in distributed algorithms for SVD (e.g. [IO16]). The typical focus of such distributed algorithms is to minimize the information that has to be communicated to obtain the same outcome as a centralized algorithm, so these algorithms are not privacy preserving—a critical challenge which we address here. The question we attack is:

> *Can parties collectively learn from distributed data and no trusted third-party, while ensuring: (1) Their data remains private, and (2) The learning is comparable, ideally identical, to a centralized setting?*

Organizations will only cooperate if they can *improve* their already existing system, and if their data can remain *private*.

Privacy in Distributed Learning. Data privacy is an emerging topic in ML. Naive solutions like data anonymization are insufficient [BS08, MEEO13]. There are two main cryptographic tools to enhance the privacy of learning algorithms: *differential privacy (DP)* and *secure multi-party computation (MPC)*. These methods differ in their use cases, security/privacy guarantees, and computation overhead. In a nutshell, DP preserves the privacy of any individual record against an *external* observer who sees the output of a query (no matter what side-information he has on the data.) This is achieved by adding noise to the output, which "flattens" any individual record's influence, thereby hiding that record. On the other hand, MPC allows mutually distrustful parties, each with private data, to compute and share a function on their joint data without leaking any other information *to each other*. The MPC privacy guarantee is also our aim, and is orthogonal to DP: MPC computes the exact output and does not protect the privacy of individual records from what might be inferrable from the output. Thus, the decision to use DP, MPC, or something else must consider the learning and privacy requirements of the application. We now argue why each of these solutions is inadequate for our purposes.

Unsuitability of DP. A fundamental constraint is that the *learning outcome of the private distributed algorithm must match the centralized[1] outcome*, because the *only* reason for the distributed parties to collaborate is if they can improve on the local learning outcome. This *renders DP unsuitable for our goals,* as the addition of noise inevitably deteriorates the learning outcome [RA12, BDMN05, RA12, WFS15, LWS15, HXZ15]. This strict accuracy restriction is important. For example, if adding privacy renders the distributed recommender system less accurate than a system one party could construct from its own data, then this party gained nothing and lost some privacy by participating in distributed learning. For completeness we include in Figs. 3(c) and 4 results confirming general observations in the literature that adding noise to obtain even moderate differential privacy results in excessive deterioration in accuracy for distributed NMF and SVD.

Insufficiency of General MPC. In theory, MPC solves our problem: run the optimization/inference algorithm on distributed data by executing some type of 'MPC byte code' on a 'distributed virtual machine.' Such an algorithm-agnostic implementation typically *incurs a high communication and computation overhead,* e.g., [NIW+13]. More recently, optimized MPC protocols tailored to private ML on distributed data were developed [KKK+16, MZ17, MR18, MG18a]. However, these rely on partially trusted third parties that take on the burden of the computation and privacy protection. Trusted third parties are a strong assumption in practice, a compromise we avoid.

1.1 Our Contributions

We propose a paradigm shift in privacy preserving distributed ML. Rather than rely on cryptography to develop (new) MPC for ML, we identify lightweight distributed cryptographic primitives and develop new learning algorithms that only communicate by means of these primitives. The primitives are cryptographically secure, leaking nothing about their inputs; however the output (typically an obfuscated function of the inputs) is announced. To quantify privacy loss from announcing the output, we adapt ideas from the noiseless privacy-preserving literature. The idea to estimate privacy loss from a leaky MPC, using privacy-preservation mechanisms, in particular DP, was recently also used in [MG18b]

---

[1] Centralized refers to the optimal (non-private) outcome where all data is aggregated for learning.

where computation is outsourced to two semi-trusted parties (one must be honest). We do not make any such requirement here.

We apply our methods to two classical ML-problems with a wide spectrum of applications: Non-negative Matrix Factorization (NMF); and, singular value decomposition (SVD). We demonstrate performance and privacy on typical applications of NMF and SVD (topic modeling, recommender systems, PCA-regression, low rank approximation).

Overview of Private Distributed NMF. We give an algorithm for private, distributed Non-negative Matrix Factorization (PD-NMF). Our algorithm allows M parties, where each party m holds input database $X^{(m)}$ (non-negative matrix), to distributedly compute an NMF for the union of their data without revealing considerable information about any individual record beyond the output of the NMF. Importantly, we guarantee that the output of the NMF is the same as a centralized NMF using the aggregated data.[2] The PD-NMF problem is formulated in Fig. 1.

PD-NMF. M mutually distrustful parties each have a non-negative $n_m \times d$ matrix $X^{(m)}$ (n_m rows over d features), for $m = 1, \ldots, M$. The parties agree on the feature-order. Given a rank k, each party must compute the same non-negative row-basis $T \in \mathbb{R}^{k \times d}$ such that:

- The sum of Frobenius reconstruction errors for each matrix $X^{(m)}$ onto the basis T plus an optional regularization term is minimized:

$$\min_T \ \tfrac{1}{2} \sum_{m=1}^{M} ||X^{(m)} - W^{(m)}T||_F^2 + \text{reg}(W, T),$$

where $W^{(m)}$ is a non-negative fit of $X^{(m)}$ to T.
- There is no trusted third party and the peer-to-peer communication is small (sub-linear in $\sum_m n_m$).
- For any document x, a coalition of parties $\{\ell_1, \ldots, \ell_j\}$ given only the communication transcript and their databases $X^{(\ell_1)}, \ldots, X^{(\ell_j)}$ cannot, in polytime, determine if $x \in X^{(m)}$, where $m \notin \{\ell_1, \ldots, \ell_j\}$.

Fig. 1. PD-NMF Problem Formulation.

Remark (On Exactness). Our approach crucially differs from DP-based approaches to private distributed learning in that we insist on the exact solution T to the NMF problem. Exactness is important. The reason party m participates in a distributed computation it to *improve their local estimate* $T^{(m)}$ to the centralized T that results from the full X. Noising the process corrupts the

---

[2] Recall that this requirement renders DP unacceptable.

estimate of T, which defeats that purpose. In practice the deterioration in T is drastic.

Toward constructing such an algorithm, we adapt an existing versatile and efficient (but non-private and non-distributed) NMF algorithm [Ho08] to the distributed scenario. We call our adapted algorithm Private Distributed NMF, PD-NMF. Our adaptation is carefully crafted so that parties running it need to *only* communicate sums of locally computed vectors; these sums are distributively computed by means of a very light-weigh cryptographic (MPC) primitive, namely 'secure multiparty sum,' denoted as SecSum. SecSum hides each party's contribution to the sum, with almost no communication overhead. The communication is $O(Mdk)$ per iteration in the peer-to-peer communication model, *independent of the database size n* (cheaper than aggregating all data to a central server). We prove that, from the same initialization, PD-NMF converges to *exactly* the same solution as the centralized NMF. Further, we develop a new private distributed initialization for PD-NMF which ensembles locally computed NMF models so that convergence is quick and to a good solution. Our distributed initialization alone matches the quality of the centralized solution.

PD-NMF communicates the sums of intermediate results. To quantify the leakage from revealing the intermediate sums, we adapt *distributional differential privacy* (DDP), also known as *noiseless DP* [BBFM12, BGKS13, BF16]. Informally, in such a notion of privacy we get a similar guarantee as in DP, i.e., indistinguishability of neighboring databases, but this guarantee is realized due to the entropy of the data. Noisless DP is similar to DP. An adversary cannot determine whether or not any given record is in the database any better than he can distinguish the two neighboring databases (with and without this record). However, noiseless DP is sensitive to both the original data distribution (indistinguishability stems from data entropy), and to prior information. For us, privacy is with respect to other participants in the distributed learning, hence the data of those participants is side-information available to the adversary trying to distinguish between possible neighbouring databases of the victim.

A major challenge is to actually estimate the distinguishing advantage (upper bounded by the distance between the neighboring distributions). In the simple one-shot mechanism considered in the strawman examples of [BBFM12, BGKS13, BF16], one can analytically compute the corresponding posterior distributions and directly calculate their distance. In distributed learning applications, even if we start with simple initial data distributions, e.g., uniform, each iteration of learning quickly removes any convenient structure in the posterior, making analytical calculations intractable.

KSDP. We propose a new *experimentally measurable* notion of distributional differential privacy, *Kolmogorov-Smirnov Distributional Privacy (KSDP)*, which is similar in spirit to DDP but uses the KS hypothesis test to quantify distance between distributions. Loosely speaking, under KSDP, we preserve privacy if an adversary cannot statistically distinguish between PD-NMF run on a database with a document x versus when the database doesn't have x. As with DDP, KSDP relies on data entropy to preserve privacy, a weaker guarantee than DP

(DP which preserves privacy regardless of data entropy). This weaker privacy is inevitable if the learning outcome must not be corrupted.

Overview of Private Distributed SVD. Let X be an $n \times d$ real-valued matrix $(n \geq d)$. The k-*truncated SVD* of X is $X_k = U_k \Sigma_k V_k^T$ where U_k, V_k are orthogonal (the top-k left and right singular vectors), and Σ_k is diagonal, (the top-k singular values). The row basis V_k^T is important for feature extraction, spectral clustering, regression, topic discovery, etc., because it gives optimal reconstruction of X: $\|X - X_k\| \leq \|X - \hat{X}\|$ for any rank-k matrix $\hat{X}$. PD-SVD asks for a private distributed algorithm to compute V_k, see Fig. 2.

PD-SVD. M mutually distrustful parties each have an $n_m \times d$ matrix $X^{(m)}$ of n_m rows over d features, sampled from an underlying distribution $\mathcal{D}$. The parties agree on the feature-order. Given a rank k: each party must compute V_k such that:

- V_k contains the optimal 'topics' (as defined above) for the full data X, where X is computed by stacking the rows of $X^{(m)}, m \in \{1, \ldots, M\}$ into a single matrix.
- There is no trusted third party and the peer-to-peer communication is small (sub-linear in $\sum_m n_m$).
- For any document x, a coalition of parties $\{\ell_1, \ldots, \ell_j\}$ given only the communication transcript and their databases $X^{(\ell_1)}, \ldots, X^{(\ell_j)}$ cannot, in polytime, determine if $x \in X^{(m)}$, where $m \notin \{\ell_1, \ldots, \ell_j\}$.

Fig. 2. PD-SVD Problem Formulation.

We use simple block power-iterations to jointly find singular values/vectors. Better numerical methods exist (see [Par98]), however our focus is to recover the centralized solution privately, and simple helps. To compute the row basis V_k, we work with the covariance matrix, $X^T X = V \Sigma^2 V^T$. It is convenient that $X^T X$ is a sum over individual covariances, $X^T X = \sum_{m=1}^M X^{(m)^T} X^{(m)}$, so linear operations on $X^T X$ can use SECSUM, and communication complexities depend on d, not $n = \sum_m n_m$. The cryprographic challenge is to reveal only V_k, and not Σ_k or U_k, as those effectively reveal the full data, or close to it. SECSUM alone can't privately compute only V_k (and hide Σ_k).

There are distributed SVD algorithms obeying a variety of security constraints. However, a persistent issue is that Σ_k is revealed, and these works do not address document privacy [WKL+16,CLZ17,HNY09,You10]. To avoid revealing Σ_k in the power iterations, we will use another lightweight cryptographic (MPC) module which we denoted as NORMEDSECSUM. (In fact, our algorithm will use both NORMEDSECSUM and the original SECSUM.) NORMEDSECSUM is similar to SECSUM, taking vectors x_m, but instead of privately sharing the sum, it shares the sum normalized by its ℓ_2-norm,

$$\text{NORMEDSECSUM}(\{\boldsymbol{x}_m\}_{m=1}^M) = \boldsymbol{s}/\|\boldsymbol{s}\|_2.$$

NORMEDSECSUM is sightly heavier than the very lightweight SECSUM. (The overhead can be brought down to hardly noticeable by pre-processing and various optimizations, see [DSZ15] and references therein.) Most importantly, the communication cost of our algorithm depends on d, not n. The privacy of PD-SVD is argued analogously to PD-NMF, using KSDP

Summary of Contributions

- We propose a shift from enclosing distributed learning algorithms inside costly MPC frameworks toward modifying learning algorithms to use only lightweight cryptographic protocols (PD-ML-Lite).
- For two landmark machine learning problems (NMF and SVD) we show that two extremely lightweight primitives suffice to recover the centralized solution (SECSUM and NORMEDSECSUM).
- We introduce Kolmogorov-Smirnov Distributional Privacy (KSDP) as an empirically estimable alternative to noiseless (aka distributional) differential privacy.
- Extensive experiments that showcase the performance of PD-NMF and PD-SVD in classical applications (topic modeling, recommender systems, PCA-regression and low rank approximation). Privacy is empirically preserved with significant learning-uplift. In contrast, differential privacy guarantees privacy but drastically deteriorates the learning outcome, implying no upside to participating in the distributed protocol.

Notation. X is the row-concatenation of $X^{(m)}$. $A_{i:}$ is the ith row; $A_{:j}$ is the jth column. $\|A\|_{1,2}$ are the ℓ_1 and ℓ_2 entry-wise norms and $\|A\|_F$ is the Frobenius norm. $[A]_+$ projects A onto the non-negative orthant by zeroing its negative entries. $\mathbf{1}_d$ is the d-dimensional vector of 1s.

2   Private Distributed NMF (PD-NMF)

Given a rank k, (locally) minimize over W, T:

$$\mathcal{E}(W,T) = \tfrac{1}{2}\|X - WT\|_F^2, \tag{1}$$

where $W \in \mathbb{R}_+^{n \times k}, T \in \mathbb{R}_+^{k \times d}$. (One can also regularize, details deferred). When either T or W is fixed, NMF reduces to non-negative least squares. We can write (1) as a sum of k rank-1 terms: Let residual R_t be the part of X to be explained by topic t, $R_t = X - \sum_{l \neq t}^k W_{:l}T_{l:}$ for $t = 1, \ldots, k$. The objective $\mathcal{E}$ becomes

$$\mathcal{E}(W,T) = \frac{1}{2k}\sum_{t=1}^k \|R_t - W_{:t}T_{t:}\|_F^2$$

Algorithm 1. PD-NMF-ITER: Private Distributed RRI-NMF, party m's view.

Input: Local data $X^{(m)}$, initial topics T, parameters $\alpha, \beta, \gamma, \delta$, SECSUM
Output: Global topics T^G

1: **repeat** until convergence
2: **for** $t \in \{0, 1, \ldots, k\}$ **do**
3:     $R_t^{(m)} \leftarrow X^{(m)} - W^{(m)}T + W_{:t}^{(m)}T_{t:}$
4:     $W_{:t}^{(m)} \leftarrow [R_t^{(m)}T_{t:}^T - \gamma \mathbf{1}_{n_m}]_+ / (\|T_{t:}\|_2^2 + \delta)$
5:     $num \leftarrow \text{SECSUM}(\{W_{:t}^{(m)T}R_t^{(m)}\}_m)$
6:     $den \leftarrow \text{SECSUM}(\{\|W_{:t}^{(m)}\|_2^2\}_m)$
7:     $T_{t:} \leftarrow [num - \alpha \mathbf{1}_d]_+ / (den + \beta)$
8:     $T_{t:} \leftarrow \arg\min_{x \geq 0, \|x\|_1 = 1} \|x - T_{t:}\|_2$

We now use a projected gradient rank one residual method (RRI-NMF) proposed in [Ho08] to minimize $\mathcal{E}$, alternating between W and T until a convergence.[3] The iterative update of each topic t is [Ho08]:

$$W_{:t} \leftarrow \frac{[R_t T_{t:}^T - \gamma \mathbf{1}_n]_+}{\|T_{t:}\|_2^2 + \delta} \qquad t = 1, \ldots, k;$$

$$T_{t:} \leftarrow \frac{[W_{:t}^T R_t - \alpha \mathbf{1}_d]_+}{\|W_{:t}\|_2^2 + \beta} \qquad t = 1, \ldots, k; \qquad (2)$$

$$T_{t:} \leftarrow \arg\min_{x \geq 0, \|x\|_1 = 1} \|x - T_{t:}\|_2 \qquad j = 1, \ldots, k$$

In the last step, projection onto the simplex can be done efficiently [Con16]. The key is that the updates of W and T decouple. The update of W is local to each party. The update of T uses a sum over rows in X. Each party evaluates its part of the sum $(W_{:t}^{(m)})^T R_t^{(m)}$), and SECSUM (see below) privately shares the sum. The observed output $W_{:t}^T R_t$ is a *sum* over *iid* rows of X which is not sensitive to specific rows. This ultimately gives privacy as X gets large.

Secure Multiparty Sum Protocol (SECSUM). The protocol SECSUM is a standard lightweight cryptographic distributed peer-to-peer protocol (MPC) among M parties $p_1, \ldots, p_M$. It takes an input from each party a vector $\boldsymbol{x}_m$ and outputs (to everyone) the sum $\sum_{m \in M} \boldsymbol{x}_m$. A party only learns this sum and no additional information about the inputs of other parties. (For details we refer to the full version).

Private Distributed RRI-NMF (PD-NMF-Iter). The update in (2) combined with SECSUM is a private and distributed iteration of RRI-NMF, denoted PD-NMF-ITER. Our final algorithm for PD-NMF in Algorithm 1 first runs PD-NMF-INIT (see later) to get initial topics T_0, and then iterates PD-NMF-ITER

---

[3] In practice, RRI-NMF and similar alternating methods [Lin07, CZA07] outperform the original multiplicative algorithms for NMF [LS01].

from T_0 until convergence. We give a simple but essential theorem on the learning outcome of PD-NMF-ITER (proof deferred), which says that our distributed algorithm mimics the centralized algorithm.

Algorithm 2. PD-SVD, party m's view.

Require: $n_m \times d$ matrix $X^{(m)}$, rank k, # iterations τ, # parties M, SECSUM and NORMEDSECSUM.
Ensure: $\hat{V}_k$: estimate of top k eigenvectors of S.
1: $S^{(m)} \leftarrow X^{(m)T}X^{(m)}$; $\hat{V}^{(m)} \leftarrow \mathcal{N}(0, \frac{1}{\sqrt{Md}})^{d \times k}$
2: $\hat{V} \leftarrow \text{SECSUM}(\{\hat{V}^{(m)}\}_m)$
3: **for** $t \in \{1, 2, \ldots, \tau\}$: **do**
4:     **for** $i \in \{1, 2, \ldots, k\}$: **do**
5:         $\hat{V}_{:i} \leftarrow \text{NORMEDSECSUM}(\{S^{(m)}\hat{V}_{:i}\}_m)$
6:     $\hat{V} \leftarrow \text{Orthonormalize}(\hat{V})$

Theorem 1. *Starting from the same initial topics T_0, PD-NMF-ITER (Algorithm 1) converges to the same solution T as the centralized RRI-NMF.*

Privately Initializing T with PD-NMF-Init. As with any iterative algorithm, RRI-NMF must be initialized. Initializing to random topics is the simplest but doesn't perform well. There are several state-of-the-art initialization algorithms [BG08, KSK12, Gil14] that are comparable in efficiency and solution quality, beating random. But, these only apply to the non-private centralized setting. We propose a new distributed initialization algorithm PD-NMF-INIT, which uses PD-NMF-ITER as a subroutine (details deferred). Hence, the privacy of PD-NMF-INIT depends on the privacy of PD-NMF-ITER. The quality of our new initialization is comparable to state-of-the-art. The key idea is that running PD-NMF-ITER from appropriately weighted local topic models using random initialization gives a very good starting point for the global topic model.

Theorem 2 (Quality and privacy of initialization). *(i) Our initialization algorithm PD-NMF-INIT is private if PD-NMF-ITER is private. (ii) The output of PD-NMF-INIT is a set of topics T_{init} that minimizes an (worst-case tight) upper bound on the global NMF-objective (details deferred).*

3 Private Distributed SVD (PD-SVD)

Let $S = X^T X = V\Sigma^2 V^T$ be the $d \times d$ covariance matrix whose eigendecomposition reveals the right-singular vectors V_k. To find the top k eigenvectors we will use block power iterations, starting with a random Gaussian initialization. This is a non-private centralized algorithm. To ensure all parties start at the same initial state, the parties agree on a pseudorandom number generator and broadcast the seed. The framework of the algorithm is similar to PD-NMF, so we give only the high-level details. The basic iteration is

$$v_{t+1} \leftarrow X^T X v_t / \|X^T X v_t\|.$$

Since $X^T X v_t = \sum_{m=1}^{M} X^{(m)^T} X^{(m)} v_t$, each party can compute its part $X^{(m)^T} X^{(m)} v_t$ and SECSUM can privately share the sum. This reveals $\|X^T X v_t\|$ the eigenvalues in Σ_k. To conceal Σ_k, we introduce a new cryptographic primitive NORMEDSECSUM in Algorithm 2 to privately compute and share the normalized sum $X^T X v_t / \|X^T X v_t\|$ (matrix-vector multiplication and rescaling are simultaneously handled by NORMEDSECSUM).

For details of NORMEDSECSUM, we refer to the full version of this work. For our implementation we we, we rely on a state-of-the-art off-the-self MPC framework called SPDZ [BDOZ10,DPSZ11,NNOB11,KPR17]. SPDZ compiles a procedural program into an arithmetic circuit over a sufficiently large finite field. Evaluating the circuit as a "distributed virtual machine" has an offline phase that is data agnostic and done independently of the online phase which is efficient (computation and communication complexity linear in M, the size of the circuit, and the input size d). We note that one can use any off-the-self MPC compiler for instantiating NORMEDSECSUM. The choice of SPDZ is for convenience as (1) the online runtime is near-optimal, and (2) newest optimizations bring the runtime of the offline (preprocessing) phase cost down to minutes. We stress that counting only the cost of the online phase is common in this context as, the preprocessing is independent of the data or the learning algorithm and can be executed at any point before the learning starts (at the cost of a linear time-memory trade-off). Nonetheless, even counting the preprocessing cost, in practice the overhead of NORMEDSECSUM will be dominated by the learning complexity.

Theorem 3 *(Proof deferred). The output of* PD-SVD *matches the centralized non-private SVD, assuming both are initialized from the same seed. Further, only the singular vector iterates are revealed at each iteration.*

4   Privacy Analysis and KSDP

To discuss privacy it is useful to define an *observable*.

Observable. Suppose a distributed mechanism $\mathcal{A}$ is executed among several parties. The party of interest uses database X; the concatenation of the remaining parties' databases is Y. Then $\mathcal{O}_{\mathcal{A},X,Y}$ is the set of objects that a coalition of adversaries observes from the communication transcript of $\mathcal{A}$.

Privacy requires that the (joint) observables of all iterations do not reveal substantial information on any individual row in X. Our goal is to estimate the information leakage from any set of observables, including the learning outcome.

Roughly, a mechanism $\mathcal{A}$ preserves privacy of any document x if its output can be simulated by an x-oblivious mechanism $\mathcal{B}$. So, $\mathcal{B}$, without access to x, can emit *all* observables $\mathcal{O}_{\mathcal{A},X,Y}$ with a comparable probability distribution to $\mathcal{A}$. Our definition is similar to the well-accepted Distributional Differential Privacy (DDP) [BGKS13, Gro14], which implies privacy of individual rows of each party's database [Kai16]. DDP is similar to DP, but uses data entropy rather than external noise to guarantee privacy. Mathematically, mechanism $\mathcal{A}$ is *distributionally differentially private* (without auxiliary information) for dataset X drawn from $\mathcal{U}$, and all individual rows $x \in X$ if for some mechanism $\mathcal{B}$,

$$\mathbb{P}[\mathcal{A}(X)] \approx_{\epsilon,\delta} \mathbb{P}[\mathcal{B}(X \setminus \{x\})],$$

where for probability density functions f, g over sample space Ω with sigma-algebra $\mathcal{S} \subseteq 2^{\Omega}$, $f \approx_{\epsilon,\delta} g$ if, $\forall \omega \in \mathcal{S}$,

$$f(\omega) \leq e^{\epsilon} g(\omega) + \delta \quad \text{and} \quad g(\omega) \leq e^{\epsilon} f(\omega) + \delta. \tag{3}$$

Adding noise to achieve DP [DR+14, BDMN05, WFS15] satisfies (3), but is invalidated as it deteriorates learning accuracy.[4] Hence, since DP is an inapplicable privacy model for our purposes, the next best thing to argue our protocol's privacy would be to theoretically compute DDP. This is intractable for complex nonlinear iterative algorithms. We take a different, experimentally validatable approach to DDP suitable for estimating privacy of (noiseless) mechanisms. We introduce *Kolmogorov-Smirnov (distributional) differential privacy*, KSDP, which may be of independent interest for situations where DDP is not-computable and noising the outcome to guarantee privacy is not a viable option.

Intuitively, the adversary tries to determine from the (high-dimensional) observable whether x is in the victim's database. A standard result is that there is a sufficient statistic $\sigma \colon \mathcal{O} \times x \to \mathbb{R}$ with maximum discriminative power. For such a statistic σ and a document x, let f be the distribution of σ with observables $\mathcal{O}_{\mathcal{A},X,Y}$ and g be the distribution of σ with observables $\mathcal{O}_{\mathcal{B},X\setminus\{x\},Y}$ (i.e. those emitted by a simulator $\mathcal{B}$ which doesn't have access to x). Equation (3) is one useful notion of similarity between PDFs f and g (composability being one of the properties), but is very difficult to satisfy, let alone prove. It is also overly strict for protecting against polynomial-time adversaries. We keep the spirit of distributional privacy, but use a different measure of similarity. Instead of working with PDFs, we propose measuring similarity between the corresponding CDFs F and G using the well-known Kolmogorov-Smirnov statistic over an interval $[a, b]$,

---

[4] Theoretical results for DP (e.g. [BBFM12]) only apply to simple mechanisms. Composition of these simple mechanisms needs to be examined case-by-case (e.g., in one-party Differentially Private NMF, [LWS15] incurr a 19% loss in learning quality when strict DP is satisfied even for $\epsilon = 0.25$). In the M-party setting due to a possible difference attack at successive iterations, each party must add noise to all observables they emit in every iteration [RA12, HXZ15]. The empirical impact is a disaster.

$$KS(F, G) \equiv \sup_{x \in [a,b]} |F(x) - G(x)|.$$

This statistic can be used in the Kolmogorov-Smirnov 2-sample test, which outputs a p-value for the probability one would observe as large a statistic if F and G were sampled from the same underlying distribution. We thus define our version of distributional privacy as follows:

KS Distributional Privacy (π-KSDP). Mechanism $\mathcal{A}$ is π−KS Distributional Private if there exists a simulator mechanism $\mathcal{B}$ s.t. for all statistics $\sigma \in \{\sigma_1, \sigma_2, \ldots\}$, and all documents $x \in X$, the KS 2-sample test run on $\text{ECDF}(\sigma(\mathcal{O}_{\mathcal{A},X,Y}, x))$ and $\text{ECDF}(\sigma(\mathcal{O}_{\mathcal{B},X \setminus \{x\},Y}, x))$ returns $p \geq \pi$.

In words, KSDP means the observables generated by a simulator that doesn't have a document x cannot be statistically distinguished from the actual algorithm running on the database containing x. The KS-test's p-value is a measure of distance between two distributions which takes number of samples into account. A high p-value means that we cannot reject that the two ECDFs are the result of sampling from the same underlying distribution. It doesn't mean that we can conclude they come from the same distribution. Although hypothesis tests with the reverse null/alternate hypothesis have been studied [Wel10], computational efficiency and interpretability are significant challenges.

The definition of π-KSDP leads to a method for measuring the privacy of a distributed mechanism (Algorithm 3). We stress that unlike DP, π-KSDP doesn't guarantee future-proof privacy against new statistics and auxiliary information. Rather it tests if a given statistic is discriminative enough to break a weaker yet meaningful distributional version of DP. In practice the most powerful statistic σ is not known. Still, we may consider a family of plausible statistics and take $\inf_\sigma \pi\text{-KSDP}(\sigma)$. An advantage of Algorithm 3 is that samples can be generated, stored, and re-used to test many different statistics quickly. Furthermore, it is suitable as a defensive algorithm for identifying sensitive documents x, which can be excluded from distributed learning if needed. Effective simulators $\mathcal{B}$ are to run $\mathcal{A}$ but either replace x by a random document, or sample n random documents to create an entirely new database. In our experiments we use such a simulator and Algorithm 3 to demonstrate that PD-NMF and PD-SVD satisfy π-KSDP.

Algorithm 3. Measuring π-KSDP.

Require: Mechanism f, set of statistics S, database X, document x, number of samples per document t.
Ensure: Minimum p-value for all statistics.
1: Determine what the *observables* of f are.
2: Generate database sub-samples $\{X_i'\}_{i=1}^t$, $X_i' \subseteq X$
3: Evaluate the mechanism $f(X_i' \cup \{x\})$ for all i.
4: Generate d.b. sub-samples $\{Y_i\}_{i=1}^t$, $Y_i \subseteq X \setminus \{x\}$
5: Evaluate the mechanism $f(Y_i)$ for all i.
6: Set $\pi \leftarrow 1$
7: **for** each $s \in S$ **do:**
8:     w/ $\leftarrow$ ECDF($\{s(f(X_i), x)\}_{i=1}^t$).
9:     w/o $\leftarrow$ ECDF($\{s(f(Y_i), x)\}_{i=1}^t$).
10:     $p \leftarrow$ KS 2 sample test on w/ and w/o.
11:     $\pi \leftarrow \min(p, \pi)$
12: **return** π

---

5   Experimental Results

On classical ML problems, we validate the accuracy and privacy of PD-NMF and PD-SVD, in comparison to the common technique of applying DP noise in each iteration.

5.1   Privacy and Accuracy of PD-NMF

We give empirical evidence to support three claims:

1. Our private initialization PD-NMF-INIT yields equivalent results to state-of-the-art non-private initialization.
2. PD-NMF produces significant learning-upflit for cooperative distributed learning versus local learning. Noise-based DP hurts the learning.
3. PD-NMF satisfies π-KSDP, while preserving the centralized learning outcome.

1. Equivalence of Initialization. We compare PD-NMF-INIT to other distributed and centralized initializations for NMF, including the state-of-the-art *non-private* initializatio nnnsvd [BG08]. We tried several data sets, varied number of parties and choices for the rank k and averaged the results over multiple trials (details deferred). The table below shows results for NMF-topic modeling using standard metrics on a held out test set [RBH15, GS04].

Algorithm	Fro. Error	Coherence	Perplexity
best of M**	8110.7	**16.9**	44.8
nnsvd	**7903.5**	**16.9**	**43.8**
random	8216.1	16.5	**43.9**
random2x**	**7919.8**	**16.9**	**43.8**
PD-NMF-INIT	**7907.9**	**17.0**	**43.8**

* Best of M initializes with the best local model
** random2x is random with twice as many iterations.

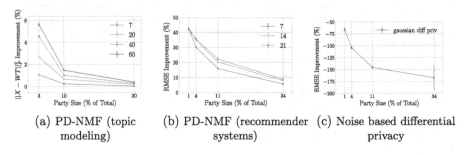

| (a) PD-NMF (topic modeling) | (b) PD-NMF (recommender systems) | (c) Noise based differential privacy |

Fig. 3. % learning-uplift for different k. (a) Topic modeling on Enron data. (b) Recommender systems on ML-1M. (c) Deterioration of learning for (ϵ, δ)-DP inside the NMF algorithm (Gaussian noise for generous parameters: $\epsilon = 0.25$ and $\delta = 0.01$) The cooperative outcome with DP is *worse* than a party's local model. (Known issue with DP, see [HXZ15, RA12]).

PD-NMF-INIT and nnsvd [BG08] are in an equivalence class above the other benchmarks. Recommender system results are qualitatively similar.

Nugget: PD-NMF-INIT is competitive with state-of-the-art *non-private* initialization schemes for NMF.

2. Improved Learning Outcome. NMF can be used for topic modeling (TM) and recommender systems (RS), we defer the details.[5] For topic modeling we use the Enron dataset and for recommender systems we use MovieLens-1M dataset [mov]. The benchmark is the RMSE achievable from local learning (averaged over parties). The % improvement in RMSE over the benchmark for PD-NMF based private distributed learning is in Fig. 3(a and b). For completeness we show the deterioration of learning outcome for noise based differential privacy in Fig. 3(c).

Nugget: Significant learning-uplift results from using the combined data, if it can be done privately. Noise based DP at a moderate level of privacy is detrimental to learning.

3. Privacy of PD-NMF. In the worst case, with 2 parties, the adversary knows the victims observables. We vary the party's size between 0.5% to 10% of all documents and $k \in \{7, 14\}$. We tried a variety of summary statistics of the observables, and report results for the most powerful statistic for each ML-problem (topic modeling on Enron data and recommender systems on MovieLens-1M).

Party Size	RS p-value	TM p-value
0.5%	0.45 ± 0.16	0.029 ± 0.02
3%	0.52 ± 0.20	0.044 ± 0.02
10%	0.48 ± 0.18	0.113 ± 0.07

Details can be found in the full version of this work. In practice, a p-value of 0.05 is sufficient to reject the null hypothesis that f (true) and g (simulator) have different distributions.

---

[5] One can adapt PD-NMF to accomodate non-observed entries.

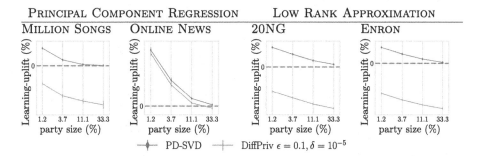

Fig. 4. Learning-uplift for distributed versus local learning. Smaller parties gain more. DP hurts.

Nugget: Privacy is preserved, even at small party sizes.

5.2   Privacy and Accuracy of PD-SVD

The results are qualitatively similar. PD-SVD is empirically private and gives significant learning-uplift. We also demonstrate that noise based DP [HR13] doesn't work in classical SVD applications. Lastly, we highlight the privacy-value of hiding Σ_k and only revealing V_k, a feature that distinguishes our work from existing private SVD.

Learning Uplift and Inapplicability of DP. We apply SVD to PCA-Regression ([Jol82]) on the Million Songs dataset [BMEWL11] and the Online News Popularity dataset [FVC15], and Low Rank Approximation ([Mar11]) on the 20NG [20n] and Enron [enr] text datasets (details are deferred to the full version). Figure 4 reports %RMSE-uplift of prediction on held out test data for the cooperative distributed V_k using PD-SVD versus a local model $V_k^{(m)}$. Importantly, in three of four experiments, differentially private SVD [HR13] with parameters $\epsilon = 0.1$, $\delta = 10^{-5}$ (generous parameters) yields worse cooperative learning than local learning!

Nugget: PD-SVD gives significant learning-uplift versus local models. Partys with more data gain less. On the other hand, differentially private SVD is DP an unattractive choice for privacy-preserving M-party distributed learning.

Measured Privacy and Value in Hiding Σ. We use π-KSDP to measure the privacy for a sample of 200 documents x, reporting p-values for the most powerful statistic tested.

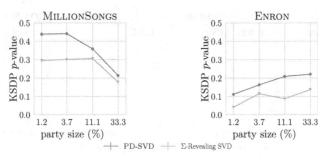

For details of the statistics, we refer to the full version of this work. We also show p-values for the MPC based secure but Σ_k-revealing SVD in [WKL+16, CLZ17].

Nugget: Privacy is preserved. Hiding Σ_k using PD-SVD adds significant value over revealing Σ_k-revealing SVD.

6   Conclusion

We proposed a new framework for distributed machine learning, which strikes a compromise between efficiency and privacy. On one end is full MPC which is impractical but guarantees almost no information-leak. On the other end is data sharing which also preserves learning outcome but loses all privacy. Our approach is in between: modify the learning algorithm so that efficient lightweight crypto (SecSum and NormedSecSum) can be used to control the information leaked through only those few shared aggregate quantities. Then, *measure* the information that is leaked.

We emphasized the learning outcome because there are significant performance gains from learning on all the data as opposed to learning locally. Smaller parties get more learning-uplift, but also risk losing more privacy. As with MPC, our algorithms preserve the learning outcome, however additional information is leaked through the aggregate outputs shared by SecSum and NormedSecSum. KSDP empirically estimates the privacy leak, which is small for PD-NMF and PD-SVD on large databases. It may be of independent interest that KSDP can also measure the privacy loss from the output of an MPC.

Tools that put the learning outcome first, and measure privacy against pre-defined post-processing functions are useful. Organizations can define post-processing methods for which they want privacy to hold. Legislation such as the GDPR describes post-processing methods, against which data must be secure.

Future research includes other empirical methods for estimating privacy, automated ways to build discriminative statistics, and a complete optimized library of elementary MPC protocols for machine learning.

References

[20n]   20 news groups dataset

[BBFM12] Balcan, M.F., Blum, A., Fine, S., Mansour, Y.: Distributed learning, communication complexity and privacy. In: Conference on Learning Theory, p. 26-1 (2012)

[BDMN05] Blum, A., Dwork, C., McSherry, F., Nissim, K.: Practical privacy: the SuLQ framework. In: Proceedings of the Twenty-Fourth ACM SIGMOD-SIGACT-SIGART Symposium on Principles of Database Systems, pp. 128–138. ACM (2005)

[BDOZ10] Bendlin, R., Damgard, I., Orlandi, C., Zakarias, S.: Semi-homomorphic encryption and multiparty computation. Cryptology ePrint Archive, Report 2010/514 (2010)

[BF16]   Bassily, R., Freund, Y.: Typical stability. arXiv preprint arXiv:1604.03336 (2016)

[BG08]   Boutsidis, C., Gallopoulos, E.: SVD based initialization: a head start for nonnegative matrix factorization. Pattern Recogn. **41**, 1350–1362 (2008)

[BGKS13] Bassily, R., Groce, A., Katz, J., Smith, A.: Coupled-worlds privacy: exploiting adversarial uncertainty in statistical data privacy. In: 2013 IEEE 54th Annual Symposium on Foundations of Computer Science (FOCS), pp. 439–448. IEEE (2013)

[BMEWL11] Bertin-Mahieux, T., Ellis, D.P.W., Whitman, B., Lamere, P.: The million song dataset. In: ISMIR (2011)

[BMPS03] Berry, M., Mezher, D., Philippe, B., Sameh, A.: Parallel computation of the singular value decomposition. Ph.D. thesis, INRIA (2003)

[BS08]   Brickell, J., Shmatikov, V.: The cost of privacy: destruction of data-mining utility in anonymized data publishing. In: SIGKDD (2008)

[CLZ17]   Chen, S., Lu, R., Zhang, J.: A flexible privacy-preserving framework for singular value decomposition under internet of things environment. CoRR, abs/1703.06659 (2017)

[Con16]   Condat, L.: Fast projection onto the simplex and the ℓ_1 ball. Math. Program. **158**, 575–585 (2016)

[CZA07]   Cichocki, A., Zdunek, R., Amari, S.: Hierarchical ALS algorithms for nonnegative matrix and 3D tensor factorization. In: Davies, M.E., James, C.J., Abdallah, S.A., Plumbley, M.D. (eds.) ICA 2007. LNCS, vol. 4666, pp. 169–176. Springer, Heidelberg (2007). https://doi.org/10.1007/978-3-540-74494-8_22

[DLCL14] Du, S.S., Liu, Y., Chen, B., Li, L.: Maxios: large scale nonnegative matrix factorization for collaborative filtering. In: NIPS 2014 Workshop on Distributed Matrix Computations (2014)

[DPSZ11] Damgard, I., Pastro, V., Smart, N.P., Zakarias, S.: Multiparty computation from somewhat homomorphic encryption. Cryptology ePrint Archive, Report 2011/535 (2011)

[DR+14]   Dwork, C., Roth, A., et al.: The algorithmic foundations of differential privacy. Found. Trends Theor. Comput. Sci. **9**, 211–407 (2014)

[DSZ15]   Demmler, D., Schneider, T., Zohner, M.: ABY - a framework for efficient mixed-protocol secure two-party computation. In: 22nd Annual Network and Distributed System Security Symposium, NDSS 2015, San Diego, California, USA, 8–11 February 2015 (2015)

[enr]   Bag of words datasets

[FVC15] Fernandes, K., Vinagre, P., Cortez, P.: A proactive intelligent decision support system for predicting the popularity of online news. In: Pereira, F., Machado, P., Costa, E., Cardoso, A. (eds.) EPIA 2015. LNCS (LNAI), vol. 9273, pp. 535–546. Springer, Cham (2015). https://doi.org/10.1007/978-3-319-23485-4_53

[Gil14] Gillis, N.: Successive nonnegative projection algorithm for robust non-negative blind source separation. SIIMS (2014)

[GNHS11] Gemulla, R., Nijkamp, E., Haas, P.J., Sismanis, Y.: Large-scale matrix factorization with distributed stochastic gradient descent. In: KDD (2011)

[Gro14] Groce, A.D.: New notions and mechanisms for statistical privacy. Ph.D. thesis, University of Maryland (2014)

[GS04] Griffiths, T.L., Steyvers, M.: Finding scientific topics. Proc. Natl. Acad. Sci. U.S.A 101(Suppl. 1), 5228–5235 (2004)

[GVL12] Golub, G.H., Van Loan, C.F.: Matrix Computations, vol. 3. JHU Press (2012)

[HNY09] Han, S., Ng, W.K., Yu, P.S.: Privacy-preserving singular value decomposition. In: Proceedings of the ICDE, March 2009

[Ho08] Ho, N.-D.: Nonnegative matrix factorization algorithms and applications. Ph.D. thesis, École Polytechnique (2008)

[HR13] Hardt, M., Roth, A.: Beyond worst-case analysis in private singular vector computation. In: Proceedings of the STOC. ACM (2013)

[HXZ15] Hua, J., Xia, C., Zhong, S.: Differentially private matrix factorization. In: IJCAI, pp. 1763–1770 (2015)

[IO16] Iwen, M.A., Ong, B.W.: A distributed and incremental SVD algorithm for agglomerative data analysis on large networks. SIAM J. Matrix Anal. Appl. 37(4), 1699–1718 (2016)

[Jol82] Jolliffe, I.T.: A note on the use of principal components in regression. Appl. Stat. 31, 300–303 (1982)

[Kai16] Kairouz, P.: The fundamental limits of statistical data privacy. Ph.D. thesis, University of Illinois at Urbana-Champaign (2016)

[KKK+16] Kim, S., Kim, J., Koo, D., Kim, Y., Yoon, H., Shin, J.: Efficient privacy-preserving matrix factorization via fully homomorphic encryption: extended abstract. In: AsiaCCS (2016)

[KPR17] Keller, M., Pastro, V., Rotaru, D.: Overdrive: making SPDZ great again. Cryptology ePrint Archive, Report 2017/1230 (2017)

[KSK12] Kumar, A., Sindhwani, V., Kambadur, P.: Fast conical hull algorithms for near-separable non-negative matrix factorization. arXiv preprint arXiv:1210.1190 (2012)

[Lin07] Lin, C.-J.: Projected gradient methods for nonnegative matrix factorization. Neural Comput. 19, 2756–2779 (2007)

[LS01] Lee, D.D., Sebastian Seung, H.: Algorithms for non-negative matrix factorization. In: NIPS (2001)

[LSS10] Limbeck, P., Suntinger, M., Schiefer, J.: SARI OpenRec - empowering recommendation systems with business events. In: DBKDA (2010)

[LWS15] Liu, Z., Wang, Y.-X., Smola, A.J.: Fast differentially private matrix factorization. CoRR (2015)

[Mar11] Markovsky, I.: Low Rank Approximation: Algorithms, Implementation, Applications. Springer, Heidelberg (2011)

[MEEO13] Malin, B.A., El Emam, K., O'keefe, C.M.: Biomedical data privacy: problems, perspectives, and recent advances. JAMIA (2013)

[MG18a] Mazloom, S., Dov Gordon, S.: Secure computation with differentially private access patterns. In: Lie, D., Mannan, M., Backes, M., Wang, X. (eds.) ACM SIGSAC Conference on Computer and Communications Security, CCS 2018, pp. 490–507. ACM (2018)

[MG18b] Mazloom, S., Dov Gordon, S.: Secure computation with differentially private access patterns. In: Proceedings of the ACM SIGSAC Conference on Computer and Communications Security, pp. 490–507 (2018)

[mov] Movielens 1m dataset

[MR18] Mohassel, P., Rindal, P.: Aby^3: a mixed protocol framework for machine learning. In: Lie, D., Mannan, M., Backes, M., Wang, X. (eds.) ACM SIGSAC Conference on Computer and Communications Security, CCS 2018, pp. 35–52. ACM (2018)

[MZ17] Mohassel, P., Zhang, Y.: SecureML: a system for scalable privacy-preserving machine learning. In: IEEE Symposium on Security and Privacy, SP 2017, pp. 19–38 (2017)

[NIW+13] Nikolaenko, V., Ioannidis, S., Weinsberg, U., Joye, M., Taft, N., Boneh, D.: Privacy-preserving matrix factorization. In: SIGSAC (2013)

[NNOB11] Nielsen, J.B., Nordholt, P.S., Orlandi, C., Burra, S.S.: A new approach to practical active-secure two-party computation. Cryptology ePrint Archive, Report 2011/091 (2011)

[Par98] Parlett, B.: The symmetric Eigenvalue Problem. SIAM (1998)

[RA12] Rajkumar, A., Agarwal, S.: A differentially private stochastic gradient descent algorithm for multiparty classification. In: Artificial Intelligence and Statistics, pp. 933–941 (2012)

[RBH15] Röder, M., Both, A., Hinneburg, A.: Exploring the space of topic coherence measures. In: Proceedings of the Eighth ACM International Conference on Web Search and Data Mining, pp. 399–408. ACM (2015)

[TMIZ19] Tsikhanovich, M., Magdon-Ismail, M., Ishaq, M., Zikas, V.: PD-ML-Lite: private distributed machine learning from lighweight cryptography. CoRR, abs/1901.07986 (2019)

[TXD03] Tang, C., Xu, Z., Dwarkadas, S.: Peer-to-peer information retrieval using self-organizing semantic overlay networks. In: SIGCOMM (2003)

[Vav09] Vavasis, S.A.: On the complexity of nonnegative matrix factorization. SIAM J. Optim. 20(3), 1364–1377 (2009)

[Wel10] Wellek, S.: Testing Statistical Hypotheses of Equivalence and Noninferiority, 2nd edn. CRC Press, Boca Raton (2010)

[WFS15] Wang, Y.-X., Fienberg, S., Smola, A.: Privacy for free: posterior sampling and stochastic gradient Monte Carlo. In: Proceedings of the 32nd International Conference on Machine Learning (ICML 2015), pp. 2493–2502 (2015)

[WKL+16] Won, H.-S., Kim, S.-P., Lee, S., Choi, M.-J., Moon, Y.-S.: Secure principal component analysis in multiple distributed nodes. Secur. Commun. Netw. 9(14), 2348–2358 (2016)

[YA09] Yi, X., Allan, J.: A comparative study of utilizing topic models for information retrieval. In: Boughanem, M., Berrut, C., Mothe, J., Soule-Dupuy, C. (eds.) ECIR 2009. LNCS, vol. 5478, pp. 29–41. Springer, Heidelberg (2009). https://doi.org/10.1007/978-3-642-00958-7_6

[You10] Youdao, N.: P4P: practical large-scale privacy-preserving distributed computation robust against malicious users. In: Proceedings of the USENEX (2010)

Crypto II: Zero-Knowledge Proofs

Code-Based Zero Knowledge PRF Arguments

Carlo Brunetta[✉], Bei Liang, and Aikaterini Mitrokotsa

Chalmers University of Technology, Gothenburg, Sweden
{brunetta,lbei,aikmitr}@chalmers.se

Abstract. Pseudo-random functions are a useful cryptographic primitive that, can be combined with zero-knowledge proof systems in order to achieve privacy-preserving identification. Libert *et al.* (ASIACRYPT 2017) has investigated the problem of proving the correct evaluation of lattice-based PRFs based on the *Learning-With-Rounding* (LWR) problem. In this paper, we go beyond lattice-based assumptions and investigate, whether we can solve the question of proving the correct evaluation of PRFs based on code-based assumptions such as the *Syndrome Decoding* problem. The answer is affirmative and we achieve it by firstly introducing a very efficient code-based PRG based on the *Regular Syndrome Decoding* problem and subsequently, we give a direct construction of a code-based PRF. Thirdly, we provide a zero-knowledge protocol for the correct evaluation of a code-based PRF, which allows a prover to convince a verifier that a given output y is indeed computed from the code-based PRF with a secret key k on an input x, *i.e.*, $y = f(k, x)$. Finally, we analytically evaluate the protocol's communication costs.

Keywords: Coding theory · Zero knowledge ·
Pseudorandom function · PRF argument · Syndrome decoding

1 Introduction

Pseudo-random functions (PRFs) is a fundamental cryptographic primitive that can be employed to authenticate users, since they generate unique pseudorandom numbers. Zero-knowledge (ZK) proofs are often used to enforce honest behaviour or prove the identity of users, while providing strong privacy guarantees. By combining pseudo-random functions with zero-knowledge proofs, it is possible to achieve privacy-preserving user identification and answer the following question:

How may a prover $\mathcal{P}$ prove to a verifier $\mathcal{V}$, the correct evaluation of a PRF function $f(k, x) = y$, without leaking any information about k?

This is a rather important question with multiple applications, *e.g.*, e-cash, unique digital signatures, non-interactive lottery and more. Although algebraic (based on number-theoretic hardness assumptions) pseudo-random functions

© Springer Nature Switzerland AG 2019
Z. Lin et al. (Eds.): ISC 2019, LNCS 11723, pp. 171–189, 2019.
https://doi.org/10.1007/978-3-030-30215-3_9

and zero-knowledge proofs, are well studied primitives; there has been comparatively *"less progress"* on these primitives based on post-quantum cryptographic assumptions such as code-based, hash-based, and multivariate-based.

Libert *et al.* [19] has recently addressed this problem based on lattice-based assumptions and more precisely, based on the *Learning-With-Rounding* (LWR) problem [4] and provide a **lattice-based** zero-knowledge PRF argument.

Code-based cryptography enables the construction of cryptographic primitives that are believed to be secure against an adversary who has at his disposal a quantum computer. More precisely, code-based cryptographic primitives are based on assumptions related to the hardness of the *Syndrome Decoding* (SD) problem [5], that has been proved to be NP-hard. Furthermore, except of their post-quantum nature, code-based cryptographic primitives offer significant advantages due to their significant algorithmic efficiency, offering several orders of complexity better than traditional cryptographic schemes.

In this paper, we focus on the construction of code-based cryptographic fundamental primitives, particularly on code-based pseudo-random generators/functions, as well as on code-based interactive zero-knowledge proof systems. We firstly introduce a code-based PRG and subsequently, we provide a direct construction of a code-based PRF. Finally, we provide a zero-knowledge protocol for the correct evaluation of the proposed code-based PRF and evaluate the protocol's communication cost.

Syndrome Decoding (SD). In this paper, we base our post-quantum cryptosystems on the hardness of the *Syndrome Decoding* (SD) problem [5], which is a commonly used assumption in code-based cryptography. Recall that the SD problem with parameters n, r, ω is stated as follows: given a uniformly random matrix $H \in \mathbb{F}_2^{r \times n}$ and a uniformly random syndrome $y \in \mathbb{F}_2^r$, find a vector (word) $x \in \mathbb{F}_2^n$ with Hamming weight ω, such that $H \cdot x^\mathsf{T} = y^\mathsf{T}$. Berlekamp, McEliece and Tilborg [5] proved that the SD problem is NP-complete, which implies that there is no polynomial-time algorithm for solving the SD problem in the worst case; however, many instances of the SD problem can be efficiently solved in the average case. Given existing results on the computing complexity for solving the SD problem (as reviewed by Chabaud and Stern [9,23]) it is the hardest to solve, when the weights of the words (*i.e.*, $x \in \mathbb{F}_2^n$) are in the neighbourhood of the Gilbert-Varshamov bound [14,24]. More precisely, we can set the weight of the words for an instance of the SD problem close to the Gilbert-Varshamov bound, such that the corresponding SD hardness assumption holds.

Considering the expensive computations required to transform binary strings into words of constant weight and length, the *Regular Syndrome Decoding* (RSD) [3], is a special case of the SD problem, where the words are restricted to *regular words*. Regular words are words of given weight w, that have a fixed number of 1's in each block of fixed size. The *Regular Syndrome Decoding* (RSD) problem is widely used in practical applications due to its high efficiency and convenience in generating words. For instance, Gaborit, Lauradoux, and Sendriern [13] used regular words to improve Fischer and Stern's code-based PRG [12]. Let us consider binary words of length n and let us divide the coordinates in w blocks of

n/w positions. A binary regular word of length n and weight w ((n, w)-regular word) has exactly one non-zero coordinate in each of these blocks. Notice that there is a reduction from the RSD to the SD problem, which implies that decoding a regular code cannot be more than about $\exp(w)$ easier than decoding a random code of the same weight.

Code-based Pseudo-random Generators/Functions. Fischer and Stern [12] proposed a simple and efficient construction of a pseudo-random generator (PRG), based on the intractability assumption for a special case of the SD problem, where $H \in \mathbb{F}_2^{\lfloor \rho n \rfloor \times n}$, $x \in \mathbb{F}_2^n$, $\omega = \lfloor \delta n \rfloor$ for some $\rho \in [0, 1]$ and $\delta \in [0, 1/2]$ such that the Gilbert-Warshamov bound denoted by $\mathsf{Bound}(\delta)$ satisfies the following condition: $\mathsf{Bound}(\delta) = -\delta \log_2 \delta - (1 - \delta) \log_2(1 - \delta) < \rho$. Thus, yielding a PRG $G_{\rho,\delta}(x) = H \cdot x^\mathsf{T}$ with domain $\mathbb{F}_2^n$ and range $\mathbb{F}_2^{\lfloor \rho n \rfloor}$. In order to obtain a PRG that outputs as many bits as we may want, Fischer and Stern [12] provided an iterative generator, which after computing $y = H \cdot x^\mathsf{T}$, separates y as $y = y_1 \| y_2$, where y_1 denotes the first $\log_2 \binom{n}{\delta n}$ bits of y and y_2 denotes the remaining bits. It outputs y_2 and uses y_1 as a new seed to compute $G_{\rho,\delta}$. We should note, that when performing this iteration, it is indispensable to have an efficient algorithm that computes a word with length n and weight $\omega = \lfloor \delta n \rfloor$ from a word of exactly $\log_2 \binom{n}{\omega}$ bits.

A pseudo-random function (PRF) is a function f_k with the property that no polynomial-time attacker, when given oracle access to f_k, can distinguish f_k from a truly random function. Goldreich, Goldwasser, and Micali [16] have shown how to generically construct a PRF from any length-doubling PRG (hence from any one-way function), known as the GGM paradigm, which requires n sequential invocations of the generator when operating on n-bit inputs. By plugging Fischer and Stern's code-based iterative PRG [12] into the sequential GGM paradigm [16], we are able to obtain a code-based PRF. However, the PRF generated with this method is maximally sequential and very inefficient, since Fischer-Stern's PRG [12] uses a quadratic algorithm to transform binary strings of length $\log_2 \binom{n}{\omega}$ into words with length n and weight ω, while this algorithm has to be executed whenever the PRG evaluation is invoked in the GGM paradigm; thus, considerably slowing down the whole process. This motivates us to explore specialized constructions of PRFs under code-based assumptions that are much more efficient, than the previously described naive solution.

Zero-knowledge Proofs for the Correct computation of Code-based PRFs. Employing a PRF as a random oracle is limited to the setting where the *"key owner"*, *i.e.* the party that evaluates the PRF, should be fully trusted. Motivated by the fact that the key should remain private in this setting, we wish to establish a method that allows the owner of the key to prove to a verifier that the given value y is indeed the correct evaluation on an input point x, without revealing the key. Zero-knowledge (ZK) proof systems are very useful in numerous protocols, where a user has to prove knowledge of some secret information (*e.g.*, his identity), without revealing this information. Constructing a ZK protocol for the correct evaluation of a code-based PRF is quite challenging.

There have been proposed ZK identification schemes [22] based on the hardness of the SD problem and its variants [2,8], as well as identity-based identification schemes [7,10]. There have also been proposed ZK proofs of plaintext knowledge based on the McEliece and the Niederreiter cryptosystems [17], as well as a ZK protocol in order to demonstrate that a given signature is generated by a certain certified user of a group, who honestly encrypts its identifying information [11]. Yet, we are not aware of any ZK protocol that can be employed to prove the correct evaluation of a code-based PRF.

Our Contribution. In this paper, we give a direct construction of PRF families based on coding theory, which is provably secure under code-based assumptions. More precisely, we take advantage of regular words, which can be very efficiently generated, and we build a new PRG by running two Fischer-Stern PRGs in parallel. Thus, avoiding the iteration needed in the Fischer-Stern PRG in order to output a bit string with doubled length. In this way, we obtain an efficient construction of PRF families from the *regular syndrome decoding* (RSD) problem [3].

Secondly, we provide a zero-knowledge protocol for the correct evaluation of our code-based PRF, which allows a prover to convince a verifier that a given output y is indeed correctly computed from the code-based PRF with a secret key k held by the prover on the input x. Such ZK protocols may be very useful in the context of oblivious PRF evaluations, which require the party who holds a PRF key to convince the other party that the key was correctly used in oblivious computations (*e.g.*, e-cash, unique digital signatures, non-interactive lottery). It is worth noting that, to the best of our knowledge, prior to our work there were few papers considering PRGs based on syndrome decoding [12,13,21] or other code-based assumptions [25], while no paper considers PRFs based on the SD assumption, let alone considering the problem of proving the correct evaluation of a code-based PRF. We believe that our results would certainly help to bring more interest into code-based cryptography and enhance its important roles in the post-quantum cryptography era.

Overview of Our Techniques. Let us consider an (n, w)-regular word of length n and weight w. We divide the coordinates in w blocks of n/w positions, and a (n, w)-regular word has exactly one non-zero coordinate in each of these blocks. If n and w are chosen such that $n/w = 2^b$, then there is a mapping $\phi_{n,w}$ from $\mathbb{F}_2^{wb}$ to the (n, w)- regular words in $\mathbb{F}_2^n$.

Let $\boldsymbol{H}_0, \boldsymbol{H}_1 \in \mathbb{F}_2^{r \times n}$ where $r = w \cdot b$ and $n = w \cdot 2^b$ and $f : \mathbb{F}_2^r \to \mathbb{F}_2^{2r}$ as:

$$f(\boldsymbol{k}) = \begin{pmatrix} \boldsymbol{H}_0 \\ \boldsymbol{H}_1 \end{pmatrix} \cdot \phi(\boldsymbol{k})^\mathsf{T} = \begin{pmatrix} \boldsymbol{H}_0 \cdot \phi(\boldsymbol{k})^\mathsf{T} \\ \boldsymbol{H}_1 \cdot \phi(\boldsymbol{k})^\mathsf{T} \end{pmatrix} = (\boldsymbol{y}_0, \boldsymbol{y}_1)^\mathsf{T}$$

For an input bit string $x \in \mathbb{F}_2^t$ and by applying the GGM paradigm, we can therefore define a code-based PRF as follows $\mathsf{PRF} : \mathbb{F}_2^r \times \mathbb{F}_2^t \to \mathbb{F}_2^r$, where:

$$\mathsf{PRF}_k(\boldsymbol{x}) = \mathsf{PRF}_k\big((x_1, \cdots, x_t)\big) = f_{x_t}(f_{x_{t-1}}(\cdots(f_{x_1}(\boldsymbol{k}))\cdots).$$

The pseudo-randomness of our code-based PRF could be reduced to the hardness of the underlying *regular syndrome decoding* (RSD) problem and the unpredictability of the Goldreich-Levin hardcore bit, similarly to [21].

Let us now explain the core idea of how we may build a zero-knowledge protocol for the correct evaluation of our proposed code-based PRF, which allows a prover to convince a verifier that a given output y is correctly computed from the PRF using a secret key k on input x, namely $y = f_{x_t}(f_{x_{t-1}}(\cdots(f_{x_1}(k))\cdots))$. Without loss of generality, let us consider the case for input length of $t = 2$. Given $x = (x_1, x_2)$, according to our PRF construction, it holds:

$$\begin{pmatrix} \boldsymbol{H}_{x_1} & 0 \\ 0 & \boldsymbol{H}_{x_2} \end{pmatrix} \begin{pmatrix} \phi(\boldsymbol{k})^\mathsf{T} \\ \phi(f_{x_1}(\boldsymbol{k}))^\mathsf{T} \end{pmatrix} = \begin{pmatrix} f_{x_1}(\boldsymbol{k})^\mathsf{T} \\ f_{x_2}(f_{x_1}(\boldsymbol{k}))^\mathsf{T} \end{pmatrix}$$

If we reveal all the intermediate results, i.e., the value $y^1 = f_{x_1}(k)$ which is exactly the seed used to compute the next GGM iteration i.e., the value $y = y^2 = f_{x_2}(y^1)$, then it is possible for a malicious verifier to compute the PRF on different inputs $x' = (x_1, 1 - x_2)$ (without knowing the secret key k), which subsequently could be used to break the pseudo-randomness of the PRF. Therefore, we have to "hide" the intermediate evaluations while proving the correctness of the PRF evaluation. This goal is accomplished by introducing a specific map ϕ^{-1} that can be used to hide all the intermediate evaluation results while maintaining the Stern's protocol format. Formally, we obtain:

$$\begin{pmatrix} \boldsymbol{H}_{x_1} & \phi^{-1} \\ 0 & \boldsymbol{H}_{x_2} \end{pmatrix} \cdot \begin{pmatrix} \phi(\boldsymbol{k})^\mathsf{T} \\ \phi(\boldsymbol{y}^1)^\mathsf{T} \end{pmatrix} = \begin{pmatrix} 0 \\ \boldsymbol{y}^\mathsf{T} \end{pmatrix}$$

By embedding the above technique into Stern's ZK protocol framework [22], we obtain an interactive ZK argument system, in which, given the input and output values x, y, the prover is able to prove that $y = \mathsf{PRF}_k(x)$ is indeed the evaluation of $f_{x_t}(f_{x_{t-1}}(\cdots(f_{x_1}(k))\cdots))$. The protocol is repeated many times to achieve negligible soundness error.

Related Work. Libert et al. [19] have investigated the problem of correctly evaluating arguments for lattice-based pseudo-random functions w.r.t. committed keys and inputs, using (interactive) zero-knowledge proofs; this is achieved by providing an abstraction of Stern's protocol [22] based on lattices. Brunetta et al. [6] further investigated the possibility of using Libert et al.'s results in order to construct more advanced primitives such as simulatable verifiable random functions (sVRF). However the following question is left open:

"Is it possible to achieve a ZK PRF argument based on other (non lattice-based) post-quantum assumptions?"

Motivated and inspired by these works, we show that it is indeed possible to construct PRF families based on coding theory assumptions and that it is possible to use the original Stern's protocol to achieve the ZK argument.

Goldreich-Goldwasser-Micali Construction. In 1986, Goldreich, Goldwasser and Micali [16] proposed a generic transformation from any PRGs that doubles the input length, into a family of PRFs. This elegant construction is the main core of our PRF and the reason of our main interest in code-based PRGs.

Code-based PRGs and Stream Ciphers. In 1996, Fischer-Stern [12] defined a simple PRG based on the *syndrome decoding* (SD) problem. A decade later, Gaborit *et al.* published a code-based stream cipher called SYND [13], which is an improvement of Fischer-Stern's PRG, revisited as a stream-cipher. Meziani *et al.* proposed 2SC [20], a code-based sponge-function stream cipher. Shortly after, Meziani *et al.* improved the SYND cipher and defined X-SYND [21], which is a stream-cipher based on the *regular syndrome decoding* (RSD) problem and of which we get inspiration for our constructions.

Stern's Protocol. In 1996, Stern [22] published a code-based identification protocol with a zero-knowledge property. Different improved versions are defined by Aguilar *et al.* [2] or Cayrel *et al.* [8] in order to reduce the soundness error. In our constructions, we have employed the original zero-knowledge identification protocol proposed by Stern [22], given the simplicity of the construction and its generality.

Paper Organisation. In Sect. 2, the paper notation and the minimal coding-theory background is reported. In Sect. 3, we present our code-based PRG construction and by applying the GGM transformation, we obtain our code-based PRF. In Sect. 4, we describe our PRF proof argument that is compatible with the Stern's protocol statements and, by applying Stern's protocol, we achieve a code-based ZK PRF argument. In Sect. 5, we describe an application scenario for our protocol and we discuss the protocol's communication cost. Finally, in Sect. 6, we summarize our results and point out to possible future directions.

2 Preliminaries

This section provides the minimal coding theory definitions needed and the notation used in the paper. We will recall some coding hard problems and we will conclude the section by reporting Stern's zero-knowledge identification protocol [22].

Let $\mathbb{N}$ be the set of positive integers and let the uniform sampling of x in a set X defined as $x \in_\$ X$. Let us denote with $|x|$ the length of the bit-representation of x. We denote with $\mathsf{I2B}_b(n)$ the map that takes an integer value n and outputs the b-bit binary representation $\boldsymbol{x} \in \mathbb{F}_2^b$. We denote with $\mathsf{B2I}(\boldsymbol{x})$ the map that takes a binary string $\boldsymbol{x}$ and outputs the corresponding integer value n.

A linear code $\mathcal{C}$ of an n-dimensional vector space over a finite field $\mathbb{F}_q$ is a k dimensional subspace where q is a prime power, k and n are integers and $0 < k < n$. The elements $\boldsymbol{y} \in \mathbb{F}_q^n$ are called *words* and, if they are part of the code, *i.e.* $\boldsymbol{y} \in \mathcal{C}$, then, they are called *codewords*. The weight of a word $\boldsymbol{x}$ is denoted as $\mathsf{wt}(\boldsymbol{x})$ and it counts the number of non-zero components of the word $\boldsymbol{x}$. A code $\mathcal{C}$ can be represented by a generator matrix $\boldsymbol{G} \in \mathbb{F}_q^{k \times n}$ as $\mathcal{C} = \{\boldsymbol{x} \cdot \boldsymbol{G} \mid \boldsymbol{x} \in \mathbb{F}_q^k\}$, where k is the number of rows and n the number of columns and the multiplication $\cdot$ is the standard matrix multiplication.

Given the vector subspace description of the code $\mathcal{C}$, the dual-code $\mathcal{C}^\perp$ is generated by a parity check matrix $\boldsymbol{H} \in \mathbb{F}_q^{(n-k) \times n}$. For the matrix $\boldsymbol{H}$, it holds

$\mathcal{C} = \{x \in \mathbb{F}_q^n \mid H \cdot x^\mathsf{T} = 0\}$. Throughout the paper, we will consider only binary codes, *i.e.* $q = 2$, and therefore, we use $\oplus$ to represent the bit-wise XOR operation.

Let us consider the integers $n, k, r \in \mathbb{N}$ and the parity check matrix $H \in \mathbb{F}_2^{r \times n}$ of the code $\mathcal{C}$ of dimension k over $\mathbb{F}_2^n$, in which we consider $r = n - k$.

Assumption 1 (Binary Syndrome Decoding (SD)). *Given a binary matrix* $H \in \mathbb{F}_2^{r \times n}$, *a binary vector* $y \in \mathbb{F}_2^r$ *and an integer* $w > 0$, *find a* **word** $x \in \mathbb{F}_2^n$ *such that* $\mathsf{wt}(x) = w$ *and* $H \cdot x^\mathsf{T} = y$.

The SD problem is known to be NP-complete [5]. We are interested in a simplified version of the SD problem in which the word x is **regular**, *i.e.* for x with weight w, it can be split into w equal-blocks of length $\frac{n}{w}$ and each of them has a single non-zero entry.

Assumption 2 (Regular Syndrome Decoding (RSD(n, r, w))). *Given a binary matrix* $H \in \mathbb{F}_2^{r \times n}$, *a binary vector* $y \in \mathbb{F}_2^r$ *and an integer* $w > 0$, *find a* **regular word** $x \in \mathbb{F}_2^n$ *such that* $\mathsf{wt}(x) = w$ *and* $H \cdot x^\mathsf{T} = y$.

Augot *et al.* [3] prove the NP-completeness of the RSD problem and we will base the security of our constructions on this specific problem.

Stern's protocol [22] is a zero-knowledge sigma-protocol that describes the language L defined as the elements $(M, y) \in \mathbb{F}_2^{r \times n} \times \mathbb{F}_2^r$ of which there exists a witness $s \in \mathbb{F}_2^n$, such that $\mathsf{wt}(s) = w$ and $M \cdot s = y$. Stern's protocol requires a commitment scheme Com and allows a prover $\mathcal{P}$ to prove to a verifier $\mathcal{V}$ the knowledge of the witness vector s given the statement (M, y).

Theorem 1 (Stern's protocol). *From the original paper [22], Stern's protocol, as reported in Fig. 1, is correct, has soundness probability of* $\frac{2}{3}$ *and it is zero-knowledge. Let* π *a permutation of the set* $\{1, \ldots, n\}$ *if we assume that* $|\pi| > n$, *and* $|\mathsf{Com}|$ *is the commitment length, then the communication cost of the protocol is:*

$$\mathsf{Cost}_{\mathsf{Stern}}(n, r) \leq \left(\underbrace{3 \cdot |\mathsf{Com}|}_{Commitment} + \overbrace{2}^{Challenge} + \underbrace{n + |\pi| + |\rho_0| + \max_{i \in \{1,2\}} |\rho_i|}_{Response} \right) bits$$

3   Code-Based PRF

In this section, inspired by Gaborit's [13] and Meziani's [21] code-based stream ciphers, we define our own simple PRG f that has double-length pseudorandom output. Furthermore, after proving that f is indeed a PRG, we present our code-based PRF obtained by employing the Goldreich-Goldwasser-Micali (GGM) transformation [16].

Let $w, b \in \mathbb{N}$ positive integers chosen such that $n = 2^b w$, $r = w \cdot b$, and the related RSD problem RSD(n, r, w) of Assumption 2 is hard. Consider the binary

---

Statement: $(M, y) \in \mathbb{F}_2^{r \times n} \times \mathbb{F}_2^r$ and witness $s \in \mathbb{F}_2^n$ with $\mathsf{wt}(s) = w$ and $M \cdot s = y$.

1. **Commitment:** $\mathcal{P}$ samples $r \in_\$ \mathbb{F}_2^n$, a permutation π of the set $\{1, \ldots, n\}$ and random values ρ_0, ρ_1, ρ_2 for the commitment scheme Com. The result of applying the permutation π to a vector $r = (r_1, \ldots, r_n)$ is $\pi(r) = (r_{\pi(1)}, \ldots, r_{\pi(n)})$. The prover $\mathcal{P}$ sends the following commitments to the verifier $\mathcal{V}$:

$$C_0 = \mathsf{Com}((\pi, M \cdot r^\mathsf{T}) \,; \rho_0) \quad C_1 = \mathsf{Com}(\pi(r) \,; \rho_1) \quad C_2 = \mathsf{Com}(\pi(r \oplus s) \,; \rho_2)$$

2. **Challenge:** $\mathcal{V}$ sends the challenge $c \in \{0, 1, 2\}$ to $\mathcal{P}$
3. **Response:** $\mathcal{P}$ sends to $\mathcal{V}$, based on the challenge c, the reply: *if* $c = 0$, $(\pi(r), \pi(s))$ and ρ_1, ρ_2; *if* $c = 1$, $(r \oplus s, \pi)$ and ρ_0, ρ_2; and *if* $c = 2$, (r, π) and ρ_0, ρ_1.

Verification: given the challenge c and the response $(\tilde{r}, \tilde{\pi})$, $\mathcal{V}$ verifies:

if $c = 0$: given ρ_1, ρ_2, $\mathcal{V}$ checks $\mathsf{wt}(\tilde{\pi}) \overset{?}{=} w$, $\mathsf{Com}(\tilde{r} \,; \rho_1) \overset{?}{=} C_1$ and $\mathsf{Com}(\tilde{r} \oplus \tilde{\pi} \,; \rho_2) \overset{?}{=} C_2$

if $c = 1$: given ρ_0, ρ_2, $\mathcal{V}$ checks $\mathsf{Com}((\tilde{\pi}, M \cdot \tilde{r}^\mathsf{T} \oplus y^\mathsf{T}; \rho_0) \overset{?}{=} C_0$ and $\mathsf{Com}(\tilde{\pi}(\tilde{r}); \rho_2) \overset{?}{=} C_2$

if $c = 2$: given ρ_0, ρ_1, $\mathcal{V}$ checks $\mathsf{Com}((\tilde{\pi}, M \cdot \tilde{r}^\mathsf{T} \,; \rho_0) \overset{?}{=} C_0$ and $\mathsf{Com}(\tilde{\pi}(\tilde{r}) \,; \rho_1) \overset{?}{=} C_1$

In each case, $\mathcal{V}$ outputs 1 if and only if all the checks are correct.

Fig. 1. Stern's protocol description.

words $s \in \mathbb{F}_2^n$ of length n and composed by w blocks of length 2^b, *i.e.* $s = (s_1, \ldots, s_w)$ such that every block s_j has weigth $\mathsf{wt}(s_j) = 1$. We are interested in maps that have binary regular words as image.

Let us define the map ϕ as the map that takes a bit-string $y \in \mathbb{F}_2^r$ and outputs a regular word $s \in \mathbb{F}_2^n$ such that $\mathsf{wt}(s) = w$ and that is computed as follows.

Firstly, the binary string y is divided into w blocks as $y = (y_1, \ldots, y_w)$ of which each block y_i is a binary string with length b. Then, for every $j \in \{1, \ldots, t\}$, we compute the integer value n_j represented by the block y_j and denote it as $\mathsf{B2I}(y_j) = n_j$. In this way, we transform the vector $(y_1, \ldots, y_w)$ into a vector of integers $(n_1, \cdots, n_w)$, where every n_j is contained in the interval $\{0, \ldots, 2^b - 1\}$. Since there are 2^b possible values for n_j, we bijectively identify every integer with a canonical vector of length 2^b. This bijection takes as input an integer n_j and outputs the canonical vector $e_{n_j+1} \in \mathbb{F}_2^{2^b}$, which is the binary vector of length 2^b, with a single 1 in position $n_j + 1$.

Finally, we transform the integer vector and obtain a vector of canonical vectors $(e_{n_1+1}, \cdots, e_{n_w+1})$ that are concatenated and output by ϕ. In summary, the map ϕ is computed as:

$$\phi(y) = \phi((y_1, \ldots, y_w)) = \left(e_{\mathsf{B2I}(y_1)+1} \| \cdots \| e_{\mathsf{B2I}(y_w)+1}\right) = s$$

It is trivial to observe that s is a regular word of length n and weigth w since s is the concatenation of w canonical vectors of length 2^b and the weight $\mathsf{wt}(s)$ is equivalent to the sum of the weight of the canonical vectors, which is w. It is important to note, that ϕ can be efficiently computed and therefore, we assume that the computational cost is constant.

For example, the vector $\boldsymbol{y} = \left(01\|11\|00\right)$ would be transformed into the regular word $\phi(\boldsymbol{y}) = \boldsymbol{s} = \left(e_2\|e_4\|e_1\right) = \left(0100\|0001\|1000\right)$.

After defining the map ϕ, we are interested in developing a pseudorandom generator (PRG) based on the RSD assumption (see Assumption 2), inspired by Meziani's [21] stream-cipher design. Let us first report both definitions.

Definition 1 (Pseudorandom Generator (PRG) [18]). *Given the positive integers $\ell_{\mathsf{in}}, \ell_{\mathsf{out}} \in \mathbb{N}$ with $\ell_{\mathsf{out}} > \ell_{\mathsf{in}}$, let $G : \{0,1\}^{\ell_{\mathsf{in}}} \to \{0,1\}^{\ell_{\mathsf{out}}}$ be a deterministic function. We say that G is a **pseudorandom generator** if the following two distributions are computationally indistinguishable:*

- *Sample a random seed $s \in \{0,1\}^{\ell_{\mathsf{in}}}$ and output $G(s)$.*
- *Sample a random string $r \in \{0,1\}^{\ell_{\mathsf{out}}}$ and output r.*

A *stream cipher* is an encryption scheme used in contexts where the messages are *streams*, *i.e.* the messages do not have a fixed-length a priori, and therefore a key-*"stream"* has to be generated and used. In order to do so, stream-ciphers are usually designed with an *initialization* algorithm that takes a key and initialize the cipher into an **internal state**. Consecutively, the cipher has an *output* algorithm that outputs a fixed-length key-stream based on the internal state and an *update* algorithm that *"evolves"* the internal state.

As described also by Fischer-Stern [12], it is natural to build stream-ciphers from PRGs: the stream cipher key is indeed the initial PRG's seed s. Then, we can compute $G(s)$ and use the first ℓ_{in} bits as the *internal state* and the remaining $\ell_{\mathsf{out}} - \ell_{\mathsf{in}}$ as the key-stream output. By iterating the PRG computation using the always different internal state, we obtain an arbitrary long key-stream.

Given the strong connection between stream ciphers and PRGs, we focus on Meziani *et al.*'s [21] code-based stream cipher, depicted in Fig. 2.

Definition 2 (X-SYND Stream Cipher [21]). *Let $w, b \in \mathbb{N}$ be positive integers and define $n = w2^b$, $r = wb$. Let $\boldsymbol{A}_0, \boldsymbol{A}_1 \in_{\$} \mathbb{F}_2^{r \times n}$ be random binary matrices. Define the **X-SYND stream cipher** as:*

- *$\mathsf{Init}(\mathsf{IV}, \boldsymbol{s})$: given an initialization vector IV and a seed $\boldsymbol{s}$ both of length $\frac{r}{2}$, let $\boldsymbol{z}^{\mathsf{T}} = \boldsymbol{A}_0 \cdot \phi\left((\boldsymbol{s}\|\mathsf{IV})\right)^{\mathsf{T}} \oplus (\boldsymbol{s}\|\mathsf{IV})^{\mathsf{T}}$ and set as initial state $\mathsf{st}_0{}^{\mathsf{T}} = \boldsymbol{A}_1 \cdot \phi(\boldsymbol{z})^{\mathsf{T}} \oplus \boldsymbol{z}^{\mathsf{T}}$;*
- *$\mathsf{Upd}(\mathsf{st}_i)$: given the internal state st_i, update the state $\mathsf{st}_{i+1}{}^{\mathsf{T}} = \boldsymbol{A}_0 \cdot \phi(\mathsf{st}_i)^{\mathsf{T}}$;*
- *$\mathsf{Out}(\mathsf{st}_i)$: given the state st_i, output the key-stream $\mathbf{k}_{i+1}{}^{\mathsf{T}} = \boldsymbol{A}_1 \cdot \phi(\mathsf{st}_i)^{\mathsf{T}}$*

Similarly to X-SYND, let $\boldsymbol{A}_0, \boldsymbol{A}_1 \in \mathbb{F}_2^{r \times n}$, where $r = w \cdot b$ and $n = w \cdot 2^b$ and the map $\phi : \mathbb{F}_2^r \to \mathbb{F}_2^n$ as before. Let us define the function $f : \mathbb{F}_2^r \to \mathbb{F}_2^{2r}$ as:

$$f(\boldsymbol{k}) = \begin{pmatrix} \boldsymbol{A}_0 \\ \boldsymbol{A}_1 \end{pmatrix} \cdot \phi(\boldsymbol{k})^{\mathsf{T}} = \begin{pmatrix} \boldsymbol{A}_0 \cdot \phi(\boldsymbol{k})^{\mathsf{T}} \\ \boldsymbol{A}_1 \cdot \phi(\boldsymbol{k})^{\mathsf{T}} \end{pmatrix} = \begin{pmatrix} \boldsymbol{y}_0 \\ \boldsymbol{y}_1 \end{pmatrix} \tag{1}$$

It has to be observed that f is indeed Meziani *et al.*'s [21] computation of the initialization and update algorithms, *i.e.* $f(\mathsf{st}_i)^{\mathsf{T}} = (\mathsf{Upd}(\mathsf{st}_i)^{\mathsf{T}}\|\mathsf{Out}(\mathsf{st}_i)^{\mathsf{T}})$.

This observation allows us to reuse Meziani *et al.* X-SYND proofs and easily prove that f is indeed a PRG.

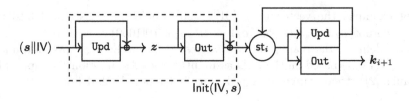

Fig. 2. A high-level representation of the X-SYND stream cipher.

Proposition 1. f *is a PRG that reduce to a* $\mathrm{RSD}(n, 2r, w)$ *problem (Assumption 2).*

Proof. We sketch the main idea of the proof in two parts, that follow the same reasoning as Meziani *et al.*'s [21] X-SYND's security proof parts.

We start by observing that since ϕ is a bijection between vectors in $\mathbb{F}_2^r$ and regular words in $\mathbb{F}_2^n$ with weight w, it is obvious that knowing a regular word solution $\boldsymbol{x}$ is equivalent of knowing the vector $\boldsymbol{k}$ such that $\phi(\boldsymbol{k}) = \boldsymbol{x}$.

Given this observation, in fact, we have an $\mathrm{RSD}(n, 2r, w)$ instance since:

$$f(\boldsymbol{k})^\mathsf{T} = \begin{pmatrix} \boldsymbol{A}_0 \\ \boldsymbol{A}_1 \end{pmatrix} \cdot \phi(\boldsymbol{k})^\mathsf{T} = \begin{pmatrix} \boldsymbol{A}_0 \\ \boldsymbol{A}_1 \end{pmatrix} \cdot \boldsymbol{x}^\mathsf{T} \in \mathrm{RSD}(n, 2r, w)$$

The second step is pseudorandomness and to prove it, we use the fact that Meziani *et al.* prove in Theorem 2 [21], using Goldreich-Levin hard-core bit theorem [15], that the map $(\mathsf{Upd}, \mathsf{Out})$ is a PRG. Given the observation that $(\mathsf{Upd}, \mathsf{Out})$ is exactly f, we can conclude that f is indeed a PRG. □

From PRG to PRF. Finally, we use our PRG f and construct a PRF. In order to do so, we use the Goldreich-Goldwasser-Micali construction [16]. For the sake of clarity, let us report the PRF definition and the GGM construction.

Definition 3 (Pseudorandom Function (PRF)). *Let S be a distribution over $\{0,1\}^\ell$ and $F_s : \{0,1\}^m \to \{0,1\}^n$ be a family of functions indexed by strings s in the support of S.*

We say $\{F_s\}$ is a pseudorandom function family if for every p.p.t. adversary D, there exists a negligible function ϵ such that:

$$|\Pr[D^{F_s}(\cdot) = 1] - \Pr[D^R(\cdot) = 1]| \leq \epsilon,$$

where s is distributed according to S, and R is a function sampled uniformly at random from the set of all functions from $\{0,1\}^m$ to $\{0,1\}^n$.

Definition 4 (GGM Construction [16]). *Let $G : \{0,1\}^\ell \to \{0,1\}^{2\ell}$ be a length-doubling PRG and $s \in \{0,1\}^\ell$ be a seed for G. Write $G(s) = (G_0(s), G_1(s))$ with $G_0, G_1 : \{0,1\}^\ell \to \{0,1\}^\ell$. Then, on input $\boldsymbol{x} \in \{0,1\}^m$, we define the* **GGM pseudorandom function** $F_s : \{0,1\}^m \to \{0,1\}^n$ *as*

$$F_s(\boldsymbol{x}) = F_s((x_1, \ldots, x_\ell)) = G_{x_\ell}(G_{x_{\ell-1}}(\cdots (G_{x_1}(s)) \cdots)) \tag{2}$$

Theorem 2. *If $G : \{0,1\}^{\ell} \to \{0,1\}^{2\ell}$ is a PRG, then $\{F_s\}$ is a PRF family.*

Having fixed a positive non-null integer $t \in \mathbb{N}$, let us define our PRF PRF : $\mathbb{F}_2^r \times \mathbb{F}_2^t \to \mathbb{F}_2^r$ as the PRF obtained by transforming our PRG f of Eq. (1) with the GGM construction of Eq. (2). For readability, we will always denote the key in subscript, *i.e.* $\mathsf{PRF}(k, x) = \mathsf{PRF}_k(x)$. Formally we have,

$$\mathsf{PRF}_k(x) = \mathsf{PRF}_k\big((x_1, \cdots, x_t)\big) = f_{x_t}\Big(f_{x_{t-1}}\big(\cdots\big(f_{x_1}(k)\big)\big)\Big)\cdots\Big) \qquad (3)$$

Corollary 1. *By Theorem 2, PRF is a code-based PRF.*

4 Code-Based Zero Knowledge PRF Argument

In this section, we describe how our PRF construction can be adapted to be compatible with Stern's protocol [22] and thus, achieve a Zero-Knowledge (ZK) PRF argument, *i.e.* can be employed to prove the correctness of a PRF evaluation. We will start from a naïve description of a Stern-like statement and explain a specific security-flow that seems not to be easily solvable. To solve the problem, we define the map ψ that will act as the inverse map ϕ^{-1} and modify accordingly the statement in order to obtain a secure Stern-like statement $\big((M, y), s\big)$.

Briefly, Stern's protocol allows a prover $\mathcal{P}$ to prove the knowledge of a witness s with weight w to a verifier $\mathcal{V}$, that holds a public statement (M, y). The statement and the witness are related to the equation $M \cdot s^{\mathsf{T}} = y^{\mathsf{T}}$.

At a first glance, we can observe that our PRG f is already defined in a Stern-like format **but** iterating the PRG requires the application of the map ϕ, which has no possible linear representation. Let us consider the GGM iterative structure and let y^i be the i-th partial evaluation of the PRF, while x_{i+1} be the next *"branching"* in the GGM construction. The $(i + 1)$-th partial evaluation is computed as $A_{x_{(i+1)}} \cdot \phi(y^i)^{\mathsf{T}} = y^{(i+1)\mathsf{T}}$. Since ϕ has no-linear representation, it is indeed impossible to re-write the equation as a single matrix $\overline{M} \in \mathbb{F}_2^{r \times n}$ that multiplies only the secret initial vector $\phi(k)$.

It is important to note that, in order to use Stern's protocol, the witness is required to have a specific weight w and therefore we will consider as witness the regular word $\phi(k)$. This observation allows us to rewrite the PRF evaluation as a system of equations that describe all the singular partial evaluations and can be directly used to run Stern's protocol. Let $k = y^0$ and $x = (x_1, \ldots, x_t)$ and $y^t = \mathsf{PRF}(k, x)$. Then, it formally holds that:

$$\begin{cases} A_{x_1} \cdot \phi(y^0)^{\mathsf{T}} = y^{1\mathsf{T}} \\ A_{x_2} \cdot \phi(y^1)^{\mathsf{T}} = y^{2\mathsf{T}} \\ \cdots \\ A_{x_t} \cdot \phi(y^{t-1})^{\mathsf{T}} = y^{t\mathsf{T}} \end{cases} \iff \begin{pmatrix} A_{x_1} & 0 & & \\ 0 & A_{x_2} & 0 & \\ & \ddots & \ddots & \ddots \\ & & 0 & A_{x_t} \end{pmatrix} \cdot \begin{pmatrix} \phi(y^0)^{\mathsf{T}} \\ \phi(y^1)^{\mathsf{T}} \\ \vdots \\ \phi(y^{t-1})^{\mathsf{T}} \end{pmatrix} = \begin{pmatrix} y^{1\mathsf{T}} \\ y^{2\mathsf{T}} \\ \vdots \\ y^{t\mathsf{T}} \end{pmatrix}$$

$$(4)$$

Unfortunately, this representation has a security-flaw that allows a malicious adversary $\mathcal{A}$ to compute the PRF on different inputs x' without requiring the knowledge of k. This flaw is not captured by the GGM transformation and Stern's protocol security model, since the problem is related to the *"composition"* of the construction and the unusual behaviour observed when naïvely merging the security models. We call this composed-protocol as **prove-on-demand** protocol, in which we can either solely compute the PRF and, in a different moment in time, request to execute the ZK arguments. Further discussion is presented in Sect. 5.

In a nutshell, let $\mathcal{A}$ be an adversary whose goal is to distinguish between our code-based PRF PRF and a random function ζ, *i.e.*, break the pseudo/randomness property and related security model. Whenever the adversary queries a value x, $\mathcal{A}$ can either ask to obtain just the value $\mathsf{PRF}(k, x)$ or to obtain the transcript of the execution of Stern's protocol, which contains $\mathsf{PRF}(k, x)$ too. It is trivial to notice that the challenger can reply to the second query type by applying the simulatable property of ZK protocols, *i.e.*, providing a simulated transcript that correctly verifies Eq. (4) and obtains a random value by evaluating ζ.

On the other hand, this naïve ZK proof gives access to $\mathcal{A}$ to **all** the partial evaluations of the GGM transformation. $\mathcal{A}$ can take, *w.l.o.g.*, the partial evaluation y^{t-1} and correctly compute $A_{1-x_t} \cdot \phi(y^{t-1})^\intercal = \mathsf{PRF}(k, x')$, which is a valid PRF evaluation of the input x' with a different t-th component. With this knowledge, $\mathcal{A}$ can query the challenger on x' and just verify if the answer is equivalent to its computation or not, therefore distinguishing between PRF and ζ. *Mutatis mutandis*, $\mathcal{A}$ can personally compute any input x' except the ones that have a different first input-bit x_1. This is because $\mathcal{A}$ does not hold the pre-computation y^0, which is exactly the secret key k.

Similarly, it is possible to find other uncommon attacks that break other security properties, *e.g.*, the soundness property for Stern's protocol. The reason of all these problems is the disclosure of the partial evaluations, that completely break the GGM transformation Theorem 2 proof. For this reason, our goal is to *"hide"* the partial evaluation, while maintaining the simple and elegant representation compliant with Stern's protocol statement.

Let us consider the map $\psi : \mathbb{F}_2^n \to \mathbb{F}_2^r$ that takes a regular word w of weight w and outputs a binary vector of length r. The main design property of ψ is to invert the map ϕ and to be representable in a linear matrix format.

First of all, let w be a regular word of length $n = w \cdot 2^b$ that representa w as the concatenation of w canonical vectors, *i.e.* $w = (e_{n_1} \mid \cdots \mid e_{n_w})$. Let $\mathsf{I2B}_b$ be the map that given an integer j, it outputs, as a row vector, the binary representation in b-bit, *i.e.*, zeros are added accordingly if necessary.

Let us consider the binary matrix ψ as:

$$\psi = \left(\underbrace{\left(\mathsf{I2B}_b(0)^{\mathsf{T}} \| \ldots \| \mathsf{I2B}_b\left(2^b - 1\right)^{\mathsf{T}}\right) \| \cdots \| \left(\mathsf{I2B}_b(0)^{\mathsf{T}} \| \ldots \| \mathsf{I2B}_b\left(2^b - 1\right)^{\mathsf{T}}\right)}_{w \text{ times}} \right) \tag{5}$$

By notation abuse, let the evaluation of the map ψ be the matrix multiplication with the matrix ψ in Eq. (5). Formally,

$$\psi(\boldsymbol{w}) = \psi \cdot \boldsymbol{w}^{\mathsf{T}} = \psi \cdot \left(\boldsymbol{e}_{n_1+1} \mid \cdots \mid \boldsymbol{e}_{n_w+1} \right)^{\mathsf{T}} = \left(\mathsf{I2B}_b(n_1) \| \ldots \| \mathsf{I2B}_b(n_t) \right)^{\mathsf{T}}$$

Lemma 1. *For all $\boldsymbol{y} \in \mathbb{F}_2^r$, it holds $(\psi \circ \phi)(\boldsymbol{y}) = \boldsymbol{y}$, i.e., ψ is the inverse of ϕ.*

Proof. Ad oculos, let $\boldsymbol{y} = (\boldsymbol{y}_1 \| \ldots \| \boldsymbol{y}_w)$.

$$(\psi \circ \phi)(\boldsymbol{y}) = \psi \left(\left(\boldsymbol{e}_{\mathsf{B2I}(\boldsymbol{y}_1)+1} \| \cdots \| \boldsymbol{e}_{\mathsf{B2I}(\boldsymbol{y}_w)+1} \right) \right)$$
$$= \left((\mathsf{I2B}_b \circ \mathsf{B2I})(\boldsymbol{y}_1) \| \ldots \| (\mathsf{I2B}_b \circ \mathsf{B2I})(\boldsymbol{y}_w) \right) = (\boldsymbol{y}_1 \| \ldots \| \boldsymbol{y}_w) = \boldsymbol{y} \quad \square$$

Given the invertibility property, we are now able to further modify and fix the naïve approach presented in Eq. (4). For every $j \in \{1, \ldots, (t-1)\}$, let us rewrite the equation by moving all the addends to the left-hand side. Formally,

$$\boldsymbol{A}_{x_i} \cdot \phi(\boldsymbol{y}^{i-1})^{\mathsf{T}} = \boldsymbol{y}^{i\mathsf{T}} \iff \boldsymbol{A}_{x_i} \cdot \phi(\boldsymbol{y}^{i-1})^{\mathsf{T}} \oplus \boldsymbol{y}^{i\mathsf{T}} = 0$$
$$\iff \boldsymbol{A}_{x_i} \cdot \phi(\boldsymbol{y}^{i-1})^{\mathsf{T}} \oplus \left(\psi \circ \phi \right)^{\mathsf{T}}(\boldsymbol{y}^i) = 0$$
$$\iff \boldsymbol{A}_{x_i} \cdot \phi(\boldsymbol{y}^{i-1})^{\mathsf{T}} \oplus \psi \cdot \phi(\boldsymbol{y}^i)^{\mathsf{T}} = 0 \tag{6}$$

By rewriting Eq. (6) in Eq. (4), define $\widehat{\boldsymbol{M}} \in \mathbb{F}_2^{tr \times tn}$ and $\widehat{\boldsymbol{s}} \in \mathbb{F}_2^{tn}, \widehat{\boldsymbol{y}} \in \mathbb{F}_2^{tr}$ as:

$$\widehat{\boldsymbol{M}} \cdot \widehat{\boldsymbol{s}} := \begin{pmatrix} \boldsymbol{A}_{x_1} & \psi & & \\ & \ddots & \ddots & \\ & & \boldsymbol{A}_{x_{t-1}} & \psi \\ & & & \boldsymbol{A}_{x_t} \end{pmatrix} \cdot \begin{pmatrix} \phi(\boldsymbol{y}^0)^{\mathsf{T}} \\ \vdots \\ \phi(\boldsymbol{y}^{t-2})^{\mathsf{T}} \\ \phi(\boldsymbol{y}^{t-1})^{\mathsf{T}} \end{pmatrix} = \begin{pmatrix} 0 \\ \vdots \\ 0 \\ \boldsymbol{y}^{t\mathsf{T}} \end{pmatrix} =: \widehat{\boldsymbol{y}} \tag{7}$$

Proposition 2. *Let $\widehat{\boldsymbol{M}}, \widehat{\boldsymbol{s}}, \widehat{\boldsymbol{y}}$ as defined in Eq. (7). The related Stern language,*

$$\hat{L} = \left\{ \left(\widehat{\boldsymbol{M}}, \widehat{\boldsymbol{y}} \right) \mid \exists \widehat{\boldsymbol{s}} : \ \mathsf{wt}(\widehat{\boldsymbol{s}}) = wt \ \wedge \ \widehat{\boldsymbol{M}} \cdot \widehat{\boldsymbol{s}} = \widehat{\boldsymbol{y}} \right\}$$

is equivalent to the PRF evaluation language for PRF of Eq. (3), i.e.,

$$L_{\mathsf{PRF}} = \{(\boldsymbol{x}, \boldsymbol{y}) \mid \exists \boldsymbol{k} : \ \mathsf{PRF}(\boldsymbol{k}, \boldsymbol{x}) = \boldsymbol{y}\}$$

Proof. Since the global parameters n, r, w are known, the matrix ψ is defined and it is trivial to observe that $\widehat{\boldsymbol{M}}$ can be reconstructed with the knowledge of the matrices $\boldsymbol{A}_0, \boldsymbol{A}_1$ and $\boldsymbol{x}$. Furthermore, since $t - 1$ components of $\widehat{\boldsymbol{y}}$ are zero, only y^t is needed to correctly reconstruct the language statement's vector. To this point, we can rewrite $\hat{L}$ as:

$$\hat{L} = \left\{ \left((A_0, A_1, x), y^t \right) \mid \exists \hat{s} : \text{wt}(\hat{s}) = wt \wedge \widehat{M} \cdot \hat{s} = \hat{y} \right\}$$

Since the PRF is defined by the matrices A_0, A_1, $y^t = \text{PRF}(k, x)$ and the matrix multiplication represents the GGM iterated PRF computations, we have

$$\hat{L} = L'_{\text{PRF}} = \{(x, y) \mid \exists \hat{s} : \text{wt}(\hat{s}) = wt \wedge \text{PRF}(k, x) = y\}$$

and we are left to prove that possessing the PRF secret key $k \in \mathbb{F}_2^r$ is equivalent to knowing all the regular-words and partial evaluations $y^j \in \mathbb{F}_2^n$ used in the GGM transformation, for all indexes $j \in \{0, \dots, (t-1)\}$.

Given that the maps ϕ and ψ are, together, a bijection between $\mathbb{F}_2^r$ and the regular word in $\mathbb{F}_2^n$ with weight w, it holds that it is irrelevant which representation is known. Trivially, the knowledge of $k = y^0$ allows the computation of all the other partial evaluations y^j for $j \in \{1, \dots, (t-1)\}$ and therefore it holds $L_{\text{PRF}} \subseteq L'_{\text{PRF}} = \hat{L}$. For the same reasons, it is possible to *"forget"* the partial evaluation and have $L_{\text{PRF}} \supseteq L'_{\text{PRF}}$. In conclusion, it holds that $\hat{L} = L_{\text{PRF}}$.   □

Corollary 2. *By Stern protocol's Theorem 1 and Proposition 2, executing Stern's protocol on $\left(\widehat{M}, \hat{s}, \hat{y} \right)$ as defined in Eq. (7), produces a Zero-Knowledge PRF argument protocol based on the code-based PRF* PRF *of Sect. 3.*

5   Theoretical Analysis for Implementation Cost

In this section, we provide an application scenario in which our protocol could be employed and we discuss the protocol's communication costs.

Let us consider an employee and an employer that are willing to sign an agreement document that guarantees special treatment for the employee. Since they do not fully trust each other, they agree on a shared document. To bind the reached agreement, they ask a notary $\mathcal{N}$ to witness the signing phase, of both the employee and employer, and *publicly commit*, by signing, the content of the agreed-document. We assume that the signed and agreed document is made public. In this way, a notary is *fully liable* and, at any moment, anyone can take the signed document and let the notary testify on the agreement's trustworthiness. This scenario is quite common, whenever we consider *physical verification* of identities or signatures while, the first number-theoretic example is given by Adleman [1] in 1983.

Let us now consider the case in which the notary $\mathcal{N}$ accepts to be liable in a *limited way*. More precisely, a verifier $\mathcal{V}$ can interact with $\mathcal{N}$ and ask to prove the agreed-document's correctness **but** $\mathcal{V}$ cannot use the interaction-transcript-of-the-protocol to further prove the document's correctness to other people.

This can be seen as the *whistle-blower's notary* problem and is depicted in Fig. 3. Let us explain the scenario in detail, while employing our ZK protocol.

The clients prepare a document x containing all the info that they are willing to publish. The notary, in possess of a secret key k, will verify the document's validity and he/she will publicly commit to the document with $y = \mathsf{PRF}_k(x)$. A verifier $\mathcal{V}$ will be able to verify the correctness of (x, y) by running the ZK PRF argument protocol with the notary $\mathcal{N}$. The zero-knowledge property imposes to the the notary that he **must** be collaborative **and guarantees** that $\mathcal{V}$ cannot use the proof-transcript and make $\mathcal{N}$ liable. This counter-intuitive second point is better understood when we change our point of view: $\mathcal{N}$ can *choose whom to prove to* and therefore he/she can interact with a trustworthy judge that is interested in the correctness of the document, while $\mathcal{N}$ can refuse to interact with strangers and avoid repercussions of any kind.

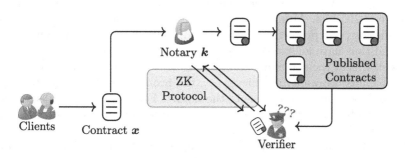

Fig. 3. The whistle-blower notary problem.

In this way, *"committing"* and *"proving"* are done in different times. The reasons of this choice find roots in the extremely different cost between *"computing"* and *"communicating"* a statement or a proof. For this reason, we classify applications, such as the one described above, that are computationally-fast but communication-costly as ***prove-on-demand*** protocols, in which the protocol's communication cost is low **until** the proof is requested.

Let us now describe *why* our protocol is a prove-on-demand protocol. We upper-bound our ZK protocol communication cost *w.r.t.* implementation principles discussed by Stern [22] and Meziani *et al.* [21].

First of all, we overestimate the length of a permutation π of the set $\{1, \ldots, n\}$ as $|\pi| = n \log_2(n)$, which is the bit-representation of the permutation's image *w.r.t.* a fixed order, *e.g.*, $\pi = \big(\mathsf{I2B}_n(\pi(1)) \| \ldots \| \mathsf{I2B}_n(\pi(n))\big)$. By employing the *random hashing technique*, as denoted by Stern, we may use a hash function Hash and commit to a message m by sampling some randomness ρ of the same length $|m|$ and commit by computing the hash value of $\big(\rho \| \rho \oplus m\big)$. To verify the decommitment, it is necessary to hold both ρ and m. In this way, the commitment's length is exactly the hash digest's length, denoted as $|\mathsf{Hash}|$.

Given $w, b \in \mathbb{N}$, the number d of Stern's protocol executions, and the PRF input space dimension t, the communication cost for our ZK PRF argument is:

$$\mathsf{Cost}(w, b, t, d) = d \cdot \mathsf{Cost}_{\mathsf{Stern}}(tw2^b, twb)$$
$$\leq d \cdot \left(3|\mathsf{Hash}| + tw \cdot \left(2^{b+1}(1 + b + \log_2(tw)) + b\right) + 2\right) \text{ bits}$$

From the X-SYND definition [21], in order to get a security level of 80 bits, the parameters are fixed as $w = 32$ and $b = 8$. We can also assume that the hash digest is $|\mathsf{Hash}| = 128$ bits. Therefore, if we consider t, d as parameters, we have:

$$\mathsf{Cost}(32, 8, t, d) = d \cdot \mathsf{Cost}_{\mathsf{Stern}}(8192t, 256t)$$
$$\leq d \cdot \left(t \cdot \left(16384 \cdot \log_2(t) + 229632\right) + 386\right) \text{ bits}$$

With these parameters, we have that our proposed PRF has a space-cost equal to $|\boldsymbol{A_0}| + |\boldsymbol{A_0}| = 2 \cdot w2^b \cdot wb$ which, in our case, is 0.5 Megabyte. The output space is 256 bits. Although the matrices used in the computations require significant cost, our protocol and proposed primitives require only binary operations and thus have an extremely low communication cost.

It is clear that the communication cost is directly proportional to the soundness probability we want to achieve, $i.e.$, the probability of a successful adversary, who may want to impersonate the notary. For example, in order to get a soundness probability of less than 2^{-80}, we have to execute the protocol at least $d \geq 137$ times.

We plot the communication cost of running our ZK PRF argument protocol, depending on the (t, d) choices in Fig. 4.

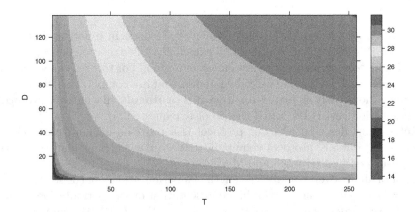

Fig. 4. A heatmap plot of $\log_2\left(\frac{\mathsf{Cost}(32,8,t,d)}{8}\right)$ in which, for every t and d, we represent the communication cost in base-2 logarithmic scale. This means that a value of 20 represents 2^{20} bytes, which is 1 Megabyte.

Regarding the PRF input space, we might consider, as a reasonable dimension, to be either $t = 128$ or $t = 256$, as the output space. In these two cases, the whole communication cost for proving the PRF evaluation would be in the order of approximately one Gigabyte.

$$\mathsf{Cost}(32, 8, 128, 137) \simeq 719.79\text{MB} \qquad \mathsf{Cost}(32, 8, 256, 137) \simeq 1508.08\text{MB}$$

Given the high-communication cost required, we would highly suggest the employment of our ZK PRF argument protocol only in *prove-on-demand* application scenarios *i.e.*, in applications where proving the PRF argument is not required frequently and thus, the communication cost, and related time, can be afforded without disrupting the application's functionality. We should note though that considering the great efficiency of the required computations, the protocol can be executed in devices with low computational abilities.

6 Conclusions and Future Work

In this paper, we construct the first zero-knowledge PRF argument based on the regular syndrome decoding assumption. Our construction starts from defining a PRG f, which directly reduces to a $\mathsf{RSD}(n, 2r, w)$ problem. By applying the GGM transformation we obtain a code-based PRF. After rewriting the GGM evaluation steps as a single linear system, we define the map ψ that consequently, allow us to rewrite the PRF evaluation in a Stern protocol statement. Finally, we obtain our code-based ZK PRF argument protocol by applying Stern's protocol.

Providing cryptographic primitives under code-based assumptions is of significant interest since code-based cryptography provides significant promise to be post-quantum secure. Furthermore, ZK PRF argument protocol can be employed to construct other code-based primitives. For instance, Brunetta *et al.*'s construction [6] would allow us to define a *simulatable verifiable random function, i.e.,* a cryptographic primitive that allows to prove non-interactively the correct PRF computation. These advanced primitives can be used to simplify complex multi-party protocols employed in applications that require sampling a pseudorandom element from a set without allowing any party to maliciously affect the result, such as e-cash, e-voting and cryptographic lotteries.

As further work, we are interested in improving the proposed protocol's efficiency. Some possible directions, we may consider is improving Stern's protocol communication cost is by employing Aguilar *et al.*'s [2] or Cayrel *et al.*'s [8] protocols that also provide lower soundness error. Another direction is to reduce the PRF's *fingerprint* by using quasi-cycle codes and not random-binary ones.

Acknowledgement. We are grateful to the anonymous reviewers for their insightful comments. This work was partially supported by the Swedish Research Council (Vetenskapsrådet) through the grant PRECIS (621-2014-4845).

References

1. Adleman, L.M.: Implementing an electronic notary public. In: Advances in Cryptology (1983)

2. Aguilar, C., Gaborit, P., Schrek, J.: A new zero-knowledge code based identification scheme with reduced communication. In: 2011 IEEE Information Theory Workshop (2011). https://doi.org/10.1109/ITW.2011.6089577

3. Augot, D., Finiasz, M., Sendrier, N.: A family of fast syndrome based cryptographic hash functions. In: Dawson, E., Vaudenay, S. (eds.) Mycrypt 2005. LNCS, vol. 3715, pp. 64–83. Springer, Heidelberg (2005). https://doi.org/10.1007/11554868_6

4. Banerjee, A., Peikert, C., Rosen, A.: Pseudorandom functions and lattices. In: Pointcheval, D., Johansson, T. (eds.) EUROCRYPT 2012. LNCS, vol. 7237, pp. 719–737. Springer, Heidelberg (2012). https://doi.org/10.1007/978-3-642-29011-4_42

5. Berlekamp, E., McEliece, R., Van Tilborg, H.: On the inherent intractability of certain coding problems (Corresp.). IEEE Transact. Inf. Theory **24**(3), 384–386 (1978)

6. Brunetta, C., Liang, B., Mitrokotsa, A.: Lattice-based simulatable VRFs: challenges and future directions. J. Internet Serv. Inf. Secur. (JISIS) **8**(4), 57–69 (2018)

7. Cayrel, P.L., Gaborit, P., Girault, M.: Identity-based identification and signature schemes using correcting codes. In: WCC, vol. 2007 (2007)

8. Cayrel, P.L., Véron, P., El Yousfi Alaoui, S.M.: A zero-knowledge identification scheme based on the q-ary syndrome decoding problem. In: Selected Areas in Cryptography (2011)

9. Chabaud, F.: On the security of some cryptosystems based on error-correcting codes. In: De Santis, A. (ed.) EUROCRYPT 1994. LNCS, vol. 950, pp. 131–139. Springer, Heidelberg (1995). https://doi.org/10.1007/BFb0053430

10. El Yousfi Alaoui, S.M., Cayrel, P.-L., Mohammed, M.: Improved identity-based identification and signature schemes using quasi-dyadic Goppa codes. In: Kim, T., Adeli, H., Robles, R.J., Balitanas, M. (eds.) ISA 2011. CCIS, vol. 200, pp. 146–155. Springer, Heidelberg (2011). https://doi.org/10.1007/978-3-642-23141-4_14

11. Ezerman, M.F., Lee, H.T., Ling, S., Nguyen, K., Wang, H.: A provably secure group signature scheme from code-based assumptions. In: Iwata, T., Cheon, J.H. (eds.) ASIACRYPT 2015. LNCS, vol. 9452, pp. 260–285. Springer, Heidelberg (2015). https://doi.org/10.1007/978-3-662-48797-6_12

12. Fischer, J.-B., Stern, J.: An efficient pseudo-random generator provably as secure as syndrome decoding. In: Maurer, U. (ed.) EUROCRYPT 1996. LNCS, vol. 1070, pp. 245–255. Springer, Heidelberg (1996). https://doi.org/10.1007/3-540-68339-9_22

13. Gaborit, P., Lauradoux, C., Sendrier, N.: SYND: a fast code-based stream cipher with a security reduction. In: 2007 IEEE International Symposium on Information Theory, June 2007. https://doi.org/10.1109/ISIT.2007.4557224

14. Gilbert, E.N.: A comparison of signalling alphabets. Bell Syst. Tech. J. **31**(3), 504–522 (1952). https://doi.org/10.1002/j.1538-7305.1952.tb01393.x

15. Goldreich, O., Levin, L.A.: A hard-core predicate for all one-way functions. In: STOC 1989. ACM (1989). https://doi.org/10.1145/73007.73010

16. Goldreich, O., Goldwasser, S., Micali, S.: How to construct random functions. J. ACM **33**(4), 792–807 (1986). https://doi.org/10.1145/6490.6503

17. Hu, R., Morozov, K., Takagi, T.: Proof of plaintext knowledge for code-based public-key encryption revisited. In: ASIA CCS 2013 (2013). https://doi.org/10.1145/2484313.2484385

18. Katz, J., Lindell, Y.: Introduction to Modern Cryptography. CRC Press, Boca Raton (2014)

19. Libert, B., Ling, S., Nguyen, K., Wang, H.: Zero-knowledge arguments for lattice-based PRFs and applications to E-Cash. In: Takagi, T., Peyrin, T. (eds.) ASIACRYPT 2017. LNCS, vol. 10626, pp. 304–335. Springer, Cham (2017). https://doi.org/10.1007/978-3-319-70700-6_11

20. Meziani, M., Cayrel, P.-L., El Yousfi Alaoui, S.M.: 2SC: An efficient code-based stream cipher. In: Kim, T., Adeli, H., Robles, R.J., Balitanas, M. (eds.) ISA 2011. CCIS, vol. 200, pp. 111–122. Springer, Heidelberg (2011). https://doi.org/10.1007/978-3-642-23141-4_11

21. Meziani, M., Hoffmann, G., Cayrel, P.-L.: Improving the performance of the SYND stream cipher. In: Mitrokotsa, A., Vaudenay, S. (eds.) AFRICACRYPT 2012. LNCS, vol. 7374, pp. 99–116. Springer, Heidelberg (2012). https://doi.org/10.1007/978-3-642-31410-0_7

22. Stern, J.: A new paradigm for public key identification. IEEE Transact. Inf. Theory **42**(6), 1757–1768 (1996). https://doi.org/10.1109/18.556672

23. Stern, J.: A method for finding codewords of small weight. In: Cohen, G., Wolfmann, J. (eds.) Coding Theory 1988. LNCS, vol. 388, pp. 106–113. Springer, Heidelberg (1989). https://doi.org/10.1007/BFb0019850

24. Varshamov, R.R.: Estimate of the number of signals in error correcting codes. Docklady Akad. Nauk, S.S.S.R. **117**, 739–741 (1957)

25. Yu, Y., Steinberger, J.: Pseudorandom Functions in Almost Constant Depth from Low-Noise LPN. In: Fischlin, M., Coron, J.-S. (eds.) EUROCRYPT 2016. LNCS, vol. 9666, pp. 154–183. Springer, Heidelberg (2016). https://doi.org/10.1007/978-3-662-49896-5_6

On New Zero-Knowledge Proofs for Lattice-Based Group Signatures with Verifier-Local Revocation

Yanhua Zhang[1(✉)], Yupu Hu[2], Qikun Zhang[1], and Huiwen Jia[3]

[1] Zhengzhou University of Light Industry, Zhengzhou 450002, China
{yhzhang,qkzhang}@zzuli.edu.cn
[2] Xidian University, Xi'an 710071, China
yphu@xidian.mail.edu.cn
[3] Guangzhou University, Guangzhou 510006, China
hwjia@gzhu.edu.cn

Abstract. For lattice-based group signatures with verifier-local revocation (VLR), a group member who issues a signature on behalf of the whole group can validly prove to the verifiers with an efficient non-interactive zero-knowledge proof protocol, from which the verifiers only come to the conclusion that the signer is a certified group member who owns a valid secret signing key and its corresponding revocation token is out of the revocation list. The first such construction was introduced by Langlois et al. (PKC 2014), furthermore, a full and corrected version was proposed in TCS 2018. However, both schemes are within the structure of *Bonsai Trees*, and thus the bit-sizes of the group public-key and the group member secret-key are proportional to $\log N$, where N is the maximum number of group members, therefore both constructions are not suitable for a large group.

In this work, we adopt a more efficient and compact identity-encoding technique which only needs a constant number of matrices to encode the group member's identity information and it saves a $\mathcal{O}(\log N)$ factor in both bit-sizes for the group public-key and the group member secret-key. In particular, a new Stern-type statistical zero-knowledge proof protocol allowing to prove the signer's validity as a valid certified group member and its revocation token correctly committed via a one-way and injective Learning With Errors (LWE) function is proposed.

Keywords: Group signatures · Lattice-based cryptography · Zero-knowledge proofs · Verifier-local revocation

1 Introduction

Group signatures (GS), as an important privacy-preserving primitive put forward by Chaum and van Heyst [7], allow the group members to issue signatures on behalf the whole group without compromising their identity information

© Springer Nature Switzerland AG 2019
Z. Lin et al. (Eds.): ISC 2019, LNCS 11723, pp. 190–208, 2019.
https://doi.org/10.1007/978-3-030-30215-3_10

(*anonymity*). Yet, given a valid message-signature pair, the opening authority can link it to the real identity of signer (*traceability*). These two appealing properties allow GS to find several real-life applications, such as in the trusted computing, digital right management, anonymous online communications, e-commerce systems, and much more.

Generally, to design an efficient GS scheme three critical cryptographic ingredients are needed: an ordinary digital signature, a CCA-secure encryption, and an efficient non-interactive zero-knowledge proof protocol. Thus to construct a theoretical secure and efficient GS scheme is a challenging work for the research community, and over the last quarter-century, various GS schemes with different security notions, different levels of efficiency and based on different assumptions have been proposed (e.g., [1–4,10,12] $\cdots$).

LATTICE-BASED GROUP SIGNATURES. Lattice-based cryptography, considered as a promising candidate for post-quantum cryptography (PQC), possessing several noticeable advantages over conventional number-theoretic cryptography (i.e., based on integer factoring or discrete logarithm problems), such as conjectured resistance against quantum computers, faster arithmetic operations and provable security under the *worst-case* hardness assumptions, has attracted significant interest since the creative works of Regev [28] and Gentry et al. [9]. In recent one decade, along with other primitives, lattice-based GS has been paid a greet attention. The first lattice-based GS construction was put forth by Gordon et al. [10], while their solution has a low efficiency due to the linear-sizes of the public key and the signature in the security parameter n and the maximum number of group members N. Camenisch et al. [5] then proposed a variant of [10] to achieve efficiency in a shorter public key and security in a stronger anonymity, but their signature size is still linear in n and N. Laguillaumie et al. [13] then overcame the linear-sizes barrier problem and provided the first logarithmic construction with relatively large parameters. Ling et al. [20] and Nguyen et al. [25] designed two more efficient lattice-based GS schemes with the signature size proportional to $\log N$ respectively. More recently, Libert et al. [16] described a lattice-based accumulator and based on which they got the first lattice-based GS that does not require any GPV trapdoors. The first lattice-based realizations with message-dependent opening and forward-secure were proposed by Libert et al. [17] and Ling et al. [22], respectively. For the lattice-based GS schemes mentioned above, all are designed for static groups and analyzed in the model of Bellare et al. [1], where no new member is allowed to join or leave after whole group's setup.

As we know, four main lattice-based GS constructions with certain dynamic features exist. In PKC 2014, Langlois et al. [14] proposed the first lattice-based GS scheme with verifier-local revocation (VLR) to support membership revocation, which only requires the verifiers to possess up-to-date group information, but not the signers. In order to fix a flaw in the revocation mechanism of [14], a full and corrected version [18] was given recently. Libert et al. [15] took the orthogonal problem of member enrollments into account and proposed a dynamic scheme in the model of Kiayias and Yong [12] and Bellare et al. [2]. Later, Ling et al. [21] added some dynamic ingredients into the static accumulator constructed in [16] to construct the first lattice-based GS scheme with full dynamicity (i.e., the members can join and leave the group at will) in the model of Bootle et al. [4]. Recently, Ling et al. [23] introduced a constant-size lattice-based GS scheme (i.e., signature size is totally independent of N), meanwhile supporting dynamic member enrollments.

As for membership revocation, the VLR mechanism is more efficient than an accumulator, especially when considering a large group. Since the VLR technique was introduced to lattice-based GS by Langlois et al. [14], several lattice-based GS schemes with VLR achieving different levels of efficiency and security notions are proposed [18, 26, 27]. But almost all of them operate within a structure of *Bonsai Trees* [6], and the bit-sizes of the group public-key and the member secret-key are proportional to $\log N$, the only exceptions are two lattice-based GS constructions with VLR [8, 29] which adopt an efficient identity-encoding technique as in [25] to encode the member's identity information and save a $\mathcal{O}(\log N)$ factor in both bit-sizes, however, the latter two GS constructions with VLR both require a series of sophisticated operations and statistical zero-knowledge proof protocols in the signing phase (i.e., strictly following the *sign-encrypt-proof* designing paradigm). Thus, these somewhat unsatisfactory state-of-affairs highlights the challenge of designing a simpler and efficient lattice-based GS scheme with VLR, specifically, an efficient statistical zero-knowledge proof protocol.

OUR CONSTRUCTIONS AND MAIN TECHNIQUES. In this work, we pay attention to the design of statistical zero-knowledge proof protocol in an efficient construction of lattice-based GS with VLR. By adopting a more efficient and compact identity-encoding technique, the bit-sizes of the group public-key and the member secret-key can save a $\mathcal{O}(\log N)$ factor in comparison with the existing lattice-based GS schemes with VLR. In particular, a new statical zero-knowledge proof protocol is introduced, and the Stern-type protocol allows the signer to prove its validity as a certified member and its revocation token is correctly committed via a one-way and injective Learning With Errors (LWE) function in zero-knowledge.

Our new Stern-type statistical zero-knowledge proof protocol mainly builds on a updatable identity-encoding technique as in [25] to encode the identity index of the group member. The group public-key only consists of a uniformly random vector $\mathbf{u} \in \mathbb{Z}_q^n$ and three random matrices $\mathbf{A}_0, \mathbf{A}_1$ and $\mathbf{A}_2$ over $\mathbb{Z}_q^{n \times m}$. For the group member $i \in \{1, 2, \cdots, N\}$, instead of generating a short trapdoor basis of a classical q-ary lattice as the secret-key of group member i, we sample a short $2m$-dimensional vector $\mathbf{e}_i = (\mathbf{e}_{i,1}, \mathbf{e}_{i,2}) \in \mathbb{Z}^{2m}$ which satisfies $\mathbf{A}_i \cdot \mathbf{e}_i = \mathbf{u} \bmod q$, where $\mathbf{A}_i = [\mathbf{A}_0 | \mathbf{A}_1 + i\mathbf{A}_2] \in \mathbb{Z}_q^{n \times 2m}$. Moreover, the member i's revocation token is constructed by $\mathbf{A}_0$ and $\mathbf{e}_{i,1}$, i.e., $\mathrm{grt}_i = \mathbf{A}_0 \cdot \mathbf{e}_{i,1} \bmod q$.

The main challenge lies in how to construct a secure and efficient Stern-type statistical zero-knowledge proof protocol to prove the above relations: (i) $[\mathbf{A}_0 | \mathbf{A}_1 + i\mathbf{A}_2] \cdot \mathbf{e}_i = \mathbf{u} \bmod q$; ($ii$) $\mathrm{grt}_i = \mathbf{A}_0 \cdot \mathbf{e}_{i,1} \bmod q$. For the relation ($ii$), we adopt the creative idea introduced by Ling et al. [18] by drawing a uniformly random matrix $\mathbf{B} \in \mathbb{Z}_q^{n \times m}$ from a random oracle and a short random vector $\mathbf{e} \in \mathbb{Z}^m$ from an LWE error distribution, then, let $\mathbf{b} = (\mathbf{B}^\top \mathbf{A}_0) \cdot \mathbf{e}_{i,1} + \mathbf{e} = \mathbf{B}^\top \mathrm{grt}_i + \mathbf{e} \bmod q$, thus, the member i's revocation token grt_i is now bound to a one-way and injective LWE function.

For the relation (i), in order to protect the anonymity of member i, the structure of $\mathbf{A}_i$ should not be given explicitly. To solve this problem, we transform $\mathbf{A}_i$ to a new form $\mathbf{A}'$ which is independent of member i's identity index, i.e., $\mathbf{A}' = [\mathbf{A}_0|\mathbf{A}_1|\mathbf{g}_{\lceil \log N \rceil} \otimes \mathbf{A}_2] \in \mathbb{Z}_q^{n \times (\lceil \log N \rceil + 2)m}$, where $\mathbf{g}_{\lceil \log N \rceil} = (1, 2^1, \cdots, 2^{\lceil \log N \rceil - 1})$ is a power-of-2 vector, let $\mathsf{bin}(i) \in \{0,1\}^{\lceil \log N \rceil}$ denote the binary representation of i, so $i = \mathbf{g}_{\lceil \log N \rceil}^\top \cdot \mathsf{bin}(i)$, $\otimes$ denotes a concatenation with vectors or matrices, a detailed definition is given latter. As a corresponding change to i's secret-key, $\mathbf{e}_i = (\mathbf{e}_{i,1}, \mathbf{e}_{i,2})$ is transformed into $\mathbf{e}'_i = (\mathbf{e}_{i,1}, \mathbf{e}_{i,2}, \mathsf{bin}(i) \otimes \mathbf{e}_{i,2}) \in \mathbb{Z}^{(\lceil \log N \rceil + 2)m}$. Thus, the relation $\mathbf{A}_i \cdot \mathbf{e}_i = \mathbf{u} \bmod q$ is now transformed into a new form, i.e., $\mathbf{A}_i \cdot \mathbf{e}_i = \mathbf{A}' \cdot \mathbf{e}'_i = \mathbf{u} \bmod q$.

Putting both the above transformations idea and the versatility of the Stern-extension argument system introduced by Ling et al. [19] together, we can construct a Stern-type interactive zero-knowledge proof protocol for the relations (i) and (ii). Furthermore, the new interactive protocol can be repeated $\omega(\log n)$ times to reduce the soundness error to a negligible value and transformed into a secure and efficient non-interactive Stern-type statistical zero-knowledge proof protocol by using the Fiat-Shamir heuristic in the random oracle model.

ORGANIZATION. In the forthcoming sections, we first recall some background on lattice-based cryptography in Sect. 2. Section 3 turns to develop a updatable identity-encoding technique, and our main Stern-type statistical zero-knowledge proof protocol is constructed in Sect. 4 and analyzed in Sect. 5.

2 Preliminaries

NOTATIONS. In this paper, the real numbers and integers are denoted by $\mathbb{R}$ and $\mathbb{Z}$, respectively. Vectors are in column form. $\mathcal{S}_k$ denotes the set of all permutations of k elements, and $\leftarrow_R$ denotes that sampling elements from a distribution uniformly at random. The Euclidean norm and infinity norm of vector $\mathbf{e}$ are denoted by $\|\mathbf{e}\|$ and $\|\mathbf{e}\|_\infty$, respectively. Given $\mathbf{e} = (e_1, e_2, \cdots, e_n) \in \mathbb{R}^n$, $\mathsf{Parse}(\mathbf{e}, k_1, k_2)$ denotes the vector $(e_{k_1}, e_{k_1+1}, \cdots, e_{k_2}) \in \mathbb{R}^{k_2 - k_1 + 1}$ for $1 \leq k_1 \leq k_2 \leq n$.

The standard notations $\mathcal{O}$ and ω are used to classify the growth of functions. All logarithms are of base 2. For an unspecified function $f(n) = \mathcal{O}(g(n) \cdot \log^c n)$ for $c > 0$, it is denoted as $f(n) = \widetilde{\mathcal{O}}(g(n))$, and notation $\mathsf{negl}(n)$ denotes a negligible function $f(n) = \mathcal{O}(n^{-c})$ for $c > 0$, and a probability is called *overwhelming* if it is $1 - \mathsf{negl}(n)$.

2.1 Lattices

Definition 1. *For integers $m \geq n \geq 1$, a prime $q \geq 2$, a matrix $\mathbf{A} \in \mathbb{Z}_q^{n \times m}$ and a vector $\mathbf{u} \in \mathbb{Z}_q^n$, define q-ary lattice and its corresponding shift (i.e., a coset of q-ary lattice):*

$$\Lambda_q^\perp(\mathbf{A}) = \{\mathbf{e} \in \mathbb{Z}^m \text{ s.t. } \mathbf{A}\mathbf{e} = \mathbf{0} \bmod q\},$$
$$\Lambda_q^{\mathbf{u}}(\mathbf{A}) = \{\mathbf{e} \in \mathbb{Z}^m \text{ s.t. } \mathbf{A}\mathbf{e} = \mathbf{u} \bmod q\}.$$

For $s > 0$, define the Gaussian function on $\mathbb{R}^m$ with center $\mathbf{c}$ as:

$$\forall \mathbf{e} \in \mathbb{R}^m, \ \rho_{s,\mathbf{c}}(\mathbf{e}) = \exp(-\pi \|\mathbf{e} - \mathbf{c}\|^2 / s^2).$$

For $\mathbf{c} \in \mathbb{R}^m$, define the discrete Gaussian distribution over Λ as:

$$\forall \mathbf{e} \in \mathbb{Z}^m, \ \mathcal{D}_{\Lambda,s,\mathbf{c}} = \rho_{s,\mathbf{c}}(\mathbf{e})/\rho_{s,\mathbf{c}}(\Lambda) = \rho_{s,\mathbf{c}}(\mathbf{e})/\textstyle\sum_{\mathbf{e} \in \Lambda} \rho_{s,\mathbf{c}}(\mathbf{e}).$$

And for convenience, we denote $\mathcal{D}_{\Lambda,s,\mathbf{c}}$ as $\mathcal{D}_{\Lambda,s}$ if $\mathbf{c} = \mathbf{0}$.

2.2 Average-Case Lattices Problems

We now recall the definitions and hardness results for three *average-case* lattices problems: the *Short Integer Solution* (SIS) problem, the *Inhomogeneous Short Integer Solution* (ISIS) problem and the *Learning With Errors* (LWE) problem.

Definition 2. *The* $\mathsf{SIS}^\infty_{n,m,q,\beta}$ *problem in infinity norm is: Given a prime* q*, a uniformly random matrix* $\mathbf{A} \in \mathbb{Z}_q^{n \times m}$ *and a real* $\beta > 0$*, to find a non-zero integer vector* $\mathbf{e} \in \mathbb{Z}^m$ *such that* $\mathbf{A} \cdot \mathbf{e} = \mathbf{0} \bmod q$*, and* $\|\mathbf{e}\|_\infty \leq \beta$*.*

Definition 3. *The* $\mathsf{ISIS}^\infty_{n,m,q,\beta}$ *problem in infinity norm is: Given a prime* q*, a uniformly random matrix* $\mathbf{A} \in \mathbb{Z}_q^{n \times m}$*, a random syndrome vector* $\mathbf{u} \in \mathbb{Z}_q^n$ *and a real* $\beta > 0$*, to find a non-zero integer vector* $\mathbf{e} \in \mathbb{Z}^m$ *such that* $\mathbf{A} \cdot \mathbf{e} = \mathbf{u} \bmod q$*, and* $\|\mathbf{e}\|_\infty \leq \beta$*.*

The ISIS problem is just an variant of SIS, and both the problems are as hard as certain *worst-case* lattice problems, such as the *Shortest Independent Vectors Problem* (SIVP).

Lemma 1 ([9,24]). *For integers* m*,* $\beta = \mathsf{poly}(n)$*,* $q \geq \beta \cdot \widetilde{\mathcal{O}}(\sqrt{n})$*, the average-case* $\mathsf{SIS}^\infty_{n,m,q,\beta}$ *problem or* $\mathsf{ISIS}^\infty_{n,m,q,\beta}$ *problem is at least as hard as the* SIVP_γ *problem in worst-case to within* $\gamma = \beta \cdot \widetilde{\mathcal{O}}(\sqrt{nm})$ *factor. In particular, if* $\beta = 1$*,* $q = \widetilde{\mathcal{O}}(n)$*,* $m = 2n\lceil \log q \rceil$*, the* $\mathsf{SIS}^\infty_{n,m,q,1}$ *problem or* $\mathsf{ISIS}^\infty_{n,m,q,1}$ *problem is at least as hard as* $\mathsf{SIVP}_{\widetilde{\mathcal{O}}(n)}$*.*

Definition 4. *The* $\mathsf{LWE}_{n,q,\chi}$ *problem is: Given a random vector* $\mathbf{s} \in \mathbb{Z}_q^n$*, a probability distribution* χ *over* $\mathbb{Z}$*, let* $\mathcal{A}_{\mathbf{s},\chi}$ *be a distribution obtained by sampling a matrix* $\mathbf{A} \in \mathbb{Z}_q^{n \times m}$*, a vector* $\mathbf{e} \leftarrow_R \chi^m$*, and outputting* $(\mathbf{A}, \mathbf{A}^\top \mathbf{s} + \mathbf{e})$*, to distinguish* $\mathcal{A}_{\mathbf{s},\chi}$ *and a uniform distribution* $\mathcal{U}$ *over* $\mathbb{Z}_q^{n \times m} \times \mathbb{Z}_q^m$*.*

Let $\beta \geq \sqrt{n} \cdot \omega(\log n)$, if q is a prime power, and χ is β-bounded distribution, then the $\mathsf{LWE}_{n,q,\chi}$ problem is as least as hard as $\mathsf{SIVP}_{\widetilde{\mathcal{O}}(nq/\beta)}$.

3   The Identity-Encoding Technique

Our construction of Stern-type statistical zero-knowledge proof protocol builds on an efficient and compact identity-encoding technique introduced by Nguyen et al. [25]. We describe it briefly. This technique takes only three public matrices (one more public matrix needed is just used to open the group signature) in group public-key (Gpk), that is, $\mathsf{Gpk} = (\mathbf{A}_0, \mathbf{A}_1, \mathbf{A}_2, \mathbf{B})$, where $\mathbf{A}_{i \in \{0,1,2\}}$, $\mathbf{B} \in \mathbb{Z}_q^{n \times m}$. To generate the secret-key for member i, it just needs to define a different matrix $\mathbf{A}_i = [\mathbf{A}_0 | \mathbf{A}_1 + i\mathbf{A}_2] \in \mathbb{Z}_q^{n \times 2m}$, where $i \in \{1, 2, \cdots, N\}$ is the group member identity index. The group secret-key (gsk) of member i is a short trapdoor basis of a classical q-ary lattice $\Lambda_q^{\perp}(\mathbf{A}_i) = \{\mathbf{e}_i \in \mathbb{Z}^{2m} \text{ s.t. } \mathbf{A}_i \cdot \mathbf{e}_i = \mathbf{0} \bmod q\}$. The maximum number of group members $N < q$ is required for the collision resistance, and this can be set simply (just setting q, a polynomial in security parameter n, big enough).

The above identity-encoding technique provides two main following benefits:

- It just needs three matrices for the identity-encoding, thus this construction provides a shorter group public-key compared with others which have the number of public matrices at least $\mathcal{O}(\log N)$.
- It shows a simple group membership relation, which allows to construct an efficient statistical zero-knowledge proof protocol for this relation.

In our VLR construction, we propose a new variant of the identity-encoding technique, the public matrix $\mathbf{B} \in \mathbb{Z}_q^{n \times m}$ is replaced by certain uniformly random vector $\mathbf{u} \leftarrow_R \mathbb{Z}_q^n$, that is, $\mathsf{Gpk} = (\mathbf{A}_0, \mathbf{A}_1, \mathbf{A}_2, \mathbf{u})$ and the group secret-key of i is not a trapdoor basis instead of a short $2m$-dimensional vector $\mathbf{e}_i = (\mathbf{e}_{i,1}, \mathbf{e}_{i,2}) \in \mathbb{Z}^{2m}$ which is in a coset of $\Lambda_q^{\perp}(\mathbf{A}_i)$, that is, $\Lambda_q^{\mathbf{u}}(\mathbf{A}_i) = \{\mathbf{e}_i \text{ s.t. } \mathbf{A}_i \cdot \mathbf{e}_i = \mathbf{u} \bmod q\}$. The revocation token of member i is constructed by $\mathbf{A}_0$ and the first part of the group secret-key, that is, the revocation token $\mathsf{grt}_i = \mathbf{A}_0 \mathbf{e}_{i,1} \bmod q \in \mathbb{Z}_q^n$.

In order to construct an efficient Stern-type statistical zero-knowledge proof protocol, we transform $\mathbf{A}_i = [\mathbf{A}_0 | \mathbf{A}_1 + i\mathbf{A}_2]$ corresponding to member i to some new form. Before do that, we first define two notations:

1. $\mathbf{g}_{\lceil \log N \rceil} = (1, 2^1, 2^2, \cdots, 2^{\lceil \log N \rceil - 1})$: a power-of-two vector, thus for any integer $i \in \{1, 2, \cdots, N\}$, $i = \mathbf{g}_{\lceil \log N \rceil}^{\top} \cdot \mathrm{bin}(i)$, where $\mathrm{bin}(i) \in \{0, 1\}^{\lceil \log N \rceil}$ denotes the binary representation of integer i.
2. $\otimes$: a concatenation with certain vectors or matrices, given $\mathbf{e}' \in \mathbb{Z}_q^m$, $\mathbf{A} \in \mathbb{Z}_q^{n \times m}$ and $\mathbf{e} = (e_1, e_2, \cdots, e_{\lceil \log N \rceil}) \in \mathbb{Z}_q^{\lceil \log N \rceil}$,

$$\mathbf{e} \otimes \mathbf{e}' = (e_1 \mathbf{e}', e_2 \mathbf{e}', \cdots, e_{\lceil \log N \rceil} \mathbf{e}') \in \mathbb{Z}_q^{m \lceil \log N \rceil},$$
$$\mathbf{e} \otimes \mathbf{A} = [e_1 \mathbf{A} | e_2 \mathbf{A} | \cdots | e_{\lceil \log N \rceil} \mathbf{A}] \in \mathbb{Z}_q^{n \times m \lceil \log N \rceil}.$$

We now transform $\mathbf{A}_i$ to certain public matrix $\mathbf{A}'$ that is independent of the identity index of member i,

$$\begin{aligned} \mathbf{A}' &= [\mathbf{A}_0 | \mathbf{A}_1 | \mathbf{A}_2 | 2\mathbf{A}_2 | \cdots | 2^{\lceil \log N \rceil - 1} \mathbf{A}_2] \\ &= [\mathbf{A}_0 | \mathbf{A}_1 | \mathbf{g}_{\lceil \log N \rceil} \otimes \mathbf{A}_2] \in \mathbb{Z}_q^{n \times (\lceil \log N \rceil + 2)m}. \end{aligned}$$

As a corresponding change to the secret-key of member i, $\mathbf{e}_i = (\mathbf{e}_{i,1}, \mathbf{e}_{i,2}) \in \mathbb{Z}^{2m}$ is transformed into $\mathbf{e}_i'$, a vector with a special structure as for $\mathbf{e}_i$,

$$\mathbf{e}_i' = (\mathbf{e}_{i,1}, \mathbf{e}_{i,2}, \text{bin}(i) \otimes \mathbf{e}_{i,2}) \in \mathbb{Z}^{(\lceil \log N \rceil + 2)m}.$$

Thus, from the above transformation, the relation $\mathbf{A}_i \cdot \mathbf{e}_i = \mathbf{u} \bmod q$ can be transformed into a new form,

$$\mathbf{A}_i \cdot \mathbf{e}_i = \mathbf{A}' \cdot \mathbf{e}_i' = \mathbf{u} \bmod q. \tag{1}$$

For the revocation mechanism, as it was stated in [18], due to some flaw in the revocation mechanism in [14] which adopts a kind of *inequality test* method to check whether the signer's revocation token belong to the given revocation list (RL) or not, a corrected technique which realizes revocation by binding signer's token grt_i to an LWE function was proposed,

$$\mathbf{b} = \mathbf{B}^\top \text{grt}_i + \mathbf{e} = (\mathbf{B}^\top \mathbf{A}_0) \cdot \mathbf{e}_{i,1} + \mathbf{e} \bmod q. \tag{2}$$

where $\mathbf{B} \in \mathbb{Z}_q^{n \times m}$ is a uniformly random matrix from a random oracle, $\mathbf{e} \in \mathbb{Z}^m$ is from the LWE error χ.

Putting both the above transformations idea and the versatility of the Stern-extension argument system introduced by Ling et al. [19] together, we can use the creative Stern-type statistical zero-knowledge proof protocol (see Sect. 4 for the details) to prove the above relations (1) and (2).

4   A New Stern-Type Interactive Protocol

In this section, we introduce a new Stern-type statistical zero-knowledge proof protocol which allows a member $\mathcal{P}$ to convince any verifier $\mathcal{V}$ that $\mathcal{P}$ is indeed a group member who has signed the message $\mathsf{m} \in \{0, 1\}^*$, i.e., $\mathcal{P}$ has a valid group secret-key, and its corresponding revocation token is correctly embedded in an LWE instance.

4.1   Some Sets and Techniques

Given $\text{id} = (d_1, d_2, \cdots, d_\ell) \in \{0, 1\}^\ell$, we now define four sets:

1. $\mathsf{B}_{2\ell}$: the set of all vectors in $\{0, 1\}^{2\ell}$ having the Hamming weight ℓ.
2. B_{3m}: the set of all vectors in $\{-1, 0, 1\}^{3m}$ having m coordinates -1, m coordinates 1, and m coordinates 0.
3. $\mathsf{Sec}_\beta(\text{id})$: the set of all vectors having the specific structure and norm, that is, $\mathbf{e} = (\mathbf{e}_1, \mathbf{e}_2, d_1\mathbf{e}_2, \cdots, d_\ell\mathbf{e}_2) \in \mathbb{Z}_q^{(\ell+2)m}$, $\|\mathbf{e}\|_\infty \leq \beta$.
4. $\mathsf{SecExt}(\text{id}^*)$: the set of all vectors having the specific structure, that is to say, $\mathbf{e} = (\mathbf{e}_1, \mathbf{e}_2, d_1\mathbf{e}_2, \cdots, d_{2\ell}\mathbf{e}_2) \in \{-1, 0, 1\}^{(2\ell+2)3m}$ for $\text{id}^* \in \mathsf{B}_{2\ell}$, an extension of id, and $\mathbf{e}_1, \mathbf{e}_2 \in \mathsf{B}_{3m}$.

Given $\mathbf{e} = (\mathbf{e}_{-1}, \mathbf{e}_0, \mathbf{e}_1, \cdots, \mathbf{e}_{2\ell}) \in \mathbb{Z}_q^{(2\ell+2)3m}$, for permutations $\pi, \varphi \in \mathcal{S}_{3m}$, $\tau \in \mathcal{S}_{2\ell}$, we define a composition $\mathcal{F}$,

$$\mathcal{F}_{\pi,\varphi,\tau}(\mathbf{e}) = (\pi(\mathbf{e}_{-1}), \varphi(\mathbf{e}_0), \varphi(\mathbf{e}_{\tau(1)}), \cdots, \varphi(\mathbf{e}_{\tau(2\ell)})).$$

In particular, given $\mathsf{id} \in \{0,1\}^\ell$, π, $\varphi \in \mathcal{S}_{3m}$, $\tau \in \mathcal{S}_{2\ell}$ and $\mathbf{e} \in \mathbb{Z}_q^{(2\ell+2)3m}$, it can be checked that,

$$\mathbf{e} \in \mathsf{SecExt}(\mathsf{id}^*) \Leftrightarrow \mathcal{F}_{\pi,\varphi,\tau}(\mathbf{e}) \in \mathsf{SecExt}(\tau(\mathsf{id}^*)),$$

where $\mathsf{id}^* \in \mathsf{B}_{2\ell}$ is an extension of id.

We recall the Decomposition-Extension (Dec-Ext) technique which was first introduced in [14,20].

Let $k = \lfloor \log\beta \rfloor + 1$ and define a sequence of integers,

$$\beta_1 = \lceil \beta/2 \rceil, \ \beta_2 = \lceil (\beta - \beta_1)/2 \rceil, \ \beta_3 = \lceil (\beta - \beta_1 - \beta_2)/2 \rceil, \cdots, \ \beta_k = 1.$$

Decomposition: Given $\mathbf{e} = (e_1, e_2, \cdots, e_m) \in \mathbb{Z}^m$, and $\|\mathbf{e}\|_\infty \leq \beta$, the goal is to represent it by k vectors in $\{-1,0,1\}^m$. The procedure Dec works as follows:

1. For index $i \in \{1, 2, \cdots, m\}$, express e_i as $\sum_{j=1}^k \beta_j e_{i,j}$, where $e_{i,j} \in \{-1,0,1\}$.
2. For each $j \in \{1, 2, \cdots, k\}$, define $\widehat{\mathbf{e}}_j = (e_{1,j}, e_{2,j}, \cdots, e_{m,j})$.

Thus, we have $\widehat{\mathbf{e}}_j \in \{-1,0,1\}^m$ and $\mathbf{e} = \sum_{j=1}^k \beta_j \widehat{\mathbf{e}}_j$.

Extension: Given $\widehat{\mathbf{e}}_j \in \{-1,0,1\}^m$, the goal is to extend it into $\mathbf{e}_j \in \mathsf{B}_{3m}$. The procedure Ext works as follows:

1. Count the numbers of coordinates -1, 0 and 1 in $\widehat{\mathbf{e}}_j$ are λ_{-1}, λ_0 and λ_1, respectively.
2. Choose a random $\mathbf{e}'_j \in \{-1,0,1\}^{2m}$ which has the numbers of coordinates -1, 0 and 1 exactly $(m - \lambda_{-1})$, $(m - \lambda_0)$ and $(m - \lambda_1)$, respectively.
3. Denote $\mathbf{e}_j = (\widehat{\mathbf{e}}_j, \mathbf{e}'_j) \in \{-1,0,1\}^{3m}$.

Thus, for all $\pi \in \mathcal{S}_{3m}$, we have $\mathbf{e} \in \mathsf{B}_{3m} \Leftrightarrow \pi(\mathbf{e}) \in \mathsf{B}_{3m}$.

Matrix Extension: Given $\mathbf{A}' = [\mathbf{A}|\mathbf{A}_0|\mathbf{A}_1|\cdots|\mathbf{A}_\ell] \in \mathbb{Z}_q^{n\times(\ell+2)m}$, the goal is to extend it into $\mathbf{A}^* \in \mathbb{Z}_q^{n\times(2\ell+2)3m}$. The procedure Matrix-Ext works as follows:

1. Add the matrix $\mathbf{0}^{n\times 2m}$ to each of component-matrices and ℓ blocks of $\mathbf{0}^{3m}$.
2. Output $\mathbf{A}^* = [\mathbf{A}|\mathbf{0}^{n\times 2m}|\mathbf{A}_0|\mathbf{0}^{n\times 2m}|\cdots|\mathbf{A}_\ell|\mathbf{0}^{n\times 2m}|\mathbf{0}^{n\times 3m\ell}]$.

4.2   The Statistical Zero-Knowledge Proof Protocol

We consider the group of $N = 2^\ell$ members, and each member is identified by a string $\mathsf{id} = (d_1, d_2, \cdots, d_\ell) \in \{0,1\}^\ell$ which is a binary representation of its index $i \in \{1, 2, \cdots, N\}$, that is, $\mathsf{id} = \mathsf{bin}(i) \in \{0,1\}^\ell$.

Let n be the security parameter, and other parameters are set as follows:

- The maximum number of group members $N = \mathsf{poly}(n)$.
- The prime modulus $q = \omega(n^2 \log n) > N$.
- The dimension $m = 2n\lceil \log q \rceil$, Gaussian parameter $s = \omega(\sqrt{n \log q \log n})$.
- The integer norm bound $\beta = \lceil s \cdot \log m \rceil$ s.t. $(4\beta + 1)^2 \leq q$.

The underlying new Stern-type statistical zero-knowledge proof protocol between the prover $\mathcal{P}$ and the verifier $\mathcal{V}$ can be summarized as follows:

1. The public inputs are $\mathbf{A}' = [\mathbf{A}_0 | \mathbf{A}_1 | \mathbf{g}_\ell \otimes \mathbf{A}_2] \in \mathbb{Z}_q^{n \times (\ell+2)m}$, $\mathbf{u} \in \mathbb{Z}_q^n$, $\mathbf{B} \in \mathbb{Z}_q^{n \times m}$, and $\mathbf{b} \in \mathbb{Z}_q^m$.
2. $\mathcal{P}$'s witnesses are $\mathbf{e}' = (\mathbf{e}'_1, \mathbf{e}'_2, \mathsf{bin}(i) \otimes \mathbf{e}'_2) \in \mathsf{Sec}_\beta(\mathsf{id})$ corresponding to a secret index $i \in \{1, 2, \cdots, N\}$, and $\mathbf{e} \in \mathbb{Z}^m$, an LWE error.
3. $\mathcal{P}$'s goal is to convince $\mathcal{V}$ in zero-knowledge that:
   a. $\mathbf{A}' \cdot \mathbf{e}' = \mathbf{u} \bmod q$ where $\mathbf{e}' \in \mathsf{Sec}_\beta(\mathsf{id})$, while keeping $\mathsf{id} = \mathsf{bin}(i) \in \{0,1\}^\ell$ secret.
   b. $\mathbf{b} = (\mathbf{B}^\top \mathbf{A}_0) \cdot \mathbf{e}'_1 + \mathbf{e} \bmod q$ where $0 < \|\mathbf{e}'_1\|_\infty, \|\mathbf{e}\|_\infty \leq \beta$.

Firstly, we sketch our group membership mechanism, that is, $\mathcal{P}$ is a certified member and its goal is showed in a. $\mathcal{P}$ does as follows:

1. Parse $\mathbf{A}' = [\mathbf{A}_0 | \mathbf{A}_1 | \mathbf{g}_\ell \otimes \mathbf{A}_2] = [\mathbf{A}_0 | \mathbf{A}_1 | \mathbf{A}_2 | 2\mathbf{A}_2 | \cdots | 2^{\ell-1}\mathbf{A}_2]$, use Matrix-Ext technique extending it to,

$$\mathbf{A}^* = [\mathbf{A}_0 | \mathbf{0}^{n \times 2m} | \mathbf{A}_1 | \mathbf{0}^{n \times 2m} | \mathbf{A}_2 | \mathbf{0}^{n \times 2m} | \cdots | 2^{\ell-1}\mathbf{A}_2 | \mathbf{0}^{n \times 2m} | \mathbf{0}^{n \times 3m\ell}].$$

2. Parse $\mathsf{id} = \mathsf{bin}(i) = (d_1, d_2, \cdots, d_\ell) \in \{0,1\}^\ell$, extend it to

$$\mathsf{id}^* = (d_1, d_2, \cdots, d_\ell, d_{\ell+1}, \cdots, d_{2\ell}) \in \mathsf{B}_{2\ell}.$$

3. Parse $\mathbf{e}' = (\mathbf{e}'_1, \mathbf{e}'_2, \mathsf{bin}(i) \otimes \mathbf{e}'_2) = (\mathbf{e}'_1, \mathbf{e}'_2, d_1\mathbf{e}'_2, d_2\mathbf{e}'_2, \cdots, d_\ell\mathbf{e}'_2)$, use Dec and Ext techniques extending $\mathbf{e}'_1$ and $\mathbf{e}'_2$ into k vectors $\mathbf{e}'_{1,1}, \mathbf{e}'_{1,2}, \cdots, \mathbf{e}'_{1,k} \in \mathsf{B}_{3m}$, and k vectors $\mathbf{e}'_{2,1}, \mathbf{e}'_{2,2}, \cdots, \mathbf{e}'_{2,k} \in \mathsf{B}_{3m}$, respectively. For each $j \in \{1, 2, \cdots, k\}$, we define a vector $\mathbf{e}'_j = (\mathbf{e}'_{1,j}, \mathbf{e}'_{2,j}, d_1\mathbf{e}'_{2,j}, d_2\mathbf{e}'_{2,j}, \cdots, d_{2\ell}\mathbf{e}'_{2,j})$, it can be checked that $\mathbf{e}'_j \in \mathsf{SecExt}(\mathsf{id}^*)$.
   Thus, $\mathcal{P}$'s goal in a is transformed into a new structure,

$$\mathbf{A}^* \cdot \left(\sum_{j=1}^k \beta_j \mathbf{e}'_j\right) = \mathbf{u} \bmod q, \text{ and } \mathbf{e}'_j \in \mathsf{SecExt}(\mathsf{id}^*). \tag{3}$$

To prove the new relation (3) in zero-knowledge, we take two steps as follows:

1. Pick k uniformly random vectors $\mathbf{r}'_1, \cdots, \mathbf{r}'_k \in \mathbb{Z}_q^{(2\ell+2)3m}$ to mask $\mathbf{e}'_1, \cdots, \mathbf{e}'_k$, it can be check that,

$$\mathbf{A}^* \cdot \left(\sum_{j=1}^k \beta_j(\mathbf{e}'_j + \mathbf{r}'_j)\right) - \mathbf{u} = \mathbf{A}^* \cdot \left(\sum_{j=1}^k \beta_j \mathbf{r}'_j\right) \bmod q.$$

2. Pick two permutations $\pi, \varphi \in \mathcal{S}_{3m}$, one permutation $\tau \in \mathcal{S}_{2\ell}$, it can be checked that,

$$\forall j \in \{1, 2, \cdots, k\}, \ \mathcal{F}_{\pi,\varphi,\tau}(\mathbf{e}'_j) \in \mathsf{SecExt}(\tau(\mathsf{id}^*)),$$

where $\mathsf{id}^* \in \mathsf{B}_{2\ell}$ is an extension of $\mathsf{id} = \mathsf{bin}(i) \in \{0,1\}^\ell$.

Secondly, we sketch our revocation mechanism, that is, $\mathcal{P}$'s revocation token is correctly embedded in an LWE instance. $\mathcal{P}$ does as follows:

1. Let $\mathbf{B}' = \mathbf{B}^\top \mathbf{A}_0 \bmod q \in \mathbb{Z}_q^{m \times m}$, $\mathbf{e}'_{j,0} = \mathsf{Parse}(\mathbf{e}'_j, 1, m)$.
2. Parse $\mathbf{e} = (e_1, e_2, \cdots, e_m) \in \mathbb{Z}^m$, use Dec and Ext techniques extending $\mathbf{e}$ into k vectors $\mathbf{e}_1, \mathbf{e}_2, \cdots, \mathbf{e}_k \in \mathsf{B}_{3m}$.
3. Let $\mathbf{B}^* = [\mathbf{B}'|\mathbf{I}^*]$ where $\mathbf{I}^* = [\mathbf{I}_m|\mathbf{0}^{n \times 2m}]$, $\mathbf{I}_m$ is the identity matrix of order m.

Thus, $\mathcal{P}$'s goal in b is transformed into a new structure,

$$
\begin{aligned}
\mathbf{b} &= \mathbf{B}' \cdot (\textstyle\sum_{j=1}^k \beta_j \mathbf{e}'_{j,0}) + \mathbf{I}^* \cdot (\textstyle\sum_{j=1}^k \beta_j \mathbf{e}_j) \\
&= \mathbf{B}^* \cdot (\textstyle\sum_{j=1}^k \beta_j (\mathbf{e}'_{j,0}, \mathbf{e}_j)) \bmod q, \ \text{and} \ \mathbf{e}_j \in \mathsf{B}_{3m}.
\end{aligned}
\tag{4}
$$

To prove the new relation (4) in zero-knowledge, we take two steps as follows:

1. Let $\mathbf{r}'_{j,0} = \mathsf{Parse}(\mathbf{r}'_j, 1, m)$.
2. Pick k uniformly random vectors $\mathbf{r}_1, \cdots, \mathbf{r}_k \in \mathbb{Z}_q^{3m}$ to mask $\mathbf{e}_1, \cdots, \mathbf{e}_k$, it can be check that,

$$
\mathbf{B}^* \cdot (\textstyle\sum_{j=1}^k \beta_j (\mathbf{e}'_{j,0} + \mathbf{r}'_{j,0}, \mathbf{e}_j + \mathbf{r}_j)) - \mathbf{b} = \mathbf{B}^* \cdot (\textstyle\sum_{j=1}^k \beta_j (\mathbf{r}'_{j,0}, \mathbf{r}_j)) \bmod q.
$$

3. Pick one permutation $\phi \in \mathcal{S}_{3m}$, it can be checked that,

$$
\forall j \in \{1, 2, \cdots, k\}, \ \phi(\mathbf{e}_j) \in \mathsf{B}_{3m}.
$$

Putting the above techniques together, we can obtain a new interactive Stern-type statistical zero-knowledge proof protocol, the details will be given bellow. Furthermore, the new Stern-type interactive protocol can be repeated $\omega(\log n)$ times to make the soundness error negligibly small and transformed into an efficient non-interactive protocol by using the Fiat-Shamir heuristic in the random oracle model.

We utilize a statistically hiding and computationally blinding *commitment scheme* (COM) proposed in [11]. For simplicity, we omit the randomness of COM. The prover $\mathcal{P}$ and the verifier $\mathcal{V}$ interact as follows:

1. Commitments: $\mathcal{P}$ randomly samples the following random objects:

$$
\begin{cases}
\mathbf{r}'_1, \mathbf{r}'_2, \cdots, \mathbf{r}'_k \in \mathbb{Z}_q^{(2\ell+2)3m}; \mathbf{r}_1, \mathbf{r}_2, \cdots, \mathbf{r}_k \in \mathbb{Z}_q^{3m}; \\
\pi_1, \pi_2, \cdots, \pi_k \in \mathcal{S}_{3m}; \varphi_1, \varphi_2, \cdots, \varphi_k \in \mathcal{S}_{3m}; \\
\phi_1, \phi_2, \cdots, \phi_k \in \mathcal{S}_{3m}; \tau \in \mathcal{S}_{2\ell}.
\end{cases}
$$

For each $j \in \{1, 2, \cdots, k\}$, let $\mathbf{r}'_{j,0} = \mathsf{Parse}(\mathbf{r}'_j, 1, m)$, $\mathcal{P}$ sends the commitment $\mathsf{CMT} = (\mathbf{c}_1, \mathbf{c}_2, \mathbf{c}_3)$ to $\mathcal{V}$, where

$$
\begin{cases}
\mathbf{c}_1 = \mathsf{COM}(\{\pi_j, \varphi_j, \phi_j\}_{j=1}^k, \tau; \mathbf{A}^* \cdot (\textstyle\sum_{j=1}^k \beta_j \mathbf{r}_j); \mathbf{B}^* \cdot (\textstyle\sum_{j=1}^k \beta_j (\mathbf{r}'_{j,0}, \mathbf{r}_j))), \\
\mathbf{c}_2 = \mathsf{COM}(\{\mathcal{F}_{\pi_j, \varphi_j, \tau}(\mathbf{r}'_j), \phi_j(\mathbf{r}_j)\}_{j=1}^k), \\
\mathbf{c}_3 = \mathsf{COM}(\{\mathcal{F}_{\pi_j, \varphi_j, \tau}(\mathbf{e}'_j + \mathbf{r}'_j), \phi_j(\mathbf{e}_j + \mathbf{r}_j)\}_{j=1}^k).
\end{cases}
$$

2. Challenge: $\mathcal{V}$ randomly chooses a challenge $\mathsf{CH} \leftarrow_R \{1, 2, 3\}$ and sends it to $\mathcal{P}$.
3. Response: Depending on CH, $\mathcal{P}$ replies as follows:
   - $\mathsf{CH} = 1$. For each $j \in \{1, 2, \cdots, k\}$, let $\mathbf{v}'_j = \mathcal{F}_{\pi_j, \varphi_j, \tau}(\mathbf{e}'_j)$, $\mathbf{w}'_j = \mathcal{F}_{\pi_j, \varphi_j, \tau}(\mathbf{r}'_j)$, $\mathbf{v}_j = \phi_j(\mathbf{e}_j)$, $\mathbf{w}_j = \phi_j(\mathbf{r}_j)$, $\mathsf{t}_{\mathsf{id}} = \tau(\mathsf{id}^*)$, define

$$\mathsf{RSP} = (\{\mathbf{v}'_j, \mathbf{w}'_j, \mathbf{v}_j, \mathbf{w}_j\}_{j=1}^k, \mathsf{t}_{\mathsf{id}}). \tag{5}$$

   - $\mathsf{CH} = 2$. For each $j \in \{1, 2, \cdots, k\}$, let $\hat{\pi}_j = \pi_j$, $\hat{\varphi}_j = \varphi_j$, $\hat{\phi}_j = \phi_j$, $\hat{\tau} = \tau$, $\mathbf{x}'_j = \mathbf{e}'_j + \mathbf{r}'_j$, $\mathbf{x}_j = \mathbf{e}_j + \mathbf{r}_j$, define

$$\mathsf{RSP} = (\{\hat{\pi}_j, \hat{\varphi}_j, \hat{\phi}_j, \mathbf{x}'_j, \mathbf{x}_j\}_{j=1}^k, \hat{\tau}). \tag{6}$$

   - $\mathsf{CH} = 3$. For each $j \in \{1, 2, \cdots, k\}$, let $\tilde{\pi}_j = \pi_j$, $\tilde{\varphi}_j = \varphi_j$, $\tilde{\phi}_j = \phi_j$, $\tilde{\tau} = \tau$, $\mathbf{h}'_j = \mathbf{r}'_j$, $\mathbf{h}_j = \mathbf{r}_j$, define

$$\mathsf{RSP} = (\{\tilde{\pi}_j, \tilde{\varphi}_j, \tilde{\phi}_j, \mathbf{h}'_j, \mathbf{h}_j\}_{j=1}^k, \tilde{\tau}). \tag{7}$$

4. Verification: Receiving RSP, $\mathcal{V}$ checks as follows:
   - $\mathsf{CH} = 1$. Check that $\mathbf{t}_{\mathsf{id}} \in \mathsf{B}_{2\ell}$, for each $j \in \{1, 2, \cdots, k\}$, $\mathbf{v}'_j \in \mathsf{SecExt}(\mathbf{t}_{\mathsf{id}})$, $\mathbf{v}_j \in \mathsf{B}_{3m}$, and that,

$$\begin{cases} \mathbf{c}_2 = \mathsf{COM}(\{\mathbf{w}'_j, \mathbf{w}_j\}_{j=1}^k), \\ \mathbf{c}_3 = \mathsf{COM}(\{\mathbf{v}'_j + \mathbf{w}'_j, \mathbf{v}_j + \mathbf{w}_j\}_{j=1}^k). \end{cases}$$

   - $\mathsf{CH} = 2$. For $j \in \{1, 2, \cdots, k\}$, let $\mathbf{x}'_{j,0} = \mathsf{Parse}(\mathbf{x}'_j, 1, m)$, and check that,

$$\begin{cases} \mathbf{c}_1 = \mathsf{COM}(\{\hat{\pi}_j, \hat{\varphi}_j, \hat{\phi}_j\}_{j=1}^k, \hat{\tau}; \mathbf{A}^*(\sum_{j=1}^k \beta_j \mathbf{x}'_j) - \mathbf{u}; \mathbf{B}^*(\sum_{j=1}^k \beta_j(\mathbf{x}'_{j,0}, \mathbf{x}_j) - \mathbf{b})), \\ \mathbf{c}_3 = \mathsf{COM}(\{\mathcal{F}_{\hat{\pi}_j, \hat{\varphi}_j, \hat{\tau}}(\mathbf{x}'_j), \hat{\phi}_j(\mathbf{x}_j)\}_{j=1}^k). \end{cases}$$

   - $\mathsf{CH} = 3$. For $j \in \{1, 2, \cdots, k\}$, let $\mathbf{h}'_{j,0} = \mathsf{Parse}(\mathbf{h}'_j, 1, m)$, and check that,

$$\begin{cases} \mathbf{c}_1 = \mathsf{COM}(\{\tilde{\pi}_j, \tilde{\varphi}_j, \tilde{\phi}_j\}_{j=1}^k, \tilde{\tau}; \mathbf{A}^* \cdot (\sum_{j=1}^k \beta_j \mathbf{h}'_j); \mathbf{B}^* \cdot (\sum_{j=1}^k \beta_j(\mathbf{h}'_{j,0}, \mathbf{h}_j))), \\ \mathbf{c}_2 = \mathsf{COM}(\{\mathcal{F}_{\tilde{\pi}_j, \tilde{\varphi}_j, \tilde{\tau}}(\mathbf{h}'_j), \tilde{\phi}_j(\mathbf{h}_j)\}_{j=1}^k). \end{cases}$$

The verifier $\mathcal{V}$ outputs 1 iff all the above conditions hold, otherwise 0.

Thus, the associated relation $\mathcal{R}(n, k, \ell, q, m, \beta)$ in the above protocol can be defined as:

$$\mathcal{R} = \left\{ \begin{array}{l} \mathbf{A}_0, \mathbf{A}_1, \mathbf{A}_2, \mathbf{B} \in \mathbb{Z}_q^{n \times m}, \mathbf{u} \in \mathbb{Z}_q^n, \mathbf{b} \in \mathbb{Z}_q^m, \mathsf{id} = \mathsf{bin}(i), \\ \mathbf{e}' = (\mathbf{e}'_1, \mathbf{e}'_2, \mathsf{bin}(i) \otimes \mathbf{e}'_2) \in \mathsf{Sec}_\beta(\mathsf{id}), \mathbf{e} \in \mathbb{Z}^m; \, s.t. \\ 0 < \|\mathbf{e}'\|_\infty, \|\mathbf{e}\|_\infty \leq \beta, \mathbf{b} = (\mathbf{B}^\top \mathbf{A}_0) \cdot \mathbf{e}'_1 + \mathbf{e} \bmod q, \\ [\mathbf{A}_0 | \mathbf{A}_1 | \mathbf{g}_\ell \otimes \mathbf{A}'_2] \cdot \mathbf{e}' = \mathbf{u} \bmod q. \end{array} \right\}$$

5   Analysis of the Protocol

Theorem 1. *Assume that* COM *is a statistically hiding and computationally binding commitment scheme, for a given commitment* CMT, *3 valid responses* RSP_1, RSP_2 *and* RSP_3 *with respect to different challenges* CH_1, CH_2 *and* CH_3, *the proposed protocol is a statistical zero-knowledge argument of knowledge for* $\mathcal{R}(n, k, \ell, q, m, \beta)$, *where each round has perfect completeness, soundness error* $2/3$, *argument of knowledge property and communication cost* $\widetilde{\mathcal{O}}(\ell n \log \beta)$.

5.1   Communication Cost

- The output of COM has bit-sizes $n \log q$, thus $\mathcal{P}$ sends 3 commitments amounting to $3n \log q$ bits.
- The challenge $\mathsf{CH} \in \{1, 2, 3\}$ can be represented by 2 bits.
- The response RSP from $\mathcal{P}$ consist of the following items:
    - One permutation in $\mathcal{S}_{2\ell}$, $3k$ permutations in $\mathcal{S}_{3m}$.
    - $2k$ vectors in $\mathbb{Z}_q^{(2\ell+2)3m}$, $2k$ vectors in $\mathbb{Z}_q^{3m}$, one vector in $\{0, 1\}^{2\ell}$.

Thus, the bit-size of RSP is bound by $\mathcal{O}(\ell m k) \log q$. Recall that $k = \lfloor \log \beta \rfloor + 1$, the communication cost of the proposed Stern-type statistical zero-knowledge protocol is bounded by $\mathcal{O}(\ell m \log \beta) \log q = \widetilde{\mathcal{O}}(\ell n \log \beta)$.

5.2   Completeness

To show that provided a tuple $(\mathbf{A}_0, \mathbf{A}_1, \mathbf{A}_2, \mathbf{u}, \mathbf{B}, \mathbf{b})$, if an honest prover $\mathcal{P}$ owns witness $(\mathsf{id} = \mathsf{bin}(i) \in \{0, 1\}^\ell, \mathbf{e}' \in \mathsf{Sec}_\beta(\mathsf{id}), \mathbf{e} \in \mathbb{Z}^m)$ and follows the proposed protocol, $\mathcal{P}$ can generate an efficient Stern-type zero-knowledge proof such that it satisfies the verification and gets accepted by $\mathcal{V}$ with a high probability.

The public inputs and witnesses are first transformed into $\mathbf{A}^*$, $\mathbf{B}^*$, id^*, and $\{\mathbf{e}'_j, \mathbf{e}_j, \mathbf{e}'_{j,0} = \mathbf{Parse}(\mathbf{e}'_j, 1, m)\}_{j=1}^k$ by $\mathcal{P}$ with the Dec, Ext and Matrix-Ext techniques, thus these new results satisfy the following new structures,

$$\mathbf{A}^* \cdot \left(\textstyle\sum_{j=1}^k \beta_j \mathbf{e}'_j\right) = \mathbf{u} \bmod q, \text{ and } \mathbf{e}'_j \in \mathsf{SecExt}(\mathsf{id}^*),$$

$$\mathbf{B}^* \cdot \left(\textstyle\sum_{j=1}^k \beta_j(\mathbf{e}'_{j,0}, \mathbf{e}_j)\right) = \mathbf{b} \bmod q, \text{ and } \mathbf{e}_j \in \mathsf{B}_{3m}.$$

Next, to show that $\mathcal{P}$ can correctly pass the verification checks for each challenge $\mathsf{CH} \in \{1, 2, 3\}$ with a high probability. Furthermore, apart from considering the checks for correct computations, it only needs to note that:

○ $\mathsf{CH} = 1$. Since $\mathsf{id} = \mathsf{bin}(i) \in \{0, 1\}^\ell$, $\mathsf{id}^* \in \mathsf{B}_{2\ell}$ is an extension of id and $\mathsf{B}_{2\ell}$ is invariant under the permutation $\tau \in \mathcal{S}_{2\ell}$, we have $\mathbf{t}_{\mathsf{id}} = \tau(\mathsf{id}^*) \in \mathsf{B}_{2\ell}$. Similarly, for $j \in \{1, 2, \cdots, k\}$, $\mathbf{e}_j \in \mathsf{B}_{3m}$, and B_{3m} is invariant under $\phi_j \in \mathcal{S}_{3m}$, we have $\mathbf{v}_j = \phi_j(\mathbf{e}_j) \in \mathsf{B}_{3m}$. As it is discussed in Sect. 4.1, we have

$$\mathbf{v}'_j = \mathcal{F}_{\pi_j, \varphi_j, \tau}(\mathbf{e}'_j) \in \mathsf{SecExt}(\tau(\mathsf{id}^*)) = \mathsf{SecExt}(\mathbf{t}_{\mathsf{id}}).$$

○ CH = 2. The key point is to check $\mathbf{c}_1$. For $j \in \{1, 2, \cdots, k\}$, $\mathcal{P}$ can pass this step by generating $\mathbf{x}'_j$, $\mathbf{r}'_j$, $\mathbf{x}_j$, $\mathbf{x}'_{j,0}$, $\mathbf{r}'_{j,0}$, $\mathbf{r}_j$ such that the following holds true:

$$\mathbf{A}^* \cdot (\textstyle\sum_{j=1}^k \beta_j \mathbf{x}'_j) - \mathbf{u} = \mathbf{A}^* \cdot (\textstyle\sum_{j=1}^k \beta_j (\mathbf{e}'_j + \mathbf{r}'_j)) - \mathbf{u}$$
$$= \mathbf{A}^* \cdot (\textstyle\sum_{j=1}^k \beta_j \mathbf{r}'_j) \bmod q,$$
$$\mathbf{B}^* \cdot (\textstyle\sum_{j=1}^k \beta_j (\mathbf{x}'_{j,0}, \mathbf{x}_j)) - \mathbf{b} = \mathbf{B}^* \cdot (\textstyle\sum_{j=1}^k \beta_j (\mathbf{e}'_{j,0} + \mathbf{r}'_{j,0}, \mathbf{e}_j + \mathbf{r}_j)) - \mathbf{b}$$
$$= \mathbf{B}^* \cdot (\textstyle\sum_{j=1}^k \beta_j (\mathbf{r}'_{j,0}, \mathbf{r}_j)) \bmod q.$$

○ CH = 3. Only need to consider the checks for correct computations and obviously these are true.

Thus, following the above discussion, the proposed protocol has perfect completeness.

5.3   Statistical Zero-Knowledge

To construct a simulator $\mathcal{S}$ who interacts with the verifier $\mathcal{V}'$ to output a simulated transcript that is statistically close to one generated by an honest prover $\mathcal{P}$ in the real interaction with a probability negligibly close to 2/3. The construction is as follows:

$\mathcal{S}$ picks a random value $\widetilde{\mathsf{CH}} \leftarrow_R \{1, 2, 3\}$, as a prediction that the verifier $\mathcal{V}'$ (maybe cheating) will not choose.

○ $\widetilde{\mathsf{CH}} = 1$. $\mathcal{S}$ works as follows:

1. Use basic linear algebra algorithm to compute k vectors $\mathbf{e}''_1, \mathbf{e}''_2, \cdots, \mathbf{e}''_k \in \mathbb{Z}_q^{(2\ell+1)3m}$ such that $\mathbf{A}^* \cdot (\sum_{j=1}^k \beta_j \mathbf{e}''_j) = \mathbf{u} \bmod q$.

2. Let $\mathbf{e}''_{j,0} = \mathsf{Parse}(\mathbf{e}''_j, 1, m)$, use linear algebra algorithm to compute k vectors $\widehat{\mathbf{e}}_1, \widehat{\mathbf{e}}_2, \cdots, \widehat{\mathbf{e}}_k \in \mathbb{Z}_q^{3m}$ such that $\mathbf{b} = \mathbf{B}^* \cdot (\sum_{j=1}^k \beta_j (\mathbf{e}''_{j,0}, \widehat{\mathbf{e}}_j)) \bmod q$.

3. Sample several random vectors and permutations,

$$\begin{cases} \mathbf{r}'_1, \mathbf{r}'_2, \cdots, \mathbf{r}'_k \in \mathbb{Z}_q^{(2\ell+2)3m}; \mathbf{r}_1, \mathbf{r}_2, \cdots, \mathbf{r}_k \in \mathbb{Z}_q^{3m}; \\ \pi_1, \pi_2, \cdots, \pi_k \in \mathcal{S}_{3m}; \varphi_1, \varphi_2, \cdots, \varphi_k \in \mathcal{S}_{3m}; \\ \phi_1, \phi_2, \cdots, \phi_k \in \mathcal{S}_{3m}; \tau \in \mathcal{S}_{2\ell}. \end{cases}$$

4. Let $\mathbf{r}'_{j,0} = \mathsf{Parse}(\mathbf{r}'_j, 1, m)$, compute $\mathsf{CMT} = (\mathbf{c}'_1, \mathbf{c}'_2, \mathbf{c}'_3)$,

$$\begin{cases} \mathbf{c}'_1 = \mathsf{COM}(\{\pi_j, \varphi_j, \phi_j\}_{j=1}^k, \tau; \mathbf{A}^* \cdot (\sum_{j=1}^k \beta_j \mathbf{r}_j); \mathbf{B}^* \cdot (\sum_{j=1}^k \beta_j (\mathbf{r}'_{j,0}, \mathbf{r}_j))), \\ \mathbf{c}'_2 = \mathsf{COM}(\{\mathcal{F}_{\pi_j, \varphi_j, \tau}(\mathbf{r}'_j), \phi_j(\mathbf{r}_j)\}_{j=1}^k), \\ \mathbf{c}'_3 = \mathsf{COM}(\{\mathcal{F}_{\pi_j, \varphi_j, \tau}(\mathbf{e}''_j + \mathbf{r}'_j), \phi_j(\mathbf{e}_j + \mathbf{r}_j)\}_{j=1}^k). \end{cases}$$

5. Send CMT to $\mathcal{V}'$.
   Receiving a challenge $\mathsf{CH} \in \{1, 2, 3\}$, $\mathcal{S}$ replies as follows:

1. $\mathsf{CH} = 1$. $\mathcal{S}$ outputs $\bot$ and aborts.
2. $\mathsf{CH} = 2$. $\mathcal{S}$ sends $\mathsf{RSP} = (\{\pi_j, \varphi_j, \phi_j, \mathbf{e}_j'' + \mathbf{r}_j, \widehat{\mathbf{e}_j} + \mathbf{r}_j\}_{j=1}^k, \tau)$.
3. $\mathsf{CH} = 3$. $\mathcal{S}$ sends $\mathsf{RSP} = (\{\pi_j, \varphi_j, \phi_j, \mathbf{r}_j', \mathbf{r}_j\}_{j=1}^k, \tau)$.

○ $\widetilde{\mathsf{CH}} = 2$. $\mathcal{S}$ works as follows:

1. Sample several random vectors and permutations,

$$
\begin{cases}
\mathbf{r}_1', \mathbf{r}_2', \cdots, \mathbf{r}_k' \in \mathbb{Z}_q^{(2\ell+2)3m}; \mathbf{r}_1, \mathbf{r}_2, \cdots, \mathbf{r}_k \in \mathbb{Z}_q^{3m}; \\
\pi_1, \pi_2, \cdots, \pi_k \in \mathcal{S}_{3m}; \varphi_1, \varphi_2, \cdots, \varphi_k \in \mathcal{S}_{3m}; \\
\phi_1, \phi_2, \cdots, \phi_k \in \mathcal{S}_{3m}; \tau \in \mathcal{S}_{2\ell}; \mathsf{id}' \in \mathsf{B}_{2\ell}; \\
\mathbf{e}_1'', \mathbf{e}_2'', \cdots, \mathbf{e}_k'' \in \mathsf{SecExt}(\mathsf{id}'); \widehat{\mathbf{e}_1}, \widehat{\mathbf{e}_2}, \cdots, \widehat{\mathbf{e}_k} \in \mathsf{B}_{3m}.
\end{cases}
$$

2. Let $\mathbf{r}_{j,0}' = \mathsf{Parse}(\mathbf{r}_j', 1, m)$, compute $\mathsf{CMT} = (\mathbf{c}_1', \mathbf{c}_2', \mathbf{c}_3')$,

$$
\begin{cases}
\mathbf{c}_1' = \mathsf{COM}(\{\pi_j, \varphi_j, \phi_j\}_{j=1}^k, \tau; \mathbf{A}^* \cdot (\sum_{j=1}^k \beta_j \mathbf{r}_j); \mathbf{B}^* \cdot (\sum_{j=1}^k \beta_j(\mathbf{r}_{j,0}', \mathbf{r}_j))), \\
\mathbf{c}_2' = \mathsf{COM}(\{\mathcal{F}_{\pi_j, \varphi_j, \tau}(\mathbf{r}_j'), \phi_j(\mathbf{r}_j)\}_{j=1}^k), \\
\mathbf{c}_3' = \mathsf{COM}(\{\mathcal{F}_{\pi_j, \varphi_j, \tau}(\mathbf{e}_j'' + \mathbf{r}_j'), \phi_j(\mathbf{e}_j + \mathbf{r}_j)\}_{j=1}^k).
\end{cases}
$$

3. Send CMT to $\mathcal{V}'$.
   Receiving a challenge $\mathsf{CH} \in \{1, 2, 3\}$, $\mathcal{S}$ replies as follows:
   1. $\mathsf{CH} = 1$. $\mathcal{S}$ sends,

   $$
   \mathsf{RSP} = (\{\mathcal{F}_{\pi_j, \varphi_j, \tau}(\mathbf{e}_j''), \mathcal{F}_{\pi_j, \varphi_j, \tau}(\mathbf{r}_j'), \phi_j(\widehat{\mathbf{e}_j}), \phi_j(\mathbf{r}_j)\}_{j=1}^k, \tau(\mathsf{id}')).
   $$

   2. $\mathsf{CH} = 2$. $\mathcal{S}$ outputs $\bot$ and aborts.
   3. $\mathsf{CH} = 3$. $\mathcal{S}$ sends $\mathsf{RSP} = (\{\pi_j, \varphi_j, \phi_j, \mathbf{r}_j', \mathbf{r}_j\}_{j=1}^k, \tau)$.

○ $\widetilde{\mathsf{CH}} = 3$. $\mathcal{S}$ works as follows:

1. Sample several random vectors and permutations,

$$
\begin{cases}
\mathbf{r}_1', \mathbf{r}_2', \cdots, \mathbf{r}_k' \in \mathbb{Z}_q^{(2\ell+2)3m}; \mathbf{r}_1, \mathbf{r}_2, \cdots, \mathbf{r}_k \in \mathbb{Z}_q^{3m}; \\
\pi_1, \pi_2, \cdots, \pi_k \in \mathcal{S}_{3m}; \varphi_1, \varphi_2, \cdots, \varphi_k \in \mathcal{S}_{3m}; \\
\phi_1, \phi_2, \cdots, \phi_k \in \mathcal{S}_{3m}; \tau \in \mathcal{S}_{2\ell}; \mathsf{id}' \in \mathsf{B}_{2\ell}; \\
\mathbf{e}_1'', \mathbf{e}_2'', \cdots, \mathbf{e}_k'' \in \mathsf{SecExt}(\mathsf{id}'); \widehat{\mathbf{e}_1}, \widehat{\mathbf{e}_2}, \cdots, \widehat{\mathbf{e}_k} \in \mathsf{B}_{3m}.
\end{cases}
$$

2. Let $\mathbf{e}_{j,0}'' = \mathsf{Parse}(\mathbf{e}_j'', 1, m)$, $\mathbf{r}_{j,0}' = \mathsf{Parse}(\mathbf{r}_j', 1, m)$, compute $\mathsf{CMT} = (\mathbf{c}_1', \mathbf{c}_2', \mathbf{c}_3')$,

$$
\begin{cases}
\mathbf{c}_1' = \mathsf{COM}(\{\pi_j, \varphi_j, \phi_j\}_{j=1}^k, \tau; \mathbf{A}^* \cdot (\sum_{j=1}^k \beta_j(\mathbf{e}_j'' + \mathbf{r}_j)) - \mathbf{u}; \\
\qquad \mathbf{B}^* \cdot (\sum_{j=1}^k \beta_j(\mathbf{e}_{j,0}'' + \mathbf{r}_{j,0}', \widehat{\mathbf{e}_j} + \mathbf{r}_j)) - \mathbf{b}), \\
\mathbf{c}_2' = \mathsf{COM}(\{\mathcal{F}_{\pi_j, \varphi_j, \tau}(\mathbf{r}_j'), \phi_j(\mathbf{r}_j)\}_{j=1}^k), \\
\mathbf{c}_3' = \mathsf{COM}(\{\mathcal{F}_{\pi_j, \varphi_j, \tau}(\mathbf{e}_j'' + \mathbf{r}_j'), \phi_j(\mathbf{e}_j + \mathbf{r}_j)\}_{j=1}^k).
\end{cases}
$$

3. Send CMT to $\mathcal{V}'$.
   Receiving a challenge $\mathsf{CH} \in \{1, 2, 3\}$, $\mathcal{S}$ replies as follows:

1. $\mathsf{CH} = 1$. $\mathcal{S}$ sends,

$$\mathsf{RSP} = (\{\mathcal{F}_{\pi_j, \varphi_j, \tau}(\mathbf{e}_j''), \mathcal{F}_{\pi_j, \varphi_j, \tau}(\mathbf{r}_j'), \phi_j(\widehat{\mathbf{e}}_j), \phi_j(\mathbf{r}_j)\}_{j=1}^k, \tau(\mathsf{id}')).$$

2. $\mathsf{CH} = 2$. $\mathcal{S}$ sends $\mathsf{RSP} = (\{\pi_j, \varphi_j, \phi_j, \mathbf{e}_j'' + \mathbf{r}_j, \widehat{\mathbf{e}}_j + \mathbf{r}_j\}_{j=1}^k, \tau)$.
3. $\mathsf{CH} = 3$. $\mathcal{S}$ outputs $\perp$ and aborts.

Based on the statistically hiding property of the commitment scheme COM, the distributions of CMT, CH and RSP are statistically close to those in the real interaction. $\mathcal{S}$ outputs $\perp$ and aborts with a probability negligibly close to $1/3$.

Furthermore, once $\mathcal{S}$ does not halt, a valid transcript will be given and the distribution of transcript is statistically close to that in the real interaction, thus, $\mathcal{S}$ can impersonate an honest prover $\mathcal{P}$ with a probability negligibly close to $2/3$.

5.4   Argument of Knowledge

To prove that the proposed protocol is an argument of knowledge for the relation $\mathcal{R}(n, k, \ell, q, m, \beta)$, it needs to show that the proposed protocol satisfies the special soundness property.

We prove that if there exists a prover $\mathcal{P}'$ (maybe cheating) who can correctly respond to three challenges $\mathsf{CH} \in \{1, 2, 3\}$ corresponding to the same commitment CMT with the public inputs $(\mathbf{A}_0, \mathbf{A}_1, \mathbf{A}_2, \mathbf{B}, \mathbf{u}, \mathbf{b})$, then there is a extractor $\mathcal{K}$ who produces $(\mathsf{id} = \mathrm{bin}(i) \in \{0, 1\}^\ell, \mathbf{e}' = (\mathbf{e}_1', \mathbf{e}_2', \mathrm{bin}(i) \otimes \mathbf{e}_2'), \mathbf{e})$ such that:

$$(\mathbf{A}_0, \mathbf{A}_1, \mathbf{A}_2, \mathbf{B}, \mathbf{u}, \mathbf{b}; \mathsf{id} = \mathrm{bin}(i), \mathbf{e}', \mathbf{e}) \in \mathcal{R}.$$

Indeed, based on 3 valid responses $\mathsf{RSP}_1, \mathsf{RSP}_2, \mathsf{RSP}_3$ given by $\mathcal{P}'$, the knowledge extractor $\mathcal{K}$ can extract the following information:

$$\begin{cases} \mathbf{t}_{\mathsf{id}} \in \mathsf{B}_{2\ell}, \forall j \in \{1, \cdots, k\}, \mathbf{v}_j' \in \mathsf{SecExt}(\mathbf{t}_{\mathsf{id}}), \mathbf{v}_j \in \mathsf{B}_{3m}, \\ \mathbf{c}_1 = \mathsf{COM}(\{\hat{\pi}_j, \hat{\varphi}_j, \hat{\phi}_j\}_{j=1}^k, \hat{\tau}; \mathbf{A}^* \cdot (\sum_{j=1}^k \beta_j \mathbf{x}_j') - \mathbf{u}; \mathbf{B}^*(\sum_{j=1}^k \beta_j(\mathbf{x}_{j,0}', \mathbf{x}_j)) - \mathbf{b}) \\ \quad = \mathsf{COM}(\{\tilde{\pi}_j, \tilde{\varphi}_j, \tilde{\phi}_j\}_{j=1}^k, \tilde{\tau}; \mathbf{A}^* \cdot (\sum_{j=1}^k \beta_j \mathbf{h}_j'); \mathbf{B}^* \cdot (\sum_{j=1}^k \beta_j(\mathbf{h}_{j,0}', \mathbf{h}_j))), \\ \mathbf{c}_2 = \mathsf{COM}(\{\mathbf{w}_j', \mathbf{w}_j\}_{j=1}^k) = \mathsf{COM}(\{\mathcal{F}_{\tilde{\pi}_j, \tilde{\varphi}_j, \tilde{\tau}}(\mathbf{h}_j'), \tilde{\phi}_j(\mathbf{h}_j)\}_{j=1}^k), \\ \mathbf{c}_3 = \mathsf{COM}(\{\mathbf{v}_j' + \mathbf{w}_j', \mathbf{v}_j + \mathbf{w}_j\}_{j=1}^k) = \mathsf{COM}(\{\mathcal{F}_{\hat{\pi}_j, \hat{\varphi}_j, \hat{\tau}}(\mathbf{x}_j'), \hat{\phi}_j(\mathbf{x}_j)\}_{j=1}^k). \end{cases}$$

Based on the computationally binding property of COM, the extractor $\mathcal{K}$ can deduce that:

$$\begin{cases} \mathbf{t}_{\mathsf{id}} \in \mathsf{B}_{2\ell}, \hat{\tau} = \tilde{\tau}, \forall j \in \{1, \cdots, k\}, \hat{\phi}_j = \tilde{\phi}_j, \hat{\pi}_j = \tilde{\pi}_j, \hat{\varphi}_j = \tilde{\varphi}_j; \\ \mathbf{A}^* \cdot (\sum_{j=1}^k \beta_j \mathbf{x}_j') - \mathbf{u} = \mathbf{A}^* \cdot (\sum_{j=1}^k \beta_j \mathbf{h}_j') \bmod q; \\ \mathbf{B}^* \cdot (\sum_{j=1}^k \beta_j(\mathbf{x}_{j,0}', \mathbf{x}_j)) - \mathbf{b} = \mathbf{B}^* \cdot (\sum_{j=1}^k \beta_j(\mathbf{h}_{j,0}', \mathbf{h}_j)); \\ \mathbf{w}_j' = \mathcal{F}_{\tilde{\pi}_j, \tilde{\varphi}_j, \tilde{\tau}}(\mathbf{h}_j'), \mathbf{v}_j' + \mathbf{w}_j' = \mathcal{F}_{\hat{\pi}_j, \hat{\varphi}_j, \hat{\tau}}(\mathbf{x}_j'), \mathbf{v}_j' \in \mathsf{SecExt}(\mathbf{t}_{\mathsf{id}}); \\ \mathbf{w}_j = \tilde{\phi}_j(\mathbf{h}_j), \mathbf{v}_j + \mathbf{w}_j = \hat{\phi}_j(\mathbf{x}_j), \mathbf{v}_j \in \mathsf{B}_{3m}. \end{cases}$$

For $j \in \{1, 2, \cdots, k\}$, let $\mathbf{e}'_j = \mathbf{x}'_j - \mathbf{h}'_j = \mathcal{F}^{-1}_{\tilde{\pi}_j, \tilde{\varphi}_j, \tilde{\tau}}(\mathbf{v}'_j)$, $\mathbf{e}_j = \mathbf{x}_j - \mathbf{h}_j = \tilde{\phi}^{-1}_j(\mathbf{v}_j)$, thus we have $\mathbf{e}'_j \in \mathsf{SecExt}(\tilde{\tau}^{-1}(\mathsf{t}_{\mathsf{id}})) = \mathsf{SecExt}(\mathsf{id}^*)$, $\mathbf{e}_j \in \mathsf{B}_{3m}$. Furthermore, let $\mathbf{e}'_{j,0} = \mathsf{Parse}(\mathbf{e}'_j, 1, m)$,

$$\begin{cases} \mathbf{A}^* \cdot (\sum_{j=1}^{k} \beta_j \mathbf{e}'_j) = \mathbf{u} \bmod q, \\ \mathbf{B}^* \cdot (\sum_{j=1}^{k} \beta_j (\mathbf{e}'_{j,0}, \mathbf{e}_j)) = \mathbf{b} \bmod q. \end{cases}$$

The knowledge extractor $\mathcal{K}$ produces $\mathsf{id} = \mathsf{bin}(i) \in \{0,1\}^{\ell}$, $\mathbf{e}' \in \mathsf{Sec}_{\beta}(\mathsf{id})$, and $\mathbf{e} \in \mathbb{Z}^m$ as follows:

1. Let $\mathsf{id}^* = (d_1, d_2, \cdots, d_{\ell}, d_{\ell+1}, \cdots, d_{2\ell}) = \tilde{\tau}^{-1}(\mathsf{t}_{\mathsf{id}})$, we obtain $\mathsf{bin}(i) = \mathsf{id} = (d_1, d_2, \cdots, d_{\ell})$ and the member index $i = \mathbf{g}_{\ell}^{\top} \cdot \mathsf{bin}(i)$ where $\mathbf{g}_{\ell} = (1, 2, \cdots, 2^{\ell-1})$.

2. Let $\mathbf{e}^* = \sum_{j=1}^{k} \beta_j \mathbf{e}'_j \in \mathbb{Z}_q^{(2\ell+2)3m}$, thus,

$$0 < \|\mathbf{e}^*\|_{\infty} \leq \sum_{j=1}^{k} \beta_j \|\mathbf{e}'_j\| \leq \beta.$$

Since $\mathbf{e}'_j \in \mathsf{SecExt}(\mathsf{id}^*)$, there exist $\mathbf{e}^*_1$, $\mathbf{e}^*_2 \in \mathbb{Z}_q^{3m}$ satisfying $\|\mathbf{e}^*_1\|_{\infty}, \|\mathbf{e}^*_2\|_{\infty} \leq \beta$, and $\mathbf{e}^* = (\mathbf{e}^*_1, \mathbf{e}^*_2, d_1 \mathbf{e}^*_2, d_2 \mathbf{e}^*_2, \cdots, d_{2\ell} \mathbf{e}^*_2)$. We set $\mathbf{e}' = (\mathbf{e}'_1, \mathbf{e}'_2, d_1 \mathbf{e}'_2, \cdots, d_{\ell} \mathbf{e}'_2) = (\mathbf{e}'_1, \mathbf{e}'_2, \mathsf{bin}(i) \otimes \mathbf{e}'_2)$, where $\mathbf{e}'_1$, $\mathbf{e}'_2$ are obtained from $\mathbf{e}^*_1$, $\mathbf{e}^*_2$ by removing the last $2m$ coordinates. Thus, $\mathbf{e}' \in \mathsf{Sec}_{\beta}(\mathsf{id})$ and

$$[\mathbf{A}_0 | \mathbf{A}_1 | \mathbf{g}_{\ell} \otimes \mathbf{A}_2] \cdot (\mathbf{e}'_1, \mathbf{e}'_2, \mathsf{bin}(i) \otimes \mathbf{e}'_2) = \mathbf{u} \bmod q.$$

3. Let $\hat{\mathbf{e}} = \sum_{j=1}^{k} \beta_j \mathbf{e}_j \in \mathbb{Z}^{3m}$, thus,

$$0 < \|\hat{\mathbf{e}}\|_{\infty} \leq \sum_{j=1}^{k} \beta_j \|\mathbf{e}_j\| \leq \beta.$$

Let $\mathbf{e} \in \mathbb{Z}^m$ be a vector obtained from $\hat{\mathbf{e}}$ by removing the last $2m$ coordinates. Thus, $\mathbf{e} \in \mathbb{Z}^m$, $0 < \|\mathbf{e}\|_{\infty} \leq \beta$ and $\mathbf{b} = (\mathbf{B}^{\top} \mathbf{A}_0) \cdot \mathbf{e}'_1 + \mathbf{e} \bmod q$.

Finally, the knowledge extractor $\mathcal{K}$ outputs,

$$\mathsf{witness} = (\mathsf{bin}(i) = \mathsf{id} \in \{0,1\}^{\ell}, \mathbf{e}' \in \mathsf{Sec}_{\beta}(\mathsf{id}), \mathbf{e} \in \mathbb{Z}^m),$$

which is a valid witness for the relation $\mathcal{R} = (n, k, \ell, m, \beta, p, t)$. This concludes the proof.

6 Conclusions

The significance of this paper consists of two aspects: firstly, we adopt an efficient and compact identity-encoding technique to encode the identity index of group member and obtain the reduced bit-sizes of the group public-key and the group member secret-key for lattice-based GS scheme with VLR; secondly, in order to prove the signer's validity as a valid certified member and its revocation token is correctly committed vis an LWE function in zero-knowledge, a new efficient Stern-type statistical zero-knowledge proof protocol is proposed. For future work, it is desirable to achieve a stronger security for lattice-based GS with VLR, at the same time accompanied by more efficient zero-knowledge proof protocols.

Acknowledgments. The authors thank the anonymous reviewers of ISC 2019 for their helpful comments and this research is supported by the National Key R&D Program of China under Grant 2017YFB0802000 and the National Natural Science Foundation of China under Grant 61772477.

References

1. Bellare, M., Micciancio, D., Warinschi, B.: Foundations of group signatures: formal definitions, simplified requirements, and a construction based on general assumptions. In: Biham, E. (ed.) EUROCRYPT 2003. LNCS, vol. 2656, pp. 614–629. Springer, Heidelberg (2003). https://doi.org/10.1007/3-540-39200-9_38
2. Bellare, M., Shi, H., Zhang, C.: Foundations of group signatures: the case of dynamic groups. In: Menezes, A. (ed.) CT-RSA 2005. LNCS, vol. 3376, pp. 136–153. Springer, Heidelberg (2005). https://doi.org/10.1007/978-3-540-30574-3_11
3. Boneh, D., Shacham, H.: Group signatures with verifier-local revocation. In: CCS, pp. 168–177. ACM (2004). https://doi.org/10.1145/1030083.1030106
4. Bootle, J., Cerulli, A., Chaidos, P., Ghadafi, E., Groth, J.: Foundations of fully dynamic group signatures. In: Manulis, M., Sadeghi, A.-R., Schneider, S. (eds.) ACNS 2016. LNCS, vol. 9696, pp. 117–136. Springer, Cham (2016). https://doi.org/10.1007/978-3-319-39555-5_7
5. Camenisch, J., Neven, G., Rückert, M.: Fully anonymous attribute tokens from lattices. In: Visconti, I., De Prisco, R. (eds.) SCN 2012. LNCS, vol. 7485, pp. 57–75. Springer, Heidelberg (2012). https://doi.org/10.1007/978-3-642-32928-9_4
6. Cash, D., Hofheinz, D., Kiltz, E., Peikert, C.: Bonsai trees, or how to delegate a lattice basis. In: Gilbert, H. (ed.) EUROCRYPT 2010. LNCS, vol. 6110, pp. 523–552. Springer, Heidelberg (2010). https://doi.org/10.1007/978-3-642-13190-5_27
7. Chaum, D., van Heyst, E.: Group signatures. In: Davies, D.W. (ed.) EUROCRYPT 1991. LNCS, vol. 547, pp. 257–265. Springer, Heidelberg (1991). https://doi.org/10.1007/3-540-46416-6_22
8. Gao, W., Hu, Y., Zhang, Y., Wang, B.: Lattice-based group signature with verifier-local revocation. J. Shanghai JiaoTong Univ. (Sci.) **22**(3), 313–321 (2017)
9. Gentry, C., Peikert, C., Vaikuntanathan, V.: Trapdoor for hard lattices and new cryptographic constructions. In: STOC, pp. 197–206. ACM (2008). https://doi.org/10.1145/1374376.1374407
10. Gordon, S.D., Katz, J., Vaikuntanathan, V.: A group signature scheme from lattice assumptions. In: Abe, M. (ed.) ASIACRYPT 2010. LNCS, vol. 6477, pp. 395–412. Springer, Heidelberg (2010). https://doi.org/10.1007/978-3-642-17373-8_23
11. Kawachi, A., Tanaka, K., Xagawa, K.: Concurrently secure identification schemes based on the worst-case hardness of lattice problems. In: Pieprzyk, J. (ed.) ASIACRYPT 2008. LNCS, vol. 5350, pp. 372–389. Springer, Heidelberg (2008). https://doi.org/10.1007/978-3-540-89255-7_23
12. Kiayias, A., Yung, M.: Secure scalable group signature with dynamic joins and separable authorities. Int. J. Secur. Netw. **1**(1/2), 24–45 (2006)
13. Laguillaumie, F., Langlois, A., Libert, B., Stehlé, D.: Lattice-based group signatures with logarithmic signature size. In: Sako, K., Sarkar, P. (eds.) ASIACRYPT 2013. LNCS, vol. 8270, pp. 41–61. Springer, Heidelberg (2013). https://doi.org/10.1007/978-3-642-42045-0_3

14. Langlois, A., Ling, S., Nguyen, K., Wang, H.: Lattice-based group signature scheme with verifier-local revocation. In: Krawczyk, H. (ed.) PKC 2014. LNCS, vol. 8383, pp. 345–361. Springer, Heidelberg (2014). https://doi.org/10.1007/978-3-642-54631-0_20

15. Libert, B., Ling, S., Mouhartem, F., Nguyen, K., Wang, H.: Signature schemes with efficient protocols and dynamic group signatures from lattice assumptions. In: Cheon, J.H., Takagi, T. (eds.) ASIACRYPT 2016. LNCS, vol. 10032, pp. 373–403. Springer, Heidelberg (2016). https://doi.org/10.1007/978-3-662-53890-6_13

16. Libert, B., Ling, S., Nguyen, K., Wang, H.: Zero-knowledge arguments for lattice-based accumulators: logarithmic-size ring signatures and group signatures without trapdoors. In: Fischlin, M., Coron, J.-S. (eds.) EUROCRYPT 2016. LNCS, vol. 9666, pp. 1–31. Springer, Heidelberg (2016). https://doi.org/10.1007/978-3-662-49896-5_1

17. Libert, B., Mouhartem, F., Nguyen, K.: A lattice-based group signature scheme with message-dependent opening. In: Manulis, M., Sadeghi, A.-R., Schneider, S. (eds.) ACNS 2016. LNCS, vol. 9696, pp. 137–155. Springer, Cham (2016). https://doi.org/10.1007/978-3-319-39555-5_8

18. Ling, S., Nguyen, K., Roux-Langlois, A., Wang, H.: A lattice-based group signature scheme with verifier-local revocation. Theor. Comput. Sci. **730**, 1–20 (2018)

19. Ling, S., Nguyen, K., Stehlé, D., Wang, H.: Improved zero-knowledge proofs of knowledge for the ISIS problem, and applications. In: Kurosawa, K., Hanaoka, G. (eds.) PKC 2013. LNCS, vol. 7778, pp. 107–124. Springer, Heidelberg (2013). https://doi.org/10.1007/978-3-642-36362-7_8

20. Ling, S., Nguyen, K., Wang, H.: Group signatures from lattices: simpler, tighter, shorter, ring-based. In: Katz, J. (ed.) PKC 2015. LNCS, vol. 9020, pp. 427–449. Springer, Heidelberg (2015). https://doi.org/10.1007/978-3-662-46447-2_19

21. Ling, S., Nguyen, K., Wang, H., Xu, Y.: Lattice-based group signatures: achieving full dynamicity with ease. In: Gollmann, D., Miyaji, A., Kikuchi, H. (eds.) ACNS 2017. LNCS, vol. 10355, pp. 293–312. Springer, Cham (2017). https://doi.org/10.1007/978-3-319-61204-1_15

22. Ling, S., Nguyen, K., Wang, H., Xu, Y.: Forward-secure group signatures from lattices (2018). https://arxiv.org/abs/1801.08323

23. Ling, S., Nguyen, K., Wang, H., Xu, Y.: Constant-size group signatures from lattices. In: Abdalla, M., Dahab, R. (eds.) PKC 2018. LNCS, vol. 10770, pp. 58–88. Springer, Cham (2018). https://doi.org/10.1007/978-3-319-76581-5_3

24. Micciancio, D., Peikert, C.: Hardness of SIS and LWE with small parameters. In: Canetti, R., Garay, J.A. (eds.) CRYPTO 2013. LNCS, vol. 8042, pp. 21–39. Springer, Heidelberg (2013). https://doi.org/10.1007/978-3-642-40041-4_2

25. Nguyen, P.Q., Zhang, J., Zhang, Z.: Simpler efficient group signatures from lattices. In: Katz, J. (ed.) PKC 2015. LNCS, vol. 9020, pp. 401–426. Springer, Heidelberg (2015). https://doi.org/10.1007/978-3-662-46447-2_18

26. Perera, M.N.S., Koshiba, T.: Zero-knowledge proof for lattice-based group signature schemes with verifier-local revocation. In: Barolli, L., Kryvinska, N., Enokido, T., Takizawa, M. (eds.) NBiS 2018. LNDECT, vol. 22, pp. 772–782. Springer, Cham (2019). https://doi.org/10.1007/978-3-319-98530-5_68

27. Perera, M.N.S., Koshiba, T.: Achieving strong security and verifier-local revocation for dynamic group signatures from lattice assumptions. In: Katsikas, S.K., Alcaraz, C. (eds.) STM 2018. LNCS, vol. 11091, pp. 3–19. Springer, Cham (2018). https://doi.org/10.1007/978-3-030-01141-3_1

28. Regev, O.: On lattices, learning with errors, random linear codes, and cryptography. In: STOC, pp. 84–93. ACM (2005). https://doi.org/10.1145/1060590.1060603
29. Zhang, Y., Hu, Y., Gao, W., Jiang, M.: Simpler efficient group signature scheme with verifier-local revocation from lattices. KSII Trans. Int. Inf. Syst. **10**(1), 414–430 (2016)

Defenses

When the Attacker Knows
a Lot: The *GAGA* Graph Anonymizer

Arash Alavi$^{(\boxtimes)}$, Rajiv Gupta, and Zhiyun Qian

University of California, Riverside, USA
aalav003@ucr.edu, {gupta,zhiyunq}@cs.ucr.edu

Abstract. When releasing graph data (e.g., social network) to public or third parties, data privacy becomes a major concern. It has been shown that state-of-the-art graph anonymization techniques suffer from a lack of strong defense against De-Anonymization (DA) attacks mostly because of the bias towards utility preservation. In this paper, we propose *GAGA*, an Efficient Genetic Algorithm for Graph Anonymization, that simultaneously delivers high anonymization and utility preservation. To address the vulnerability against DA attacks especially when the adversary can re-identify the victim not only based on some information about the neighbors of a victim but also some knowledge on the structure of the neighbors of the victim's neighbors, *GAGA* puts the concept of *k(d)-neighborhood-anonymity* into action by developing the first general algorithm for any *d* distance neighborhood. *GAGA* also addresses the challenge of applying minimum number of changes to the original graph to preserve data utilities via an effective and efficient genetic algorithm. Results of our evaluation show that *GAGA* anonymizes the graphs in a way that it is more resistant to modern DA attacks than existing techniques – *GAGA* (with $d = 3$) improves the defense against DA techniques by reducing the DA rate by at least a factor of 2.7× in comparison to the baseline. At the same time it preserves the data utilities to a very high degree – it is the best technique for preserving 11 out of 16 utilities. Finally, *GAGA* provides application-oriented level of control to users via different tunable parameters.

Keywords: Graph anonymization · Data privacy · Network security

1 Introduction

Social network data are routinely released for different purposes such as advertising, academic research, medical diagnosis, criminology, etc. Since these data contain sensitive information about the users, when releasing such data to the public or third parties, data privacy is a major concern. To achieve privacy preservation, various graph anonymization techniques have been proposed to anonymize the social graph data before its release [4,13,17,23,28,29].

© Springer Nature Switzerland AG 2019
Z. Lin et al. (Eds.): ISC 2019, LNCS 11723, pp. 211–230, 2019.
https://doi.org/10.1007/978-3-030-30215-3_11

The main drawback of existing anonymization techniques is that they trade-off anonymization with utility preservation. Previous works including [4,17,23, 28,29] evaluated their approaches only in terms of data utility performance and lack a complete evaluation of their ability to withstand modern De-Anonymization (DA) attacks [10,14,22,24,27]. As shown in [11], existing graph anonymization techniques not only produce anonymized graphs that are *susceptible to DA attacks*, they also *make more than the minimum required changes* to the original graph even though applying minimum number of changes is their primary objective.

In this paper, we propose *GAGA*, an Efficient Genetic Algorithm for Graph Anonymization, that simultaneously achieves high anonymization via utility preservation. *GAGA* defends against modern DA attacks as follows:

– **$K(d)$-neighborhood-anonymity for any d** is supported by *GAGA* to provide defense against modern DA attacks. Existing anonymization techniques have been found to be ineffective against modern DA attacks especially when the attacker has complex knowledge about the structure of some-order neighbors (e.g., neighbors of neighbors) of a victim, which can be obtained by the attackers by either modifying the social network graph before releasing by creating fake users and linking to victim and its neighbors (active attack) or by trying to find themselves in the released graph and from this and many other auxiliary graphs (e.g., other social networks) discover the structure of neighbors of the victim (passive attack).

At the same time, the combination of various features enables *GAGA* to preserve utilities and to give more application-oriented level of control to its users (researchers, advertisers, developers, etc.) as follows:

– **Edge switching** is supported by *GAGA* to preserve *degree* and its related utilities (e.g., *role extraction*) since *edge switch* is the only known technique that can effectively preserve these utilities [11]. Therefore, in contrast to most anonymization techniques that add some fake edges to the original graph, *GAGA* gives higher priority to edge switching over edge adding or removing. Meanwhile it has been observed that *k-neighborhood-anonymity* based algorithm is generally the best approach to partially or conditionally preserve other utilities. Thus, to cover as much as possible utilities, *GAGA* applies *edge switch* to the *k(d)-neighborhood-anonymity* model. The genetic algorithm further minimizes the number of edge switches for better utility preservation.

– **Controls via k and d** are provided by *GAGA* allowing application-oriented level of control by its users. If defending against modern DA attacks is desired, larger values of k and d are used. If merely utility preservation is demanded, small values of k and d are used.

– **Controls via genetic algorithm (GA)** are also provided by *GAGA*. GA is effective and efficient for solving optimization problems (here, applying minimum number of changes). Besides, its tunable parameters allow not only control over solutions quality in terms of preserving utility but also runtime performance of the tool (albeit, graph anoymization is usually an offline process). These parameters include: initial population size; number of switches

(s), adds, and removes (mutation rate) in each GA iteration; probabilities that control the search space; finding local maxima (a set of good enough solutions) as opposed to the global maximum (best solutions).

Our evaluation leads to the following key conclusions.

- First our comparison of *GAGA* with existing anonymization techniques with respect to multiple DA attacks, for a subgraph of Facebook friendship network, shows that *GAGA* is the best for defending against all DA attacks when it employs $d = 3$-neighborhood structures. We set *Union Cluster* [25] as our evaluation baseline and show that *GAGA* improves the defense against DA techniques by reducing the rate of successfully de-anonymized users by at least a factor of 2.7× when $d = 3$ in comparison to the baseline and leads to zero de-identified users in some cases.
- Second our comparison of *GAGA* with existing anonymization approaches, for a real world input graph, shows that under 16 graph and application utility metrics, *GAGA* is overall the best at preserving utilities – it is the best for 11 out of 16 utilities and close to the best for the remaining 5.
- Finally, our comparison of *GAGA* with Zhou and Pei's [29] work that uses $d = 1$-neighborhood anonymity model shows that *GAGA* incurs only 69% of the cost of Zhou and Pei's approach when it also employs $d = 1$-neighborhood structures, indicating that previous works cannot preserve most utilities though this is their primary objective.

The remainder of the paper is organized as follows. We discuss background and motivate our work in Sect. 2. Section 3 presents the details of *GAGA*. Section 4 evaluates *GAGA* and compares it with state-of-the-art techniques. We discuss related work in Sect. 5. The paper ends with conclusions in Sect. 6.

2   Background and Motivation

Preserving data privacy has been widely studied. One of the main approaches used to preserve data privacy is based upon the concept of anonymity. Graphs and databases have played an important role in this domain [1–3, 18, 20]. In this paper we address the data privacy preservation in graphs, specifically for graphs representing social networks. A number of graph anonymization techniques have been proposed to preserve users' privacy. We discuss the limitations of these techniques first from the perspective of defense against DA attacks and then from the perspective of utility preservation to motivate our approach.

As a concrete motivating example, consider the sample graph shown in Fig. 1. The social graph on the left side is going to be publicly published. Assume that an adversary knows that Alice has 2 friends and each of them has 4 friends, then the vertex representing Alice can be re-identified uniquely in the network (black vertex in Fig. 1). The reason is that no other vertices have the same 2-neighborhood graph to the 2-neighborhood graph for Alice. Existing graph anonymization techniques fail to anonymize this example graph so that an adversary cannot re-identify any user certainly. The *k-degree-anonymity* based algorithm in [17] removes/adds edges from/to the original graph to create a graph in which for every vertex there are at least $k − 1$ other vertices with the same degree. Based on *k-degree-anonymity*, the graph is *2-degree-anonymized*. In the other approach, *k-neighborhood-anonymity* based algorithm in [29] adds edges to the original graph to create a graph in which for every vertex there are at least $k − 1$ other vertices with the same *1-neighborhood* graphs. Based on *k-neighborhood-anonymity*, the graph is *2-neighborhood-anonymized*. Hence, the existing *k-anonymity* approaches are inadequate when the attacker has more complex knowledge about the neighborhood structures.

Based upon the above discussion, we conclude that we must support $k(d)$-neighborhood-anonymity for any d, instead of k-degree-anonymity or k-neighborhood-anonymity for d = 1-neighborhood considered in prior works. That is, our approach will provide an algorithm that efficiently enables d-neighborhood privacy preservation for any d to protect against attacks that use complex neighborhood acknowledgements of the target vertex.

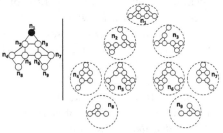

Fig. 1. Graph to be publicly published on the left and *2-neighborhood* structures for each vertex on the right. Black vertex represents Alice.

Next we consider the issue of utility preservation. *SecGraph* introduced by Ji et al. [11], evaluates different anonymization algorithms using various utilities. According to their study, *k-neighborhood-anonymity* preserves most of the graph and application utilities. The one application utility which *k-neighborhood-anonymity* algorithm cannot preserve is the *role extraction* utility where it considers the uniqueness of each vertex based on their structure in the graph. Among all anonymization algorithms, the *Rand Switch* approach introduced in [28] where existing pair of edges are switched randomly n times, is the only one that can preserve *role extraction*.

Because of the above reason, in this paper we give higher priority to edge switching over edge adding and removing since *edge switching* can effectively preserve degree and its related utilities (e.g., role extraction) leading to preserving more utilities. We further apply *edge switching* to the $k(d)$-neighborhood-anonymity model and use Genetic Algorithm as the main approach for utility preservation.

Summary: With more knowledge about the local neighborhood structures in a social network, an adversary has more chances to re-identify some victims. We show that existing anonymization techniques not only do not present a complete model to *defend against DA attacks*, specially structure-based attacks, but also

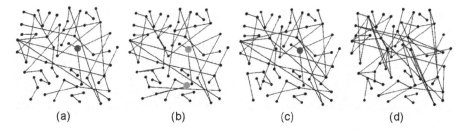

Fig. 2. Sample social network graph (a) Original graph to be publicly published, bigger colored node shows the victim vertex (b) Anonymized graph using our approach with $k = 2$ and $d = 2$, bigger colored nodes show the victim vertex and the vertex with similar 2-neighborhood (c) Anonymized graph using *k-degree Anonymization* in [17] with $k = 2$ (d) Anonymized graph using *Random Walk Anonymization* in [21] with $r = 2$. (Color figure online)

they *make more than the minimum required changes.* In contrast, an additional goal of our approach is applying fewer changes and thus providing a better trade-off between anonymization and utility preservation. As a motivating example, Fig. 2(a) depicts the original graph, and the anonymized graphs generated by our approach, *k-degree Anonymization,* and *Random Walk Anonymization* techniques using the minimum values for the parameters of each approach ($k = 2$ and $d = 2$ for our approach, $k = 2$ for *k-degree Anonymization,* and $r = 2$ for *Random Walk Anonymization*). Assume an adversary knows that a user has 3 friends and only one of them has another friend, then the user can be re-identified easily (colored bigger vertex in Fig. 2(a)), since this is the only user with that friendship neighborhood structure.

(Our Approach). In Fig. 2(b), our approach applies minimum number of changes of 3 edges switches and 1 edge removal to the original graph (i.e., we preserve degrees for all vertices except for only two vertices). We anonymize the graph in a way that for each vertex there is at least one other vertex with similar *2-neighborhood* structure (i.e., there is another user with similar *2-neighborhood* friendship to the target user *2-neighborhood* depicted with two colored vertices which reduces the re-identification chance by 50%). Note that for simplicity of presentation, we consider $k = 2$ and $d = 2$. Larger values of k and d reduce the attacker's chance of success.

(K-Degree Anonymization). In Fig. 2(c), by applying slightly more changes compared to our approach, the *k-degree-anonymity* concept introduced in [17] is achieved which is weaker in comparison to *k(d)-neighborhood-anonymity.* This means that for each vertex there is at least one other vertex with similar degree which is already satisfied with our approach. Hence, the adversary can still re-identify the target user easily.

(Random Walk Anonymization). In Fig. 2(d), while introducing much more noise compared to our approach, this technique only ensures some level of link privacy. The reason of comparing our approach with *Random Walk Anonymization* technique is that it is the only graph anonymization technique which takes the concept of neighborhoods structures into consideration. That is, in social network graph G, replace an edge *(u, v)* by the edge *(u, z)* where z denotes the terminus point of a random walk algorithm. As a result, noise is introduced into the graph leading to huge data loss.

3   GAGA

In this section, we present an Efficient Genetic Algorithm for Graph Anonymization (*GAGA*). *GAGA* creates an optimal anonymized graph by applying minimum number of changes to the original graph in comparison to existing approaches which make the graph less responsive to various queries. *GAGA* can preserve data privacy against many complicated DA attacks. To achieve these goals we use Genetic algorithm (GA) as the main approach. Our reasoning is that first, Genetic Algorithms are very effective in achieving optimal or near-optimal solutions in a variety of single- and multi-objective problems (e.g., classification, game theory, bioinformatics, etc.). Hence, achieving an optimal anonymized graph as a two-fold optimization problem (i.e., achieving a *k(d)-neighborhood-anonymized* graph and applying minimum number of changes simultaneously) fits a genetic algorithm-based model very well. Second, different tunable parameters in genetic algorithm helps to avoid leaving some areas of the search space undiscovered, resulting in widening the search space more that the other approaches. In this section, we describe how we apply GA to the graph anonymization problem. Figure 3 shows an overview of *GAGA*. Now we discuss each step of GA that we used in *GAGA*:

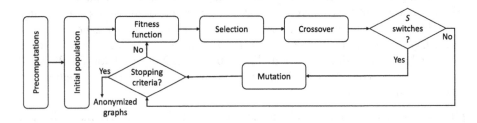

Fig. 3. *GAGA* overview.

3.1   Precomputation Step

Before applying the GA to the original graph, we perform precomputations that evaluate the original graph so that we can choose the best parameters to create the optimal *k(d)-neighborhood-anonymized* graph. As a result, the original graph is categorized as one of: *good*, *bad*, or *ugly* scenarios. In the *good* scenario, the original graph is close to a *k(d)-neighborhood-anonymized* solution and hence it needs a small number of changes. In the *bad* scenario, many vertices do not satisfy the *k(d)-neighborhood-anonymity* and hence the original graph needs changes to large number of vertices. In the *ugly* scenario, few vertices violate the *k(d)-neighborhood-anonymity* but they have a very different neighborhood compared to other vertices; hence it requires huge changes to a small number of vertices. Our precomputations involve the following steps:

Step 1. Percentage of Violating Vertices: We identify the vertices that violate the *k(d)-neighborhood-anonymity* (i.e., there are less than k − 1 other vertices with similar *d-neighborhood* to the *d-neighborhood* of these violating vertices) and compute the percentage of violating vertices. A low percentage of violating vertices means that by applying some changes to a small group of vertices, we can create a *k(d)-neighborhood-anonymized* graph. We further observe that the changes can be small or big themselves. Hence, we consider a threshold value (T_{pv}) and if the percentage is below the threshold value, we consider the graph as one of the *good* ones (i.e., small changes to small number of vertices are required) or an *ugly* one (i.e., big changes to small number of vertices are required). If the percentage is above the threshold value, we consider the graph as *bad* (i.e., some changes to large number of vertices are required).

Step 2. Violating Vertices' Neighborhoods Analysis: After the previous step, the original graph is categorized as *good/ugly* or *bad*. To distinguish between *good* and *ugly* scenarios, we analyze the neighborhoods around violating vertices and compare them with the neighborhoods of vertices that satisfy the *k(d)-neighborhood-anonymity*. If some of the violating vertices have a very different neighborhood than others (we simply compare degrees for this purpose), we categorize the graph as *ugly*. Otherwise, we categorize the graph as *good*. To analyze the rate of difference, we again define a threshold value (T_u) so that if the value is above the threshold we consider the graph as *ugly* scenario. Otherwise, if the value is below the threshold, we consider the graph as *good* scenario. We illustrate the scenarios using three sample graphs in Fig. 4. The treatment for each of three scenarios is described next:

Good Scenario. In the *good* scenario, in the beginning of the GA process, we focus only on violating vertices according to a probability and apply the GA to them. For this purpose, we select the vertices –selection in GA– from violating vertices to apply the changes (switches, adds, removes) –mutation in GA– so the number of violating vertices will decrease. As we proceed forward towards the end of the process, we select some vertices from other non violating vertices and apply the changes to them based on a probability. This increases the probability of searching more areas of the search space causing the graph to become $k(d)$-neighborhood-anonymized faster.

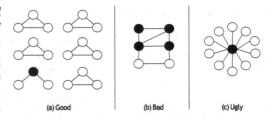

Fig. 4. Black vertices represent the violating vertices. Assume that $k = 2$, $d = 1$, and $T_{pv} = 10\%$; i.e., the graph is $2(1)$-neighborhood-anonymized if for each vertex of the graph, there is at least one other vertex with similar (1)-neighborhood graph. (a) *Good scenario*: 5% of vertices violate the $2(1)$-neighborhood-anonymity. (b) *Bad scenario*: 66% of vertices violate the $2(1)$-neighborhood-anonymity. (c) *Ugly scenario*: 9% of vertices violate the $2(1)$-neighborhood-anonymity but the violating vertex has a very different neighborhood than other vertices.

Bad Scenario. In the *bad* scenario, there is no advantage to focus only on violating vertices neighborhoods. So we apply the GA to the whole graph. For this purpose, we select the vertices –selection in GA– from all the vertices in graph to apply the changes. In comparison to the *good* scenario, the *bad* scenario, in general requires more changes and thus more time to create the $k(d)$-neighborhood-anonymized graph. As we will see in Sect. 4, even in *bad* scenarios, our results are much more efficient in terms of minimum number of changes and hence utility preservation compared to the existing techniques.

Ugly Scenario. In the *ugly* scenario, we again focus on violating vertices in the beginning of the GA process like in *good* scenario but we apply more changes in each step of GA compared to *good* scenario so that the graph becomes $k(d)$-neighborhood-anonymized faster. Again, as we move forward, we select some vertices from other non-violating vertices to increase the probability of searching more areas of the search space.

3.2   Initial Population

In this step we randomly apply edge switches on the original graph to create a fixed number of chromosomes as the initial population. We present chromosome representation details in Sect. 3.6. As we discussed earlier, we create a larger initial population in *bad* scenarios compared to the *good* and *ugly* scenarios.

3.3   Fitness Function and Selection

For each chromosome, the fitness value – which defines how good a solution the chromosome represents – is computed and the chromosomes are selected for reproduction based on their fitness values. Therefore, first, we need to define a function which computes the distance between the modified graph and the original graph (fitness function) and second, we need a function to compute the distance between the modified graph and the solution of a *k(d)-neighborhood-anonymized* graph (selection function). We define the fitness function as below:

$$fitness(G, \tilde{G}) = \frac{1}{size((E \backslash \tilde{E}) \cup (\tilde{E} \backslash E))} \tag{1}$$

Given the original graph $G(V, E)$, V is the set of vertices and E is the set of edges in G, and the modified graph $\tilde{G}(\tilde{V}, \tilde{E})$, we evaluate the distance between the modified graph and the original graph by computing the number of edges in the union of relative complement of E in $\tilde{E}$ and relative complement of $\tilde{E}$ in E. Finally, we consider the inverse of the computed number of different edges so that a graph with higher fitness value has fewer changes. After we compute the fitness values, we use roulette wheel selection so that the chromosomes with a higher fitness value will be more likely to be selected. With this method, in each step of GA we select those chromosomes which need fewer modifications to the original graph. As we discussed earlier, we need to define a selection function as well. We define the selection function as the inverse of the number of vertices in the graph that do not satisfy the *k(d)-neighborhood-anonimity* concept for a given k and d. Using this selection function, in each step of GA, we select those chromosomes which are closer to the solution.

3.4   Crossover and Mutation

Crossover and mutation are the two basic processes in GA. Crossover process copies individual strings (also called parent chromosomes) into a tentative new population for genetic operations and mutation is used to preserve the diversity from one generation to the next. Mutation prevents the GA from becoming trapped in a local optima. For crossover, the main function we employ is *edge switch* as follows. Given graph $G(V, E)$ and a pair of edges $(u, v) \in E$ and $(w, z) \in E$ such that $(u, w) \notin E$ and $(v, z) \notin E$, we remove edges (u, v) and (w, z) and we add edges (u, w) and (v, z) to the graph. Note that *edge switch* can be considered as the process of combining the parent chromosomes where the parents are the chromosome and a copy of itself.

For mutation, we remove/add one or some number of random edges to some chromosomes. Specifically in our GA, first we try to perform *edge switch* for a certain number of times (s in Fig. 3). If we fail to reach to a solution by applying s edge switches, then we start to remove/add one or some number of random edges to some chromosomes to create the new generation and then we repeat the GA for the new generation. If it is a *good* scenario, we remove/add very small number of edges in each step and if it is a *bad* scenario, we remove/add greater number of edges in each step. To decide whether to add or remove edges, if the selected vertex has a degree higher than average graph degree, we remove an edge while if the vertex degree is lower than average degree, we add an edge.

3.5 Checking Stopping Criteria

GAGA always returns at least one *k(d)-neighborhood-anonymized* graph as the solution by trying to apply minimum number of changes (switches, adds, removes) to the original graph. Therefore, in general we only have one stopping criteria except for invalid cases\inputs i.e. suppose a graph $G(V, E)$ with $|V| = n$ is given and a *k(d)-neighborhood-anonymized* graph is requested for some $k > n$. The problem has no solution unless we add fake vertices. *GAGA* does not introduce any fake vertices as in some previous works [6,16]. As noted in [29], adding fake vertices is not desirable because this can change the global structure of the original graph. By maintaining the original utilities of the published social network, *GAGA* ensures that the changes are likely to have little or no impact on solutions to many applications/queries.

3.6 Implementation Highlights

We implemented *GAGA* in Java. The implementation challenges are as follows.

Chromosomal Representation. As discussed earlier, we need to represent the graph in an effective way such that *k(d)-neighborhood-anonymity* concept can be put into action and the d distance neighborhood for each vertex can be easily considered. For this purpose, we represent the graph as a *HashMap* structure where each key represents a vertex of the graph and the value represents the *d-neighborhood* structure around the vertex.

Thresholds and Parameters. As we discussed, k and d are the main parameters of *GAGA* which provide the data owners some application-oriented level of control over achieving the desired level of data preservation and anonymization. Besides the k and d parameters, *GAGA* contains other thresholds and parameters used in GA: initial population size, s as the number of maximum edge switches before remove/add one or some number of random edges, thresholds T_{pv} and T_u to categorize the scenario of the graph, a parameter to indicate finding local maxima as opposed to the global maximum for scenarios where the user/data owner can tolerate some number of violating vertices. *GAGA* receives the above parameters as the input.

Graph Isomorphism Test. The graph isomorphism tests are frequently conducted in the selection phase of GA. For this purpose, we used the VF2 algorithm introduced in [7] as a (sub)graph isomorphism algorithm with efficient performance specially for large graphs. Since the nature of any isomorphism test is that it takes time, we perform multiple level of prechecks to avoid applying the algorithm as much as possible. As a simple example, when two subgraphs have different number of vertices (or edges), or different degree sequences, we do not apply the VF2 algorithm.

4 Experimental Evaluation

In this section, first, we evaluate the effectiveness of *GAGA* against the existing De-Anonymization (DA) attacks using real world graph. Second, we evaluate *GAGA* under various utility metrics and compare the results with the state-of-the-art graph anonymization approaches. Finally, we compare the performance of *GAGA* with work by Zhou and Pei [29]. All the experiments were conducted on a PC running Ubuntu 16.04 with an Intel Core i7-4770 CPU running at 3.4 GHz and 23 GB RAM.

4.1 Evaluating *GAGA* against DA attacks

As discussed in Sect. 2, Ji et al. [11] implemented the *SecGraph* tool to conduct analysis and evaluation of existing anonymization techniques. In this subsection, we compare *GAGA* with the state-of-the-art anonymization techniques using *SecGraph* against different DA attacks.

Dataset and DA Attacks. We use Facebook friendship network collected from survey participants using the Facebook app [15] consisting of 61 nodes and 270 undirected edges representing the friendship between users. We evaluate the anonymization approaches against the following five practical DA attacks: **(1) Narayanan and Shmatikov** [22]: They proposed a re-identification algorithm to de-anonymize the graph based on the graph topology. Here the attacker, in addition to having detailed information about a very small number of members of the target network, also has access to the data of another graph (a subgraph from the target graph or another social network). Thus, the power of the attack depends on the level of the attacker's access to auxiliary networks; **(2) Srivatsa and Hicks** [24]: They presented an approach to re-identify the mobility traces. They used the social network data of the participating users as the auxiliary information. They used heuristic based approach on Distance Vector, Randomized Spanning Trees, and Recursive Subgraph Matching to propagate the DA; **(3) Yartseva and Grossglauser** [27]: They proposed a simple percolation-based graph matching algorithm that incrementally maps every pair of node with at least r (predefined threshold) neighboring mapped pairs. They also showed that the approach used in [22] has a sharp phase transition in performance as a function of the seed set size. That is, when the seed set size is below a certain threshold, the algorithm fails almost completely. When the number of seeds exceeds the threshold, they achieve a high success rate. This is again consistent with the evaluation of [22] which shows that the power of the attack depends on how large the auxiliary networks are; **(4) Korula and Lattanzi** [14]: They presented a similar approach to [27] where they use an initial set of links of users across different networks as the seed set and map a pair of users with the most number of neighboring mapped pairs; **(5) Ji et al.** [12]: They proposed two DA attack frameworks, namely De-Anonymization and Adaptive De-Anonymization. The later attack is used to de-anonymize data without the knowledge of the overlap size between the anonymized data and the auxiliary data. In their attack, besides the vertices' local properties, they incorporate global properties as well.

Our evaluation methodology is basically the same as in [11]. We compare *GAGA* with the following anonymization techniques: *Add/Del* approach introduced in [17] which adds k randomly chosen edges followed by deletion of other k randomly chosen edges. *Deferentially Private Graph Model (DP)* proposed in [23], in which a partitioned privacy technique is employed to achieve differential privacy. *K-Degree Anonymization (KDA)* technique presented in [17], in which some edges are added to or removed from the original graph so that each vertex has at least k − 1 other vertices with the same degree. *Random Walk Anonymization (RW)* approach proposed in [21], where the graph is perturbed with replacing the edges by random walk paths in order to provide link privacy. *t-Means Clustering Algorithm (t-Means Cluster)* introduced in [25], uses conventional t-Means algorithm to create clusters with size of at least k. *Union-Split Clustering (Union Cluster)* technique presented in [25], is similar to *t-Means Clustering Algorithm* while cluster centers are not chosen arbitrarily to bypass the variability in clustering results.

We present the results in Table 1. The criteria for parameters settings for each anonymization technique are the same to settings as in [11] which follows the same settings in original works. That is for *Union Cluster*, k is the size of each cluster; for *Add/Del*, f is the fraction of edges to be modified; for *KDA*, k is the anonymization parameter indicating the number of similar nodes with respect to degree; for *DP*, ε is the parameter that determines the amount of noises that must be injected into the graph where a larger value of ε means that it is easier to identify the source of the graph structure and hence a lower level of graph privacy is preserved; for *t-Means Cluster*, t is the parameter which shows the minimum size of each cluster; for *RW*, r is the number of steps; and finally, for *GAGA*, k indicates the number of similar nodes with respect to neighborhood structures and d shows the level of *d-neighborhood*. For DA attacks, we randomly sample a graph with probability $s = 80\%$ and $s = 90\%$ from the original graph as the auxiliary graph and then we apply the graph anonymization approaches to obtain the anonymized graphs. A larger value for s results in successfully de-anonymizing more users since with a large s, the anonymized graph and the auxiliary graph are likely to have similar structures. We also feed each DA technique 20 pre-identified seed mappings. Then we use the auxiliary graph to de-anonymize the anonymized graph. We use *Union Cluster* as the baseline for our evaluation. For each anonymization technique, *SecGraph* provides the number of successfully de-anonymized users – this number for *Union Cluster* is given in parenthesis. For rest of the techniques, Table 1 provides the factor by which number of successfully de-anonymized users is reduced in comparison to the baseline. **Note that *GAGA* is the optimal solution against all DA attacks (bold values in Table 1) as for all DA attacks *GAGA* offers the most defense – in fact the number of de-anonymized users is either 0 (perfect defense) or 1 (near perfect) of 50–57. *GAGA* (wih d = 3) reduces the de-anonymization rate by at least a factor of 2.7× over the baseline. A factor of ∞ means no user has been de-anonymized successfully.** Larger values of d make *GAGA* more powerful against DA attacks.

Table 1. Comparing *GAGA*'s preservation of privacy with existing approaches introduced in [11] against five DA attacks. Using Union Cluster as the baseline, the factor by which number of de-anonymized users is reduced by each other technique is presented.

DA	s	Union cluster (k = 5)	Add/Del (f = 0.23)	KDA (k = 5)	DP (ε = 10)	t-Means cluster (t = 5)	RW (r = 2)	GAGA (k = 5, d = 1)	(k = 5, d = 2)	(k = 5, d = 3)
Ji et al. [12]	0.8	1 (2 of 42)	1.1×	1.1×	1.2×	1.3×	1.8×	1.5×	2.3×	**2.7× (1 of 57)**
	0.9	1 (2 of 37)	1.1×	1.1×	-	1.4×	-	1.4×	2.2×	**3.1× (1 of 57)**
Korula and Lattanzi [14]	0.8	1 (2 of 48)	1.2×	1.2×	1.2×	1.2×	1.3×	1.5×	∞	**∞ (0 of 51)**
	0.9	1 (2 of 45)	0.9×	1.2×	-	1.1×	-	1.2×	2.5×	**∞ (0 of 50)**
Narayanan and Shmatikov [22]	0.8	1 (3 of 51)	0.8×	1×	1×	1.6×	1.4×	1.5×	**3.1×**	**3.1× (1 of 53)**
	0.9	1 (3 of 44)	0.8×	1×	-	1.5×	-	1.5×	3.3×	**3.6× (1 of 53)**
Srivatsa and Hicks [24]	0.8	1 (2 of 42)	1.1 ×	1.1×	1.2×	1.3×	1.6×	1.5×	1.9×	**2.7× (1 of 57)**
	0.9	1 (2 of 38)	1×	1.1×	-	1.3×	-	1.4×	1.9×	**3× (1 of 57)**
Yartseva and Grossglauser [27]	0.8	1 (4 of 52)	1.4×	1.7×	1.8×	2×	2.2×	2.1×	3.6×	**4× (1 of 52)**
	0.9	1 (4 of 44)	1.3×	1.5×	-	1.7×	-	2×	3.9×	**4.7× (1 of 52)**

This is because each DA attack uses a combination of structural properties/semantics while each anonymization technique usually focuses on one structural property/semantic (e.g., vertex degree in *KDA* [17] or *1-neighborhood-anonymity* in [29]). However in *GAGA* we use *k(d)-neighborhood-anonymity* for any *d-neighborhood* which makes all complex neighborhoods structures similar to at least $k - 1$ other neighborhoods structures followed by other structural properties/semantics changes. Note that no values for *DP* and *RW* when $s = 90\%$ are given because the anonymized graphs obtained in these two cases do not have enough edges; however, we are able to report the results for them when $s = 80\%$.

4.2 Evaluating *GAGA* for Utilities

Now we compare *GAGA* with the state-of-the-art anonymization techniques using *SecGraph* from the graph and application utility preservation perspective.

Dataset and utility metrics. We use DBLP co-authorship network [15] consisting of 8734 nodes and 10100 undirected edges representing the co-authorship where two authors are connected if they publish at least one paper together. We apply the same graph anonymization approaches that we used in previous subsection along with *GAGA* to anonymize the original graph and then measure how each data utility is preserved in the anonymized graph compared to the original graph. We use the following 16 popular graph and application utility metrics to measure the utility preservation:

Authorities Score: which is the sum of the scores of the hubs of all of the vertex predecessors. *Betweenness Centrality:* which indicates the centrality of a vertex. It is equal to the number of shortest paths from all vertices to all others that go through the specific vertex. *Closeness Centrality:* which is defined as the inverse of the average distance to all accessible vertices. *Community*

Detection: a communication in a graph is a set of vertices where there are more connections between the members of the set than the members to the rest of the graph. *SecGraph* uses the hierarchical agglomeration algorithm introduced in [26] to measure the *Community Detection.* **Degree:** which indicates the degree distribution of the graph. **Effective Diameter:** which is the minimum number of hops in which some fraction (say, 90%) of all connected pairs of vertices can reach each other. **EigenVector:** let A be the adjacency matrix of a graph G, the *EigenVector* is a non-zero vector v such that $Av = \lambda v$, where λ is a scalar multiplier. **Hubs Score:** which is the sum of the authorities scores of all of the vertex successors. **Infectiousness:** which measures the number of users infected by a disease in a infectious diseases spreading model where each user transmits the disease to its neighbors with some infection rate. **Joint Degree:** which indicates the joint degree distribution of the graph. **Local Clustering Coefficient:** which quantifies how close the vertex neighbors are to being a complete graph. **Network Constraint:** which measures the extent to which a network is directly or indirectly concentrated in a single contact. **Network Resilience:** which is the number of vertices in the largest connected cluster when vertices are removed from the graph in the degree decreasing order. **Page Rank:** which computes the ranking of the vertices in the graph. **Role Extraction:** which automatically determines the underlying roles in the graph and assigns a mixed-membership of the roles to each vertex to summarize the behavior of the vertices. *SecGraph* uses the approach in [9] to measure the *Role Extraction.* **Secure Routing:** to address the security vulnerabilities of P2P systems, Marti et al. [19] proposed an algorithm to leverage trust relationships given by social links. *SecGraph* uses their approach to measure the *Secure Routing* utility metric.

Table 2 presents the results and provides the parameters that were used for each approach. Each value in the table represents one of the following: *Cosine Similarity* in case of Authorities Score, Betweenness Centrality, Closeness Centrality, Degree, Hubs Score, Infectiousness, Joint Degree, Local Clustering Coefficient, Network Constraint, Network Resilience, Page Rank, Role Extraction, and Secure Routing; *Ratios* in case of Effective Diameter and EigenVector; and *Jaccard Similarity* in case of Community Detection between the anonymized and original graphs.

For *GAGA*, we set $k = 5$ and $d = 1$ and hence as a result, 297 edge adds and 307 edge removes (including 145 edge switches in total) have been applied to the graph. Accordingly, we set the similar parameters for other approaches so that the number of changes to the original graph can be compared with *GAGA* fairly. For example, we used the same $k = 5$ and $t = 5$ for *KDA*, *Union Cluster*, and *t-Means Cluster* accordingly. For *Add/Del*, we set f to 0.06, that is because 297 edge adds, and 307 edge removes in *GAGA* map to $307 + 297$ edge adds/deletes for *Add/Del*. We also used a reasonable value for ε in *DP* that is the same value in original work, as we mentioned earlier larger value of ε means smaller changes to the graph so we set ε to the reasonable value of 10. For *RW*, we set r to the minimum value of 2. In general, our evaluation results are consistent with

Table 2. Comparing the utility preservation of *GAGA* with the utility preservation of existing approaches introduced in [11] with respect to various utilities.

Utility	Add/Del (f = 0.06)	DP (ε = 10)	GAGA (k = 5, d = 1)	KDA (k = 5)	RW (r = 2)	t-Means cluster (t = 5)	Union cluster (k = 5)
Authorities score	0.4995	0.324	**0.7079**	0.4013	0.3792	0.6773	0.6976
Betweenness centrality	0.8256	0.762	**0.9606**	0.8459	0.8247	0.9378	0.8755
Closeness centrality	0.9123	0.785	0.9604	0.9788	0.8612	0.9632	0.9832
Community detection	0.3926	0.1766	0.8783	0.8747	0.2933	0.5324	0.9103
Degree	0.9877	0.9265	**0.9998**	0.9979	0.9648	0.9972	0.9989
Effective diameter	0.9559	0.6268	**0.9632**	0.9205	1.7626	0.9394	0.9629
EigenVector	0.8562	0.4443	**0.9927**	0.6573	0.5573	0.9598	0.9909
Hubs score	0.6844	0.2971	**0.7259**	0.5274	0.3967	0.6997	0.686
Infectiousness	0.8033	0.8675	0.8393	0.8364	0.7093	0.8513	0.8622
Joint degree	0.7645	0.6102	**0.9875**	0.7713	0.2679	0.6832	0.7943
Local clustering coefficient	0.9846	0.9074	**0.9977**	0.997	0.9561	0.9909	0.9939
Network constraint	0.9885	0.9777	0.9992	0.9999	0.987	0.9994	0.9999
Network resilience	0.9989	0.9954	0.9997	0.9999	0.9913	0.9999	0.9999
Page rank	0.3722	0.3323	**0.3766**	0.3681	0.3625	0.3758	0.3742
Role extraction	0.5519	0.2271	**0.6685**	0.3134	0.2418	0.5282	0.6248
Secure routing	1.0346	1.1149	**1.0024**	1.007	0.9571	0.9505	1.1717

the results presented in [11]: most of the graph and application utilities can be partially or conditionally preserved with most anonymization algorithms.

Despite the fact that no anonymization scheme is optimal to preserve all utilities, note that for most of the utilities (11 out of 16 highlighted as bold values in Table 2) *GAGA* is the best approach to preserve these utilities. For some other utilities, *Union Cluster* and *KDA* have good performance. However, as we discussed in the previous subsection, *Union Cluster* and *KDA* are very vulnerable to DA attacks. This makes *GAGA* the most efficient practical approach which can preserve most of the utilities and at the same time also defend well against modern DA attacks.

4.3   *GAGA* vs. Zhou and Pei [29]

As we discussed in Sect. 2, Zhou and Pei [29] presented the *k-neighborhood-anonymity* model to preserve users' privacy against some neighborhood attacks. They evaluated the anonymization cost of their approach using various data sets generated by the R-MAT graph model [5]. To compare our work with Zhou and Pei's work, we used the same model with the same default parameters to generate the same data sets. Figure 5 compares the anonymization cost of *GAGA* with their work. Recall that as discussed earlier, Zhou and Pei [29] only support *1-neighborhood* and only apply edge addition to the original graph. However, *GAGA* supports any *d* and applies three different changes to the graph: switch, add, and remove. Therefore, to compare the cost of *GAGA* to their approach

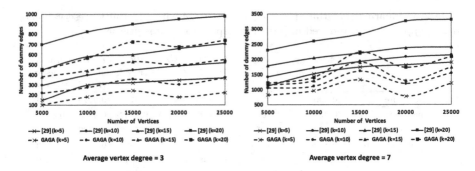

Fig. 5. Comparing the cost of *GAGA* with the cost of Zhou and Pei [29] on various data sets.

we use $d = 1$ and we compute the sum of all edge additions and deletions that *GAGA* applies to the original graph. The results show that in all cases *GAGA* is far more efficient in terms of the anonymization cost (i.e., number of changes to the original graph) than Zhou and Pei's approach when obtaining the same level of privacy preservation. Notice how our approach is efficient even for denser graphs where the average vertex degree is 7 – while the number of dummy edges for Zhou and Pei varies from around 1100 to 3300, the total number of edge adds and removes applied by *GAGA* varies only from 830 to 2230.

We present the results in further detail in Table 3. The first column shows the number of vertices used to generate the graphs using R-MAT graph model. For brevity, we report only the cases of 5,000 and 25,000 vertices. The third and eighth column give the number of violating vertices along with the corresponding scenario with respect to different k values (g is the *good* scenario, b is the *bad* scenario, and u is the *ugly* scenario). We give the average degree of violating vertices in fourth and ninth column. A high average degree means that some violating vertices have much higher degree than the graph's average degree (3 or 7) and as a result greater number of removes than adds are needed to anonymize the graph.

Note that since Zhou and Pei [29] only consider $d = 1$ scenario, the degree of the vertices can be considered as a good parameter to represent the structure of neighborhoods. Thus, we also present the average degree for violating vertices in the tested data sets. Since in *GAGA* we consider *k(d)-neighborhood Anonymization* for any *d-neighborhood*, degree is not a good parameter to represent the complex structure of *d*-neighborhoods. Thus, we report the number of adds, and removes (including edges switches). Finally, we compare the anonymization cost of *GAGA* with Zhou and Pei's [29] cost in the "Avg. (*GAGA cost* ÷ Zhou and Pei [29] cost)" column. **In all cases, our approach is more efficient. On average, our approach incurs only 69% of the cost of Zhou and Pei's approach in terms of number of changes to the original graph.**

Table 3. *GAGA* anonymization cost on various data sets.

Num. of vertices	k	Average vertex degree = 3					Average vertex degree = 7				
		Num. of violating vertices (scenario)	Avg. deg. of violating vertices	Num. of adds	Num. of removes	Avg. (GAGA cost ÷ Zhou and Pei [29] cost) (%)	Num. of violating vertices (scenario)	Avg. deg. of violating vertices	Num. of adds	Num. of removes	Avg. (GAGA cost ÷ Zhou and Pei [29] cost) (%)
5000	5	36(g)	16	39	63	64	321(b)	24	217	614	67
25000	5	116(u)	25	97	129		700(b)	38	388	825	
5000	10	115(b)	14	103	120	72	429(b)	22	315	744	71
25000	10	178(u)	23	177	194		1009(b)	34	457	1093	
5000	15	184(b)	12	175	209	81	505(b)	21	339	827	68
25000	15	284(u)	21	241	309		1187(b)	32	528	1207	
5000	20	217(b)	11	192	261	72	553(b)	20	397	829	61
25000	20	354(u)	19	317	422		1299(b)	32	659	1421	

5   Related Work

As we discussed in Sect. 2, several graph anonymization techniques have been proposed. Casas-Roma et al. [4] compare *random-based* algorithm [8] and *k-degree-anonymity* algorithm [17] in terms of graph and risk assessment metrics and it was shown that *k-degree-anonymity* is more effective. The evaluation was limited to 3 small data sets, moreover, only 6 metrics to measure the graph utility preservation are used and no DA attacks were considered in the evaluation. The sole use of degrees in representing graphs and characterizing anonymization introduces limitations. First, it makes anonymization vulnerable to attacks that use more complex graph characteristics such as neighborhood structure of a target vertex. Second, a graph is represented by degree sequence which is not desirable since two different graphs can have same degree sequence. To overcome the limitations of *k-degree-anonymity*, Zhou and Pei [29] introduced the concept of *k-neighborhood-anonymity* [29] that considers graph structure. As we discussed, they only consider $d = 1\text{-}neighborhood$ which is not efficient for complex DA attacks. Finally, Ji et al. [11] implemented the *SecGraph* tool to analyze existing anonymization techniques in terms of data utility and vulnerability against modern DA attacks. They conclude that it is a big challenge to effectively anonymize graphs with desired data utility preservation and without enabling adversaries to utilize these data utilities to perform modern DA attacks. Therefore in this paper, aiming to address the limitations in *k-anonymity* graph anonymization techniques, we implemented and evaluated *GAGA* that not only provides defense against modern DA attacks, but also preserves most of the utilities.

6   Conclusions

In this paper we addressed the limitations in graph anonymization techniques. We proposed, implemented, and evaluated *GAGA*, an efficient genetic algorithm for graph anonymization. Our results show that *GAGA* is highly effective and has a better trade-off between anonymization and utility preservation compared to existing techniques.

First, by applying the concept of *k(d)-neighborhood Anonymization* for any *d*, *GAGA* preserves data privacy against the modern DA attacks. Second, with the help of genetic algorithm and giving higher priority to edge switching over edge adding and removing, *GAGA* preserves the graph and application utilities. Moreover, *GAGA* gives application-oriented level of control on anonymization and utility preservation to the users/data owners via selection of k and d parameters. There are other parameters and thresholds (*GA initial population*, s, T_{pv}, T_u, etc.) used in *GAGA*. These could be further tuned to obtain the optimal solutions for any graph.

Acknowledgement. This work is supported by NSF grant CCF-1617424 to the University of California Riverside.

References

1. Aggarwal, C.C., Yu, P.S.: Privacy-Preserving Data Mining: Models and Algorithms, 1st edn. Springer, Boston (2008). https://doi.org/10.1007/978-0-387-70992-5
2. Atzori, M.: Weak *k*-anonymity: a low-distortion model for protecting privacy. In: Katsikas, S.K., López, J., Backes, M., Gritzalis, S., Preneel, B. (eds.) ISC 2006. LNCS, vol. 4176, pp. 60–71. Springer, Heidelberg (2006). https://doi.org/10.1007/11836810_5
3. Bayardo, R.J., Agrawal, R.: Data privacy through optimal k-anonymization. In: 21st International Conference on Data Engineering (ICDE 2005), pp. 217–228, April 2005. https://doi.org/10.1109/ICDE.2005.42
4. Casas-Roma, J., Herrera-Joancomartí, J., Torra, V.: Comparing random-based and *k*-anonymity-based algorithms for graph anonymization. In: Torra, V., Narukawa, Y., López, B., Villaret, M. (eds.) MDAI 2012. LNCS (LNAI), vol. 7647, pp. 197–209. Springer, Heidelberg (2012). https://doi.org/10.1007/978-3-642-34620-0_19
5. Chakrabarti, D., Zhan, Y., Faloutsos, C.: R-MAT: a recursive model for graph mining, pp. 442–446. https://doi.org/10.1137/1.9781611972740.43
6. Chester, S., Kapron, B., Ramesh, G., Srivastava, G., Thomo, A., Venkatesh, S.: Why Waldo befriended the dummy? K-anonymization of social networks with pseudo-nodes. Soc. Netw. Anal. Min. **3**(3), 381–399 (2013). https://doi.org/10.1007/s13278-012-0084-6
7. Cordella, L.P., Foggia, P., Sansone, C., Vento, M.: A (sub)graph isomorphism algorithm for matching large graphs. IEEE Trans. Pattern Anal. Mach. Intell. **26**(10), 1367–1372 (2004). https://doi.org/10.1109/TPAMI.2004.75
8. Hay, M., Miklau, G., Jensen, D., Weis, P., Srivastava, S.: Anonymizing social networks. Technical report, Science (2007)

9. Henderson, K., et al.: Rolx: structural role extraction & mining in large graphs. In: SIGKDD, pp. 1231–1239. ACM, New York (2012). https://doi.org/10.1145/2339530.2339723

10. Ji, S., Li, W., Gong, N.Z., Mittal, P., Beyah, R.A.: On your social network deanonymizablity: quantification and large scale evaluation with seed knowledge. In: NDSS (2015)

11. Ji, S., Li, W., Mittal, P., Hu, X., Beyah, R.: SecGraph: a uniform and open-source evaluation system for graph data anonymization and de-anonymization. In: Proceedings of the 24th USENIX Conference on Security Symposium, SEC 2015, pp. 303–318. USENIX Association, Berkeley (2015)

12. Ji, S., Li, W., Srivatsa, M., He, J.S., Beyah, R.: Structure based data de-anonymization of social networks and mobility traces. In: Chow, S.S.M., Camenisch, J., Hui, L.C.K., Yiu, S.M. (eds.) ISC 2014. LNCS, vol. 8783, pp. 237–254. Springer, Cham (2014). https://doi.org/10.1007/978-3-319-13257-0_14

13. Jia, J., Wang, B., Gong, N.Z.: Random walk based fake account detection in online social networks. In: 2017 47th Annual IEEE/IFIP International Conference on Dependable Systems and Networks (DSN), pp. 273–284, June 2017. https://doi.org/10.1109/DSN.2017.55

14. Korula, N., Lattanzi, S.: An efficient reconciliation algorithm for social networks. Proc. VLDB Endow. **7**(5), 377–388 (2014). https://doi.org/10.14778/2732269.2732274

15. Leskovec, J., Krevl, A.: SNAP datasets: stanford large network dataset collection, June 2014. http://snap.stanford.edu/data

16. Li, N., Zhang, N., Das, S.K.: Relationship privacy preservation in publishing online social networks. In: 2011 IEEE Third International Conference on Privacy, Security, Risk and Trust and 2011 IEEE Third International Conference on Social Computing, pp. 443–450, October 2011. https://doi.org/10.1109/PASSAT/SocialCom.2011.191

17. Liu, K., Terzi, E.: Towards identity anonymization on graphs. In: Proceedings of the 2008 ACM SIGMOD International Conference on Management of Data, SIGMOD 2008, pp. 93–106. ACM, New York (2008). https://doi.org/10.1145/1376616.1376629

18. Machanavajjhala, A., Kifer, D., Gehrke, J., Venkitasubramaniam, M.: L-diversity: privacy beyond k-anonymity. ACM Trans. Knowl. Discov. Data **1**(1) (2007). https://doi.org/10.1145/1217299.1217302

19. Marti, S., Ganesan, P., Garcia-Molina, H.: SPROUT: P2P routing with social networks. In: Lindner, W., Mesiti, M., Türker, C., Tzitzikas, Y., Vakali, A.I. (eds.) EDBT 2004. LNCS, vol. 3268, pp. 425–435. Springer, Heidelberg (2004). https://doi.org/10.1007/978-3-540-30192-9_42

20. Meyerson, A., Williams, R.: On the complexity of optimal k-anonymity. In: Proceedings of the Twenty-Third ACM SIGMOD-SIGACT-SIGART Symposium on Principles of Database Systems, PODS 2004, pp. 223–228. ACM, New York (2004). https://doi.org/10.1145/1055558.1055591

21. Mittal, P., Papamanthou, C., Song, D.: Preserving link privacy in social network based systems. In: NDSS (2013)

22. Narayanan, A., Shmatikov, V.: De-anonymizing social networks. In: 2009 30th IEEE Symposium on Security and Privacy, pp. 173–187, May 2009. https://doi.org/10.1109/SP.2009.22

23. Sala, A., Zhao, X., Wilson, C., Zheng, H., Zhao, B.Y.: Sharing graphs using differentially private graph models. In: Proceedings of the 2011 ACM SIGCOMM Conference on Internet Measurement Conference, IMC 2011, pp. 81–98. ACM, New York (2011). https://doi.org/10.1145/2068816.2068825

24. Srivatsa, M., Hicks, M.: Deanonymizing mobility traces: using social network as a side-channel. In: Proceedings of the 2012 ACM Conference on Computer and Communications Security, CCS 2012, pp. 628–637. ACM, New York (2012). https://doi.org/10.1145/2382196.2382262

25. Thompson, B., Yao, D.: The union-split algorithm and cluster-based anonymization of social networks. In: Proceedings of the 4th International Symposium on Information, Computer, and Communications Security, ASIACCS 2009, pp. 218–227. ACM, New York (2009). https://doi.org/10.1145/1533057.1533088

26. Yang, J., Leskovec, J.: Overlapping community detection at scale: a nonnegative matrix factorization approach. In: Proceedings of the Sixth ACM International Conference on Web Search and Data Mining, WSDM 2013, pp. 587–596. ACM, New York (2013). https://doi.org/10.1145/2433396.2433471

27. Yartseva, L., Grossglauser, M.: On the performance of percolation graph matching. In: Proceedings of the First ACM Conference on Online Social Networks, COSN 2013, pp. 119–130. ACM, New York (2013). https://doi.org/10.1145/2512938.2512952

28. Ying, X., Wu, X.: Randomizing social networks: a spectrum preserving approach, pp. 739–750. https://doi.org/10.1137/1.9781611972788.67

29. Zhou, B., Pei, J.: Preserving privacy in social networks against neighborhood attacks. In: Proceedings of the 2008 IEEE 24th International Conference on Data Engineering, ICDE 2008, pp. 506–515. IEEE Computer Society, Washington, DC (2008). https://doi.org/10.1109/ICDE.2008.4497459

Mitigation Techniques for Attacks on 1-Dimensional Databases that Support Range Queries

Evangelia Anna Markatou$^{(\boxtimes)}$ and Roberto Tamassia

Brown University, Providence, RI 02912, USA
markatou@brown.edu, rt@cs.brown.edu

Abstract. In recent years, a number of attacks have been developed that can reconstruct encrypted one-dimensional databases that support range queries under the persistent passive adversary model. These attacks allow an (honest but curious) adversary (such as the cloud provider) to find the order of the elements in the database and, in some cases, to even *reconstruct* the database itself.

In this paper we present two mitigation techniques to make it harder for the adversary to reconstruct the database. The first technique makes it impossible for an adversary to reconstruct the values stored in the database with an error smaller than k, for k chosen by the client. By fine-tuning k, the user can increase the adversary's error at will.

The second technique is targeted towards adversaries who have managed to learn the distribution of the queries issued. Such adversaries may be able to reconstruct most of the database after seeing a very small (i.e. poly-logarithmic) number of queries. To neutralize such adversaries, our technique turns the database to a circular buffer. All known techniques that exploit knowledge of distribution fail, and no technique can determine which record is first (or last) based on access pattern leakage.

Keywords: Searchable encryption · Encrypted databases · Leakage-abuse attacks · Mitigation

1 Introduction

Currently, many organizations outsource their data, and sometimes their entire information technology infrastructure to the cloud. This is a reasonable choice as the cloud is a reliable, inexpensive, and generally safe place to store an organization's data. However, although storing data on the cloud usually provides protection from outside attackers, it may expose the data to the prying eyes of curious insiders within the provider. Thus, an additional security measure is to store encrypted data on the cloud and to support queries on the data using searchable encryption. This additional encryption step ensures that the data can not be seen in plaintext by a curious cloud provider.

© Springer Nature Switzerland AG 2019
Z. Lin et al. (Eds.): ISC 2019, LNCS 11723, pp. 231–251, 2019.
https://doi.org/10.1007/978-3-030-30215-3_12

1.1   Reconstruction Attacks on Encrypted Databases

Although, at a first glance, searchable encryption appears to guarantee the confidentiality of the data, unfortunately, this is not the case. Recent papers have demonstrated several attacks against encrypted databases that allow for range queries on the data. These attacks leak various amounts of information about the data, in some cases even achieving full database reconstruction.

For example, consider an encrypted one-dimensional database whose values are from a set of N consecutive integers. Kellaris, Kollios, Nissim, and O'Neill [24] have demonstrated that they can achieve full database reconstruction after observing the (encrypted) answers to $O(N^4 \log N)$ range queries. More recently, Grubbs, Lacharité, Minaud, and Paterson [20] have improved in this result and have shown how to achieve full database reconstruction from $O(N^2 \log N)$ queries. To make matters worse, they have also shown that approximate database reconstruction (i.e., reconstruction of most database elements with an asymptotically small error) can be done from a poly-logarithmic number of queries. Although approximate database reconstruction recovers only a portion of the database, this portion could be large enough for the attacker and may reveal sensitive data stored in the database.

The literature presents plenty of attacks on other various types of leakage as well. For example, Kornaropoulos, Papamanthou and Tamassia [25] have developed an approximate reconstruction attack utilizing leakage from k-nearest neighbor queries. Grubbs, Lacharité, Minaud, and Paterson [19] utilize volume leakage from responses to range queries to achieve full database reconstruction. Grubbs, Ristenpart, and Shmatikov [21] present a snapshot attack that can break the claimed security guarantees of encrypted databases.

All this previous research suggests that even if the database is stored encrypted, database reconstruction may be possible in reasonable time. Having realized that current searchable encryption approaches provide little protection against powerful attackers such as *honest but curious cloud providers*, in this paper we take a slightly different approach and explore whether it is possible to make the task of the attacker a bit more difficult by introducing some form of *noise* or some kind of error by *changing* the queries issued by the clients. For example, when a client issues query $[a, b]$, our methods issue query $[a', b']$ (where $a \neq a'$ and/or $b \neq b'$) or our methods issue multiple queries. The choice of a' and b' is done in such as way so as to *obfuscate* the real query that the clients want to issue and thus *confuse* the attacker. So far, all attacks either assume that the client issues queries uniformly at random [20,24] or that the adversary has access to all possible query responses [19,28].

1.2   Contributions

After defining our encrypted database model (Sect. 2) and reviewing related work (Sect. 3), we present two *obfuscation* techniques to mitigate reconstruction attacks on encrypted databases from the observation of the answers to one-dimensional range queries. These techniques, which we call *blocked queries* and *wrap-around queries*, are summarized below.

- **Blocked Queries or BQ (Sect. 4)**

  Our first technique modifies the queries issued by the client. The client selects an integer parameter k. When the client wants to issue a query $[a, b]$, BQ rounds a down to the nearest smaller multiple of k, and rounds b up to the nearest larger multiple of k minus 1. That is, the client issues modified query:

  $$[k \cdot \lfloor a/k \rfloor, k \cdot \lceil (b+1)/k \rceil - 1].$$

  In this way, the adversary can only *approximately* reconstruct the database. Indeed, we will show that for each record r_i which corresponds to value v_i, the adversary can estimate v_i only up to an error of k.

  The client can pick k as they desire. Note that k introduces a trade-off between communication complexity and security: the higher the value of k, the higher the error in the adversary's approximation, but also the larger the range being queried, which can increase the communication complexity.

- **Wrap-around Queries or WQ (Sect. 5)**

  Our second approach focuses on the scenario where the adversary knows the distribution of the queries. Indeed, a large body of previous work on attacks (including [20] and [24]) assumes that clients issue queries *uniformly at random* (or that the query distribution is known). Using this assumption, previous work managed to achieve (almost) full database reconstruction in poly-logarithmic time with only a very small amount of error of $O(1/\log N)$. Therefore, protecting the privacy of the data in settings when the adversary knows the distribution of the queries is of paramount importance.

  To obfuscate the database results, when the query distribution is known, we use a four-pronged approach:

  - We introduce the notion of *wrap-around* queries. In normal queries $[a, b]$ we always assume that $a \leq b$. In contrary, in *wrap-around* queries $[a, b]$ we assume that $a > b$.

    In such cases the result of a *wrap around* query $[a, b]$ is the union of the results of normal queries $[a, N]$ and $[1, b]$. That is, a *wrap-around* query, as the name goes, *wraps around* the end of the value range (i.e. N) and continues from the beginning (i.e. 1).

    One may imagine that wrap-around queries treat the data not as a vector (from 1 to N) but as a cyclic buffer. The size of the buffer is still N, but the start of the cyclic buffer is not known. Actually, in a cyclic buffer, much like in a circle, there is no start (or end for that matter).

  - Approximately each time a client issues query $[a, b]$, WQ issues a second query: $[a', b']$.[1] The purpose of this second query is to confuse the adversary who will not be able to say whether the original query were $[a, b]$ or $[a', b']$. Note, that query $[a', b']$ has to be a bit more sophisticated. Indeed, queries $[a', b']$ are taken from a suitable distribution so that when one combines all queries $[a, b]$ and $[a', b']$, the probability of each value $v_i \in [1, N]$ being queried is the same for all i. In this way, no value v_i

---

[1] Depending on the distribution, WQ may need to issue several queries. For the purposes of discussion, at this point we assume that just one extra query $[a', b']$ is issued.

is more popular than the other values, removing asymmetries previously exploited by adversaries.[2]

- Range queries $[a, b]$ are issued as singleton queries $[a, a]$, $[a + 1, a + 1]$, $[a+2, a+2]$, ... $[b, b]$. In this way the attacker will not be able to distinguish normal queries (which would have been issued as a single query) from wrapped-around ones (which would otherwise have been issued as two queries: $[a, N]$ and $[1, b]$).
- We always issue range queries in pairs. We deconstruct all range queries into singleton queries as above, and shuffle the singleton queries of each range query. We then issue all the singleton queries to the server.[3]

Approach BQ aims to introduce an error in the reconstruction of any database. This makes exact reconstruction impossible for any adversary exploiting access pattern leakage. We note that method WQ aims to render unusable a large number of current attacks on encrypted databases, that assume that they know the query distribution. Indeed, using WQ, we break the main assumption that attacks have made so far: The assumption that when queries are issued uniformly at random, some database values appear more frequently than others.

Kellaris et al. [24] and Grubbs et al. [20] present attacks that inherently depend on the client issuing queries following some distribution. These attacks no longer work when WQ is deployed.

2 Model

We consider a client that stores information on a database hosted by a server. The client issues one-dimensional range queries to the server using tokens, and the server returns responses to such queries. Specifically, we consider a database consisting a collection of n records, where each record (r, x) comprises a unique identifier, r, from some set R, and an integer value, x, from some interval of N consecutive integers (e.g., $X = [0, \ldots, N-1]$ or $X = [1, \ldots, N]$). For a record (r, x) of the database, we use the notation $x = val(r)$ to indicate the value x associated with identifier r.

We now introduce "normal" queries, which the user can issue, and "wrap-around" queries, which they cannot.

Definition 1 (Normal Query). *A range query $[a, b]$ such that $a \leq b$, is called a* normal query. *It returns the set of all matching identifiers, $M = \{r \in R : val(r) \in [a, b]\}$.*

Definition 2 (Wrap-around Query). *A range query $[a, b]$, where $a > b$, is called a* wrap-around query. *It returns the set of all matching identifiers, $M = \{r \in R : val(r) \geq a \text{ or } val(r) \leq b\}$.*

---

[2] Actually, the same should be true for all combinations of values v_i and v_j as we will later show.

[3] If we issued queries one by one, the last query issued would always be a normal query.

The *adversarial model* we consider is a persistent passive adversary, able to observe all communication between the client and the server. The adversary aims to recover information about $val(r)$ for the different $r \in R$. In this paper, we consider adversaries that are only exploiting access pattern leakage. Any other leakage that could potentially be exploited is out of the scope of the paper. More specifically, every time the user issues a query, the adversary can detect how many records are included in the response and their ciphertexts.

Definition 3 (Access Pattern Leakage). *If whenever the server responds to a query, the adversary observes the set of all matching identifiers, we say that the scheme allows for access pattern leakage.*

Definition 4 (Communication Complexity). *We consider the communication complexity of a scheme as the number of queries issued by the client and the number of records returned by the server.*

3 Related Work

We have been able to search on encrypted data since the 1980s with *private multiparty computation* [37], and *oblivious random access memory (ORAM)* [15]. However, the first paper to consider searching on encrypted data explicitly is by Song, Wagner and Perrig [35] in 2000. Since then, a number of papers have been published on the topic presenting techniques with various leakage profiles, often followed by attacks.

There exist a number of cryptographic techniques that allow searching on encrypted data. These techniques fall broadly in the following categories: *homomorphic encryption* [12,13,36], *oblivious random access memory* [15,17], *private multiparty-computation* [16,37], *searchable encryption* [5–9,14,23], and *property-preserving encryption* [1–3,31].

Generally, the techniques based on oblivious random access memory and homomorphic encryption give stronger security guarantees, but are fairly slow. Techniques based on property-preserving encryption are fairly efficient, but can have some limitations with regards to security [2]. Searchable encryption lies between the two, being faster than oblivious random access memory and homomorphic encryption based techniques, and allowing for stronger security guarantees than property-preserving encryption based techniques. Using searchable encryption or property preserving encryption, the client can perform a variety of queries on their data: from index-based search queries [8,9,23] to more complex ones [10,11,32,33].

In this paper, we focus on access pattern leakage, which is leaked by most systems based on searchable encryption or property preserving encryption [24]. There are a number of attacks that exploit the above leakage. This work started with a seminal paper by Kellaris et al. [24]. They showed that a passive persistent adversary can fully reconstruct a database by observing encrypted range queries and their responses, given a client who performs queries uniformly at random. A few attack papers followed building on this work [20,28,29]. There are also other attacks that focus on slightly different types of leakage. For example, Kornaropoulos et al. [25] utilize leakage from k-nearest neighborhood queries and Grubbs et al. [19] utilize volume leakage. Grubbs et al. [21] also present a snapshot attack.

While most of the above attack papers assume that the client issues queries uniformly at random, in recent work, Kornaropoulos et al. [26,27] develop distribution-agnostic reconstruction attacks for range and k-nearest neighbor (k-NN) queries. Other attacks in the area assume a more active adversary or that the encryption scheme reveals more properties [4,22,34,38]. There has been some work on mitigating these attacks [10], but it does not prevent asymmetries caused by the client's query distribution. One could use techniques based on ORAM [15,17] or fully homomorphic encryption [12,13] to prevent (most of) the above attacks. However, these techniques are quite expensive and not very practical.

4   Blocked Queries

In this section, we present our BQ technique (Fig. 1 and Algorithm 1) which aims to introduce an error to any adversary's reconstruction of the database. Without loss of generality, we assume that the range of possible database values, N, is a multiple of a positive integer k, which is a parameter of the scheme. When the client issues query $[a, b]$, the BQ system issues the superset query

$$[k \cdot \lfloor a/k \rfloor, k \cdot \lceil (b+1)/k \rceil - 1].$$

This way, no two queries can overlap in fewer than k positions, even if $a = b$ in one of them.

Algorithm 1. $BQ(a, b, k)$

1: Return $\left[k \cdot \lfloor a/k \rfloor, k \cdot \lceil \frac{b+1}{k} \rceil - 1\right]$

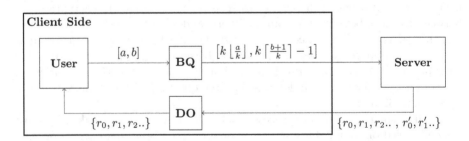

Fig. 1. The BQ technique: when the client wishes to issue a query BQ extends the query to ask for noise values. Once the server responds, the de-obfuscation module (DO) removes any extra identifiers.

4.1   Analysis

Lemma 1. *Let R_a be the set of records with value in the interval $[a \cdot k, (a + 1) \cdot k)$, for some integer a, $0 \leq a < N/k$. If one element of R_a is in a query response, all elements of R_a will also be in the query response.*

Proof. The proof is by contradiction. Let r_1 and r_2 be two records whose values v_1 and v_2 are both in $[a \cdot k, (a + 1) \cdot k)$. Suppose there exists some adversary that can deduce that $v_1 < v_2$. The only leakage we consider here is access pattern leakage. In order for the adversary to distinguish between r_1 and r_2, they must observe some query response, say $[c, d]$, which breaks the symmetry. That means that $[c, d]$ returns only one of the two values r_1 or r_2. In order for that to happen an endpoint of the query must fall between v_1 and v_2.

However, c has to be a multiple of k, and d has to be a multiple of k minus 1. Note that $|v_1 - v_2| \leq k - 1$. Additionally, there is only one multiple of k in $[a \cdot k, (a + 1) \cdot k)$. Thus, c is either equal to $a \cdot k$ or c is outside $[a \cdot k, (a + 1) \cdot k)$ and d is either equal to $(a + 1) \cdot k$ or d is outside $[a \cdot k, (a + 1) \cdot k)$. We conclude that neither c nor d can fall between v_1 and v_2, and thus, no query can return exactly one of v_1 and v_2. $\square$

Definition 5 (Database D_k). *Let D be a database containing a set of records, (r, x), that the user wishes to store. We construct database D_k by transforming record (r, x) into $\left(r, \lfloor \frac{x}{k} \rfloor\right)$. See an example in Fig. 2.*

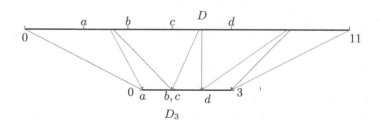

Fig. 2. Example of modified database, D_3, for a database $D = \{a, b, c, d\}$ with values from range $[0, 11]$

Lemma 2. *No adversary A can distinguish between the real database D, and D_k using access pattern leakage.*

Proof. Let A be an adversary that can distinguish between the real database D, and D_k using access pattern leakage. That means that there exists some query response that can be observed when a user queries D that cannot be observed when they query D_k, or there exists some query response that can be observed when a user queries D_k that cannot be observed when they query D.

Let $[a, b]$ be a query whose results can be observed when a user queries D that cannot be observed when they query D_k. If we issue query $[\frac{a}{k}, \frac{b+1}{k} - 1]$ to D_k, we get the same result. Let $[a, b]$ be a query whose results can be observed when a user queries D_k that cannot be observed when they query D. However, query $[a \cdot k, (b + 1) \cdot k - 1]$ to D results in the same response. Thus, adversary A has no way of breaking the symmetry between database D and D_k using access pattern leakage.   □

Theorem 1. *Consider a user that issues range queries on an encrypted database D with integer values from interval $[0, \ldots, N - 1]$ and adopts the blocked queries mitigation scheme (Algorithm 1). Let k be an integer parameter such that N is multiple of k. Using access pattern leakage, no adversary can identify a range of size smaller than k where any database value belongs in.*

Proof. Suppose there exists some adversary, A, that can identify a range of values smaller than k, where some $val(r)$ belongs. Let $v_1 = val(r)$. Suppose $v_1 \in [a \cdot k, a \cdot (k+1)]$. Suppose that A determines that $v_1 \in [a \cdot k, b)$. Now suppose that there is some record, whose value v_2 is in $[b, a \cdot (k + 1)]$. Adversary A could break the symmetry between v_1 and v_2, because A has different information for the two values. Thus, A could break the symmetry between databases D and D_k. This leads to a contradiction by Lemma 2.   □

4.2   Communication Overhead

An important point to address is how much the BQ technique increases the communication complexity. When the user wishes to issue query $[a, b]$, we issue instead query $[k \cdot \lfloor a/k \rfloor, k \cdot \lceil (b+1)/k \rceil - 1]$. The user asked us to query $b - a$ values in the database, and at most, we will query $b - a + 2k$ values in the database.

Let $\bar{s}$ be the average query size that the client issues. Using our scheme, the client can introduce an error of k to the adversary's reconstruction, while the fraction of the size of the noise to normal traffic is bounded by $\frac{2k}{\bar{s}}$. The overhead of this scheme depends a lot on the choice of k, and the query distribution that the user picks. For example, if the user picks queries uniformly at random, the average query size is

$$\frac{2}{N(N + 1)} \sum_{i=1}^{N} i(N - i + 1) = \frac{2}{N(N + 1)} \frac{(N + 2)N(N + 1)}{6} = \frac{N + 2}{3}.$$

Thus, the fraction of noisy records to normal ones is $\frac{6k}{N+2}$. If $\frac{N}{k}$ is a constant, then the multiplicative communication overhead of this scheme is also a constant, while the adversary's reconstruction error is proportional to N.

The trivial mitigation strategy would be to ask for the whole database back on every query. This is equivalent to setting $k = N$. Our scheme allows the user to reduce the communication overhead by making a trade-off on security. Generally, as long as $k << N/6$, the scheme is more efficient over the trivial scheme.

5   Wrap-Around Queries

An assumption commonly made in the literature on attacks on encrypted databases is that the adversary knows the query distribution. In particular, for 1D range queries, the distribution is often assumed to be "uniform at random," i.e., all queries $[a, b], a \leq b$, have the same probability of being issued. To defend against these adversaries, in this section, we present our second mitigation scheme, *wrap-around queries*, schematically illustrated in Fig. 3.

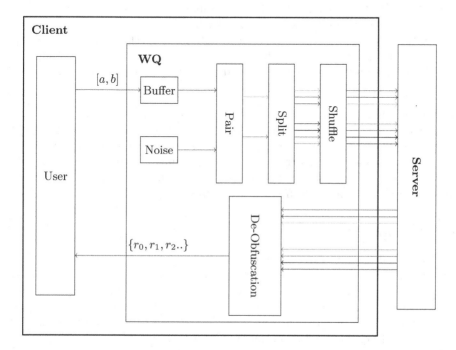

Fig. 3. The wrap-around queries module receives queries from the client and adds them to a buffer. It periodically constructs a pair of queries that contains both noise (i.e., fictitious queries) and real queries. Each query in the pair is further split into singleton queries (i.e., queries spanning a single value). Then, the singleton queries from each range query are shuffled. The shuffled queries are sent to the server. The de-obfuscation component receives the answers to the queries in the pair from the server, filters out the answers to noise, and reassembles the remaining singleton answers into answers to the original queries, which it forwards to the client.

This scheme turns the linear range of possible database values into a cyclic range with no discernible beginning and end in the eyes of the adversary. As the user issues queries according to a fixed probability distribution, we add fictitious queries that correspond to a "complementary" distribution. Thus, we convert the original query stream into one uniformly distributed over the cyclic range, hence removing any asymmetries on the number of times database values are present in query answers. As a result, we prevent the adversary from distinguishing among any two cyclic shifts of the database using the access pattern leakage.

5.1   Key Ideas

The wrap-around queries technique depends on three key ideas:

1. Our technique issues additional queries to introduce noise. Approximately, every time the client issues a query, we issue one or more additional fictitious queries. The fictitious queries may be normal queries (i.e., $[a', b']$ where $a' \leq b'$) or wrap-around queries (i.e., $[a', b']$ where $a' > b'$).
2. Our technique issues queries in pairs. To determine if a slot in the pair contains a noise or a normal query, we flip a coin.
3. Whenever a query $[a, b]$ is to be issued, we issue a series of *singleton queries* $[a, a], [a + 1, a + 1] \ldots [b, b]$, instead.

This technique essentially changes the ordered vector of values $[1, N]$ into a circular buffer of N values that has no start and no end. This change (from a vector to a circular buffer) renders a persistent passive adversary unable to determine which identifier corresponds to the minimum (or maximum) value. In addition, the fictitious queries follow such a distribution so that all individual values $val(r_i)$ have the same frequency of appearance.

5.2   Example

We illustrate how the wrap-around queries scheme works with an example. Suppose we have a database of size 5 and the user issues queries that are uniformly distributed. Let S_n be the set of normal queries that the client can issue (i.e. $[a, b]$ where $a \leq b$) and let S_w be the set of wrap-around queries that the client cannot issue (i.e. $[a, b]$ where $a > b$). The set S_n contains 15 queries and the set S_w contains 10 queries. All these queries are shown in Table 1.

Table 1. All possible cyclic queries on five elements: (a) normal queries; (b) wrap-around queries

(a) Normal					(b) Wrap-around				
$[1, 1]$	$[2, 2]$	$[3, 3]$	$[4, 4]$	$[5, 5]$	-	-	-	-	-
$[1, 2]$	$[2, 3]$	$[3, 4]$	$[4, 5]$	-	-	-	-	-	$[5, 1]$
$[1, 3]$	$[2, 4]$	$[3, 5]$	-	-	-	-	-	$[4, 1]$	$[5, 2]$
$[1, 4]$	$[2, 5]$	-	-	-	-	-	$[3, 1]$	$[4, 2]$	$[5, 3]$
$[1, 5]$	-	-	-	-	-	$[2, 1]$	$[3, 2]$	$[4, 3]$	$[5, 4]$

We use a buffer, B, to store the queries that the user wishes to issue. Let's acquire a biased coin that returns heads with probability $\frac{15}{25}$ and tails with probability $\frac{10}{25}$. We flip the biased coin twice. On heads, we pick a range query from buffer B (if the buffer is empty we choose a normal query from S_n uniformly at random) and on tails we pick a fictitious query, which is a wrap-around query selected uniformly at random from S_w. Thus, after each coin flip, we add a query to the pair. Once the pair is formed, we deconstruct all queries into a series of singleton queries, shuffle the singletons, and issue them to the server. Once the server responds, we identify the responses corresponding to real queries and send them to the user.

In Table 2, we show how many times each single value (from 1 to 5) is expected to be included in a query in the pair. The probability of value 1 appearing in a query in the pair is $15/25 \cdot 5/15 + 10/25 \cdot 10/10 = 3/5$. The probability of value 3 appearing in a query in a given slot in the pair is $15/25 \cdot 9/15 + 10/25 \cdot 6/10 = 3/5$: exactly the same as the probability of value 1. The same happens for all values: the probability of a value i to appear in a query in a given slot is $3/5$: the same probability for all values i.[4] Thus, all values have the same probability of being included in a query in a slot.

Table 2. All values in the database appear with the same frequency in the query results. In this table we show in how many queries each value appears. That is, value "1" appears in 5 normal queries and 10 wrap-around queries (a total of 15). Similarly, value "2" appears 8 times in normal queries and 7 times in wrap-around queries (a total of 15). Each values appears 15 times in the normal and wrap-around queries combined.

Value	Appearances	Normal queries
1	5	$[1, 1], [1, 2], [1, 3], [1, 4], [1, 5]$
2	8	$[1, 2], [1, 3], [1, 4], [1, 5], [2, 2], [2, 3], [2, 4], [2, 5]$
3	9	$[1, 3], [1, 4] [1, 5], [2, 3], [2, 4], [2, 5], [3, 3], [3, 4], [3, 5]$
4	8	$[1, 4], [1, 5], [2, 4], [2, 5], [3, 4], [3, 5], [4, 4], [4, 5]$
5	5	$[1, 5], [2, 5], [3, 5], [4, 5], [5, 5]$
Value	Appearances	Wrap-around queries
1	10	$[5, 1], [4, 1], [3, 1], [2, 1], [5, 2], [4, 2], [3, 2], [5, 3], [4, 3], [5, 4]$
2	7	$[5, 2], [4, 2], [3, 2], [5, 3], [4, 3], [5, 4], [2, 1]$
3	6	$[2, 1], [3, 1], [3, 2], [4, 3], [5, 3], [5, 4]$
4	7	$[2, 1], [3, 1], [4, 1], [3, 2], [4, 2], [4, 3], [5, 4]$
5	10	$[2, 1], [3, 1], [4, 1], [5, 1], [3, 2], [4, 2], [5, 2], [4, 3], [5, 3], [5, 4]$

5.3 Algorithm

In this section, we present Algorithm 2, WQ, which performs a generic version of our wrap-around mitigation scheme. The algorithm takes the following inputs:

---

[4] The reader might wonder that since there are five values (1 to 5), then each value should have probability $1/5$ (not $3/5$) to appear in the query results. We should note however that these queries are *range* queries that return more than one value.

- *buffer*: a buffer that contains the queries that the client wishes to issue;
- *coin*: a random coin with given fixed probabilities for heads and tails;
- S_n: set of normal queries;
- S_w: set of wrap-around queries;
- N: size of the database.

Note that inputs *coin*, S_n, and S_w depend on the probability distribution of the user's queries.

Algorithm WQ operates as follows. As long as there are still queries in *buffer*, WQ generates a new pair of queries. For each slot in the pair, we flip *coin*, and depending on the result, either a normal or a wrap-around query takes up the slot. If *coin* instructs that a normal query takes up the slot, we pop one from *buffer*. If *buffer* is empty, we just pick a normal query uniformly at random. If *coin* instructs that a wrap-around query takes up the slot, we pick one uniformly at random. Each query is then split into singleton queries, and a random permutation of the singletons is added to the pair slot.

Once the pair is full, we query the server. We discard any answers to wrap-around or fake queries, and return the rest to the client.

Algorithm 2. $WQ(buffer, coin, S_n, S_w, N)$

1: **while** $|buffer| > 0$ **do**
2:      $pair = []$
3:      **for** two rounds **do**
4:          Flip *coin*
5:          **if** *coin* $= 1$ **then**
6:              $[a, b] = buffer.\mathsf{pop}()$
7:              // If *buffer* is empty, pick query $[a, b]$ uniformly at random from S_n
8:          **else**
9:              Pick query $[a, b]$ uniformly at random from S_w
10:
11:          $singletons = []$
12:          **for** $i \in range(a, b)$ **do**
13:              Add query $[i, i]$ to *singletons*
14:          Add a random permutation of *singletons* to *pair*
15:
16:      Issue all queries from *pair* to server
17:
18:      **if** *pair* contained a user query **then**
19:          Return the relevant server's responses to the user.

5.4   Uniform Query Distribution

For the case of a user that issues uniformly distributed range queries, Algorithm 2 is specialized by selecting a biased coin, c, with probability

$$Pr(c = 1) = \frac{N(N+1)}{2N^2} = 1 - Pr(c = 0),$$

which yields Algorithm 3, WQU.

Algorithm 3. $WQU(buffer, N)$

1: Let c be a biased coin with $Pr(c = 1) = \frac{N(N+1)}{2N^2} = 1 - Pr(c = 0)$
2: Let S_n be the set of queries $[i, j]$ such that $1 \leq i \leq j \leq N$
3: Let S_w be the set of queries $[i, j]$ such that $1 \leq j < i \leq N$
4: Execute $WQ(buffer, c, S_n, S_w, N)$ (Algorithm 2)

We now analyze the security properties of Algorithm 3.

Lemma 3. *When using Algorithm 3, a slot of the pair contains each query with the same probability.*

Proof. Table 3 shows all possible queries.

Table 3. All possible queries: Note that the blue queries are normal, and the red ones are wrap-around.

$[1, 1]$	$[1, 2]$	$\ldots$	$[1, N - 1]$	$[1, N]$
$[2, 1]$	$[2, 2]$	$\ldots$	$[2, N - 1]$	$[2, N]$
$[3, 1]$	$[3, 2]$	$\ldots$	$[3, N - 1]$	$[3, N]$
$\ldots$	$\ldots$	$\ldots$	$\ldots$	$\ldots$
$[N - 1, 1]$	$[N - 1, 2]$	$\ldots$	$[N - 1, N - 1]$	$[N - 1, N]$
$[N, 1]$	$[N, 2]$	$\ldots$	$[N, N - 1]$	$[N, N]$

Let q_1 be a normal query. Note that there are $\frac{N(N+1)}{2}$ normal queries. In a given pair slot, query q_1 is issued with probability

$$\frac{N(N+1)}{2N^2} \cdot \frac{1}{\frac{N(N+1)}{2}} = \frac{1}{N^2}.$$

Now, let q_2 be a wrap-around query. Note that there are $N^2 - \frac{N(N+1)}{2}$ wrap-around queries. In a given pair slot, query q_2 is issued with probability

$$\frac{N^2 - \frac{N(N+1)}{2}}{N^2} \cdot \left(\frac{1}{N^2 - \frac{N(N+1)}{2}}\right) = \frac{N(N-1)}{2N^2} \cdot \left(\frac{2}{N(N-1)}\right) = \frac{1}{N^2}$$

Thus, all queries are issued with the same probability $\frac{1}{N^2}$. $\square$

Lemma 4. *When using Algorithm 3, each value in the database has the same probability of being in a given pair slot.*

Proof. Lemma 3 shows that all queries are issued with the same probability.

Let's look at all the queries that query some value, say v. There are N queries that start at v and contain v.

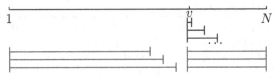

$$[v, v], [v, v+1], [v, v+2] \ldots [v, v-3], [v, v-2], [v, v-1]$$

There are $N - 1$ queries that start at $v - 1$ and contain v:

$$[v-1, v], [v-1, v+1], [v-1, v+2] \ldots [v-1, v-3], [v-1, v-2]$$

There are $N - 2$ queries that start at $v - 2$ and contain v:

$$[v-2, v], [v-2, v+1], [v-2, v+2] \ldots [v-2, v-3]$$

Thus, there are $N + N - 1 + N - 2 + \ldots + 1 = \frac{N(N+1)}{2}$ queries that query value v. So, for any v there are $\frac{N(N+1)}{2}$ queries that query it. Since all queries are issued with the same probability (Lemma 3), all values v have the same probability of being queried in given a slot pair. □

Lemma 5. *When using Algorithm 3, every contiguous set of points of size s has the same probability of being queried in a given pair slot.*

Proof. Let's look at some set of records S, and at the queries that return all elements of the set. Suppose that the smallest value of an element in S is v_{min} and the largest is v_{max}. There are $N - s$ queries that return all elements of S and start at v_{min}.

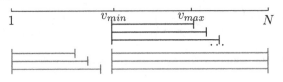

$$[v_{min}, v_{max}], [v_{min}, v_{max} + 1], [v_{min}, v_{max} + 2] \ldots$$
$$[v_{min}, v_{min} - 3], [v_{min}, v_{min} - 2], [v_{min}, v_{min} - 1].$$

Similarly to Lemma 4, there are $\frac{(N-s)(N-s+1)}{2}$ queries that return all points from S. Thus, for any set of size s there are $\frac{(N-s)(N-s+1)}{2}$ queries that return all its elements. $\qquad\square$

Definition 6 (Database D_{shift_s}). *Let D be a database with integer values from an interval of size N and let s be an integer. We define database D_{shift_s} as the set of records $(r, x + s(mod\ N))$, for all records $(r, x) \in D$. That is, we cyclically shift the values of all records by s.*

The following theorem summarizes the security property of wrap-around queries method for a uniform query distribution.

Theorem 2. *Consider a user that issues uniformly distributed range queries on an encrypted database D with integer values from an interval of size N and adopts the wrap-around mitigation scheme (Algorithm 3). For any integer s, a passive persistent adversary who observes the noisy query stream produced by the algorithm and the corresponding query results cannot distinguish with probability greater than $1/2$ between database D and database D_{shift_s} using access pattern leakage and knowledge of the user's query distribution.*

Proof. Suppose there exists some adversary that can distinguish between D and D_{shift_s} with probability greater than $1/2$. The adversary has two weapons: (*i*) the fact that a user that issues uniformly distributed range queries, and (*ii*) access pattern leakage. As long as there are queries that the user wants to send out, Algorithm 3 will create pairs of queries to send to the server.

Algorithm 3 issues range queries as a random permutation of singleton queries. Note that the random permutation is necessary, as otherwise we leak the order of the records and the distances between them on a single query. We have to send the queries in pairs. If we sent only one query at a time, the adversary would know that the last query we sent was a normal query.

1. Let us first examine the access pattern leakage: Algorithm 3 will eventually issue all queries $[a, b]$ for $a, b \in [1, N]$ regardless of whether the database stored is D or D_{shift_s}. Now, because Algorithm 3 issues both normal and wrap-around queries, we can map a query from D to a query from D_{shift_s} with the same response. Query $[a, b]$ on database D produces the same response as query $[a + s(mod\ N), b + s(mod\ N)]$ on database D_{shift_s}. Thus, the adversary cannot get any information out of the access pattern leakage as the two databases produce the same sets of responses.
2. Now, let us examine what the adversary can accomplish using the knowledge that the user issues uniformly distributed range queries. The adversary might try to use this knowledge since due to the uniformity of queries, the frequency with which values of the database appear in query answers varies. To be exact, elements in the middle of the database have a higher chance of being

queried than elements in the ends. However, Algorithm 3, ensures that any set of contiguous points of a certain size is equally likely to be in a pair slot (Lemma 5). Thus, there are no asymmetries that the adversary could exploit to deduce which database is which.

Thus, neither uniformity nor access pattern leakage can help the adversary break the symmetry between the two databases, and the best they can do is guess, which succeeds with probability 1/2. □

Corollary 1. *Consider a user that issues uniformly distributed range queries on an encrypted database D with integer values from an interval of size N and adopts the wrap-around mitigation scheme (Algorithm 3). The adversary is unable to infer which record has the minimum (or maximum) value with probability greater than 1/n, where n is the size of the database.*

Notably, after all their observations the adversary gains no knowledge on which record is the first one.

5.5   Truncated Uniform Distribution

The wrap-around queries mitigation technique can be extended to work with any fixed query distribution. Indeed, from any fixed distribution, we can construct a complementary distribution such that an adversary who observes the resulting noisy query stream sees the equivalent of a uniform distribution over the queries for a cyclic buffer (Table 3).

In this section, we consider a client who issues queries of up to size t uniformly at random, i.e., a truncated uniform distribution. This is in line with related work [26, 27] that also considers a client who focuses on queries of small size.

In this case, we can instruct our mitigation scheme to also only send queries of size up to t. That is, the only queries allowed (for both the client and the algorithm) are of the form $[a, b]$, where: if the query is normal ($a \leq b$): $b - a$ has to be smaller or equal to t, else if the query is a wrap-around query: $b + N - a$ has to be smaller or equal to t.

The new algorithm, Algorithm 4, WQT, has to use a new biased coin, and modified S_n and S_w sets. The new biased coin will return 1 with probability $\frac{2N-t+1}{2N}$. We set S_n to the set of normal queries $[a, b]$, where $b - a \leq t$, and S_w to the set of wrap-around queries $[a, b]$, where $b + N - a \leq t$.

Algorithm 4. $WQT(buffer, N, t)$

1: Let c be a biased coin with $Pr(c = 1) = \frac{2N-t+1}{2N} = 1 - Pr(c = 0)$
2: Let S_n be the set of queries $[i, j]$ such that $1 \leq i \leq j \leq N$ and $j - i \leq t$
3: Let S_w be the set of queries $[i, j]$ such that $1 \leq j < i \leq N$ and $j + N - i \leq t$
4: Execute $WQ(buffer, c, S_n, S_w, N)$ (Algorithm 2)

We now analyze the security properties of Algorithm 4.

Lemma 6. *When using Algorithm 4, a slot of the pair contains each query with the same probability.*

Proof. There are $\sum_{i=0}^{t-1} N - i = \frac{1}{2}t(2N - t + 1)$ normal queries, and $\sum_{i=0}^{t-1} i = \frac{1}{2}t(t-1)$ wrap-around queries. In a given pair slot, a normal query and a wrap-around query are issued with probability

$$\frac{2N - t + 1}{2N} \cdot \frac{2}{t(2N - t + 1)} = \frac{1}{Nt} \text{ and } \left(1 - \frac{2N - t + 1}{2N}\right) \cdot \frac{2}{t(t-1)} = \frac{1}{tN},$$

respectively. Thus, all queries are issued with the same probability.   □

Lemma 7. *When using Algorithm 4, every contiguous set of points of size s has the same probability of being queried in a given pair slot.*

Proof. For any set of size $s \leq t$, the proof follows as in Lemma 5 supported by Lemma 6, there are $\frac{(N-s)(N-s+1)}{2}$ queries that return all its elements. For any set of size $s > t$ there are 0 queries that return all its elements.

Theorem 3. *Consider a user that issues uniformly distributed range queries of size smaller than t, on an encrypted database D with integer values from an interval of size N and adopts the wrap-around mitigation scheme (Algorithm 4). For any integer s, a passive persistent adversary who observes the noisy query stream produced by the algorithm and the corresponding query results cannot distinguish with probability greater than $1/2$ between database D and database D_{shift_s} using access pattern leakage and knowledge of the user's query distribution.*

The proof follows as in Theorem 2 supported by Lemma 7.

5.6   Communication Overhead

In order to analyze the communication overhead introduced by the wrap-around queries mitigation method, we consider a client who performs queries up to size t uniformly at random and employs Algorithm 4, WQT. Note that for the special case $t = N$, we have a uniform query distribution.

The communication overhead depends heavily on the underlying database. The protocol is most efficient on *dense* databases. Here, we have overhead from singleton queries and from wrap-around queries as before. In the setting of a dense database, there is at least one record for every value queried. Thus, the multiplicative overhead introduced is at most 2×.

Let us now consider the overhead introduced from wrap-around queries. The average size of a normal query is $\frac{\sum_{i=1}^{t} i(N-i+1)}{\sum_{i=1}^{t} N-i+1} = \frac{(t+1)(3N-2t+2)}{3(2N-t+1)}$, and the average size of a wrap-around query is $\frac{2\sum_{i=0}^{t-1} i(i+1)}{t(t-1)} = \frac{2(t+1)}{3}$.

Thus, the issued queries' average size is:

$$\frac{2N-t+1}{2N}\frac{(t+1)(3N-2t+2)}{3(2N-t+1)}+\frac{t-1}{2N}\frac{2(t+1)}{3}=\frac{t+1}{2}.$$

Now, the multiplicative overhead of the query, denoted with m, is the ratio between the new average query size and the average size of normal queries:

$$m = \frac{\frac{t+1}{2}}{\frac{(t+1)(3N-2t+2)}{3(2N-t+1)}} = \frac{3}{2} \cdot \frac{2N-t+1}{3N-2t+2}.$$

Note that depending on the choice of t. we have $1 \leq m < 1.5$, hence the smaller t, the smaller the overhead. Thus, the communication overhead varies between $1\times$ and $3\times$, depending on t and how many records are on each value. The more records per value, the smaller the proportional overhead.

5.7 Defending Against Current Attacks

The WQ technique makes the adversary's job more difficult in two ways:

1. It removes asymmetries due to the client's query distribution: Exploiting these asymmetries has been a focus of Kellaris et al. [24] in their seminal paper on attacks. Grubbs et al. [20] present a very elegant algorithm as well that exploits this uniformity assumption. As we remove the asymmetries, these attacks can no longer reconstruct the database.
2. More importantly, it turns the database into a cyclic buffer in the eyes of any adversary: No adversary exploiting access pattern leakage can tell which element is the first (or last) in the database. So, even if an adversary can reconstruct the shape of the database, they won't be able to recover the actual record values, unless they have access to auxiliary information.

5.8 Observations

Encryption schemes that allow for range queries can be costly. It's interesting to note that when running Algorithm 2, the server is never queried for a range that is larger than 1. Thus, a lot of the formerly required machinery is no longer necessary, the server can just store an encrypted dictionary.

Regarding storage complexity, Algorithm 2 issues singleton queries from two range queries. This can require a lot of storage. To reduce this complexity, we can run Algorithm 2 in a streaming fashion. Specifically, instead of constructing and storing *pair*, we can use techniques for block ciphers with arbitrary block size to perform the pseudorandom permutation in sub-linear (in N) space, see for example [18, 30].

6 Conclusion

In recent years, a number of attacks have been developed to fully or approximately reconstruct encrypted databases from the information leakage of encrypted range queries and their responses. In an effort to mitigate the attacks, this paper presents two approaches to help better protect the confidentiality of user data. Our first approach, blocked queries, introduces an error to the reconstruction of the database by any adversary. Our second approach, wrap-around queries, is aimed specifically at a broad class of attacks that assume the user queries the database uniformly at random. This approach removes exploitable asymmetries in query answers caused by uniformity, thus reducing the capability of such attacks.

Acknowledgments. We are grateful to Arkady Yerukhimovich for valuable comments and suggestions.

References

1. Agrawal, R., Kiernan, J., Srikant, R., Xu, Y.: Order preserving encryption for numeric data. In: Proceedings of the ACM International Conference on Management of Data, SIGMOD (2004)
2. Bellare, M., Boldyreva, A., O'Neill, A.: Deterministic and efficiently searchable encryption. In: Menezes, A. (ed.) CRYPTO 2007. LNCS, vol. 4622, pp. 535–552. Springer, Heidelberg (2007). https://doi.org/10.1007/978-3-540-74143-5_30
3. Boldyreva, A., Chenette, N., Lee, Y., O'Neill, A.: Order-preserving symmetric encryption. In: Joux, A. (ed.) EUROCRYPT 2009. LNCS, vol. 5479, pp. 224–241. Springer, Heidelberg (2009). https://doi.org/10.1007/978-3-642-01001-9_13
4. Cash, D., Grubbs, P., Perry, J., Ristenpart, T.: Leakage-abuse attacks against searchable encryption. In: Proceedings of the ACM Conference on Computer and Communications Security, CCS (2015)
5. Cash, D., Jarecki, S., Jutla, C., Krawczyk, H., Roşu, M.-C., Steiner, M.: Highly-scalable searchable symmetric encryption with support for Boolean queries. In: Canetti, R., Garay, J.A. (eds.) CRYPTO 2013. LNCS, vol. 8042, pp. 353–373. Springer, Heidelberg (2013). https://doi.org/10.1007/978-3-642-40041-4_20
6. Chang, Y.-C., Mitzenmacher, M.: Privacy preserving keyword searches on remote encrypted data. In: Ioannidis, J., Keromytis, A., Yung, M. (eds.) ACNS 2005. LNCS, vol. 3531, pp. 442–455. Springer, Heidelberg (2005). https://doi.org/10.1007/11496137_30
7. Chase, M., Kamara, S.: Structured encryption and controlled disclosure. In: Abe, M. (ed.) ASIACRYPT 2010. LNCS, vol. 6477, pp. 577–594. Springer, Heidelberg (2010). https://doi.org/10.1007/978-3-642-17373-8_33
8. Curtmola, R., Garay, J., Kamara, S., Ostrovsky, R.: Searchable symmetric encryption: Improved definitions and efficient constructions. In: Proceedings of the ACM Conference on Computer and Communications Security, CCS (2006)
9. Curtmola, R., Garay, J., Kamara, S., Ostrovsky, R.: Searchable symmetric encryption: improved definitions and efficient constructions. J. Comput. Secur. **19**(5), 895–934 (2011)
10. Demertzis, I., Papadopoulos, S., Papapetrou, O., Deligiannakis, A., Garofalakis, M.: Practical private range search revisited. In: Proceedings of the ACM International Conference on Management of Data, SIGMOD (2016)

11. Faber, S., Jarecki, S., Krawczyk, H., Nguyen, Q., Rosu, M., Steiner, M.: Rich queries on encrypted data: beyond exact matches. In: Pernul, G., Ryan, P.Y.A., Weippl, E. (eds.) ESORICS 2015. LNCS, vol. 9327, pp. 123–145. Springer, Cham (2015). https://doi.org/10.1007/978-3-319-24177-7_7
12. Gentry, C.: Computing arbitrary functions of encrypted data. Commun. ACM **53**, 97–105 (2010)
13. Gentry, C., Boneh, D.: A Fully Homomorphic Encryption Scheme, vol. 20, no. 09. Stanford university, Stanford (2009)
14. Goh, E.J.: Secure indexes. Cryptology ePrint Archive, Report 2003/216 (2003). https://eprint.iacr.org/2003/216
15. Goldreich, O.: Towards a theory of software protection and simulation by oblivious RAMs. In: Proceedings of the ACM Symposium on Theory of Computing, STOC (1987)
16. Goldreich, O., Micali, S., Wigderson, A.: How to play any mental game. In: Proceedings of the ACM Symposium on Theory of Computing, STOC (1987)
17. Goldreich, O., Ostrovsky, R.: Software protection and simulation on oblivious rams. J. ACM (JACM) **43**(3), 431–473 (1996)
18. Granboulan, L., Pornin, T.: Perfect block ciphers with small blocks. In: Biryukov, A. (ed.) FSE 2007. LNCS, vol. 4593, pp. 452–465. Springer, Heidelberg (2007). https://doi.org/10.1007/978-3-540-74619-5_28
19. Grubbs, P., Lacharite, M.S., Minaud, B., Paterson, K.G.: Pump up the volume: practical database reconstruction from volume leakage on range queries. In: Proceedings of the ACM Conference on Computer and Communications Security, CCS (2018)
20. Grubbs, P., Lacharité, M.S., Minaud, B., Paterson, K.G.: Learning to reconstruct: statistical learning theory and encrypted database attacks. Cryptology ePrint Archive, Report 2019/011 (2019). https://eprint.iacr.org/2019/011
21. Grubbs, P., Ristenpart, T., Shmatikov, V.: Why your encrypted database is not secure. In: Proceedings of the Workshop on Hot Topics in Operating Systems, HotOS (2017)
22. Grubbs, P., Sekniqi, K., Bindschaedler, V., Naveed, M., Ristenpart, T.: Leakage-abuse attacks against order-revealing encryption. In: Proceedings of IEEE Symposium on Security and Privacy, SP (2017)
23. Kamara, S., Papamanthou, C., Roeder, T.: Dynamic searchable symmetric encryption. In: Proceedings of the 2012 ACM Conference on Computer and Communications Security, CCS (2012)
24. Kellaris, G., Kollios, G., Nissim, K., O'Neill, A.: Generic attacks on secure outsourced databases. In: Proceedings of the ACM Conference on Computer and Communications Security, CCS (2016)
25. Kornaropoulos, E.M., Papamanthou, C., Tamassia, R.: Data recovery on encrypted databases with k-nearest neighbor query leakage. In: Proceedings of the IEEE Symposium on Security and Privacy, SP (2019)
26. Kornaropoulos, E.M., Papamanthou, C., Tamassia, R.: The state of the uniform: attacks on encrypted databases beyond the uniform query distribution. Cryptology ePrint Archive, Report 2019/441 (2019). https://eprint.iacr.org/2019/441
27. Kornaropoulos, E.M., Papamanthou, C., Tamassia, R.: The state of the uniform: attacks on encrypted databases beyond the uniform query distribution. In: Proceedings of the IEEE Symposium on Security and Privacy, SP (2020, to appear)
28. Lacharité, M.S., Minaud, B., Paterson, K.G.: Improved reconstruction attacks on encrypted data using range query leakage. In: Proceedings of the IEEE Symposium on Security and Privacy, SP (2018)

29. Markatou, E.A., Tamassia, R.: Full database reconstruction with access and search pattern leakage. Cryptology ePrint Archive, Report 2019/395 (2019). https://eprint.iacr.org/2019/395

30. Morris, B., Rogaway, P., Stegers, T.: Deterministic encryption with the Thorp shuffle. J. Cryptol. **31**(2), 521–536 (2018)

31. Pandey, O., Rouselakis, Y.: Property preserving symmetric encryption. In: Pointcheval, D., Johansson, T. (eds.) EUROCRYPT 2012. LNCS, vol. 7237, pp. 375–391. Springer, Heidelberg (2012). https://doi.org/10.1007/978-3-642-29011-4_23

32. Pappas, V., et al.: Blind seer: a scalable private DBMS. In: Proceedings of the IEEE Symposium on Security and Privacy, SP (2014)

33. Poddar, R., Boelter, T., Popa, R.A.: Arx: a strongly encrypted database system. IACR Cryptology ePrint Archive 2016/591 (2016)

34. Pouliot, D., Wright, C.V.: The shadow nemesis: inference attacks on efficiently deployable, efficiently searchable encryption. In: Proceedings of the ACM Conference on Computer and Communications Security, CCS (2016)

35. Song, D.X., Wagner, D., Perrig, A.: Practical techniques for searches on encrypted data. In: Proceeding of IEEE Symposium on Security and Privacy, SP (2000)

36. Vaikuntanathan, V.: Computing blindfolded: new developments in fully homomorphic encryption. In: Proceedings of the IEEE Symposium on Foundations of Computer Science, FOCS (2011)

37. Yao, A.C.: Protocols for secure computations. In: Proceedings of the IEEE Symposium on Foundations of Computer Science, FOCS (1982)

38. Zhang, Y., Katz, J., Papamanthou, C.: All your queries are belong to us: the power of file-injection attacks on searchable encryption. In: Proceeding of the USENIX Security Symposium (2016)

Web Security

Getting Under Alexa's Umbrella: Infiltration Attacks Against Internet Top Domain Lists

Walter Rweyemamu[(✉)], Tobias Lauinger, Christo Wilson, William Robertson, and Engin Kirda

Northeastern University, Boston, MA, USA
walter@iseclab.org

Abstract. Top domain rankings such as Alexa are frequently used in security research. Typical uses include selecting popular websites for measurement studies, and obtaining a sample of presumably "benign" domains for model training or whitelisting purposes in security systems. Consequently, an inappropriate use of these rankings can result in unwanted biases or vulnerabilities. This paper demonstrates that it is feasible to infiltrate two domain rankings with very little effort. For a domain with no real visitors, an attacker can maintain a rank in Alexa's top 100 k domains, for instance, with seven fake users and a total of 217 fake visits per day. To remove malicious domains, multiple research studies retained only domains that had been ranked for at least one year. We find that even those domains contain entries labelled as malicious. Our results suggest that researchers should refrain from using these domain rankings to model benign behaviour.

1 Introduction

Many security researchers rely on "top site" rankings [26] such as the lists compiled by Alexa [2] and Umbrella [4]. For example, researchers use domains from these lists to train or evaluate proposed security systems, or they whitelist ranked domains to improve classifier performance [7,9,13,17,18,21]. In doing so, they assume that the "most popular" domains are benign.

This assumption is problematic because prior research has shown evidence for malicious domains in Alexa's ranking [19,20,23]. Some researchers have taken additional precautions to address this concern, such as checking whether domains are blacklisted [9,13], or retaining only domains that have been ranked for long time periods [7,18,24]. To date there is no consensus on which method should be used, and we are unaware of any study that has investigated whether the latter method effectively removes malicious domains.

In the first part of this paper, we survey how often domains have been ranked in Alexa and Umbrella over the course of one year, and contrast their presence with their blacklist status. We find that even Alexa's top 10 k contains a domain labelled as malicious, but consistently ranked year-round. The full Alexa list

© Springer Nature Switzerland AG 2019
Z. Lin et al. (Eds.): ISC 2019, LNCS 11723, pp. 255–276, 2019.
https://doi.org/10.1007/978-3-030-30215-3_13

contains 27 malicious domains (Umbrella: 292) during the entire year. These results indicate that the duration of a domain's presence in a top ranking alone is not a reliable indicator for benignness.

While researchers might not trust the *domains* listed in the rankings because some of them are known to be malicious, a common assumption appears to be that the *ranking* itself is reliable. Under this assumption, rankings contain malicious domains because these domains receive visits from real users, not because the ranking was manipulated. For example, Nadji et al. justify their whitelisting of the Alexa top 10 k by arguing that *"If an attacker is aware of our whitelisting strategy there is little room for abuse. For an attacker to abuse our whitelisting strategy to evade our analysis, they would have to commandeer and point a whitelisted domain to their malicious infrastructure"* [21]. However, in anecdotal reports users claim to successfully bolster their own website rank by faking visits [8,10,27], and a cursory exploration of list infiltration attacks in prior work [16,26] cast doubt on how resilient these lists are to manipulation.

In the second part of this paper, we conduct a systematic study of list infiltration attacks for both Alexa and Umbrella, and demonstrate that such attacks can be carried out with negligible resources. We find that maintaining a rank in the top 100 k domains requires approximately 217 requests per day from seven fake users for Alexa, and 24 k requests from spoofed source IP addresses for Umbrella, for domains that do not receive any real visitors. An Alexa rank of around 500 k could even be obtained *manually*, by a single user, by installing Alexa's toolbar and visiting 15–30 pages per day. As an illustration of the research impact of such attacks, our experimental domains with fake ranks have begun attracting crawler traffic, including various research crawlers from university networks.

Since we control all (fake) traffic to our experimental domains, we can quantify the extent of the *weekend effect*. This phenomenon, first mentioned by Scheitle et al. [26], is a temporary change in the rankings of Alexa and Umbrella that reoccurs every weekend, presumably due to different Internet traffic patterns compared to the workweek. To date, it is unknown how much Alexa domains with constant traffic change their ranks over time. We find that domains with constant (fake) traffic considerably improve their ranks during the weekend, such as from 448 k to 299 k, or from 88 k to 61 k in Alexa, and in Umbrella from 379 k to 230 k, or from 160 k to 72 k. Conversely, an Alexa rank of 84 k during the weekend requires roughly two fake users (62 fake URL visits) fewer than a similar rank during the workweek. This result implies that weekend ranks are based on less traffic, thus less reliable and more susceptible to fluctuation.

Overall, this paper sheds light on several aspects of top domain lists that researchers should account for when using these lists in their work. Specifically, we make the following contributions:

- We demonstrate infiltration attacks for Alexa and Umbrella where attackers add new domains to the rankings even though these domains do not receive any real visitors.

- Through controlled experiments, we measure the impact of (fake) traffic characteristics, and notably quantify the differences between weekday and weekend ranks.
- We analyse (real) web traffic to our experimental domains, and show that once ranked, domains start receiving regular visits from crawlers in various university networks.
- We are the first to assess a mitigation strategy against malicious domains in the rankings used in prior work, and find that it fails to fully eliminate malicious domains.

2 Background and Related Work

In this paper, we often refer to entries of rankings or lists, which can lead to confusion as to a "high" rank being good or bad. As a convention, a *higher* rank is a *better, numerically lower* rank, towards the top of the list with the most popular entries.

2.1 Use of Top Lists in Security Research

Top domain lists are frequently used in research as observed by Le Pochat et al. [16], who found 102 papers using the Alexa ranking at the four highest tier security conferences between 2015 and 2018. Furthermore, Scheitle et al. [26] reference 68 studies using the Alexa Top Sites published at the top measurement, security, and systems conferences in 2017 alone. Researchers typically use these rankings in one of two ways.

Designating the "largest" Websites. Especially for measurement studies, researchers often seek to cover a representative set of websites so that their findings can be considered relevant with respect to the browsing habits of typical users [11,15,22,28]. When researchers select domains for their popularity, it is less of a concern whether the domains are compromised or malicious. Similarly, while attackers might manipulate the ranks of their domains to make them appear more popular, this is likely not a major concern for measurement results aggregated over a large number of domains, as long as the extent of rank manipulation remains moderate relative to the frequency of the measured property.

Designating "benign" Websites. Many security papers need labelled training and evaluation data for detection mechanisms. Some researchers resort to domain rankings and use popular domains as an approximation of "benign" websites. For example, Lever et al. [18] obtain the malicious domains contacted by malware samples by filtering out domains that have been present in the Alexa top 10 k for at least one year (except for several commonly abused dynamic DNS domains). Similarly, Rahbarinia et al. [24] detect malware control domains after labeling domains as benign when they have appeared in the Alexa top 1 M for one year. Alrwais et al. [7] study bulletproof hosting in AS sub-allocations and create a "noisy" set of benign allocations from domains that have been present in the Alexa top 50 k for two years. While these papers aim to reduce the likelihood of ranked domains being malicious by requiring them to be ranked for a long time period, we are not aware of any study showing that this is indeed a sound approach. Other papers such as EXPOSURE [9] or IceShield [13] vet ranked domains through blacklists. Unfortunately, many authors do not make such an effort. WarningBird, for example, whitelists the Alexa top 1 k "to reduce false-positive rates" of a URL classifier [17].

Several prior studies have reported evidence that malicious domains exist in the Alexa ranking. Li et al. [20] mention a fake antivirus campaign on a website ranked 2,404 on Alexa. Pitsillidis et al. [23] detect a 1–2% overlap between blacklists and the Alexa top 1 M (even though they consider them false positives of the blacklists). Lever et al. report that "more than 100 ... domains were ranked in the top 10,000 by Alexa on the day they were added to the blacklist" [19].

2.2   List Compilation Methodology

In this paper, we consider two measurement-based top site lists: Amazon Alexa Top Sites [2], which is the most popular list in research [26], and Cisco Umbrella Top 1 Million [4], a more recent list ranking arbitrary (sub)domains instead of websites. Table 1 summarises the data sources and popularity model of these lists.

Table 1. Data sources of common top site lists.

Ranking	Data source	List contents
Alexa	Browser toolbar	Typed-in website domains
Umbrella	DNS resolver	Resolved (sub)domains

Alexa. The data for the Alexa ranking originates primarily from "millions of users" [3] who have installed the Alexa browser toolbar and share their browsing history with Alexa. Its website documents Alexa's methodology as follows: The installed browser toolbar records all URLs that are visited from the address bar of the browser window, meaning that third-party resources such as advertisements or tracking code are ignored. Only blogs and personal homepage subdomains are ranked separately from the main domain. Domains are ranked according to a combination of the number of users visiting the site, and the unique URLs on that site visited by each user. While the ranking is updated daily, the (API) data is smoothed over a 3-month time window. Ranks below 100 k are not statistically meaningful because the data collected about those domains is too scarce [3, 5]. The ranking is available through an API, on the website and as a CSV download [1], with noticeable differences (Sect. 4.3).

Umbrella. The Umbrella rankings are derived from incoming DNS lookups observed in Cisco's Umbrella Global Network and the OpenDNS service, which amount to over 100 B daily requests from 65 M users in 165 countries [4]. Consequently, the list reflects the popularity of domains used in any Internet protocol, not only web traffic. Umbrella states that ranks are based on unique client IPs looking up each domain [14]. However, our findings in Sect. 4.4 differ.

2.3   Related Work

Recently, Scheitle et al. [26] studied the contents and stability of Internet top domain lists such as Alexa and Umbrella. Additionally, they demonstrated rank manipulation with a successful attack against Umbrella, obtaining ranks of up to 30 k on a Friday, and 17 k on a Sunday using the same traffic characteristics. The authors attributed this rank difference to the *weekend effect*, that is, a decrease in traffic to other ranked domains during the weekend.

In prior work, we studied potential consequences of the weekend effect in Alexa and Umbrella, such as different country and website category distributions of the ranked domains on weekdays and the weekend [25]. Furthermore, we observed the presence of clusters of alphabetically ordered domains in Alexa and Umbrella, which we speculated to be due to these domains being considered equivalent in terms of observed traffic.

Le Pochat et al. [16] described multiple list infiltration attacks against various top domain lists. Regarding Alexa, Le Pochat et al. proposed two different attacks. Their first attack variant involved installing the Alexa browser toolbar in real browser instances, where they were able to obtain a rank of 345 k with only nine fake requests. The second attack variant targeted Alexa Certify, a paid service to directly measure website visits using a tracking script provided by Alexa. Le Pochat et al. also studied whether domains ranked by Alexa and Umbrella are malicious according to Google Safe Browsing.

This paper contrasts and extends on prior work in the following ways:

- We extend Scheitle et al. by introducing an attack against Alexa.
- We are the first to analyse the crawler traffic received by domains with fake ranks.
- We improve the attack technique against Alexa by Le Pochat et al. where instead of installing the Alexa extension in real browser sessions, we submitted fake browsing traffic to Alexa's internal API, a more scalable approach. In contrast to Le Pochat et al. who do not mention some parameters of their attack, we document in detail the parameters involved in the attack such as the number of distinct URLs, and distinct fake users (AIDs), to explore their effect, and allow for comparisons with later work.
- We measure the magnitude of the weekend effect by comparing weekday and weekend ranks of experimental domains with identical amounts of (fake) traffic.
- We experimentally confirm the hypothesis that the alphabetically ordered domains are equivalent in terms of observed traffic, as speculated by our earlier work.

– We extend the malicious domain analysis by Le Pochat et al. who considered only a single snapshot of the rankings, by investigating how long malicious domains remain ranked, and whether all domains ranked for one year are benign.

3   Domain Longevity and Maliciousness

To obtain a set of *benign* domains, several researchers have selected domains ranked by Alexa for one or more years [7,18,24]. The rationale behind this approach is that malicious domains are often active for only a few days before they are blacklisted [12].

3.1   Longevity of Ranked Domains

We begin our analysis of this strategy by studying how often domains appear in the ranking. This analysis is based on ranking CSVs downloaded from Alexa and Umbrella each day for a duration of one year, beginning with the ranking for 14 October 2017. While either ranking contains exactly 1 M domains each day, over the 365 days, Alexa included a total of 24 M unique domains (Fig. 1a), and Umbrella over 7 M domains (Fig. 1b). This implies that the rankings are very unstable. A large portion of the domains remain ranked for a short time only, before being replaced with new domains. For example, Fig. 1c and d show that only 6.1 % and 20.3% of Alexa and Umbrella domains, respectively, were listed on more than 50 (not necessarily consecutive) days. An implication of this instability is that fewer than 93 k domains in Alexa, and just over 303 k domains in Umbrella, were ranked consistently every day over the one-year period. Over 90% of Alexa list entries, and almost 70% of Umbrella entries on any given day will leave the ranking at least once within one year.

Note that several years before our study, Rahbarinia et al. [24] found a much larger number of 459 k domains had been present in the Alexa ranking during 365 consecutive days. We believe that this is due to a change in Alexa's ranking in January 2018, first reported by Scheitle et al. [26]. Before that date, presumably due to smoothing, Alexa's ranking was relatively stable. During our experiments (Sect. 4.3), we found that as of late 2018, Alexa was not applying any smoothing to the ranks found in the CSV download, resulting in a less stable ranking.

Often, researchers use only a list prefix such as the top 10 k or 100 k instead of the full ranking. Furthermore, Alexa cautions that ranks below 100 k are not statistically meaningful [3,5]. Figure 1a and b show that shorter list prefixes are increasingly more stable. Around 48 % of the Alexa top 1 k, and 63 % of the Umbrella top 1 k domains, for instance, were ranked in the top 1 k every day. An exception are the Umbrella top 10 and top 100, which are less stable than the top 1 k, or the corresponding list prefixes in Alexa. This is due in part to the weekend effect, which causes domains that are much more popular during the weekend to enter the shorter list prefixes and displace other domains. As a result, neither of these domains is present in the short list prefixes during 365 consecutive days.

<table>
<tr><th colspan="5">(a) Alexa (absolute numbers)</th></tr>
</table>

Prefix	All Domains total (∪)	1 y (∩)	Malicious total	1 y
10	16	6	0	0
100	181	63	0	0
1 k	2,972	483	36	0
10 k	36,679	3,935	493	1
100 k	1,005,275	25,708	15,907	13
1 M	24,161,278	92,832	65,755	27

(b) Umbrella (absolute numbers)

Prefix	All Domains total (∪)	1 y (∩)	Malicious total	1 y
10	22	5	0	0
100	157	51	0	0
1 k	1,670	634	0	0
10 k	22,207	5,089	17	0
100 k	386,493	39,074	858	43
1 M	7,065,560	303,057	34,974	292

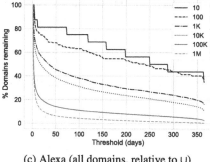

(c) Alexa (all domains, relative to ∪)

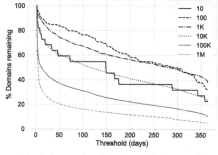

(d) Umbrella (all domains, relative to ∪)

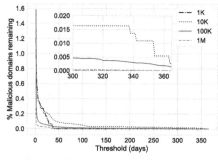

(e) Alexa (malicious domains, relative to ∪ of all domains)

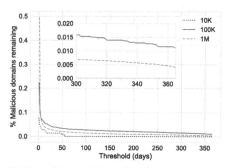

(f) Umbrella (malicious domains, relative to ∪ of all domains)

Fig. 1. Number of days domains were ranked by Alexa and Umbrella in the year since 14 October 2017. Out of the 1 M domains that appeared in the Alexa top 100 k, only 25.7 k were ranked in this prefix for the entire year. Requiring domains to be ranked consistently for one year removes a majority of malicious domains, but 27 in Alexa, and 292 in Umbrella remain.

3.2 Maliciousness of Ranked Domains

To determine the maliciousness of ranked domains, we looked up their status in Google Safe Browsing in the last week of October 2018. Maliciousness after the year had already elapsed, we do not know about their maliciousness at the time they were ranked. For example, our methodology does not detect domains that were temporarily compromised and subsequently cleaned up. Furthermore, we cannot distinguish compromised domains from those that are intentionally malicious. Yet, our methodology models the strategy used by researchers who first compile a list of presumably "benign" domains and then collect data from these domains, such as downloading "benign" websites and extracting features for model training. In this scenario, it is critical that these domains not be malicious at the time data is collected from them.

In relative terms, a very small fraction of domains that were ranked on any of the 365 days are labelled as malicious – 65,755 out of 24 M domains in Alexa, and 34,974 out of 7 M domains in Umbrella. The top 100 in Alexa, and the top 1 k domains in Umbrella do not contain any domain labelled as malicious. Malicious domains do exist in the Alexa top 1 k and the Umbrella top 10 k, but they appear on no more than 37 and 54 days, respectively. All longer list prefixes contain malicious domains even among those that were ranked every day for one year. Out of the almost 93 k domains in Alexa that were ranked every day, 27 are malicious according to Safe Browsing; they were all marked as "social engineering" or "unwanted software." However, Alexa contained six "malware" domains ranked for over 300 days, out of which two were just one and two days away from the 365-day threshold. In Umbrella, 292 out of 304 k domains ranked the entire year were labelled as malicious: 231 as "unwanted software," 33 as "malware," and 28 as "social engineering."

The ratio of consistently ranked malicious domains over all malicious domains is lower than the ratio of consistently ranked domains over all domains, which suggests that malicious domains leave the ranking faster than benign domains. Yet, at a time scale of one year, the strategy of retaining only domains consistently ranked for a longer time period reduces, but does not completely eliminate malicious domains. A small number of malicious domains may be acceptable in some scenarios, such as when aggregating over large numbers of domains. However, mislabelled training data in a machine learning context (i.e., a few examples labelled as benign despite being malicious) could have a disproportionate effect on classifier performance. Another issue is that requiring domains to be ranked continuously significantly decreases the number (and diversity) of domains, as a domain's absence for a single day, or during each weekend, would cause it to be eliminated from the final set of domains.

4   Infiltration Attacks

Both Alexa and Umbrella exhibit strong weekend effects, visible in different domains being popular during the weekend as opposed to the workweek [25, 26]. These periodic changes suggest that changes in observed traffic have a direct and immediate impact on the ranking. Consequently, it may be possible for attackers to manipulate the ranks of existing domains, or to infiltrate the lists with new domains. We ran controlled experiments with the primary goal of showing that such attacks are indeed feasible. Since we controlled the (fake) traffic to our domains, we were able to quantify the extent of the weekend effect by comparing weekday and weekend ranks. Further, we explored the effect of various attack parameters, especially when they have an influence on the cost of the attack. We did so by running multiple independent experiments in parallel, one with a reference domain, and additional experiments with separate domains that vary one attack parameter each. We used newly registered domains to avoid any bias due to prior activity. We also created several control domains that were registered but not used in any experiment. To observe the effect of being ranked, we logged incoming web requests on our domains.

4.1 Ethical Considerations

Since our experiments involved domain lists that were in active use, we needed to consider and minimise potential risks due to our activities. To that end, we carefully designed a research protocol prior to starting our experiments.

The main risk was that consumers of the lists would receive invalid data if our experiments were to succeed. We reduced the impact of this risk in the following ways:

– *Limit the number of fake domains used concurrently.* At any time, each ranking contained no more than ten of our domains. This is a negligible fraction compared to the full one million entries of each list.
– *Limit the maximum rank we attempt to achieve.* Since Alexa cautions that the bottom 900 k ranks are not statistically meaningful [3,5], we need to infiltrate the top 100 k domains to show that the attack can result in a significant rank. However, once a domain crosses that threshold both during the workweek and the weekend, we do not seek any higher rank. Our highest ranks were around 60 k (during the weekend), and we never had more than three domains ranked in the top 100 k at the same time. Our experiments barely impact consumers of the most popular domains.
– *Limit the duration of the experiments.* Due to the strong weekend effect, and to quantify natural rank fluctuation, we need to test each attack parameter for at least one week. Once a stable attack parameter has been found and confirmed, we end the experiment and the domain disappears from the ranking within one or two days, in line with the fast responsivity of the lists. As an exception, we maintained a 200 k Alexa rank for one reference domain that we used to explore long-term effects, convergence between the Alexa rank shown on the website and in the CSV file, and to observe website crawling during an extended period of seven months.
– *Use newly-registered domains under our control.* The experimental domains and their mostly empty websites do not harm any potential visitor. The experiments are not aimed at directing human visitors to our websites. This probability is minuscule since the domains only appear in the ranking among a million other sites and are not advertised elsewhere. Neither we nor any third party unduly benefits from the fake ranks of our experiments.

Our approach involved sending fake data to Alexa and Umbrella. We do not consider overloading their systems as a major risk, as those systems are designed to handle very large numbers of users. For example, Umbrella reports a total of 100 B requests per day [4], whereas our experiments never exceeded more than 42 k requests per day. Similarly, Alexa claims millions of toolbar users [3], and we simulated no more than a dozen daily toolbar users with moderate browsing behaviour. To err on the side of caution, we perform our experiments in an open way from IP ranges in our institutional network. We place a message with contact information on our experimental domains, but have not received any inquiries.

We did not seek IRB approval because our experiments do not involve human data, and our IRB does not review ethics beyond human subjects research.

We strictly followed this protocol throughout our experiments. Given these precautions, we believe that any short-term risks are outweighed by the long-term benefit of showing that the lists can be manipulated with little effort. Furthermore, by raising awareness for the limitations of the lists, our findings may prevent future harm to consumers of the lists.

4.2   Alphabetically Sorted Clusters

Our earlier study showed that the Alexa and Umbrella rankings contained long sequences of alphabetically sorted domains [25]. When considering any sequence of at least 42 alphabetically sorted domains as a cluster, more than 54% of list entries in Alexa, and more than 91% in Umbrella were part of such a cluster.

We hypothesised that these clusters correspond to domains that the list publishers cannot distinguish based on their traffic characteristics. Our experiments support this hypothesis, as domains with identical fake traffic were ranked in the same cluster. Furthermore, in Umbrella, subdomains appear to cause their parent domain to be ranked, too. Since our experiments involved only one subdomain per parent domain, and we did not fake any visits to the parent domain, both the subdomain and the parent domain always appeared in the same cluster.

In our experiments, we take advantage of clustering in two ways. First, if two domains with different traffic parameters appear in the same cluster, we know that their traffic is considered equivalent by the list publisher, and the different parameter is likely irrelevant. Second, inside each cluster, the position of a domain is determined only by its lexicographical ordering. This means that it is possible to place a domain at the beginning of the cluster, and thus obtain a minor improvement of the domain's rank, by selecting a name beginning with zeroes. This also reduces the rank distance between similar experimental domains, and makes our tables easier to read.

4.3   Alexa

Alexa primarily collects data from users who install the Alexa toolbar in their browser and give consent to share their browsing history with Alexa. The presumably most straightforward approach for attackers would be to install the toolbar in real browsers and use automation tools to create fake browsing sessions. However, this approach is somewhat expensive to scale, and it is more complicated to vary variables such as screen size and network delays that are collected by Alexa. Another option is to reverse-engineer the browser toolbar, understand its data collection and communication behaviour, and use its internal remote APIs to send fake toolbar traffic to Alexa, without actually visiting any website. We pursue the latter approach for better control of experimental conditions.

When the toolbar is first installed, it requests a new user identifier (AID) from Alexa's servers, and the user must consent to the data collection. We did not automate this process, as only a limited number of AIDs were necessary for our experiments. Instead, we generated AIDs manually and extracted the identifier as well as cookies from the browser profile. When active, the toolbar downloads configuration from Alexa and sends a request with metadata each time the URL in the address bar changes. The data sent to Alexa includes the current and previous URL, the page load time, response status code, the window and tab IDs, a request counter, the screen resolution and the browser window width. While the toolbar collects additional information, it does not seem related to website ranking, thus we do not investigate further. Simply recording an API message and replaying it multiple times does not result in a rank, as Alexa appears to do semantic checks. Therefore, we implemented a script that emulates the toolbar's communication behaviour by increasing counters as necessary, and randomising fields such as the page load time. From Alexa's website, we gather that both the number of users and the number of unique pages visited on a domain may influence its rank. We implement our script such that it can emulate browsing sessions consisting of visits to a predefined list of pages on our experimental domain, optionally interleaved with fake visits to unrelated non-experimental websites. Fake visits consist in data being submitted to Alexa's toolbar API. We do not connect to any of these "visited" domains.

For our experiments, we use newly registered domains with a website that contains only a brief sentence with contact information. We run multiple experiments in parallel, one as a baseline, and others where we vary different parameters to observe their effect. The parameters we consider are the number of users (AIDs), the number of unique pages "visited" on our websites, whether the fake browsing session includes any visits to non-experimental websites, and the number of browsing sessions per user. To create lists of pages to visit on our website, we concatenate random dictionary words to simulate a directory structure; these pages do not actually exist. When an experiment calls for the inclusion of visits to non-experimental websites, we pick domains from the Alexa top 100. Our limited experiments are unlikely to have a noticeable effect on the ranking of domains that are already highly popular.

Attack Parameters. In our experiments until end of June 2018, we found that the number of identical browsing sessions did not matter; one or two fake visits per unique URL had the same effect as twenty repetitions, provided all other parameters were the same. In fact, when the number of repetitions was too high, the domain lost its rank. However, Alexa does not appear to permanently block traffic from the associated source IP addresses or AIDs. Similarly, interleaving fake visits to the experimental domain with visits to non-experimental websites did not seem to have any effect on whether or not the experimental domain could obtain a rank. A working website was not a requisite either, as submitting fake visits for a domain without any DNS A record resulted in a normal rank.

Since summer 2018, several details appear to have changed. In our more recent experiments, two repetitions per unique URL were necessary in order to *obtain* a rank for a new domain for the first time, whereas a single visit per URL was sufficient to *maintain* the rank on the following days. Similarly, our newer experiments required us to interleave fake visits to our experimental domain with approximately half as many fake visits to other domains. We do not know whether these changes happened in response to the disclosure of the attack by Le Pochat et al. [16]. With minimal changes, attacks can still be carried out successfully.

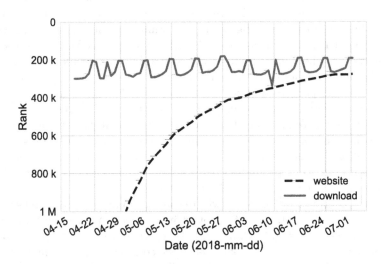

Fig. 2. Alexa ranks for the baseline domain (two AIDs, 21 pages). The rank on the website appears to be smoothed; it starts at 7.2 M and slowly converges to the more immediate rank from the CSV file download. Weekend ranks, with constant fake traffic, are around 74 k better than workweek ranks.

We use as the baseline a domain with fake traffic from two AIDs visiting 21 pages each (the front page and twenty deeper pages). With constant fake traffic, such a domain reaches a median rank of 270 k during the workweek, and a median rank of 196 k during the weekend, as shown in Fig. 2. The ranks found in Alexa's CSV file appear to be immediate and have little long-term variation. The same domain's rank on Alexa's website starts at 7.2 M and gradually approaches the rank from the CSV file; it appears to be smoothed. Alexa's API returns values similar to those found on the website.

Visits to more unique pages on the experimental domain have a moderate effect on the domain's rank. In our experiment, increasing the baseline from 21 to 41 page visits resulted in a slightly better rank than the baseline, 241 k during the week instead of 263 k. Further increasing to 81 page visits yielded a rank of 220 k instead of the same-day baseline rank of 259 k.

In comparison, emulating more unique toolbar users (AIDs) has a much higher impact on the rank. To explore this effect in detail, we designed a separate experiment. We created eight domain names to be "visited" by one to eight AIDs. Each domain had a long prefix of zeroes so that it would be placed on top of its respective alphabetically sorted cluster in the ranking (see Sect. 4.2). We used all AIDs from a single IP address, but in sequence such that only one AID was active at any time. Each AID ran between one and eight sessions, where each session consisted of visits to 21 pages on the respective experimental domain, as well as an average of 10 pages on unrelated domains. Initially, each session consisted of two repetitions, and we later reduced them to one repetition without any discernible impact on the ranks. We experimentally determined that Alexa used midnight UTC as the cutoff time for rank computations, thus we scheduled our experiments accordingly. The duration of a single session with one repetition was approximately ten minutes, plus random delays between sessions.

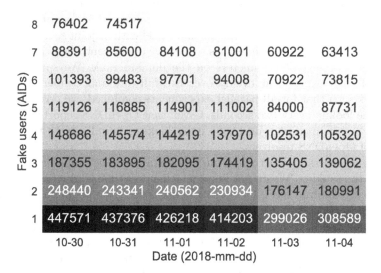

Fig. 3. The impact of fake users (requesting 21 pages each) on the Alexa rank. Dates refer to when the fake traffic was sent. A rank in the top 100 k requires visits from 6–7 fake users during the workweek, and 5 users on the weekend. A *single* toolbar user's traffic causes ranks in the top 500 k.

The domain visited by two AIDs had the same effective settings as the baseline domain, and resulted in comparable ranks, as shown in Fig. 3. Using only one AID resulted in a rank of about 448 k, which means that a domain can be ranked in Alexa's top 500 k based on traffic from *a single user*. This suggests that the data used by Alexa to compute the lower ranks is quite fragile. The high volatility of the ranking underscores this issue (Sect. 3.1).

A domain visited by eight users achieves a weekday rank of around 75 k. Data for this domain is only available for two days because we disabled this part of the experiment when the high rank appeared in Alexa's ranking, following our guidelines from Sect. 4.1. A rank in the top 100 k, which are considered more reliable by Alexa [3,5], requires between five and seven users, depending on the day. Their fake visits correspond to 155–217 API requests, made from a single IP address in one to two hours. None of these requirements represent any significant cost for an attacker.

4.4   Umbrella

The Umbrella ranking is derived from DNS lookups using the OpenDNS resolver. Since the resolver is available for public use, attackers can repeatedly look up their own domain to make it appear more popular than it actually is. A blog post about the ranking suggests that the number of source IP addresses may influence the rank more than the total number of lookups [14]. To test this hypothesis experimentally, we obtained permission to utilise four unused network prefixes of our institution for outgoing DNS lookups, totalling 24.5 k possible source IP addresses. We run multiple experiments in parallel with disjoint sets of source IPs and independent, fresh domain names to observe under controlled circumstances the influence of several parameters on the domain rank. We spread out the lookups of each experiment evenly over the full day and deliberately choose parameters such that for all parallel experiments combined, we do not exceed a limit of one lookup every two seconds. Given that OpenDNS reports 100 B daily requests [4], our maximum of 42,000 daily lookups is unlikely to threaten the stability of OpenDNS resolvers.

During a successful experiment, our domain appears in Umbrella's next daily update of the ranking. We do not know which cutoff time Umbrella uses to split their data stream into days. Our results suggest that the beginning and end of our experiments are not perfectly aligned with Umbrella's notion of a day, as the first and last days' ranks are always significantly worse than the ranks in between (which are based on 24 h of lookups). For this reason, and to observe "natural" rank fluctuations, we run our experiments with constant lookups for about one week. We then discard the ranks of the first and last day, retaining only those in between that we consider "stable".

Many domains in the ranking appear in alphabetically sorted clusters (Sect. 4.2). We leverage this characteristic to improve the ranks of our experimental domains by looking up a 0000000000 subdomain, which results in the subdomain being placed at the beginning of the cluster, and the parent domain further down in the alphabetical order of the same cluster. A secondary effect of

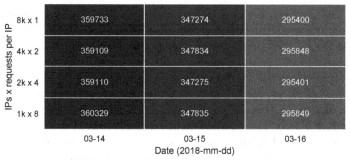

(a) Effect of traffic parameters (top to bottom): Baseline, four times more lookups, longer DNS A record TTL, non-existing domain.

(b) Identical total lookups sent from varying number of source IPs.

(c) Rank in the top 100 k, and a reference domain for comparison.

Fig. 4. Ranks obtained in the Umbrella experiments sending lookups to OpenDNS. Adjacent ranks correspond to domains in a single cluster. Minor rank differences for similar traffic parameters denote different clusters, likely due to sampling or packet loss. Two lookups sent from 12 k IP addresses result in a 123 k Thursday rank, and 72 k on Sunday.

this approach is that two list entries result from lookups of just one domain. We did not expand this technique to deeper subdomain levels so as not to unnecessarily pollute the list, but it is a possibility for attackers.

Attack Parameters. After an initial exploratory experiment to find a successful combination of parameters that resulted in a (low) rank, we designed three subsequent experiments to determine how the size of the source IP pool, the number of lookups, the TTL of the domain's DNS A record, and the resolvability of the domain influence the resulting rank. In the first experiment, the baseline corresponds to 2 k source IPs each making three daily lookups, using a domain name that resolves to an A record with a 3 h TTL. As shown in Fig. 4a, looking up a domain name with a 12 h TTL, or a name that cannot be resolved, results in subdomain ranks comparable to the baseline, between 536 k and 907 k depending on the day of the week.

Contrarily, quadrupling the number of lookups from the same number of source IPs results in a higher rank between 227 k and 351 k.

This finding contradicts our intuition and public documentation [14] that the Umbrella ranking may be based on source IPs rather than lookup counts. To investigate, we designed another experiment with four conditions, a domain looked up once from 8 k source IPs, twice from 4 k IPs, four times from 2 k IPs, and eight times from 1 k IPs, respectively. All four domains achieved nearly identical ranks, as visible in Fig. 4b. However, this does not mean that more lookups can be directly substituted for the same number of source IP addresses. In a separate experiment, 1 k source IPs making two lookups each did not result in a rank, whereas 2 k source IPs with one lookup did. Similarly, making two lookups each from 12 k source IPs resulted in a rank between 72 k and 123 k (Fig. 4c), considerably better than the same total number of lookups using only 2 k source IPs (Fig. 4a, 227 k to 351 k). We hypothesise that Umbrella's ranking is based on a potentially non-linear combination of source IPs and lookup counts, where source IPs have a higher weight. However, this is hardly a hurdle for attackers, as DNS is based on UDP, and source IPs can be spoofed. An attacker can place a domain in Umbrella's top 100 k with about 24 k daily DNS lookups, or potentially even fewer by spoofing more than the 12 k source IPs we had available in our experiment. The technical complexity and cost for an attacker, given a network location that does not filter spoofed source IPs, are very low.

4.5   Limitations

In our experiments, we refrained from pursuing ranks that were significantly higher than 100 k, in line with our ethical guidelines (Sect. 4.1). Prior work has demonstrated attacks for ranks as high as 31 k in Alexa (using a different technique [16]), and 17 k in Umbrella (using a similar technique [26]), thus it appears reasonable to assume that attackers could reach even higher ranks. To the best of our knowledge, all prior work (including our efforts) only showed that new domains can be added to the ranking, rather than manipulating the ranks of domains already present on the list. It is conceivable that list publishers treat long-term entries differently from new entries, though it seems unlikely, given the extent of change that we observed in the rankings.

4.6   The Weekend Effect

Prior work has shown that both Alexa and Umbrella periodically and temporarily change their composition during each weekend compared to the workweek. One manifestation of this phenomenon is that different sites are popular during the weekend [26]. However, we also show that the lists appear to be based on less traffic data during the weekend. Since our experiments use constant traffic parameters, any rank increase of the experimental domains from the workweek to the weekend must be due to other ranked domains receiving less traffic. All of our domains received better ranks on Saturday and Sunday. In general, this effect was more pronounced in the lower ranks. For example, our one-AID domain in Alexa increased its rank from 448 k on Tuesday to 299 k on Saturday, whereas the seven-AID domain only increased from 88 k to 61 k. Similarly, Umbrella ranked a domain with three lookups from 2 k IP addresses at 885 k on Wednesday, and at 536 k on Sunday, a difference of 349 k ranks, more than one third the length of the list.

For attackers, this means that rank manipulation is less costly during the weekend, as comparable ranks can be obtained with fewer resources. For example, weekend attacks at the operating points in Fig. 3 typically require two fake users less than during the workweek.

We cannot determine whether these rank changes correctly mirror the extent of websites receiving fewer visitors during the weekend, or if they are amplified by fewer Alexa toolbar or OpenDNS users being active during the weekend. In either case, they show that the influence of a single user on the composition of the domain ranking grows during the weekend, rendering the ranking less reliable.

4.7   The Aftermath

To immediately observe the impact of a domain being ranked, we logged all web requests to our test domains. Before being ranked, most domains received no requests. We registered these domains many weeks before first using them, and observed only very rare visits from crawlers such as one likely associated with the DomainTools service. Presumably, these crawlers discovered the domains through .pw zone files, as our domains were not referenced elsewhere. Once ranked, our domains started receiving regular visits from crawlers. Table 2 shows that an Alexa rank has a much higher impact on crawler traffic than an Umbrella rank. Our domain in the Umbrella top 100 k received at most four web requests on any day, whereas the two Alexa domains received at least 10–13 requests each day, with a maximum of 174. By the end of June 2018, we had observed 125 distinct crawlers.

To estimate the number of distinct crawlers, we identify them by the Autonomous System (AS) of their IP address, which unlike user agent strings cannot be faked easily. We group together multiple ASes used by Amazon cloud services. This approach is clearly an underestimation of the number of crawlers, whereas counting crawlers by the number of distinct source IP addresses would

Table 2. Daily web requests to experimental domains while ranked.

Domain/experiment	Ranked	Min	Avg/day	Max
none (control)	0 days	0	0	0
Umbrella 100 k	7 days	1	1.9	4
Alexa 200 k (reference)	60 days	13	35.1	174
Alexa 100 k	9 days	10	27.8	42

likely overestimate their number due to IP changes in residential networks, and deliberate IP changes or IP pooling in cloud-based crawlers. Furthermore, this would complicate detection of recurring crawlers.

Table 3. Twelve out of 125 web Crawlers observed on the experimental Alexa Reference Domain (until end of June 2018). URLs visited: Homepage/robots.txt/experimental URLs/other URLs

Crawler/AS Name	First delay	Active days	Periodicity	Requests per visit	URLs visited
Google	1.7 days	59	Daily	1.5	●/●/○/●
Amazon	1.8 days	47	Appr. daily	5.4	●/●/●/●
SPRINT-SDC, PL	1.8 days	13	Irregular	26.8	○/○/○/●
Symantec	35.6 days	3	Occasional	1.0	●/○/○/○
Cisco Ironport	1.8 days	2	Once	2.0	●/○/○/○
Trend Micro	39.2 days	1	Once	1.0	●/○/○/○
McAfee	1.6 days	1	Once	2.0	●/○/○/○
University of Michigan	2.6 days	58	Daily	2.0	●/○/○/○
RWTH Aachen	6.2 days	10	Irregular	1.0	●/○/○/○
University of Sydney	13.4 days	2	Twice	1.0	●/○/○/○
Colgate University	10.1 days	1	Once	1.0	●/○/○/○
KU Leuven	29.6 days	1	Once	1.0	●/○/○/○

Table 3 shows a selection of crawlers identified by their AS name, and the types and periodicity of requests they made. Some crawlers visited our domains only once, close to the date the domains entered the ranking. These crawls included vendors of software security products, likely to assess the type and maliciousness of the websites. Our domains also received visits from crawlers evidently looking for potential vulnerabilities on our websites, such as unprotected configuration files, database backups, management scripts and vulnerable web applications. As these crawls came from residential access networks, we suspect they were not benign security surveys.

Only one crawler requested the fake pages our script sent to Alexa. To the best of our knowledge, these URLs do not appear publicly in any data released by Alexa, thus we assume this crawler was affiliated with Alexa. Except for the front page, these pages do not exist, and result in HTTP 404 errors for the crawler. We did not notice any impact on our domain ranks after the visit.

We observed a number of crawls originating from university networks, including U. Michigan, RWTH Aachen, and a crawl from KU Leuven that we were able to attribute to a concurrent study of domain lists and attacks through the detailed time and user agent description in their paper [16].

Some, but not all, crawlers request `robots.txt`, a convention for websites to tell crawlers which areas may or may not be visited, or indexed by search engines. None of the identified research crawlers respected the convention.

Our websites were highly ranked in Alexa and Umbrella, but do not have any real visitors. The fact that they were already included in research studies shows that the risk of infiltration is real, albeit we do not believe that our limited experiments skewed parallel research efforts in any significant way.

5   Discussion

We assess the likelihood and consequences of manipulation from the perspective of potential attacker motivations.

Distort Empirical Measurements Such as Web Crawls. Since many security web crawls use top domain lists as their seed, if attackers manage to manipulate the ranks of existing domains, or add additional domains to the lists, they could create artificial scenario, and skew aggregate results [16]. We argue that this risk is relatively low, especially for academic research, as the prospect of financial gain for attackers is somewhat remote. Vandalism may occur, but there is hope that it would be transient in nature, limited in scope, and could be mitigated by combining multiple data sources.

Intentional distortion of measurements is likely a minor risk, yet it could happen accidentally, as a side effect of other motivations that are more lucrative to attackers.

Bypass Security Mechanisms. Some research prototypes [9,17] use features of domains from top domain lists as benign examples for training purposes, or they outright whitelist any domain found on the list. The threat intelligence feed Umbrella Investigate API [6] includes domain ranks; infiltration could make a domain appear more benign than it actually is. Thus, attackers may infiltrate top domain lists to evade detection or bypass such security mechanisms.

In contrast to the vandalism discussed above, it is easier to see how an attacker could financially benefit from a bypass attack, thus we argue that it is a medium-high risk. Fortunately, these systems usually do not depend on a specific source for their list of benign websites, and may not need any rank data at all.

Malicious infiltration of the lists could be addressed by obtaining lists of benign websites from more trustworthy sources and validating them before use, such as by using only domains in the intersection of multiple lists from different sources, and cross-checking them against blacklists, as proposed by Le Pochat et al. [16].

Furthermore, as discussed in Sect. 3, several research studies compiled lists of presumed "benign" domains from Alexa by retaining only domains ranked for at least one year. While not perfect (e.g., this strategy cannot rule out long-lived domains compromised by attackers), it imposes an additional cost on attackers, namely a one-year preparation period for successful attacks.

Increase the Value of a Domain, Gain More Visibility and More Visitors Through a Better (Fake) Ranking. Several online services provide independent estimates for potential sale prices of domain names, and some of them factor in domain rankings. Attackers could manipulate their domain's ranking to artificially inflate the domain valuation. As an extreme example, worthofweb.com estimates an unrealistic $ 21,000 value for one of our test domains, even though it does not receive any real visitors and was initially purchased for $ 0.50. While it is unlikely that such an estimate would be used as the sole basis for sale price negotiation, in general rank manipulation could lead to the incorrect belief of more visitors, thus a higher sale price. Similarly, a better rank may lead to higher prices that can be charged for advertising campaigns.

Rank manipulation is, in fact, not a hypothetical risk. Unscrupulous website owners can buy an "Alexa rank boost" from a range of online services, which we do not name to avoid promoting them. Some of these services promise to direct real web traffic to the website, whereas others reassure prospective customers that *"(...) We send alexa desired data to alexa system directly to improve alexa rank. So there won't be any increase in your web traffic and thus no impact on your website."* A rank of 100 k is advertised at about $ 40 per month, with the highest offered target rank of 1 k costing $ 3,300. Some of these services have been in operation for more than six years, citing customer feedback such as *"I sold my site finally at the price 3 times as previous"* and *"It helps me in talking about the ad prices."* Given the existence of these services, it is likely that rank manipulation is already occurring in practice, but we are not aware of any proven technique to detect manipulations of top domain lists from a list consumer perspective.

6   Conclusion

We have demonstrated that attackers can place domains in Alexa's and Umbrella's domain rankings, even though these domains do not receive any real visitors. Though the lists may not have been designed to withstand attacks, they are frequently used in research in ways that they were not designed for (e.g., [7,9,13,17,18,21]). Our research shows these attacks take up negligible resources, and are trivial to execute. A rank in the Alexa top 100 k, for instance, requires a total of 217 fake visits from seven fake toolbar users. This poses a threat to security systems that assume the most popular domains to be benign. Before using domain rankings for such a purpose, some researchers have sanitised them by discarding all domains ranked for less than one year. However, our analysis has shown that this step does not fully eliminate malicious domains. Furthermore, the limited cost of infiltration attacks means that determined attackers can circumvent such measures by mounting long-term attacks. We recommend that researchers reconsider using these rankings when rank manipulation or maliciousness could have a negative impact on their research. Detecting rank manipulation attempts, both from a list provider and list consumer perspective, is an interesting and important topic for future work.

Acknowledgements. We thank David Choffnes and Northeastern University's ITS for assisting the authors in obtaining permission to use the university's IP space. We also thank Ahmet Buyukkayhan for running Google Safe Browsing experiments on our behalf. This work was funded by Secure Business Austria and the National Science Foundation under grants IIS-1553088 and CNS-1703454.

References

1. Alexa top 1 million download. http://s3.amazonaws.com/alexa-static/top-1m.csv.zip
2. Amazon Alexa top sites. https://www.alexa.com/topsites
3. Are there known biases in Alexa's traffic data? https://support.alexa.com/hc/en-us/articles/200461920-Are-there-known-biases-in-Alexa-s-traffic-data-
4. Cisco Umbrella top 1 million. https://s3-us-west-1.amazonaws.com/umbrella-static/index.html
5. How are Alexa's traffic rankings determined? https://support.alexa.com/hc/en-us/articles/200449744-How-are-Alexa-s-traffic-rankings-determined-
6. Umbrella investigate API documentation. https://investigate-api.readme.io/docs/top-million-domains
7. Alrwais, S., et al.: Under the shadow of sunshine: understanding and detecting bulletproof hosting on legitimate service provider networks. In: Security & Privacy Symposium (2017)
8. Baker, L.: Manipulating Alexa traffic ratings (2006). https://www.searchenginejournal.com/manipulating-alexa-traffic-rankings/3044/
9. Bilge, L., Kirda, E., Kruegel, C., Balduzzi, M.: EXPOSURE: finding malicious domains using passive DNS analysis. In: NDSS (2011)
10. Digital Point Forums: Alexa is a scam? (2010). https://forums.digitalpoint.com/threads/alexa-is-a-scam.2016206/
11. Englehardt, S., Narayanan, A.: Online tracking: a 1-million-site measurement and analysis. In: CCS (2016)
12. Hao, S., et al.: Understanding the domain registration behavior of spammers. In: IMC (2013)
13. Heiderich, M., Frosch, T., Holz, T.: ICESHIELD: detection and mitigation of malicious websites with a frozen DOM. In: Sommer, R., Balzarotti, D., Maier, G. (eds.) RAID 2011. LNCS, vol. 6961, pp. 281–300. Springer, Heidelberg (2011). https://doi.org/10.1007/978-3-642-23644-0_15
14. Hubbard, D.: Cisco umbrella 1 million (2016). https://umbrella.cisco.com/blog/2016/12/14/cisco-umbrella-1-million/
15. Larisch, J., Choffnes, D., Levin, D., Maggs, B.M., Mislove, A., Wilson, C.: CRLite: a scalable system for pushing all TLS revocations to all browsers. In: Security & Privacy Symposium (2017)

16. Le Pochat, V., van Goethem, T., Tajalizadehkhoob, S., Korczynski, M., Joosen, W.: Tranco: a research-oriented top sites ranking hardened against manipulation. In: NDSS (2019)

17. Lee, S., Kim, J.: WarningBird: detecting suspicious URLs in Twitter stream. In: NDSS (2011)

18. Lever, C., Kotzias, P., Balzarotti, D., Caballero, J., Antonakakis, M.: A lustrum of malware network communication: evolution and insights. In: Security & Privacy Symposium (2017)

19. Lever, C., Walls, R.J., Nadji, Y., Dagon, D., McDaniel, P., Antonakakis, M.: Domain-Z: 28 registrations later. In: Security & Privacy Symposium (2016)

20. Li, Z., Zhang, K., Xie, Y., Yu, F., Wang, X.: Knowing your enemy: understanding and detecting malicious web advertising. In: CCS (2012)

21. Nadji, Y., Antonakakis, M., Perdisci, R., Lee, W.: Connected colors: unveiling the structure of criminal networks. In: Stolfo, S.J., Stavrou, A., Wright, C.V. (eds.) RAID 2013. LNCS, vol. 8145, pp. 390–410. Springer, Heidelberg (2013). https://doi.org/10.1007/978-3-642-41284-4_20

22. Pearce, P., Ensafi, R., Li, F., Feamster, N., Paxson, V.: Augur: Internet-wide detection of connectivity disruptions. In: Security & Privacy Symposium (2017)

23. Pitsillidis, A., Kanich, C., Voelker, G.M., Levchenko, K., Savage, S.: Taster's choice: a comparative analysis of spam feeds. In: IMC (2012)

24. Rahbarinia, B., Perdisci, R., Antonakakis, M.: Segugio: efficient behavior-based tracking of malware-control domains in large ISP networks. In: DSN (2015)

25. Rweyemamu, W., Lauinger, T., Wilson, C., Robertson, W., Kirda, E.: Clustering and the weekend effect: recommendations for the use of top domain lists in security research. In: Choffnes, D., Barcellos, M. (eds.) PAM 2019. LNCS, vol. 11419, pp. 161–177. Springer, Cham (2019). https://doi.org/10.1007/978-3-030-15986-3_11

26. Scheitle, Q., et al.: A long way to the top: significance, structure, and stability of Internet top lists. In: IMC (2018)

27. SEO Chat Forums: Alexa ranking is fake? (2004). http://forums.seochat.com/alexa-ranking-49/alexa-ranking-fake-10828.html

28. Starov, O., Nikiforakis, N.: XHOUND: Quantifying the fingerprintability of browser extensions. In: Security & Privacy Symposium (2017)

Truth in Web Mining: Measuring the Profitability and the Imposed Overheads of Cryptojacking

Panagiotis Papadopoulos[1(✉)], Panagiotis Ilia[2], and Evangelos Markatos[1]

[1] University of Crete/FORTH, Heraklion, Greece
{panpap,markatos}@ics.forth.gr
[2] University of Illinois at Chicago, Chicago, USA
pilia@uic.edu

Abstract. In recent years, we have been observing a new paradigm of attacks, the so-called cryptojacking attacks. Given the lower-risk/lower-effort nature of cryptojacking, the number of such incidents in 2018 were nearly double of those of ransomware attacks. Apart from the cryptojackers, web-cryptomining library providers also enabled benign publishers to use this mechanism as an alternative monetization schema for web in the era of declined ad revenues. In spite of the buzz raised around web-cryptomining, it is not yet known *what is the profitability of web-cryptomining and what is the actual cost it imposes on the user side.*

In this paper, we respond to this exact question by measuring the overhead imposed to the user with regards to power consumption, resources utilization, network traffic, device temperature and user experience. We compare those overheads along with the profitability of web-cryptomining to the ones imposed by advertising to examine if web-cryptomining can become a viable alternative revenue stream for websites. Our results show that web-cryptomining can reach the profitability of advertising under specific circumstances, but users need to sustain a significant cost on their devices.

Keywords: Cryptomining · Cost of in-browser mining ·
Digital advertising · Cryptojacking

1 Introduction

The last 15 months, we observe on the web the uncommon case of a new conceptual type of attack cropping up in cybersecurity. This new type of attack is the well-known cryptojacking, which had a 35% share of all web threats [19] last year. Specifically, when ransomware attacks declined by 45% in fourth quarter of 2018 in comparison to the first quarter of the same year, cryptojacking attack incidents quadrupled by 450% in the same time-frame [25].

Despite of the reduction in cryptocurrency prices, cryptojacking continues to be prevalent on the web [42] due to the minimal effort it requires from the

© Springer Nature Switzerland AG 2019
Z. Lin et al. (Eds.): ISC 2019, LNCS 11723, pp. 277–296, 2019.
https://doi.org/10.1007/978-3-030-30215-3_14

attackers. The concept behind this category is pretty simple: When a user visits a website, their system resources get abused by the attacker to mine cryptocurrency for as long user has the tab open (and in some cases even for longer [44]). Malicious miners have shown up in mobile devices, cloud infrastructure, IoT gadgets and game consoles [36], or even critical infrastructure [37].

Of course, in-browser mining is not a new idea. The compatibility of JavaScript miners with all modern browsers gave motivation for web coin mining attempts since the very early days of Bitcoin, back in 2011 [35]. However, the increased mining difficulty of Bitcoin was the primary factor that led such approaches to failure. Yet, the emergence of altcoins with features like transaction speed, mining speed and distributed mining, became the growth factor for some coins (e.g., Monero [7] grew from 13$ to 300$ within 2017 [20]) and was the catalyst for the incarnation of JavaScript-based coin mining [29].

Coinhive [6], was the first JavaScript-based in-browser mining library (September 2017), which promoted web-cryptomining as an alternative revenue stream for publishers. And indeed, we observed a significant [1,12,15] number of benign content providers deploying mining libraries in their websites (e.g., The PirateBay [11]). Of course the increased growth of cryptomining did not create opportunities only for benign publishers, but cyber-attackers as well. Several incidents have been reported the last couple of years with popular and prestigious websites [18,22,30,32,34] being infected, thus forcing their visitors to mine cryptocoins. Although there are many existing works studying the prevalence or proposing detection mechanisms and countermeasures on cryptojacking [27,28,55], yet some interesting questions still remain unaddressed: *What is the actual cost of web-cryptomining on the user side? What is the profitability for the attacker or the benign publisher? Can it become an alternative web monetization scheme for benign publishers?*

In this study, we aim to tackle these exact questions; we conduct the first full-scale analysis of the profitability and costs of web-cryptominingon the user-side, in an attempt to shed light in this newly emerged technology, and explore if/to what degree it can replace ads on the web. Specifically, we estimate the possible revenues based on advertising and web-cryptomining, aiming to determine under what circumstances a miner-supported website can reach the profits from digital advertising. To achieve that, we collect a large dataset of ad- and miner-supported websites, and we develop WebTestbench: a sensor-based testbed to measure the resource utilization of both monetization models and compare the imposed user-side costs. In particular, with WebTestbench we measure (i) the utilization of system resources such as CPU and main memory, (ii) the degradation of the user experience due to the mining workload, (iii) the energy consumption and how this affects battery-operated devices (e.g., laptops, tablets, smartphones), (iv) system temperature and how overheating affects the user's device and (v) network and how this can affect a possible Internet data-plan.

To summarize, the main contributions of this paper are the following:

(i) We study the profitability of web-based cryptocurrency mining, while questioning its ability to become a reliable monetization method for web services.

Our results show that for the average duration of a website visit, ads are at least 5.5× more profitable than web-cryptomining. However, a miner-supported website can produce higher revenues if the visitor keeps their tab open for longer than 5.53 min, when there are no more ads served. Based on these findings, a hybrid approach that leverages both ad and cryptomining would allow publishers to receive the maximum possible profit.

(ii) We design a methodology to assess the resource utilization patterns of in-browser cryptominers on the visitor's device. We implement our approach into the WebTestbench framework[1] and we investigate what costs these utilization patterns impose on the visitor's side with regards to the user experience, and energy consumption and battery autonomy.

(iii) We collect a large dataset of around 200 K ad- and miner- supported websites that include different web-cryptomining libraries. We use this dataset as input for the WebTestbench framework and we compare the resource utilization and costs of the two monetization models. Our results show that while browsing a miner-supported website, the visitor's CPU gets utilized 59× more than while visiting an ad-supported website, thus increasing the temperature (52.8%) and power consumption (2×) of their device.

2 Background

2.1 In-Browser Mining

Web-based mining is a method of cryptocurrency mining that happens inside a browser, using a script delivered from a website. The first attempts of in-browser Bitcoin (or Ethereum) mining failed due to the increased mining difficulty. However, the rise of alternative crypto-coins (altcoins) that provide distributed mining, increased mining speed and ASIC (Application-Specific Integrated Circuit) resistance, made distributed CPU (i.e, x86, x86-64, ARM) based mining very effective, even when using commodity hardware, and opened new potential funding avenues on the web. The large growth of web-cryptomining started with the release of Coinhive's JavaScript-based Monero miner [6] in September 2017[2]. After Coinhive, many more companies launched their own web mining services [56]. Such miners compute hashes as a Proof-of-Work, and can be easily included in any website, thus enabling publishers to utilize visiting users' CPUs as an alternative monetization mechanism.

Upon visiting a miner-supported website, the user receives a mining library along with the website's content. Usually these libraries are provided by third parties or mining service providers (MSP), who are responsible for (i) maintaining the source code, (ii) controlling the synchronization of computations, (iii) collecting the computed hashes and (iv) pay the publishers. Upon rendering, a miner

---

[1] Open-source: https://github.com/panpap/webTestbench.

[2] Months after this paper's submission, Coinhive announced that it shuts down its operations after 2 years due to the hard fork and algorithm update of the Monero network [5].

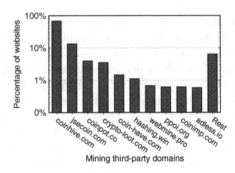

Fig. 1. Cryptomining market share per third party library in our dataset. Coinhive owns the dominant share (69%) when JSEcoin follows with 13%.

establishes a persistent connection with the remote MSP (e.g., coinhive.com) to communicate with the service/mining pool. Through this channel, the miner receives periodically PoW tasks and reports back the computed hashes.

2.2 Cryptojacking

The so-called Drive-by Mining, or *cryptojacking*, takes place either (i) directly: when the publisher of a website performs web-cryptomining without the consent of their visitors[3], or (ii) indirectly: by compromising embedded third party libraries or by delivering malicious mining code through the ad ecosystem [21]. For example, the compromisation of a single screen reader third party (i.e., Browsealoud [43]) resulted in infecting more than 4000 websites that were using it. Victims of cryptojacking have been several popular and prestigious websites [18, 22, 30, 32, 34].

3 Data Collection and Analysis

To gather the necessary data for our study, we collect several miner blacklists [59] including the ones used by the 5 most popular mine-blocking browser extensions[4]. By merging these blacklists we compose a list of 3610 unique entries of mining libraries and keywords. Then, we use these entries to query PublicWWW archive [51], and we collect a total of 107511 mine-including domains. It should be noted that the domains we collected are ranked in the range from 1353 to 960540 in the Alexa rank of popular websites, and that the majority of them are based in the USA, Russia and Brazil.

The mining websites we collected, include more than 27 different third party miners, such as Coinhive, CryptoLoot, JSEcoin and CoinHave. In Fig. 1, we

---

[3] Contrary to digital advertising where the visitors can discern ad-impressions, in web-cryptomining it is not easy to perceive the existence of a running miner.

[4] Coin-Blocker, No Mining, MinerBlock, noMiner and CoinBlock.

Table 1. Summary of our dataset

Type	Amount
Blacklist entries	3610
Miner-supported websites	107511
Ad-supported websites	100000
Unique third-party miners	27

present the portion of websites in our dataset that use each one of these libraries. As seen, besides the large variety of mining libraries, there is a monopolistic phenomenon in the market of cryptominers, with Coinhive owning the dominant share (69%). From the rest of the libraries only JSEcoin miner surpasses 10%.

Apart from miner-supported websites, we also collected an equal number of ad-supported ones, which are among the same popularity ranking range. Then, by using the blacklist of Ghostery adblocker, we enumerated all the ad-slots in these websites. We found the average number of ad-slots per website to be 3.4. Finally, Table 1 summarizes the contents of our dataset.

3.1 WebTestbench Framework for Utilization Analysis

To measure the costs each domain in our dataset imposes on the user, we designed and developed WebTestbench: a web measuring testbed. A high-level overview of the architecture of WebTestbench is presented in Fig. 2. The WebTestbench framework follows an extensible modular design, and consists of several measuring components that work in a plug-and-play manner. Each such component is able to monitor utilization patterns across different system resources (e.g., memory, CPU, etc.). The main components of our platform currently include:

A. **crawler component**, which runs the browser (i.e., Google Chrome) in a headless mode. The crawling is responsible of stopping and purging *any* state after a website probe (e.g., set cookies, cache, local storage, registered service workers, etc.), and listening to the commands of the main controller (i.e., next visiting website, time interval, etc.).
B. **main controller**, which takes as input a list of domains and the visiting time per website. It is responsible for scheduling the execution of the monitoring components.
C. **monitoring platform**, which is responsible for the per time interval execution of the monitoring modules. This platform was build in order to be easily expandable in case of future additional modules.

For the scope of this analysis, we developed 6 different modules to measure the utilization that miners perform in 6 different system resources:

1. memory activity (physical and virtual), by using the `psrecord` utility [53] and attaching to the crawling browser tab's pid.

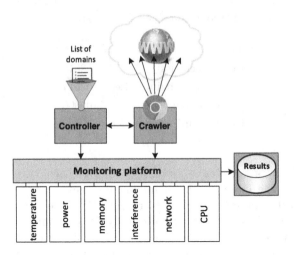

Fig. 2. High level overview of our measurement testbed. A Chrome-based platform fetches each website for a specific time, and its different components measure the resources.

2. CPU utilization per core, by using the linux process status tool (`ps`).
3. system temperature (overall and per core), by leveraging the Linux monitoring sensors (`lm_sensors` [54]).
4. network traffic, by capturing (i) the network packets through `tcpdump` and (ii) the HTTP requests in the application layer along with their metadata (e.g., timing, initiator, transferred bytes, type, status code).
5. process interference, to infer the degradation of user experience caused by the heavy CPU utilization of mining processes. This module consists of a CPU intensive benchmarking that includes multi-threaded MD5 hash calculations.
6. energy consumption, by utilizing an external Phidget21 power sensing package [50]. Phidget enable us to accurately measure the energy consumption of the 3 ATX power-supply lines (+12.0a, +12.0b +5.0, +3.3 V)[5]. The 12.0 Va line powers the processor, the 5.0 V line powers the memory, and the 3.3 V line powers the rest of the peripherals on the motherboard.

3.2   Methodology

In order to explore the different resource utilization patterns for miner- and ad-supported websites, we load our domain dataset in WebTestbench and we fetch each landing page for a certain amount of time. During this period the network monitoring module captures all outgoing HTTP(S) requests of the analyzed website. Additionally, the modules responsible for measuring the energy consumption, the CPU and memory utilization and the temperature, report the sensors' values in a per second interval. By the end of this first phase, WebTestbench

---

[5] Instrumented in a similar way as in other studies [49].

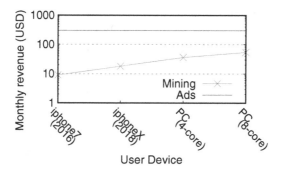

Fig. 3. Estimation of monthly profit for a website with 100 K visitors and average visit duration of 1 min. Visitors with mid-rage 8-core PCs (300 H/s) provide 5.5× less revenue to the publisher than when having 3 ads in the website.

erases any existing browser state and re-fetches the same website. This time, the only simultaneously running process is the interference measuring module which reports its progress at the end of the second phase.

4 Profitability and Cost Analysis

In this section, we explore the profitability of cryptomining for the owner of the mining module (i.e., publisher or cryptojacker) and the cost this imposes on the users. For the following experiments, we use a Linux desktop equipped with a Hyper-Threading Quad-core Intel I7-3770 operating at 3.90 GHz, with 8 MB SmartCache, 8 GB RAM and an Intel 82567 1GbE network interface.

4.1 Profitability of In-Browser Mining

In the first set of experiments, we explore the profitability of in-browser miners and compare it to the current digital advertising model. Thereby, in the first experiment we simulate the monthly profit of the two strategies for a website of moderate popularity: 100,000 visitors per month. Studies have measured the average duration of a website visit being around 1 min [38].

For this experiment, we use the popular Monero mining library of Coinhive and in order to measure the highest possible revenues for the miner's owner we assume the maximum rate this library provided ever: 0.0001468 XMR/1M hashes. This means that the miner's owner would get 0.0001468 Monero (XMR) per 1 million calculated hashes. Given the volatility of crypto-coin values against fiat money, in our simulations, we use the mean value of Monero across last year (2018): 1 Monero = 205 USD. Apart from the visit duration, the amount of total calculated hashes of a website depends on the computation power of the visitors' devices. Thus, in this experiment, in order to cover a wider range of CPU hashrate capabilities, we use 4 different levels of computation rates

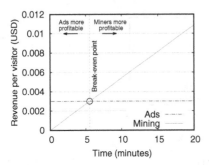

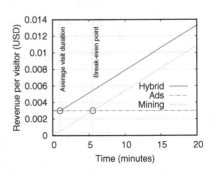

Fig. 4. Revenue per visitor. A publisher makes higher profit from mining than using ads (3 ad-slots) when the visitor (mid-rage 8-core PC) has his tab open for duration > 5.53 min.

Fig. 5. Revenue per visitor according to a hybrid approach. The revenue is bounded either before or after the break-even point, to be always higher or equal to both ads and web-cryptomining

based on [10]: the rate of 50 Hash/s (e.g., iPhone7), 90 Hash/s (e.g., iPhoneX), 200 Hash/s (e.g., 4-core PC) and 300 Hash/s (e.g., 8-core PC).

In the same experiment, we also compute the monthly revenue in case of a benign publisher when leverages instead of web-cryptomining, the advertising model to monetize their content. The most popular medium for personalized ad-buying nowadays [14] is the programmatic instantaneous auctions. The average number of ad-slots in an ad-supported website is 3 and the median charge price per ad impression as measured in previous studies [46,47] is 1 CPM[6] (Cost per thousand of impressions).

As can be seen in Fig. 3, for the average duration of a user's visit, the miner achieves an average computation rate from visitors of as high as 300 Hash/s. We see however that the website produces 5.5× more revenue when using ads instead of web-cryptomining[7]. In addition, we see that as the visitor's hardware improves, the distance between these two monetization methods becomes smaller. This means that in the future web mining can be capable of providing comparable profits for the publishers.

It is apparent, that for a miner-supported website, *time matters*. Indeed, recent studies [1] show that the majority of miner-supported websites provide content that can keep the visitor on the website for a long time. Such content includes video or movie streaming, flash games, etc. Of course, in web-cryptomining, the user does not need to interact with the website's content per se. As such, numerous deceiving methods (e.g., via service workers [13,44] or pop-unders [57]) are currently used, aiming to allow the embedded miner to work in the background for as long as possible.

---

[6] Advertiser pays 1 US dollar every 1000 successfully rendered impressions.

[7] Our simulation results have been also verified by real world experiments [8].

Table 2. Distribution of the average CPU Utilization for the different monetization methods. The median miner-supported website utilizes 59× more the user's CPU than the median ad-supported website.

Type	10th Perc.	Median	90th Perc.
Advertising	3.33%	9.71%	17.19%
Mining	560.11%	574.01%	580.71%

In the next experiment, we set out to identify the minimum time the website needs to remain open inside a tab of a visitor's browser in order to make higher profits than when using ads. In Fig. 4 we simulate the revenue per visitor for a website running in the background, and we use the same hash-rate levels as above. In order to produce revenues higher than when ads are delivered, the website must remain open in the user's browser for a duration longer than 5.53 min. When on background, the website does not receive fresh ads, since no new ad-auctions take place. In Fig. 4 we see that it is more profitable to use ads on the left of the break-even point, but when moving on the right of break-even point, web-cryptomining generate higher income.

To mitigate that, one could use a hybrid model to combine both. Specifically, as shown in Fig. 5, websites can utilize ads to generate a basic revenue from the visitor and move to web-cryptomining when she switches to different browser tab (e.g., after 1 min). This way, publishers can continue making profit when their websites become idle. So a publisher's revenue when using ads is given by R_A (1), when using web-cryptomining by R_M (2), and when using the hybrid model by R_H (3), where t_0 is the average duration of a visit.

$$for\ t \in (0, t_0):\ R_A(t) = C_1 \tag{1}$$

$$for\ t \in [t_0, \infty):\ R_M(t) = C_2 * t \tag{2}$$

$$R_H(t) = C_1 + C_2 * (t - t_0) \tag{3}$$

As can be seen in Fig. 5, the revenue produced by the hybrid approach is always higher or equal to both ads and web-cryptomining.

4.2 Costs on the User Experience

After estimating the possible revenues of cryptomining, it is time to measure the costs this method imposes on the user and see how do these compare to the costs a website imposes when it uses ads to monetize its content.

CPU and Memory Utilization: In this set of experiments, we explore the average CPU and memory utilization by mining-supported websites. Note at this point, that the intense of mining is tunable. The majority of mining libraries enable their controller to fine tune the number of threads and the throttling of the miner. In this experiment we fetch each website in our two subsets for 3 min using WebTestbench and we extract the distribution of its CPU utilization

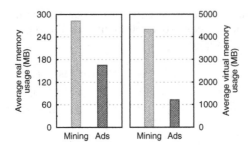

Fig. 6. Distribution of average real and virtual memory utilization through time. Miner-supported websites although reserve (3.59×) larger chunks of virtual memory, require 1.7× more MBytes of real memory than ad-supported websites.

through time. In Table 2 we report the average values for the median, the 10th and 90th percentiles. As we see, the median miner-supported website utilizes the visitor's CPU up to 59× more than an ad-supported website. We also measure the utilization of the visitor's main memory. In Fig. 6 we plot the average values for both real and virtual memory activity. As expected, miners do not utilize memory as heavy as CPU. On average the miner-supported websites require 1.7× more space in real memory than the ad-supported websites.

Network Activity: Next, we measure the network utilization of the average mining-supported website. As discussed in Sect. 2, a mining library needs to periodically communicate with a remote third party server (i.e., the MSP's server) in order to report the calculated hashes but also to obtain the next PoW. This communication in the vast majority of the libraries in our dataset takes place through a special persistent channel that allows bidirectional communication. To assess the network activity of web miners, we use the network capturing module of WebTestbench and we monitor the traffic of each (ad- and miner-supported) website for 3 min.

Based on the used third-party mining library, we isolate the web socket communication between its in-browser mining module and the remote MSP server. In order to compare this PoW-related communication of miners with the corresponding ad-related traffic of ad-supported websites, we utilize the open-source blacklist of the Disconnect browser extension to isolate all advertising related content. In Fig. 7, we plot the distribution of the total transmitted volume of bytes per website for the visit duration of 3 min. Although the web socket communication of miners consists of small packets of 186 Bytes on average, we see that in total the median PoW-related communication of miner-supported websites transmitted 22.8 KBytes, when the median ad-traffic volume[8] of ad-supported websites was 6.7 KBytes. This means that the median miner-generated traffic volume is 3.4× larger than the median ad-generated. In this experiment, we see that the network utilization patterns depend not only on the

---

[8] Traffic that ad-related domains transmit to the user's browser (includes: impressions, ad/tracking related scripts, etc.).

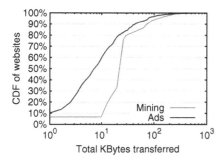

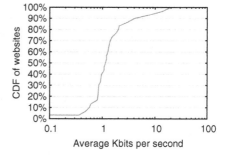

Fig. 7. Distribution of the transmitted volume of bytes per website for a visit duration of 3 min. The median miner-generated traffic volume is 3.4× larger than the median ad-generated.

Fig. 8. Distribution of transmitted bit rate per miner-supported website in our dataset. The median in-browser miner communicates with its MSP by transmitting 1,168 bits per second.

throttling of the miner but also on the different implementations. For example, while using the same portion of CPU, the miner of coinhive.com transmits on average 0.6 packets/s, webmine.cz: 2.2 packets/s, cryptoloot.com: 4.7 packets/s and jsecoin.com: 1.3 packets/s.

In Fig. 8, we plot the distribution of the average data transfer rate per miner-supported website in our dataset. As shown, for the median case, the communication between the miner and the MSP has a transfer rate of 1 Kbit per second (or 142 Bytes/s). As in the previous experiment, the rate highly depends on the mining library, with some of them reaching up to 14 Kbit per second. At this point, recall that the PoW-related communication between the miner and the MSP holds for as long as the miner is running, and as shown in Fig. 4, a miner must run for longer than 5.53 min to produce revenues higher than ads. This means that for the median case, the total volume of transferred bytes will exceed 46 KBytes.

In the case of a user who use consumption-based Internet service pricing[9] the monetary cost imposed is 0.000219$ per minute on average when browsing a miner-supported website. On the other hand, a publisher who includes a coinhive miner in its website earns 0.000409$ per minute from that user (considering that the user provides a hash rate of 227 Hash/s as in [8]). Hence, we see that users with metered connections, when they visit miner-related websites, pay a monetization cost that is 53% less than the revenue of the publisher.

Power Efficiency: Of course the intensive resource utilization of cryptominers affects also the power consumption of the visitor's device, which has a direct impact on its battery autonomy. In the next experiment, we measure the power consumed by (i) main memory and (ii) CPU and network adapter components of the user's device while visiting miner- and ad- supported websites for a 3 min duration. In Table 3, we report the average median, 10th and 90th percentile

---

[9] Considering the average prices per byte in USA and Europe [2,16,58].

Table 3. Distribution of the average consumption of power for the different monetization methods. The median miner-supported website forces the user's device to consume more power than the median ad-supported website: 2.08× and 1.14× more power for the CPU and the memory component, respectively.

Component	Type	10th Percentile	Median	90th Percentile
CPU & network adapter	Advertising	31.88 W	32.39 W	34.17 W
	Mining	63.35 W	67.60 W	71.22 W
Main memory	Advertising	4.37 W	4.46 W	5.35 W
	Mining	4.76 W	4.99 W	5.67 W

values for all websites in our dataset. As shown, there is a slightly increased (1.14× more than ad-supported websites) consumption of the memory component in miner-supported websites. However, we see that the heavy computation load of cryptominers significantly increases the CPUs and network adapters consumption, making miner-supported websites consume 2.08× more energy than ad-supported websites! This means that a laptop able to support 7 h of consecutive traditional ad supported browsing, would support 3.36 h of mining-supported browsing.

System Temperature: The increased electricity powering of the visitor's system results to an increased thermal radiation. During the above experiment, we measure the distribution of the per-core temperatures while visiting each website in our dataset for 3 min. In Fig. 9 we present the average results for the percentiles: 10th, 25th, 50th, 75th, 90th. As we can observe, the core temperatures for miner-supported websites are constantly above the optimal range of 45–60 °C [33]. In particular, the visitor's system operates for most of the time in the range of 43–50 °C while visiting ad-supported websites. When the visited website includes a miner, the average temperature of the cores reaches up to 52.8% higher, in the range of 73–77 °C, when in 10% of the cases it may reach higher than 84 °C.

To that end, with regards to the costs imposed to the user, high temperatures may lead to degraded system performance and poor user experience. Apart from that, constantly running a commodity device (e.g., mobile phone, laptop or desktop PC) at high temperatures, without a proper cooling mechanism, may significantly decrease the hardware's lifespan in the long term or even cause physical damage by thermal expansion.

Impact on Multi-tab Browsing and Parallel Processes: The heavy utilization of the visitor's CPU can affect the overall user's experience not only in the visited website, but in parallel processes and browser tabs, too. Indeed, for as long as the browser tab of a mining-supported website is open, the multi-threaded computations of the miner leaves limited processing power for the rest of the running applications. To make matters worse, as part of a PC's own

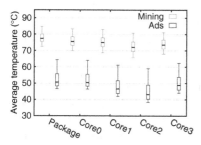

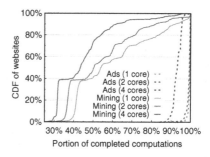

Fig. 9. Distribution of average temperatures per system's core. When the visited site has miner, the average temperature of the cores may reach up to 52.8% higher (73–77 °C) than when with ads.

Fig. 10. Impact of background running miner- and ad-supported websites to a user's process. When the majority of ad-supported websites have negligible effect in other processes, the median embedded miner causes a performance degradation of up to 57% to a parallel running process.

cooling system, the motherboard, in case of increased temperatures, may instruct the CPU component to slow down, or even force the system to shut down [4].

To assess how these factors may affect parallel running processes in the visitor's device, we use the interference measuring module of WebTestbench and we measure the performance overhead caused by background running miners. This module introduces computation workloads to the system to emulate a parallel running process of the user. Specifically, WebTestbench fetches each website in our dataset for the average visit duration (i.e., 1 min), in parallel conducts multi-threaded MD5 hash calculations, and in the end reports the number of calculated hashes. To test the performance of parallel processing under different computation workloads, we visit each website using 3 setups for the MD5 process, utilizing in parallel 1, 2, and 4 cores of the CPU. In addition, we run the MD5 process alone for 1 min to measure the maximum completed operations.

In Fig. 10, we plot the distribution of completed operations per website. As expected, when there is a miner-supported website running in the user's browser, the performance of the user's processes that run in parallel is severely affected. In particular, we see that the median miner-supported website forces the parallel process (depending on its computation intensity) to run in 54%, 50% or even 43% of its optimal performance, thus causing a performance degradation of 46% to 57%! Additionally, we see a 39% of miners greedily utilizing all the system's CPU resources causing a performance reduction of 67% to the parallel process.

Additionally, we measure the interference that ad-supported websites introduce to the parallel processes. As expected, the impact is minimal and practically only processes with full CPU utilization are affected, facing performance degradation of less than 10% for the majority of websites. This is mainly the result of JavaScript code responsible for ad serving, user tracking, analytics, etc.

Such severe performance degradation when the user is visiting a mining-supported website can cause glitches, or even crushes to parallel applications (like movie playback, video games), thus ravaging the user's experience. Of course, this performance degradation does not only affect parallel running applications but also mining operations from other open browser tabs. Indeed, a miner can achieve full utilization when the user has visited the miner-supported *website1*. However, when the user opens a second miner-supported *website2*, the utilization for both, as well as the revenues for *publisher1* and *publisher2*, drop to a half. It is easy thus to anticipate, that **the scalability of cryptomining is limited since the more websites rely on web-cryptomining for funding, the less revenues will be generated for their publishers.** While this monetization model has that apparent drawback, in digital advertising each ad-supported website is totally independent from any parallel open browser tabs.

5   Discussion

User Awareness: The recent years, directives like GDPR aim to bring transparency on the web. Website owners need to request user's consent before placing any cookies on the user side but also clearly present in a privacy policy statement what they do and with whom they share the user's data.

The lack of similar policies and directives regarding the proper use of cryptomining has raised a big controversy regarding the lack of transparency in miner-supported websites [9,31]. Many miner-supported websites do not inform the user about the existence of a miner, neither ask for the visitor's consent to utilize their system's resources for cryptocurrency mining.

In one of the first law cases about web-based mining, the Attorney General Hoffman stated that "*no website should tap into a person's computer processing power without clearly notifying the person and giving them the chance to opt out*" [26]. As a result, whenever a user visits a website and she is not aware about the background web-cryptomining, irrespectively whether the mining code has been legitimately deployed by the publisher or a malicious actor that hijacked the website, this is considered as a *cryptojacking* attempt.

Letting the Users Choose: Since both digital advertising [23,46] and web-cryptomining impose costs on the user, a new paradigm could be to inform the user about these costs and give them the option to choose which of the two monetization schemes is more suitable for them (as already happens with paywalls [17,48]). In the case of advertising, the costs are associated with the network bandwidth and the privacy implications of targeted advertising [3,41,45], while the cost of web-cryptomining is associated with higher energy consumption (and battery drainage, overheating, etc.). A viable option for publishers would be to inform the users about these costs, and provide two different versions of their website (i.e., one that serve ads and one that uses cryptoming), thus allowing the user to choose between the two schemes. Indeed, such examples have already tested by various publishers [52].

Of course there are users using ad-blockers who may also deploy mine-blockers (e.g., Coin-Blocker, No Mining, CoinBlock, etc.) to avoid both approaches. However, publishers will eventually deny access to such users (similar to what already happened with ad-blocking users [39]) in an attempt to mitigate declining revenues.

6   Related Work

Eskandari et al. [15], in one of the first web mining related studies, analyzes the existing in-browser mining approaches. In particular, they measured the growth of cryptomining by looking for mining libraries in Internet archive services. In addition, they collected a set of 33 K websites by querying for popular mining projects the Censys.io BigQuery dataset, and they studied the CPU utilization of the included miners. In [1] authors analyze the top 100,000 websites for cryptocurrency mining scripts in an attempt to measure the adoption of cryptominers in the web. The analysis revealed 220 of these websites using cryptomining scripts with their aggregated audience being around 500 million people. The content of these hosting websites were usually content that could keep the user on the website for long, and specifically movie/video/tv streaming (22.27%), file sharing (17.73%), Adult (10%) and News & Media (7.73%).

In [27], authors propose OUTGUARD: a system for automated cryptojacking detection. This system uses an SVN classification model which uses as input features like CPU usage, page execution time, iframe source loads, etc., and the accuracy it achieves reaches 97.9% TPR and 1.1% FPR. Authors run a prototype of their system across Alexa Top 1M sites and they found 3,600 new cases of cryptojacking. Konoth et al. in [28] analyze Alexa Top 1 Million websites studying the prevalence and profitability of cryptojacking (or drive-by mining). Authors identified 20 active cryptomining campaigns and evaluate current blacklist-based countermeasures. The ineffectiveness of these approaches motivated authors to propose *MineSweeper*: a detection approach that leverages cryptographic functions identified through static analysis and monitoring of cache events during run time. Similarly, in [55], authors study the prevalence (measured as low as 0.08%) of cryptomining as a monetization model for publishers. They identify and classify mining websites in the three largest TLDs and the Alexa Top 1M (over 138M domains). They also discuss the inadequacy of block lists and present a WebAssembly-based fingerprinting method to identify miners. Their approach was able to identify 82% more mining websites than NoCoin filter list.

In [24], authors leverage inherent characteristics of cryptojacking scripts to build *CMTracker*: a behavior based detector to automatically track cryptocurrency web mining scripts and their related domains. They discovered 2770 unique cryptojacking samples in a dataset with Alexa top 100 K sites. They estimate the cost of these miners to be more than 278 K kWh extra power per day, and earnings of at least 59K USD/day for the attackers. Finally, they study the evasiveness of cryptojacking scripts with 26% of them use code obfuscation. They tested the detectability of these obfuscation-using scripts using VirusTotal and they saw that only 28% of them could be detected by at least one anti-virus engine.

7   Summary and Conclusion

In this paper, we measure the costs cryptominers impose on the user side by analyzing the utilization patterns of miner-deploying websites on the visitor's system resources (e.g., CPU, memory, network). We study the impact of these utilization patterns (i) on the visitor's device by measuring the system's power consumption and temperature, and also (ii) on the visitor's experience while running other applications in parallel. As a next step, we investigate the ability of web-cryptomining to become a reliable alternative monetization model for benign web publishers.

The findings of our analysis can be summarized as follows:

- for the average duration of a web visit, website generates more than 5.5× higher revenues by including 3 ad impressions than by including a cryptominer.
- to produce higher revenues with a miner than with ads, the user's browser tab must remain open for a duration longer than 5.53 min or use a hybrid approach.
- the median miner-deploying website utilizes up to 59× more of the visitor's CPU and require 1.7× more space in real memory than ad-supported websites.
- the transfer rate of the median miner-MSP communication is 1 Kbit/s. For a user with a metered Internet connection, the monetary cost imposed is on average 0.000219$ per minute, when the publisher from the same user earns 0.000409$ per minute.
- the median miner-generated traffic volume is 3.4× larger than the corresponding ad-generated.
- a visit to an average miner-deploying website consumes on average 2.08× more energy than to an average ad-supported website.
- a visitor's system operates in up to 52.8% higher temperatures when visiting a website with miner than when with ads.
- In-browser miners severely affect parallel running processes. The median miner-deploying website when running in the background may degrade even 57% of the performance of parallel running applications.

After completing our analysis, we see that web-cryptomining can indeed constitute an alternative monetization mechanism for specific categories of benign publishers after obtaining consent from the visitors. In these days, where EU regulators [40] aim to reform the way user data are being collected and processed for targeted advertising, cryptomining provides a privacy-preserving monetization model that requires zero data from the users. However, this study shows that the intensive resource utilization of web-cryptomining libraries imposes a significant cost on the user's device, thus accelerating the deterioration of its hardware. To make matters worse, this *heavy utilization also limits the scalability and profitability of web-cryptomining, since the more websites adopt miners the less portion of resources each of them can acquire from a user that keeps multiple tabs open.* By using a hybrid approach, publishers could increase their profits by monetizing with ads at the beginning and then switch to mining to leverage the time when their websites reside in idle tabs.

Acknowledgements. The research leading to these results has received funding from European Union's Marie Sklodowska-Curie grant agreement 690972 (PROTA-SIS) and Horizon 2020 Research & Innovation Programme under grant agreement 786669 (REACT). This work has been also supported by the EU H2020-SU-ICT-03-2018 Project No. 830929 CyberSec4Europe (cybersec4europe.eu). The paper reflects only the authors' view and the Agency and the Commission are not responsible for any use that may be made of the information it contains.

References

1. AdGuard Research: Cryptocurrency mining affects over 500 million people. And they have no idea it is happening (2017). https://adguard.com/en/blog/crypto-mining-fever/
2. AT&T: Create your mobile share advantage plan (2018). https://www.att.com/shop/wireless/data-plans.html
3. Bashir, M.A., Arshad, S., Robertson, W., Wilson, C.: Tracing information flows between ad exchanges using retargeted ads. In: Proceedings of 2016 USENIX Security Conference, SEC 2016 (2016)
4. Bates, P.: How heat affects your computer, and should you be worried? https://www.makeuseof.com/tag/how-heat-affects-your-computer-and-should-you-be-worried/
5. Catalin Cimpanu: Coinhive cryptojacking service to shut down in March 2019 (2019). https://www.zdnet.com/article/coinhive-cryptojacking-service-to-shut-down-in-march-2019/
6. Coinhive: Monetize your business with your users' CPU power. https://coinhive.com/#javascript-api
7. CoinWarz: Monero network hashrate chart and graph. https://www.coinwarz.com/network-hashrate-charts/monero-network-hashrate-chart
8. Maxence Cornet: Coinhive review: embeddable javascript crypto miner - 3 days in (2017). https://medium.com/@MaxenceCornet/coinhive-review-embeddable-javascript-crypto-miner-806f7024cde8
9. Cryptocurrency Posters. The ethics of Javascript mining (2019). https://www.cryptocurrencyposters.com/the-ethics-of-javascript-mining/
10. CryptoMining24.net: CPU for monero (2017). https://cryptomining24.net/cpu-for-monero/
11. Van der Sar, E.: The pirate bay website runs a cryptocurrency miner (updated). https://torrentfreak.com/the-pirate-bay-website-runs-a-cryptocurrency-miner-170916/
12. Desai, D., Gandhi, D., Sadique, M., Ghule, M.: Cryptomining is here to stay in the enterprise. https://www.zscaler.com/blogs/research/ryptomining-here-stay-enterprise
13. Dorsey, B.: Browser as botnet, or the coming war on your web browser. Radical Networks (2018)
14. eMarketer Podcast: Emarketer releases new us programmatic ad spending figures (2017). https://www.emarketer.com/Article/eMarketer-Releases-New-US-Programmatic-Ad-Spending-Figures/1016698

15. Eskandari, S., Leoutsarakos, A., Mursch, T., Clark, J.: A first look at browser-based cryptojacking. In: Proceedings of IEEE S&B'18, S&B'18 (2018)
16. FANDOM Lifestyle Community: Prepaid data SIM card wiki - Spain (2017). http://prepaid-data-sim-card.wikia.com/wiki/Spain
17. Filloux, F.: Paid or ad-supported: pick one model, and stick with it (2016). https://mondaynote.com/paid-or-ad-supported-pick-one-model-and-stick-with-it-a0c7f8db8db8
18. Fung, B.: Hackers have turned politifact's website into a trap for your pc (2017). https://www.washingtonpost.com/news/the-switch/wp/2017/10/13/hackers-have-turned-politifacts-website-into-a-trap-for-your-pc/
19. Gately, E.: Webroot: beware the worst malware of 2018. https://www.channelpartnersonline.com/2018/10/30/webroot-beware-of-the-worst-malware-of-2018/
20. Global Coin Report: Here's how monero (XMR) gets to $1,000 (2018). https://globalcoinreport.com/heres-monero-xmr-gets-1000/
21. Goodin, D.: Ad network uses advanced malware technique to conceal CPU-draining mining ads. https://arstechnica.com/information-technology/2018/02/ad-network-uses-advanced-malware-technique-to-conceal-cpu-draining-mining-ads/
22. Greenfield, P.: Government websites hit by cryptocurrency mining malware (2018). https://www.theguardian.com/technology/2018/feb/11/government-websites-hit-by-cryptocurrency-mining-malware
23. Gui, J., Mcilroy, S., Nagappan, M., Halfond, W.G.J.: Truth in advertising: the hidden cost of mobile ads for software developers. In Proceedings of the 37th International Conference on Software Engineering, ICSE 2015 (2015)
24. Hong, G., et al.: How you get shot in the back: a systematical study about cryptojacking in the real world. In Proceedings of the 2018 ACM SIGSAC Conference on Computer and Communications Security, pp. 1701–1713. ACM (2018)
25. IBM Security: IBM x-force report: ransomware doesn't pay in 2018 as cybercriminals turn to cryptojacking for profit. https://newsroom.ibm.com/2019-02-26-IBM-X-Force-Report-Ransomware-Doesnt-Pay-in-2018-as-Cybercriminals-Turn-to-Cryptojacking-for-Profit
26. Steve, C., Hoffman, L.J., Jacobson, J.S.: New jersey division of consumer affairs obtains settlement with developer of bitcoin-mining software found to have accessed new jersey computers without users' knowledge or consent (2015). http://nj.gov/oag/newsreleases15/pr20150526b.html
27. Kharraz, A., et al.: Outguard: Detecting in-browser covert cryptocurrency mining in the wild. In Proceedings of 2019 World Wide Web Conference, WWW 2019 (2019)
28. Konoth, R.K., et al.: Minesweeper: an in-depth look into drive-by cryptocurrency mining and its defense. In Proceedings of the 2018 ACM SIGSAC Conference on Computer and Communications Security, CCS 2018 (2018)
29. Leyden, J.: More and more websites are mining crypto-coins in your browser to pay their bills, line pockets. https://www.theregister.co.uk/2017/10/13/crypto_mining/
30. Leyden. J.: Real mad-quid: murky cryptojacking menace that smacked ronaldo site grows. http://www.theregister.co.uk/2017/10/10/cryptojacking/
31. Leyden, J.: Security opt-in cryptomining script coinhive 'barely used' say researchers (2018). https://www.theregister.co.uk/2018/02/27/ethical_coinhive/
32. Lomas, N.: Cryptojacking attack hits 4,000 websites, including UK's data watchdog (2018). https://techcrunch.com/2018/02/12/ico-snafu/

33. Martin, J.: What's the best CPU temperature? (2018). https://www.techadvisor. co.uk/how-to/desktop-pc/cpu-temp-3498564/
34. McCarthy, K.: Cbs's showtime caught mining crypto-coins in viewers' web browsers. http://www.theregister.co.uk/2017/09/25/showtime_hit_with_coinmining_script/
35. Nadolny, D.: Bitcoin plus miner. https://wordpress.org/plugins/bitcoin-plus-miner/
36. Newman, L.H.: The year cryptojacking ate the web (2018). https://www.wired. com/story/cryptojacking-took-over-internet/
37. Newman, L.H.: Now cryptojacking threatens critical infrastructure, too (2019). https://www.wired.com/story/cryptojacking-critical-infrastructure/
38. Nielsen, J.: How long do users stay on web pages? https://www.nngroup.com/ articles/how-long-do-users-stay-on-web-pages/
39. Nithyanand, R., et al.: Adblocking and counter blocking: a slice of the arms race. In 6th USENIX Workshop on Free and Open Communications on the Internet (FOCI 16), Austin, TX. USENIX Association (2016)
40. Official Journal of the European Union: Directive 95/46/ec (general data protection regulation). http://eur-lex.europa.eu/legal-content/EN/TXT/PDF/? uri=CELEX:32016R0679
41. Olejnik, L., Tran, M.-D., Castelluccia, C.: Selling off user privacy at auction. In: 21st Annual Network and Distributed System Security Symposium, NDSS 2014, San Diego, California, USA, 23–26 February, 2014 (2014)
42. Osborne, C.: Ransomware has been abandoned in favor of cryptojacking attacks against the enterprise (2019). https://www.zdnet.com/article/ransomware-has-been-abandoned-in-favor-of-cryptojacking-attacks-against-the-enterprise/
43. Paganini, P.: Thousands of websites worldwide hijacked by cryptocurrency mining code due browsealoud plugin hack (2018). https://securityaffairs.co/wordpress/ 68966/hacking/browsealoud-plugin-hack.html
44. Papadopoulos, P., Ilia, P., Polychronakis, M., Markatos, E.P., Ioannidis, S., Vasiliadis G.: Master of web puppets: abusing web browsers for persistent and stealthy computation. In: Proceedings of the Network and Distributed System Security Symposium, NDSS 2019 (2019)
45. Papadopoulos, P., Kourtellis, N., Markatos, E.: Cookie synchronization: everything you always wanted to know but were afraid to ask. In: The World Wide Web Conference, WWW 2019, pp. 1432–1442. ACM, New York (2019)
46. Papadopoulos, P., Kourtellis, N., Markatos, E.P.: The cost of digital advertisement: comparing user and advertiser views. In: Proceedings of the 2018 World Wide Web Conference, WWW 2018, pp. 1479–1489. International World Wide Web Conferences Steering Committee Republic and Canton of Geneva, Switzerland (2018)
47. Papadopoulos, P., Kourtellis, N., Rodriguez, P.R., Laoutaris, N.: If you are not paying for it, you are the product: how much do advertisers pay to reach you? In: Proceedings of Internet Measurement Conference, IMC 2017 (2017)
48. Papadopoulos, P., Snyder, P., Livshits, B.: Another brick in the paywall: the popularity and privacy implications of paywalls. CoRR, abs/1903.01406 (2019)
49. Papadopoulos, P., Vasiliadis, G., Christou, G., Markatos, E., Ioannidis, S.: No sugar but all the taste! memory encryption without architectural support. In: Foley, S.N., Gollmann, D., Snekkenes, E. (eds.) ESORICS 2017. LNCS, vol. 10493, pp. 362–380. Springer, Cham (2017). https://doi.org/10.1007/978-3-319-66399-9_20
50. Phidgets Inc.: What is a phidget? https://www.phidgets.com/docs21/What_is_a_ Phidget

51. PublicWWW: Source code search engine (2019). https://publicwww.com/
52. Robertson, A.: Salon asks ad-blocking users to opt into cryptocurrency mining instead (2018). https://www.theverge.com/2018/2/13/17008158/salon-suppress-ads-cryptocurrency-mining-coinhive-monero-beta-testing
53. Robitaille, T.: psrecord: record the CPU and memory activity of a process. https://github.com/astrofrog/psrecord
54. Roeck, G.: Overview of the lm-sensors package. https://github.com/groeck/lm-sensors
55. Rüth, J., Zimmermann, T., Wolsing, K., Hohlfeld, O.: Digging into browser-based crypto mining. In: Proceedings of the Internet Measurement Conference 2018, IMC 2018, pp. 70–76. ACM, New York (2018)
56. ShafayI: Javascript mining — best coinhive alternative for 2019 (2019). https://coinogle.com/javascript-mining/
57. Tung, L.: Windows: this sneaky cryptominer hides behind taskbar even after you exit browser (2017). https://www.zdnet.com/article/windows-this-sneaky-cryptominer-hides-behind-taskbar-even-after-you-exit-browser/
58. WhistleOut Inc.: Compare the best cell phone plans (2018). https://www.whistleout.com/CellPhones
59. zerodot1: Coinblockerlists - simple lists that can help to prevent illegal mining in the browser or other applications (2019). https://zerodot1.gitlab.io/CoinBlockerListsWeb/index.html

Side Channels

LightSense: A Novel Side Channel for Zero-permission Mobile User Tracking

Quanqi Ye[1]([envelope]), Yan Zhang[2], Guangdong Bai[3], Naipeng Dong[4],
Zhenkai Liang[4], Jin Song Dong[4], and Haoyu Wang[5]

[1] Advanced Digital Sciences Centre, Singapore, Singapore
`quanqi.ye@adsc-create.edu.sg`
[2] University of Science and Technology of China, Hefei, China
`zhangyan.aq@gmail.com`
[3] The University of Queensland, Brisbane, Australia
`g.bai@uq.edu.au`
[4] National University of Singapore, Singapore, Singapore
{`dcsdn,dcsdjs`}`@nus.edu.sg`, `liangzk@comp.nus.edu.sg`
[5] Beijing University of Posts and Telecommunications, Beijing, China
`haoyuwang@bupt.edu.cn`

Abstract. Android devices are equipped with various sensors. Permissions from users must be explicitly granted for apps to obtain sensitive information, e.g., geographic location. However, some of the sensors are considered trivial such that no permission control is enforced over them, e.g., the ambient light sensor. In this work, we present a novel side channel, i.e. the ambient light sensor, that can be used to track the mobile users. We develop a location tracking system with off-line trained route identification models using the values from the attacker's own ambient light sensor. The system can then be used to track a user's geographic location. The experiment results show that our route identification models achieve a high accuracy of over 91% in user's route identification and our tracking system achieves an accuracy at about 64% in real-time tracking the user with estimation error at about 70 m. Our system out-performs the state-of-the-art works with other side channels. Our work shows that with merely the values from the ambient light sensor of user's mobile phone that requires zero-permission to access, the geographic routes that the users have taken and their real-time locations can be identified with machine learning techniques in high accuracy.

1 Introduction

Mobile phones nowadays are equipped with many powerful sensors. The mobile sensing techniques bring in great convenience for app developers to enrich the functionalities of mobile apps, e.g., the Location-Based-Services (LBSs). However, it also introduces security and privacy issues. The data collected by such apps might appear to be innocuous, but malicious apps could use it for other purposes. Recent reports show that the location information the malicious apps

© Springer Nature Switzerland AG 2019
Z. Lin et al. (Eds.): ISC 2019, LNCS 11723, pp. 299–318, 2019.
https://doi.org/10.1007/978-3-030-30215-3_15

collect may reveal the user's occupation or personal activities which poses severe privacy infringement to them [6,16]. On the other hand, multiple incidents of massive personal private data leakage happen from time to time [11,18,33]. Therefore, mobile users are becoming increasingly concerned about what data the mobile apps can collect and whether the collected data can be used to infringe their privacies.

Android operating system (Android for short) uses a permission model to regulate apps' access to sensitive data. For example, if an app needs to access a user's geographical locations, it needs to explicitly declare the *ACCESS_FINE_LOCATION* permission in its manifest file. When a user installs the app on the mobile phone, a request to the permission will be shown to the user for approval. The user can either choose to accept the permission request and installs the app or simply decline the request. Android 6.0 (API level 23) and the above enforce runtime permission mechanism [3]. User can choose to approve or deny the access request to sensitive data during runtime when the app actually needs to access the sensitive data. In this way, a user can control the permissions granted to the apps in a more flexible way.

However, although most privacy-sensitive resources, e.g., geographical location, have been guarded by permissions, there are still some resources that are considered as innocuous and available to all apps without being guarded by any permission. The ambient light information is one of such resources. It can be detected by the ambient light sensor. The value of the ambient light sensor is a double precision number representing the ambient brightness level. Reading the value of ambient light sensor from the app does not need any permission in all versions of Android. Furthermore, almost all newly manufactured mobile phones come with this sensor to provide the feature of automatically adjusting the screen brightness level according to the ambient brightness level. For example, when the user is standing under the sun, the screen brightness will be automatically increased so that the content displayed on screen becomes more readable.

In this work, we present a novel side channel (i.e., ambient light sensor) and we show that even the user denies the app from accessing the location information, the malicious apps on the mobile phone can still infer the location information of the mobile user from this side channel. This novel side channel can be used in the attacks to track the mobile users' locations in urban area.

The victims can be those who are walking texting, runners or hikers putting their mobile phones in the armband, and bikers who rest the mobile phones on the phone brackets etc. It can also be applied in the scenarios where the mobile phone is not covered (e.g., resting on bracket for navigation). Furthermore, it is already not a news that the number of people who are texting while walking and causing traffic accidents is so large [24] that many cities in the world (e.g., Washington D.C.) have built "phone lanes" dedicated to people that are text walking [20]. Potentially, there are many victims affected by this side channel.

Taking advantages of machine learning techniques, the seemingly innocuous values collected from the ambient light sensor can be used to track the mobile users of the routes that they go through and even locate the user along the routes in real-time. Specifically, we prove that using this novel side channel, i.e., the ambient light sensor, an attacker is able to achieve the following two goals.

1. **Route Identification.** Given the known set of routes the victim[1] might go through, the attacker can identify which routes the victim has gone through with the ambient light sensor values from the victim's mobile phone.
2. **Real-time Location Tracking.** Given the known area where the victim might be travelling on, the attacker can infer the location of the victim in a real-time manner with the ambient light sensor values from the victim's mobile phone.

In order to achieve the above two goals, we first collect the values from the ambient light sensor on the experimental routes without interacting with victims. Then, we train models using machine learning algorithms off-line with the collected data. The trained models are later used to identify the routes that the user has gone through. After that, based on the route identification approach, we develop a location tracking system that can be used to track the user in real-time. We highlight that the above approach relies solely on the ambient light sensor whose values are available to all apps in Android without any permission. On one hand, this guarantees the stealthiness of the attack if an attacker applied the above approach. On the other hand, although combined sensor can provide more information and achieve better accuracy, by using a single sensor, we can evaluate "how much" information can be leaked just from the light sensor alone. Thus, we have a baseline on how severe is the privacy leakage from this side channel. This attack is also flexible as it can be launched as a targeted attack or a large scale attack (e.g., phishing by location-based advertisement services [15]).

Our evaluation shows that this approach can achieve a high overall accuracy of about 91% in route identification and accuracy of about 64% in real-time tracking the victim with estimation error at about 70 m, which outperforms other existing the state-of-the-art works with other side channels (See Sect. 6).

1.1   Our Contributions

We summarize our contributions in the following.

- We discover and prove a novel side-channel, i.e., ambient light, that can be used to track mobile users. To the best of our knowledge, we are the first to show that the ambient light sensors on Android mobile devices can be used to track the mobile users.
- We develop a location tracking system using machine learning techniques to track the mobile users.
- The results in the real-world experiments suggest that our system achieves a much higher accuracy with less estimation error than previous similar works (Sect. 6) with other side channels.

---

[1] We use "victim" and the aforementioned "user" interchangeably in this paper.

2   Threat Models and Challenges

We assume that the attacker has managed to have his malicious app installed on the victim's mobile device. This is practical and easy to achieve as the attacker can develop a malicious app and disguise it as an useful utility app that does not require any special permission (e.g., a stock price watching app). He can then wait for the victims to install his app. The malicious app can monitor victim's light sensor in the background and continuously collects the values from the ambient light sensor. It does not require any special permission that needs to be granted by the user. The collected data can be stored in its private storage. Starting from Android 4.4, apps do not need any permission to store data in an app's own private storage [4]. The user may not even notice that he/she is being tracked. However, the malicious app does need the Internet connection to transmit the collected data to the attacker. To achieve this, the malicious app can request the Internet permission. For Android operating system with API level higher than 23, the Internet permission request is granted automatically if the user chooses to install an app which requests the Internet permission and it is hidden from users by default [2]. The Internet permission is classified under normal permissions category and normal permissions can not be revoked by users. Although the Internet permission is still listed on the permissions requested in the system setting menu after the app has been installed, users seldom care about what permissions an app has requested and seldom check the permission list. Even though the users may check the permission list, they might not consider the Internet permission as a suspicious permission request, given that the Internet permission is such a common permission request that 83% of apps request full network access permission [26].

The attacker can even remove the Internet permission request to make the app really zero-permission. This can be achieved by delegating the network communication task to the default browser in the system. When the app has data to upload to the attacker's server, it can generate an `intent` with a URL and attaches the data in the query string for system browser [21]. Then the app prompts a dialog for the user to update the app. Upon clicking the buttons, browser is launched, the URL requested with the data embedded is passed to the attacker's server. After the server has received the data, it redirects the browser to the app's homepage. In this way, the user would not even notice that the data has been smuggled to the attacker's server and the malicious app does not need the Internet permission at all. The only limitation of this approach is that the maximum length of the query string is browser-specific. Different browsers have different limits for the length of their URLs. The discussion of Chromium[2] suggests that the length of character it can handle is 2 Mb [5]. 2 Mb is enough for smuggling about 6 full days' data if the malicious app generates and transmits one value (4 bytes per value) per second.

---

[2] Chromium is the open-source version of Chrome (the default browser of Android [1]).

2.1   Challenges

We summarize major challenges to track a user with light sensor as follows.

1. **Routes explosion.** The area might be too big for the attacker to sample every distinct route in that area.
2. **Brightness level variations.** The attacker might sample the routes, for example, with a different angle of phone placement or in a different weather or time of day, which has different environment brightness levels, than the victim.
3. **Speed variations.** The attacker might travel in a different speed from the user. For example, the speed differences between walking and bicycling.

   We discuss the solutions to the first challenge in Sects. 3.1 and 3.3, the second challenge in Sect. 3.3 and the third challenge in Sect. 3.3.

3   Route Identification

The attack has two stages in total - off-line state and attack stage. The first stage includes off-line training and system building, the second stage is the attack.

- **Off-line Stage.** This stage is shown in Fig. 1. During the off-line training step, the attacker collects the ambient light values of all the routes segments (see Sect. 3.1) in an area using the attacker's own mobile phone. The attacker then trains the machine learning models and builds the tracking system on his server with the collected data. This step can be conducted without the victim's interaction and without data from the victim's mobile phone at all.
- **Attack Stage.** This stage is shown in Fig. 2. The second stage is the attacking stage which needs the victim to have a malicious zero-permission app installed on his/her mobile phone (see Sect. 2). The malicious app will send the victim mobile phone's ambient light sensor values (e.g., one value per second) via the Internet to a server under the attacker's control. The attacker can then use the values received from victim's mobile phone as the input to the system built in the first step to infer the routes the victim travels and tracks the user.

3.1   Tracking User in an Area

When the user is on a long route with multiple junctions, there are two problems that we need to solve in order to successfully track the user. First, the total number of long routes would be large because of the combinations of multiple choices at each junction. Collecting data of all the long routes spanning multiple junctions will cost a lot of time in the off-line model training phase. Sometimes, it is even an impossible task for the attacker to collect data for every distinct long route if there are too many junctions (Challenge 1 in Sect. 2.1).

Second, some long routes might share the same route segments between junctions. For instance, a route starting from point A to point C and a route starting

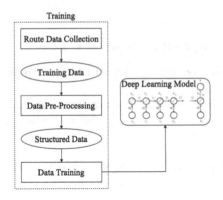

Fig. 1. Steps of route identification

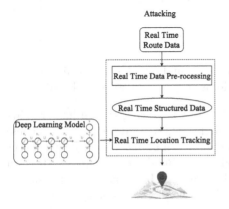

Fig. 2. Real-time tracking system overview

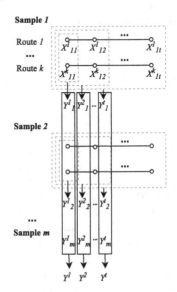

Fig. 3. An example of experiment routes

Fig. 4. Recomposition of time series

from point A to point D share the same route segment from point A to point B while they differ with route segment from point B to point C and route segment from point B to point D. The shared segments between two long routes (i.e., segment A to B) will lower the classification accuracy of two long routes (i.e., route A to C and route A to D) due to the fact that the shared segments increases similarity of the two long routes and reduces their distinguishability.

In order to solve these two problems, instead of collecting the data from all the routes in an area to train the models to identify the routes, we sample only the route segments separated by junctions. We collect the training datasets for each short route segment and train multiple models that identify different short route segments with the time series collected from them. Our system will automatically select the models that are used to identify the subsequent short route segments to fit the victim's data when the victim is at a junction. For more details, see Sect. 4.2.

In this way, we transfer the problem of identifying a long route into identifying several consecutive route segments separated by junctions. This significantly reduces the overheads in collecting the data in order to train the route identification models. Together with the approach we introduced in Sect. 3.3, we solve the first challenge in Sect. 2.1.

At the same time, this approach also solves the problem of low accuracies due to overlapping of route segments. Because the datasets for different long routes have overlapping route segments, while this approach has no overlapped route segments between each other.

Furthermore, it also greatly improves the scalability of our system. New route segments and new data can be easily added to our system by just training models for the new route segments without the need to retrain all the models, because our approach tracks the victims on a long route by tracking the short route segments connected by junctions that the victim takes. Additionally, adding new routes does not decrease the accuracies of our system because the accuracy depends on individual route segments rather than the combined long route.

3.2   Data Collection for Route Identification

We select multiple route segments on campus to conduct our experiments. Figure 3 shows one of the examples of the route segments from the same starting point to the same end point. For each route segment, we sample M times of the ambient light sensor values, which form the training datasets.

In order to capture all the possible brightness conditions where the victims might be travelling with, the M time samplings are carried out on different days with different weather and in different time of a day. The data is collected at a high data sampling rate of 100 times per second. Therefore, our datasets for the route segments cover the weather variations and different environment brightness due to different time of the day, which can reflect the real-world scenarios where the victim might be travelling in.

Suppose there are K route segments in our experiment areas, the final dataset we collect is $X = \{X^1, X^2, \ldots, X^K\}$ which contains K sub-datasets. The training datasets for route segment k can be denoted as $X^k = \{x_1^k, x_2^k, \ldots, x_m^k, \ldots, x_M^k\}$ ($1 \leq k \leq K, 1 \leq m \leq M$), where $x_m^k = (x_{m1}^k, x_{m2}^k, \ldots, x_{mt}^k)$ is the time series with a length of t for the m-th sample of route segment k. Note that the length of each sample t is not a constant value, it might vary due to the route segment length and the speed of the traveler.

3.3   Data Preprocessing

The raw data we collected in the last step can not be applied in training the models directly. We need to perform the following four steps of preprocessing to the data in the datasets, namely normalisation, time series alignment, time series resampling, and speed resampling.

Normalization. The raw data is collected in different weather and times of the day. Therefore, the absolute values of light intensity might vary greatly. Moreover, even in the same weather, the range of the raw data we collect might be very wide, e.g., in the sun and in the shade. Normalizing the raw data removes the effects of weather and also speeds up the convergence of the training processes.

The normalization process is as follows. First, for each value in a time series (in a single sample), we subtract from it the mean value of all the values of that time series. Second, we divide the value derived in the first step by the standard deviation of all the values in that time series.

We highlight that the normalization to the datasets removes the absolute values of the light intensity and the numbers in the datasets after normalization only reflect the light variation patterns along the routes which are not related to the absolute light intensity values. It thus removes the effects of phone placement angle, weather, time of day where the absolute values of the light intensity might be different. As long as it is the same route, the light variation patterns along that route will not change with different angles of phone placement, different weather and times of the day. Thus, the normalization to the datasets enables our models and systems to work on different angles of phone placement, different weather and time of the day, because they work on recognizing the light variation patterns along the routes rather than the absolute light values. The second challenge is resolved. Practicability and scalability of our approach are also greatly improved.

Time Series Alignment. When we are collecting data, we can not guarantee that every sample has exactly the same number of sampled values in a time series (for a single sample), i.e., same length in every time series. We can neither guarantee that the length of the time series collected from victim's mobile phone are exactly the same length as the ones in our training datasets. Therefore, we need to align the time series to make them the same length.

First, for the training datasets of the route segments, we find the longest time series in the training datasets and we record the length of this time series. For the rest of the time series in the training datasets, we repeat their last values until the lengths of them are the same as the length of the longest time series. After this step, all the time series of the routes in the training datasets are in the same length. Then, for the time series in testing datasets, if the time series are shorter than the length of the time series in its corresponding training datasets (same route), we again repeat the last value in that time series of the testing datasets until they have the same length as in their corresponding training datasets. If the time series in testing datasets are longer than the length of the times series in its corresponding training datasets, we do an average downsampling [27] to testing datasets making them same length as the corresponding training datasets.

After this step, the length of every time series in the training datasets and the testing datasets of a same route have the same length.

Time Series Resampling. We resample all the datasets at a sampling rate of one value per second. We take the median value of all the values within same second as the resampled ambient light sensor value for that second. Time series resampling benefits our approach in the following three aspects. **First**, during the data collection, we have a high data sampling rate at 100 times per second. However, the values in one second might not change much and thus there are a lot of duplicated values in the collected datasets. The time series resampling help us speed up the training processes and it makes our model converge more quickly. **Second**, the cars or buses go by might introduce noises to the time series. Such noises sometimes might not last for the whole second. The resampling help us remove such noises in the data. **Third**, it enables the attacker to have more samples by resampling the sampled datasets. Thus, this can reduces the overhead of sampling the light sensors values of the route segments. It also improves the scalability of the attack and make it easier to launch this attack.

Speed Resampling. The training datasets collected by the attacker might have different speed from the victim's testing datasets, e.g., walking v.s. bicycling. In order to solve this challenge (Challenge 2 in Sect. 2.1), we perform resampling to the training datasets to get different datasets representing different speeds. We use the speed in the original training datasets as our baseline speed, then we perform resampling to the training datasets to get the datasets for different speeds. In our models, we resample the datasets into two new datasets. Therefore, we have in total 3 different datasets for training different models. We let the speed of our original datasets to be v. The speeds of the three different datasets are $0.5v$, v and $2v$ datasets. More fine-grained speed samples can be generated according to attacker's need.

For the $0.5v$ datasets, we repeat the value in one second in the original datasets into two seconds (the original datasets have been data preprocessed, which has one value per second). For example, one of the time series of the original datasets is $X = \{x_1, x_2, \ldots, x_t\}$ where t is the length of the time series of t seconds. Then, after speed resampling into $0.5v$, the time series becomes $X' = \{x_1, x_1, x_2, x_2, \ldots, x_t, x_t\}$. In this way, the length of the time series is two times of the original one but the route length is the same. Thus, the speed is reduced by half to be $0.5v$. Similarly, to get the datasets of $2v$, we get one value every two seconds from the original datasets. We resample the original time series $X = \{x_1, x_2, x_3, x_4 \ldots, x_{t-1}, x_t\}$ into $X' = \{x_2, x_4, \ldots, x_t\}$. The length of the time series is half of the original time series but the route length is still the same. Thus, the speed becomes two times of the original speed ($2v$). We highlight that we use a high sampling rate for the data collection (100 times per second). Therefore, the resampling does not lose much "information" of routes.

Therefore, after this step, there are different datasets for a route segment corresponding to different speeds. The datasets for the same speed of different route segments starting from the same junctions have the same length. Therefore, we have solved the third challenge in Sect. 2.1. It also enables our models to track victims on different travelling patterns, e.g., walking, running, biking etc.

3.4 RNN Model with a Gated Recurrent Unit

We employ Recurrent Neural Network (RNN) [12,29] with a Gated Recurrent Unit (GRU) [31,34] as the engine of our route identification models and real-time location tracking system. RNN is one of the most popular deep learning methods for analyzing sequence information, especially time series data. An RNN module consists of an input layer, one or multiple hidden layers and one output layer [14]. The current output of the RNN module not only depends on the current input, but also depends on the previous computations from previous inputs. It performs the same calculation for every element of a sequence (time series in our case). The structure of a one-hidden-layered RNN is shown in Fig. 5. The calculations of the hidden units and the output units iterate over all elements in a time series with the following equations:

$$h_t = tanh(Ux_t + Wh_{t-1} + b) \tag{1}$$
$$o_t = tanh(Vh_t + c) \tag{2}$$

where $tanh$ is an activation function [17,19], U, W and V are corresponding parameters that need to be trained.

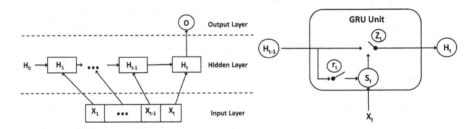

Fig. 5. One-hidden-layer RNN module   **Fig. 6.** The structure of a GRU

In practice the output of a standard RNN can only make use of the information in a few steps back due to the vanishing gradient problem [9,28]. In order to learn longer-term dependencies, we change the way in calculating the hidden units by using Gated Recurrent Units (GRUs). The calculation structure of a hidden unit h_t of GRU is shown in Fig. 6, where h_t is computed based on x_t and h_{t-1} with a gating mechanism. The reset gate r_t in GRU determines how to combine the new input x_t with the previous memory h_{t-1} in computing s_t, where s_t is a "candidate" hidden state. The calculation of h_t uses the update gate z_t to define how much of the previous memories to keep around.

Detailed equations for calculating a GRU hidden unit are shown as follows:

$$z_t = \sigma(x_t U^z + h_{t-1} W^z + b^z) \tag{3}$$
$$r_t = \sigma(x_t U^r + h_{t-1} W^r + b^r) \tag{4}$$
$$s_t = tanh(x_t U^s + (h_{t-1} \odot r_t) W^s + b^s) \tag{5}$$
$$h_t = (1 - z_t) \odot s_t + z_t \odot h_{t-1} \tag{6}$$

where the function $\sigma(x) = max(0, min(1, x * 0.2 + 0.5))$ is the hard sigmoid and $\odot$ denotes component-wise multiplication.

Overall, our route identification algorithm first performs data preprocessing on the raw time series data and then the preprocessed data is fed into the deep learning module to train proper models. Given a testing route sample under classification, the outputs of the RNN module provide K probabilities with each showing the probability of the current route sample being route i (i from 1 to K is a route whose data has been collected as training data). The system then decides the most likely route the testing sample to be by the one with highest probability.

3.5   Models Training

We use the route segments between point A and point B in Fig. 7 as an example to demonstrate the model training process. There are three route segments - route segment 4, route segment 5 and route segment 6, respectively. For the datasets of the route segments starting from same junction (A) in the same speed, let us say their lengths of each time series after data preprocessing are t. That means there are t seconds with t values in every time series of every route segment starting from point A to point B after data preprocessing. We thus train t models, each of which identifies 3 classes (one class per route segment). The first model accepts time series of length 1, the second model accepts time series of length 2, and so on until the t-th model accepts time series of length t. The overall process of this example is shown in Fig. 4.

Suppose that there are M samples for each route segment starting from point A to point B. The time series of the first sample of route segment 4 is $X_1^4 = \{X_{11}^4, X_{12}^4, \ldots, X_{1t}^4\}$; the time series of the first sample of route segment 5 is $X_1^5 = \{X_{11}^5, X_{12}^5, \ldots, X_{1t}^5\}$ and the time series of the first sample of route segment 6 is $X_1^6 = \{X_{11}^6, X_{12}^6, \ldots, X_{1t}^6\}$. We follow the same notation conventions as in Sect. 3.2 where the k in X_m^k denotes the route segment ID, m denotes the m-th sampling to the route segment. Similarly to notation in Sect. 3.2, t in X_{mt}^k is the length of the longest time series after data preprocessing. Then, we let $Y_1^1 = \{\{X_{11}^4\}, \{X_{11}^5\}, \{X_{11}^6\}\}$, $Y_1^2 = \{\{X_{11}^4, X_{12}^4\}, \{X_{11}^5, X_{12}^5\}, \{X_{11}^6, X_{12}^6\}\}, \ldots,$ $Y_1^i = \{\{X_{11}^4, X_{12}^4, \ldots, X_{1i}^4\}, \{X_{11}^5, X_{12}^5, \ldots, X_{1i}^5\}, \{X_{11}^6, X_{12}^6, \ldots, X_{1i}^6\}\}, \ldots, Y_1^t = \{X_1^4, X_1^5, \ldots, X_1^6\}$ $(1 \leq i \leq t)$. The set Y_1^i $(1 \leq i \leq t)$ represents the time series of the first sample of length i for all the route segments starting from point A to point B in the same speed. Similarly, we can derive set $Y_m^i = \{X_m^4, X_m^5, X_m^6\}$, $(1 \leq m \leq M, 1 \leq i \leq t)$ which represents the time series of the m-th sample of length i for all the route segments starting from point A to point B. Finally, we have $Y^1 = \{Y_1^1, Y_2^1, \ldots, Y_M^1\}$, $Y^2 = \{Y_1^2, Y_2^2, \ldots, Y_M^2\}$, $\ldots,$ $Y^i = \{Y_1^i, Y_2^i, \ldots, Y_M^i\}$ and so on until $Y^t = \{Y_1^t, Y_2^t, \ldots, Y_M^t\}$ $(1 \leq i \leq t)$. Each of such set Y^i is of length M (the total number of sampling for each route segment). Finally, for each dataset of Y^i where i ranges from 1 to t, we train a model that accepts length i time series (where i ranges from 1 to t) and identifies (or classifies) route segments 4, 5 and 6 starting from point A at the same speed. We repeat the above process for each junction and speed in both directions.

In summary, after this training step, we have trained t models for every speed at every junctions in both directions, where t is the length of the longest time series among all the samples for the route segments sharing the same starting junction after data preprocessing.

4   Applying Light Sensor in Real-Time Tracking

The fact that light sensor is giving out user's location information can even be applied to track the user in real-time if user's starting location is known. It is a matter of time that the attacker can eventually build a system using the light sensor values to track the users in real-time whose accuracy is comparable to GPS. In the following, we take the first step towards this goal trying to apply light sensor values in real-time tracking the users. Our system shows that this goal is practical and feasible.

The overall flow of our system is shown in Fig. 2. The left-hand side are the route identification models trained in Sect. 3. The right-hand side is the actual attacking. With the real-time values from the ambient light sensor of the victim's mobile phone, the system on attacker's server first preprocesses the data. Then the preprocessed structured data is fed into the off-line trained models. Finally, based on the trained models, our system outputs the route segments that the victim is on and infer the victim's location in real-time.

4.1   Real-Time Location Estimation

At the attacking steps (shown in Sect. 2), the data from the victim's mobile ambient light sensor is transmitted to attacker's server in real-time. The attacker performs normalization and time series resampling in the same way as in Sect. 3.3. Then, the preprocessed datasets are sent to our models for identifying.

In our training datasets, the GPS locations are also recorded. Note that after the data preprocessing steps in the model training stage, all the time series for route segments starting from the same junctions in the same direction with the same speed have the same length. The average GPS location for each second is calculated over all the GPS locations at that same second in training datasets. For example, let $G_m^k = \{g_{m1}^k, g_{m2}^k, \ldots, g_{mt}^k\}$ represent the GPS locations of route segment k from the first second to the t-th second at the m-th sample in the training datasets, where $g_{mt}^k = \{g_{mt1}^k, g_{mt2}^k, \ldots, g_{mtr}^k\}$ and r is the sampling rate meaning that there are r samples in a second. Recall that the sampling rate of our datasets is 100 times per second. Thus in our case, $r = 100$.

We let $\overline{g_{mt}^k}$ be the median value of all the values in the set g_{mt}^k, and we use it as the average GPS location for the value of the t-th second for route segment k of the m-th sample. Therefore, the set of average locations at the m-th sample of route segment k can be represented as $\overline{G_m^k} = \{\overline{g_{m1}^k}, \overline{g_{m2}^k}, \ldots, \overline{g_{mt}^k}\}$. Remark that after the data preprocessing, all the samples have the same length t (the length of the longest time series) and it is the same for every sample from 1 to M. After that, we let $F_t^k = \{\overline{g_{1t}^k}, \overline{g_{2t}^k}, \ldots, \overline{g_{Mt}^k}\}$ be the set of locations at the t-th second of all M samples for route segment k. The average location at the t-th second of all M samples for route segment k is thus $\overline{F_t^k}$ which is the average value of all the elements in the set F_t^k. Finally, we can have the set of average locations for a route segment k across all M samples for every second which is $\overline{G^k} = \{\overline{F_1^k}, \overline{F_2^k}, \ldots, \overline{F_i^k}, \ldots, \overline{F_t^k}\}, (1 \leq i \leq t)$.

If there are t values after real-time data preprocessing at the attacking stage, the t values are feed into the model that accepts length t time series. The system then outputs the identification result indicating the victim is currently on which route segment. The result means that the victim is on that identified route segment and she has travelled for t seconds. Thus, our real-time tracking system outputs the average GPS location at t-th second of the identified route segment.

4.2 Handover at Junction

When the victim is tracked until s/he reaches the junction, based on the victim's history (previous travelled route segments and directions), the system resets the time series to length zero and automatically switches to the models of the route segments starting from that junction to identify the new route segment using the new preprocessed time series from the victim's mobile phone. For example, if the victim is travelling on route segment 3 from junction E to junction C as shown in Fig. 7. When the victim has come to the end of route segment 3, our system automatically uses the models that identifies (classifies) route segments 7, 8 and 9 to fit the new values coming from victim's light sensor. Then based on the outputted results of the models, the system selects the new route segment which best fits the new light sensor values and outputs the estimated real-time locations of the victim. In this way, the long route the victim travels which spanning over multiple junctions can be identified accurately and efficiently by identifying multiple connected route segments.

5 Evaluation

We have collected two sets of data in two areas in two different cities at different latitudes. One area is near the Equator and the other is in the Northern Hemisphere at temperate zone. We refer to the first and second datasets as dataset Q (Q area) and dataset T (T area) respectively in the rest of this section. The map of these two areas are shown in Figs. 7 and 8.

In Fig. 7, the joining point of lines represents a junction. There are 5 junctions from A to E. Between two adjacent junctions, there are multiple route segments represented by solid lines. There are in total 9 route segments in the area separated by the 5 junctions. Each route segment is labelled with a route segment ID which ranges from 1 to 9. The total combinations of long route can be up to 15 without circle from point A to point E. The datasets for this area are collected by two persons. One of them samples the routes segments from 1 to 9, and the other samples the data for the long routes in a different speed from the first person for testing our real-time location tracking system. The datasets for

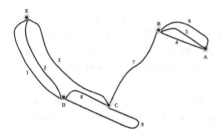

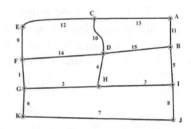

Fig. 7. Area near Equator (Q)   **Fig. 8.** Area in temperate zone (T)

the route segments are collected using the approach we introduced in Sect. 3.2. Every route segment has been sampled at least for 30 times for each direction and the long routes are sampled once. The datasets are collected using a Nexus 5 mobile phone with a bicycle.

For the area in Fig. 8, there are totally 11 junctions with 15 route segments. Each of the route segment is assigned a route segment ID ranging from 1 to 15. There are already 18 different long routes for a user to travel from junction A to junction K without going backwards. The total combinations of the long routes that a user can take are too many for the attacker if he wants to sample every long route to train the models. Similar to the datasets in the area of Fig. 7, there are two persons collecting data for the area in Fig. 8. One collects all the data for route segments from 1 to segments 15, and the other collects datasets once for randomly selected long routes used for testing our real-time tracking system. Every route segment is sampled at least 30 times for each of the directions. For the sake of diversity, we use another Nexus 5 mobile phone, which is different from the one that is used to collect data for Q area, to sample the data in area T with bicycles. We summarize the statistics of our datasets in Table 1.

5.1 Route Segments Identification Evaluation

The datasets are first preprocessed and then be fed into the machine learning models for training and testing. We set the number of hidden unit of our RNN models as 10 in our experiments and the number of input unit as 1 because we only fit the model with the values from light sensor (one feature used). We apply a 2-hidden-layer GRU module to capture higher-level feature interactions between different time steps.

We further apply 5-fold cross validation in estimating how accurately the machine learning models we trained perform in practice. The datasets are randomly partitioned into 5 similar sized sub-samples. This process is repeated 5 times, with each of the 5 sub-samples used once in each validation as the validation data and we use the remaining 4 sub-samples as the training data. The accuracies of all the testing results from the validations are shown in Table 2.

The Start and End for accuracies of Q area (Table 2a) specify the travelling directions of the victim. For example, the accuracy in Table 2a in the first row

Table 1. The datasets in two areas

(a) Summaries for Q Area and T Area

Area	Q	T
# Segments	9	15
# Junctions	5	11
# Volunteers	2	2
# Sampled Times	60	60

(b) Route Segments Length for Q Area and T Area

Area ID	Length in m Q	T
1	248	71
2	230	90
3	292	50
4	131	70
5	132	70
6	177	76
7	155	140
8	123	77
9	285	92
10	N.A.	96
11	N.A.	90
12	N.A.	83
13	N.A.	63
14	N.A.	90
15	N.A.	57

Table 2. Route segments identification

(a) Accuracies for Area Q

Start	End	#Routes	Accuracy%
A	B	3	99.2
B	A	3	96
C	D	2	98.8
D	C	2	98.8
D	E	2	100
E	D	2	96.3

(b) Accuracies for Area T

Start	#Routes	Accuracy%
A	2	91.7
B	3	83.3
C	3	94.4
D	4	79.2
E	2	91.7
F	3	88.9
G	3	72.2
H	3	83.3
I	3	72.2
J	2	100.0
K	2	66.7

with starting junction to be A and ending junction to be B means that the victim starts travelling at junction A and travels towards B and the victim has 3 route segments to choose to travel on. The accuracy for identifying these three route segments is 99.2%. In Table 2b, the start column specifies the starting junction of the victim and the number of routes specifies how many route segments that he/she can travel on. The overall result in Table 2 shows that the route segment identification is very accurate. The accuracy shows our approach is effective. The results also prove that the light sensor values can be used to differentiate and identify route segments. As the route identification evaluation shows, we have achieved the first goal proposed in Sect. 1.

5.2 Real-Time Location Tracking Evaluation

Figure 9 shows four results of the estimation errors of the long route experiments. Figure 9a to d show the system predictions and the estimation errors in meters of the long route experiments respectively. The vertical red solid lines in Fig. 9 show us the time when the user actually reaches the end of a route segment and a junction, while the vertical green dashed lines show us the system's predictions of the time that the victim reaches the junction. The real-time location estimation errors, i.e., the distance between the user's real location and the predicted location are also shown in Fig. 9 with blue solid line. For example, in Fig. 9a, our

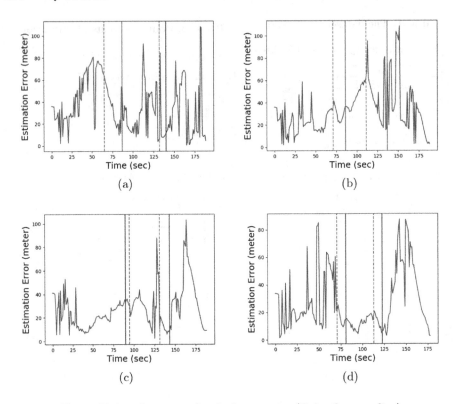

Fig. 9. Estimation errors for the long routes (Color figure online)

system predicts that the user has arrived at the first junction at about 62nd second while the user actually reaches the first junction at about the 79th second. Our system prediction result leads the actual result roughly by 17 s. The largest estimation error shown in Fig. 9a is about 140 m while the average estimation errors is much lower at about 40 m to 50 m.

The overall accuracies in Fig. 9a, b, c and d are 75.66%, 66.67%, 58.73% and 53.16% respectively. The average accuracy for the long route experiments in Fig. 9 is 63.56%. This means that about 63.56% of the time (e.g. 63 s out of 100 s), the system can locate the user on the correct route. Figure 10 shows the average and distribution of errors for Fig. 9. Figure 10a shows the average estimation error of the four estimation errors from Fig. 9a to d. On the whole, the trend of the average error is quite stable. The overall average error is around 70 m. From Fig. 10b and c, we can see that 80% of the errors is less than 50 m. From Fig. 9a to d we know that the times of user that reaches the end of the first route segment is around 70th second to 80th second and the time that the user reaches the second route segment is around 130th second to 140th second.

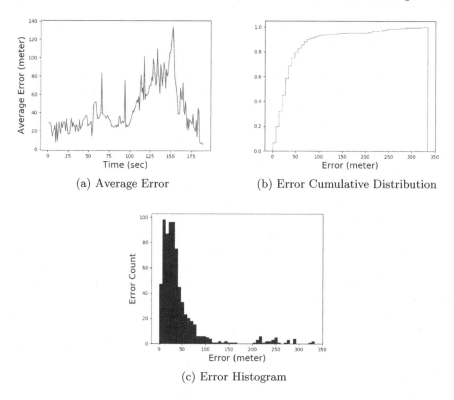

(a) Average Error

(b) Error Cumulative Distribution

(c) Error Histogram

Fig. 10. Average and distribution errors for the long routes

6   Related Work

Most of the previous discovered side channels on mobile platform are motion related sensors (i.e., gyroscope, accelerometer). Our work is most related to PowerSpy [22]. In [22], the authors discover that the power consumption speed can be used to infer user's location. Similarly, we both identify a side channel that leaks user's location information. Unlike [22], this paper uses a different side channel and algorithm to tell the location in a more fine-grained scale (e.g., within 70 m). Moreover, we have enhanced our approach to perform a random route real-time location tracking while in [22], it only reports real-time location tracking on one specified known route with only estimation error. Our evaluation, which is similar to the one in [22], shows that our approach achieves a higher accuracy in both route identification (91% v.s. 85%) and real-time user tracking (64%), and lower estimation error (~70 m v.s. ~1 km). The work in Elastic Pathing [10] also presents a side channel for mobile users. They propose to use merely speed information to track the route of the mobile users. However, unlike this work, it is based on a different attack model and algorithm. In addition, our system achieves much higher accuracies (91% v.s. 26%) while much lower estimation errors (~70m v.s. ~500 m).

The following works [13,23,25] use motion sensors such as gyroscope, accelerometer, to infer the route of a user. They adopt similar techniques. First, by using the motion sensors to infer the trajectory or shape of the route the user travels. Then, assuming the city of the user is known, they try to find the same shape of route from the maps and infer the route from the matches. These works differ in the techniques to match the shape of routes inferred from the motion sensors to the shapes of route on maps. While our approach is significantly different from theirs in that we only rely on the ambient light sensor which itself is totally not designed for helping navigation or tracking after user. More importantly, light sensor itself does not reveal any information on user's motion while accelerometer or gyroscope in some sense reveals user's motion.

In this paper [36], the authors discover a side channel using mobile phone's microphone. When user is using voice navigation, the length of the speech can be used to infer the navigation information and thus infer the route the user travels. Unlike our work, this work focus on inferring the secrets from the public resources of Android while our work mainly presents and proves that light sensor is indeed a novel side channel that is leaking mobile user's location information. In the paper [30], the authors using innocuous permissions to steal sensitive information from audio sensor. In this paper [7], the authors using mobile phone's camera and microphone to fingerprinting the locations. Unlike the above two paper, we do not rely on sensor permissions and we can identify not only the routes the user travels but also track the user location on that route.

This paper also relates to covert channel information leakage. These papers [8, 32,35] present covert channels that leak the authenticators which allow the attackers to steal user's credentials via different approaches. This paper is similar to them in that a new covert channel is identified that can be used to compromise users' privacy. This paper differs from them where the approach for exploiting and extracting information to compromise users' privacy is different.

7 Conclusion

This work presents a novel side channel of ambient light that can be used to track the mobile users. We developed a location tracking system that can identify the routes the user travels and tracks the user in real-time with the ambient light sensor. The experiments show that our tracking system works at high accuracy and outperforms other similar works.

Acknowledgement. This paper is supported by the National Research Foundation, Prime Minister's Office, Singapore under its National cybersecurity R&D Program (TSUNAMi project, Award No. NRF2014NCR-NCR001-21) and administered by the National Cybersecurity R&D Directorate, and the National Natural Science Foundation of China (No. 61702045).

References

1. The chromium projects. https://www.chromium.org/
2. Normal permissions. https://developer.android.com/guide/topics/permissions/normal-permissions.html
3. Requesting permissions at run time. https://developer.android.com/training/permissions/requesting.html
4. Stroage options. https://developer.android.com/guide/topics/data/data-storage.html#AccessingExtFiles
5. Loading large urls kills the renderer, January 2011. https://bugs.chromium.org/p/chromium/issues/detail?id=69227
6. Why location privacy matters, Feburary 2017. https://thetinhat.com/blog/thoughts/location-privacy.html
7. Azizyan, M., Constandache, I., Roy Choudhury, R.: Surroundsense: mobile phone localization via ambience fingerprinting. In: Proceedings of the 15th Annual International Conference on Mobile Computing and Networking, pp. 261–272. ACM (2009)
8. Bai, G., et al.: All your sessions are belong to us: investigating authenticator leakage through backup channels on android. In: 2015 20th International Conference on Engineering of Complex Computer Systems (ICECCS), pp. 60–69. IEEE (2015)
9. Bengio, Y., Simard, P., Frasconi, P.: Learning long-term dependencies with gradient descent is difficult. IEEE Trans. Neural Netw. 5(2), 157–166 (1994)
10. Gao, X., Firner, B., Sugrim, S., Kaiser-Pendergrast, V., Yang, Y., Lindqvist, J.: Elastic pathing: your speed is enough to track you. In: Proceedings of the 2014 ACM International Joint Conference on Pervasive and Ubiquitous Computing, pp. 975–986. ACM (2014)
11. Goodin, D.: Yahoo says half a billion accounts breached by nation-sponsored hackers, September 2016. https://arstechnica.com/information-technology/2016/09/yahoo-says-half-a-billion-accounts-breached-by-nation-sponsored-hackers/
12. Gregor, K., Danihelka, I., Graves, A., Rezende, D.J., Wierstra, D.: Draw: a recurrent neural network for image generation. arXiv preprint arXiv:1502.04623 (2015)
13. Han, J., Owusu, E., Nguyen, L.T., Perrig, A., Zhang, J.: Accomplice: location inference using accelerometers on smartphones. In: 2012 Fourth International Conference on Communication Systems and Networks (COMSNETS), pp. 1–9. IEEE (2012)
14. Haykin, S.: Neural Networks: A Comprehensive Foundation. Prentice Hall PTR, Upper Saddle River (1994)
15. Help, G.A.: About targeting geographic locations. https://support.google.com/google-ads/answer/2453995?hl=en
16. Iqbal, M.U., Lim, S.: Privacy implications of automated gps tracking and profiling. IEEE Technol. Soc. Mag. 29(2), 39–46 (2010)
17. Karlik, B., Olgac, A.V.: Performance analysis of various activation functions in generalized mlp architectures of neural networks. Int. J. Artif. Intell. Expert Syst. 1(4), 111–122 (2011)
18. Lawler, R.: Equifax security breach leaks personal info of 143 million us consumers. https://www.engadget.com/2017/09/07/equifax-hack-143-million/
19. Leshno, M., Lin, V.Y., Pinkus, A., Schocken, S.: Multilayer feedforward networks with a nonpolynomial activation function can approximate any function. Neural Netw. 6(6), 861–867 (1993)

20. Levy, K.: Here's what happens when cellphone users get their own lane on the sidewalk, July 2014. https://www.businessinsider.com/cellphone-walking-lane-2014-7/?IR=T

21. Masinter, L., Berners-Lee, T., Fielding, R.T.: Uniform resource identifier (uri): generic syntax. RFC 3986 (2005). https://tools.ietf.org/html/rfc3986

22. Michalevsky, Y., Schulman, A., Veerapandian, G.A., Boneh, D., Nakibly, G.: Powerspy: location tracking using mobile device power analysis. In: USENIX Security Symposium, pp. 785–800 (2015)

23. Narain, S., Vo-Huu, T.D., Block, K., Noubir, G.: Inferring user routes and locations using zero-permission mobile sensors. In: Security and Privacy (SP), pp. 397–413. IEEE (2016)

24. Nasar, J.L., Troyer, D.: Pedestrian injuries due to mobile phone use in public places. Accid. Anal. Prev. **57**, 91–95 (2013)

25. Nawaz, S., Mascolo, C.: Mining users' significant driving routes with low-power sensors. In: Proceedings of the 12th ACM Conference on Embedded Network Sensor Systems, pp. 236–250. ACM (2014)

26. Olmstead, K., Atkinson, M.: Apps permissions in the google play store (2015). http://www.pewinternet.org/2015/11/10/an-analysis-of-android-app-permissions/

27. Paris, S., Durand, F.: A fast approximation of the bilateral filter using a signal processing approach. In: Leonardis, A., Bischof, H., Pinz, A. (eds.) ECCV 2006. LNCS, vol. 3954, pp. 568–580. Springer, Heidelberg (2006). https://doi.org/10.1007/11744085_44

28. Pascanu, R., Mikolov, T., Bengio, Y.: On the difficulty of training recurrent neural networks. In: International Conference on Machine Learning, pp. 1310–1318 (2013)

29. Sak, H., Senior, A., Beaufays, F.: Long short-term memory recurrent neural network architectures for large scale acoustic modeling. In: Fifteenth Annual Conference of the International Speech Communication Association (2014)

30. Schlegel, R., Zhang, K., Zhou, X., Intwala, M., Kapadia, A., Wang, X.: Soundcomber: a stealthy and context-aware sound trojan for smartphones. In: NDSS, vol. 11, pp. 17–33 (2011)

31. Tang, D., Qin, B., Liu, T.: Document modeling with gated recurrent neural network for sentiment classification. In: EMNLP, pp. 1422–1432 (2015)

32. Wang, K., Bai, G., Dong, N., Dong, J.S.: A framework for formal analysis of privacy on SSO protocols. In: Lin, X., Ghorbani, A., Ren, K., Zhu, S., Zhang, A. (eds.) SecureComm 2017. LNICST, vol. 238, pp. 763–777. Springer, Cham (2018). https://doi.org/10.1007/978-3-319-78813-5_41

33. Whittaker, Z.: 198 million americans hit by 'largest ever' voter records leak, Jun 2017. http://www.zdnet.com/article/security-lapse-exposes-198-million-united-states-voter-records/

34. Wu, Z., King, S.: Investigating gated recurrent networks for speech synthesis. In: 2016 IEEE International Conference on Acoustics, Speech and Signal Processing (ICASSP), pp. 5140–5144. IEEE (2016)

35. Ye, Q., Bai, G., Wang, K., Dong, J.S.: Formal analysis of a single sign-on protocol implementation for android. In: 2015 20th International Conference on Engineering of Complex Computer Systems (ICECCS), pp. 90–99. IEEE (2015)

36. Zhou, X., et al.: Identity, location, disease and more: inferring your secrets from android public resources. In: Proceedings of the 2013 ACM SIGSAC Conference on Computer & Communications Security, pp. 1017–1028. ACM (2013)

Robust Covert Channels Based on DRAM Power Consumption

Thales Bandiera Paiva[1(✉)], Javier Navaridas[2], and Routo Terada[1]

[1] Institute of Mathematics and Statistics,
University of Sao Paulo, Sao Paulo, Brazil
{tpaiva,rt}@ime.usp.br

[2] School of Computer Science, University of Manchester, Manchester, UK
javier.navaridas@manchester.ac.uk

Abstract. To improve the energy efficiency of computing systems, modern CPUs provide registers that give estimates on the power consumption. However, the ability to read the power consumption introduces one class of security concerns called covert channels, which are communication channels that enable one process to transmit a message to another one in a system where these processes were meant to be isolated. Our contribution consists in the first covert channel in which messages are transmitted by modulating the DRAM power consumption. The channel implementation outperforms similar proposals, achieving 1800 bps with 10% error, and 2400 bps with 15% error, when running on a notebook and on a desktop platforms, respectively, To test its robustness against application interference, we considered the channel's performance when running concurrently with different benchmarks: MRBench, Terasort and LINPACK. When running on the notebook, the channel is fairly robust, achieving between 300 and 600 bps with around 10% error depending on the workload considered.

Keywords: Covert channel · Intel RAPL · Power consumption

1 Introduction

Power consumption is a major concern for both small embedded devices and huge clusters. In the first case, the low battery life is a major hardware constraint, while in the second, the amount of power needed by HPC environments can make its use unfeasible, or at least unprofitable. To improve the energy efficiency of computing systems, it is important to be able to measure and profile the power consumption. One common solution is to use external power measuring tools, such as Watt's Up Pro Power Meter, or PowerMon 2 [2]. Another solution is to use internal power measurement interfaces such as Running Average Power Limit

T. B. Paiva is supported by CAPES. R. Terada is supported by CNPq grant number 442014/2014-7.

(RAPL), introduced by Intel on SandyBridge chips, or the AMD Application Power Management.

The RAPL components provide a software interface for the user to obtain estimates on the processor's power consumption based on models validated by Intel. Since its inception, researchers have studied how accurately RAPL measurements correspond to real power consumption and how one can use this interface to efficiently profile an application energy usage [5,24]. Two security concerns that comes with the ability to measure power consumption in software are side-channel attacks and covert channels. With respect to RAPL components, side-channel attacks were first studied by Mantel et al. [16], while covert channels were first considered by Miedl and Thiele [20].

A covert channel enables two processes called the Trojan and the spy to communicate in a system where they are meant to be isolated [13]. As such, this type of channel is a central tool in data exfiltration, where an attacker wants to recover some secret information from a target system without leaving any trace. Figure 1 illustrates the use of a covert channel.

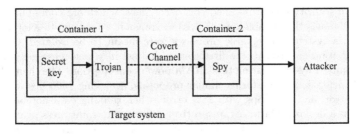

Fig. 1. In this setup, the Trojan and spy run on different isolated containers of the target system. The Trojan obtains some secret information, but because of the system's security policy, unauthorized applications in the container where the secret key reside cannot access the Internet. The Trojan then uses a covert channel to transmit the secret key to the spy process, which has access to the Internet and therefore can transmit the secret key to the attacker.

To successfully build a covert channel, the spy and the Trojan must have access to some shared resource, but not the usual ones such as shared memory, files, or network, because communication over these ones could be detected by security auditors or explicitly prohibited by isolation mechanisms. There are numerous examples of covert channels. Some recent constructions are based on inaudible audio [4], branch predictors [7], core temperature [17], and cache coherence protocols [26].

The US Department of Defense standard Trusted Computer System Evaluation Criteria (TCSEC) [23] defines a high bandwidth covert channel as one which can transmit at rates higher than 100 bps. To protect systems against information leakage, it is important to lower, to 0 if possible, the bandwidths of known covert channels. This can be done by introducing noise, lowering the rate in which the channel can be modulated, or preventing the processes from accessing the resources in which covert channels are based.

In this work, we investigate the possibility of building a covert channel using the DRAM power consumption estimates given by the Intel RAPL interface. In Linux, these estimates can be read using the `powercap` module without any special privileges. Our main motivation is that, for devising mechanisms to protect the systems against these channels without compromises to energy efficiency, it is necessary to understand the true risk posed by these RAPL covert channels.

Contribution. We present the first covert channel based on the RAPL measurement registers for the DRAM power consumption. This covert channel can transmit at 2400 bps, with error rates around 15%. We tested the channel performance under two platforms: a notebook and a desktop computer. The channel robustness against application interference was evaluated under three different workloads: MRBench, Terasort and LINPACK. The channel appears to be much more robust against interference than previous work. In particular, under the notebook setup, the channel achieved high bandwidths between 300 and 600 bps with error rates close to 10%, depending on the workload considered. On the desktop, the covert channel achieves 400 bps under MRBench or Terasort workload with 10% error rate, but it is not reliable when LINPACK is running.

This paper is organized as follows. Section 2 reviews relevant side and covert channels based on power consumption. The threat model and experimental setup are presented in Sect. 3. In Sect. 4, we show how to modulate CPU and DRAM power usage and discuss how the benchmarks affect the power consumption. The algorithms for Trojan and spy are presented in Sect. 5. The performance evaluation of the covert channel is done in Sect. 6. In Sect. 7, we consider two methods to achieve higher transmission rates. Section 8 consists of a discussion on our results. We finish with the conclusion and discussion of possible future work in Sect. 9.

2   Related Work

2.1   Side-Channel Attacks

In a side-channel attack, an attacker obtains secret information by observing or measuring the system when some critical computation is running. Side-channel attacks are one of the main problems faced when implementing cryptographic primitives, since the mathematical security models usually abstract away software, hardware, and implementation details.

In 1999, Kocher et al. [12] presented two powerful techniques for side-channel analysis of cryptographic schemes: SPA (simple power analysis) and DPA (differential power analysis). Both of these attacks work by measuring the power trace of a system when it is performing some cryptographic computation. When performing an SPA, the attacker tries to recover some secret information by directly interpreting the power trace. In contrast, in a DPA, the attacker uses statistical analysis to correlate the power consumption to the data processed. As such, DPA can better eliminate noise in the measurements. Power analysis

322   T. B. Paiva et al.

has been used to attack widely used schemes such as AES [15], RSA [18], and Elliptic Curves [3].

The main limitation of the attacks mentioned above is that direct access to the hardware is needed to perform the measurements. Therefore, it makes them less practical than side-channel attacks based on timing [12] or cache [8,27]. There are some examples of power analysis attacks that do not use dedicated hardware against mobile devices [19,25], where the power information is obtained by monitoring the device's battery.

Closely related to our research is the work by Mantel et al. [16] that shows, to the best of our knowledge, the first energy consumption side-channel attack using the software-based measurements provided by the RAPL interface. In this work, the authors mount a key distinguishing attack against a popular implementation of the RSA cryptosystem. The authors reported that, with only 25 energy consumption observations, an attacker can distinguish between two RSA keys with 99% of success.

2.2 Covert Channels

One of the first covert channels related to power usage was introduced in 2006 by Murdoch [21]. In this work, the Trojan, running on a server, modulates a message as the usage of a device to heat it up or cool it down. The spy then recovers the message by observing the clock skew on timestamps of the collected responses from the server that were caused by differences in temperature. The capacity of Murdoch's channel was later estimated as 20.5 bph (bits per hour) by Zander et al. [28].

In 2015, two covert channels directly based on power consumption and measurement were proposed. Guri et al. [9] showed a covert channel achieving between 1 and 8 bph between two separated desktop computers, where the Trojan modulates the heat dissipation, and the spy decodes the message using its hardware's native heat sensors. In 2015, Masti et al [17] showed how to use the CPU core temperature measurements to build a covert channel. One very interesting property of this covert channel is that it can transmit information between applications running in two different cores because the temperature in one core (which runs the Trojan), affects the temperature of the cores close to it (which may be running the spy). Their channel implementation achieves a throughput of up to 12.5 bps. Their result was improved to 50 bps by Bartolini et al. [1], and latter by Long et al. [14] to 160 bps with close to 0% error rate, and 600 bps with around 15% error rate.

In 2018, Miedl and Thiele [20] presented the first construction of a covert channel based on the processor's power consumption. Their channel implementation is completely based on the CPU power consumption. They considered two platforms for their experiments: a Lenovo notebook with an Intel Core i7 quad-core processor, and server rack based on an Intel Xeon octa-core. Surprisingly, for their channel implementation, the power covert channel showed a lower error rate when running in the notebook than in the server. Using the notebook, the channel achieved 1000 bps with an error rate of a little less than 15%. Miedl and Thiele [20] did not consider the RAPL registers for the DRAM power when building the covert channels.

3 Threat Model and Experimental Setup

3.1 Threat Model

Our threat model is very similar to the one considered by Miedl and Thiele [20] when building covert channels based on RAPL CPU power measurements. The spy process can read the RAPL power consumption estimates on the PP0 and DRAM domains. In Linux, the spy can use the `powercap` module to read the power consumption provided by the RAPL registers. This does not require any privileged permission.

The spy runs in two phases. First it records the power consumption in a certain time interval, and then it analyses the data to decode the message. The Trojan is a simple, possibly multi-thread, C program that uses simple memory operations, and does not have access to the RAPL measurements. It does not explicitly communicate with the spy, neither has access to the Internet.

3.2 Experimental Setup

In the following sections, we describe experiments and results which are highly dependent on the architecture of our experimental environments. We tested the covert channel in two environments, which are described next.

Notebook setup The notebook considered is an HP Pavilion 14-v064br. This notebook has 8 GB of RAM and an Intel Haswell i5-4210U CPU with base frequency of 1.70 GHz. This CPU has two cores and supports 4 threads. The sizes of the caches L1, L2, and L3, are, respectively, 32K, 256K, and 3 MB.

Desktop setup This environment consists of a 16 GB of RAM computer provided with an Intel Coffee Lake i7-8700 CPU with base frequency of 3.20 GHz. This CPU has two 6 and supports 12 threads. The sizes of the caches L1, L2, and L3, are, respectively, 32K, 256K, and 12 MB.

RAPL offers power measurements on four domains: Package, PP0, PP1, and DRAM. The Package domain corresponds the CPU package, which contains the cores, cache, memory controller and possibly processor graphics. PP0 (Power Plane 0) corresponds to the power consumption of the cores, and PP1 (Power Plane 1) contains the processor graphics component consumption. Not surprisingly, the DRAM domain measures the DRAM power consumption. The RAPL registers are updated at a frequency of about 1000 Hz [10]. Figure 2 illustrates the RAPL domains for the notebook setup.

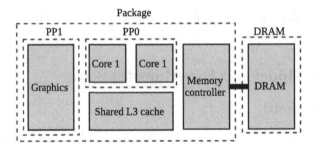

Fig. 2. The four domains for which one can measure power consumption using the RAPL interface on an Intel Haswell i5 4210U, which is our notebook's CPU.

4 Power Consumption Profiles

In this section, we perform some experiments to get a grasp on how different processes affect power consumption. For now on, we are interested only in PP0 and DRAM domains.

4.1 Modulating CPU and DRAM Power

To analyze the power consumption profile of CPU-bound tasks, we ran a simple loop computing a trigonometric function with different number of threads. The result can be seen in the upper part of Fig. 3. We can see 4 distinguishable power consumption profiles (excluding the idle power consumption), corresponding to using 1 to 4 threads. The power consumption using 4 and 5 threads are somewhat indistinguishable, which is no surprise since our machine only supports 4 hardware hyperthreads.

For the power consumption profile of memory-bound tasks, we measured the DRAM power consumption when running `memset` to set different sizes of memory chunks. We chose to use `memset` in this work because, among other memory operations like `memcpy` and `memchr`, its impact on the DRAM power consumption was the easiest to control in our tests. The bottom part of Fig. 3 shows our results. We can clearly see that power consumption and time to complete increase together with the size of the memory chunk used.

4.2 Benchmarks' Profiles

When evaluating the covert channel with respect to the robustness against application interference, we consider three benchmarks: MRBench [11], Terasort [22], and LINPACK [6]. The parameters used can be found at https://www.ime.usp.br/~tpaiva/.

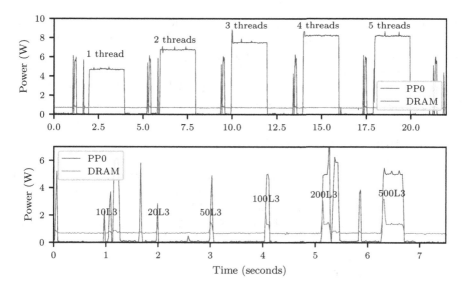

Fig. 3. Power consumption profiles of CPU-bound tasks with different number of threads (top) and of the `memset` operation when setting different sizes of memory chunks, with respect to L3 cache's size, considering the notebook setup.

Figure 4 shows the power consumption of the first 30 s of each benchmark. We can see that MRBench and Terasort affect power consumption in a similar way, although MRBench appears to stress the DRAM power slightly more. LIN-PACK has a very interesting profile. In the first 5 s it uses all hardware threads

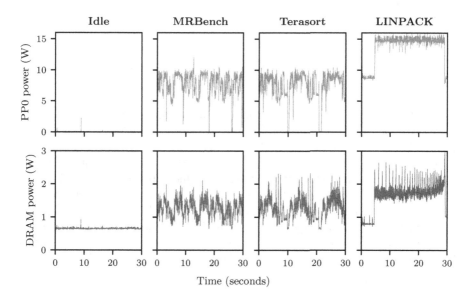

Fig. 4. Power consumption profiles of the benchmarks considering the notebook setup.

consistently, affecting the CPU power, but without affecting much the DRAM power. After this period, it starts stressing the DRAM power, and the CPU power also increases by a considerable margin.

It is important to notice that DRAM power usage appears to imply CPU power usage, but not the opposite. This makes DRAM power, in theory, less prone to noise, making it useful for building robust covert channels.

5 Building the Covert Channels

This section describes the algorithms for building the covert channels based on power consumption. The algorithms do not depend on whether the channel is based on the power consumption by the CPU or by the DRAM. We begin by describing the behavior of the Trojan process, that modulates the power consumption. Then we discuss how a spy process can decode the message using the power measurement samples. We finish this section with a brief discussion on strategies to synchronize the two processes.

5.1 Trojan: Modulating Power Consumption

Suppose we want to encode a binary message $M = (m_1, \ldots, m_n)$. Let A be the CPU or DRAM intensive task we want to use to encode the message. Suppose we want to transmit r bits per second. Let t_s be the time when the transmission is initiated. The algorithm for transmitting the message is given next.

1. Set $i \leftarrow 1$.
2. If $m_i = 1$, run the intensive task A, keeping control of the current time t_c, while

$$t_c - t_s < i \times 1/r. \tag{1}$$

3. If $m_i = 0$, wait until $t_c - t_s < i \times 1/r$
4. Do $i \leftarrow i + 1$.
5. Go to step 2 if $i \leq n$, otherwise finish.

One of the critical steps in the modulating algorithm is given by Eq. 1, which ensures that the transmission is always synchronized with the time when the transmission was initiated. This makes the decoding step easier.

Figure 5 shows the transmission of the same 20-bit message using CPU and DRAM-based Trojans, transmitting at 100 bps. One important observation with respect to the CPU power modulation shown in Fig. 5 is that the processor needs some time to go from high to low power consumption. This behavior can be seen in the transmission of the 3rd, 8th, and 16th bits. Therefore when implementing the covert channel, one can consider to make the CPU-intensive task stop earlier when going from a 1 to a 0 bit to lower the probability of a decoding error.

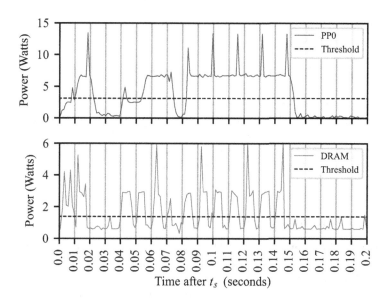

Fig. 5. Example of two Trojans, one using CPU-based modulation (top) and the other using memory-based modulation (bottom), transmitting at 100 bps.

5.2 Spy: Demodulating Power Consumption

Let $T = (t_1, \ldots, t_N)$, be a sequence of time points where a power measurement occurs, and $P = (p_1, \ldots, p_N)$ be the sequence of corresponding observed values. That is, the i-th measurement was made at time t_i and the observed power consumption was p_i. Suppose that t_s, the time when the message starts being transmitted, and the number of bits to be transmitted n, are known. In Sect. 5.4, we discuss briefly how t_s and n can be obtained by the spy process. As in the previous section, let r be the known transmission rate, that is, the number of bits per second that the Trojan process is programmed to transmit. Then the spy process runs the following algorithm.

1. Set $i \leftarrow 1$.
2. Let

$$S_i \leftarrow \left\{ j \in \{1, \ldots, N\} : \frac{(i-1)}{r} \le t_j - t_s < \frac{i}{r} \right\},$$

that is, S_i contains the indexes of the time measurements when, ideally, the power measurements samples correspond to the transmission of the i-th message bit.
3. Let

$$\overline{P_i} \leftarrow \frac{1}{|S_i|} \sum_{j \in S_i} p_j,$$

that is, $\overline{P_i}$ is the average of the power measurements that correspond to the i-th message bit.

4. If $\overline{P_i} \geq \overline{P}$, where $\overline{P}$ is some precomputed threshold, then set $\hat{m}_i \leftarrow 1$.
5. Else, set $\hat{m}_i \leftarrow 0$.
6. Do $i \leftarrow i + 1$.
7. If $i \leq n$, go to step 2. If not, return the decoded message $\hat{M} = (\hat{m}_1, \ldots, \hat{m}_n)$.

It is important to note that this algorithm stays valid even if n is not defined. This could be the case when the Trojan never stops streaming the user's private data. Figure 5 can help us visualize the decoding process, considering $t_s = 0, r = 100, N = 20$, and message $M = (11001110111111100000)$. The thresholds $\overline{P}$ shown in the figure depend on the type of Trojan used to encode the message.

5.3   Computing the Threshold $\overline{P}$

A simple method for computing the threshold $\overline{P}$ is to run simulations on the target system to learn the distributions of the m_i's' when given P_i's. If the attacker does not have access to the target system beforehand to run the simulations, but he knows that each element of the message is independent and equally distributed over 0 and 1, he can compute the threshold $\overline{P}$ as the average of a large number of P_i's. If the attacker does not have access to the target system, nor does the message bits are independent and equally distributed, the Trojan and spy can use a protocol which starts by sending an encoding of a known message so that the spy can learn the threshold $\overline{P}$ specific for the target system.

5.4   Synchronizing the Trojan and the Spy Processes

It is important, for the decoding algorithm to work correctly, that the spy knows at what time the message starts being transmitted, denoted as t_s. If the Trojan and the spy share a clock, the instant t_s can be hardcoded in them. But in a more interesting setting, where, for example, the Trojan and spy are running in different Virtual Machines, the assumption of a shared clock is strong.

Let M_{sync} be a binary message of length n_{sync} hardcoded in both Trojan and spy. The Trojan and the spy can use the following protocol for synchronization.

Trojan:
1. To transmit a message M, the Trojan simply transmits (M_{sync}, M) using the encoding algorithm from Sect. 5.1.

Spy:
1. Read the power consumption registers continually at sample rate T.
2. For each time sample t, try to decode the first n_{sync} bits using $t_s = t$, and compare the result with M_{sync}, which is known a priori.
3. If the number of errors is above some threshold (e.g. 15%), discard t and try the next time sample.
4. Else, use $t_s = t$ to decode (M_{sync}, M) and obtain the message M.

To lower the error rates, when the spy finds a good value in step 4, it can try time samples close to t to find the one which gives the lower error rate with respect to M_{sync}. We call this variant the maximum likelihood syncing, and it is the one used in the experiments in Sect. 6.

It is also important, for finite n, for the spy to know the message length n. The simplest solution is to allow only messages of a fixed length, but it may be too restrictive. One solution is to use the first $\lceil \log n_{max} \rceil$ bits to represent the length of the message that will be transmitted, where n_{max} is the maximum message length allowed.

6   Evaluation of the Covert Channels

We now evaluate the performance of our covert channels with respect to the transmission rate and robustness against application interference.

6.1   Bit Error Rate

In Sect. 4, we show that it is possible to distinguish between power consumption profiles of the memset when the size of the memory chunks use are sufficiently different. But, to implement a binary channel, we only need to distinguish between two DRAM power consumption states: doing nothing and memset some sufficiently large memory chunk. The size of this memory chunk must be small enough to enable high rate communication, but also large enough to be distinguishable from the baseline DRAM power consumption.

To find good sizes for the memory chunk, we ran Trojans simulations using memory chunks of different sizes considering the notebook and desktop setups. For the notebook, we considered 2, 5, and 10 times its L3 size. For the desktop, we considered two sequential memset operations on memory chunks of sizes 0.8, 1, and 1.5 times its L3 cache size.

The simulations consisted in a Trojan process transmitting 10 different 1000 bits random messages at increasing rates. The spy used the first 100 bits for synchronization using the maximum likelihood algorithm discussed in Sect. 5.4., and then decoded the remaining bits. The decoding threshold $\overline{P}$ is dynamically computed as the average of the power samples.[1] The first column of Fig. 6 (Baseline) shows the results of our experiments.

We can see that the larger memory chunks are useful when the transmission rate is lower, because it makes it easier to distinguish between 0's and 1's. However, for higher transmission rates, larger sizes do not work very well because operations on them are slow, which cause synchronization problems.

This simple channel implementation is capable of achieving high transmission rates, without big differences between the two setups. For example, it can transmit at 400 bps with almost 0% error rate, and at 600 bps with less than 10% error rate.

---

[1] Notice that this works because the binary messages are random, thus we expected them to have a similar number of 0's and 1's.

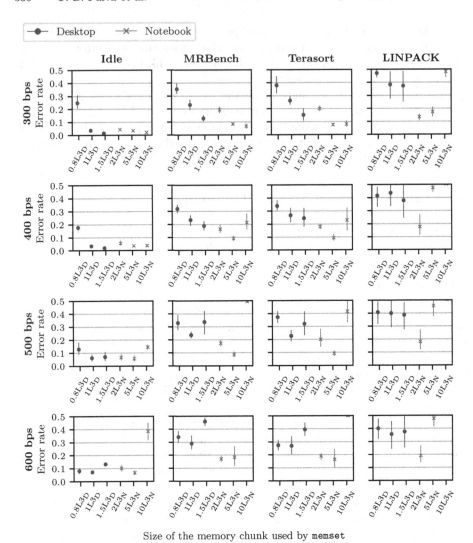

Fig. 6. Error rates for DRAM-based Trojans transmitting at increasing rates when the underlying system is under different workloads. $L3_D$ and $L3_N$ denote the L3 cache sizes of the desktop and notebook platforms, respectively.

6.2 Robustness of the Channels

To assess the robustness of the covert channels with respect to application interference, we considered the channels' performance under 3 different workloads: MRBench [11], Terasort [22], and LINPACK [6]. For each workload, we tested the DRAM-based Trojans using the parameters considered in the previous section.

The results are shown in the corresponding columns of Fig. 6. Under the desktop setup, the channel tolerates MRBench and Terasort with around 15% error rate at 300 bps, but LINPACK makes the channel very unreliable. With respect to the notebook setup, the DRAM-based Trojan appears to be fairly robust, achieving 500 bps at error rates close to 10% under MRBench and Terasort, and 300 bps under the LINPACK workload with less than 15% error.

It is interesting to see that LINPACK is the one to affect the channel the most, which is not surprising given its power consumption profile presented in Sect. 4.2.

7 Achieving Higher Transmission Rates

7.1 Using Better Decoding Algorithms

Since the maximum RAPL sample rate is currently fixed at $T = 1000$ samples per second, the number of samples per transmission gets lower as the transmission rate increases. Therefore, to achieve higher transmission rates, we have to extract as much information as we can from the samples. Unfortunately, using only the mean of the samples for each transmitted bit gives us too little information, which prevented us from reliably achieving transmission rates higher than 600 bits in the previous section.

One alternative to the simple decoder we have been using until now is to use clustering algorithms such as Support Vector Machines or Random Forests. We propose to use the whole set of samples corresponding to the transmission of each bit as features. More formally, let σ be a small integer, T be the RAPL sample rate, r be the Trojan's transmission rate, and c_i be the center of the time interval dedicated to the transmission of the i-th message bit. Then to decode the i-th message bit, the spy uses the σ power samples taken at time points which are the closest to c_i. In our experiments, we observed that $\sigma = \max(\lceil T/r \rceil, 4)$ is a good choice. With this setup, since we always feed at least 4 power samples to the classifier, it can perform much better at rates such as 1000 bits per second, where using $\lceil T/r \rceil$ would yield only 1 power sample.

The first row of Fig. 7 (1 bit per symbol)[2] shows the error rates for the transmission of binary messages using DRAM based Trojans, under different workloads, when the spy uses the Random Forests classifier. Again, in our experiment, we ran 10 independent transmissions of a message of 1000 bits for each transmission rate and workload. To train the classifier, we used an initial message of 5000 bits with the correct labels. We consider that the synchronization step is already done, that is, the value of t_s is known a priori.

We can see that by using Random Forests we can achieve much higher transmission rates. Under both setups, the Trojan achieved 800 bps with error rates lower than 10%. When running on the notebook, the Trojan even achieved 1000 bps with around 10% error rate. Again, the channel is more robust when running in the notebook platform, where it is able to transmit at 600 bps under MRBench and Terasort with 10% error rate. This makes the Random Forests decoder a better choice than our previous decoding algorithm, at the expense of

---

[2] That is, the binary case.

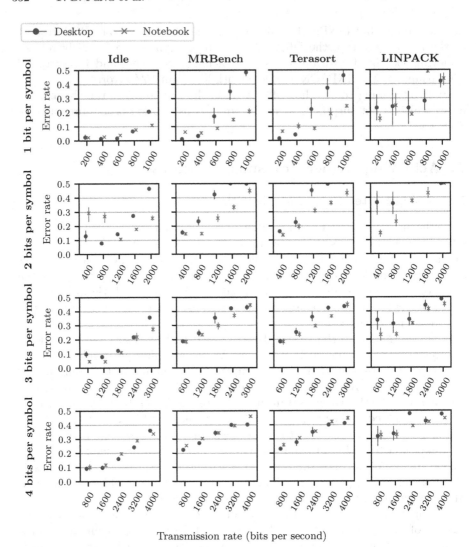

Fig. 7. Error rates for different transmission rates and workloads when transmitting 2, 3, and 4 bits at a time using DRAM-based Trojans combined with CPU-based power consumption states.

a more complex spy process, and the need of a possibly large initial predefined message to train the classifier.

7.2 Encoding Multiple Bits

In this section we investigate the possibility of transmitting non-binary symbols per power modulation. Our main observation is that, from DRAM power consumption samples, it is possible to distinguish, although with some error, the size of the memory chunk set by memset.

Figure 8 illustrates four memory power consumption states representing symbols a, b, c, and d. Under the notebook setup, these symbols correspond to the memset operation on memory chunks of size 0, 1.5, 3, and 6 times the platform's L3 size, respectively. Similarly, under the desktop setup, they correspond to two sequential memset operations using 0, 0.8, 1.2, and 1.4 times the corresponding L3 size. Notice that, if we want to transmit at high rates, we cannot use memset over too large chunks of memory because the operation cannot take more time than the inverse of the transmission rate, otherwise we get synchronization problems.

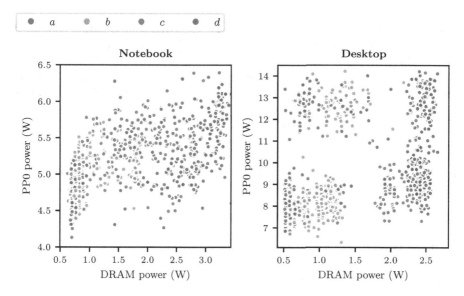

Fig. 8. Power consumption states representing 4 different symbols (2 bits), considering a random message of 1000 symbols transmitted at 200 symbols per second.

Recall Fig. 3, where we can see distinct power consumption profiles corresponding to different operations. One straightforward algorithm to encode 4 bits at once, that is, 4 bits per symbol, when modulating one symbol message is to use 4 threads: 1 thread is responsible for modulating the DRAM power consumption, and the other 3 modulate only the PP0 power consumption. The behavior of the encoding algorithm is shown in Table 1. For example, to transmit the bits 1010, one thread does a memset operation on a memory chunk 3 times the size of L3 cache, and 2 threads perform a CPU-bound task for a predefined time interval. Notice that in a system with more cores, we expect the number of symbols we can distinguish to be larger, since it has more power consumption states.

Table 1. Encoding 4 bits per transmitted symbol combining CPU and DRAM power consumption states under the notebook setup. For the desktop, we used 0.8, 1.2, and 1.4 times L3, correspondingly.

		DRAM power states			
		Do nothing	memset 1.5L3	memset 3L3	memset 6L3
CPU power states	Do nothing	0000	0001	0010	0011
	1 thread	0100	0101	0110	0111
	2 threads	1000	1001	1010	1011
	3 threads	1100	1101	1110	1111

Figure 7 shows the error rates observed for the DRAM modulation combined with the CPU modulation for different workloads. Notice that for 2 bits per symbol, there is no need for a CPU power modulation thread, since there are 4 distinguishable memory power consumption states. We can see that, under the desktop setup, it was possible to transmit at 2400 bps using 4 bits per symbol at error rates close to 15%. Furthermore, under both setups, it is possible to transmit at 1800 bits per second with error rates around 10%.

It is important to note that the robustness of the channel is better when using 1 and 2 bits per symbol, since there is no need for CPU-power modulation threads, which are less robust with respect to application interference. For more than 2 bits per symbol, the robustness of the channel under both setups is very similar.

8   Discussion

Using the DRAM power modulation alone enables us to build a covert channel implementation with the following very desirable properties.

1. It can transmit at high rates with low error rates, as defined by TCSEC [23].
2. It uses simple algorithms for encoding and decoding.
3. It is robust against application interference.

One important feature of DRAM power is that, by manipulating memory chunks of different sizes, we get different power consumption profiles. This can yield a potentially large number of distinguishable states. Further study using other classifiers can help us estimate the number of useful states.

Combining the DRAM and CPU power states, we achieved the throughput of 1800 bps with 10% error, and 2400 with 15% error under the notebook and desktop setups, respectively. This significantly improves upon Miedl and Thiele's results [20], in which only CPU power modulation is considered, as shown in Table 2.

Table 2. Comparison between our covert channel and the one by Miedl and Thiele [20].

Miedl and Thiele [20]			Our work		
Processor	Transfer rate	Error rate	Processor	Transfer rate	Error rate
Intel Xeon E5-2690 (octa-core)	200 bps	≈15%	Intel Core i7-8700 (hexa-core)	2400 bps	≈15%
Intel Core i7-4710MQ (quad-core)	1000 bps	≈15%	Intel Core i5-4210U (dual-core)	1800 bps	≈10%

It is important to emphasize that both our platforms have lower numbers of cores than the corresponding ones used by Miedl and Thiele's. It is reasonable to expect the throughput to be even higher in a machine with more cores, since it has more power states. However our results suggest that in a system with more cores, the covert channel robustness against application interference is significantly compromised, in particular under workloads similar to LINPACK.

Our implementation also improves upon Miedl and Thiele's work with respect to the robustness against application interference, mainly because the way memset with large memory chunks affects the DRAM power profile appears to be very different than other common applications. Furthermore, understanding which benchmarks affect the quality of this covert channel can shed some light on countermeasures against side-channel attacks.

The data and source code are publicly available at https://www.ime.usp.br/~tpaiva/.

9   Conclusion and Future Work

In this paper, we introduce a new method for building covert channels which uses the DRAM power consumption estimates given by the processor's internal power measuring registers. We evaluate in detail the performance of the covert channel with respect to throughput, error rate, and robustness against application interference.

We show how to combine DRAM and CPU power consumption states to achieve higher transmission rates. Using this method, our channel implementation improves upon similar proposals, with respect to bandwidth and robustness against application interference. Using more complex encoding and decoding techniques, higher transmission rates with lower error rates may be achieved.

A simple countermeasure to these covert channels is to prohibit applications from reading the power consumption, but this may be to restrictive. Another possible solution would be to allow applications to read the consumption only at low rates. However, further research is needed to find which sampling rates are secure but also give useful information to applications.

For future work, it is interesting to derive a capacity bound for the DRAM-based covert channel as Miedl and Thiele [20] consider for the CPU-based one. It would also be interesting to consider error correction codes to lower the error rates. Another possible extension of this work would be to compare the bandwidth and error rates of the channel when running in different environments.

Acknowledgments. This study was financed in part by the Coordenação de Aperfeiçoamento de Pessoal de Nível Superior - Brasil (CAPES) - Finance Code 001. This research is part of the INCT of the Future Internet for Smart Cities funded by CNPq proc. 465446/2014-0, Coordenação de Aperfeiçoamento de Pessoal de Nível Superior –Brasil (CAPES) – Finance Code 001, FAPESP proc. 14/50937-1, and FAPESP proc. 15/24485-9. Dr. Navaridas is supported by EuroEXA, funded by the European Union's Horizon 2020 programme under Grant Agreement 754337. Part of this paper was written while T. B. Paiva was attending the Escuela de Ciencias Informáticas 2018 supported by a travel grant given by the Computer Science Department of Universidad de Buenos Aires.

References

1. Bartolini, D.B., Miedl, P., Thiele, L.: On the capacity of thermal covert channels in multicores. In: Proceedings of the Eleventh European Conference on Computer Systems, p. 24. ACM (2016)
2. Bedard, D., Fowler, R., Linn, M., Porterfield, A.: PowerMon 2: fine-grained, integrated power measurement. Renaissance Computing Institute, Technical Report TR-09-04 (2009)
3. Coron, J.-S.: Resistance against differential power analysis for elliptic curve cryptosystems. In: Koç, Ç.K., Paar, C. (eds.) CHES 1999. LNCS, vol. 1717, pp. 292–302. Springer, Heidelberg (1999). https://doi.org/10.1007/3-540-48059-5_25
4. Deshotels, L.: Inaudible sound as a covert channel in mobile devices. In: WOOT (2014)
5. Desrochers, S., Paradis, C., Weaver, V.M.: A validation of DRAM RAPL power measurements. In: Proceedings of the Second International Symposium on Memory Systems, pp. 455–470. ACM (2016)
6. Dongarra, J.J.: Performance of various computers using standard linear equations software (2018). http://www.netlib.org/benchmark/performance.ps
7. Evtyushkin, D., Ponomarev, D., Abu-Ghazaleh, N.: Covert channels through branch predictors: a feasibility study. In: Proceedings of the Fourth Workshop on Hardware and Architectural Support for Security and Privacy, p. 5. ACM (2015)
8. Gruss, D., Maurice, C., Wagner, K., Mangard, S.: Flush+Flush: a fast and stealthy cache attack. In: Caballero, J., Zurutuza, U., Rodríguez, R.J. (eds.) DIMVA 2016. LNCS, vol. 9721, pp. 279–299. Springer, Cham (2016). https://doi.org/10.1007/978-3-319-40667-1_14
9. Guri, M., Monitz, M., Mirski, Y., Elovici, Y.: BitWhisper: covert signaling channel between air-gapped computers using thermal manipulations. In: 2015 IEEE 28th Computer Security Foundations Symposium, pp. 276–289, July 2015. https://doi.org/10.1109/CSF.2015.26
10. Intel: Intel® 64 and IA-32 architectures software developer's manual. Intel (2019). https://software.intel.com/sites/default/files/managed/22/0d/335592-sdm-vol-4.pdf

11. Kim, K., Jeon, K., Han, H., Kim, S.G., Jung, H., Yeom, H.Y.: MRBench: a benchmark for MapReduce framework. In: 14th IEEE International Conference on Parallel and Distributed Systems, ICPADS 2008, pp. 11–18. IEEE (2008)
12. Kocher, P., Jaffe, J., Jun, B.: Differential power analysis. In: Wiener, M. (ed.) CRYPTO 1999. LNCS, vol. 1666, pp. 388–397. Springer, Heidelberg (1999). https://doi.org/10.1007/3-540-48405-1_25
13. Lampson, B.W.: A note on the confinement problem. Commun. ACM **16**(10), 613–615 (1973)
14. Long, Z., Wang, X., Jiang, Y., Cui, G., Zhang, L., Mak, T.: Improving the efficiency of thermal covert channels in multi-/many-core systems. In: 2018 Design, Automation & Test in Europe Conference & Exhibition (DATE), pp. 1459–1464. IEEE (2018)
15. Mangard, S.: A simple power-analysis (SPA) attack on implementations of the AES key expansion. In: Lee, P.J., Lim, C.H. (eds.) ICISC 2002. LNCS, vol. 2587, pp. 343–358. Springer, Heidelberg (2003). https://doi.org/10.1007/3-540-36552-4_24
16. Mantel, H., Schickel, J., Weber, A., Weber, F.: How secure is green IT? The case of software-based energy side channels. In: Lopez, J., Zhou, J., Soriano, M. (eds.) ESORICS 2018. LNCS, vol. 11098, pp. 218–239. Springer, Cham (2018). https://doi.org/10.1007/978-3-319-99073-6_11
17. Masti, R.J., Rai, D., Ranganathan, A., Müller, C., Thiele, L., Capkun, S.: Thermal covert channels on multi-core platforms. In: USENIX Security Symposium, pp. 865–880 (2015)
18. Messerges, T.S., Dabbish, E.A., Sloan, R.H.: Power analysis attacks of modular exponentiation in smartcards. In: Koç, Ç.K., Paar, C. (eds.) CHES 1999. LNCS, vol. 1717, pp. 144–157. Springer, Heidelberg (1999). https://doi.org/10.1007/3-540-48059-5_14
19. Michalevsky, Y., Schulman, A., Veerapandian, G.A., Boneh, D., Nakibly, G.: PowerSpy: location tracking using mobile device power analysis. In: 24th USENIX Security Symposium, USENIX Security 2015, pp. 785–800 (2015)
20. Miedl, P., Thiele, L.: The security risks of power measurements in multicores. In: 33rd ACM/SIGAPP Symposium on Applied Computing, SAC 2018, pp. 1585–1592. ETH Zurich (2018)
21. Murdoch, S.J.: Hot or not: revealing hidden services by their clock skew. In: Proceedings of the 13th ACM Conference on Computer and Communications Security, pp. 27–36. ACM (2006)
22. O'Malley, O.: Terabyte sort on apache Hadoop, pp. 1–3. Yahoo, May 2008. http://sortbenchmark.org/Yahoo-Hadoop.pdf
23. United States Department of Defense: Trusted Computer System Evaluation Criteria (Orange Book). Technical report, National Computer Security Center (1985)
24. Weaver, V.M., et al.: Measuring energy and power with PAPI. In: 2012 41st International Conference on Parallel Processing Workshops (ICPPW), pp. 262–268. IEEE (2012)
25. Yan, L., Guo, Y., Chen, X., Mei, H.: A study on power side channels on mobile devices. In: Proceedings of the 7th Asia-Pacific Symposium on Internetware, pp. 30–38. ACM (2015)
26. Yao, F., Doroslovacki, M., Venkataramani, G.: Are coherence protocol states vulnerable to information leakage? In: 2018 IEEE International Symposium on High Performance Computer Architecture (HPCA), pp. 168–179. IEEE (2018)

27. Yarom, Y., Falkner, K.: FLUSH+RELOAD: a high resolution, low noise, L3 cache side-channel attack. In: 23rd USENIX Security Symposium, USENIX Security 2014, pp. 719–732 (2014)
28. Zander, S., Branch, P., Armitage, G.: Capacity of temperature-based covert channels. IEEE Commun. Lett. **15**(1), 82–84 (2011)

Malware Analysis

Barnum: Detecting Document Malware via Control Flow Anomalies in Hardware Traces

Carter Yagemann[1(✉)], Salmin Sultana[2], Li Chen[2], and Wenke Lee[1]

[1] Georgia Institute of Technology, Atlanta, GA 30332, USA
yagemann@gatech.edu, wenke@cc.gatech.edu
[2] Security and Privacy Research, Intel Labs, Hillsboro, OR 97124, USA
{salmin.sultana,li.chen}@intel.com

Abstract. This paper proposes Barnum, an offline control flow attack detection system that applies deep learning on hardware execution traces to model a program's behavior and detect control flow anomalies. Our implementation analyzes document readers to detect exploits and ABI abuse. Recent work has proposed using deep learning based control flow classification to build more robust and scalable detection systems. These proposals, however, were not evaluated against different kinds of control flow attacks, programs, and adversarial perturbations.

We investigate anomaly detection approaches to improve the security coverage and scalability of control flow attack detection. Barnum is an end-to-end system consisting of three major components: (1) trace collection, (2) behavior modeling, and (3) anomaly detection via binary classification. It utilizes Intel® Processor Trace for low overhead execution tracing and applies deep learning on the basic block sequences reconstructed from the trace to train a normal program behavior model. Based on the path prediction accuracy of the model, Barnum then determines a decision boundary to classify benign vs. malicious executions.

We evaluate against 8 families of attacks to Adobe Acrobat Reader and 9 to Microsoft Word on Windows 7. Both readers are complex programs with over 50 dynamically linked libraries, just-in-time compiled code and frequent network I/O. Barnum shows its effectiveness with 0% false positive and 2.4% false negative on a dataset of 1,250 benign and 1,639 malicious PDFs. Barnum is robust against evasion techniques as it successfully detects 500 adversarially perturbed PDFs.

Keywords: Malware · Automated analysis · Classification · Deep-learning

1 Introduction

Control flow hijack attacks are still prevalent with nearly one million new exploit malware being reported in Q2, 2018 [3]. These attacks typically exploit memory corruption vulnerabilities to redirect the target program's control flow and gain

© Springer Nature Switzerland AG 2019
Z. Lin et al. (Eds.): ISC 2019, LNCS 11723, pp. 341–359, 2019.
https://doi.org/10.1007/978-3-030-30215-3_17

arbitrary code execution. They continue to exist despite protection mechanisms like control flow integrity (CFI) and code-pointer integrity (CPI) [22] due to compromises between accuracy and performance.

A serious concern to these systems is that they have been proven to only detect deviations from their models, which does not account for all control flow anomalies. Beyond exploits, over 97% of document malware rely on macros and ABIs that do not violate program integrity [29,34]. *Such abuse requires anomaly detection rather than integrity enforcement to detect and analyze.*

In this context, neural networks able to automatically learn features show great promise in detecting complex malware with high accuracy and scalability. Deep learning based malware detection has mostly focused on analyzing executable files and runtime ABI calls. The static analysis approaches use the headers, instruction opcodes, or raw bytes of an executable file to build models and classify the file before execution [10,35,36]. The dynamic approaches profile user or kernel ABI call sequences during execution [19,21,39]. Despite their potential, these classifiers are vulnerable to adversarial attacks [15,17,37].

We investigate anomaly detection approaches to build a robust offline system to detect control flow attacks. To be particular, we want to extend detection to unknown attacks against binaries that lack source code such as commercial off-the-shelf software, third-party libraries, and legacy programs. For security use cases, anomaly detection is more suitable than classification, since it is neither practical nor scalable to create behavior models for all possible attacks. In this paper, we describe Barnum, an anomaly detection based system that applies deep learning on hardware execution traces to build a per-application behavioral model and detect control flow attacks. The recent advancement in deep learning behavior modeling and hardware execution tracing enables us to efficiently trace many executions of a program with different inputs and build an automated system to identify expected behaviors from this vast volume of data.

We utilize Intel® Processor Trace (Intel® PT), a low overhead tracing feature in the CPU, to get the complete control flow audit of a program execution. Intel® PT records the non-deterministic control flow transfers, contextual, timing, etc. information, which combined with the program binary can be used to reconstruct the executed instruction sequences. We summarize the instructions into *basic blocks* (BBs), a sequence of linear instructions ending with a branching instruction, and assign each BB a unique BBID, creating a long sequence. We develop a hypervisor-based framework that makes the trace collection and processing secure and portable across OSes. Utilizing low level tracing also adds to the portability of Barnum across different OSes and hardware.

Barnum divides the control flow attack detection into two layers: (1) control flow modeling and (2) anomaly detection via binary classification. First, we train the normal behavior model of a program via self-supervised learning on benign traces. We then apply this model on unlabeled traces to predict the next BBIDs and use the prediction accuracy and confidence to learn the classification threshold of benign vs. anomalous traces.

We evaluate Barnum against 8 families of attacks (labeled by AVClass [42]) to Adobe Acrobat Reader and 9 to Microsoft Word on Windows 7. Both readers are complex programs with over 50 dynamically linked libraries, frequent use of just-in-time (JIT) compilation, network I/O for auto-updating and fetching remote content, and have known bugs that have been successfully exploited in the wild by attackers. Barnum shows its effectiveness with 0% false positive (FP) and 2.4% false negative (FN) on a dataset of 1,250 benign and 1,639 malicious PDFs and 0% FP, 10% FN on 200 benign and 379 malicious Word documents. The latter dataset is more challenging because 94% of the samples rely on ABI abuse, not exploits, which is outside the scope of related dynamic analysis systems. 2 detected Word malware samples are fully undetected on VirusTotal (VT). Barnum is able to handle programs that utilize JIT compilation by observing the control flow into and out of JIT regions without having to analyze the JIT code execution. Additionally, we use Mimicus [45] to perturb 500 malicious samples and confirm that the performance of Barnum does not degrade.

To summarize, we make the following contributions:

- We develop an offline anomaly detection based control flow attack detection system that applies deep learning on fine-grained control flow traces of an application. We describe the design challenges and architecture of Barnum.
- We utilize Intel® PT to collect control flow traces. The *hypervisor based* processing of *low level traces* make Barnum secure and portable across systems.
- We represent the control flow trace as a sequence of basic blocks and develop a multi-layer system to model program behavior for anomaly detection.
- We extensively evaluate Barnum against 8 families of attacks to Adobe Reader and 9 to Microsoft Word on Windows 7 64 bit. The experimental results show 0% FP, 2.4% FN and 0% FP, 10% FN to classify benign and malicious PDF and Word documents, respectively. We show that Barnum is resilient to adversarial attacks like Mimicus.

The rest of the paper is organized as follows: the next section describes the problem and provides background information. Section 3 details the design of Barnum. Our evaluation of Barnum on document malware is presented in Sect. 4. Section 5 covers related work and we conclude in Sect. 6.

All the Barnum source code, malware hashes, and data for reproducing results are available at the project homepage[1] or by contacting the first author.

2   Problem and Background

This section describes the problem Barnum is designed to address. We discuss our assumptions in the context of our adversary model and evaluation scenarios.

---

[1] https://tinyurl.com/y27clrfl.

2.1   Threat Model and Assumptions

In this work, our goal is to detect document malware via control flow anomalies. Most attacks against programs rely to some degree on changing the execution flow of the target program. Although it is possible to construct data-only attacks [8], most adversaries still rely on techniques like Return-Oriented-Programming to craft exploit payloads [6]. With this in mind, we consider a target program that may contain memory corruption vulnerabilities that an adversary can exploit to run a control flow manipulation attack. We also consider patterns like ABI abuse, which do not violate integrity. For example, a malicious script may invoke one ABI to save a file followed by another to execute it. This is allowed by the software specification, but is not the typical usage pattern.

We also assume that the libraries imported by the program contain vulnerabilities and that there may be dynamic code generation, even when the program is not under attack. For example, Adobe Acrobat Reader performs just-in-time (JIT) compilation on JavaScript.

2.2   Document Malware

We focus on offline analysis rather than online detection or prevention. We rely on dynamic analysis that, similar to related systems [38], executes the given sample for a fixed duration of time. It is possible for malware to employ techniques that detect the analysis environment [12,31] or delay execution beyond the observed time frame [20]. However, unlike general executables, malicious *documents* begin in a viewer program and rely on either scripts or malformed elements (e.g. CVE-2018-4990) to gain control. Thus, their options for environment detection are limited and can in themselves create a detectable signal. If the viewer is closed before the malware has gained control, the attack will be prematurely terminated. Thus, *document* malware cannot stall or inject benign activity for the durations general malware can. *Therefore we acknowledge the known limitations of virtualized dynamic analysis, but argue the compromises are reasonable for the document malware context.*

An additional challenge to document malware analysis is that even when an application is under attack, most of the overall activity can still be benign. For example, a trace of Acrobat Reader opening a malicious PDF will contain behaviors like creating the GUI, which our analysis must be robust to.

Lastly, not all document malware rely on exploits. While many do use vulnerabilities in the document viewer to hijack the program execution, some rely instead on combining the provided ABIs in abusive ways. For example, several PDF malware use `exportDataObject` to save and execute an attachment. The user is warned about such behavior with a message window, but if they click accept or disable the warning, the attack will succeed. Since ABI abuse does not violate control flow integrity (i.e. the program is functioning as intended), mechanisms like CFI and memory safety are not appropriate solutions. These ABI invocations, however, are reflected in the resulting control flow trace and hence, still create a signal. In Sect. 4 we show that compared to exploits, ABI abuse is harder for Barnum to detect, but is still distinguishable in many cases.

3 Design

Figure 1 shows the system architecture of Barnum. It consists of three major components: (1) execution trace collection, (2) program behavior modeling, and (3) anomaly detection via binary classification. Barnum is evaluated on document malware targeting Acrobat Reader and Microsoft Word on Windows 7, but due to its OS and program agnostic design, the methodology can easily be expanded to cover other programs that process discrete inputs, such as web services.

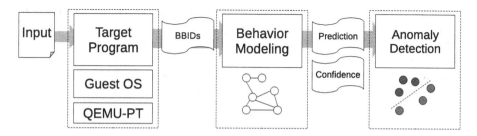

Fig. 1. Barnum has three components: (1) trace collection, (2) behavior modeling, and (3) anomaly detection.

3.1 Control Flow Tracing

The analysis of a program input begins with the collection of a trace. For this component, there are several design challenges that need to be addressed: *(a) how do we efficiently generate traces of the program execution, (b) since we need a trusted component to collect traces, how does it bridge the semantic gap to the rest of the system, and (c) how do we collect the traces and process them into a useful representation?* Underpinning this is the obvious security requirement that traces must be complete, untampered with, and difficult to evade.

Efficient Tracing. We need an efficient and secure way to collect control flow traces so we can analyze document malware. For this reason, we decide to leverage Intel® PT at the hypervisor level. Intel® PT is a hardware tracing feature found in recent Intel® CPUs. Using Intel® PT, developers can trace the CPU to get a rich stream of data including branching taken-not-taken (TNT), target instruction pointer (TIP) for indirect calls and jumps, power events, hardware interrupts, etc. These events are recorded asynchronously as a stream of packets directly into memory. The CPU guarantees that packets will be recorded in the correct order upon instruction retirement. In other words, an Intel® PT trace only records what is actually executed. Due to its asynchronous nature, Intel® PT introduces minimal performance overhead; under 4% in our measurements. This is several orders of magnitude faster than approaches like binary instrumentation, allowing Barnum to analyze and classify more samples.

Semantic Gap. Intel® PT has built-in filtering options to control what is traced. Of particular interest to this work are CR3 and current privilege level (CPL) filtering. As these names imply, they configure Intel® PT to only enable tracing when a particular value is loaded into the CR3 register and when the CPU is in a particular CPL. We combine these filters to trace only the user space activity of our target process. We use a configurable agent inside the virtual machine (VM) to start the target program and open the document sample.

One caveat to this approach is we need a way to associate CR3 values with processes. To overcome this challenge, we leverage virtual machine introspection (VMI) to monitor the guest kernel's process list.

For security and portability, we control Intel® PT from a hypervisor and configure it to write the trace into reserved memory. Since the hypervisor has exclusive control over the Intel® PT configuration, the traces are ensured to be complete and untampered with. The trace is then saved to storage for analysis.

Data Preprocessing. Unfortunately, an Intel® PT trace alone does not tell the full story about the program control flow. For example, TNT packets record a single 1/0 bit for conditionals, which is insufficient to detect loops. To construct meaningful representations of the control flow, we need the corresponding instructions so we can calculate all the branch targets. This requires additional sideband data. Specifically, we use VMI to read the memory mapping from the guest kernel's data structures and recover the executable pages *immediately before opening the document sample.* Thus, we only miss dynamically generated code or late loaded libraries. Once collected, we combine the program binary with the Intel® PT trace to reconstruct the exact sequence of instructions executed and their corresponding addresses. We then use the memory mapping to normalize addresses as offsets within libraries and executables.

We summarize the instructions into basic blocks (BBs), defined as a sequence of linear instructions ending with a branching instruction (i.e. indirect calls and jumps, direct branches, and returns) and assign each basic block a universally unique *BBID*. We represent the control flow trace as a long sequence of BBIDs for program behavior modeling. Our implementation extends kAFL [41] to support user space tracing and we use `libipt` [1] for trace decoding.

Just-In-Time Compilation. For many programs, dynamic code generation occurs due to JIT compilation of scripting languages like JavaScript. Since it is not feasible to enumerate a representative set of possible scripts for documents, we instead elect to disregard this code in our analysis. When the program jumps into a code region that is dynamically generated, we stop disassembling the Intel® PT trace until the execution returns to a region that was not dynamically generated,

Last Instr	inc	movzx	icall	pop	ret	push	push	icall	pop	pop	pop	ret	pop	inc
Subseq #1	701	224	612	968	511	332	172	82	179	20	721	33	422	187
Subseq #2	701	224	612	968	511	332	172	82	179	20	721	33	422	187
Subseq #3	701	224	612	968	511	332	172	82	179	20	721	33	422	187
Subseq #4	701	224	612	968	511	332	172	82	179	20	721	33	442	187

Fig. 2. An example of sub-sequencing the BBIDs for a sliding window of size 3. The cells contain BBIDs and the top row is the last instruction in each BB. Each row shows a subsequence contained in the same 14 BBIDs. The lighter cells are the features and the darker cells are the labels.

upon which we resume disassembly. This means that while we do not attempt to analyze the control flow inside the JIT code, we still capture the points at which the program enters and exits it. Similarly, while we do not record kernel space, the trace captures where entries and exits occur. This allows us to observe the boundary between these worlds, which is sufficient to detect patterns like ROP chains and shellcode injection because programs typically have a binding layer that the control flow always passes through [33]. In other words, observing transitions that do not go through the binding layer of the program, enter system libraries directly from JIT code, etc., are indicative of an attack.

3.2 Control Flow Behavior Modeling of a Program

To model the normal control flow of a target program, we have to address the following: *(a) how do we slice the long BBID sequence into manageable subsequences, (b) what model should we use to represent normal control flow paths, and (c) what do we do about code coverage?*

Data Slicing. Since control flow hijacking only occurs at indirect calls, jumps, and returns, we only need to analyze subsequences that end on one of these instructions. Figure 2 shows how we use a fixed sliding window with variable width steps so that each frame ends on such instructions. The next BBID after the frame will become its label, which we discuss later. The optimal window size is experimentally found to be 32 BBIDs for our model.

Deep Learning Model Selection. While we have the intuition that knowing past control flow is useful for predicting future execution, shadow stacks being one such example, it is not trivial to utilize this history to achieve accurate predictions. Using heuristics would be neither practical nor scalable. Instead, we turn to machine learning (ML) to find these patterns automatically.

We structure our behavior model as a supervised learning problem where, given a fixed window of past BBIDs, we want to predict the next BBID. In machine learning terms, the features are the sequence of past BBIDs and the label is the next BBID in the trace. As we explain earlier, we do not directly analyze JIT code. Therefore, the max number of BBIDs is fixed and can be over-approximated. Since the trace encodes both the features and labels, this type of learning falls into the subcategory of *self-supervised learning*. *The advantage of this approach is it does not require manual ground truth annotation, allowing for better scalability. This is essential given how much data Intel® PT generates.* To train a program behavior model, we only use traces from the benign dataset since we want to learn paths under normal conditions.

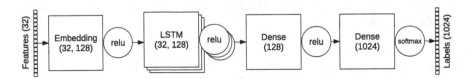

Fig. 3. The layers, shapes, and activations of our model. Recall that the subsequence length is 32, hence 32 features. Not shown is a 50% dropout between the two dense neural layers. We bucket the BBID predictions into 1,024 labels to reduce model size.

Since our features are temporally related, we center our model around recurrent neural networks, specifically Long Short Term Memory (LSTM). Our model consists of an embedding layer followed by three LSTM layers and a final dense neural network, as shown in Fig. 3. We find the exact layout and hyperparameters experimentally. To reduce model size and improve runtime performance, we map the BBIDs to buckets, which shrinks the input and output spaces. To find the ideal number of buckets, we start with each BBID being its own bucket (i.e. no reduction) and merge buckets until accuracy degrades. For our datasets, the ideal number is 1024. We decide not to use classical ML models like n-gram because small n values miss features and large values produce sparsity leading to performance degradation. In short, picking n is hard whereas deep learning simplifies feature selection. The ability of LSTM to automatically extract both long and short-term features makes it well suited to our context. By contrast, convolutional neural networks have yet to demonstrate higher accuracy, but are known to be susceptible to minimal perturbations [4]. In Sect. 4, we evaluate simpler approaches to this problem to demonstrate the added value of our ML technique.

Code Coverage. A legitimate concern is whether the training dataset can cover all possible benign execution paths of a target program. This is known as the *code coverage* problem [11]. Code coverage is known to be difficult to guarantee, especially when source code is not available. We approximate the coverage of our dataset in Sect. 4 by counting the number of executed instructions.

3.3   Anomaly Detection

Now that we have trained a behavior model to predict normal control flow paths, we move on to the third major component of Barnum: anomaly detection. The major challenge here is how to go from path prediction to anomaly detection. We use the accuracy and confidence of the model on benign traces to determine a decision boundary for classifying benign vs. anomalous executions. Given the BBID subsequences for a trace and the behavior model, we feed each subsequence into the model, get the prediction and confidence for the next BBID, and check whether the prediction is correct or not. This process results a sequential list of ⟨*confidence percentage, prediction correctness*⟩ tuples. Since Barnum is a dynamic analysis framework that records traces for a fixed duration of time, for a given trace, we average the prediction accuracy and confidence corresponding to wrong predictions. This gives us two dimensions to examine with our intuition being that *wrong* predictions with *high* confidence are a signal for anomalies.

Given these dimensions, we create a linear decision boundary to express a threshold. Any data points above the threshold are considered normal while points below the threshold are anomalous. It is possible to use other kernels to express the decision threshold, but in practice we find a linear boundary to be sufficient to achieve high classification accuracy.

4 Evaluation

In this section, we present our evaluation results for Barnum. Specifically, we evaluate each of the three components of Barnum in the context of analyzing document malware targeting Adobe Acrobat Reader 9.3 and Microsoft Word 2010 on 64 bit Windows 7. We analyze two distinct programs to demonstrate Barnum is not overly tailored to a particular program.

4.1 Overview

To evaluate Barnum, we ask several questions:

- **Path prediction.** How well can Barnum learn the control flow of complex programs like Acrobat Reader? How does it compare to simpler methods like rote learning?
- **Document malware classification.** How accurately can Barnum classify previously unseen traces to separate benign and malicious documents? How does it compare to other related work in malware classification?
- **Resource consumption.** How much memory and storage does Barnum consume to analyze samples? How long does it take to perform analysis?

4.2 Datasets and Experimental Setup

For our PDF dataset, we consider 3,660 samples, of which 1,250 are benign and 2,410 are malicious. These samples are picked randomly from a malware feed spanning several years. The benign samples are from several sources including past conference proceedings and the 2013 Contagio dataset [30]. We confirm that our benign documents contain embedded JavaScript, Flash, and Shockwave so simply detecting active content will not trivially lead to accurate classification.

For our malicious dataset, we start with 2,410 malicious samples that match known signatures from anti-virus companies. Since our system is built on runtime tracing, we have to manually verify that these samples exhibit their malicious behavior in our target VM. For example, some malicious PDFs carry exploits for particular versions of Acrobat Reader and will not perform any malicious activity if this requirement is not satisfied. We use older program versions to maximize the chance of triggering the malware, but even then there are unreliable exploits that simply crash. Lastly, some attacks are embedded in remote content that the document references. Once the hosting server is taken down, the document becomes benign. After manual filtering, our malicious dataset contains 1,639 samples; about 68% of the original set. In the context of evaluating dynamic malware analysis systems, this is typical. For comparison, PlatPal [48] had only 320 malware after filtering, of which their system detected 75.9%.

PDF							
pdfjsc	perferd	name	singleton	tiff	swrort	pidief	pdfka
2	2	4	7	10	99	201	1,314

Word								
powload	emotet	powdow	sagent	valyria	sload	donoff	obfuse	singleton
3	5	8	8	23	25	33	61	206

Fig. 4. AVClass label counts. Singleton labels are merged into a single category.

In total, AVClass produces 8 unique labels for this dataset with 7 samples producing no family label (i.e. AVClass classifies them as singletons). The distribution is shown in Fig. 4. We also randomly perturb 500 of our malicious samples using Mimicus [45] to evaluate the robustness of Barnum.

To demonstrate that Barnum is not tailored to Acrobat Reader, we also evaluate a dataset of 200 benign and 379 malicious Word documents. AVClass produces 9 unique labels for this dataset with *206 samples classified as singletons*. The high number of singletons is due to low detection rates and matches to signatures with uninformative names on VT. For example, 19 malware are detected by 3 or less of the 60 anti-virus products used by VT and 2 samples are fully undetected at the time of writing. Several matched signatures are simply named *heuristic*. In short, our Microsoft Word dataset is more challenging for existing anti-virus than the PDF dataset.

A point worth stressing is *Barnum handles Acrobat Reader and Microsoft Word without modifying any lines of source code*. We only adjust two settings to select which program the agent starts and the process name to trace.

Our experiments are performed on a single desktop with an Intel® i7-6700K CPU and Nvidia 1080-Ti GPU. The GPU is only used by the behavior model.

4.3 Baseline for Comparing PDF Detection

Most existing solutions for PDF malware analysis examine static features extracted from the document [9, 26, 28]. These systems are very accurate (>95%), but are also known to be vulnerable to perturbations like the one proposed in Mimicus. For dynamic analysis, solutions like CWXDetector [47] achieve upwards of 93% detection, but have limitations like not being able to detect exploit based attacks [40, 44, 46] or code reuse [25]. A more recent work, Plat-Pal [48], avoids these limitations, but only detects 75.9% of their 320 samples as malicious or suspicious. We compare Barnum accordingly:

1. We compare the behavior model to a database that performs rote learning to measure the value our LSTM model adds to Barnum.
2. We show that our detection accuracy is better than CWXDetector and Plat-Pal, which also perform dynamic analysis on PDF malware.
3. We show that our detection is robust against Mimicus [45], which evades systems based on static document input features.

	[25]		[47]		[48]		**Barnum**	
TP	91.7%	(917)	93.2%	(6,781)	75.9%	(243)	**97.8%**	(1,600)
FN	8.3%	(83)	6.8%	(497)	24.1%	(77)	**2.4%**	(39)
TN	100%	(994)	100%	(7,278)	100%	(1,030)	100%	(375)
FP	0%	(0)	0%	(0)	0%	(0)	0%	(0)

Fig. 5. Comparison of Barnum against related dynamic PDF analysis systems in terms of true positive (TP), false negative (FN), true negative (TN), and false positive (FP) rates. Values are shown as counts and percentages. Barnum has the best TP and FN.

A comparison of our results to related work is presented in Fig. 5.

4.4 Path Prediction for PDF Dataset

To evaluate the accuracy of our behavior model, we randomly split our benign PDF samples into a training set of 875 and a testing set of 375. Recall that we do not use the malicious PDFs in this stage of the pipeline.

We also use these same sets to train and test a model based on rote learning. Specifically, for each subsequence given to the rote learner during training, it looks up the corresponding row in its database and increments the label (i.e. the next BBID that follows the subsequence) by one. This creates a database that counts how often each label occurs for any subsequence seen during training. To conserve memory, we store this database in Redis, which uses a compressed key-value encoding and only create rows for subsequences seen during training. For testing, the model checks if it has seen the given subsequence before. If it has, it makes a weighted random guess based on the counts of all the possible labels. If the subsequence never occurred in training, it makes a completely random guess.

Note that we can adjust the learning capacity of the LSTM model by adding and removing nodes, which impacts accuracy and in-memory size. For comparison, we adjust the LSTM to achieve the same accuracy as the rote learner. Under this condition, the rote learner's database takes up 2,030 MB of memory whereas the LSTM model only needs 2.7 MB. In short, back-propagation enables LSTM to extract the most important patterns instead of memorizing everything.

4.5   Training Coverage of PDF Dataset

As part of the evaluation for our behavior model, we consider how well our benign PDF training dataset covers Acrobat Reader. First, we measure the novelty each additional trace adds to training. Specifically, for each trace, we extract the BBID subsequences and calculate the percentage that do not occur in previous traces. The result is summarized in Fig. 6(a). Note that within a single trace, if the same subsequence occurs multiple times, it is only considered once in the percentage calculation. As the figure shows, by the end of training we are still encountering traces where 15% of the subsequences are new. Unfortunately, the plot also appears to fit a power curve. If this trend is accurate, it implies that while getting decent coverage is doable, achieving excellent coverage is hard. Recent work in ML theory supports our finding [16]. However, even with only 875 benign training traces, we achieve better detection accuracy than the related work considered in Fig. 5.

In addition to the previous metric, we also consider code coverage in terms of how many unique instructions we encounter across Acrobat Reader and all its loaded libraries. The result is summarized in Fig. 6(b). Note that this figure is shown in log scale. We successfully cover 100% of the instructions in

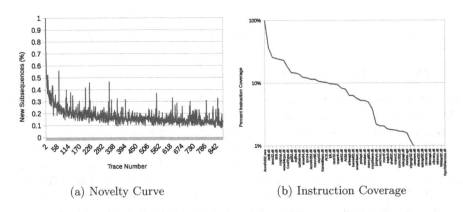

|(a) Novelty Curve|(b) Instruction Coverage|

Fig. 6. The percentage of new subsequences appearing in each subsequent trace (left) and the coverage of instructions by library (right) for the Acrobat Reader dataset. Note that we do not expect full coverage of third-party libraries.

`AcroRd32.exe`, but on closer inspection we notice this binary is fairly small; only a few thousand machine instructions. It is likely that this is mostly bootstrapping logic and the core functionality is actually located in `AcroRd32.dll`, where we cover only 12% of the instructions. This low coverage is not surprising given all the features Acrobat Reader contains that we do not invoke like automatic updating and document editing tools. It is unclear to what degree (if any) adding more traces would increase coverage. Similarly, low coverage in libraries is expected since no program uses every function in every linked library. Interestingly, we cover 37% of `ntdll.dll`, which is used to interact with the Windows kernel.

4.6 Anomaly Detection for PDF Dataset

As described in Sect. 3, once Barnum has a model trained for predicting the normal paths of our target program, it can be used by the next layer to perform binary classification between normal and anomalous traces. To start, we take our benign training samples and calculate the behavior model's average accuracy and misprediction confidence for each. We then set a threshold expressed as a linear decision boundary such that all these samples fall on one side. This becomes the normal side. Anything that falls on the other side is an anomaly. Figure 7(a) shows that Barnum classifies the PDFs with 0% false positive and 2.4% false negative. *This translates to 98.1% accuracy, 100% precision, and 97.6% recall.* These results are significantly better than CWXDetector (6.8% false negative) and PlatPal (24.1% false negative). In Fig. 7(b), we show the ROC curve for different thresholds.

To investigate, we randomly pick some misclassified samples and manually analyze them. Our finding is the malicious samples near the threshold boundary tend to abuse the Acrobat Reader ABIs (e.g. calling ABIs to save and execute an attachment) whereas those further from the boundary use exploits. For example,

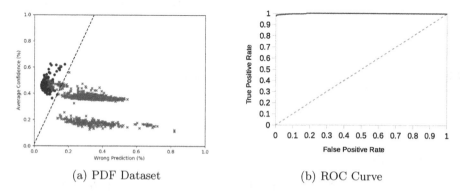

(a) PDF Dataset   (b) ROC Curve

Fig. 7. Classification of our testing PDF dataset of 375 benign, 1,639 malicious, and 500 Mimicus perturbed PDFs. At 0% false positive, the false negative rate is 2.4%. The accuracy is not degraded by Mimicus.

all the `pdfka` traces contain an indirect transfer that appears hundreds of times, which is mispredicted by the model, causing this family to fall further from the decision boundary. The transfer site does not appear in any other traces and we believe it is indicative of an exploit against Acrobat Reader's TIFF parser (CVE-2010-0188). We could not find or create a benign PDF that invokes the same path.

To further demonstrate the value of Barnum, we randomly pick 500 samples from our set of 1,639 malicious PDFs and perturb them using Mimicus [45]. This is an evasion technique that adds additional DOM elements before the PDF trailer and modifies meta-data fields (e.g. author) to change the sample's appearance without altering its runtime behavior. As a result, it is effective against systems that rely on static features of the input document. Since Mimicus guarantees that the runtime behavior (e.g. exploit) is preserved, it is not effective against dynamic systems like Barnum. However, we *do not* claim that our system cannot be evaded just because it resists Mimicus. Rather, the point of including these samples is to show that *Barnum achieves accuracy that is comparable to systems based on static features while also achieving robustness comparable to dynamic systems.* For the adversary, changing the malicious PDF's behavior is more difficult than manipulating the static document features used by existing solutions because the former requires tweaking the exploit, without breaking it, while the latter is achievable with DOM element appends and meta-data tweaks.

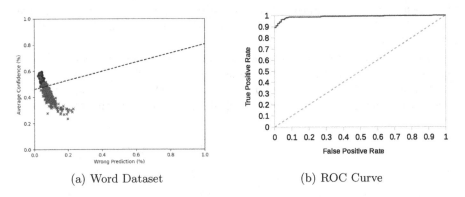

(a) Word Dataset   (b) ROC Curve

Fig. 8. Barnum classifies 100 benign and 379 malicious Word documents with 0% false positive and 10% false negative. The right figure shows the ROC curve.

4.7   Anomaly Detection for Word Dataset

To demonstrate that Barnum is not limited to Adobe Acrobat Reader, we also evaluate a set of 100 benign training, 100 testing, and 379 malicious Word documents using Microsoft Word 2010. The resulting classification and ROC curve are shown in Fig. 8. Barnum achieves 0% false positive and 10% false negative rates on this dataset. The lower performance compared to the PDF dataset is due to most of the attacks relying on macros. Only 25 of the Word malware do not contain macros. Exploits are more prevalent in the PDF dataset and easier for Barnum to detect because their control flow overlaps less with benign traces. If we consider only the 25 Word samples without macros, our system's accuracy becomes 100% with no false positives or negatives. Two recent related work, ALDOCX [32] and the work by Bearden et al. [5], achieve lower false negative rates; 5.6% and 3.7% respectively. However, they use static document features, making them vulnerable to evasion techniques like Mimicus.

4.8 Runtime and Space Performance

The majority of our runtime cost comes from training the behavior model and using it to make predictions. It takes 3 epochs and 1.5 days to train on 875 benign PDFs. The low number of epochs is due to traces being long and repetitive, meaning fewer iterations are needed to converge. At test time, about 25% of the runtime is preprocessing, 75% is querying the path prediction model, and less than 1% is calculating the classification decision. Testing 1,783 PDFs takes 5.7 hours, which equates to about 7,500 samples per day per GPU. Traces are 30 MB on average when saved to storage (i.e. at rest).

5 Related Work

In this section, we summarize the related work in anomaly detection and document malware analysis.

5.1 Machine Learning Based Malware Detection

Anomaly detection has been applied to numerous domains such as networking [14,24], videos [27], and programs [13]. More recently, researchers have started exploring the value machine learning can add to anomaly detection [2,7]. LSTM in particular models anomalies well because it can handle sequences.

Barnum relates most closely to HeNet [7] in that both systems apply deep-learning on hardware traces to detect control flow attacks. Our work, however, surpasses HeNet in several regards. First, HeNet focuses solely on detecting exploit based attacks whereas Barnum expands its scope to include other attacks such as ABI abuse. Second, HeNet directly encodes its traces as images and uses transfer learning, whereas our behavior model is trained from scratch on BBIDs. While transfer learning makes training faster, training from scratch ensures that the layers only inherit deep latent features of trace data. Transfer learning cannot make this guarantee. Third, HeNet has not been extensively evaluated against a large dataset or adversarial inputs.

5.2   Document Malware

The proposals for document malware classification fall into two broad categories: analysis of static input features and dynamic execution. Analysis based on static input features has received the most attention [9,18,23,28,43] because it is faster, easier to scale, and takes advantage of the formal format structure of documents. Unfortunately, while they have solved problems like de-obfuscating scripts, they are known to be vulnerable to ML evasion techniques [45,49]. As we demonstrate in Sect. 4, since Barnum is based on control flow, altering the static structure is not enough to evade our system. Although we cannot claim our system cannot be evaded, evading our system is harder than evading systems based on input features because doing so requires alteration of the exploit.

On the other hand, there are fewer systems that classify documents based on dynamic behavior [26,47]. Most interesting is PlatPal [48], which runs a PDF in two different OSes and uses differential analysis to detect exploitation. Unfortunately, this approach is error prone due to sources of nondeterminism and subtle differences between implementations of the same program for different OS. It is also expensive due to the need for two virtual machines per sample.

6   Conclusion

This work introduces a methodology for collecting, modeling, and detecting control flow anomalies in an OS and program agnostic manner. We present Barnum, a prototype end-to-end system for collecting and analyzing traces of document editors opening benign and malicious PDF and Microsoft Word documents on Windows 7. We show that Barnum can classify documents with higher accuracy than other dynamic analysis frameworks and resists perturbations that thwart systems using static input feature.

Acknowledgement. This research was supported, in part, by the Intel Science and Technology Center for Adversary-Resilient Security Analytics. Some malware samples were provided by the Georgia Tech Research Institute Apiary framework. Any opinions, findings, and conclusions in this paper are those of the authors only and do not necessarily reflect the views of our sponsors.

References

1. 01org: libipt (2018). https://github.com/01org/processor-trace
2. Aditham, S., Ranganathan, N., Katkoori, S.: LSTM-based memory profiling for predicting data attacks in distributed big data systems. In: 2017 IEEE International Parallel and Distributed Processing Symposium Workshops (IPDPSW), pp. 1259–1267. IEEE (2017)
3. C.B., et al.: McAfee Labs Threat Report. Technical report, McAfee Labs, September 2018
4. Athalye, A., Carlini, N., Wagner, D.: Obfuscated gradients give a false sense of security: circumventing defenses to adversarial examples. arXiv preprint arXiv:1802.00420 (2018)

5. Bearden, R., Lo, D.C.T.: Automated microsoft office macro malware detection using machine learning. In: 2017 IEEE International Conference on Big Data (Big Data), pp. 4448–4452. IEEE (2017)
6. Carlini, N., Wagner, D.: ROP is still dangerous: breaking modern defenses. In: Proceedings of the 23rd USENIX Conference on Security Symposium (2014)
7. Chen, L., Sultana, S., Sahita, R.: HeNet: a deep learning approach on Intel processor trace for effective exploit detection. arXiv preprint arXiv:1801.02318 (2018)
8. Chen, S., Xu, J., Sezer, E.C., Gauriar, P., Iyer, R.K.: Non-control-data attacks are realistic threats. In: Proceedings of the 14th USENIX Security Symposium (2005)
9. Corona, I., Maiorca, D., Ariu, D., Giacinto, G.: LuxOR: detection of malicious PDF-embedded Javascript code through discriminant analysis of API references. In: Proceedings of the 2014 Workshop on Artificial Intelligent and Security Workshop, pp. 47–57. ACM (2014)
10. Davis, A., Wolff, M.: Deep learning on disassembly data. In: BlackHat USA (2015)
11. Fallah, F., Devadas, S., Keutzer, K.: OCCOM-efficient computation of observability-based code coverage metrics for functional verification. IEEE Trans. Comput.-Aided Des. Integr. Circ. Syst. **20**(8), 1003–1015 (2001)
12. Ferrie, P.: Attacks on more virtual machine emulators. Symantec Technol. Exch. **55**, 1–17 (2007)
13. Gao, D., Reiter, M.K., Song, D.: On gray-box program tracking for anomaly detection, p. 24. Department of Electrical and Computing Engineering (2004)
14. Garcia-Teodoro, P., Diaz-Verdejo, J., Maciá-Fernández, G., Vázquez, E.: Anomaly-based network intrusion detection: techniques, systems and challenges. Comput. Secur. **28**(1–2), 18–28 (2009)
15. Grosse, K., Papernot, N., Manoharan, P., Backes, M., McDaniel, P.D.: Adversarial perturbations against deep neural networks for malware classification. CoRR abs/1606.04435 (2016)
16. Hestness, J., et al.: Deep learning scaling is predictable, empirically. arXiv preprint arXiv:1712.00409 (2017)
17. Hu, W., Tan, Y.: Black-box attacks against RNN based malware detection algorithms. CoRR abs/1705.08131 (2017)
18. Karademir, S., Dean, T., Leblanc, S.: Using clone detection to find malware in acrobat files. In: Proceedings of the 2013 Conference of the Center for Advanced Studies on Collaborative Research, pp. 70–80. IBM Corporation (2013)
19. Kim, G., Yi, H., Lee, J., Paek, Y., Yoon, S.: LSTM-Based System-Call Language Modeling and Robust Ensemble Method for Designing Host-Based Intrusion Detection Systems. CoRR abs/1611.01726 (2016)
20. Kolbitsch, C., Kirda, E., Kruegel, C.: The power of procrastination: detection and mitigation of execution-stalling malicious code. In: Proceedings of the 18th ACM Conference on Computer and Communications Security, pp. 285–296. ACM (2011)
21. Kolosnjaji, B., Zarras, A., Webster, G., Eckert, C.: Deep Learning for Classification of Malware System Call Sequences, pp. 137–149 (2016)
22. Kuznetsov, V., Szekeres, L., Payer, M., Candea, G., Sekar, R., Song, D.: Code-pointer integrity. In: Proceedings of the 11th USENIX Conference on Operating Systems Design and Implementation (2014)
23. Laskov, P., Šrndić, N.: Static detection of malicious Javascript-bearing PDF documents. In: Proceedings of the 27th Annual Computer Security Applications Conference, pp. 373–382. ACM (2011)
24. Lazarevic, A., Ertoz, L., Kumar, V., Ozgur, A., Srivastava, J.: A comparative study of anomaly detection schemes in network intrusion detection. In: Proceedings of the 2003 SIAM International Conference on Data Mining, pp. 25–36. SIAM (2003)

25. Liu, D., Wang, H., Stavrou, A.: Detecting malicious Javascript in PDF through document instrumentation. In: 2014 44th Annual IEEE/IFIP International Conference on Dependable Systems and Networks (DSN), pp. 100–111. IEEE (2014)

26. Lu, X., Zhuge, J., Wang, R., Cao, Y., Chen, Y.: De-obfuscation and detection of malicious PDF files with high accuracy. In: 2013 46th Hawaii International Conference on System Sciences (HICSS), pp. 4890–4899. IEEE (2013)

27. Mahadevan, V., Li, W., Bhalodia, V., Vasconcelos, N.: Anomaly detection in crowded scenes. In: 2010 IEEE Conference on Computer Vision and Pattern Recognition (CVPR), pp. 1975–1981. IEEE (2010)

28. Maiorca, D., Giacinto, G., Corona, I.: A pattern recognition system for malicious PDF files detection. In: Perner, P. (ed.) MLDM 2012. LNCS (LNAI), vol. 7376, pp. 510–524. Springer, Heidelberg (2012). https://doi.org/10.1007/978-3-642-31537-4_40

29. Microsoft: New feature in office 2016 can block macros and help prevent infection (2016). https://cloudblogs.microsoft.com/microsoftsecure/2016/03/22/new-feature-in-office-2016-can-block-macros-and-help-prevent-infection/

30. Mila: 16,800 clean and 11,960 malicious files for signature testing and research (2013). http://contagiodump.blogspot.com/2013/03/16800-clean-and-11960-malicious-files.html

31. Miramirkhani, N., Appini, M.P., Nikiforakis, N., Polychronakis, M.: Spotless sandboxes: evading malware analysis systems using wear-and-tear artifacts. In: 2017 IEEE Symposium on Security and Privacy (SP), pp. 1009–1024. IEEE (2017)

32. Nissim, N., Cohen, A., Elovici, Y.: ALDOCX: detection of unknown malicious microsoft office documents using designated active learning methods based on new structural feature extraction methodology. IEEE Trans. Inf. Forensics Secur. **12**(3), 631–646 (2017)

33. Niu, B., Tan, G.: RockJIT: securing just-in-time compilation using modular control-flow integrity. In: Proceedings of the 21st ACM SIGSAC Conference on Computer and Communications Security (2014)

34. Proofpoint: The human factor report 2016 (2016). https://www.proofpoint.com/sites/default/files/human-factor-report-2016.pdf

35. Raff, E., Barker, J., Sylvester, J., Brandon, R., Catanzaro, B., Nicholas, C.: Malware Detection by Eating a Whole EXE. ArXiv e-prints, October 2017

36. Raff, E., Sylvester, J., Nicholas, C.: Learning the PE Header. Malware Detection with Minimal Domain Knowledge, ArXiv e-prints, September 2017

37. Rosenberg, I., Shabtai, A., Rokach, L., Elovici, Y.: Generic black-box end-to-end attack against RNNs and other API calls based malware classifiers. ArXiv e-prints, July 2017

38. Sandbox, C.: Cuckoo sandbox (2018). https://cuckoosandbox.org/

39. Saxe, J., Berlin, K.: Deep neural network based malware detection using two dimensional binary program features. In: International Conference on Malicious and Unwanted Software (MALWARE), pp. 11–20, October 2015

40. Schmitt, F., Gassen, J., Gerhards-Padilla, E.: PDF scrutinizer: detecting Javascript-based attacks in PDF documents. In: 2012 Tenth Annual International Conference on Privacy, Security and Trust, pp. 104–111. IEEE (2012)

41. Schumilo, S., Aschermann, C., Gawlik, R., Schinzel, S., Holz, T.: KAFL: hardware-assisted feedback fuzzing for OS Kernels. In: 26th USENIX Security Symposium, USENIX Security 2017, pp. 167–182. USENIX Association (2017)

42. Sebastián, M., Rivera, R., Kotzias, P., Caballero, J.: AVCLASS: a tool for massive malware labeling. In: Monrose, F., Dacier, M., Blanc, G., Garcia-Alfaro, J. (eds.) RAID 2016. LNCS, vol. 9854, pp. 230–253. Springer, Cham (2016). https://doi.org/10.1007/978-3-319-45719-2_11

43. Smutz, C., Stavrou, A.: Malicious PDF detection using metadata and structural features. In: Proceedings of the 28th Annual Computer Security Applications Conference, pp. 239–248. ACM (2012)

44. Snow, K.Z., Krishnan, S., Monrose, F., Provos, N.: SHELLOS: enabling fast detection and forensic analysis of code injection attacks. In: USENIX Security Symposium, pp. 183–200 (2011)

45. Šrndic, N., Laskov, P.: Mimicus: a library for adversarial classifier evasion (2016)

46. Tzermias, Z., Sykiotakis, G., Polychronakis, M., Markatos, E.P.: Combining static and dynamic analysis for the detection of malicious documents. In: Proceedings of the Fourth European Workshop on System Security, p. 4. ACM (2011)

47. Willems, C., Freiling, F.C., Holz, T.: Using memory management to detect and extract illegitimate code for malware analysis. In: Proceedings of the 28th Annual Computer Security Applications Conference, pp. 179–188. ACM (2012)

48. Xu, M., Kim, T.: PlatPal: detecting malicious documents with platform diversity. In: 26th USENIX Security Symposium, USENIX Security 2017, pp. 271–287. USENIX Association (2017)

49. Xu, W., Qi, Y., Evans, D.: Automatically evading classifiers. In: Proceedings of the 2016 Network and Distributed Systems Symposium (2016)

An Analysis of Malware Trends in Enterprise Networks

Abbas Acar[1]([✉]), Long Lu[2], A. Selcuk Uluagac[1], and Engin Kirda[2]

[1] Florida International University, Miami, USA
{aacar001,suluagac}@fiu.edu
[2] Northeastern University, Boston, USA
l.lu@northeastern.edu,ek@ccs.neu.edu

Abstract. We present an empirical and large-scale analysis of malware samples captured from two different enterprises from 2017 to early 2018. Particularly, we perform threat vector, social-engineering, vulnerability and time-series analysis on our dataset. Unlike existing malware studies, our analysis is specifically focused on the recent enterprise malware samples. First of all, based on our analysis on the combined datasets of two enterprises, our results confirm the general consensus that AV-only solutions are not enough for real-time defenses in enterprise settings because on average 40% of the malware samples, when first appeared, are not detected by most AVs on VirusTotal or not uploaded to VT at all (i.e., never seen in the wild yet). Moreover, our analysis also shows that enterprise users transfer documents more than executables and other types of files. Therefore, attackers embed malicious codes into documents to download and install the actual malicious payload instead of sending malicious payload directly or using vulnerability exploits. Moreover, we also found that financial matters (e.g., purchase orders and invoices) are still the most common subject seen in Business Email Compromise (BEC) scams that aim to trick employees. Finally, based on our analysis on the timestamps of captured malware samples, we found that 93% of the malware samples were delivered on weekdays. Our further analysis also showed that while the malware samples that require user interaction such as macro-based malware samples have been captured during the working hours of the employees, the massive malware attacks are triggered during the off-times of the employees to be able to silently spread over the networks.

Keywords: Enterprises · Malware · Network

1 Introduction

Despite its ever-evolving nature, malware still is the most frequently encountered cyber threat in the world [6], severely impacting both enterprise and home networks. The damage caused may vary depending on the type of malware and digital assets accessible on the victim's network. Generally, a user has one or a

Z. Lin et al. (Eds.): ISC 2019, LNCS 11723, pp. 360–380, 2019.
https://doi.org/10.1007/978-3-030-30215-3_18

few devices connected to home network, while the number of systems connected to an enterprise network can vary from hundreds to thousands with a variety of security policies in place. This complexity of the enterprise networks brings new challenges for securing valuable assets on such networks.

Reports [8] show that enterprise and home users are exposed to different types of attacks because of their distinct day-to-day usage patterns. Therefore, attacks may also differ from each other in several ways. First, since attacks on enterprise networks can be very profitable, attackers can be extra motivated to use more sophisticated, advanced, and persistent methods (i.e., targeted attacks). Second, since enterprises prefer defense-in-depth approaches, which pose some restrictions on the use of the Internet and email for personal purposes, enterprise users may face less number of attacks but a wider variety of malware threats than the personal computer users [8]. Last but not least, as the attack surface is much larger on enterprise networks, with one insecure vector on the network (e.g., a misconfigured router), attackers can access the data of multiple users, and potentially stay undetected for longer periods of time.

Even though malware detection is a well-studied topic in the literature, only a few works [19, 20, 23, 24] have focused on malware samples encountered in real-world enterprises. These studies analyze security logs in order to extract intelligence on malware discovered in a specific enterprise. In another work [18], suspicious emails and malicious attachments were examined. Compared to these studies, in this work, we analyze the samples captured on-site inside two different enterprises, i.e., not only email attachments but also file downloads. Our work aims to shed some light on what kind of malware is seen in typical, high-profile enterprises today, what the infection vectors look like, and what trends do attacks follow.

In this study, we have access to a dataset of ≈3.6 million samples collected from two enterprises from 2017 to early 2018 (we call Organization A and Organization B to avoid disclosing their identity and security weaknesses). Particularly, all the file downloads and email attachments of the employers from two high-profile, global enterprises are collected and analyzed. Among all the samples, only 2,942 of them have been detected as malicious, and among malicious samples, the dataset includes 122 unique samples that have never been seen in the wild (i.e., not on VirusTotal (VT)), even as of the writing of this paper[1].

Moreover, this dataset has several unique features that other studies in literature do not have:

1. *The samples are captured on-site inside companies.* Previous studies in the literature of malware research use datasets of malware that were captured in the wild, or shared by AV companies. Hence, the malware being analyzed does not have any context for how and when the infection took place. However, our dataset has been captured through the sensors deployed on the real-world networks of two enterprises.
2. *Both the behavioral analysis and Virus Total (VT) reports have been obtained during both the time of capture (i.e., just after the sample has been captured).*

---

[1] July 2018.

To the best of our knowledge, we are not aware of any study using such a unique dataset.

3. *The samples are analyzed using an advanced behavioral analysis module that we have access to*[2] This module is able to detect 2,920 different malicious activities of the malicious samples and the list is always updated with newly discovered malicious behaviors.

We leverage this dataset to perform the empirical analysis of malware samples collected from two organizations. We characterize our analysis under five categories.

- **Overall characteristics analysis:** In this, we analyze the overall statistics of both benign and malicious files in the dataset to understand the characteristics of files received and sent by enterprise employers during their daily routines.
- **Threat vector analysis:** In this, we analyze the document types of malware used as a threat vector to infect the enterprise networks in our study.
- **Social-engineering analysis:** In this, we analyze the file names of the malware, and the content of the malware instances to understand how users are motivated to click on the malicious artifact.
- **Vulnerability analysis:** In this, we analyze the samples that have been labeled with a CVE number in terms of their distribution over time.
- **Time-series analysis:** In this, we analyze the distribution of malicious samples over time to understand the logic behind the time management of attackers.

1. On average, one out of two malicious samples in our dataset were not detected by AVs on VT while almost one out of five malicious samples were not found on VT during the time of capture of the sample.
2. Documents are the most frequently used file types in both enterprises with the frequency of 72% and 36%, respectively for Enterprise-A and Enterprise-B. However, our further threat vector analysis showed that the file type distribution of malicious files is same as all files. While the most malicious file types are documents , executable and jar are the most common two file types used in malicious samples received in Enterprise B.
3. Our threat vector analysis showed that 34% of all malware samples are received in the format of *jar* and those malware samples are labeled as being part of massive phishing email campaigns by both AVs, and the dynamic analysis module we had access to.
4. Our social-engineering analysis showed that 51% of the malicious documents are related to a financial matter (e.g., purchase order, invoice) noting that financial subjects are the most used subjects in BEC scams. However, contrary to reports [6], we also found that 23% of all document-based malware samples are organizational-looking (e.g., attached CV) files.

---

[2] We explain the details of the analysis module in Sect. 3.

5. Our vulnerability analysis revealed that 80% of the malware samples exploiting any CVE vulnerability are using the CVEs released in the year of 2017. This shows that attackers follow recent exploits, and use them more than they use older exploits. We also verified other works [18] that all of the samples utilizing an exploit has been captured after their publish date.

6. Finally, our time-series analysis revealed that as one would expect, the number of received malware during the work hours is a lot more than those captured during off times – assuming that the employees work from 8 am to 5 pm during weekdays. In contrast, there have been reports [9,13] that have shown that some large-scale, non-human interaction requiring attacks occurred during the weekend.

2   Scope, Dataset, and Privacy

In this section, we explain the scope of the paper and the characteristics of our dataset.

2.1   Scope

Enterprise malware is not well-studied in literature because gaining access to malware samples captured by enterprises is generally difficult. However, understanding the nature of the threats that enterprise users have been exposed to during their daily works is important as such threats may result in catastrophic outcomes.

Table 1. Summary of our dataset collected from two different organizations.

Organization	Time interval	# Samples	Malicious samples (%)
A	Jan 2017–Feb 2018	3,192,452	243 (0.008 %)
B	Feb 2017–Jan 2018	463,476	2,699 (0.582 %)
Total	Jan 2017–Feb 2018	3,655,928	2,942 (0.081 %)

Compared to home users, as a part of their daily work, the enterprise users receive and send a lot more files, especially documents. Email is the most common way of communicating and transferring files, which makes it also the most common threat vector [2,5]. However, other than allowing us to have access to email attachments and file downloads, our dataset does not include information related to the infection vector. That is, we do not have access to the contents of the emails, email headers (e.g., from, to, subject), or security logs inside the enterprise. Clearly, such information would greatly help to an analysis like ours in this work, but such information is typically difficult to acquire because of privacy concerns.

2.2 Dataset

Every file downloaded, including email attachments from two enterprises during one year, have been captured through the sensors deployed at the organizations. Sensors scan the incoming and outgoing network traffic, the traffic within the network, as well as the host activity on the network. As the sensors are directly installed on end-users' systems, they have access to the unencrypted payload. Samples are sent to the back-end of the security company that we gained access to, and all the samples are analyzed in an isolated sandbox during the time of the capture.

Our dataset includes reports of both benign and malicious samples, which are indexed based on their hashes and as well as the raw malicious files. Moreover, we have access to reports generated at different times. Both behavioral analysis results and VT results of all files have been generated at the instant of the capture. Moreover, since VT results may change over time, we also checked the VT results during the time of the experiment.[3] Particularly, the dataset includes the analysis result of $\approx$3.65 million samples (3.2M from A and 450K from B), which have been captured from two organizations, namely A and B[4], starting from January 2017 to February 2018. The maliciousness occurrences of samples collected from A is 0.582 %, i.e., almost every 6 files out of a thousand files an employee in the organization works on are malicious, and it is much less than 1 in a thousand in organization B. As we mentioned earlier, we also have the raw binaries of 2940 malicious samples. In the following sections, we analyze the characteristics of the malicious samples in more detail. Table 1 is the summary of main characteristics of our dataset.

1. Behavioral analysis results:
   (a) Metadata
       i. Timestamp
       ii. Hash (i.e., SHA1)
       iii. File type
       iv. Mime type
   (b) The list of malicious behaviors
2. VT results
   (a) VT result (e.g., detection ratio, label) at the instant of the capture
   (b) VT result during the time of the experiment[5]
3. Malicious raw binaries

2.3 Privacy

Note that even though we have the privilege of having a unique, real-world attack datasets from two high-profile organizations, due to privacy policies, our analysis has some limitations. In particular, we could not correlate the captured data, and some features that are unique to the enterprises (e.g., such as the industrial sector that they are active in).

---

[3] July 2018.

[4] For privacy reasons, we do not disclose the company names.

[5] July 2018.

3   Analysis of Samples

In this section, we explain our analysis methods, results and labeling procedure. Particularly, we used two types of analysis results to label the samples: An advanced Dynamic Analysis (DA) module that was provided to us, and Virus-Total (VT).

Dynamic Analysis Module Reports. The DA module is an advanced malware detection and analysis module that runs the samples in a sandbox and monitors their behaviors. It is capable of running the sample in an appropriate environment for different file types. For example, if the sample is an executable or document file (e.g., word, pdf), it is directly run in the proper OS (e.g., Windows) environment and its behaviors are monitored. However, if it is, for example, an archive file (e.g., zip, jar), it will be decompressed first, and then executed. In addition, if it is an HTML or URL type of sample, it will be executed in an instrumented or emulated browser. A malware sample, sometimes, can run inside more than one environment. For example, a JavaScript file can be executed by loading it in a browser as well as run directly on the operating system. While the sample reveals malicious behavior in an environment, it may not reveal in another environment. In total, 2,920 different malicious sub-behaviors under 35 total categories (e.g., evasion, packer, macro, signature) are extracted. A sample is tested against all these malicious behaviors. If the sample shows a particular malicious behavior, that specific behavior has been added to the report. The report includes all of the malicious behaviors that have been revealed by the sample. A sample report that is generated after monitoring the behaviors of the sample is given in Appendix A.

After acquiring the reports of malicious behaviors and sub-behaviors, in order to classify the sample, every malicious behavior category (e.g., evasion, packer) is converted into a boolean value according to the detection of the malicious sub-behavior from that category. After that, every value is multiplied with its unique weight and summed. The final result is called a "score". If the score of a sample is less than 30, it is labeled as benign. If it is larger than 70, the sample is labeled as malicious. Samples with a score between 30 and 70 are labeled as suspicious. Note that we improve this simple classification by re-labeling the samples using the strategy in Table 2.

Table 2. Ground truth labeling strategy. DA score has been obtained through the dynamic analysis module and VT positives is the number of AV detection of the given sample on VT.

VT positives

DA module	Malicious(>3)	Benign(<=3)	NotFound
Malicious(>70)	❶-Malicious (2,685)	❷-Suspicious (128)	❸-Malicious (127)
Suspicious([30,70])	❼-Malicious (128)	❽-Suspicious (449)	❾-Suspicious (92)
Benign(<30)	❹-Suspicious (285)	❺-Benign (~3.6 M)	❻-Benign (20,628)

VirusTotal Reports. We also checked the analysis results of the samples on VT. As our dataset is dominated by the samples labeled as benign by our DA module, the number of benign samples with 0 score are 99.8% (≈3.65M) of all samples. Therefore, we randomly selected a subset of benign samples, and checked those samples on VT. We observed that none are on VT – hence, not detected by AVs. However, we also checked all other 19,867 unique samples with any type of malicious behavior (i.e., score > 0) detected by our dynamic analysis on VT. In order to avoid false positives of VT, we chose the threshold detection number of 3 [21]. That is, if a sample is detected by more than 3 AVs on VT, we say that the sample is labeled as malicious by VT. Otherwise, it is labeled as benign by VT.

Ground Truth. In order to obtain a ground truth for the labels of the samples in our dataset, we use both the reports generated by the DA module and VT. Even though there is a consensus on some of the files, there are also inconsistencies between the DA module and VT. We follow the strategy in Table 2 in order to re-label the samples. In particular, if labels from both the dynamic analysis engine and VT match (❶ and ❺), the sample is labeled with the result of both tests, while if they contradict each other (❷ and ❹), we label them as suspicious. Moreover, not all of the samples were found on VT, where we had only DA module reports. For those (❸ and ❻), if it is not labeled suspicious (i.e., the score is not in [30, 70]) by the DA module, we labeled that sample with the result of that one report. Finally, if the sample is labeled by the DA module as suspicious, and found malicious by VT (❼), we label it as malicious. However, if there is no consensus between the DA module and VT, we label it as suspicious. ❽ and ❾ are labeled as suspicious because either there are not enough reports, or the samples are not exhibiting enough malicious behavior. The analysis of suspicious files has been left as a future work as the scope of this paper is to characterize the malicious files.

At the end of this labeling procedure, we classified every sample as either malicious, suspicious, or benign. In total, we have ≈3.6M benign, 3,767 suspicious, and 2,940 malicious samples. Note that in this classification, we used the most recent reports generated by VT, where we have also the VT reports generated during the time of capture.

4   Results

In this section, we present the results from a more detailed analysis and share our findings and insights. First, we analyze the overall characteristics of the dataset. Second, we analyze the file types of malicious samples to understand the threat landscape and infection vectors used in attacks. Third, we investigate the malicious documents in detail to understand the social-engineering techniques used to trick users. Fourth, we study the exploits and the corresponding CVEs found in our dataset. Finally, we compare the data from two organizations and discover the commonalities and differences from the time-series distribution of malware samples.

Table 3. Number of unique unclassified and undetected malware samples.

Organization	Class	AV label	AV detection during the time of capture	As of analysis (7/24/2018)
A and B	Malicious	Undetected	1,318 (47.7%)	121 (4.4%)
A and B	Malicious	Unclassified	514 (18.6%)	122 (4.4%)

4.1 Overall Characteristics Analysis

Unique Malicious Samples. We obtained the hashes of 2,940 malware samples. We observed 2,766 unique samples in total. These samples were checked on VirusTotal (VT) both at the time of capture and at the time of this analysis. We call a sample: (1) *unclassified* if it is not found on VT; (2) *undetected* if it is found on VT and detected by fewer than 3 anti-virus software (AV) on VT. We found that, at the time of capture, a small fraction of the unique samples already existed on VT and were detected by AVs; 47.7% of them existed on VT but were not detected by AVs (i.e., undetected); 18.6% of them had never been submitted to VT (i.e., unclassified). It is worth noting that AVs on VT are regularly updated with signatures of newly discovered malware. We found that the numbers of undetected and unclassified samples drop significantly months later at the time of this analysis. We also observed that most of those unclassified samples are in the format of the document. This result underlines the delayed detection by AVs and thus the unsuitability of AVs for immediate detection of malware attacks at their onset. Table 3 shows the sample counts and percentages of undetected and unclassified samples at the two different times.

Summary of Findings-1: As shown in Table 3, *at the capture time, almost one out of two malicious samples (1,318/2,763) in our dataset were not detected by AVs; almost one out of five malicious samples (514/2,763) had not been submitted to VT.* This shows the ineffectiveness of the AVs in real-time malware detection. However, AVs can still be useful as the first line of defense in the defense-in-depth solutions deployed in enterprises, in order to quickly filter out the previously discovered/reported malware samples. Moreover, we also found that AVs evolve over time by adding more samples to their database. The percentage of both undetected and unclassified samples dropped to 4.4% at the time of this analysis (i.e., months after the initial malware captures). However, there were still 121 unique malicious samples undetected by AVs and 122 unique samples never submitted to VT at that time. Note that unclassified and undetected files refer to different files, so in total, we can interpret it as 243 files can not be detected by AVs. Moreover, we also note that as we did not perform analysis on historical VT reports.

File Type Distribution. The types of samples are detected and reported by the DA module. Figure 1 shows the distribution of file types among all the samples in Organization A and B. The most common file type used in both A and B

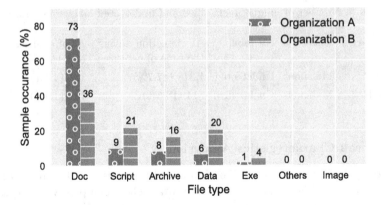

Fig. 1. File type distribution among all samples (≈3.65M samples), including both benign and malicious samples from Organization A and B. The figure shows that documents (e.g., doc, pdf) are the most common file types observed in enterprise networks whereas the executable file types are a lot less common.

is a document, as expected, with frequencies of 73% and 36% for organizations A and B, respectively. Since the number of benign samples is a lot more than the number of malicious samples, the distribution is dominated by benign samples. However, as this is also known to attackers, they can use documents to carry or hide a malicious payload in order to bypass detection heuristics based on file types. Moreover, it is also interesting to see that scripts such as JavaScript or PowerShell scripts are commonly used in these organizations for benign purposes. Although we have no visibility into what exactly scripts are used for, we can reasonably expect that may serve the purpose of automating workflows. We expect that the attackers may increasingly utilize scripts in order to infect enterprise computers and networks. Finally, we also observed that executable are much less common (respectively 1% 4% for A and B) than document-based samples. Therefore, considering that malicious payloads often exist in the form executables, it is more likely for executables propagated in company networks, especially from untrusted sources, to be malicious than documents.

Malware Type Distribution. In order to better understand the threat landscape in organizations, we also analyzed the types of malware samples in our dataset. The distribution of malware types observed in A and B is illustrated in Fig. 2.

We used the malware labels reported by the DA module. If a sample was undetected and unclassified by the DA module, we fetched the most recent labels from VT. We note that a sample often has different labels assigned by different AVs on VT and many of them tend to use overly generic labels (e.g., trojan). We picked more specific and descriptive labels, such as those from Microsoft and Kaspersky.

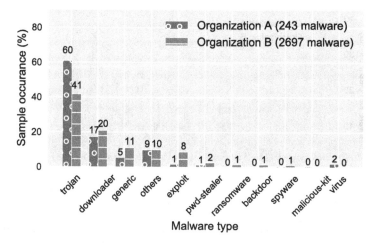

Fig. 2. Top-10 malware types in our dataset, where trojan is the most common malware type for both A and B. Moreover, downloaders are a lot more common than exploits, which shows that attackers prefers simpler methods like macro-based malwares over more advanced vulnerabilities.

Summary of Findings-2: The top-10 malware types in our dataset are shown in Fig. 2. The most common malware type in our dataset is trojan for both A and B. Trojan is a generic name and mostly used for labeling samples that are not associated with any malware family or do not contain enough malware family information. Therefore, as expected, the number of trojan samples is more than other types in both A and B. In the second place, we see the downloaders, counting for 17% and 20% of malware found in A and B, respectively. The downloaders are usually embedded to documents and infect the system by downloading and installing more malware at a later stage of infection. This hidden malware is more difficult to catch due to their limited and conditional exposure. Therefore, the methods based only on static analysis are not able to extract these samples, echoing the need for combining both static and dynamic analysis for malware discovery. The fourth in both Organization A and B is exploit, meaning that samples showing the behavior of a publicly disclosed CVE. *As shown in Fig. 2 compared to downloaders and trojans, we observe that both organizations receive less number of exploits.* This result matches the findings reported by some security companies [2,11]. It shows that the attackers are more often using simple methods (e.g., embedding malware using document macros) than employing advanced vulnerabilities. This is because the former is much less complex to carry out than the latter while still yielding good results on unwary or security-unconscious users in enterprises.

Average Malware Counts per Day. We analyzed how the capture/appearance of malware varies over time and if it exhibits any patterns. Figure 3

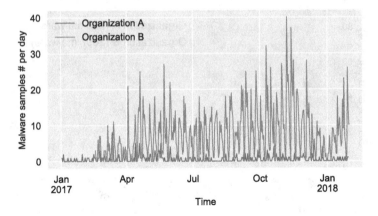

Fig. 3. The number of malicious samples captured per day. On average, A received 0.6 malicious and 8K benign samples per day while B received 7.7 malicious and 1300 benign samples.

shows the number of malicious samples captured per day in our dataset during the course of a year (Jan. 2017 to Jan. 2018).

Summary of Findings-3. According to Fig. 3, the number of malicious samples per day varies in the range from 0 to 8 for Organization A throughout the whole period whereas the same number fluctuates significantly and topped at 40 per day for Organization B. *On average, A received 0.6 malicious and 8K benign samples (downloads and email attachments) per day while B received 7.7 malicious and 1,300 benign samples per day.* B has seen 80 times more malicious samples than A. This discrepancy indicates that the risks of attacks and malware infection can vary a lot across different organizations and industry sectors, revealing attacks being driven by nature and potential value of the target businesses. Moreover, we tried to identify the cause to the spikes in Fig. 3. But we could not find any major security events or reports for those dates. We suspect that the spikes were resulted from some hidden attacks targeting that particular organization or sector.

4.2   Threat Vector Analysis

Attackers use not only executable files but also other types of files such as MS office documents (e.g. docx, xlsx) or archive files (e.g., jar, zip) to spread malware. Using documents, the attackers can embed the malicious code and run within a document itself. This embedding can happen in the form of, for instance, macros in MS Office documents and JavaScript (JS) in pdf files. Since MS Office 2016, macros have been disabled by default in documents [10]. Similarly, JS code has been disabled by default in PDF readers. Therefore, unlike executables, the malicious code does not execute in the first place when a user opens the document. Instead, the user is asked to "enable active content". To adapt to such security countermeasures, attackers now try to convince users to enable the macros and scripts using social-engineering techniques, e.g., showing images with fake warnings for users to "Enable content". When accompanied by very convincing messages or emails, users may easily fall for these tricks. Once the macros have been enabled, the embedded malicious code is triggered, which goes on to download and run the actual malware or full malicious payload. Moreover, Java (jar) archive files have been widely used and have seen a surge in recent malicious email campaigns [3], where the malicious payload is compressed (zip or rar) and attached to the email. This file format is preferred by the attackers as it is relatively less-known file type for malicious files. Plus, it benefits from the cross-platform nature of Java. In addition to macros and JS, we also observed other types of scripts. For example, PowerShell scripts have been used to infect Windows PC. In Fig. 4, we plot the 10 most malicious file types used in A and B, among which 6 are common between A and B.

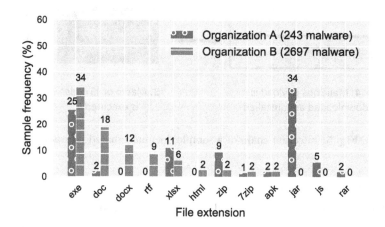

Fig. 4. Most malicious file types in A and B, where 6 of them are common.

Summary of Findings-4. Figure 1 shows that 73% and 36% of the files observed on the company networks are document-based files, compared to only 1% and 4% for executable files, for A and B, respectively. We found that Java archive files are the most common file type used in malware samples targeting B while executable files are the most common for A. Both types of files require manual actions to be triggered. Malware written in Java can run on any platform that has JVM (Java Virtual Machine) installed, i.e., does not require the knowledge of the system that the victim is using. Therefore, they are highly preferred for phishing email campaigns. We also saw the samples of commercial RAT (Remote Access Trojan), such as Jrat, Adwind, Jaraut. *For B, we observed that 34% of all malware samples are jar files and we also saw that all of the Java malware samples are labeled as part of phishing email campaigns by AVs. Therefore, one can reasonably suspect that the list of emails of A may have been leaked*

to attackers. Moreover, our results confirm the findings of the other reports [2,11]
that document-based malicious files are still highly preferred by attackers as they
are often considered safe by the average users.

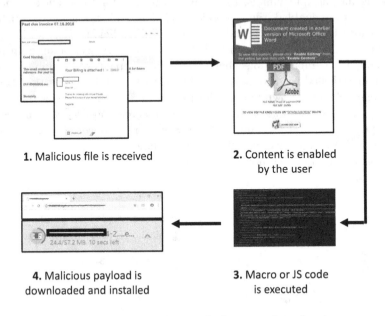

1. Malicious file is received   **2.** Content is enabled
                                              by the user

4. Malicious payload is   **3.** Macro or JS code
downloaded and installed   is executed

Fig. 5. Infection chain of a sample document-based malware.

4.3 Social-Engineering Analysis

According to recent reports published by Microsoft [8], there is a recent transition
from exploits to macro-based malware to infect endpoints. In our dataset, we
observed 1,370 malicious documents while there is only 158 samples associated
with a publicly known vulnerability. Even though macros have been disabled
by default since 2016, it continues to be a common threat vector for massive
pishing campaigns like Locky, Cerber [7]. This still poses threats mainly because
people fall victim to social engineering tricks, and in turn, grant permissions to
malicious samples. Therefore, it is important to understand and prevent social-
engineering techniques used by the attackers.

What happens if a user is tricked to enable the macros or JavaScript in
pdf documents? In order to find out, we also run the samples in an isolated
environment and observed their behaviors. Figure 5 shows the infection chain of
document-based malware samples. Malicious documents are usually received as
an attachment to emails, which direct users to enable dynamic content or scripts.
When a user does so, the code runs, downloads the actual malicious payload,
and then installs it on the victim's system.

Method. In order to understand the social-engineering techniques used by
attackers, we performed the following analysis. First, we analyzed the file names

of the samples when received by the victim. Since the samples in our dataset were renamed using their hash values, we fetched the original filenames of the documents from the VirusTotal's database. Second, we also analyzed the subject of the document as inferred from file names and actual file content. Based on inferred subjects, we categorized all the documents into several categories. We observed that some of the samples only include "content enable" images and do not have a meaningful file name. We categorized them as No-content files.

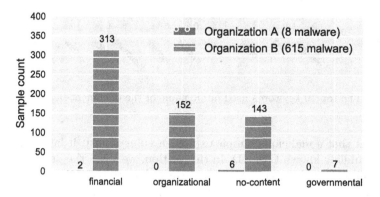

Fig. 6. Distribution of the subject in malicious documents. *51% (313/615) of the malicious documents Organization B received have been shown as related to a financial matter, while it is hard to comment on Organization A, as it has a very limited number of samples (36 samples.)*

Summary of Findings-5. The subject distribution is shown in Fig. 6. *51% (313/615) of the malicious documents Organization B received have been shown as related to a financial matter, which is similar to the results reported by Symantec* [12] *showing that financial subjects are the most used in business email compromise (BEC) scams. However, unreported in* [11] *, we found that 23% of all document-based malware pretends to be usual business files of various kinds. For example, emails related procurement orders and resumes are highly common in the malicious documents found in B. In order to better understand the techniques used by attackers, we also analyzed the file subject in more details and plotted the counts for each subject word (Fig. 7). The most commonly used keyword is "resume", accompanied by a name (e.g., "Rebecca-Resume.doc"). Other commonly used phrases are mostly related to finance such as "order", "invoice", or "payment". Moreover, their acronyms like "PO", "RTQ", "INV" etc. are also mostly preferred to trick the victim.*

4.4 Vulnerability Analysis

Newly discovered and reported vulnerabilities in software are assigned an ID, called CVE, as a uniform reference among vendors and security researchers. If

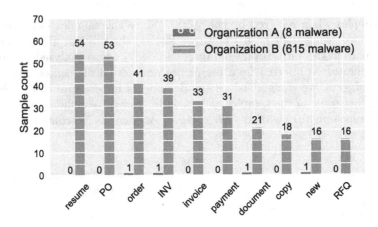

Fig. 7. The top 10 keywords used in file name of the document-based malwares.

AVs detect that a malicious sample exploits a vulnerability, it labels the sample with its publicly known CVE ID. In this section, we share the details about the vulnerabilities found in the samples and their characteristics.

Method. In order to tag the malware samples with a CVE identifier, we used three sources. The first one is our DA module. It matches the vulnerability behavior with the malware's behavior i.e., if the particular behavior is observed, the sample is labeled with the given CVE instead of malware type related to that behavior. Second, we used the labels provided by Microsoft and Kaspersky on VT. We observed 158 samples in total that use at least one vulnerability with a CVE. We observed a discrepancy between the samples labeled by them. For instance, five samples are tagged as the exploit of CVE-2014-1761 by Kaspersky and as CVE-2012-0158 by Microsoft. We counted those samples twice, which does not affect the overall results much due to the small numbers of such cases.

Table 4. List of CVEs in our dataset. *Publish Date, Affected product,* and *Vulnerability Type* are taken from [4]. *First seen on VT* and *Capture Time* are the respective dates for the first sample in our dataset. *AV detection ratio* is the average detection ratio of all samples tagged with a specific *CVE ID*.

CVE ID	Publish Date	First seen on VT	Capture Time	Count	Affected product	Vulnerability Type	AV detection ratio
2010-3333	2010-11-09	2017-05-09	2017-05-09	2	MS Office	Remote Code Execution	30/56
2012-0158	2012-04-10	2017-03-22	2017-03-22	22	MS Office	Remote Code Execution	32/58
2014-1761	2014-03-25	2017-08-21	2017-08-21	5	MS Office	Memory corruption	30/59
2015-1641	2015-04-14	2017-10-04	2017-10-10	5	MS Office	Memory corruption	31/59
2015-2545	2015-09-08	2017-09-08	2017-09-08	1	MS Office	Remote Code Execution	27/59
2017-0199	2017-04-12	2017-05-23	2017-05-23	64	MS Office	Remote Code Execution	31/58
2017-8570	2017-07-11	2017-08-30	2017-08-30	6	MS Office	Remote Code Execution	29/60
2017-8759	2017-09-12	2017-09-14	2017-09-19	33	MS .NET Framework	Remote Code Execution	27/59
2017-11882	2017-11-14	2017-11-22	2017-11-22	23	MS Office	Memory corruption	33/59

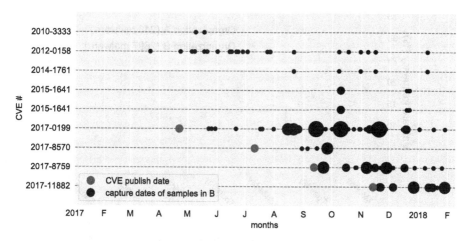

Fig. 8. Distribution of CVEs in our dataset over time. The size of the circle is proportional with the sample count at that time interval.

Summary of Findings-6. Table 4 shows the list of nine CVEs found in our dataset. Publish date, affected product, and vulnerability type are taken from [4]. First seen on VT and capture time are the respective dates for the first sample in our dataset. AV detection ratio is the average detection ratio of all samples tagged with a specific CVE ID. As shown in Table 4, *80% of the exploits are targeting the CVEs released in the year of 2017. This shows that attackers tend to use recent exploits for better results.* This is because many systems now automatically patch known vulnerabilities within a short window (e.g., a few months). The chances for a successful exploit is higher if more recent vulnerabilities are targeted than older vulnerabilities. This also shows that attackers are fast in following and leveraging new CVEs.

Moreover, we also saw that malware using CVE-2017-8759 appeared only two days after its release date. The first sample exploiting CVE-2017-8570 was captured 50 days after its public release. In general, we observed that *a sample exploiting a vulnerability can be seen in the wild after a period of a few months or even just days since the vulnerability disclosure.* Therefore, it is important to patch vulnerabilities as soon as possible. On the other hand, when we analyzed the samples for Organization B, we saw that *on average, B received the samples exploiting vulnerabilities three months after their disclosure dates.*

Figure 8 shows the distribution of exploits in our dataset over time in terms of their captured dates and initial disclosure dates. *In a similar work [18], it was shown that none of the exploits were used before their public disclosure. We also verify that all of the samples utilizing an exploit were been captured after the CVE disclosure dates.*

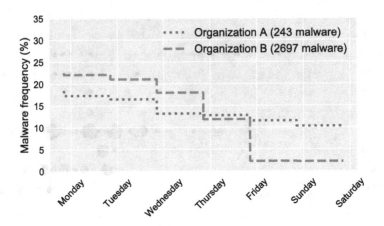

Fig. 9. Number of malware received per the days of the week.

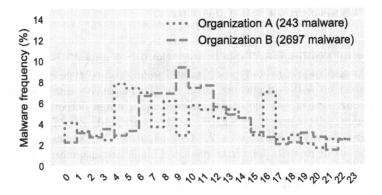

Fig. 10. Number of malware received per hours of the day.

4.5 Time Series Analysis of Malicious Samples

Attackers use many different techniques to trick users. Some of these tricks depend on proper timing. For example, employees may receive the malicious samples at a certain time of the day, or specifically on some days. In this section, we analyze these timing-related factors from the victim's perspective. We use the capture time of the malicious samples in our time series analysis.

Working Hours vs. Off-Times. According to the reports [1], the largest number of security threats are detected on weekdays, i.e., when employees are working on their computers. In order to verify if this pattern exists in our dataset, we plot the distribution of malicious samples frequency for each day of the week in Fig. 10 and for each hour during the day in Fig. 9.

Summary of Findings-7. Based on Figs. 9 and 10, *the number of received malware during the work hours is a lot bigger than that number for off-hours, assuming employees work from 8 am to 5 pm on weekdays.* However, there are also reports [9] and some massive attacks [13] contradicting with our finding. Especially, the attacks utilizing a vulnerability prefer weekends as they may want to spread over the network without being detected. However, the malware that require to be enabled by the victim are going to prefer working hours.

5   Related Work

Malware detection has been an active research area for years. There have been numerous studies [14–16, 22] working with large-scale malware dataset with the sizes of the datasets changing from a hundred thousand to millions and on different problems such as detection, clustering, indexing, etc. In all these studies, the samples captured different sources and were brought together for evaluating the proposed method, or collected in the wild, where the target entity is unknown. However, in practice, while it is known that home and enterprise users are known to have different threat landscapes, it is not clear if different enterprises actually have been targeted by different types of threats. In our study, we perform an analysis of such a dataset and provide the characterization of malicious samples captured from two different enterprises.

Enterprise Malware Detection. In the literature, there are only a few works [17,19,20,23,24] about enterprise malware. All of these studies analyze security logs in order to extract some intelligence related to malware encounters occurred in a specific enterprise. In another work [18], the authors analyze suspicious email collected from two members of an NGO, where both the content of the emails, and malicious email attachments were used for the analysis. Compared to the datasets used in these studies, our dataset was collected from specific commercial enterprises from 2017 to early 2018 and the samples were analyzed during the capture time with both a DA analysis module as well as VT. Note that to date, there have not been many scientific works that have reported on what kind of malware high-profile organizations are faced on a daily basis. In this paper, we aim to bridge that gap.

6   Conclusion

In this work, we presented an analysis of malware samples captured from two different enterprises from 2017 to early 2018. First, as one would expect, our analysis on the combined dataset showed that only-AV solutions are not effective in real-time defense because on average, 40% of the malware samples were either not detected at all, or have never been seen in the wild yet during the incident. Second, as employees in a typical enterprise work with more documents than executables, attackers mostly use documents as an attack vector. Hence, frameworks that allow the processing of documents in the cloud would provide better protection against many such attacks. In our vulnerability analysis, we also found that attackers use recently disclosed CVEs more than older disclosures. Additionally, after our social-engineering analysis, we also found that financial issues are still the most common subject used in social-engineering attacks against the enterprises that we analyzed.

Acknowledgments. The authors would like to thank the anonymous reviewers and our shepherd Dr. Yajin Zhou for their comments and suggestions, which significantly improve the quality and presentation of this paper. This work was partially supported by US National Science Foundation under the grant numbers NSF CNS-1514142, NSF CNS-1703454, NSF-CNS-1718116, NSF-CAREER-CNS-1453647, and ONR (Cyber-Phys).

A   A Sample Malicious Behaviours Report Generated by the DA Module

The list of malicious behaviours extracted via the DA module from a given sample:

"Anomaly: Found suspicious security descriptors for lowering the integrity level",
"Autostart: Registering for autostart during Windows boot",
"Evasion: Potentially malicious application/program",
"Evasion: Potentially malicious application/program (MMX stalling code detected)",
"Evasion: Targeting anti-analysis/reverse engineering",
"Evasion: Trying to enumerate security products installed on the system from WMI",
"Execution: Anomalous execution of VBScript file",
"Execution: Attempt to download / exec with javascript / vbscript code",
"Family: EICAR test sample",
"Packer: Potentially unwanted application/program (VMProtect)",
"Steal: Targeting Firefox Browser Password",
"Steal: Targeting Internet Explorer Browser Password",
"Steal: Targeting Opera Browser Password",
"Steal: Targeting Outlook Mail Password",
"Steal: Targeting Windows Saved Credential",
"Stealth: Creating executables masquerading as browser clients",
"Stealth: Creating executables masquerading as files from a Java installation",
"Stealth: Creating hidden executable files",
"Stealth: Modifying attributes to hide files"

B   Massive Malware Attacks in Our Dataset

The following is the list of most frequently captured malware samples in our dataset (Table 5).

Table 5. Massive malware attacks in our dataset.

Attack	Type	A-count	B-count	Infection	What it does
Donoff	Downloader	28	445	Email	Downloads Cerber
Skeeyah	Trojan	55	207	Email	Opens a backdoor
Tiggre	Trojan	13	120	Malicious website	Mines cryptocurrency
Madeba	Trojan	1	89	Email	Downloads another malware
Dynamer	Trojan	56	103	Dropped by other malware	Downloads another malware
Fareit	Spyware	39	87	Dropped by other malware	Steals sensitive information
Bluteal	Trojan	0	45	Dropped by other malware	Gives remote access
Occamy	Trojan	2	37	Dropped by other malware	Steals sensitive information
Locky	Ransomware	0	31	Email	Encrypts files
Nemucod	Ransomware	38	45	Email	Encrypts files

References

1. 2017 Q2 quarterly threat report. https://www.esentire.com/resources/knowledge/2017-q2-quarterly-threat-report/. Accessed 28 Sept 2018
2. 2017 state of malware. https://www.malwarebytes.com/pdf/white-papers/CTNT-Q4-17.pdf?aliId=91372483. Accessed 25 Sept 2018
3. Combating a spate of java malware with machine learning in real-time. https://cloudblogs.microsoft.com/microsoftsecure/2017/04/20/combating-a-wave-of-java-malware-with-machine-learning-in-real-time/. Accessed 17 Sept 2018
4. CVE details. The ultimate security vulnerbility datasource. https://www.cvedetails.com/. Accessed 20 Sept 2018
5. Data Breach Investigations Report (DBIR). https://www.verizonenterprise.com/resources/reports/rp_DBIR_2018_Report_en_xg.pdf. Accessed 20 Sept 2018
6. ENISA threat landscape report 2017. https://www.enisa.europa.eu/publications/enisa-threat-landscape-report-2017/at_download/fullReport. Accessed 23 Sept 2018
7. Fireeye warns 'massive' locky ransomware campaign hits America. https://blog.knowbe4.com/fireeye-warns-massive-locky-ransomware-campaign-hits-america. Accessed 25 Sept 2018
8. Microsoft security intelligence report volume 20—July through December 2015. http://download.microsoft.com/download/E/8/B/E8B5CEE5-9FF6-4419-B7BF-698D2604E2B2/Microsoft_Security_Intelligence_Report_Volume_20_English.pdf. Accessed 23 Sept 2018
9. More cyber-attacks occur on weekends than a weekday, study reveals. http://www.eweek.com/security/more-cyber-attacks-occur-on-weekends-than-a-weekday-study-reveals. Accessed 28 Sept 2018

10. New feature in office 2016 can block macros and help prevent infection. https://cloudblogs.microsoft.com/microsoftsecure/2016/03/22/new-feature-in-office-2016-can-block-macros-and-help-prevent-infection/. Accessed 17 Sept 2018

11. Symantec 2017 internet security threat report. https://www.symantec.com/content/dam/symantec/docs/reports/istr-22-2017-en.pdf. Accessed 25 Sept 2018

12. Symantec 2017 internet security threat report. https://www.symantec.com/content/dam/symantec/docs/reports/istr-23-2018-en.pdf. Accessed 16 Oct 2018

13. What is wannacry ransomware and why is it attacking global computers?. https://www.theguardian.com/technology/2017/may/12/nhs-ransomware-cyber-attack-what-is-wanacrypt0r-20. Accessed 25 Sept 2018

14. Bayer, U., Comparetti, P.M., Hlauschek, C., Kruegel, C., Kirda, E.: Scalable, behavior-based malware clustering. In: NDSS, vol. 9, pp. 8–11. Citeseer (2009)

15. Hu, X., Chiueh, T.C., Shin, K.G.: Large-scale malware indexing using function-call graphs. In: Proceedings of the 16th ACM Conference on Computer and Communications Security, pp. 611–620. ACM (2009)

16. Invernizzi, L., et al.: Nazca: detecting malware distribution in large-scale networks. In: NDSS, vol. 14, pp. 23–26 (2014)

17. Kotzias, P., Bilge, L., Vervier, P.A., Caballero, J.: Mind your own business: a longitudinal study of threats and vulnerabilities in enterprises. In: NDSS (2019)

18. Le Blond, S., Uritesc, A., Gilbert, C., Chua, Z.L., Saxena, P., Kirda, E.: A look at targeted attacks through the lense of an NGO. In: USENIX Security Symposium, pp. 543–558 (2014)

19. Li, Z., Oprea, A.: Operational security log analytics for enterprise breach detection. In: 2016 IEEE Cybersecurity Development (SecDev), pp. 15–22, November 2016. https://doi.org/10.1109/SecDev.2016.015

20. Oprea, A., Li, Z., Yen, T., Chin, S.H., Alrwais, S.: Detection of early-stage enterprise infection by mining large-scale log data. In: 2015 45th Annual IEEE/IFIP International Conference on Dependable Systems and Networks, pp. 45–56, June 2015. https://doi.org/10.1109/DSN.2015.14

21. Perdisci, R., Lanzi, A., Lee, W.: McBoost: boosting scalability in malware collection and analysis using statistical classification of executables. In: 2008 Annual Computer Security Applications Conference (ACSAC), pp. 301–310. IEEE (2008)

22. Tamersoy, A., Roundy, K., Chau, D.H.: Guilt by association: large scale malware detection by mining file-relation graphs. In: Proceedings of the 20th ACM SIGKDD International Conference on Knowledge Discovery and Data Mining, pp. 1524–1533. ACM (2014)

23. Yen, T.F., Heorhiadi, V., Oprea, A., Reiter, M.K., Juels, A.: An epidemiological study of malware encounters in a large enterprise. In: Proceedings of the 2014 ACM SIGSAC Conference on Computer and Communications Security, CCS 2014, pp. 1117–1130. ACM, New York (2014). https://doi.org/10.1145/2660267.2660330

24. Yen, T.F., et al.: Beehive: large-scale log analysis for detecting suspicious activity in enterprise networks. In: Proceedings of the 29th Annual Computer Security Applications Conference, ACSAC 2013, pp. 199–208, ACM, New York (2013). https://doi.org/10.1145/2523649.2523670

L(a)ying in (Test)Bed
How Biased Datasets Produce Impractical Results for Actual Malware Families' Classification

Tamy Beppler, Marcus Botacin, Fabrício J. O. Ceschin, Luiz E. S. Oliveira, and André Grégio[✉]

Federal University of Paraná (UFPR), Curitiba, PR, Brazil
{tebeppler,mfbotacin,fjoceschin,lesoliveira,gregio}@inf.ufpr.br

Abstract. The number of malware variants released daily turned manual analysis into an impractical task. Although potentially faster, automated analysis techniques (e.g., static and dynamic) have shortcomings that are exploited by malware authors to thwart each of them, i.e., prevent malicious software from being detected or classified accordingly. Researchers then invested in traditional machine learning algorithms to try to produce efficient, effective classification methods. The produced models are also prone to errors and attacks. Novel representations of the "subject" were proposed to overcome previous limitations, such as malware textures. In this paper, our initial proposal was to evaluate the application of texture analysis for malware classification using samples collected in-the-wild in order to compare them with state-of-the-art results. During our tests, we discovered that texture analysis may be unfeasible for the task at hand, if we use the same malware representation employed by other authors. Furthermore, we also discovered that naive premises associated to the selection of samples in the datasets caused the introduction of biases that, in the end, produced unreal results. Finally, our tests with a broader unfiltered dataset show that texture analysis may be impractical for correct malware classification in a real world scenario, in which there is a great variety of families and some of them make use of quite sophisticate obfuscation techniques.

Keywords: Malware classification · Texture analysis · Malware visualization

1 Introduction

Malware is one of the biggest threats to networked systems. Despite the myriad of defensive tools and techniques, malware writers constantly evolve their code to prevent detection. A multitude of variants emerge from automated malware creation toolkits that, even resulting in samples with few differences from each

This study was financed in part by the Coordenação de Aperfeiçoamento de Pessoal de Nível Superior - Brasil (CAPES) - Finance Code 001.

© Springer Nature Switzerland AG 2019
Z. Lin et al. (Eds.): ISC 2019, LNCS 11723, pp. 381–401, 2019.
https://doi.org/10.1007/978-3-030-30215-3_19

other, are capable of accomplishing undetectable artifacts [2]. Due to that, security researchers are stuck in an eternal arms race with malware developers, so as to discover new ways for protection whereas understanding incoming menaces.

Classifying a file as malicious requires knowing its features. Analysis techniques are used to extract features that can be used to further malware categorization (by intent, functionality, damage etc.) and better understanding of the threats they pose. However, current malware detection techniques are slow to react to new attacks and threats, since they are based on overwhelming static and/or dynamic analysis to obtain and match malicious patterns against files. To gain speed, Nataraj et al. [20] proposed the use of texture analysis—fast, accurate, and resilient to obfuscation techniques, according to the authors—to change the malware classification problem into an image recognition one.

Image processing techniques are largely used in many fields because they accomplish high precision for pattern recognition [36] tasks. By converting a binary file into a gray-scale texture, we can recognize a pattern for each family of files, thus potentially allowing for malware classification. The goal of this paper is to evaluate state-of-the-art texture analysis techniques for malware classification in a real-life, larger dataset, as well as to validate the claim of resilience against obfuscation. Our main contributions are threefold: (i) we analyze the literature on texture-based malware classification; (ii) we evaluate texture analysis techniques from literature in a publicly available malware dataset, and then in a private, broader, imbalanced dataset composed of malware samples collected in the wild; (iii) we compare these literature texture-based techniques for malware classification regarding the dataset used and the setup of the experiment, in order to discuss our discovery of biased results due to improper testing.

The remainder of this paper is organized as follows. In Sect. 2 we present the background and related work on texture analysis and malware classification. In Sect. 3, we show the methodology adopted for our experiments. In Sect. 4, we describe our tests and analyze the obtained results. In Sect. 5, we discuss our findings. Finally, in Sect. 6, we present the concluding remarks.

2   Background and Related Work

There are several ways to represent malicious software. Representation enables the extraction of distinctive features, which allow further classification. It is expected that samples from the same family have similar features. One representation may be the source code or instructions' flow, from which features can be obtained by static analysis. Another representation possible is the malicious program execution trace or the set/sequence of functions or system calls launched in runtime, from which features are extracted by dynamic analysis. The former prevents infection and evasion because the analysis is performed without execution and, according to [20], offers more complete coverage. However, static analysis may fail under binary obfuscation, such as the packing present in approximately 80% of malware samples [19]. Accomplishing wider code coverage may also be difficult if the malware developer uses opaque constants [18]. Both anti-analysis techniques increase the processing and memory costs, making static analysis unfeasible. The latter actually runs the sample in a controlled environment so as to obtain the execution behavior. Thus, dynamic analysis does not suffer from the same obfuscation techniques (packing, compressing, and encryption of original binary) than static, becoming more effective in certain cases [20]. However, it suffers from other evasion techniques, such as anti-emulation/virtualization, stalling, sleeping, and others, being slower and highly resource consuming. Combined, hybrid approaches were proposed to address the limitations of static and dynamic analysis, but the achieved results were similar in quality and worse in computational cost [6]. Therefore, a different way to extract malware features should be used to avoid evasion and obfuscation techniques, and, in an ideal case, be fast and cost less computing resources.

Malware Texture Analysis. Many applications use features extracted from textures to improve classification and recognition problems [3,5,31]. Conti et al. [4] mapped large binary objects by classifying regions using texture analysis and claimed that it can be used for malware identification. Based on that, Nataraj et al. [20] proposed an orthogonal approach using texture representations of malware for classification purposes. Similar to static analysis, texture analysis examines the binary without execution, i.e., it does not suffer with infection, evasion techniques, and obfuscation techniques, according to the claims of [20]. The texture representation preserves similar features even in obfuscated binary and, according to Zhang et al. [36], image recognition methods may improve malware detection. An image texture is a block of pixels with repeated patterns. In a malware texture representation, each byte of the binary file is converted to its correspondent value in a gray-scale image with fixed width and the binary's size divided by the fixed width as height. In Fig. 1, we show that samples from the same family may be similar among themselves, but distinctive from other families.

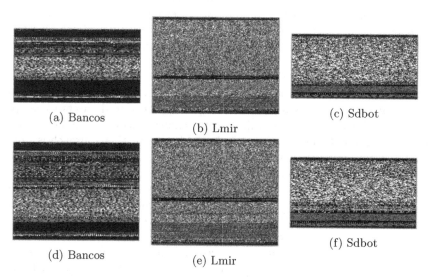

(a) Bancos   (b) Lmir   (c) Sdbot

(d) Bancos   (e) Lmir   (f) Sdbot

Fig. 1. Malware variant textures of different families from our dataset.

Although textures seem promising, since many authors use their analysis considering only similarities within families, not all samples produce textures that allow their comparison with other family members. Indeed, many samples neither are related to their families, nor distinguishable from other families' samples. It clearly difficults correct malware classification, as we can observe in Fig. 2, which illustrates selected samples harder to distinguish from the same dataset of Fig. 1. This observation makes us realize that the overwhelmingly great results presented in literature might have issues.

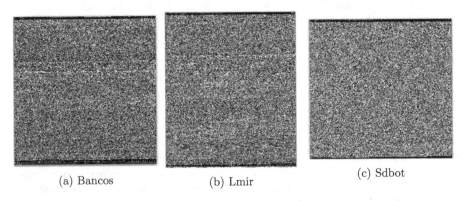

(a) Bancos   (b) Lmir   (c) Sdbot

Fig. 2. Other textures of variants from already seen families from our dataset.

Classification Techniques. Nataraj et al. [20] first proposed texture analysis for malware classification—they showed that it is possible to identify patterns among samples from the same family after converting their binaries into gray-scale textures. Using GIST descriptor and K-nearest neighbor (KNN) with euclidean distance, achieve 98% of accuracy. The authors affirm that it is a fast approach and agnostic to platform (while usually malware analysis techniques are made for a specific operational system). The possible disadvantages are binary section reallocation or insertion of amount redundant data. After that, the authors used Host-Rx, Malheur, and VX Heaven datasets to compare texture and dynamic analysis [22]. Texture analysis achieves similar accuracy 4,000 times faster than dynamic analysis. Additionally, this approach is said to be resilient to obfuscation techniques. Following the same strategy, Makandar and Patrot [15] use GIST and Gabor Wavelet Transform (GWT) descriptors to select features, and Artificial Neural Network (ANN) for malware classification with 96.35% accuracy rate on Malheur dataset. Makandar et al. [12] use Support Vector Machine (SVM) on the same dataset with accuracy of 89.68%.

Nataraj [19] proposed texture and signal analysis to try to discover unknown attacks due to the combination of orthogonal methods, since it is more difficult/expensive to build malware that evade all detection schemes. Applying GIST descriptor and KNN classifier to different platform datasets, the accuracy rate are 97.4%, 98.37%, 83.27% e 84.55% for Malimg (Windows), Malheur (Windows), VxShare (Linux) and Malgenome (Android) respectively. Kosmidis and Kalloniatis [8] followed the same approach with different machine learning classifiers (Decision Trees - DT, Nearest Centroid - NC, Stochastic Gradient Descent - SGD, Perceptron, Multilayer Perceptron - MLP and Random Forest - RF) to find the best solution for texture analysis. All of them achieve more than 87% on Malimg Dataset (the best was Random Forest; accuracy: 91.6%).

Luo and Lo [11] compared GIST to LBP with different classifiers (SVM, KNN and TensorFlow, a library for machine learning). LBP provided better accuracy in all cases, achieving 93.17% with TensorFlow. Discrete Wavelet Transform descriptor is used by Makandar and Patrot [14] with KNN and SVM classifiers. On Malimg Dataset it produced 98.8% accuracy rate with SVM and 98.84% with KNN. The authors changed the size of textures in [16] and with SVM classifier achieve accuracy of 98.53% on Malimg Dataset and 91.05% on Malheur dataset.

Convolutional Neural Networks (CNN) were used for malware texture classification by Yue [35] and it results in 98.63% accuracy rate on Malimg Dataset. Singh [30] used the Residual Networks (ResNet) architecture with 152 layers on his own dataset achieving 98.21% accuracy rate and, on Malimg Dataset, 96.08%. Rezende et al. [27] utilize CNN with Visual Geometry Group with 16 layers (VGG-16) architecture pre-trained on the ImageNet Dataset to extract features and, to classification, SVM that results in 92.97% of accuracy on Virus-Sign Dataset. SVM was also used in Makandar and Patrot [17], but the features were extracted with GWT on Malimg Dataset, the accuracy rate was 75.11%, and 89.11% when using KNN at the same conditions. CNN was also used by Yakura et al. [34] on VX Heavens dataset, resulting on 49.03% of accuracy. The same classifier was used by Kabanga and Kim [7] but they achieve 98% of accuracy on Malimg Dataset. The authors affirm that a small change on the image, even that invisible to a human, could cause a misclassification of image.

We observed that the descriptor affects accuracy rate [11]: the same dataset and classifiers used in [20] and [14] with different descriptors resulted in distinct accuracy rate. Although it is not possible to properly compare all research due to differences in datasets and resizing, we show the accuracy rate per classifier using GIST (Fig. 3) and other descriptors (Fig. 4). KNN performed better with other descriptors than LBP and GWT, followed by RF (only tested with GIST). SVM presented the worst results (except when applied in a reduced dataset) and may be considered inadequate to classify textures of these datasets.

Furthermore, as mentioned earlier, some classifiers select features automatically, i.e. do not need texture descriptors. Figure 5 displays the accuracy rate of CNN used on literature in different datasets. CNN with more layers (increasing depths) presents better accuracy, but exploding/vanishing of gradients and degradation problem may appear in deeper CNN [30]. Before select features, many authors resize the initial texture. Each malware binary has different size, which request resizing to use some descriptors. This size of input texture could interfere on classification results. Nataraj et al. [21] opt to set 64×64 as resizing value because a lesser value do not result in a robust signature and larger,

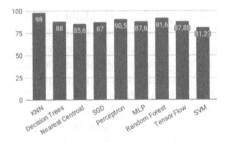

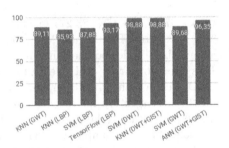

Fig. 3. Classification accuracy using GIST descriptor by classifier.

Fig. 4. Classification accuracy using different descriptors by classifier.

increase computational complexity. However, this value is attributed empirically and there are none consent about the best one. The differences between worst and best accuracy rate achieved with set values from literature are shown in Fig. 6. This graphic show us that, despite the better accuracy uses square of 64×64, it would be more prudent consider the resizing of 224×224 because it has lower variation and maintain a high accuracy rate in all cases.

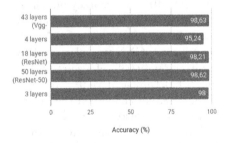

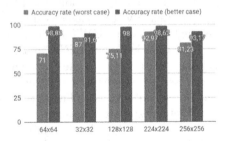

Fig. 5. Accuracy rate from different CNN architectures.

Fig. 6. Best and worst accuracy by resizing value.

For fair comparison, all studies should use the same dataset. We found eight different datasets used to malware texture classification. The most used is Malimg [20] (9,342 samples converted to textures distributed in 25 malware families). Table 1 exhibits basic information of each dataset and their achieved accuracy, and shows that the dataset with more families has a decrease of accuracy rate. It is worth to emphasize that each work applied different techniques, descriptors, and classifiers, which interfere with obtained results.

Considering only the classifier: KNN was used in [11,13,14,17,19,20,22], achieving the best result of literature in [13]; SVM was used in [11,12,14,16,17], with the same result as KNN in [14]; a comparison of many classifiers is in [8]; ANN is used in recent research [7,15,26,30,34]. Table 2 shows the state-of-the-art in malware texture classification and respective techniques and results.

Table 1. Datasets from literature used for malware families classification.

Dataset Name	Samples	Families	Accuracy (%)	Dataset Name	Samples	Families	Accuracy (%)
Host-Rx	393	6	95.14	MalGenome	1094	13	97.40
Malheur	3131	24	89.68 a 98.37	VXShare	568	8	83.27
VX Heaven	63002	531	72.80	Singh 2017	44945	20	95.24 a 98.21
Malimg	9342	25	75.11 a 98.88	VirusSign	10136	20	92.97

3   Methodology

To evaluate texture-based techniques, we follow Nataraj et al. methodology [9], illustrated in Fig. 7. The methodology steps are as follows.

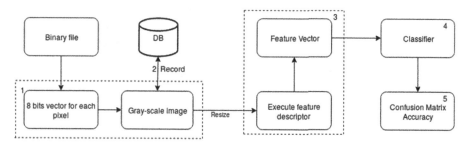

Fig. 7. Steps for malware texture classification.

Step 1: **Conversion of binary files into digital images:** each byte from binary file represents one gray-scale pixel (0, black; 255, white), following a defined width [19], while the heights vary according to the file size. This step is really fast, for instance to convert our dataset took 0.0163 s by sample.

Step 2: **Dataset organization:** before classification, we divide the samples into families according to the labels from VirusTotal [32]. We select the labels for our dataset with AVClass [29], similar to [19], in which the selected label is a common label between six antivirus (AV) vendors (AVClass uses all AV vendors).

Step 3: **Extraction of feature vector:** we compute the features from all samples after re-sizing their produced images, as suggested in [19]. To do so, we compared two descriptors (GIST and LBP) and performed a resize of 128×128, since it presented better results in our preliminary experiments when compared to the resize scales used in literature.

Step 4: **Supervised classification:** after the extraction of the feature vectors, we can classify the produced textures. In this paper, we used the same traditional classifiers of literature, and for the CNN algorithm we used the ResNet architecture from [26].

Table 2. Techniques used for malware classification based on texture analysis (n/i: no information available; ✗: no descriptor).

Ref.	Scale	Descriptor	Classifier	Accuracy (%)	Dataset
[20]	n/i	GIST	KNN	98.00	Malimg
[22]	64 × 64	GIST	KNN	95.14	Host-Rx
				97.57	Malheur
				72.80	VX Heaven
[15]	64 × 64	GWT + GIST	ANN	96.35	Malheur
[12]	n/i	GWT	SVM	89.68	Malheur
[19]	64 × 64	GIST	KNN	97.40	Malimg
				98.37	Malheur
				97.40	MalGenome
				83.27	VXShare
[13]	n/i	DWT, GIST	KNN	98.88	Malimg
[8]	32 × 32	GIST	DT	88.00	Malimg
			NC	85.60	
			SGD	87.00	
			Perceptron	90.50	
			MLP	87.80	
			RF	91.60	
[35]	n/i	✗	CNN	98.63	Malimg
[11]	n/i	LBP	CNN	93.17	Malimg
			SVM	87.88	
			KNN	85.93	
		GIST	CNN	87.88	
			SVM	81.23	
			KNN	82.83	
[14]	64 × 64	DWT	KNN	98.84	Malimg
			SVM	98.88	
[16]	256 × 256	DWT	SVM	91.05	Malheur
				92.53	Malimg
[30]	32 × 32	✗	CNN	95.24	Malshare+
			CNN (ResNet)	98.21	VirusShare + VirusTotal
			CNN (ResNet)	96.08	Malimg
[26]	224 × 224	✗	CNN (ResNet)	98.62	Malimg
[27]	224 × 224	✗	SVM	92.97	VirusSign
[34]	64 × 64	✗	CNN	49.03	VX Heaven
[17]	128 × 128	GWT	KNN	89.11	Malimg
			SVM	75.11	
[7]	128 × 128	✗	CNN	98.00	Malimg

Step 5: **Results visualization:** we used common classification metrics to show the obtained results. We opt to use accuracy rate, widely utilized in the literature, and confusion matrix, to better visualization of accuracy and error for each family.

Experimental Setup. We performed all experiments, but CNN, on a desktop computer (Ubuntu 16.04 LTS, Intel Core i5-650, 3 GHz 4 MB Cache and 4 GB RAM). CNN ran on a server (Ubuntu 14.04.3 LTS, Intel Xeon E5620, 2.4 GHz, 12 MB Cache, 32 GB RAM). An image descriptor is applied for extraction of meaning features only. In this research, we use a global (GIST [24]) and a local (LBP [23]) descriptor. The first is the most used in literature for malware texture classification, but global descriptors may lose information and classify incorrectly when redundant data is added or there is relocation of sections [20]. To address that, a local descriptor is used, LBP, which is widely used and well-known local descriptors due to its easy implementation and good results for texture-based classification. Both descriptors are used to extract features in a feature vector of textures with resizing of 128×128. We used `pyleargist` library to implement our GIST descriptor with 20 filters and 320 as dimension, and `scikit-image` [33] to our LBP descriptor, which is divided into 3 × 3 blocks (thus evaluating 8 neighbors), and applies the *uniform* method (rotation invariant and gray-scale).

Regarding the classification algorithms used here, we set the same parameters used in literature or, if not mentioned, the default from `scikit-learn` [25]. For the CNN classifier, we opt to use the technique proposed by Rezende et al. [26], since it achieves one of the highest accuracy rates and presents enough information to replicate the experiment. Our classification metrics were implemented with the `sklearn.metrics` module—accuracy rate and confusion matrices came from the `accuracy_score` and `confusion_matrix` functions, respectively. We selected data for training and testing with 10-fold cross-validation.

Datasets. We use two datasets, a publicly available one (Malimg) and a private, locally collected in our lab along the years. We do that because, for fair evaluation, we must have reliable, unbiased, not manipulated, correctly labeled datasets. The only way to maximize our chances of meeting these requirements is to use a public dataset already scrutinized and composed of few families to validate our preliminary premises and, after that, confirm if the hypothesis still holds when we use a private, bigger, unfiltered dataset closer to a real scenario. For our dataset (collected along the years), we follow Rossow et al. recommended practices for security experiments [28] and Li et al. advices on watching for biases in data selection [10]. Malimg [20] consists of 9,342 textures distributed into 25 malware families, and the dataset description is shown in Table 3. We found thirteen related work that used this public dataset in their experiments. Our local dataset consists of 19,979 unique malware distributed into 5,715 families, which we re-labeled with AVClass [29] on VirusTotal [32] labels. These samples were collected by a partner CSIRT and shared with our lab[1] since 2007. In Table 4 we show an excerpt of our dataset containing the most representative families (with at least 50 samples each). In our experiments, we used the whole dataset as well as some of its subgroups.

Table 3. Malimg dataset. Notice that variants may be in distinct families and that the two Allaple families correspond to almost half of the dataset.

	Class	Family	# variants	%
1	Worm	Allaple.L	1591	17.03
2	Worm	Allaple.A	2949	31.57
3	Worm	Yuner.A	800	08.56
4	PWS	Lolyda.AA 1	213	02.28
5	PWS	Lolyda.AA 2	184	01.97
6	PWS	Lolyda.AA 3	123	01.32
7	Trojan	C2Lop.P	146	01.56
8	Trojan	C2Lop.gen!G	200	02.14
9	Dialer	Instantaccess	431	04.61
10	Trojan Downloader	Swizzor.gen!I	132	01.41
11	Trojan Downloader	Swizzor.gen!E	128	01.37
12	Worm	VB.AT	408	04.37
13	Rogue	Fakerean	381	04.09
14	Trojan	Alueron.gen!J	198	02.12
15	Trojan	Malex.gen!J	136	01.46
16	PWS	Lolyda.AT	159	01.70
17	Dialer	Adialer.C	125	01.34
18	Trojan Downloader	Wintrim.BX	97	01.04
19	Dialer	Dialplatform.B	177	01.89
20	Trojan Downloader	Dontovo.A	162	01.73
21	Trojan Downloader	Obfuscator.AD	142	01.52
22	Backdoor	Agent.FYI	116	01.24
23	Worm:AutoIT	Autorun.K	106	01.13
24	Backdoor	Rbot!gen	158	01.69
25	Trojan	Skintrim.N	80	00.86

---

[1] Additional information about samples will be available after acceptance to do not violate the conference blindness requirement.

Table 4. Description of an excerpt of our dataset (families with samples ≥50).

	Class	Family	# variants	%
1	Backdoor	Agobot	202	02,86
2	Backdoor	Aimbot	73	01,03
3	Worm	Bagle	138	01,96
4	Trojan Banker	Banbra	75	01,06
5	Trojan	Bancos	327	04,63
6	Trojan Downloader	Banload	215	03,05
7	Backdoor	Bifrose	128	01,81
8	Trojan	Constructor	110	01,56
9	Trojan Downloader	Dadobra	145	02,05
10	Trojan	Delf	1267	17,96
11	Trojan Downloader	Dyfuca	84	01,19
12	Trojan	Goldun	58	00,82
13	Trojan	Harnig	58	00,82
14	Virus	Hllc	61	00,86
15	Virus	Hllo	60	00,85
16	Backdoor	Hupigon	332	04,71
17	Trojan Downloader	Inservice	115	01,63
18	Backdoor	Ircbot	151	02,14
19	Trojan Downloader	Istbar	199	02,82
20	Worm	Kelvir	82	01,16
21	Trojan PSW	Ldpinch	123	01,74
22	Trojan PSW	Lineage	101	01,43
23	Trojan	Lmir	410	05,81
24	Trojan	Lowzones	60	00,85
25	Worm	Mytob	86	01,22
26	Trojan	Nsanti	50	00,71
27	Backdoor	Pcclient	79	01,12
28	Trojan PSW	Qqpass	123	01,74
29	Trojan	Qqrob	58	00,82
30	Backdoor	Ranky	72	01,02
31	Backdoor	Rbot	909	12,88
32	Virus	Score	120	01,70
33	Backdoor	Sdbot	685	09,71
34	Worm	Spybot	122	01,73
35	Trojan Downloader	Swizzor	56	00,79
36	Backdoor	Wootbot	63	00,89
37	Trojan	Zlob	59	00,84

4   Experiments and Results

In this section, we reproduce literature experiments using both publicized datasets and our malware collection and evaluate classifiers resistance to obfuscation.

Reproducing Literature Results. To validate reported literature results, we first reproduced their experiments using the same dataset (Malimg) and parameters described in the considered papers (GIST and LBP descriptors and 32×32, 64×64 and 128×128 (standard) texture's scales). The first experiment consists on identifying the best algorithm and feature extractors for texture classification. Table 5 shows the accuracy rate for all algorithms and feature extractors applied to the complete Malimg dataset. The higher accuracy rates (above 90%) for all classifiers are achieved using the GIST descriptor. The CNN classifier without a descriptor also achieves high accuracy.

Table 5. Texture descriptors & classifiers accuracy evaluation. GIST descriptor achieves higher detection rates than LBP in most classifiers. ([1]: direct mapping without texture descriptor; [2]: resize from literature; [3]: standardized scale).

Classifier	CNN[1]	KNN	DT	RF	NC	SVM	SGD	Perceptron	MLP
GIST[2]	N/A	96.97	93.06	95.23	91.33	95.23	91.44	90.03	95.99
LBP[2]	N/A	85.59	69.34	78.66	47.02	53.41	37.38	30.88	71.07
GIST[3]	N/A	97.94	96.32	97.83	96.42	95.88	94.58	91.33	96.42
LBP[3]	N/A	95.77	92.96	95.67	84.72	51.25	40.41	66.41	83.31
N/A	98.57	N/A	N/A	N/A	N/A	N/A	N/A	N/A	N/A

Understanding Classifier's Errors. While some combinations of feature extractors and classifiers achieve high accuracy results in the complete Malimg dataset, most combinations do not present accuracy results high enough to be considered practical in actual contexts, due to either the low TP rates or high FP rates, which contradicts published literature results.

To understand classifier's errors, we performed an in-depth investigation on how they classified each malware sample. We discovered that all classifiers errors occur on malware families that are very similar among themselves, thus producing very similar texture patterns. Table 6 shows that both RF and CNN classifier confuse the families `Swizzor.gen!E` (Fig. 8) and `Swizzor.gen!I` (Fig. 9).

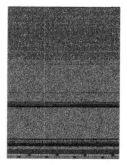 

Table 6. RF & CNN confusion matrices: classifiers mix samples from `Swizzor.gen!E` and `Swizzor.gen!I` families.

Samples	S.gen!E	S.gen!I	Allaple
S.gen!E	**99**	48	0
S.gen!I	48	38	0
Allaple	0	0	**100**

Fig. 8. `Swizzor.gen!E`   **Fig. 9.** `Swizzor.gen!I`

The classifier's confusion between similar families suggests that current texture-based approaches are only able to detect completely distinguishable families, as already pointed out by studies in other scenarios [10]. Therefore, we repeated our experiments, but now limiting the dataset to the samples used in [13], with no conflict between similar families. Table 7 shows accuracy rates for distinct classifiers and feature extractors combinations. The GIST descriptor keeps overperforming LBP for most scenarios, as in the complete dataset, but now achieving an accuracy of 100%. LBP classifiers also increased their rates, showing that similar families is an issue for all types of classifiers and feature extractors.

Table 7. Texture descriptors & classifiers accuracy evaluation. GIST descriptor achieves higher detection rates than LBP for most classifiers: 100% of accuracy happens due to the selection of dissimilar families for the experiment. ([1]direct mapping without texture descriptor; [2]literature resizing; [3]standard scale).

Classifier	CNN[1]	KNN	DT	RF	NC	SVM	SGD	Perceptron	MLP
GIST[2]	N/A	100.00	99.81	99.81	97.91	99.81	99.43	91.63	99.81
LBP[2]	N/A	99.24	96.77	99.05	71.10	78.90	73.76	86.50	90.87
GIST[3]	N/A	100.00	99.81	100.00	99.05	100.00	100.00	100.00	100.00
LBP[3]	N/A	99.43	98.67	99.43	94.68	78.52	78.33	87.26	91.44
N/A	99.87	N/A	N/A	N/A	N/A	N/A	N/A	N/A	N/A

These experiments results show that current texture-based approaches present best results when the considered malware families are clearly different, which is not acknowledge in the literature, thus highlighting the need for more granular and real-world considerations when developing and evaluating malware solutions.

Extending Evaluations to Other Datasets. Given the previous findings that the ability of existing texture-based classifiers is strongly tied to datasets having no similar families, we hypothesized that classifiers would not perform well when working with a real-world dataset, which is very imbalanced, thus presenting some families with multiple samples and other with a very limited number of samples. To test this hypothesis, we considered a dataset of Brazilian malware samples daily collected from a CSIRT institution and submitted all samples to classification procedures by the same classifiers and feature extractors from the previous tests. Table 8 shows accuracy results for all combinations of feature extractors and classifiers and, as hypothesized, all of them resulted in very low accuracy rates in this scenario closer to reality.

Table 8. Texture descriptors & classifiers accuracy evaluation. GIST descriptor achieves higher detection rates than LBP in most classifiers. Accuracy rate decreases significantly when using a scenario closer to reality. ([1]: resize from literature; [2]: standardized scale).

Classifier	KNN	DT	RF	NC	SVM	SGD	Perceptron	MLP
GIST[1]	34.36	14.46	18.87	04.10	27.90	11.08	10.05	29.85
LBP[1]	13.13	08.00	10.46	01.13	16.31	06.46	00.00	16.00
GIST[2]	35.08	19.49	23.18	03.69	28.51	13.33	04.10	29.54
LBP[2]	13.64	11.59	15.49	01.44	16.61	01.03	00.51	21.44

Since the experiments supported our hypothesis on the limits of applying texture-based classification in real scenarios, we investigated further to understand the practical factors limiting classification performance. We first discovered that classification rates were underscored due to families' clusters having too few samples. To mitigate this effect, we limited our real-world dataset to a set of 37 families that have at least 50 different samples each. We highlight that such number of distinct families is still higher than the ones from the publicized datasets. Table 9 shows classification accuracy for all algorithms and feature extractors using this new dataset. As expected, accuracy increased for all classifiers, but it is still not enough for operating in an actual scenario.

Table 9. Texture descriptors & classifiers accuracy evaluation. GIST descriptor achieves higher detection rates than LBP in most classifiers. Accuracy rate unsatisfying even when discarding small families. ([1]: direct mapping without texture descriptor; [2]: resize from literature; [3]: standardized scale).

Classifier	CNN[1]	KNN	DT	RF	NC	SVM	SGD	Perceptron	MLP
GIST[2]	N/A	49.13	26.09	38.84	10.72	32.32	12.03	17.39	38.98
LBP[2]	N/A	23.77	15.51	23.77	07.10	20.43	13.19	03.48	22.46
GIST[3]	N/A	48.84	29.13	43.04	15.36	35.36	26.09	20.87	41.01
LBP[3]	N/A	30.43	22.90	31.16	12.46	21.88	10.29	08.26	26.67
N/A	45.52	N/A	N/A	N/A	N/A	N/A	N/A	N/A	N/A

We also discovered that the number of families was also a factor for classifiers' rates underscoring. Therefore, we limited our dataset to the 10 most prevalent malware families, randomly choosing 100 samples from each one of them. Table 10 shows accuracy for all combinations of classifiers and texture extractors. In this new, limited dataset, classifiers achieved almost 80% of accuracy, which is a significant accuracy rate (but limited in number of families).

Table 10. Texture descriptors & classifiers accuracy evaluation. GIST descriptor achieves higher detection rates than LBP in most classifiers. Accuracy rate increases with balanced dataset and fewer families. ([1]: direct mapping without texture descriptor; [2]: resize from literature; [3]: standardized scale).

Classifier	CNN[1]	KNN	DT	RF	NC	SVM	SGD	Perceptron	MLP
GIST[2]	N/A	78.00	59.00	70.00	54.00	69.00	62.00	58.00	72.00
LBP[2]	N/A	63.00	37.00	46.00	43.00	43.00	11.00	13.00	41.00
GIST[3]	N/A	78.00	73.00	70.00	63.00	61.00	57.00	52.00	66.00
LBP[3]	N/A	67.00	52.00	64.00	32.00	34.00	12.00	10.00	43.00
N/A	76.50	N/A	N/A	N/A	N/A	N/A	N/A	N/A	N/A

Finally, to highlight that current texture-based malware classifier's effectiveness is limited to few malware families, we again limited our dataset, now to only the top 8 most prevalent malware families. Table 11 presents accuracy results for distinct combinations of classifiers and feature descriptors. As hypothesized, accuracy keeps increasing, now reaching scores greater than 84%.

Table 11. Texture descriptors & classifiers accuracy evaluation. GIST descriptor achieves higher detection rates than LBP in most classifiers. Accuracy rate increases with fewer families. ([1]: direct mapping without texture descriptor; [2]: resize from literature; [3]: standardized scale).

Classifier	CNN[1]	KNN	DT	RF	NC	SVM	SGD	Perceptron	MLP
GIST[2]	N/A	87.50	66.25	81.25	67.50	66.25	68.75	57.50	77.50
LBP[2]	N/A	62.50	42.50	50.00	37.50	53.75	23.75	27.50	47.50
GIST[3]	N/A	88.75	75.00	86.25	77.50	68.75	70.00	51.25	81.25
LBP[3]	N/A	76.25	67.50	77.50	47.50	46.25	35.00	66.25	52.50
N/A	84.75	N/A	N/A	N/A	N/A	N/A	N/A	N/A	N/A

Overall, our experiments indicate that: (i) KNN and CNN are the best malware texture classifiers; (ii) a 128 × 128 scale produces the greatest accuracy results; and (iii) the use of GIST results in greatest accuracy rates. On the one hand, our findings support the experiments conclusions from literature. On the other hand, we highlighted that these results do not hold true for actual scenarios, since current approaches are not fully capable of handling imbalanced dataset and a large number of families. Improving texture-based classifiers to handle these cases and make them practical is currently an open research question not acknowledge by the existing literature.

Evaluating Obfuscation Resistance. In addition to dataset imbalances, approaches tackling real-world scenarios will also face challenges to classify malware samples due to sample's characteristics themselves. For instance, statistics [1] report that more than 80% of malware files use some obfuscation techniques to avoid malware detection. The literature in texture-based malware classification reports that these approaches are resilient to obfuscation techniques [20] (in [19], UPX is used to demonstrate this resilience), but since they use static binary information for classification, it is doubtful that these approaches are able to correctly disambiguate obfuscated code. To test this hypothesis, we repeated all experiments now considering obfuscated binary versions. Based in the previous findings, we limited the dataset to the top 8 most prevalent malware families, a malware family range which previous experiments showed that texture-based malware detection is effective.

Evaluating Compression Resistance. In our first experiment we compressed all binaries with the popular ZIP and TAR.GZ tools, since compression reduces all redundancy that might allow family characterization. In addition, distributing compressed files via mail attachments is a popular strategy leveraged by attackers during their phishing campaigns, thus it constitute a real-world scenario. Table 12 presents accuracy results for ZIP-compressed files and Table 13 presents accuracy results for TAR.GZ-compressed files.

Table 12. Texture descriptors & classifiers accuracy evaluation. GIST descriptor achieves higher detection rates than LBP in most classifiers. Accuracy rate decreases with ZIP. ([1]: direct mapping without texture descriptor; [2]: resize from literature; [3]: standardized scale).

Classifier	CNN[1]	KNN	DT	RF	NC	SVM	SGD	Perceptron	MLP
GIST[2]	N/A	65.00	42.50	52.50	40.00	53.75	31.25	23.75	51.25
LBP[2]	N/A	28.75	23.75	32.25	30.00	18.75	16.25	12.50	30.00
GIST[3]	N/A	60.00	42.50	57.50	45.00	43.75	30.00	31.25	56.25
LBP[3]	N/A	30.00	35.00	35.00	30.00	26.25	13.75	12.50	20.00
N/A	45.75	N/A	N/A	N/A	N/A	N/A	N/A	N/A	N/A

All classifier were affected by binary compression and reduced their accuracy rates. The best classifier score lowered from 88% in the previous evaluation to 65% in the compressed dataset. The CNN classifier achieved only 45,75% in the ZIP dataset and 42,13% in the TAR.GZ dataset. These results are even more impacting when considered that we limited our evaluation to only the 8 most well-classified families. Therefore, these results suggests that texture-based classifiers are unable to distinguish armored samples, as following discussed.

Table 13. Texture descriptors & classifiers accuracy evaluation. GIST descriptor achieves higher detection rates than LBP in most classifiers. Accuracy rate decreases with TAR.GZ. ([1]: direct mapping without texture descriptor; [2]: resize from literature; [3]: standardized scale).

Classifier	CNN[1]	KNN	DT	RF	NC	SVM	SGD	Perceptron	MLP
GIST[2]	N/A	66.25	40.00	53.75	40.00	50.00	25.00	30.00	58.75
LBP[2]	N/A	27.50	23.75	31.25	31.25	22.50	12.50	12.50	37.50
GIST[3]	N/A	66.25	48.75	56.25	55.00	48.75	16.25	31.25	53.75
LBP[3]	N/A	31.25	36.25	40.00	30.00	25.00	12.50	12.50	21.25
N/A	42.13	N/A	N/A	N/A	N/A	N/A	N/A	N/A	N/A

Evaluating Packing Resistance. More than compression, malware samples can be distributed in completely modified versions, which can be done, for instance, by using a packer. To evaluate the impact of packing in texture-based malware classifiers, we packed all samples using The Ultimate Packer for eXecutables (UPX), a popular and open-source packing solution. The compression provided by UPX is greater than GZIP and it adds a decompression module to the executable [1], which makes samples to look like even more similar.

Table 14 shows classification accuracy for the distinct combinations of classifiers and feature descriptors. As hypothesized, classification accuracy is significantly reduced, as the textures now represents the packing structure and not the packed code. More specifically, the classification accuracy is almost the same for all classifiers. Our exploratory analysis identified that it happens because all samples are grouped to the same family, as shown in Fig. 10. Therefore, the percentage of correctly labeled samples refers to the only ones that truly belong to the attributed family. In practice, malware samples can leverage packing solutions even more sophisticated than UPX, thus highlighting the need of developing more obfuscation-resistant texture-based malware classifiers.

Table 14. Texture descriptors & classifiers accuracy evaluation. GIST descriptor achieves higher detection rates than LBP in most classifiers. It is not possible to classify malware compressed with UPX. ([1]: direct mapping without texture descriptor; [2]: resize from literature; [3]: standardized scale).

Classifier	CNN	KNN	DT	RF	NC	SVM	SGD	Perceptron	MLP
GIST[1]	N/A	12.99	12.99	12.99	12.99	12.99	12.99	12.99	12.99
LBP[1]	N/A	12.99	12.99	12.99	12.99	12.99	12.99	12.99	12.99
GIST[2]	N/A	12.99	12.99	12.99	12.99	12.99	12.99	12.99	12.99
LBP[2]	N/A	12.99	12.99	12.99	12.99	12.99	12.99	12.99	11.69
N/A	12.50	N/A	N/A	N/A	N/A	N/A	N/A	N/A	N/A

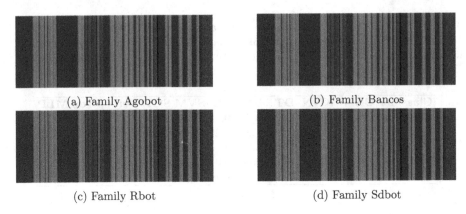

(a) Family Agobot

(b) Family Bancos

(c) Family Rbot

(d) Family Sdbot

Fig. 10. Variants texture from different families of compressed with UPX.

5 Discussion

In this section, we summarize our main findings and point future directions for the development of texture-based malware classifiers.

Representing a File as a Texture Is Challenging. Although the creation of a new representation may ease some tasks, it creates new challenges. Representing a binary file as a texture requires defining: (i) an appropriate scale, which directly affects classification results; (ii) a dimensional representation (1D, 2D, 3D), which may imply in information loss if the binary file is too large; and (iii) padding texture, in the case where a binary file is too small. Therefore, future developments in texture classification should also focus in advancing representations and pre-processing steps in addition to providing new texture descriptors.

Biased Datasets Cannot be Generalized. Whereas we were able to reproduce literature results using the publicized datasets, we were not able to achieve high accuracy in a dataset of malware samples collected in-the-wild, despite the generalization claims made in literature reports. Further investigations revealed that the described texture descriptors were able to classify only some malware families. These families were present in the publicized datasets but not in our real-world collection, which highlights the need of breaking down detection accuracy by malware families when reporting experiments results, otherwise reported results cannot be generalized to other contexts, as here demonstrated.

Handling Obfuscation is Still a Challenge. Despite claims of approaches' resistance to obfuscation, our experiments revealed that obfuscating malware binaries is still an effective measure to bypass detection mechanisms. Even samples previously classified correctly were mistakenly classified after being packed with popular packers, such as UPX. The major reason for classifiers wrongly labelling samples is that packing solutions produce similar code patternsregardless of the embedded payload, thus leading to the same textures. Therefore, future work should consider packed code in their developments and evaluations, otherwise the developed solutions might be impractical in actual scenarios.

6 Conclusion

Texture-based malware classification can be performed leveraging multiple approaches, with multiple scales, descriptors and classifiers. In this paper we presented an evaluation of the effectiveness of these approaches to identify the usage scenarios for which they are most suited. Our experiments considered both global (GIST) and local (LBP) descriptors and a multitude of classifiers (e.g., KNN, DT, RF, CNN). We were able to reproduce literature experiments using their publicized datasets and identified that the 128×128 scale produces higher results than other scales and that the GIST detector achieves higher detection rates than LBP. However, we were not able to achieve similar detection rates when evaluating a real dataset of malware samples collected in-the-wild. Further investigations revealed that the reported literature results hold true for only some malware families, which are prevalent in publicized datasets but not on our real collection, thus reinforcing the need of presenting detection results broken down by malware families. Moreover, we notice that despite literature claims, obfuscation is still an effective technique to bypass detection. As a future work, we plan to develop new malware representation strategies, such as considering 3D textures instead of 2D ones to reduce information loss in conversion procedures, towards making texture-based malware classifiers practical in actual scenarios.

References

1. Al-Anezi, M.M.K.: Generic packing detection using several complexity analysis for accurate malware detection. Int. J. Adv. Comput. Sci. **5**(1) (2014)
2. Awad, R.A., Sayre, K.D.: Automatic clustering of malware variants. In: Intelligence and Security Informatics (ISI), pp. 298–303. IEEE (2016)
3. Bertolini, D., Oliveira, L.S., Justino, E., Sabourin, R.: Texture-based descriptors for writer identification and verification. Expert Syst. Appl. **40**, 2069–2080 (2013)
4. Conti, G., et al.: Automated mapping of large binary objects using primitive fragment type classification. Digit. Investig. **7**, S3–S12 (2010)
5. Costa, Y.M., Oliveira, L., Koerich, A.L., Gouyon, F., Martins, J.: Music genre classification using LBP textural features. Signal Process. **92**, 2723–2737 (2012)
6. Damodaran, A., Di Troia, F., Visaggio, C.A., Austin, T.H., Stamp, M.: A comparison of static, dynamic, and hybrid analysis for malware detection. J. Comput. Virol. Hack. Tech. **13**, 1–12 (2017)
7. Kabanga, E.K., Kim, C.H.: Malware images classification using convolutional neural network. J. Comput. Commun. **6**, 153 (2017)
8. Kosmidis, K., Kalloniatis, C.: Machine learning and images for malware detection and classification. In: Pan-Hellenic Conference on Informatics. ACM (2017)

9. Laks: Sarvam blog (2014). http://sarvamblog.blogspot.com.br
10. Li, P., Liu, L., Gao, D., Reiter, M.K.: On challenges in evaluating malware clustering. In: Jha, S., Sommer, R., Kreibich, C. (eds.) RAID 2010. LNCS, vol. 6307, pp. 238–255. Springer, Heidelberg (2010). https://doi.org/10.1007/978-3-642-15512-3_13
11. Luo, J.S., Lo, D.C.T.: Binary malware image classification using machine learning with local binary pattern. In: IEEE Big Data (2017)
12. Makandar, A., Patrot, A.: Malware analysis and classification using artificial neural network. In: I-TACT (2015)
13. Makandar, A., Patrot, A.: An approach to analysis of malware using supervised learning classification. In: International Conference on Recent Trends in Engineering, Science and Technology (2016)
14. Makandar, A., Patrot, A.: Malware class recognition using image processing techniques. In: ICDMAI (2017)
15. Makandar, A., Patrot, A.: Malware image analysis and classification using support vector machine. Int. J. Trends CS Eng. **4**, 01–03 (2015)
16. Makandar, A., Patrot, A.: Wavelet statistical feature based malware class recognition and classification using supervised learning classifier. Orient. J. CS Technol. **10**, 400–406 (2017)
17. Makandar, A., Patrot, A.: Trojan malware image pattern classification. In: Guru, D.S., Vasudev, T., Chethan, H.K., Sharath Kumar, Y.H. (eds.) Proceedings of International Conference on Cognition and Recognition. LNNS, vol. 14, pp. 253–262. Springer, Singapore (2018). https://doi.org/10.1007/978-981-10-5146-3_24
18. Moser, A., Kruegel, C., Kirda, E.: Limits of static analysis for malware detection. In: 23rd Annual Computer Security Applications Conference (2007)
19. Nataraj, L.: A signal processing approach to malware analysis. UCSB (2015)
20. Nataraj, L., Karthikeyan, S., Jacob, G., Manjunath, B.: Malware images: visualization and automatic classification. In: International Symposium on Visualization for Cyber Security. ACM (2011)
21. Nataraj, L., Kirat, D., Manjunath, B., Vigna, G.: SARVAM: search and retrieval of malware. In: ACSAC NGMAD (2013)
22. Nataraj, L., Yegneswaran, V., Porras, P., Zhang, J.: A comparative assessment of malware classification using binary texture analysis and dynamic analysis. In: Workshop on Security and AI. ACM (2011)
23. Ojala, T., Pietikainen, M., Maenpaa, T.: Multiresolution gray-scale and rotation invariant texture classification with local binary patterns. Trans. Pattern Anal. Mach. Intell. **24**, 971–987 (2002)
24. Oliva, A., Torralba, A.: Modeling the shape of the scene: a holistic representation of the spatial envelope. Int. J. Comput. Vis. **42**, 145–175 (2001)
25. Pedregosa, F., et al.: Scikit-learn: machine learning in Python. J. ML Res. **12**, 2825–2830 (2011)
26. Rezende, E., Ruppert, G., Carvalho, T., Ramos, F., de Geus, P.: Malicious software classification using transfer learning of ResNet-50 deep neural network. In: ICMLA (2017)
27. Rezende, E., Ruppert, G., Carvalho, T., Theophilo, A., Ramos, F., Geus, P.: Malicious software classification using VGG16 deep neural network's bottleneck features. In: Latifi, S. (ed.) Information Technology - New Generations. AISC, vol. 738, pp. 51–59. Springer, Cham (2018). https://doi.org/10.1007/978-3-319-77028-4_9
28. Rossow, C., et al.: Prudent practices for designing malware experiments: status quo and outlook. In: S&P. IEEE (2012)

29. Sebastián, M., Rivera, R., Kotzias, P., Caballero, J.: AVCLASS: a tool for massive malware labeling. In: Monrose, F., Dacier, M., Blanc, G., Garcia-Alfaro, J. (eds.) RAID 2016. LNCS, vol. 9854, pp. 230–253. Springer, Cham (2016). https://doi.org/10.1007/978-3-319-45719-2_11

30. Singh, A.: Malware classification using image representation. Master's thesis. Indian Institute of Technology Kanpur (2017)

31. Thakare, V.S., Patil, N.N., Sonawane, J.S.: Survey on image texture classification techniques. Int. J. Adv. Technol. **4**, 97–104 (2013)

32. VirusTotal: Virustotal (2017). https://www.virustotal.com/#/home/upload

33. van der Walt, S., et al.: The scikit-image contributors: scikit-image: image processing in Python. PeerJ (2014)

34. Yakura, H., Shinozaki, S., Nishimura, R., Oyama, Y., Sakuma, J.: Malware analysis of imaged binary samples by convolutional neural network with attention mechanism. In: Conference on Data and Application Security and Privacy, CODASPY 2018. ACM (2018)

35. Yue, S.: Imbalanced malware images classification: a CNN based approach. CoRR (2017). http://arxiv.org/abs/1708.08042

36. Zhang, J., Qin, Z., Yin, H., Ou, L., Xiao, S., Hu, Y.: Malware variant detection using opcode image recognition with small training sets. In: ICCCN. IEEE (2016)

Automated Reconstruction of Control Logic for Programmable Logic Controller Forensics

Syed Ali Qasim[1]($\boxtimes$), Juan Lopez Jr.[2], and Irfan Ahmed[1]

[1] Virginia Commonwealth University, Richmond, VA 23284, USA
{qasimsa,iahmed3}@vcu.edu
[2] Oak Ridge National Lab, Oak Ridge, TN 37830, USA
lopezj@ornl.gov

Abstract. This paper presents Similo, an automated scalable framework for control logic forensics in industrial control systems. Similo is designed to investigate denial of engineering operations (DEO) attacks, recently demonstrated to hide malicious control logic in a programmable logic controller (PLC) at field sites from an engineering software (at control center). The network traffic (if captured) contains substantial evidence to investigate DEO attacks including manipulation of control logic. Laddis, a state-of-the-art forensic approach for DEO attacks, is a binary-logic decompiler for the Allen-Bradley's RSLogix engineering software and MicroLogix 1400 PLC. It is developed with extensive manual reverse engineering effort of the underlying proprietary network protocol and the binary control logic. Unfortunately, Laddis is not scalable and requires similar efforts to extend on other engineering software/PLCs. The proposed solution, Similo, is based on the observation that engineering software of different vendors are equipped with decompilers. Similo is a virtual-PLC framework that integrates the decompilers with their respective (previously-captured) ICS network traffic of control logic. It recovers the binary logic into a high-level source code (of the programming languages defined by IEC 61131-3 standard) automatically. Similo can work with both proprietary/open protocols without requiring protocol specifications and the binary formats of control logic. Thus, it is scalable to different ICS vendors. We evaluate Similo on three PLCs of two ICS vendors, i.e. MicroLogix 1400, MicroLogix 1100, and Modicon M221. These PLCs support proprietary protocols and the control logics written in two programming languages: Ladder Logic and Instruction List. The evaluation results show that Similo can accurately reconstruct a control logic from an ICS network traffic and can be used to investigate the DEO attacks effectively.

Keywords: Control system · SCADA · Forensics · PLC · ICS

© Springer Nature Switzerland AG 2019
Z. Lin et al. (Eds.): ISC 2019, LNCS 11723, pp. 402–422, 2019.
https://doi.org/10.1007/978-3-030-30215-3_20

1 Introduction

Industrial control systems (ICS) monitor and control our critical infrastructures such as nuclear plant and gas pipelines. These systems were originally designed to be isolated environments with limited access to the outer world. Increasingly, they are now connected to the Internet and corporate networks, thereby making them vulnerable to cyber attacks [3,10,18,19].

Unfortunately, the current forensic capabilities are insufficient to investigate cyberattacks on ICS environments because these environments are significantly different from traditional IT systems [1,2]. They are connected with physical processes, have the critical requirement of high availability, and use resource-constrained computing devices, legacy operating system, and proprietary network protocols.

An ICS consists of control center and field sites. The control center runs ICS services such as human machine interface (HMI), historian, and engineering workstation. The fields sites have physical process, and computing devices such as sensors, actuators, and programmable logic controllers (PLCs). A PLC maintains a desired actuator state by a control logic and observing the current state of a physical processes using sensor data. The PLC also communicates the sensor data and actuator state to control center over a communication channel.

Recently, Senthivel *et al.* [16] present a new class of ICS attacks, namely, denial of engineering operations attack (DEO). In DEO I, an attacker compromises a control logic of a target PLC. When an engineering software attempts to retrieve the control logic from the compromised PLC, it intercepts the traffic via man-in-the-middle attack and replaces/removes the malicious logic from the control logic in the network traffic before forwarding it to the software. Hence, the engineering software receives a normal (non-malicious) control logic. In DEO II, which is a variant of DEO I, the attacker replaces a legitimate instruction in a control logic with noise data such as 0xFFFFFF to make the engineering software malfunction.

The ICS network traffic contains substantial evidence to investigate DEO attacks including manipulation of control logic. The challenge is to reconstruct and transform the binary control logic (in the traffic dump) into its high-level source code. The closest effort in this direction is Laddis [16], which is a binary-logic decompiler for the Allen-Bradley's RSLogix engineering software and MicroLogix PLC series. Unfortunately, Laddis is not scalable and requires manual reverse engineering to extend on other engineering software/PLCs.

This paper presents Similo to recover a control logic from an ICS network traffic automatically. Similo is based on the observation that engineering software of different vendors are equipped with a decompiler that transforms a binary control logic into a high-level language source-code. Similo is an automated and scalable framework (for control logic forensics), which utilizes the *upload* function of an engineering software to integrate a previously-captured network traffic dump of a control logic with a decompiler in the engineering software. The framework does not require manual reverse engineering efforts for proprietary protocols and binary control logic. Thus, it is scalable.

We evaluate `Similo` on 113 control logic programs at three different levels: packet-level, functional-level and source-code-level of control logic. We use the engineering software of two different vendors, Allen-Bradley and Modicon, and three PLCs supporting two IEC 61131-3 programming languages i.e., Instruction List and Ladder Logic and two proprietary protocols i.e., PCCC, and M221 proprietary layer encapsulated in Modbus. The evaluation results show that `Similo` can engage an engineering software using an ICS network traffic dump of a control logic including session establishment, echo messages and transferring of the control logic in the traffic dump to an engineering software. This results in a correct reconstruction and transformation of a control logic into a source-code. We further recreate DEO attacks on these PLCs and engineering software and utilize `Similo` to investigate them successfully.

2   Background

2.1   Control Logic

Programmable Logic Controller. PLCs are embedded devices that reside on field-sites to control and monitor physical processes directly. A PLC has input and output modules. The input module connects input devices such as sensors that provide temperature and pressure in a pipeline, level of liquid in a tank, etc. The output module connects with actuators to maintain the desired state of a physical process. The control logic in a PLC processes the input to set the output. A PLC also supports network communication (such as Ethernet or serial port) to communicate with the ICS services in control center such as engineering software.

PLC Programming. IEC 61131-3 defines five languages to write a control logic. These languages can be divided into two categories, (i) Textual, and (ii) Graphical. Structured text, and Instruction list are textual while Ladder Logic, Functional Block Diagram, and Sequential Function Chart are graphical. Note that for the purpose of evaluation, we select one language from each category i.e Ladder logic (graphical) and Instruction List (textual).

Ladder Logic. Ladder logic is a graphical language and is derived from Relay Logic. The program is defined in the form of a graphical diagram. A horizontal line in a Ladder logic program is called *rung*. A rung comprises of a number of input and output instructions. An instruction defines an operation to be performed by the processor [4].

Figure 1a is a ladder logic program consisting of one rung and two instructions: (1) *XIC* (Examine if closed) on left is associated with the input address *I:0/0*, (2) *TON* (timer on delay) on right. The timer instruction has three attributes, (i) time base (the unit of time, 1.0 means one second). (ii) Preset (maximum time to wait). (iii) Accumulator (the time that has passed). It also has two control bits, *EN* (enable) and *DN*(Done).

When the program executes and the *XIC* is true, it will start the timer and *EN* will become true. The preset is 6 and the time-base is one second. When the

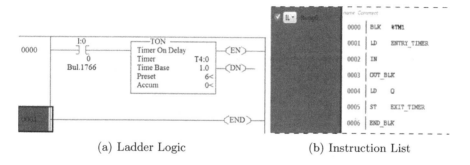

(a) Ladder Logic   (b) Instruction List

Fig. 1. Different representations of a timer program (Color figure online)

timer completes 6 s, the *DN* bit turns to true and the accumulator is changed to the preset value.

Instruction List. Unlike Ladder Logic, Instruction List resembles assembly language consisting of sequence of instructions. Figure 1b shows an equivalent program in Fig. 1a. The first instruction *BLK* is the start of the timer function block. The second instruction, *LD* (load operator) looks for close edge contact, which is associated with the input *%I0.0*. The contact is closed when bit *%I0.0* is 1. The following instructions are as follows: *IN* represents the input of Timer function block; *Out_BLK* wires the output of timer; *Q* represents the output of timer, and it becomes 1 when the timer expires; *ST* is store operator, which is equivalent to a coil in ladder logic and takes the value of previous logic and is used to store output. Finally, *END_BLK* represents the end of the timer function block [12].

When the program executes and *LD* is true, it sets *IN* true and starts the timer. The timer has a time-base of 1 s and preset of 6 s. When the timer completes 6 s, it sets *Q* (output of timer) true and then both *LD* and *Q* go into *ST*. *LD* and *Q* are in series. When both *LD* and *Q* are true, it will turn the output *ST* true.

2.2 Denial of Engineering Operations (DEO) Attack

Recently, Senthivel *et al.* [16] present denial of engineering operation (DEO) attacks that jeopardize an engineering software's capabilities to perform remote-maintenance on a PLC. They demonstrate the attacks on Allen-Bradley MicroLogix 1400-B and RSlogix 500 (engineering software).

(1) DEO Attack I. In DEO I (Fig. 2), an attacker performs a man-in-the-middle between a target PLC and an engineering workstation (the computer running an engineering software). When the control engineer downloads a control logic program to a compromised PLC, the attacker intercepts the communications and infects this control logic by replacing some part of the code with malicious logic before forwarding it to the PLC. Similarly, when the control engineer tries to upload the control logic from the PLC, the attacker intercepts the

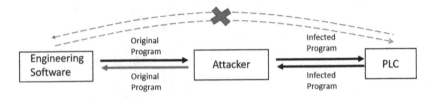

Fig. 2. DEO Attack I: hiding infected ladder logic from the engineering software

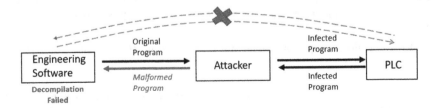

Fig. 3. DEO Attack II: crashing the decompiler running on Engineering software

traffic and replaces the infected logic with the original code. In this way, the control engineer remains unaware of the malicious control logic running on the PLC.

Consider the ladder logic program in Fig. 1a, the timer controls the yellow light in a traffic light signal. The attacker modifies the preset value from 6 s to 80 s when the program is downloaded to the PLC of the signal. When a control engineer attempts to retrieve the program from the PLC, the attacker intercepts the traffic and change the preset back to its original value i.e., 6.

(2) DEO Attack II. DEO II is similar to the DEO 1 in that the attacker performs a man-in-middle between the engineering workstation and PLC, intercepts the communication, and manipulate the traffic as it passes through the attacker's machine. However, in DEO II (Fig. 3), the attacker replaces the original code with random (noise) data such as 0xFFFF. When an engineering software receives the malformed logic, it fails to decompile.

2.3   Challenges in DEO Forensic Investigation

For a forensic investigation of DEO attacks, the network traffic (if captured) contains substantial evidence including manipulation of control logic. The challenge is to reconstruct and transform the binary control logic (in the traffic dump) into its high-level source code. Unfortunately, binary control-logic does not have a standard open format (such as Linux ELF) to allow a generic decompiler. ICS vendors define their binary control-logic representations. Often, each vendor has multiple binary representations across their different engineering software to program different types of PLCs.

Recall that IEC 61131-3 standard defines five programming languages for PLCs (such as Structured Text, and Ladder Logic) [9]. An engineering software often supports only one or two languages. Thus, binary logic must be transformed into their respective high-level languages for forensic investigation, making the transformation more challenging. Lastly, the engineering software and PLCs communicate using different ICS protocols that may be proprietary or may use an open protocol with an embedded proprietary protocol layer. Thus, reconstruction of binary control logic from a network traffic capture requires extensive manual reverse engineering of the proprietary protocols.

The closest effort in this direction to develop forensic investigation capabilities for control logic is `Laddis` [16], which is a binary-logic decompiler for the Allen-Bradley's RSLogix engineering software and MicroLogix PLC series. `Laddis` is developed with the manual reverse engineering of the PCCC protocol and the binary representation of the high-level ladder logic program written in RSLogix. Unfortunately, `Laddis` is not scalable and requires similar efforts to extend on other engineering software/PLCs.

3   Problem Statement

Given an ICS network traffic dump of a control logic, our goal is to reconstruct and transform the binary control logic (in the traffic dump) into its high-level source code. Considering the challenges outlined in Sect. 2.3, a practical solution should address at least two basic requirements:

Automation. The solution must be automated to achieve a high-level source code of a low-level binary control logic in a network traffic without human intervention including reverse engineering of a proprietary ICS protocol and a binary representation of a high-level control logic.

Scalability. The solution must be scalable to multiple vendor products including engineering software (used to create a control logic), proprietary ICS protocols, and PLCs.

4   Similo - A Virtual PLC Framework

4.1   Overview of Similo

We observe that engineering software of different vendors are equipped with decompilers that can transform a binary control logic into a high-level language source-code. We propose to integrate a decompiler in engineering software with a previously-captured network traffic dump of a control logic to obtain the source-code of the control logic. Our solution is `Similo`, an automated and scalable virtual-PLC framework that does not require manual reverse engineering. `Similo` utilizes the *upload* function of an engineering software to achieve the integration.

Upload Function. The *upload* is a required functionality (used by control engineers) to retrieve a binary control logic from a PLC remotely, which further triggers a decompiler in engineering software to achieve high-level source code of the control logic.

Generally, when a control engineer runs the *upload* command in engineering software, it starts a series of request-response messages between a PLC and an engineering software such as session-establishment messages, echo messages, and control logic messages. Engineering software first establishes a session with a PLC and then, sends read-request messages to the PLC to read the memory locations of a control logic. In response, PLC sends the data on the requested memory locations (i.e., control logic) to the engineering software in the payload of response messages. After receiving an entire binary control logic, engineering software passes it to the decompiler to trigger decompilation process, which in turn produces the source code in a high-level language.

Virtual-PLC Framework. To develop `Similo`, we assess the communication behavior of the *upload* function of two engineering software, RSLogix 500 and SoMachine-Basic with three PLCs, Allen-Bradley's MicroLogix 1400 and MicroLogix 1100, and Schneider Electric's Modicon M221. We make two interesting observations that show that the communication behavior is deterministic: first, an engineering software always makes a small number of unique requests to retrieve the control logic from a PLC; second, if we send an associated response message from a previous network dump as reply to a request message from engineering software, the next request message from the software will be same as the next request message in the network traffic dump.

Based on these observations, we design `Similo` using the *upload* function. Recall that engineering software uses the *upload* function to retrieve control logic from a PLC memory. `Similo` on the other hand retrieves control logic from a network traffic (captured during the transfer of the logic). It consists of a virtual-PLC that responds to the *upload* function queries using a previous network traffic dump of a control logic. It handles dynamic protocol fields in the request-response messages automatically, making it scalable to different PLCs, proprietary protocols and engineering software. For this paper, we test `Similo` successfully on three different PLCs (Micrologix 1400, MicroLogix 1100 and Modicon M221), two ICS protocols (ENIP, and Modbus) and two engineering software (RsLogix, and SoMachineBasic).

`Similo` consists of two phases: training, and testing. The training phase provides understanding of dynamic header fields of messages using benign pcap files while the testing phase engages an engineering software to respond to the request messages using the response messages in a network traffic (under investigation) including updating the header fields.

4.2   Learning/Training Phase

Figure 4 presents an overview of the training phase, which consists pairing, comparison and grouping, and optimization steps for identifying dynamic header fields in request-response messages.

Pairing. Pairing is the first step to identify an instance of a message in a set of two benign pcap files from different sessions that contain same control logic. We assume that the header values of dynamic fields change across multiple sessions.

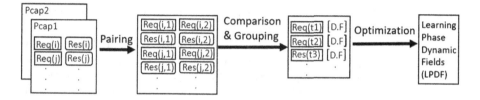

Fig. 4. Overview of learning/training phase

However, their contents (control logic) remain the same since same control logic is used on both pcap files. We use two properties of a message to find same message instance in the pcap files: (1) message length and (2) message content similarity.

Ideally, we have to compare each message of the first pcap file with all messages of the second pcap file to find the best match. However, we optimize this approach by finding a match with 85% threshold (based on our initial experiments) i.e if the length of two messages is same and the similarity is more than 85%, they are considered same and paired together. In our experience, this approach decreases the time taken for learning significantly without affecting the functionality of Similo. Note that pairing is used for initial screening of pcap files and does not assume to achieve 100% accuracy for finding same messages. The results of pairing are further refined in later stages. Figure 4 show the pairing process, where *Req (i, 1)* and *Res (i, 1)* is a request response pair from pcap1 and *Req (i, 2)* and *Res (i, 2)* is a pair from pcap2.

Comparison and Grouping. After pairing similar messages, Similo performs differential analysis on each pair, i.e comparing two messages character by character and records the indices (i.e., locations of bytes) where the values are different. During our experiments, we found that the length of header fields vary in different request messages due to which the offsets of dynamic fields also vary. In order to tackle this, Similo groups messages based on length such that all the messages in one group will have the same header size and structure. There after Similo find the differences of all message pairs in one group which are further processed to get the dynamic fields.

Optimization. In this process, the differences identified between the message pairs in each group are compared with one another and only those indices are selected that are present in more than 50% of messages. Since the initial pairing is not 100% accurate, there is a chance that other than the dynamic header fields, some paired messages may also have little differences in payload too. So the optimization process filters the differences present in payload. For example if the differential analysis of three message pairs of length X has resulted in the following dynamic field indices: *(0, 1, 4, 9, 19), (0, 3, 4, 15), (1, 3, 4, 22)* the resultant would be *(0, 1, 3, 4)*, which will represent the offsets of dynamic fields in all the messages in group X. The optimized indices are further divided in different groups based on the adjacency and each group represents one dynamic field such as transaction ID, length etc. These dynamic fields might be incomplete/partially filled but that problem is solved during the testing phase.

After these steps, Similo gets the indices of dynamic fields in all the request-response messages present in one set of pcap files. The same process is repeated with other pcap files and finally the results of all the files are again compared and analyzed using the majority rule and the information and the resulting dynamic fields, referred to as Learning Phase Dynamic Fields (LPDF), are used in testing phase.

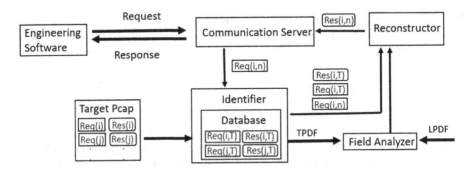

Fig. 5. Overview of testing phase

4.3   Testing Phase

Figure 5 shows an overview of the testing phase. After completing the training phase, Similo takes a target pcap file, extracts request and response messages, and then, stores them in database in the form of request and response pairs. Afterwards, it starts the communication server and waits for the message from the engineering software initiated by the *upload* function. Upon receiving a request, the communication server forwards it to the Identifier. The identifier performs two tasks. First, it finds the same request message (based on content) in the database. Second, it compares the two messages and identifies the dynamic fields between these two request messages. We call them training phase dynamic fields (TPDF).

The identification is similar to pairing since it uses message length and content similarity. However, at this stage, we have information about the dynamic fields from the learning phase. Note that the dynamic fields are present in the header and the later part contains the control logic. For every request message with the same length as of the new request message, instead of comparing the whole message, the identifier only compares the part that lies beyond the last dynamic field determined by learning phase.

The grouping of messages based on length helps Similo in performing the look up efficiently. The identifier selects the request message with highest similarity with a new request message. It then, passes the request along with the

	Learning phase dynamic fields	Testing phase dynamic fields	Combined dynamic fields
Overlap	((0,1,2),(6,7))	((2,3),(9))	((0,1,2,3),(6,7))
Adjacent	((0,1,2),(6,7))	((3),(9))	((0,1,2,3),(6,7))
Confined	((0,1,2),(6,7))	((1),(9))	((0,1,2)(6,7))

Fig. 6. Accumulation example of dynamic fields in learning and testing phases

request-response pair from the database to *Reconstructor*. Similarly, the testing phase dynamic fields are passed to Field analyzer.

Field Analyzer. We know the location and tentative size of dynamic fields in a message, however we still have to ascertain the boundary of the fields. To find complete fields, field analyzer compares the dynamic fields from learning phase with the dynamic fields from the testing phase. Specifically, if any dynamic field from the TPDF overlaps, is adjacent to, or is confined in any dynamic field from the LPDF, Field analyzer combines it with the dynamic field from learning phase otherwise it discards it. Figure 6 explains the working of Field Analyzer. In the first case two fields were identified in the testing phase i.e *(2, 3)* and *(9)*. Since *(2, 3)* is overlapping one of the LPDF, it is combined with it resulting in *(0, 1, 2, 3)* where as *(9)* is not overlapping, adjacent or confined in any of the LPDF so it is discarded. Similarly the second and third case explains the Adjacent and Confined scenarios.

It is still possible that even after this combination some fields are partly empty. That means the values at those indices remain same in both sessions, thus we do not need to change them for reconstructing the response message. The final dynamic fields are forwarded to Reconstructor.

Reconstructor. It is the last component in Similo, which takes request-response messages from the target pcap and the dynamic field offsets from the Field analyzer. The dynamic fields in a target request message are mapped to its paired response message. If the values are same, reconstructor changes the values of dynamic fields in the response message according to the values in the new request message and forwards this message to the communication server. The communication server then sends this response message to the engineering software and waits for next request and so on. This process finally makes the engineering software to recover the control logic from the network dump.

5   Implementation

We have implemented Similo in python and used scapy [14] for network packet manipulation. During the learning phase, Similo makes dictionaries from the pcap files. The request and response messages are filtered on the basis of IP address and port. The transport layer payloads of request and response messages are converted to hex streams and used as keys and values.

To calculate similarity, we use SequenceMatcher from difflib library [8]. Furthermore, `Similo` compares both sets of requests and response messages present in each tuple, character by character and the differences are stored in a dictionary, where length of request message represents the key and value is a list of arrays of differences generating from each comparison. These differences are later processed to get the offsets of dynamic fields within a packet via Optimization.

The optimization uses a majority rule to separate the protocol related dynamic fields from the rest. For each message type (based on length), it calculates the number of instances of each offset. If an offset appears in majority (more than 50% or user defined threshold), it is considered as part of dynamic field and used in the testing phase, otherwise, it's ignored.

During our research, we found that generally, the PLCs have fixed ports for communicating with the engineering software e.g Allen-Bradley MicroLogix 1100 and 1400 use port 44818, Modicon M221 uses port 502. Thus, in the testing phase, using the socket library, `Similo` opens a server socket (communication server) using socket on the default ports of real PLCs and waits for message from the engineering software. After getting a target pcap file from the user, it generates the database i.e dictionary using the method explained.

The identifier is a search function that takes a request message from the server *Req (i, n)* and iterates on the database keys to finds same request message with different dynamic fields *(req_t)*. For this purpose, it uses the length and similarity of static fields. After finding same request from the target pcap *Req(i, T)*, it compares these two requests to find the differences. The Identifier then passes the *Req (i, n)*, *Req (i, T)* and *Res (i, T)* to the reconstructor and *TPDF* to the Field analyzer.

The field analyzer function takes two inputs: LPDF, and *TPDF*. It iterates over both of them and if any *TPDF* fields are adjacent, overlap or one is confined in the boundary of a LPDF, it combines the two, otherwise, it ignores the *TPDF* (Fig. 6). The output of this function is an array of arrays containing dynamic field offsets. Finally the Reconstructor function takes the *Req(i, n)*, *Req(i, T)* and *Res (i, T)* from the Identifier and the final set of dynamic fields from the Field analyzer. It maps the dynamic fields in *Req (i, T)* on *Res (i, T)* to check if the values of dynamic field in the request and response message are same. If it is true, it edits the *Res (i, T)* by changing the value of dynamic fields according to the new request *R(i, n)* and forwards the new response message to the communication server, which then sends it to the engineering software.

6   Evaluation

Lab Setup. We evaluate `Similo` on three PLCs Allen-Bradley MicroLogix 1400 Series B, Allen Bradley MicroLogix 1100 Series B, and Schneider Electric Modicon M221. The engineering softwares used for the first two PLC is RSLogix 500 V9.2.01 and M221 is evaluated on SoMachine Basic v 1.6 and v 1.4. Both programming software run on Windows 7 virtual machine (VM) and the virtual-

PLC runs on a VM with Ubuntu v 16.04. The engineering software, PLCs and virtual-PLC all were connected via Ethernet.

Experiment Methodology. A typical experiment includes capturing the network traffic when an engineering software uploads a control logic from a real PLC. Similo uses the pcap files and communicates with the engineering software to recover the control logic. At the end, two programs are compared in the engineering software manually to find accuracy of the virtual PLC.

Dataset. For the evaluation of the PLCs, Allen-Bradley MicroLogix 1400 and MicroLogix 1100, we use 39 and 22 different Ladder logic programs respectively. For Modicon M221, we use 52 Instruction List programs. These programs were written for different physical processes such as traffic light, hot water tank, elevator, gas pipeline, and vending machines, and are of varying complexity and sizes. Tables 1, 2 and 3 show the features of the datasets for MicroLogix 1400 and 1100, and Modicon M221 respectively.

Table 1. Dataset summary of Ladder logic programs for MicroLogix 1100

File information		Rung				Instruction			
File size (KB)	# of files	Min	Max	Total	Avg.	Min	Max	Total	Avg
0–40	16	2	17	90	5.62	3	48	240	15
41–60	1	4	4	4	4	12	12	12	12
61–80	4	8	63	145	36.25	25	245	543	135.75
81–100	1	13	13	13	13	37	37	37	37
Total	**22**	–	–	**252**	–	–	–	**832**	–

Table 2. Dataset summary of Ladder logic programs for MicroLogix 1400

File information		Rung				Instruction			
File size (KB)	# of files	Min	Max	Total	Avg.	Min	Max	Total	Avg
20–40	21	1	17	99	4.71	1	48	276	13.14
41–60	8	4	48	93	10.33	4	53	344	38.88
61–80	7	8	63	149	22.57	28	245	577	96.166
81–100	2	13	15	28	14	15	37	52	26
101–120	1	10	10	10	10	23	23	23	23
Total	**39**	–	–	**379**	–	–	–	**1272**	–

Table 3. Dataset summary of Instruction List programs for Modicon M221

File information		Rung				Instruction			
File size (KB)	# of files	Min	Max	Total	Avg.	Min	Max	Total	Avg
60–80	30	1	3	72	2.4	2	23	793	26.4
80–100	14	2	27	107	7.64	7	112	463	33
100–130	4	8	14	43	10.75	20	72	153	38.2
130+	4	12	26	63	16	36	118	269	67.2
Total	**52**	–	–	**286**	–	–	–	**1678**	–

6.1   Virtual PLC as a Device

Similo establishes and maintains a connection with engineering software as a real PLC. We evaluate it with two engineering software i.e RSlogix and SoMachine Basic and conclude that both software recognize Similo as a device and does not distinguish between real PLC and Similo. Figure 1 shows the outcome of the experiments where Similo is recognized as a real MicroLogix 1100, MicroLogix 1400 and Modicon M221 PLC. The experiments are performed as follows.

To connect Allen-Bradley MicroLogix 1100 and 1400 to the engineering workstation, the user has to manually configure a driver in the RSlinx Classic. For Ethernet communication the user can select either EtherNet/IP driver or Ethernet devices driver. In case of Ethernet device driver the user has to give the IP address of the PLC device while EtherNet/IP driver searches the subnet to discover the PLC devices. In our experiments we configured Ethernet devices driver (AB_ETH-1) and gave it the IP address of Similo as shown in red circles in Fig. 7a and b, Rslinx classic identified Similo as a real MicroLogix 1100 and MicroLogix 1400 PLCs.

Similarly, in SoMachine Basic, user can either give the IP address of the PLC or browse the subnet with the help of refresh devices function available (marked in the figure). In our experiment we provide SoMachine Basic the IP address of Similo. Figure 7c shows that SoMachine Basic identified Similo as a real PLC (TM221CE16R).

6.2   Function-Level Accuracy

To successfully imitate a real PLC, Similo has to perform three tasks i.e. (i) establish a connection with the engineering software (ii) handle non-control logic messages such as echo, and (iii) upon receiving an *upload* request from the engineering software, correctly uploading the control logic (present in the pcap file). In this section, we evaluate the ability of Similo to establish and maintain a stable connection with the engineering software and upload the correct control logic to the engineering software.

(a) Similo recognized as MicroLogix 1100 by Rockwell Automation's RSLogix 500

(b) Similo recognized as MicroLogix 1400 by Rockwell Automation's RSLogix 500

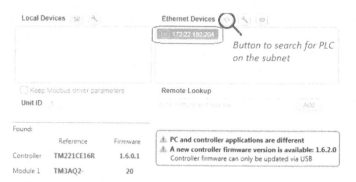

(c) Similo recognized as Modicon M221 by Schneider Electric's SoMachine Basic

Fig. 7. Similo recognized as a real PLC (MicroLogix 1100 and 1400 and Modicon M221) by two engineering software, RSLogix 500 and SoMachine Basic (Color figure online)

Session Establishment and Maintenance. Note that apart from the transferring control logic, engineering software also sends ping (echo) messages and other functional commands to PLC. To test the robustness of Similo in establishing and maintaining the connection, we perform the following experiment. Both RSLogix 500 and SoMachine Basic initiates a connection with Similo and keeps it open for few minute without requesting for an upload. During these experiments, Similo maintained the connection successfully in 113 cases.

Transfer Accuracy. After establishing and maintaining the session successfully, the next task of Similo is to upload a given control logic in network traffic correctly. As mentioned in Sect. 4, the *upload* function of engineering software sends a series of read requests to the PLC. In the beginning the engineering software gets the program storage information/metadata of the control logic from the PLC, then it starts reading the control logic binary from the PLC memory. During the upload process, upon receiving the request message, Similo searches for a response message in its database and sends the reply after editing the dynamic/session dependant fields.

At this stage, any changes other than the dynamic fields can disrupt the connection between the engineering software and PLC or damage the integrity of control logic. Our experiments show that Similo identified and edited the dynamic fields successfully while preserving the integrity of control logic being uploaded. Furthermore, we analyze Similo's capability to reverse-engineer the ICS proprietary protocols. To evaluate the accuracy of Similo, we manually calculated the number of rungs and instructions in each of the 113 control logic files and transferred them one by one with Similo to the engineering software. After each upload, the program was compared with the original files to see if the number of rungs and instructions are the same. To further check the integrity of control logic transferred by Similo, the instructions in original and Similo-transferred control logic were compared manually to check their order on the rung. Similarly, the values of other variables, such as timer preset, and timer base were also compared with the original program.

MicroLogix 1400. For Allen-Bradley MicroLogix 1400 PLC, 39 ladder-logic programs containing 379 rungs and 1272 instructions were uploaded. Similo showed 100% accuracy in establishing connection, basic communication and control logic upload. Moreover, in all cases, the original programs and the ones uploaded by Similo were identical. Table 4 shows the transfer accuracy of Similo.

MicroLogix 1100. To evaluate the accuracy of Similo on MicroLogix 1100, we used 22 ladder-logic programs of varying complexities containing 252 rungs and 832 instructions. Similo was able to upload all programs with 100% transfer accuracy.

Modicon M221. Modicon M221 was evaluated using 52 different programs in Instruction-list, comprising of 286 rungs and 1678 instructions. These programs varied in terms of complexity ranging from as minimum as one rung and two instructions per program to more than 20 rungs and 100+ instructions per program. During our experiments Similo showed 100% accuracy in uploading the control logic from the pcap files.

Table 4. Transfer accuracy of Similo

PLC	# of control logic files uploaded	Original program		Similo output		Accuracy %
		Rungs	Instructions	Rungs	Instructions	
MicroLogix 1100	22	252	832	252	832	100%
MicroLogix 1400	39	379	1272	379	1272	100%
Modicon M221	52	286	1678	286	1678	100%

6.3   Packet-Level Accuracy

One of the main heuristics in developing Similo is the deterministic behaviour of engineering software. The engineering software uses same set of messages to initiate a connection or request for upload. Thus, keeping the deterministic behaviour of the engineering software in mind, if Similo has a complete network traffic of a previous session, it can use it to communicate with the engineering software with a high probability that all request-messages from engineering software can be found in the network traffic. The results from our experiments strengthens this theory.

This section evaluates Similo's ability to identify a given request-message in the database (target pcap file). Table 5 shows the results of packet-level accuracy of Similo. During the process of uploading 52 control logic programs as Modicon M221, Similo received 8800 request messages from the engineering software. Out of these, 8776 message of same as length and average similarity of 99.99% were present in the database. For the remaining 24 messages, Similo selected the request message with the closest length. In this case the average similarity of the messages selected by Similo is 0.58%. Although this similarity is not perfect, but the engineering software accepted the response message from Similo without crashing or giving errors and the overall behaviour of the communication does not change. Similarly, for MicroLogix 1400, while uploading 39 control logic files, Similo received 4219 messages and all of these were present in the database with average similarity of 100%. For MicroLogix 1100, during the upload process, Similo received 1639 and all of them were present in the database (target pcap files) with 100% accuracy.

Table 5. Packet-level accuracy of Similo

PLC	No. of files	Request messages received	Request messages present in DB		Request messages not present in DB	
			No.	Avg. similarity %	No.	Avg. similarity %
MicroLogix 1100	22	1639	1639	100%	0	-
MicroLogix 1400	39	4219	4219	100%	0	-
Modicon M221	52	8800	8776	99.99%	24	56.39%

6.4   Forensic Analysis Using Similo

To evaluate Similo for a forensic analysis of a real cyberattack, we used two denial of engineering operations (DEO) attacks for Allen-Bradley MicroLogix 1400, presented by Senthival et al. [16]. This section contains the attack summary and execution details along with a forensic analysis using Similo.

DEO Attack I: Hiding Infected Ladder Logic (Running in the PLC) from Engineering Software. In the first attack, the attacker performs a man-in-the-middle between PLC and the engineering workstation (computer running the engineering software). When a ladder logic program is downloaded to the PLC, the attacker replaces some portion of the original program with malicious logic. When a control engineer attempts to retrieve the program running on the PLC, the attacker intercepts the communication and replaces the infected logic with the original logic. In this way, the engineering software shows the original program and the attacker deceives the engineer successfully.

Attack Execution. To achieve the man-in-the-middle, we used ARP poisoning via Ettercap. The program used for this attack was designed to control the traffic light. It contains three timers, each controlling one of the signal lights (red, orange, green). The goal of the attack is to make a change in the timing of green light. The timer instruction consists of three parameters i.e base, preset and accumulated. The preset value controls the amount of time. So to achieve the goal, when the Control engineer downloads this program to the PLC (MicroLogix 1400), using a custom built Ettercap filter, we change the value of preset from 20 to 80. Now the green light will stay ON for 80 s instead of 20. Similarly when the control engineer uploads the ladder logic program from the PLC, we replace the preset value back to 20 and the control engineer only sees the original program on the engineering software. Thus, the PLC runs the infected ladder logic but the Control engineering is not aware of this infection.

Forensic Analysis. To investigate the DEO attack, we use Similo to recover both instances of the control logic in a network traffic capture i.e., one between the engineering software to the attacker, and the other between attacker and the PLC. We utilize MAC addresses to separate the network traffic. Figures 8 and 9 show the recovered instances of the control logic, one is original where the other is manipulated by the attacker by changing the timer preset value from 20 to 80.

DEO Attack II: Crashing an Engineering Software. In the second DEO attack, the attacker performs a man-in-the-middle between the PLC and the workstation. Whenever a control engineer tries to upload a ladder logic program from a target PLC, the attacker intercepts the traffic and modifies the ladder logic instructions by adding random noise such as the sequence of 0xFF bytes. Apparently, it fails the decompilation process in engineering software. This DEO

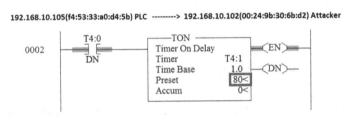

Fig. 8. Control logic from PLC to attacker (Color figure online)

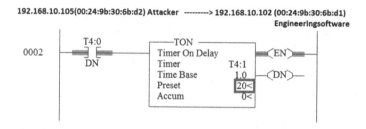

Fig. 9. Control logic from attacker to engineering workstation (Color figure online)

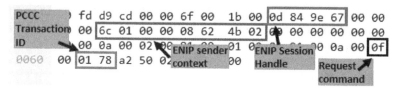

(a) Request message from the engineering software

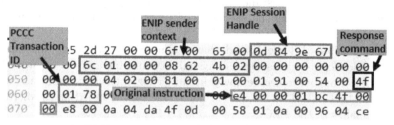

(b) Response message from PLC to attacker

(c) Malformed response from attacker to Engineering software

Fig. 10. Request and response packets that crash the decompiler

attack is a denial of service, which jeopardizes a control engineer's capability to retrieve the program running on the PLC using engineering software.

Attack Execution. Similar to the first attack, the attacker uses ARP poisoning (with Ettercap) to achieve man-in-the-middle. When a control engineer tries to upload the code from a target PLC, the attacker intercepts the communication and replaces a genuine instruction with a malfunctioning one. Figure 10b and c show the original and malformed messages.

Forensic Analysis. To investigate the DEO attack, we use MAC addresses to separate the two instance of the control logic, and then utilize `Similo` to attempt to recover the control logic. To identify malformed control logic packet between engineering software and attacker, we initiate the *upload* function. However, the malformed packet disrupts the engineering software and makes it unavailable for further communication with `Similo`. `Similo` identifies the packet that has caused the disruption since no further communication is possible after the packet is transmitted. Figure 10 shows response message from both benign and manipulated control logic. Figure 10(c) is identified by `Similo`.

To recover the second (malicious) instance of the control logic between the attacker and infected PLC, `Similo` utilizes the *upload* function again and transmit the control logic to the engineering software successfully, resulting in the recovery of the logic to high-level source code.

7   Related Work

When a PLC is compromised by an adversary, it can have disastrous effect on ICS infrastructures. For instance, Stuxnet damages a nuclear plant physically and it does so by changing the frequency of a motor drive controlling the speed of a centrifuge [6].

Valentine *et al.* [17] mentioned that a simple intentional or unintentional error in ladder logic can disrupt the availability and integrity of a target PLC. For example, if output coil is removed in ladder logic, the code will still compile and run on the PLC. However, it will not trigger an intended alarm disrupting the functionality of the PLC.

Kotler *et al.* [11] say due to limited resources installing an additional program on PLC to check the control logic programs is difficult and it will put extra computational burden on the PLC. The authors propose a method using formal verification to detect malicious or faulty PLC programs. They used NuSMV to perform the formal verification. Cheung *et al.* proposed [7] a model based intrusion detection technique for SCADA network that monitors Modbus TCP.

Patel *et al.* recognize [13] that many private protocols exists in SCADA networks. Since most of these proprietary protocols are designed to maximize performance only few of them have built-in security features like message authentication. Attackers can use reverse engineering approach to get the communication and network information.

Beresford *et al.* [5] presented different way to attack Siemens Simatic S7 PLC by reverse engineering and modifying International Standards Organization Transport Service Access Point protocol (the standard protocol for communicating with and programming all S7 Programmable Logic Controllers made by Siemens). Using a replay attack the attacker can perform all the tasks a normal engineering software do like turning off the CPU, disabling memory protection and uploading new project files to the PLC.

After the attack there are very few tools that can analyze the network capture and extract the control logic transferred during the attack. Moreover the available tools focus on one protocol or control logic language. Senthivel *et al.* [15]

made Cutter, a tool to extract the PCCC traffic from network capture. This tool parses the pcap files according to protocol specific tags. Cutter only extracts the PCCC data from the files so the authors made another tool Laddis, which decompiles the files extracted by cutter to get the high level control logic code from binaries. These tools are developed entirely on reverse engineering and are only limited to PCCC protocol extraction and decompilation. This raises the need of a generic tool which can use network dump to get the high level presentation of control logic and Similo tries to solve that problem.

8   Conclusion

We presented a fully-automated framework Similo to recover a control logic from an ICS network traffic. Similo integrated a previously captured ICS traffic with the decompiler and handled dynamic header fields automatically without manual reverse engineering. We evaluated Similo on three different PLCs and two protocols of two different ICS vendors to show that Similo supported multiple vendors successfully. Furthermore, Similo was evaluated on the denial of engineering operations attacks and recovered the malicious and original control logic from the network traffic accurately.

References

1. Ahmed, I., Obermeier, S., Naedele, M., Richard III, G.G.: SCADA systems: challenges for forensic investigators. Computer **45**(12), 44–51 (2012)
2. Ahmed, I., Obermeier, S., Sudhakaran, S., Roussev, V.: Programmable logic controller forensics. IEEE Secur. Priv. **15**(6), 18–24 (2017)
3. Ahmed, I., Roussev, V., Johnson, W., Senthivel, S., Sudhakaran, S.: A SCADA system testbed for cybersecurity and forensic research and pedagogy. In: Proceedings of the 2nd Annual Industrial Control System Security Workshop (ICSS) (2016)
4. Allen-Bradley: User manual. https://literature.rockwellautomation.com/idc/groups/literature/documents/um/1763-um001_-en-p.pdf
5. Beresford, D.: Exploiting Siemens Simatic S7 PLCs (2011)
6. Chen, T.M., Abu-Nimeh, S.: Lessons from Stuxnet. Computer **44**(4), 91–93 (2011)
7. Cheung, S., Dutertre, B., Fong, M., Lindqvist, U., Skinner, K., Valdes, A.: Using model-based intrusion detection for SCADA networks. In: Proceedings of the SCADA Security Scientific Symposium, Miami Beach, Florida, January 2007
8. difflib. https://docs.python.org/3/library/difflib.html
9. IEC: IEC 61131-3. https://www.sis.se/api/document/preview/562735/
10. Kalle, S., Ameen, N., Yoo, H., Ahmed, I.: CLIK on PLCs! Attacking control logic with decompilation and virtual PLC. In: Proceeding of the 2019 NDSS Workshop on Binary Analysis Research (BAR) (2019)
11. Kottler, S., Khayamy, M., Hasan, S.R., Elkeelany, O.: Formal verification of ladder logic programs using NuSMV. In: SoutheastCon 2017, pp. 1–5 (2017)
12. Modicon: SoMachine Basic - Generic Functions Library Guide. https://www.schneider-electric.com/en/download/document/EIO0000001474/
13. Patel, S.C., Bhatt, G.D., Graham, J.H.: Improving the cyber security of SCADA communication networks. Commun. ACM **52**(7), 139–142 (2009)

14. Scapy. https://scapy.net/
15. Senthivel, S., Ahmed, I., Roussev, V.: SCADA network forensics of the PCCC protocol. Digit. Investig. **22**(S), S57–S65 (2017)
16. Senthivel, S., Dhungana, S., Yoo, H., Ahmed, I., Roussev, V.: Denial of engineering operations attacks in industrial control systems. In: Proceedings of the Eighth ACM Conference on Data and Application Security and Privacy, CODASPY 2018, pp. 319–329. ACM, New York (2018)
17. Valentine, S., Farkas, C.: Software security: application-level vulnerabilities in SCADA systems. In: 2011 IEEE International Conference on Information Reuse Integration, pp. 498–499, August 2011. https://doi.org/10.1109/IRI.2011.6009603
18. Yoo, H., Ahmed, I.: Control logic injection attacks on industrial control systems. In: Dhillon, G., Karlsson, F., Hedström, K., Zúquete, A. (eds.) SEC 2019. IFIPAICT, vol. 562, pp. 33–48. Springer, Cham (2019). https://doi.org/10.1007/978-3-030-22312-0_3
19. Yoo, H., Kalle, S., Smith, J., Ahmed, I.: Overshadow PLC to detect remote control-logic injection attacks. In: Perdisci, R., Maurice, C., Giacinto, G., Almgren, M. (eds.) DIMVA 2019. LNCS, vol. 11543, pp. 109–132. Springer, Cham (2019). https://doi.org/10.1007/978-3-030-22038-9_6

Crypto III: Signatures and Authentication

Secure Stern Signatures in Quantum Random Oracle Model

Hanwen Feng, Jianwei Liu, and Qianhong Wu[✉]

School of Cyber Science and Technology, Beihang University, Beijing, China
{feng_hanwen,liujianwei,qianhong.wu}@buaa.edu.cn

Abstract. The Stern signatures are a class of lattice-based signatures constructed from Stern protocols, a special class of sigma protocols, admitting diverse functionalities with good asymptotic efficiency. However, the post-quantum security of existing Stern signatures is unclear, since they are built via the Fiat-Shamir transformation, which has not been proved to be secure in the quantum random oracle model (QROM). The goal of this paper is to find an alternative transformation for constructing post-quantum secure Stern signatures.

The Unruh transformation (Eurocrypt 2015) is an alternative that can build secure signatures in QROM from post-quantum secure sigma protocols. Unfortunately, its proof relies on the *2-special soundness* of the underlying sigma protocol, while Stern protocols are *3-special sound*. We fill this gap by providing an extended proof for the Unruh transformation. Specifically, we prove that it is still secure in the QROM even if the underlying sigma protocols are *k-special sound*, where $k > 2$ could be an arbitrary integer. Observing that Stern protocols are post-quantum secure sigma protocols with 3-special soundness, our proof implies a generic method to obtain secure Stern signatures in the QROM.

Keywords: Quantum random oracles · Signatures · Lattice-based cryptography

1 Introduction

Stern protocols are a class of sigma protocols and originally designed as an code-based identification scheme [25]. They were recently taken as powerful tools for proving a wide range of relations appearing in lattice-based cryptography [20]. From some specifically designed Stern protocols, a number of lattice-based signatures, e.g. group signature (GS) schemes [15,16] and ring signature (RS) schemes [18,28], are proposed through some protocol-to-signature transformation such as the Fiat-Shamir transformation [9], and we call them Stern signatures. These signature schemes have significant efficiency improvements over the other lattice-based GS and RS implementations [5,10] not from Stern protocols. In addition, many desirable properties of GS, e.g., full dynamicity [21] and forward security [23], are firstly implemented in the lattice setting, with the appropriate Stern signatures.

© Springer Nature Switzerland AG 2019
Z. Lin et al. (Eds.): ISC 2019, LNCS 11723, pp. 425–444, 2019.
https://doi.org/10.1007/978-3-030-30215-3_21

While the main motivation of building cryptographic schemes on lattices is to achieve post-quantum security, existing Stern signatures are not guaranteed to be secure against quantum adversaries. This is due to that all of them are built via the Fiat-Shamir transformation. In the classical world, this transformation could give a secure signature in the Random Oracle Model (ROM), and its security proof relies on the abilities of rewinding Turing Machines and adaptively programming random oracles. However, these abilities seem not available in the quantum setting. Since a quantum attacker can evaluate a hash function on some superposition state, the random oracle in the quantum world should also be able to respond superposition queries. While the classical simulation technique of random oracles requires the simulator to know the value of each query before responding, this technique will lead to a failure response to a superposition query, since knowing the value of a superposition state also disturbs this state. This fact sparks the notion of quantum random oracle model (QROM) in which superposition queries are allowed. Moreover, in the QROM, a black-box security proof for Fiat-Shamir has been ruled out by Ambainis *et al.* [2].

The existing methods to build post-quantum secure signatures include new security proofs for the Fiat-Shamir [14,24,27] and the Unruh transformation [26]. Due to the negative result on the general proof of the Fiat-Shamir [2], the known new proofs only works under very specific conditions. Specifically, Unruh [27] and Kiltz *et al.* [14] showed that the Fiat-Shamir could give a non-interactive zero-knowledge (NIZK) proof system if the underlying sigma protocol has the *statistical standard soundness*. Furthermore, to achieve a secure signature, the hard instance generator is required to be *dual-mode* [27] or *lossy* [14]. Recently, Liu and Zhandry [24] showed that the Fiat-Shamir could also contribute a secure signature when the sigma protocol is *computational standard special sound*, but their proof requires the *lossy functions* or *separability* of the underlying protocol. Unruh transformation [26] is the only known post-quantum secure alternative. It can build a secure signature in the QROM from arbitrary sigma protocol with the *standard special soundness*. Observing the standard special soundness is the common requirement in all above methods, however, Stern protocols do not have the property, and thus none of these methods are guaranteed to be applicable to these protocols.

In this paper, we fill the gap between the Stern protocols and post-quantum secure Stern signatures, by providing a generic transformation that works for all Stern protocols.

1.1   Our Contributions

Our main contribution can be summarized in the following informal theorem.

Theorem 1 (informal). *If there is a sigma protocol Σ for a relation R that is complete, k-special sound and honest-verifier zero-knowledge (HVZK) against quantum attackers, then there is an efficient non-interactive zero-knowledge proof of knowledge (NIZKPoK) Ψ for R in the QROM. There is an efficient method to build post-quantum secure Stern signatures.*

Sigma protocols are a class of three-message proof systems, in which each transcript is a triple (commitment, challenge, response). Differently from previous works [14,26,27], we work on a sigma protocol with the k-special soundness. Consider k valid transcripts for a statement $s.t.$ all of them share the same commitment but have pair-wise distinct challenges. The k-special soundness states that a witness for the statement can be extracted from all the k transcripts. We call sigma protocols with completeness, HVZK property and k-special soundness *generalized sigma protocols*. Sigma protocols with the 2-special soundness, a.k.a. *standard special soundness*, are called *standard sigma protocol* and required in previous works [14,26,27]. We observe that there are many important sigma protocols only have the k-special soundness for $k > 2$. For example, all Stern protocols have 3-special soundness, and the OR-composition of sigma protocols [6,8] and one-out-of-many proofs [12] also give k-special sound protocol where $k > 2$. Therefore, it is of great value to work on generalized sigma protocols.

We provide a generic framework for constructing an NIZKPoK from an arbitrary generalized sigma protocol. Our starting point is Unruh's work [26], which provides a generic framework called Unruh transformation for constructing an NIZKPoK in the QROM from an arbitrary standard sigma protocol. Specifically, we prove the Unruh transformation is still secure even if the underlying sigma protocol is an arbitrary generalized sigma protocol. We believe our work is necessary, since the original proofs in [26] are closely related to the standard special soundness, and some previous results that apply to sigma protocols with the standard special soundness do not apply to ones with k-special soundness for $k > 2$. A convincing example is the well-known OR-composition technique [8] of sigma protocols, which works well with standard sigma protocols but cannot even get a proof system with arbitrary generalized sigma protocols.

The most important application of our work is to construct post-quantum secure Stern signatures. With Stern protocols, many important lattice-based signature schemes have been proposed via the Fiat-Shamir, such as the first logarithmic ring signature [18], the first dynamic group signature [16], the first constant-size group signature [22] and so on. We analyze the post-quantum security of Stern protocols, and show that they are generalized sigma protocols with 3-special soundness against quantum adversaries. Therefore, all existing Stern signatures can be modified to ones with post-quantum security by replacing the Fiat-Shamir with the Unruh transformation. Obviously, our result will also support the subsequent Stern signatures achieving post-quantum security. In addition, some related schemes, such as group encryptions [17] and compact e-cash schemes [19], are also constructed from Stern protocols and their security proofs rely on the corresponding NIZKPoK. We believe our results will be helpful for strengthening their post-quantum security.

Our Techniques. We show the existence of NIZKPoK from the generalized sigma protocols, by proving the Unruh transformation is secure when the underlying protocol is an arbitrary generalized sigma protocol. Recall the original results of the Unruh transformation. It can give an non-interactive zero-knowledge proof system $\Psi = (\mathcal{P}, \mathcal{V})$ with online-extractability, if the underlying sigma protocol is complete, 2-special sound and HVZK. The online-extractability says that the witness can be extracted from one valid proof without rewinding the prover for multiple times, and it indicates Ψ is a proof of knowledge. Specifically, the 2-special soundness is required in [26] to prove the online-extractability, while it is not necessary in proving other properties. To make the Unruh transformation work well with general sigma protocols, we need to remove the dependence of online-extractability on the 2-special soundness.

The idea behind the original proof [26] for online-extractability is presenting a reduction that can use a successful adversary $\mathcal{A}$ to break the randomness of a random oracle H. Concretely, a non-interactive proof in Unruh's construction consists of many transcripts of the underlying sigma protocols. We denote the proof by $((com_i)_{[t]}, (ch_{i,j}, h_{i,j})_{[t] \times [m]}, (resp_i)_{[t]})$, where com_i is a commitment, $(ch_{i,j})_{j \in [m]}$ is a sequence of challenges for the commitment com_i, and $resp_i$ is a response to some challenge under com_i. Unruh's construction uses two random oracles, H and G. Let $J_1 | \cdots | J_t = H((com_i)_{[t]}, (ch_{i,j}, h_{i,j})_{[t] \times [m]})$. A valid proof should satisfies the following conditions: (i) for all $i \in [t]$, $(com_i, ch_{i,J_i}, resp_i)$ is valid transcript for a statement x; and (ii) $h_{i,J_i} = G(resp_i)$. We say an adversary $\mathcal{A}$ succeeds if he can generate a valid proof for a false statement x. Consider the standard sigma protocol, for a false statement x, there is at most one index j_i^* for each com_i s.t. $(com_i, ch_{i,j_i^*}, resp_i)$ is valid. It means that $\mathcal{A}$ can predicate the output of H as $j_1^* | \cdots | j_t^*$, and of course the advantage of $\mathcal{A}$ is negligible. However, the k-special soundness enables a malicious prover to create $k-1$ tuples, for each i, $(com_i, ch_{i,j}, resp_{i,j})_{[k-1]}$ that can be accepted. Thus, $\mathcal{A}$ need not to predicate a concrete output value of the random oracle, and original proof does not work for this case. We overcome this problem by proving it is still hard for an adversary to predicate the output range of the random oracle. Namely, it is hard to find an element d s.t. $H(d) \in \mathbb{J}$, where $\mathbb{J}$ is unique determined by d without H and $|\mathbb{J}|$ is negligible in the size of all possible outputs of H. We complete this proof by reducing it to another problem that finding a point d s.t. $\mathcal{B}(d) = 1$ for a random function $\mathcal{B}$ where each $\mathcal{B}(d)$ is distributed as $\Pr[\mathcal{B}(d) = 1] = 2^{-t(\log m - \log(k-1))}$. The hardness of latter problem can be derived from Lemma 7 in [26].

2   Preliminaries

2.1   Notations

For sets, we use $[i, n]$ to denote the set $\{i, i+1, \cdots, n\}$ and abbreviate it as $[n]$ if $i = 1$. We use $(a_i)_{[n]}$ to denote the sequence $(a_1, \cdots, a_n)$.

We say a function $f(n)$ is negligible in n if $\lim_{n \to \infty} n^c f(n) = 0$ for any constant $c > 0$, denoted by $f(n) \in \text{negl}(n)$. A function $f(n)$ is a non-negligible function in n if $f(n) \notin \text{negl}(n)$. We use $\lambda \in \mathbb{N}$ to denote the security parameter, and say that two distributions ϕ and φ are statistical close, denoted by $\phi \approx \varphi$, if their statistical distance belongs to $\text{negl}(\lambda)$.

For arrow using, $x \hookleftarrow X$ or $X \hookrightarrow x$ denotes that sampling x from the uniform distribution over X or sampling x from distribution X, which is determined by the case X is either a set or a distribution; $a \hookleftarrow b$ or $b \hookrightarrow a$ denotes that a is an image of b under some map; $a \leftarrow \mathcal{T}(b)$ or $\mathcal{T}(b) \rightarrow a$ denotes that a is an output of the algorithm $\mathcal{T}(b)$; $\mathsf{A} \Longleftrightarrow \mathsf{B}$ denotes that the events A and B are equivalent.

2.2   Quantum Random Oracle

Since in real world hash functions are executed offline, a quantum attacker can evaluate a hash function on some quantum superposition states, e.g, $|\varphi\rangle = \sum c_i |k_i\rangle$ where $(|k_i\rangle)$ are basis kets. To adapt to the capabilities of quantum attackers, the random oracle in the quantum world should allow the adversary to issue superposition queries, thus called quantum random oracle. The typical simulation technique for random oracle is to maintain a hash table, which requires the simulator knows the value of each query. However, since the simulator has to *measure* the query before responding it, this technique would *destroy* this superposition state and obtain the state $|k_i\rangle$ with probability $|c_i|^2$. Therefore, new techniques for designing or analyzing cryptographic schemes in the QROM are developed [4, 26, 29].

The following lemma says that it is infeasible for any oracle algorithm (with quantum computing ability, possibly) within bounded queries to find a non-zero point (i.e., d *s.t.* $\mathcal{B}(d) = 1$) for a sufficiently sparse random function $\mathcal{B}$.

Lemma 1 ([26])**.** *Let* $\eta \in [0,1]$ *be a fixed number. Let* $\mathcal{B} : \mathbb{D} \rightarrow \{0,1\}$ *be a random function, s.t. for each* $d \in \mathbb{D}$, $\mathcal{B}(d)$ *is independently distributed with Bernoulli distribution* $\Pr[\mathcal{B}(d) = 1] = \eta$. *Let* $\mathcal{A}$ *be an algorithm that performs at almost* q *queries (that could be quantum superposition queries) to* $\mathcal{B}$. *Then* $\Pr[\mathcal{B}(d) = 1 : d \leftarrow \mathcal{A}^{\mathcal{B}}()] \leq 2(q+1)\sqrt{\eta}$.

The following lemma states that a truly random function and a proper polynomial are indistinguishable for an attacker within queries of bounded times. Since it allows the attacker to make superposition queries, this lemma also implies an alternative method to simulate a random oracle in the quantum world.

Lemma 2 ([29])**.** *A 2q-wise independent function is perfectly indistinguishable from a random function, for any algorithm performing at most* q *queries. And a uniformly random polynomial function with at least degree* $2q - 1$ *is 2q-wise independent.*

2.3   Non-interactive Zero-Knowledge Proof of Knowledge

A non-interactive proof protocol $\Psi = (\mathcal{P}, \mathcal{V})$ for a relation R can be described as $(\pi \leftarrow \mathcal{P}^H(x, w), \nu \leftarrow \mathcal{V}^H(x, \pi))$, in which, the prover $\mathcal{P}$ and the verifier $\mathcal{V}$ are PPT algorithms, H is a random oracle, x is the statement, w is the witness *s.t.* $(x, w) \in R$, and $\nu \in \{0, 1\}$. Let $\mathcal{R}$ be the uniform distribution of random oracles.

Completeness property states that a proof produced by an honest prover will always be accepted by an honest verifier.

Definition 1 (Completeness, [26]). $\Psi = (\mathcal{P}, \mathcal{V})$ *is complete, if for any* $(x, w) \in R$, $H \leftarrow \mathcal{R}$, $\pi \leftarrow \mathcal{P}^H(x, w)$, *we have that* $1 \leftarrow \mathcal{V}^H(x, \pi)$ *with overwhelming probability.*

Zero-knowledge property says that a malicious verifier cannot infer anything except validity of the statement through adaptively getting proofs from the prover.

Definition 2 (Zero-knowledge, [26]). $\Psi = (\mathcal{P}, \mathcal{V})$ *is zero-knowledge, if there is a pair of algorithms* $(\mathcal{S}_P, \mathcal{S}_O)$ *(called simulator), s.t. for any quantum-polynomial-time algorithm* $\mathcal{A}$, *we have that*

$$|\Pr[b = 1 : H \hookleftarrow \mathcal{R}, b \leftarrow \mathcal{A}^{H,\mathcal{P}}()]| - |\Pr[b = 1 : H \leftarrow \mathcal{S}_O, b \leftarrow \mathcal{A}^{H,\mathcal{S}_P}()|$$

is negligible.

Knowledge-soundness captures that if a prover can produce a valid proof with the probability greater than the soundness error, then there is an extractor that can extract a witness by interacting with the prover. A non-interactive protocol is an NIZKPoK if it is complete, zero-knowledge and knowledge-sound.

The *online-extractability* is a special case of *knowledge soundness*. It captures that the extractor can extract a witness from a valid proof, without rewinding the prover. In quantum setting, the extractor in this property is allowed to get the circuit description of the random oracles, which are generated by a simulator $\mathcal{S}_O$.

Definition 3 (Online-extractability, [26]). $\Psi = (\mathcal{P}, \mathcal{V})$ *is online extractable w.r.t* $\mathcal{S}_O$, *if there is a PPT extractor* $\mathcal{E}$ *s.t. for any quantum-polynomial-time adversary* $\mathcal{A}$, *we have that*

$$\Pr[\nu = 1 \land (x, w) \notin R : H \leftarrow \mathcal{S}_O, (x, \pi) \leftarrow \mathcal{A}^H, \nu \leftarrow \mathcal{V}^H(x, \pi), w \leftarrow \mathcal{E}(H, x, \pi)]$$

is negligible.

The following property says the online-extractability still holds when the adversary can adaptively get many simulated proofs.

Definition 4 (Simulation-sound online-extractability, [26]). $\Psi = (\mathcal{P}, \mathcal{V})$ *is simulation-sound online-extractable, if there is a polynomial-time algorithm* $\mathcal{E}$ *(called extractor) s.t. for any quantum-polynomial-time algorithm* $\mathcal{A}$,

$$\Pr[\nu = 1 \land (x, \pi) \notin \mathbb{X} \land (x, w) \notin R :$$
$$H \leftarrow \mathcal{S}_O, (x, \pi) \leftarrow \mathcal{A}^{H,\mathcal{S}_P}, \nu \leftarrow \mathcal{V}^H(x, \pi), w \leftarrow \mathcal{E}(H, x, \pi)]$$

is negligible. $\mathbb{X}$ *denotes the set of all proofs produced by* $\mathcal{S}_P$.

3 Online-Extractable NIZK Proof in QROM from Generalized Sigma Protocols

The Unruh transformation [26] is a generic framework to construct an online-extractable NIZK proof system from a standard sigma protocol. In this section, we show how to construct a non-interactive proof system from an arbitrary generalized sigma protocol by using the Unruh transformation, and prove that it is still an NIZK proof system with online-extractability.

3.1 Generalized Sigma Protocols

Sigma protocols [8] are a certain class of three-message proof systems, existing for many relations and admitting very generic operations. A sigma protocol Σ for a relation R can be described by a tuple $(D_{com}, D_{ch}, D_{resp}, P_{\Sigma}^1, P_{\Sigma}^2, V_{\Sigma})$, in which D_{com}, D_{ch} and D_{resp} are the domains of the messages; $(P_{\Sigma}^1, P_{\Sigma}^2)$ are two PPT algorithms that share the same state and constitute a prover; and V_{Σ} is a PPT verifier. We denote the statement by x and the witness by w. The first message is called *commitment*, that is $com \leftarrow P_{\Sigma}^1(x, w)$. The second message is called *challenge*, that is uniformly picked from D_{ch}: $ch \hookleftarrow D_{ch}$ by the verifier V. The last message is called *response*, that is sent by the prover: $resp \leftarrow P_{\Sigma}^2(x, w, com, ch)$. Finally, the verifier checks whether the proof is valid: $\nu \leftarrow V(x, com, ch, resp)$, where $\nu = 0$ denotes that the proof is invalid, and $\nu = 1$ denotes the opposite case.

We consider the sigma protocols with the completeness, the honest-verifier zero-knowledge (HVZK) property, and the (computational) k-special soundness. We call them *generalized sigma protocols*. The properties are defined as follows.

Definition 5. *For a sigma protocol $\Sigma = (D_{com}, D_{ch}, D_{resp}, P_{\Sigma}^1, P_{\Sigma}^2, V_{\Sigma})$,*

1. **Completeness:** *If P, V follow the protocol on input x and private input w to P s.t. $(x, w) \in R$, the verifier accepts this proof with overwhelming probability.*
2. **(computational) k-special soundness:** *Let $k \geq 2$ be a certain positive integer. Let $(com, ch_1, resp_1), \cdots, (com, ch_k, resp_k)$ be valid proofs for some statement x, that are produced by an arbitrary quantum-polynomial-time adversary $\mathcal{A}$, where $ch_1, \cdots, ch_k$ are pairwise distinct. There is a PPT algorithm E_{Σ} that takes the k valid proofs as inputs and outputs a witness w s.t. $(x, w) \in R$ with overwhelming probability. Specifically, 2-special soundness is also known as **standard special soundness**.*
3. **Honest-verifier zero-knowledge (HVZK):** *There is a PPT algorithm S_{Σ} s.t. for any quantum-polynomial-time adversary $\mathcal{A}$, for all $(x, w) \in R$,*

$$| \Pr[b = 1 : com \leftarrow P_{\Sigma}^1(x, w), ch \hookleftarrow D_{ch}, resp \leftarrow P_{\Sigma}^2(com, ch, x, w),$$
$$b \leftarrow \mathcal{A}(com, ch, resp)]| - | \Pr[b = 1 : (com, ch, resp) \leftarrow S_{\Sigma}(x), b \leftarrow \mathcal{A}(com, ch, resp)]|$$

is negligible.

Generalized sigma protocols with 2-special soundness are called the standard sigma protocols. As most sigma protocols are 2-special sound, many researches [6,24,26] only consider the standard sigma protocols, ignoring the sigma protocols with k-special soundness. However, the two properties are not identical. From their definitions, in the standard sigma protocols, a malicious prover can only answer to a certain challenge for a forged commitment, which also known as *optimal soundness* [7]. k-special soundness does not necessarily have *optimal soundness* property. This difference makes the well-known OR-composition [8] method not applicable to non-standard sigma protocols. Therefore, any conclusions that apply to standard sigma protocols must be rigorously justified when they are promoted to generalized sigma protocols.

3.2   Non-interactive Protocol from General Sigma Protocols

Now we turn to show how to build a non-interactive proof system from an arbitrary generalized sigma protocol, through the Unruh transformation.

In the Unruh transformation, the prover needs to produce several commitments $(com_i)_{[t]}$, generate various responses to at least k pairwise distinct challenge elements for each commitment com_i, hide all responses using a random oracle $G : D_{resp} \rightharpoonup D_{resp}$, and only open one response $resp_{i,J_i}$ for each com_i, where J_i is determined by another random oracle H. Since responses for different challenges under the same commitment are already contained (although hidden) in the proof, it is possible to extract the witness without rewinding the prover. The verification of this protocol is quite straightforward. The verifier first computes the $(J_i)_{[t]}$, and checks (i) whether $V_\Sigma(com_i, ch_{i,J_i}, resp_{i,J_i}) = 1$ for all $i \in [t]$, (ii) whether h_{i,J_i} is honestly generated from $resp_{i,J_i}$ for all $i \in [t]$, and (iii) whether all challenge elements for the same commitment are pairwise distinct. A more detailed description is given as follows.

Description of the Protocol. Let $\Sigma = (D_{com}, D_{ch}, D_{resp}, P_\Sigma^1, P_\Sigma^2, V_\Sigma)$ be an arbitrary generalized sigma protocol with k-special soundness, cf. Definition 5. Let t and $m \geq k$ be positive integers. In this protocol, t is the number of times $\mathcal{P}$ needs to run the algorithm P_Σ^1, and m is the number of challenges that $\mathcal{P}$ needs to answer under each commitment generated by P_Σ^1. Let $H : \{0,1\}^{\leq \ell} \rightharpoonup \{1, \cdots, m\}^t$ for some large enough $\ell \in \mathbb{N}$ and $G : D_{resp} \rightharpoonup D_{resp}$ be two hash functions, which are modeled as random oracles when analyzing security. The non-interactive protocol $\Psi = (\mathcal{P}, \mathcal{V})$ is built as shown in Fig. 1. We remark Ψ is exactly the Unruh's construction [26], with the exception that we require $m > k$ to make it compatible with the generalized sigma protocols. The requirement is necessary for the online-extractability.

3.3   Analysis of the Unruh Transformation

The non-interactive protocol Ψ has been shown to be a online-extractable NIZK proof system if the underlying sigma protocol is a standard sigma protocol [26].

$\mathcal{P}$:
Input $(x, w) \in R$
For $i = 1$ to t do
  $com_i \leftarrow P_\Sigma^1(x, w)$
  For $j = 1$ to m do
    $ch_{i,j} \leftarrow D_{ch}/\{ch_{i,1}, \cdots ch_{i,j-1}\}$
    $resp_{i,j} \leftarrow P_\Sigma^2(com_i, ch_{i,j}, x, w)$
For $i = 1$ to t do
  For $j = 1$ to m do
    $h_{i,j} = G(resp_{i,j})$
$J_1|\cdots|J_t :=$
$H(x, (com_i)_{[t]}, (ch_{i,j})_{[t]\times[m]}, (h_{i,j})_{[t]\times[m]})$
For all i, set $resp_i := resp_{i,J_i}$
Return $\pi :=$
$((com_i)_{[t]}, (ch_{i,j})_{[t]\times[m]}, (h_{i,j})_{[t]\times[m]}, (resp_i)_{[t]})$

$\mathcal{V}$:
Input: (x, π)
$J_1|\cdots|J_t :=$
$H(x, (com_i)_{[t]}, (ch_{i,j})_{[t]\times[m]}, (h_{i,j})_{[t]\times[m]})$
For $i = 1$ to t do
  Check $ch_{i,1}, \cdots, ch_{i,m}$ pairwise distinct
For $i = 1$ to t do
  Check $V_\Sigma(x, com_i, ch_{i,J_i}, resp_i) = 1$
For $i = 1$ to t do
  Check $h_{i,J_i} = G(resp_i)$
If all checks succeed Then
Return 1

Fig. 1. Non-interactive protocol from arbitrary generalized sigma protocols

In the original proof, the standard soundness is necessary for proving the online-extractability but not for others properties. In this section, we review the results on completeness and zero-knowledge property of the Unruh transformation, and provide a new proof for online-extractability which removes the dependence on the standard soundness.

Already Known Properties. For the completeness of the security analysis, we present the already known results on the properties of a non-interactive protocol Ψ constructed from an arbitrary generalized sigma protocol. These properties, including completeness, zero-knowledge property and non-malleability, are proved in [26], without requiring soundness property of the underlying sigma protocol.

The completeness comes the completeness of the sigma protocol.

Lemma 3 (Completeness [26]). *If Σ is complete, Ψ is complete.*

The main challenge in proving zero-knowledge is to simulate and reprogram quantum random oracles. In the [26], the simulator is a two-stage algorithm $(\mathcal{S}_P, \mathcal{S}_O)$. $\mathcal{S}_O$ initializes the two random oracles H and G as two random polynomial functions p_H and p_G, the degree of which are greater than $2q_H - 1$ and $2q_G - 1$, respectively. As stated in Lemma 2, the polynomial function p_G (and p_H) cannot be distinguished with a random function for any algorithm performing at most q_G (and q_H) queries. $\mathcal{S}_P$ gets the description of p_H and p_G, and can program them by replacing with other functions. By constructing such a simulator $(\mathcal{S}_P, \mathcal{S}_O)$, the zero-knowledge property can be proved.

Lemma 4 (Zero-knowledge [26]). *Let Σ be a sigma protocol with correctness and HVZK property. And the output of P_Σ^2 has superlogarithmic mini-entropy. Let Ψ be a non-interactive protocol constructed from the sigma protocol Σ, as in*

$\mathcal{E}$:
Input $G = p_G$, H, x, $\pi = ((com_i)_{[t]}, (ch_{i,j})_{[t] \times [m]}, (h_{i,j})_{[t] \times [m]}, (resp_i)_{[t]})$
$J_1 | \cdots | J_t := H(x, (com_i)_{[t]}, (ch_{i,j})_{[t] \times [m]}, (h_{i,j})_{[t] \times [m]})$
For $i = 1$ to t do
$\quad CU = \{(com_i, ch_{i,J_i}, resp_{i,J_i})\}$
$\quad$ For $j = 1$ to m except J_i do
$\quad\quad$ For each $resp'_{i,j} \in p_G^{-1}(h_{i,j})$ do
$\quad\quad\quad$ If $V_\Sigma(com_i, ch_{i,h}, resp) = 1$ Then
$\quad\quad\quad\quad CU = CU \cup \{((com_i, ch_{i,j}, resp'_{i,j}))\}$, break
$\quad$ If $|CU| = k$ Then
$\quad\quad$ Extract $(com_i, ch_{i,j_1}, resp_{i,j_1}, \ldots, ch_{i,j_k}, resp_{i,j_k}) \leftarrow CU$
$\quad\quad$ Return $E_\Sigma(com_i, ch_{i,j_1}, resp_{i,j_1}, \ldots, ch_{i,j_k}, resp_{i,j_k})$.

Fig. 2. Extractor for the NIZK proof system

Fig. 1. Assume that the tuple $((com_i)_{[t]}, (ch_{i,j})_{[t] \times [m]}, (h_{i,j})_{[t] \times [m]})$ produced by $\mathcal{P}$ also has superlogarithmic min-entropy. Then, Ψ is zero-knowledge.

Non-malleability captures that an attacker with access to the simulation S_P cannot produce a new proof by just modifying the response of a simulated proof.

Lemma 5 (Non-malleability [26]). *Let $\mathcal{A}$ be any quantum-polynomial-time attacker. Let q_G be the upper bound for the number of queries to G made by $\mathcal{A}$, S_P and $\mathcal{V}$ together. Let n be the upper bound for the number of invocations to S_P. Let κ be the lower bound for the collision-entropy of the tuple $((com_i)_{[t]}, (ch_{i,j})_{[t] \times [m]}, (h_{i,j})_{[t] \times [m]})$. The set of all simulation proofs generated by S_P is denoted by $\mathbb{X}$. Let MallSim denote the event*

$$[\pi^{half} = \pi^{*half} : (G, H) \leftarrow S_O, (x, \pi = (\pi^{half}, (resp_{i,J_i})_{[t]})) \leftarrow \mathcal{A}^{G,H,S_P},$$
$$(x, \pi^* = (\pi^{*half}, (resp^*_{i,J^*_i})_{[t]}) \in \mathbb{X}, 1 \leftarrow \mathcal{V}^{G,H}(x, \pi))],$$

where π^{half} denotes $((com_i)_{[t]}, (ch_{i,j})_{[t] \times [m]}, (h_{i,j})_{[t] \times [m]})$. Then, we have

$$\Pr[MallSim] \leq \frac{n(n+1)}{2} 2^{-\kappa} + \mathcal{O}((q_G + 1)^3 2^{-\ell_{resp}}),$$

where the ℓ_{resp} is the upper bound of the bit length of $resp_{i,J_i}$.

Online-Extractability. To prove the online-extractability, we first construct an extractor $\mathcal{E}$ as shown in Fig. 2. $\mathcal{E}$ takes an input as the description of p_G. Here, p_G is a polynomial over $GF(2^{\ell_{resp}})$, and $p_G^{-1}(h_{i,j})$ is the set of preimages of $h_{i,j}$ under G. From previous results [3], the inverse function p_G^{-1} can be efficiently computed. $\mathcal{E}$ can use the inverse function p_G^{-1} to recover different responses under at least k pair-wise-distinct challenges for one commitment, from a proof π for statement x, and extract a witness w by running the extractor E_Σ of the sigma protocol.

Now, we show Ψ is online-extractable w.r.t. the extractor $\mathcal{E}$. For clarity, we also use the following definitions, which are presented in [26] and will be useful in the following context.

Definition 6. *For a sigma protocol $\Sigma = (D_{com}, D_{ch}, D_{resp}, P^1_\Sigma, P^2_\Sigma, V_\Sigma)$, a tuple $(com, ch, resp)$ is Σ-valid iff $V_\Sigma(com, ch, resp) = 1$. Let RE be a finite subset of D_{resp}, we call a tuple (com, ch, RE) is set-valid iff there is at least one element $resp' \in RE$ s.t. $(com, ch, resp')$ is Σ-valid. We call $(com, ch, resp)$ (or $(com, ch, RE))$ Σ-invalid (or set-invalid) if it is not Σ-valid (or set-valid).*

The following theorem implies the online extractability of Ψ. It states that, no quantum-polynomial-time adversary has the ability to produce a valid proof from which is not possible to extract other $k-1$ valid responses for distinct $k-1$ challenges under the same commitment. Thus, the extractor can always get k valid responses from a valid proof π, and can use E_Σ to extract the witness.

Theorem 2 (Online-extractability). *Let G be an arbitrary distributed function, and let $H : \{0,1\}^{\leq \ell} \to \{0,1\}^{t \log m}$ be uniformly random (and independent of G). Then for any algorithm $\mathcal{A}^{G,H}$, it is hard to find x and $\pi = ((com_i)_{[t]}, (ch_{i,j})_{[t] \times [m]}, (h_{i,j})_{[t] \times [m]}, (resp_i)_{[t]})$ which satisfies the following conditions:*

i. $\forall i,\ h_{i,J_i} = G(resp_i)$ *where* $J_1|\cdots|J_t := H(x, (com_i)_{[t]}, (ch_{i,j})_{[t] \times [m]}, (h_{i,j})_{[t] \times [m]})$;

ii. $(com_i, ch_{i,J_i}, resp_i)$ *is Σ-valid, $\forall i$;*

iii. For each i, define $\mathbb{J}_i := \{j | (com_i, ch_{i,j}, G^{-1}(h_{i,j}))$ is set-valid$\}$, then $|\mathbb{J}_i| \leq k-1$.

Concretely, if $\mathcal{A}$ issues at most q_H queries to $H()$, it can find such a pair (x, π) with probability at most $2(q_H + 1)2^{-t(\log m - \log(k-1))/2}$.

Proof. For clarity, the statement we are going to prove will be stronger than that specified in this theorem. In detail, we consider

1. a stronger attacker $\mathcal{A}_1$: G is a fixed function and $\mathcal{A}_1$ can get the full description of it, instead of only getting access to an oracle G;
2. and a weaker goal: the attacker need to output a tuple $(x, (com_i)_{[t]}, (ch_{i,j})_{[t] \times [m]}, (h_{i,j})_{[t] \times [m]})$ along with $(\mathbb{J}_i)$ s.t. $|\mathbb{J}_i| \leq k-1$ for each i and $H(x, (com_i)_{[t]}, (ch_{i,j})_{[t] \times [m]}, (h_{i,j})_{[t] \times [m]}) \in \mathbb{J}_1 \times \cdots \times \mathbb{J}_t$.

Here, $\mathbb{J}_i$ is defined as in the condition (iii). It is obvious that if there is an algorithm $\mathcal{A}$ that can output a tuple satisfying the conditions (i) (ii) (iii), then there must be an algorithm $\mathcal{A}_1$ achieving *the weaker goal*. Thus, it is enough to prove that *the weaker goal* is still hard for *the stronger attacker*. To accomplish that, we first divide the *the weaker goal* into two stages:

1. Find a tuple $(x, (com_i)_{[t]}, (ch_{i,j})_{[t] \times [m]}, (h_{i,j})_{[t] \times [m]})$, s.t. for each i, the cardinality of the set $\mathbb{J}_i$ is at most $k-1$;

2. Make it hold that $H(x, (com_i)_{[t]}, (ch_{i,j})_{[t] \times [m]}, (h_{i,j})_{[t] \times [m]}) \in \mathbb{J}_1 \times \cdots \times \mathbb{J}_t$.

We use $\mathbb{T}$ to denote the set of all tuples satisfying the requirement in the first stage. We observe that the first stage can be achieved by running the prover algorithm $\mathcal{P}$ of Ψ, and for each i and all $j \neq J_i$ replacing $h_{i,j}$ with random elements. Without lost of generality, we assume that $\mathcal{A}_1$ can find an element $d \in \mathbb{T}$. So, it is sufficient to prove the hardness for finding a tuple $d \in \mathbb{T}$ satisfying the requirement in the second stage, i.e.,

$$H(d) \in \mathbb{J}_1 \times \cdots \times \mathbb{J}_t. \tag{1}$$

Now, we consider a deterministic algorithm $\mathcal{F}$, which takes an input as a set $\mathbb{J}_i$ with size as most $k - 1$ and outputs a set $\bar{\mathbb{J}}_i$ s.t. $\mathbb{J}_i \subset \bar{\mathbb{J}}_i$ and $|\bar{\mathbb{J}}_i| = k - 1$. We note such an algorithm $\mathcal{F}$ can be trivially constructed by orderly adding new elements to the original set. For example, let $k = 5$, $\mathbb{J}_1 = \{2, 5\}$, $\mathbb{J}_2 = \{1, 3, 4\}$, then we can get $\bar{\mathbb{J}}_1$ by adding 1,3 to $\mathbb{J}_1$, and get $\bar{\mathbb{J}}_2$ by adding 2 to $\mathbb{J}_2$. With this notation, we modify the requirement in the second state to a weaker variant:

$$H(d) \in \bar{\mathbb{J}}_1 \times \cdots \times \bar{\mathbb{J}}_t. \tag{2}$$

Since $\mathbb{J}_i \subset \bar{\mathbb{J}}_i$ for $i \in [t]$, an element $d \in \mathbb{T}$ that satisfies Eq. 1 also meets the weaker requirement described by Eq. 2. Thus, we can show the hardness of finding a $d \in \mathbb{T}$ satisfying Eq. 1, by proving the infeasibility of finding a $d \in \mathbb{T}$ satisfying Eq. 2.

Let $\mathcal{B} : \mathbb{T} \to \{0, 1\}$ be a random function with that all $\mathcal{B}(d)$ is independently distributed as $\Pr[\mathcal{B}(d) = 1] = 2^{-(t(\log m - \log(k-1)))}$. Using the function $\mathcal{B}$, we can build a function $H_B : \{0, 1\}^* \to \{0, 1\}^{t \log m}$ as

$$H_B(d) = \begin{cases} y \hookleftarrow \{0, 1\}^{t \log m}, \text{if } d \notin \mathbb{T}; \\ y \hookleftarrow \bar{\mathbb{J}}_1 \times \cdots \times \bar{\mathbb{J}}_t, \text{if } d \in \mathbb{T} \text{ and } \mathcal{B}(d) = 1; \\ y \hookleftarrow \{0, 1\}^{t \log m} \backslash (\bar{\mathbb{J}}_1 \times \cdots \times \bar{\mathbb{J}}_t), \text{if } d \in \mathbb{T} \text{ and } \mathcal{B}(d) \neq 1. \end{cases} \tag{3}$$

Since $\mathcal{B}(d) = 1$ with probability $2^{t(\log m - \log(k-1))}$, it is easy to see that H_B is a uniform random function. In other words, H_B has the same distribution with H, and we can replace H with H_B, without raising any advantages of $\mathcal{A}_1$. In this case, if $\mathcal{A}_1^{H_B}$ outputs an element $d \in \mathbb{T}$ satisfying the requirement in the second stage, $\mathcal{A}_1^{H_B}$ also finds an element $d \in \mathbb{T}$ s.t. $\mathcal{B}(d) = 1$. Basing on this fact, we can build an algorithm $\mathcal{S}$, which constructs a function H_B by getting access to $\mathcal{B}()$, and provides an access to it for $\mathcal{A}_1$. $\mathcal{S}_H$ will output what $\mathcal{A}_1^{H_B}$ outputs. Recalling the Lemma 1, the probability $\Pr[\mathcal{B}(d) = 1 : d \leftarrow \mathcal{S}^\mathcal{B}()]$ is at most $2(q' + 1)\sqrt{\eta}$, where q' is the number of queries issued to $\mathcal{B}()$ and η is the probability with which $\mathcal{B}(d) = 1$. Note that $\mathcal{S}$ does not need to query all values of $\mathcal{B}$. Instead, $\mathcal{S}$ performs queries to $\mathcal{B}$ only when $\mathcal{A}_1$ issues queries to H'_B. Therefore, we have $q' = q_H$, and thus the probability with which $\mathcal{A}_1^{H_B}$ can find an element $d \in \mathbb{T}$ satisfying $\mathcal{B}(d) = 1$ is at most $2(q_H + 1)2^{-t(\log m - \log(k-1))/2}$. This is what we want to prove.

The simulation-sound online-extractability is implied by the online-extractability and the non-malleability.

Theorem 3 (Simulation-sound online-extractability). *Let Σ be a sigma protocol with k-special soundness property. Let $\Psi = (\mathcal{P}, \mathcal{V})$ be a protocol described in Fig. 1 using Σ. Let $(\mathcal{S}_P, \mathcal{S}_O)$ be its corresponding simulator and $\mathcal{E}$ be the extractor. Assume the tuple $((com_i)_{[t]}, (ch_{i,j})_{[t] \times [m]}, (h_{i,j})_{[t] \times [m]})$ produced by $\mathcal{S}_P$ has superlogarithmic collision-entropy, and the ranges of H and G have super-polynomial sizes. Then Ψ is simulation-sound online-extractable with $\mathcal{E}$, with respect to $(\mathcal{S}_P, \mathcal{S}_O)$.*

Proof. The definition of this property is stated in Definition 4. For clarity, we define the following events:

- ShouldEx: $\nu = 1 \wedge (x, \pi) \notin \mathbb{X}$, which denotes that the output of $\mathcal{A}$ is a valid proof and not contained in the set $\mathbb{X}$ of simulated proofs.
- ExFail: ShouldEx $\wedge$ $(x, w) \notin R$, which denotes that the output of $\mathcal{A}$ belong to ShouldEx, but the extractor fails to extract the witness for x.
- E_1, E_2 and E_3 denote that the output of $\mathcal{A}$ satisfies the condition of Theorem 2 (i), (ii) and (iii), respectively.
- MallSim, defined as in Lemma 5.

Let H_0 be the initial state of H, and H_1 be the state of H after (x, π) produced by $\mathcal{A}$.

This proof starts from a simple observation: the event ExFail $\wedge$ ¬MallSim $\wedge$ ¬E_3 happens with negligible probability. In detail, ensured by ¬MallSim, $\forall (x^*, \pi^*) \in \mathbb{X}$, it holds that $(x, \pi^{half}) \neq (x^*, \pi^{*half})$ (π^{half} is defined as in Lemma 5). Thus, the random oracle H is never reprogrammed at (x, π^{half}) (as stated in [26], $\mathcal{S}_P$ only programs H at points that $\mathcal{S}_P$ outputs). It implies that $H_0(x, \pi^{half}) = H_1(x, \pi^{half})$. Ensured by ¬$E_3$, there must be at least k pairs $(ch_{i,j_\tau}, resp_{i,j_\tau})_{\tau \in [k]}$ for some i, where $(ch_{i,j_\tau})_{\tau \in [k]}$ are pairwise distinct. Then, the extractor $\mathcal{E}$ can get a witness w by running $w \leftarrow E_\Sigma(com_i, ch_{i,j_1}, resp_{i,j_1}, \ldots, ch_{i,j_k}, resp_{i,j_k})$. In this case, the event $(x, w) \notin R$ happens only with ϵ_Σ, which is the failure probability of the extractor algorithm in the underlying sigma protocol. In other words, we have $\Pr[\text{ExFail} | \neg \text{MallSim} \wedge \neg E_3] \leq \epsilon_\Sigma$, which also implies

$$\Pr[\text{ExFail} \wedge \neg \text{MallSim} \wedge \neg E_3] \leq \epsilon_\Sigma. \tag{4}$$

Another useful observation is that ExFail $\Rightarrow E_1 \wedge E_2$, which is due to that in ExFail the output of $\mathcal{A}$ is valid and every valid proof satisfies condition (i) and (ii) in Theorem 2. From the two observations, the result of this theorem can deduced via the following probability analysis.

$$\Pr[\text{ExFail}] = \Pr[\text{ExFail} \wedge \neg \text{MallSim}] + \Pr[\text{ExFail} \wedge \text{MallSim}]$$
$$\leq \Pr[\text{ExFail} \wedge E_1 \wedge E_2 \wedge \neg \text{MallSim}] + \Pr[\text{MallSim}]$$
$$= \Pr[\text{ExFail} \wedge E_1 \wedge E_2 \wedge E_3 \neg \text{MallSim}] +$$
$$\Pr[\text{ExFail} \wedge E_1 \wedge E_2 \wedge \neg E_3 \neg \text{MallSim}] + \Pr[\text{MallSim}]$$
$$\leq \Pr[E_1 \wedge E_2 \wedge E_3] + \Pr[\text{ExFail} \wedge \neg E_3 \wedge \neg \text{MallSim}] + \Pr[\text{MallSim}].$$

Lemma 5 and Theorem 2 already imply that $\Pr[E_1 \wedge E_2 \wedge E_3]$ and $\Pr[\texttt{MallSim}]$ are both negligible. Since $\Pr[\texttt{ExFail} \wedge \neg E_3 \wedge \neg \texttt{MallSim}]$ is also negligible as shown in Eq. 4, $\Pr[\texttt{ExFail}]$ is negligible. We have completed this proof.

We have showed that Ψ is zero-knowledge and online-extractable if the outputs of P_{Σ}^2, $\mathcal{P}$ and $\mathcal{S}_P$ have superlogarithmic min-entropy or collision-entropy. Unruh [26] has showed the conditions are not really restrictions on the underlying sigma protocols. In detail, we can make every sigma protocol satisfies these requirements by padding superlogarithmic random bits to the commitments and responses, and modifying the V_{Σ} to ignore these random bits. As a conclusion, we have the following results.

Corollary 1. *Let Σ be a sigma protocol with completeness, k-special soundness, and HVZK property. Then, there exists an NIZK proof system with simulation-sound online-extractability with respect to Σ.*

4   Secure Stern Signatures in QROM

4.1   Stern Protocol

Stern protocols were originally proposed for demonstrating the possession of a short vector w.r.t. a syndrome matrix, i.e. proving there is a vector $\mathbf{x} \in \{-1, 0, 1\}^d$ *s.t.* $\mathbf{M} \cdot \mathbf{x} = \mathbf{v}$ for a public matrix $\mathbf{M}$ and a vector $\mathbf{v}$. In recent years, they are adapted to the lattice setting, and are extended to prove the possession of a secret vector belonging to a specific designed set $\mathbb{V} \subset \{-1, 0, 1\}^d$. It has been shown that many relations in lattice-based cryptography can be transformed into this form [17, 19]. We define such a relation as Stern relation in the following, and present a Stern protocol for it.

Definition 7 (Stern Relation). *Let $\mathbb{V} \subset \{-1, 0, 1\}^d$, n, d, q are positive integers, the Stern relation is defined as*

$$R_S = \{(\mathbf{M} \in \mathbb{Z}_q^{n \times d}, \mathbf{v} \in \mathbb{Z}_q^n); \mathbf{x} \in \{-1, 0, 1\}^d : \mathbf{M} \cdot \mathbf{x} = \mathbf{v} \bmod q, \mathbf{x} \in \mathbb{V}\}.$$

Permutations are the main techniques used in Stern protocols. To handle a Stern relation, we need an *eligible set of permutations* (ESP) as in Definition 8 for the set $\mathbb{V}$.

Definition 8 (Eligible Set of Permutations (ESP)). *Let $\mathbb{S}$ be a finite set s.t. each element $\varphi \in \mathbb{S}$ can be associated with a permutation Φ_{φ} over d elements. We call $\mathbb{E}_S = \{\Phi_{\varphi} | \varphi \in \mathbb{S}\}$ is an **eligible set of permutations** for $\mathbb{V}$, if*

$$\begin{cases} \mathbf{x} \in \mathbb{V} \iff \Phi_{\varphi}(\mathbf{x}) \in \mathbb{V}; \\ \text{if } \mathbf{x} \in \mathbb{V} \text{ and } \varphi \text{ is uniform in } \mathbb{S}, \text{ then } \Phi_{\varphi}(\mathbf{x}) \text{ is uniform in } \mathbb{V}. \end{cases}$$

For the Stern relation R_S with an ESP $\mathbb{E}_S$, Libert *et al.* [19] presented a Stern protocol, to demonstrate the knowledge of $\mathbf{x}$ for the public tuple $(\mathbf{M}, \mathbf{v})$. They also proved that the protocol is a zero-knowledge argument of knowledge (ZKAoK) in the classical setting. A detail description for the protocol is introduced in Appendix A. The results about the Stern protocol are summarized in the following lemma.

Lemma 6 ([19]). *Assuming there is an ESP $\mathbb{E}_S = \{\Phi_\varphi | \varphi \in \mathbb{S}\}$ for the set $\mathbb{V}$ of the Stern relation R_S, there is a statistical ZKAoK for R_S, with perfect completeness, soundness error $2/3$, and proof size of $\widetilde{\mathcal{O}}(d \cdot \log q)$.*

Stern Protocol in the Quantum Setting. While the Stern protocol has been proved to be a ZKAoK in the classical world, the use of computational binding commitment scheme in Stern protocols may lead to some negative result in the quantum world, as discussed in [2]. In the following, we show that it is still a generalized sigma protocol with 3-special soundness. The result is inherently implied by the proof provided in [19] for Lemma 6.

Completeness is easy to be verified in both the classical world and the quantum world. To prove that this protocol is an argument of knowledge, Libert *et al.* firstly proves the 3-special soundness [19], and then use techniques in [11] to complete the proof. Since the 3-special soundness can be reduced to the computational binding property of the lattice-based commitment scheme [13] without using rewinding techniques, it is also solid in the quantum world. We also note that there is a quantum attack on computational binding commitment scheme [2], that is a quantum-polynomial-time algorithm [2] that can open a commitment value to an arbitrary value. However, it does not mean this algorithm can open one commitment to two values at the same time. Concretely, two open values for the same commitment of [13] will give a solution to the SIS problem [1], which is conjectured to be hard for quantum computers. Thus, this attack will not break the 3-special soundness of Stern protocols.

To prove the zero-knowledge property, basing on the hiding property of COM, Libert *et al.* [19] firstly constructs a PPT simulator $\mathcal{S}$, which can answer to the challenge $ch \neq \bar{ch}$ for the commitment generated according to the guess $\bar{ch}$. We remark $\mathcal{S}$ is built without rewindable access to the prover and based on the hiding property of the lattice-based commitment scheme. Thus, this protocol is HVZK in the quantum world.

From the argument above, it is easy to see the quantum security of Stern protocols, as summarized in Corollary 2.

Corollary 2. *Let R_S be the Stern relation defined in Definition 7, and $\{\Phi_\varphi | \varphi \in \mathbb{S}\}$ be an ESP for the set $\mathbb{V}$. There is a post-quantum secure generalized sigma protocol for R_S with 3-special soundness. The proof size is $\widetilde{\mathcal{O}}(d \cdot \log q)$.*

4.2 General Stern Signatures

As suggested in [26], there is a typical framework for constructing a signature scheme from a hard instance generator for a relation R and an NIZKPoK $\Psi =$

$(\mathcal{P}, \mathcal{V})$ for R. Here, the hard instance generator is an algorithm to generate an instance (x, w) of R and no quantum-polynomial-time adversary can compute a witness w' s.t. $(x, w') \in R$ if only given x. A proof can be bound to a particular message, by including the message in the statement to be proven but ignoring the message when determining whether the statement hashes a witness or not. Formally, the signature scheme $(KeyGen, Sign, Verify)$ can be constructed as follows.

1. $KeyGen(1^\lambda)$: Run $(x, w) \leftarrow G(1^\lambda)$. Set $pk := x$ and $sk := (x, w)$.
2. $Sign(sk, m)$: Run $\pi \leftarrow P((x, m), w)$, and return $\sigma = \pi$.
3. $Verify(pk, \sigma, m)$: Run $\nu \leftarrow V(x, \pi)$, and return ν.

For the signature scheme $(KeyGen, Sign, Verify)$, we have

Theorem 4 ([26]). *If Ψ is zero-knowledge and simulation-sound online-extractable, and Gen is a hard instance generator against quantum-polynomial-time adversaries, the signature scheme (KeyGen, Sign, Verify) is strongly unforgeable.*

The general Stern signatures are built under this framework, by implementing R with R_S, Gen with a hard instance generator for R_S, and Ψ with an NIZKPoK constructed from the Stern protocol. In the existing Stern signatures, the NIZKPoK (in the ROM) is constructed by applying the Fiat-Shamir to a Stern protocol. Observing the hard instances generators in these schemes are lattice-based, an intuitive is to replace the Fiat-Shamir with an alternative NIZKPoK in the QROM. Since the Stern protocol for the relation R_S is a generalized sigma protocol with 3-special soundness, as shown in Theorem 2, there will be an NIZK poof system with simulation-sound online-extractability for R_S from Corollary 2. Then, we can build a secure Stern signature in this way.

We remark that many Stern signatures such as group signatures and ring signatures are designed for diverse functionalities, and their security definitions are beyond the strong unforgeability. An ad-hoc observation is that the original security proofs for these advanced security properties only require of the underlying non-interactive proof system to have the zero-knowledge property and the simulation-sound property. For example, the group signature scheme presented in [18] considers the *full-anonymity* and the *full-traceability*. The former requires the underlying non-interactive protocol is simulation-sound and zero-knowledge, and the latter requires the simulation-soundness. Since applying the Unruh transform to the Stern protocols will give a post-quantum secure NIZK proof system with simulation soundness, we can also get a post-quantum secure group signature. Therefore, modifying the existing Stern signatures with the online-extractable NIZK proof system will be helpful to make them secure against quantum adversaries.

Efficiency of Stern Signatures. Now, we consider the efficiency of the secure Stern signatures. We remark that the size of a signature is dominated by its corresponding non-interactive proof. Thus, considering the proof size is enough.

It is easy to verify that a Stern protocol is originally compatible with the requirements in Lemma 4 and Theorem 3, which means that a Stern protocol can be taken as the underlying sigma protocol of the construction in Fig. 1, without any modification. Formally, we have the following corollary.

Corollary 3. *Let Σ be a Stern protocol for $\mathcal{L}$ with proof size c. Let $t = \omega(\log \lambda)$ and $m = 3$. Then, the non-interactive proof system $\Psi = (\mathcal{P}, \mathcal{V})$ in Fig. 1 is an NIZK proof system with simulation-sound online-extractability. The proof size is $3t \cdot c$.*

Then, we consider the computation cost of the post-quantum secure Stern signatures. Since our modification is only replacing the Fiat-Shamir with the Unruh transformation, comparing the overhead of the prover and the verifier between the two proof system will suffice. Assume the computation cost of the P_Σ^1, P_Σ^2, and V_Σ, of the underlying Stern protocol, are u, v, and w, respectively. Since the overhead of computing a hash function is much smaller than the computation cost of the three algorithms, we just ignore it when analyzing. Then, the prover's computation cost of the NIZK proof system is $t \cdot (u + 3v)$, and the verifier's cost is $t \cdot w$. Compared to the NIZK proof system from the Fiat-Shamir transform, in which the prover's computation cost is almost $t(u + v)$ and the verifier's cost is also $t \cdot w$, our modification will not cause significant efficiency loss.

Acknowledgment. This paper is supported by the National Key Research and Development Program of China through project 2017YFB0802502, by the National Cryptography Development Fund through project MMJJ20170106, by the National Natural Science Foundation of China through projects 61672083, 61532021, 61472429, 61402029, 61702028 and 61571024, by the Beijing Natural Science Foundation through project 4132056.

A   Stern Protocols

Let COM be the string commitment scheme from [13], which is statistically hiding and computational binding and based on the SIS assumptions [1]. Assuming there is an ESP $\mathbb{E}_S = \{\Phi_\varphi | \varphi \in \mathbb{S}\}$ for the set $\mathbb{V}$ of the Stern relation R_S, there is a sigma protocol as in Fig. 3 for R_S.

In a high level, this protocol is derived by two main techniques, *permutation* and *masking*.

- *permutation*: to prove the witness $\mathbf{x} \in \mathbb{V}$, the prover randomly samples $\varphi \leftarrow \mathbb{S}$ that is associated with a permutation Φ_φ, and computes $\Phi_\varphi(\mathbf{x})$. The prover can convince the verifier that $\mathbf{x} \in \mathbb{V}$ in zero-knowledge by leaking $\Phi_\varphi(\mathbf{x})$, since from the properties of Φ_φ as in Definition 8, we have

$$\Phi_\varphi(\mathbf{x}) \in \mathbb{V} \Longleftrightarrow \mathbf{x} \in \mathbb{V}.$$

- *masking*: to prove the knowledge of $\mathbf{x}$ *s.t.* $\mathbf{M} \cdot \mathbf{x} = \mathbf{v} \bmod q$, the prover samples $\mathbf{r} \leftarrow \mathbb{Z}_q^d$, and demonstrates $\mathbf{M} \cdot (\mathbf{r} + \mathbf{x}) = \mathbf{M} \cdot \mathbf{r} + \mathbf{v} \bmod q$ instead.

1. P_Σ^1: The prover samples $\varphi \hookleftarrow \mathbb{S}$, $\mathbf{r}_1 \hookleftarrow \mathbb{Z}_q^d$ and randomness number ρ_1, ρ_2, ρ_3 for COM, then computes $\mathbf{z} = \mathbf{x} + \mathbf{r}$. Then prover sends the following commitments $com = (C_1, C_2, C_3)$ to the verifier, where $C_1 = \mathrm{COM}(\varphi, \mathbf{M} \cdot \mathbf{r} \bmod q; \rho_1)$, $C_2 = \mathrm{COM}(\Phi_\varphi(\mathbf{r}); \rho_2)$, and $C_3 = \mathrm{COM}(\Phi_\varphi(\mathbf{z}); \rho_3)$.
2. The verifier sends a challenge $ch \hookleftarrow \{1, 2, 3\}$ to the prover.
3. P_Σ^2: Acordding to the received challenge ch, the prover sends $resp$, as follows;
   - $ch = 1$: $resp = (\alpha, \zeta, \rho_2, \rho_3)$, where $\alpha = \Phi_\varphi(\mathbf{x})$ and $\zeta = \Phi_\varphi(\mathbf{r})$.
   - $ch = 2$: $resp = (\iota, \mathbf{e}, \rho_1, \rho_3)$, where $\iota = \varphi$ and $\mathbf{e} = \mathbf{z}$.
   - $ch = 3$: $resp = (\psi, \mathbf{f}, \rho_1, \rho_2)$, where $\psi = \varphi$ and $\mathbf{f} = \mathbf{r}$.
 * V_Σ: After receiving $resp$, the verifier performs the following procedures;
   - $ch = 1$: check that $\alpha \in \mathbb{V}$, $\mathrm{COM}(\alpha + \zeta; \rho_3) = C_3$, and $\mathrm{COM}(\zeta; \rho_2) = C_2$.
   - $ch = 2$: check that $C_1 = \mathrm{COM}(\iota, \mathbf{M} \cdot \mathbf{e} - \mathbf{v} \bmod q; \rho_1)$; and $C_3 = \mathrm{COM}(\Phi_\iota(\mathbf{e}); \rho_3)$
   - $ch = 3$: check that $C_1 = \mathrm{COM}(\psi, \mathbf{M} \cdot \mathbf{f}; \rho_1)$ and $C_2 = \mathrm{COM}(\Phi_\psi(f); \rho_2)$.
   Then returns 1 if all conditions hold in each case.

Fig. 3. The general Stern protocol

The two techniques give an intuitive reason why the Stern protocol has HVZK property. The 3-special soundness can be easily checked by computing a witness from three tuples with the same commitment. We refer interested readers to [19] for a detailed proof.

References

1. Ajtai, M.: Generating hard instances of lattice problems (extended abstract). In: the 28th ACM STOC, pp. 99–108. ACM (1996)
2. Ambainis, A., Rosmanis, A., Unruh, D.: Quantum attacks on classical proof systems: the hardness of quantum rewinding. In: FOCS 2014, pp. 474–483. IEEE Computer Society (2014)
3. Ben-Or, M.: Probabilistic algorithms in finite fields. In: FOCS 1981, pp. 394–398 (1981)
4. Boneh, D., Dagdelen, Ö., Fischlin, M., Lehmann, A., Schaffner, C., Zhandry, M.: Random oracles in a quantum world. In: Lee, D.H., Wang, X. (eds.) ASIACRYPT 2011. LNCS, vol. 7073, pp. 41–69. Springer, Heidelberg (2011). https://doi.org/10.1007/978-3-642-25385-0_3
5. Brakerski, Z., Kalai, Y.T.: A framework for efficient signatures, ring signatures and identity based encryption in the standard model. IACR Cryptology ePrint Archive 2010, 86 (2010)

6. Ciampi, M., Persiano, G., Scafuro, A., Siniscalchi, L., Visconti, I.: Improved OR-composition of sigma-protocols. In: Kushilevitz, E., Malkin, T. (eds.) TCC 2016. LNCS, vol. 9563, pp. 112–141. Springer, Heidelberg (2016). https://doi.org/10.1007/978-3-662-49099-0_5

7. Ciampi, M., Persiano, G., Siniscalchi, L., Visconti, I.: A transform for NIZK almost as efficient and general as the Fiat-Shamir transform without programmable random oracles. In: Kushilevitz, E., Malkin, T. (eds.) TCC 2016. LNCS, vol. 9563, pp. 83–111. Springer, Heidelberg (2016). https://doi.org/10.1007/978-3-662-49099-0_4

8. Cramer, R., Damgård, I., Schoenmakers, B.: Proofs of partial knowledge and simplified design of witness hiding protocols. In: Desmedt, Y.G. (ed.) CRYPTO 1994. LNCS, vol. 839, pp. 174–187. Springer, Heidelberg (1994). https://doi.org/10.1007/3-540-48658-5_19

9. Fiat, A., Shamir, A.: How to prove yourself: practical solutions to identification and signature problems. In: Odlyzko, A.M. (ed.) CRYPTO 1986. LNCS, vol. 263, pp. 186–194. Springer, Heidelberg (1987). https://doi.org/10.1007/3-540-47721-7_12

10. Gordon, S.D., Katz, J., Vaikuntanathan, V.: A group signature scheme from lattice assumptions. In: Abe, M. (ed.) ASIACRYPT 2010. LNCS, vol. 6477, pp. 395–412. Springer, Heidelberg (2010). https://doi.org/10.1007/978-3-642-17373-8_23

11. Groth, J.: Evaluating security of voting schemes in the universal composability framework. In: Jakobsson, M., Yung, M., Zhou, J. (eds.) ACNS 2004. LNCS, vol. 3089, pp. 46–60. Springer, Heidelberg (2004). https://doi.org/10.1007/978-3-540-24852-1_4

12. Groth, J., Kohlweiss, M.: One-out-of-many proofs: or how to leak a secret and spend a coin. In: Oswald, E., Fischlin, M. (eds.) EUROCRYPT 2015. LNCS, vol. 9057, pp. 253–280. Springer, Heidelberg (2015). https://doi.org/10.1007/978-3-662-46803-6_9

13. Kawachi, A., Tanaka, K., Xagawa, K.: Concurrently secure identification schemes based on the worst-case hardness of lattice problems. In: Pieprzyk, J. (ed.) ASIACRYPT 2008. LNCS, vol. 5350, pp. 372–389. Springer, Heidelberg (2008). https://doi.org/10.1007/978-3-540-89255-7_23

14. Kiltz, E., Lyubashevsky, V., Schaffner, C.: A concrete treatment of Fiat-Shamir signatures in the quantum random-oracle model. In: Nielsen, J.B., Rijmen, V. (eds.) EUROCRYPT 2018. LNCS, vol. 10822, pp. 552–586. Springer, Cham (2018). https://doi.org/10.1007/978-3-319-78372-7_18

15. Langlois, A., Ling, S., Nguyen, K., Wang, H.: Lattice-based group signature scheme with verifier-local revocation. In: Krawczyk, H. (ed.) PKC 2014. LNCS, vol. 8383, pp. 345–361. Springer, Heidelberg (2014). https://doi.org/10.1007/978-3-642-54631-0_20

16. Libert, B., Ling, S., Mouhartem, F., Nguyen, K., Wang, H.: Signature schemes with efficient protocols and dynamic group signatures from lattice assumptions. In: Cheon, J.H., Takagi, T. (eds.) ASIACRYPT 2016. LNCS, vol. 10032, pp. 373–403. Springer, Heidelberg (2016). https://doi.org/10.1007/978-3-662-53890-6_13

17. Libert, B., Ling, S., Mouhartem, F., Nguyen, K., Wang, H.: Zero-knowledge arguments for matrix-vector relations and lattice-based group encryption. In: Cheon, J.H., Takagi, T. (eds.) ASIACRYPT 2016. LNCS, vol. 10032, pp. 101–131. Springer, Heidelberg (2016). https://doi.org/10.1007/978-3-662-53890-6_4

18. Libert, B., Ling, S., Nguyen, K., Wang, H.: Zero-knowledge arguments for lattice-based accumulators: logarithmic-size ring signatures and group signatures without trapdoors. In: Fischlin, M., Coron, J.-S. (eds.) EUROCRYPT 2016. LNCS, vol. 9666, pp. 1–31. Springer, Heidelberg (2016). https://doi.org/10.1007/978-3-662-49896-5_1

19. Libert, B., Ling, S., Nguyen, K., Wang, H.: Zero-knowledge arguments for lattice-based PRFs and applications to e-cash. In: Takagi, T., Peyrin, T. (eds.) ASIACRYPT 2017. LNCS, vol. 10626, pp. 304–335. Springer, Cham (2017). https://doi.org/10.1007/978-3-319-70700-6_11

20. Ling, S., Nguyen, K., Stehlé, D., Wang, H.: Improved zero-knowledge proofs of knowledge for the ISIS problem, and applications. In: Kurosawa, K., Hanaoka, G. (eds.) PKC 2013. LNCS, vol. 7778, pp. 107–124. Springer, Heidelberg (2013). https://doi.org/10.1007/978-3-642-36362-7_8

21. Ling, S., Nguyen, K., Wang, H., Xu, Y.: Lattice-based group signatures: achieving full dynamicity with ease. In: Gollmann, D., Miyaji, A., Kikuchi, H. (eds.) ACNS 2017. LNCS, vol. 10355, pp. 293–312. Springer, Cham (2017). https://doi.org/10.1007/978-3-319-61204-1_15

22. Ling, S., Nguyen, K., Wang, H., Xu, Y.: Constant-size group signatures from lattices. In: Abdalla, M., Dahab, R. (eds.) PKC 2018. LNCS, vol. 10770, pp. 58–88. Springer, Cham (2018). https://doi.org/10.1007/978-3-319-76581-5_3

23. Ling, S., Nguyen, K., Wang, H., Xu, Y.: Forward-secure group signatures from lattices. CoRR abs/1801.08323 (2018)

24. Liu, Q., Zhandry, M.: Revisiting post-quantum Fiat-Shamir. IACR Cryptology ePrint Archive 2019, 262 (2019)

25. Stern, J.: A new paradigm for public key identification. IEEE Trans. Inf. Theory **42**(6), 1757–1768 (1996)

26. Unruh, D.: Non-interactive zero-knowledge proofs in the quantum random oracle model. In: Oswald, E., Fischlin, M. (eds.) EUROCRYPT 2015. LNCS, vol. 9057, pp. 755–784. Springer, Heidelberg (2015). https://doi.org/10.1007/978-3-662-46803-6_25

27. Unruh, D.: Post-quantum security of Fiat-Shamir. In: Takagi, T., Peyrin, T. (eds.) ASIACRYPT 2017. LNCS, vol. 10624, pp. 65–95. Springer, Cham (2017). https://doi.org/10.1007/978-3-319-70694-8_3

28. Yang, R., Au, M.H., Lai, J., Xu, Q., Yu, Z.: Lattice-based techniques for accountable anonymity: composition of abstract Stern's protocols and weak PRF with efficient protocols from LWR. IACR Cryptology ePrint Archive 2017, 781 (2017)

29. Zhandry, M.: Secure identity-based encryption in the quantum random oracle model. In: Safavi-Naini, R., Canetti, R. (eds.) CRYPTO 2012. LNCS, vol. 7417, pp. 758–775. Springer, Heidelberg (2012). https://doi.org/10.1007/978-3-642-32009-5_44

Adding Linkability to Ring Signatures with One-Time Signatures

Xueli Wang[1,2,3], Yu Chen[1,2,3,4(✉)], and Xuecheng Ma[1,3]

[1] State Key Laboratory of Information Security,
Institute of Information Engineering, Chinese Academy of Sciences,
Beijing 100093, China
{wangxueli,maxuecheng}@iie.ac.cn, cycosmic@gmail.com
[2] State Key Laboratory of Cryptology, P.O. Box 5159, Beijing 100878, China
[3] School of Cyber Security, University of Chinese Academy of Sciences,
Beijing 101408, China
[4] Ant Financial, Hangzhou 310012, China

Abstract. We propose a generic construction that adds linkability to any ring signature scheme with one-time signature scheme. Our construction has both theoretical and practical interest. In theory, the construction gives a formal and cleaner description for constructing linkable ring signature from ring signature directly. In practice, the transformation incurs a tiny overhead in size and running time. By instantiating our construction using the ring signature scheme [13] and the one-time signature scheme [12], we obtain a lattice-based linkable ring signature scheme whose signature size is logarithmic in the number of ring members. This scheme is practical, especially the signature size is very short: for 2^{30} ring members and 100 bit security, our signature size is only 4 MB.

In addition, when proving the likability we develop a new proof technique in the random oracle model, which might be of independent interest.

Keywords: Ring signature · Linkable ring signature · Generic construction · Lattice-based

1 Introduction

Ring signature (RS) was first proposed by Rivest et al. [22], which allows a signer to sign a message on behalf of a self-formed group. RS provides not only unforgeability but also anonymity. Unforgeability requires an adversary cannot forge a signature on behalf of a ring which he does not know any secret key of ring members. Anonymity requires signatures do not leak any information about the identity of the signer, which can be categorized into two types: anonymity against probabilistic polynomial adversary and anonymity against unbounded adversary.

As an extension of RS, Liu et al. [18] first proposed the concept of linkable ring signature (LRS). LRS requires three properties: anonymity, linkability and

© Springer Nature Switzerland AG 2019
Z. Lin et al. (Eds.): ISC 2019, LNCS 11723, pp. 445–464, 2019.
https://doi.org/10.1007/978-3-030-30215-3_22

nonslanderability. Anonymity is the same as that of RS. Linkability requires that if a signer signs twice, then a public procedure can link the two signatures to the same signer. Nonslanderability requires a user should not be entrapped that he has signed twice. Due to the security of LRS, it is widely used in many privacy-preserving scenarios which require accountable anonymity. For instance, LRS can be applied in e-voting system [26] to ensure that the voters can vote anonymously and will not repeat their votes. In a more popular setting, cryptocurrency, LRS plays a crucial role in providing anonymity of spenders while defeating the double-spending attack, and hence LRS has received much attention with the rise of Monero [21] and other cryptocurrencies based on CryptoNote protocol [23].

The richer functionality of LRS makes it suited for a wide range of privacy-preserving applications, but also renders it relatively complicated to realize. The only known generic construction of LRS is proposed by Franklin and Zhang [14], but the linkability of their work is restricted to the same message, which may not be suited for cryptocurrency. In addition, there are some existing works that proposed a RS scheme firstly and then extended it to the linkable version, such as [3,19,26], but these transformations are not generic. In light of the state of affairs described above, we are motivated to consider the generic construction of LRS, in particular, whether LRS can be built from RS. From a theoretical point of view, one is interested in the weakest assumptions needed for LRS. From a practical point of view, it is highly desirable to obtain general methods for constructing LRS rather than designing from scratch each time.

1.1 Our Contributions

In this paper, we give an affirmative answer to the above question. The contribution of this paper is threefold:

- We give a generic construction that adds linkability to any RS scheme with one-time signature (OTS) scheme. The construction achieves a lower bound of the complexity that constructing LRS scheme since RS is an arguably weaker primitive compared to chameleon hash plus function (CH^+) which is used as the underlying primitive by a recent generic construction of LRS [19]. In particular, the requirement for the underlying RS schemes is mild: the space of public keys $\hat{PK}$ has some group structure $(\hat{PK}, \odot)$ (e.g. additive group with $+$) and the distribution of public keys generated by the key generation algorithm should be statistically close to the uniform distribution over $\hat{PK}$, which are naturally satisfied by most of RS schemes [1,5,6,13,15,16]. Moreover, almost all the known RS schemes [5,6,8–10,15,16,22] provide the anonymity against unbounded adversaries but LRS schemes with the anonymity against unbounded adversaries are only given in [17,18,25] recently. Our transformation preserves the same anonymity of the underlying RS schemes and hence it can be used to enrich LRS schemes with the anonymity against unbounded adversaries. Finally, our transformation introduces a small overhead on the size and running time compared to the underlying RS schemes.

- We develop a new proof approach to reduce the linkability of LRS to the unforgeability of RS, which can bridge the gap between all public keys must be generated honestly in security definition of RS and generated by adversaries in reduction. Although this approach may do not help in proving many other existing LRS schemes, it gives inspiration for designing other LRS schemes from RS schemes with other primitives. In addition, we believe the new proof approach might be of independent interest in the random oracle model.
- By instantiating our generic transformation based on the RS scheme in [13] and the OTS scheme Dilithium[1] [12], we obtain a lattice-based LRS scheme whose signature size is logarithmic in the number of ring members. Compared with the underlying primitive CH^+ of [19], which only can be used to construct LRS scheme with linear signature size, RS schemes can be instantiated with logarithmic signature size and transformed to LRS schemes with the same size by our construction. Hence, the signature size of our scheme is very short even for a large ring, for 2^{30} ring members and 100 bit security, our signature size is only 4 MB comparing to 166 MB[2] in the prior shortest lattice-based LRS scheme [27]. In addition, the experimental results demonstrate the concrete scheme is practical.

1.2 Technique Overview

To describe our construction, it is instructive to recall the generic construction of LRS in [19], which is called Raptor. In [19], they introduced the concept of CH^+ and gave a generic construction of LRS based on CH^+ and OTS. In the key generation procedure, the signer generates a hash key hk and its trapdoor td, and a key pair (ovk, osk) of OTS. Then, the user computes the public key pk by masking hk with the hash value $H(ovk)$, and sets the secret key $sk = (td, ovk, osk)$. In the signing procedure, the signer s firstly reconstructs a new set of hash keys $\{hk'_i = pk_i \oplus H(ovk_i)\}_{i \in [N]}$, where N is the number of ring members and s is the index of the signer, then runs the signing algorithm of RS on the set of public keys $\{hk'_i\}_{i \in [N]}$ to get the ring signature $\hat{\sigma}$. Finally, the signer runs the signing algorithm of OTS to sign the message $(\hat{\sigma}, \{hk'_i\}_{i \in [N]}, ovk_s)$ with the secret key osk_s and gets the one-time signature $\tilde{\sigma}$. The final signature σ is set as $(\hat{\sigma}, \tilde{\sigma}, ovk)$. In the security proof, the anonymity and linkability are reduced to the associated properties of CH^+ and the nonslanderability is reduced to the unforgeability of OTS. However, there is a gap in the proof of linkability. The linkability is based on the collision-resistance of CH^+, but the proof fails to embed the challenge hk_c of collision-resistance into the output of the linkability game. See Appendix A for details on these issues.

Inspired by the idea in [19], we give a generic construction of LRS from RS directly, rather than from CH^+. The security proof of our scheme is not trivial, especially it is difficult to reduce the linkability of LRS to the unforgeability

---

[1] Dilithium is a signature scheme, we use it as a OTS scheme.
[2] The signature size is from [16], the RS scheme in [16] is the major component of [27] and they have the same asymptotic size.

of RS. The reason is that in the security definition of unforgeability, a valid signature forgery must be generated with respect to a ring of which the adversary does not have any associated secret keys, but this condition is hard to achieve by the forgery contained in the output of linkability game for our construction. We resolve it by developing a new proof approach.

Construction Sketch. In the key generation procedure, the user firstly generates the key pair $(\hat{pk}, \hat{sk})$ and (ovk, osk) of LRS and OTS respectively. Then, he computes the public key $pk = \hat{pk} \odot H(ovk)$ and sets the secret key $sk = (\hat{sk}, osk, ovk)$. In the signing procedure, if the signer signs a message m on the ring $T = \{pk_i\}_{i \in [N]}$, he firstly reconstructs a new ring $\hat{T}' = \{\hat{pk}'_i\}_{i \in [N]}$, where $\hat{pk}'_i$ is equal to $pk_i \odot (H(ovk_s))^{-1}$, where $(H(ovk_s))^{-1}$ is the inverse element of $H(ovk_s)$ in the group $\hat{PK}$. It is easy to see that $\hat{pk}_i = \hat{pk}'_i$ only when $i = s$ and hence the signer knows the associated secret key $\hat{sk}_s$ of $\hat{pk}'_s$. Then, he runs RS.Sign on $\hat{T}'$ with $\hat{sk}_s$ to get the ring signature $\hat{\sigma}$. Finally, the signer runs OTS.Sign on the message $(\hat{\sigma}, T, ovk_s)$ with the secret key osk_s, then he gets the one-time signature $\tilde{\sigma}$ and sets the final signature $\sigma = (\hat{\sigma}, \tilde{\sigma}, ovk_s)$, where ovk_s acts as the linkability tag.

Proof Sketch. We will omit the proofs of anonymity and nonslanderability and just sketch the new proof approach here. As described above, the linkability of our construction is reduced to the unforgeability of underlying RS schemes. Suppose there exists an adversary $\mathcal{A}$ that breaks the linkability of our LRS scheme. Then, we construct an adversary $\mathcal{B}$ that breaks the unforgeability of underlying RS scheme by using $\mathcal{A}$. If $\mathcal{A}$ succeeds, i.e., $\mathcal{A}$ outputs $N + 1$ unlinked valid signatures for the same ring whose size is N, then at least one of the signatures, denoted as σ^*, contains the linkability tag which is not used in the key generation procedure. $\hat{\sigma}^*$ contained in σ^* is set as the output of $\mathcal{B}$. The core problem that we face in reduction is how to simulate the public key for $\mathcal{A}$ to make $\hat{\sigma}^*$ is generated on the ring $\hat{T}'$ which $\mathcal{B}$ does not know the secret keys. At a high level, we resolve this problem by fixing every $\hat{pk}' \in \hat{T}'$ for $\mathcal{B}$ in advance instead of making it generated by $\mathcal{A}$. More specifically, $\mathcal{A}$ and $\mathcal{B}$ have access to the joining oracle $\mathcal{O}_{\text{join}}$ and $\hat{\mathcal{O}}_{\text{join}}$ respectively, where $\mathcal{O}_{\text{join}}$ and $\hat{\mathcal{O}}_{\text{join}}$ output public keys of LRS and RS at random. For every query to $\mathcal{O}_{\text{join}}$ made by $\mathcal{A}$, $\mathcal{B}$ should query $\hat{\mathcal{O}}_{\text{join}}$ twice to get two public keys $\hat{pk}, \hat{pk}''$. $\hat{pk}$ is used to simulate the response of $\mathcal{O}_{\text{join}}$, and $\hat{pk}''$ is used to fix the elements in $\hat{T}'$. By the programmability of H, we generate pk in two different ways using $\hat{pk}, \hat{pk}''$ respectively: $pk = \hat{pk} \odot h = \hat{pk}'' \odot h'$, where h' is chosen randomly and programmed as the output of the Ith H-query, h is computed by the above equation and programmed as the output of the H-query whose input is associated ovk. If the input of the Ith H-query is ovk_s, then the forgery of RS contained in the output of $\mathcal{A}$ is generated on the public keys output by $\hat{\mathcal{O}}_{\text{join}}$ which $\mathcal{B}$ does not know the secret keys. The real execution of $\mathcal{O}_{\text{join}}$ is depicted in Fig. 1 and the simulation of $\mathcal{O}_{\text{join}}$ is depicted in Fig. 2.

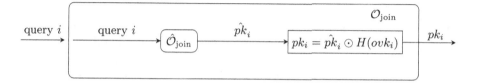

Fig. 1. Real $\mathcal{O}_{\mathrm{join}}$

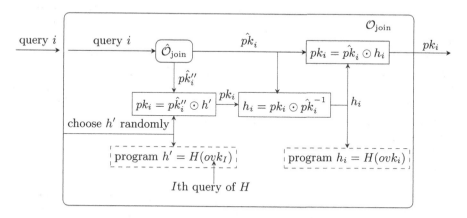

Fig. 2. Simulation of $\mathcal{O}_{\mathrm{join}}$

1.3 Related Work

Ring Signature. Abe et al. [1] showed how to construct a RS scheme from a three-move sigma protocol based signature scheme and presented the first RS scheme under the discrete-logarithm assumption whose public keys are group elements. Groth and Kohlweiss [15] proposed a RS scheme whose signature size grows logarithmically in the number of ring members from a sigma protocol for a homomorphic commitment. They instantiated their scheme with Pedersen commitment and set the public keys as the commitments to 0. Bose et al. [5] gave a generic technique to convert a compatible signature scheme to a RS scheme whose signature size is independent of the number of ring members and instantiated it from Full Boneh-Boyen signature. Brakerski and Kalai [6] proposed the first lattice-based RS scheme from ring trapdoor functions whose public keys are matrices over a group. Libert et al. [16] proposed the first lattice-based RS scheme whose signature size is logarithmic in the number of ring members. The scheme is from zero-knowledge arguments for lattice-based accumulators and the public keys of it are binary strings. We show that all of the above RS schemes satisfy the requirements of our transformation, and hence they can be extended to the LRS schemes directly by using our generic construction.

Linkable Ring Signature. Tsang and Wei [26] extended the generic RS constructions in [10] to their linkable version, but their schemes are under a weak security model which does not consider the nonslanderability. Chow et al. [7] proposed escrowed linkability of RS which can be used in spontaneous traceable signature and anonymous verifiably encrypted signature. Yuen et al. [28] proposed a LRS scheme whose signature size is square root of the number of ring members. Sun et al. [24] presented an accumulator-based LRS scheme whose signature size is independent of the number of ring members. Yang et al. [27] presented a construction of weak-PRF from LWR and designed a LRS scheme based on lattice by combining with an accumulator scheme in [16] and the supporting ZKAoKs. Zhang et al. [29] proposed an anonymous post-quantum cryptocash which contains an ideal lattice-based LRS scheme. Baum et al. [4] proposed a LRS scheme based on module lattice, which is mainly constructed from a lattice-based collision-resistant hash function. At the same time, Torres et al. [25] proposed a post-quantum one-time LRS scheme, which generalized a practical lattice-based digital signature BLISS [11] to LRS and is successfully applied to the privacy protection protocol which is called lattice ringCT v1.0. Recently, Backes et al. [3] proposed the first construction of logarithmic-size ring signatures which do not rely on a trusted setup or the random oracle heuristic and extended their scheme to the setting of linkable ring signatures.

Note 1. The issues we discovered about Raptor exist in the previous eprint version, available at https://eprint.iacr.org/2018/857 (version: 20180921:135633). We have communicated with the authors of Raptor, they confirmed our findings and the issues have been discovered independently by them as well. They shared with us their revised version which does not have the same flaws.

2   Preliminary

2.1   Notations

We use $\mathbb{N}$, $\mathbb{Z}$ and $\mathbb{R}$ to denote the set of natural numbers, integers and real numbers respectively. For $N \in \mathbb{N}$, we define $[N]$ as shorthand for the set $\{1, ..., N\}$. If S is a set then $s \leftarrow S$ denotes the operation of uniformly sampling an element s from S at random. We use the same notation to sample s from a distribution S. If S is an algorithm, the same notation is used to denote the algorithm outputs s. We denote a negligible function by $\mathsf{negl}(\lambda)$, which is a function $g(\lambda) = O(\lambda^c)$ for some constant c. We use lower-case bold letters and upper-case bold letters to denote vectors and matrices (e.g. $\mathbf{x}$ and $\mathbf{A}$). We denote the Euclidean norm of a vector $\mathbf{x} = (x_0, ..., x_{n-1})$ and a polynomial $f(x) = a_0 + a_1 X + \cdots + a_{n-1} X^{n-1}$ in variable X as $||\mathbf{x}|| = \sqrt{\sum_{i=0}^{n-1} x_i^2}$ and $||f|| = \sqrt{\sum_{i=0}^{n=1} a_i^2}$. For a vector $\mathbf{f} = (f_0, \cdots, f_{n-1})$ of polynomials, $||\mathbf{f}|| = \sqrt{\sum_{i=0}^{n-1} ||f_i||^2}$. The infinity norm of f is $||f||_\infty = \max_i |a_i|$. Let q be an odd prime integer and assume $q \equiv 5 \bmod 8$. We define the rings $R = \mathbb{Z}[X]/\langle X^d + 1 \rangle$ and $R_q = \mathbb{Z}_q[X]/\langle X^d + 1 \rangle$, where $d > 1$ is a power of 2. We denote the set of integers $\{a, a+1, \cdots, b-1, b\}$ by $[a, b]$. We use $D_{v,\sigma}$ to denote the discrete normal distribution centered at v with standard deviation σ. We write D_σ as shorthand for $v = 0$.

2.2 Ring Signature

A RS scheme consists of four algorithms (Setup, KeyGen, Sign, Vrfy):

- Setup(1^λ): On input the security parameter 1^λ, outputs public parameter pp. We assume pp is an implicit input to all the algorithms listed below.
- KeyGen(pp): On input the public parameter pp, outputs secret key sk and public key pk.
- Sign(sk, m, T): On input the secret key sk, a signing message m and a set of public keys T, outputs a signature σ.
- Vrfy(T, m, σ): On input the set of public keys T, signing message m and signature σ, outputs *accept/reject*.

Correctness. For any security parameter λ, any $\{pk_i, sk_i\}_{i \in [N]}$ output by KeyGen, any $s \in [N]$, and any message m, we have Vrfy($T, m,$ Sign(sk_s, m, T)) = *accept*, where $T = \{pk_i\}_{i \in [N]}$.

Before introducing the security definitions of RS, we first assume there are three oracles as following:

- Joining oracle $pk \leftarrow \mathcal{O}_{\text{join}}(\bot)$: $\mathcal{O}_{\text{join}}$ generates a new user and returns the public key pk of the new user.
- Corruption oracle $sk \leftarrow \mathcal{O}_{\text{corrupt}}(pk)$: On input a public key pk which is a output of $\mathcal{O}_{\text{join}}$, returns the associated secret key sk.
- Signing oracle $\sigma \leftarrow \mathcal{O}_{\text{sign}}(T, m, pk_s)$: On input a set of public keys T, message m and the public key of the signer $pk_s \in T$, returns a valid signature σ on m and T.

Anonymity. Anonymity can be defined by the following game between an adversary $\mathcal{A}$ and a challenger $\mathcal{CH}$:

1. Setup: $\mathcal{CH}$ runs Setup with security parameter 1^λ and sends the public parameter pp to $\mathcal{A}$.
2. Query: $\mathcal{A}$ is allowed to make queries to $\mathcal{O}_{\text{join}}$ according to any adaptive strategy.
3. Challenge: $\mathcal{A}$ picks a set of public keys $T = \{pk_i\}_{i \in [N]}$ and a message m. $\mathcal{A}$ sends (T, m) to $\mathcal{CH}$. $\mathcal{CH}$ picks $s \in [N]$ and runs $\sigma \leftarrow$ Sign(sk_s, m, T). $\mathcal{CH}$ sends σ to $\mathcal{A}$.
4. Output: $\mathcal{A}$ outputs a guess $s^* \in [N]$.

$\mathcal{A}$ wins if $s^* = s$. The advantage of $\mathcal{A}$ is defined by $\text{Adv}_{\mathcal{A}}^{\text{anon}} = |\Pr[s^* = s] - \frac{1}{N}|$.

Definition 1. *A RS scheme is said to be anonymous (resp. anonymous against unbounded adversaries) if for any PPT adversary (unbounded adversary) $\mathcal{A}$, $\text{Adv}_{\mathcal{A}}^{\text{anon}}$ is negligible in λ.*

Unforgeability. Unforgeability is defined by the following game between an adversary $\mathcal{A}$ and a challenger $\mathcal{CH}$.

1. Setup: $\mathcal{CH}$ runs Setup with security parameter 1^λ and sends the public parameter pp to $\mathcal{A}$.
2. Query: $\mathcal{A}$ is allowed to make queries to $\mathcal{O}_{\text{join}}, \mathcal{O}_{\text{corrupt}}$ and $\mathcal{O}_{\text{sign}}$ according to any adaptive strategy.
3. Output: $\mathcal{A}$ outputs a forgery (m^*, σ^*, T^*).

$\mathcal{A}$ wins if

- Vrfy$(m^*, \sigma^*, T^*) = accept$;
- all of the public keys in T^* are query outputs of $\mathcal{O}_{\text{join}}$;
- no public key in T^* has been input to $\mathcal{O}_{\text{corrupt}}$; and
- (m^*, T^*) has not been queried to $\mathcal{O}_{\text{sign}}$.

The advantage of $\mathcal{A}$, denoted as $\mathsf{Adv}_{\mathcal{A}}^{\text{forge}}$, is defined by the probability that $\mathcal{A}$ wins in the above game.

Definition 2. *A RS scheme is said to be unforgeable if for any PPT adversary $\mathcal{A}$, $\mathsf{Adv}_{\mathcal{A}}^{\text{forge}}$ is negligible in λ.*

2.3   Linkable Ring Signature

A LRS scheme consists of five algorithms (Setup, KeyGen, Sign, Vrfy, Link):

- Setup(1^λ): On input the security parameter 1^λ, outputs public parameter pp. We assume pp is an implicit input to all the algorithms listed below.
- KeyGen(pp): On input the public parameter pp, outputs secret key sk and public key pk.
- Sign(sk, m, T): On input the secret key sk, a signing message m and a set of public keys T, outputs a signature σ.
- Vrfy(T, m, σ): On input the set of public keys T, the signing message m and the signature σ, outputs *accept/reject*.
- Link$(m_1, m_2, \sigma_1, \sigma_2, T_1, T_2)$: On input two sets of public keys T_1, T_2, two signing messages m_1, m_2 and their signatures σ_1, σ_2, outputs *linked/unlinked*.

Correctness. For any security parameter 1^λ, any $\{pk_i, sk_i\}_{i \in [N]}$ output by KeyGen, any $s \in [N]$, and any message m, we have Vrfy$(T, m, \mathsf{Sign}(sk_s, m, T)) = accept$ where $T = \{pk_i\}_{i \in [N]}$.

Anonymity. Anonymity of LRS is the same as that of RS.

Linkability. The linkability of LRS is used to go against the dishonest signers. The intuition of linkability is that a signer cannot generate two valid unlinked signatures. It can be translated into that the users in a ring with size N cannot produce $N + 1$ valid signatures and any two of them are unlinkable. Linkability can be defined by the following game between an adversary $\mathcal{A}$ and a challenger $\mathcal{CH}$:

1. Setup: $\mathcal{CH}$ runs Setup with security parameter 1^λ and sends the public parameter pp to $\mathcal{A}$.
2. Query: $\mathcal{A}$ is allowed to make queries to $\mathcal{O}_{\text{join}}$, $\mathcal{O}_{\text{corrupt}}$, $\mathcal{O}_{\text{sign}}$ according to any adaptive strategy.
3. Output: $\mathcal{A}$ outputs $N + 1$ messages/signature pairs $\{T, m_i, \sigma_i\}_{i \in [N+1]}$, where T is a set of public keys with size N.

$\mathcal{A}$ wins if

- all public keys in T are query outputs of $\mathcal{O}_{\text{join}}$;
- $\mathsf{Vrfy}(m_i, \sigma_i, T) = accept$ for all $i \in [N + 1]$;
- $\mathsf{Link}(m_i, m_j, \sigma_i, \sigma_j) = unlinked$ for all $i, j \in [N + 1]$ and $i \neq j$.

The advantage of $\mathcal{A}$, denoted as $\mathsf{Adv}_{\mathcal{A}}^{\text{link}}$, is defined by the probability that $\mathcal{A}$ wins in the above game.

Definition 3. *A LRS scheme is said to be linkable if for any PPT adversary $\mathcal{A}$, $\mathsf{Adv}_{\mathcal{A}}^{\text{link}}$ is negligible in λ.*

Nonslanderability. Nonsladerabiliy can be defined by the following game between an adversary $\mathcal{A}$ and a challenger $\mathcal{CH}$:

1. Setup: $\mathcal{CH}$ runs Setup with security parameter 1^λ and sends the public parameter pp to $\mathcal{A}$.
2. Query: $\mathcal{A}$ is allowed to make queries to $\mathcal{O}_{\text{join}}$, $\mathcal{O}_{\text{corrupt}}$, $\mathcal{O}_{\text{sign}}$ according to any adaptive strategy.
3. Challenge: $\mathcal{A}$ gives $\mathcal{CH}$ a set of public keys T, a message m and a public key $pk_s \in T$. $\mathcal{CH}$ runs $\mathsf{Sign}(sk_s, m, T)$ and returns the signature σ to $\mathcal{A}$.
4. Output: $\mathcal{A}$ outputs a messages/signature pair (m^*, σ^*, T^*).

$\mathcal{A}$ wins if

- $\mathsf{Vrfy}(m^*, \sigma^*, T^*) = accept$;
- pk_s is not queried by $\mathcal{A}$ to $\mathcal{O}_{\text{corrupt}}$ and as an ring member to $\mathcal{O}_{\text{sign}}$;
- all public keys in T and T^* are query outputs of $\mathcal{O}_{\text{join}}$; and
- $\mathsf{Link}(m, m^*, \sigma, \sigma^*) = linked$.

The advantage of $\mathcal{A}$, denoted as $\mathsf{Adv}_{\mathcal{A}}^{\text{slander}}$, is defined by the probability that $\mathcal{A}$ wins in the above game.

Definition 4 (Nonslanderability). *A LRS scheme is said to be nonslanderable if for any PPT adversary $\mathcal{A}$, $\mathsf{Adv}_{\mathcal{A}}^{\text{slander}}$ is negligible in λ.*

We adopt the same definitions of linkability and nonslanderability as in [2]. Typically, the linkability definition in [2] allows the adversary to make polynomially many queries to $\mathcal{O}_{\text{corrupt}}$ which is necessary because in the definition of unforgeability the adversary has the same ability.

Hence, the *unforgeability* of LRS can be implied by the linkability and the nonslanderability according to [2].

2.4   Assumption and Rejection Sampling

For the sake of completeness, we state the following lattice assumption, commitment scheme in [13] and rejection sampling lemma.

Definition 5 (Module-SIS$_{n,m,q,\theta}$). *Let $R_q = \mathbb{Z}_q[X]/\langle X^d + 1\rangle$. Given $\mathbf{A} \leftarrow R_q^{n \times m}$, find $\mathbf{x} \in R_q^m$ such that $\mathbf{Ax} = \mathbf{0}$ mod q and $0 < ||\mathbf{x}|| \le \theta$.*

Lemma 1 ([20]). *Let V be a subset of $\mathbb{Z}^d$ where all the elements have norms less T, and h be a probability distribution over V. Define the following algorithms:*

$\mathcal{A}: v \leftarrow h; \mathbf{z} \leftarrow D_{v,\sigma}^d;$ *output $(\mathbf{z}, v)$ with probability* $\min\{\frac{D_\sigma^d(\mathbf{z})}{MD_{\mathbf{v},\sigma}^d(\mathbf{z})}, 1\}$

$\mathcal{F}: v \leftarrow h; \mathbf{z} \leftarrow D_\sigma^d;$ *output $(\mathbf{z}, v)$ with probability $\frac{1}{M}$,*

where $\sigma = 12T$ and $M = e^{1 + \frac{1}{288}}$. Then the output of algorithm $\mathcal{A}$ is within statistical distance $2^{-100}/M$ of the output of $\mathcal{F}$. Moreover, the probability that $\mathcal{A}$ outputs something is more than $\frac{1 - 2^{-100}}{M}$.

2.5   Commitment Scheme

Definition 6. *Let $R_q = \mathbb{Z}_q[X]/\langle X^d + 1\rangle$, $S_{\mathbf{r}}(\epsilon_{\mathbf{r}}) = \{\mathbf{r} \in R_q^m : ||\mathbf{r}||_\infty \le \epsilon_{\mathbf{r}}\}$ be the randomness domain with χ as the probability distribution of $\mathbf{r}$ on $S_{\mathbf{r}}(\epsilon_{\mathbf{r}})$ for a positive real number $\epsilon_{\mathbf{r}}$, and $S_M(\epsilon_M) = \{\mathbf{m} \in R_q^v : ||\mathbf{m}||_\infty \le \epsilon_M\}$ be the message domain for a positive real number ϵ_M for $m, v \in \mathbb{Z}^+$. The commitment of a message vector $\mathbf{m} = (m_1, ..., m_v) \in S_M(\epsilon_M)$ using a randomness $\mathbf{r} \in S_{\mathbf{r}}$ is given as*

$$\text{Com}_{ck}(\mathbf{m}; \mathbf{r}) = \mathbf{G} \cdot (\mathbf{r}; m_1, \cdots, m_v)^{\text{T}} \in R_q^n$$

where $ck = \mathbf{G} \leftarrow R_q^{n \times (m+v)}$ and it is used as the commitment key.

3   Generic Construction of Linkable Ring Signature

3.1   Construction

The generic construction is based on two primitives: (1) a ring signature scheme RS = (Setup, KeyGen, Sign, Vrfy); (2) a one-time signature scheme OTS = (KeyGen, Sign, Vrfy).

- Setup(1^λ): On input the security parameter 1^λ, this algorithm runs $\hat{pp} \leftarrow$ RS.Setup(1^λ). It also chooses a hash function $H : OVK \rightarrow \hat{PK}$, where OVK and $\hat{PK}$ are public key spaces of OTS and RS respectively. Finally, it outputs public parameter $pp = \hat{pp}$. We assume pp is an implicit input to all the algorithms listed below.
- KeyGen(pp): On input the public parameter pp, runs $(\hat{pk}, \hat{sk}) \leftarrow$ RS.KeyGen($\hat{pp}$). Then, the algorithm runs $(ovk, osk) \leftarrow$ OTS.KeyGen. It returns public key $pk = \hat{pk} \odot H(ovk)$ and secret key $sk = (\hat{sk}, osk, ovk)$.
- Sign(sk_s, m, T): On input the secret key sk_s, a signing message m and a set of public keys $T = \{pk_i\}_{i \in [N]}$, computes $\hat{pk}'_i = pk_i \odot (H(ovk_s))^{-1}$ for $i \in [N]$ and sets $\hat{T}' = \{\hat{pk}'_i\}_{i \in [N]}$. Next, the algorithm runs

$$\hat{\sigma} \leftarrow \text{RS.Sign}(\hat{sk}_s, m, \hat{T}'),$$
$$\tilde{\sigma} \leftarrow \text{OTS.Sign}(osk_s, \hat{\sigma}, T, ovk_s).$$

  Finally, it returns the signature $\sigma = (\hat{\sigma}, \tilde{\sigma}, ovk_s)$.
- Vrfy(T, m, σ): On input the set of public keys T, a signing message m and the signature σ, this algorithm first parses σ as $\sigma = (\hat{\sigma}, \tilde{\sigma}, ovk)$ and computes $\hat{pk}'_i = pk_i \odot (H(ovk))^{-1}$ for $i \in [N]$. Next, it runs RS.Vrfy($\hat{T}' = \{\hat{pk}'_i\}_{i \in [N]}, m, \hat{\sigma}$) and OTS.Vrfy($ovk, (\hat{\sigma}, T, ovk), \tilde{\sigma}$). Finally, it outputs $accept$ if RS.Vrfy returns $accept$ and OTS.Vrfy returns $accept$; otherwise outputs $reject$.
- Link($m_1, m_2, \sigma_1, \sigma_2, T_1, T_2$): On input two sets of public keys T_1, T_2, two signing messages m_1, m_2 and their signatures σ_1, σ_2, runs Vrfy(m_1, σ_1, T_1) and Vrfy(m_2, σ_2, T_2). If Vrfy(m_1, σ_1, T_1) = $reject$ or Vrfy(m_2, σ_2, T_2) = $reject$, it aborts. Otherwise, the algorithm parses σ_1 and σ_2 as $\sigma_1 = (\hat{\sigma}_1, \tilde{\sigma}_1, ovk_1)$ and $\sigma_2 = (\hat{\sigma}_2, \tilde{\sigma}_2, ovk_2)$, and compares ovk_1 and ovk_2. If $ovk_1 = ovk_2$, then outputs $linked$; otherwise outputs $unlinked$.

3.2 Security

Theorem 1. *Our LRS scheme is anonymous (resp. anonymous against unbounded adversary) if the underlying RS scheme is anonymous (resp. anonymous against unbounded adversary).*

Proof. If there exists an adversary $\mathcal{A}$ with oracle access to $\mathcal{O}_{\text{join}}$ can break the anonymity of LRS, then we can construct an adversary $\mathcal{B}$ with oracles access to $\hat{\mathcal{O}}_{\text{join}}, \hat{\mathcal{O}}_{\text{sign}}$ to break the anonymity of RS with the same advantage, where $\hat{\mathcal{O}}_{\text{join}}$ and $\hat{\mathcal{O}}_{\text{sign}}$ are oracles in security games of RS.

Given a signature $\hat{\sigma}$ on the set of public keys T and a message m chosen by $\mathcal{B}$, $\mathcal{B}$ interacts with $\mathcal{A}$ with the aim to guess the signer s.

1. Setup: Given the public parameter $\hat{pp}$, $\mathcal{B}$ selects a hash function $H : OVK \rightarrow \hat{PK}$, where H is modeled as random oracle and OVK and $\hat{PK}$ are public key spaces of OTS and RS respectively. $\mathcal{B}$ then sends $pp = \hat{pp}$ to $\mathcal{A}$.

2. Oracle simulation: $\mathcal{A}$ is allowed to access the joining oracle $\mathcal{O}_{\text{join}}$: $\mathcal{B}$ runs $(ovk, osk) \leftarrow$OTS. KeyGen at first. Upon receiving a joining query, $\mathcal{B}$ queries $\hat{\mathcal{O}}_{\text{join}}$ to obtain a public key $\hat{pk}$ of RS, computes $pk = \hat{pk} \odot H(ovk)$. $\mathcal{B}$ then sends pk to $\mathcal{A}$.

   The only difference between this simulation and the real game is that in this simulation, every pk is generated by the same ovk. This simulation is indistinguishable from the real game. According to the distribution of $\hat{pk}$ is close to the uniform distribution over $\hat{PK}$, we can get that $\hat{pk} \odot H(ovk)$ is also close to the uniform distribution no matter which ovk is chosen since $\hat{pk} \in \hat{PK}$. Hence, pk generated in two games are both close to the uniform distribution over $\hat{PK}$.

3. Challenge: Received $(T = \{pk_i\}_{i\in[N]}, m)$ from $\mathcal{A}$, $\mathcal{B}$ computes $\hat{pk}'_i = pk_i \odot (H(ovk))^{-1}$ for all $i \in [N]$ and sets $\hat{T}' = \{\hat{pk}'_i\}_{i\in[N]}$. $\mathcal{B}$ then sends $(\hat{T}', m)$ to $\mathcal{CH}$ and received a signature $\hat{\sigma}$ (signed by $\hat{pk}_s \in \hat{T}$ which is chosen by $\mathcal{CH}$). $\mathcal{B}$ runs $\tilde{\sigma} \leftarrow$OTS.Sign$(osk, \hat{\sigma}, T, ovk)$ and sends $\sigma = (\hat{\sigma}, \tilde{\sigma}, ovk)$ to $\mathcal{A}$.

4. Output: $\mathcal{A}$ outputs the index s^*.

Finally, $\mathcal{B}$ forwards s^* to $\mathcal{CH}$. $\mathcal{A}$ essentially guesses which index is used to generate $\hat{\sigma}$ since $\tilde{\sigma}, ovk$ are identical no matter which index $\mathcal{CH}$ has chosen. If $\mathcal{A}$ succeeds, $\mathcal{B}$ also succeeds due to $\mathcal{B}$ is also aim to guess which index is used to generate $\hat{\sigma}$. We have $\text{Adv}_{\mathcal{A}}^{\text{anon}} = \text{Adv}_{\mathcal{B}}^{\text{anon}}$.

Theorem 2. *Our LRS scheme is linkable in the random oracle model if the underlying RS is unforgeable.*

Proof. We proceed via a sequence of games. Let S_i be the event that $\mathcal{A}$ succeeds in Game i.

Game 0. This is the standard linkability game for LRS. $\mathcal{CH}$ interacts with $\mathcal{A}$ as below:

1. Setup: $\mathcal{CH}$ runs $\hat{pp} \leftarrow$RS.Setup(1^λ), selects a hash function $H : OVK \to \hat{PK}$, where H is modeled as random oracle and OVK and $\hat{PK}$ are public key spaces of OTS and RS respectively. $\mathcal{CH}$ then sends $pp = \hat{pp}$ to $\mathcal{A}$.

2. Oracle simulation: $\mathcal{A}$ is allowed to access the following four oracles:

   Random oracle H: To make our proof explicit, we separate the queries of H as two categories: querying directly and querying in $\mathcal{O}_{\text{join}}$ and $\mathcal{O}_{\text{sign}}$. $\mathcal{CH}$ initializes an empty set RO. Upon receiving a random oracle query i, if it has been queried, $\mathcal{CH}$ returns associated output in RO; else, $\mathcal{CH}$ picks $h_i \leftarrow \hat{PK}$ at random, sends h_i to $\mathcal{A}$ and stores the pair of (i, h_i) in RO.

   Joining oracle $\mathcal{O}_{\text{join}}$: $\mathcal{CH}$ initializes an empty set JO. Upon receiving a joining query, $\mathcal{CH}$ runs $(\hat{pk}, \hat{sk}) \leftarrow$RS.KeyGen and $(ovk, osk) \leftarrow$OTS.KeyGen, computes $pk = \hat{pk} \odot H(ovk)$, sets $sk = (\hat{sk}, osk, ovk)$. $\mathcal{CH}$ then sends pk to $\mathcal{A}$ and stores pk in JO.

   Corruption oracle $\mathcal{O}_{\text{corrupt}}$: Upon receiving a corruption query pk, $\mathcal{CH}$ sends associated sk to $\mathcal{A}$ if $pk \in JO$; else, $\mathcal{CH}$ return $\perp$.

Signing oracle $\mathcal{O}_{sign}$: Upon receiving a signing query $(T = \{pk_i\}_{i\in[N]}, m, pk_s \in T)$, $\mathcal{CH}$ computes $\hat{pk}'_i = pk_i \odot (H(ovk_s))^{-1}$ for $i \in [N]$, sets $\hat{T}' = \{\hat{pk}'_i\}_{i\in[N]}$, runs $\hat{\sigma} \leftarrow$ RS.Sign$(\hat{sk}_s, m, \hat{T}')$ and $\tilde{\sigma} \leftarrow$ OTS.Sign$(osk_s, \hat{\sigma}, T, ovk_s)$. $\mathcal{CH}$ then sends $\sigma = (\hat{\sigma}, \tilde{\sigma}, ovk_s)$ to $\mathcal{A}$.

3. Outputs: $\mathcal{A}$ outputs $N + 1$ message/signature pairs $\{m_i, \sigma_i\}_{i\in[N+1]}$ on the same set of public keys $T = \{pk_i\}_{i\in[N]}$.

According to the definition, we have $\mathsf{Adv}_{\mathcal{A}}^{\mathrm{link}} = \Pr[S_0]$.

Game 1. Same as Game 0 except that in $\mathcal{O}_{join}$ of oracle simulation stage, $\mathcal{CH}$ additionally choose $h' \leftarrow \hat{PK}$ at first before receiving queries. This change is purely conceptual and thus we have $\Pr[S_1] = \Pr[S_0]$.

Game 2. Same as Game 1 except that in H of oracle simulation stage, $\mathcal{CH}$ chooses a index $I \leftarrow [1, ..., q_h]$, where q_h is the maximum number of times $\mathcal{A}$ directly queries H, then $\mathcal{CH}$ programs the output of the Ith query as h'.

By the programmability of H, and h' is chosen uniformly and independently, we have $\Pr[S_2] = \Pr[S_1]$.

Game 3. Same as Game 2 except that in $\mathcal{O}_{join}$ of oracle simulation stage, $\mathcal{CH}$ additionally runs $(\hat{pk}'', \hat{sk}'') \leftarrow$ RS.KeyGen and computes h such that $\hat{pk} \odot h = \hat{pk}'' \odot h'$ upon receiving a joining query. $\mathcal{CH}$ then sends $pk = \hat{pk} \odot h$ to $\mathcal{A}$. Due to the distribution of $\hat{pk}$ is close to the uniform distribution over $\hat{PK}$, hence $\Pr[S_3] = \Pr[S_2]$.

Game 4. Same as Game 3 except that in H of oracle simulation stage, $\mathcal{CH}$ programs the output of the query on ovk (querying in $\mathcal{O}_{join}$) as corresponding h which is computed in Game 3. By the programmability of H, we have $\Pr[S_4] = \Pr[S_3]$.

Lemma 2. *If the RS is unforgeable, then the probability that any adversary wins in Game 4 is negligible in λ.*

If $\mathcal{A}$ wins in Game 4, then we can construct an adversary $\mathcal{B}$ with oracles access to $\hat{\mathcal{O}}_{join}$, $\hat{\mathcal{O}}_{corrupt}$ and $\hat{\mathcal{O}}_{sign}$ to break the unforgeability of RS with the advantage $q_h \cdot \mathsf{Adv}_{\mathcal{A}}^{\mathrm{forge}}$, implying $\Pr[S_4]$ must be negligible, where $\hat{\mathcal{O}}_{join}, \hat{\mathcal{O}}_{corrupt}$ and $\hat{\mathcal{O}}_{sign}$ are oracles in security games of RS.

$\mathcal{B}$ interacts with $\mathcal{A}$ in Game 4 with the aim to output $(m^*, \sigma^*, \hat{T}^*)$ satisfying the conditions in Definition 4.

1. Setup: Given the public parameter $\hat{pp}$, $\mathcal{B}$ selects a hash function $H : OVK \rightarrow \hat{PK}$, where H is modeled as random oracle and OVK and $\hat{PK}$ are public key spaces of OTS and RS respectively. $\mathcal{B}$ then sends $pp = \hat{pp}$ to $\mathcal{A}$.
2. Oracle simulation:

   Random oracle H: To make our proof explicit, we separate the queries of H as two categories: querying directly and querying in $\mathcal{O}_{join}$ and $\mathcal{O}_{sign}$. $\mathcal{B}$ initializes an empty set RO, chooses a index $I \leftarrow [1, ..., q_h]$, where q_h is the maximum number of times $\mathcal{A}$ directly queries H. $\mathcal{A}$ then programs the output

of the Ith query as h' and stores them in RO. On receiving a random oracle query i, if it has been queried, $\mathcal{A}$ returns associated output in RO; otherwise, $\mathcal{B}$ programs the output as associated h if it is the query on ovk (querying in $\mathcal{O}_{\mathsf{join}}$), else $\mathcal{B}$ picks $h_i \leftarrow \hat{PK}$, sends h_i to $\mathcal{A}$ and stores the pair (i, h_i) in RO. Joining oracle $\mathcal{O}_{\mathsf{join}}$: $\mathcal{B}$ initializes an empty set JO and chooses $h' \leftarrow \hat{PK}$. Upon receiving a joining query from $\mathcal{A}$, $\mathcal{B}$ queries $\hat{\mathcal{O}}_{\mathsf{join}}$ twice to get two public keys $\hat{pk}, \hat{pk}''$, computes h such that $\hat{pk} \odot h = \hat{pk}'' \odot h'$, runs $(ovk, osk) \leftarrow$ OTS.KeyGen. $\mathcal{B}$ then sends $pk = \hat{pk} \odot h$ to $\mathcal{A}$ and stores pk in JO.
Corruption oracle $\mathcal{O}_{\mathsf{corrupt}}$: Upon receiving a corruption query pk, $\mathcal{B}$ queries the oracle $\hat{\mathcal{O}}_{\mathsf{corrupt}}$ on input $\hat{pk}$ to obtain $\hat{sk}$ if $pk \in JO$; else $\mathcal{B}$ returns $\perp$. $\mathcal{B}$ then sends $sk = (\hat{sk}, ovk, osk)$ to $\mathcal{A}$.
Signing oracle $\mathcal{O}_{\mathsf{sign}}$: Upon receiving a signing query $(T = \{pk_i\}_{i \in [N]}, m, pk_s \in T)$, $\mathcal{B}$ queries the oracle $\hat{\mathcal{O}}_{\mathsf{sign}}$ on input $(\hat{T}' = \{\hat{pk}'_i = pk_i \odot h_i^{-1}\}_{i \in [N]}, m, \hat{pk}_s \in \hat{T}')$ to get a signature $\hat{\sigma}$, runs $\tilde{\sigma} \leftarrow$ OTS.Sign$(osk_s, \hat{\sigma}, T, ovk_s)$. $\mathcal{B}$ then sends $\sigma = (\hat{\sigma}, \tilde{\sigma}, ovk_s)$ to $\mathcal{A}$.

3. Output: $\mathcal{A}$ outputs $N + 1$ message/signature pairs $\{m_i, \sigma_i\}_{i \in [N+1]}$ on the same set of public keys $T = \{pk_i\}_{i \in [N]}$ and wins in Game 4.

Upon receiving $\{m_i, \sigma_i, T = \{pk_j\}_{j \in [N]}\}_{i \in [N+1]}$, $\mathcal{B}$ parses every signature σ_i as $\sigma_i = (\hat{\sigma}_i, \tilde{\sigma}_i, ovk_i)$. Since $\mathcal{A}$ outputs $N + 1$ unlinked signatures on N public keys, so there exits at least one of ovk_i in σ_i which is not produced by $\mathcal{O}_{\mathsf{join}}$. We assume it is ovk^*. Hence, the probability of $\hat{pk}_j^* = pk_j \odot (H(ovk^*))^{-1}$ has been input to $\hat{\mathcal{O}}_{\mathsf{corrupt}}$ and $\hat{\mathcal{O}}_{\mathsf{sign}}$ is negligible for all $j \in [N]$. Furthermore, if ovk^* is the Ith query of H, which happens with probability at least $\frac{1}{q_h}$, then $\{\hat{pk}_j^*\}_{j \in [N]}$ are all query outputs of $\hat{\mathcal{O}}_{\mathsf{join}}$. Hence, $\mathcal{B}$ can outputs a successful forgery $(m^*, \hat{\sigma}^*, \hat{T}^* = \{\hat{pk}_j^*\}_{j \in [N]})$ if $H(ovk^*) = h'$; else it returns $\perp$.

It is straightforward to verify that $\mathcal{B}$'s simulation for Game 4 is perfect, we can conclude $\Pr[S_4] = q_h \cdot \mathsf{Adv}_{\mathcal{B}}^{\mathsf{forge}}$. Putting all the above together, the theorem immediately follows.

Theorem 3. *Our LRS is nonslanderable in the random oracle model if the underlying one-time signature is unforgeable.*

Proof. The proof of nonslanderability is trivial. Due to the page limitation, we omit the details of this proof and just provide a brief sketch here. We embedded the challenge ovk of unforgeability into the challenge $\sigma = (\hat{\sigma}, \tilde{\sigma}, ovk)$ of nonslanderability by querying the one-time signature $\tilde{\sigma}$ on input the message $(\hat{\sigma}, T, ovk)$ and programming the random oracle H. If the unforgeability is broken, that is the adversary outputs (T^*, m^*, σ^*) which satisfies $\mathsf{Link}(\sigma^*, \sigma, m^*, m, T^*, T) = linked$. Then, $((\hat{\sigma}^*, T^*, ovk^*), \tilde{\sigma}^*)$ is a valid forgery of OTS, where $\hat{\sigma}^*, \tilde{\sigma}^*, ovk^*$ are contained in $\sigma^* = (\hat{\sigma}^*, \tilde{\sigma}^*, ovk^*)$.

4   Instantiation

We give an instantiation of our construction by using the RS in [13] and the (one-time) signature Dilithium [12].

- Setup(1^λ): On input 1^λ, select the commitment key $ck = \mathbf{G} \leftarrow R_q^{n \times (m+k\beta)}$, two hash functions $H : \{0,1\}^* \to \mathcal{C}$ and $H' : \{0,1\}^* \to R_q^n$, where $k = \log_\beta N$, $\mathcal{C} = \{X^\omega : 0 \leq \omega \leq 2d - 1\}$ is the challenge space.
- KeyGen(pp): On input public parameter pp, select $r_i \leftarrow \{-M, ..., M\}^d$ for $i \in [m]$ and set $\mathbf{r} = (r_1, ..., r_m)$, compute $\mathbf{c} = \text{Com}_{ck}(\mathbf{0}; \mathbf{r})$, where $\mathbf{0}$ is the all-zero vector, set $\hat{pk} = \mathbf{c}$, $\hat{sk} = \mathbf{r}$, run $(ovk, osk) \leftarrow \text{Dilithium.KeyGen}(1^\lambda)$. Output $pk = \hat{pk} + H'(ovk)$, $sk = (\hat{sk}, osk, ovk)$.
- Sign(sk_s, m, T): On input the secret key sk_s, a signing message m and a set of public keys $T = \{pk_i\}_{i \in [N]}$
  1. Compute $\hat{pk}'_i = pk_i - H'(ovk_s)$ for each $i \in [N]$ and set $\hat{T}' = \{\hat{pk}'_i\}_{i \in [N]}$.
  2. Sample $a_{0,1}, ..., a_{k-1,\beta-1} \leftarrow D^d_{12\sqrt{k}}$, compute $a_{j,0} = -\sum_{i=1}^{\beta-1} a_{j,i}$ for $j = 0, ..., k-1$, select $r_{b,i}, r_{c,i} \leftarrow \{-M, ..., M\}^d$ for $i \in [m]$ and set $\mathbf{r}_b = (r_{b,1}, ..., r_{b,m}), \mathbf{r}_c = (r_{c,1}, ..., r_{c,m})$, sample $r_{a,i}, r_{d,i} \leftarrow D^d_{12M\sqrt{2md}}$ for $i \in [m]$ and set $\mathbf{r}_a = (r_{a,1}, ..., r_{a,m})$, $\mathbf{r}_d = (r_{d,1}, ..., r_{d,m})$, compute $A = \text{Com}_{ck}(a_{0,0}, ..., a_{k-1,\beta-1}; \mathbf{r}_a)$, $B = \text{Com}_{ck}(\delta_{s_0,0}, ..., \delta_{s_{k-1},\beta-1}; \mathbf{r}_b)$, $C = \text{Com}_{ck}(\{a_{j,i}(1 - 2\delta_{j,i})\}_{j,i=0}^{k-1,\beta-1}; \mathbf{r}_c)$, $D = \text{Com}_{ck}(-a_{0,0}^2, ..., -a_{k-1,\beta-1}^2; \mathbf{r}_d)$, where $\delta_{j,i}$ is Kronecker's delta, $\delta_{j,i} = 1$ if $j = i$ and $\delta_{j,i} = 0$ otherwise. Sample $\rho_{j,i} \leftarrow D^{md}_{12M\sqrt{3md/k}}$ for $i \in [m]$ and set $\rho_j = (\rho_{j,1}, ..., \rho_{j,m})$, compute $E_j = \sum_{i=0}^{N-1} p_{i,j} c_i + \text{Com}(\mathbf{0}; \rho_j)$ for $j = 0, ..., k-1$, where $p_{i,j}$ is computed by $p_i(x) = \prod_{j=0}^{k-1}(x \cdot \delta_{s_j,i_j} + a_{j,i_j}) = \prod_{j=0}^{k-1} x \cdot \delta_{s_j,i_j} + \sum_{j=0}^{k-1} p_{i,j} x^j = \delta_{s,i} x^k + \sum_{j=0}^{k-1} p_{i,j} x^j, i \in [N]$. Compute $x = H'(ck, m, \hat{T}', A, B, C, D, \{E_j\}_{j=0}^{k-1})$, $f_{j,i} = x \cdot \delta_{s_j,i_j} + a_{j,i_j}, \forall j, \forall i \neq 0$, $\mathbf{z}_b = x \cdot \mathbf{r}_b + \mathbf{r}_a$, $\mathbf{z}_c = x \cdot \mathbf{r}_c + \mathbf{r}_d$, $\mathbf{z} = x^k \cdot \hat{sk}_s - \sum_{j=0}^{k-1} x^j \cdot \rho_j$. Set CMT $= (A, B, C, D, \{E_j\}_{j=0}^{j=k-1})$ and RSP $= (\{f_{j,i}\}_{j=0,i=1}^{k-1,\beta-1}, \mathbf{z}, \mathbf{z}_b, \mathbf{z}_c)$.
  3. Repeat step 2 L times in parallel and get $\{\text{CMT}_l\}_{l \in [L]}$, $\mathbf{x} = \{x_l\}_{l \in [L]}$ and $\{\text{RSP}_l\}_{l \in [L]}$. If $\text{RSP}_l \neq \perp$ for all $l \in [L]$, set $\hat{\sigma} = (\{\text{CMT}_l\}_{l \in [L]}, \mathbf{x}, \{\text{RSP}_l\}_{l \in [L]})$. Otherwise, go to Step 2 (repeat at most $\frac{-\lambda}{\log(1-1/\mathcal{M}^2)}$).
  4. Run $\hat{\sigma} \leftarrow \text{Dilithium.Sign}(osk, (\hat{\sigma}, T, ovk_s))$.
  5. Output $\sigma = (\hat{\sigma}, \tilde{\sigma}, ovk_s)$.
- Vrfy(T, m, σ): On input the set of public keys $T = \{pk_i\}_{i \in [N]}$, a signing message m and the signature σ, parse σ as $\sigma = (\hat{\sigma}, \tilde{\sigma}, ovk)$ and compute $\hat{pk}'_i = pk_i - H(ovk)$ for each $i \in [N]$, then
  1. For every $(\text{CMT}_l, x_l, \text{RSP}_l)$, $l \in [L]$ Check whether
     - $f_{j,0} = x - \sum_{i=1}^{\beta-1} f_{j,i}$ for $j = 0, ..., k-1$
     - $xB + A = \text{Com}_{ck}(f_{0,0}, ..., f_{k-1,\beta-1}; \mathbf{z}_b)$
     - $xC + D = \text{Com}_{ck}(f_{0,0}(x - f_{0,0}), ..., f_{k-1,\beta-1}(x - f_{k-1,\beta-1}); \mathbf{z}_c)$
     - $\|f_{j,i}\| \leq 60\sqrt{dk}, \forall j, \forall i \neq 0$ and $\|f_{j,0}\| \leq 60\sqrt{dk(\beta-1)}, \forall j$
     - $\|\mathbf{z}\|, \|\mathbf{z}_s\|, \|\mathbf{z}_c\| \leq 24\sqrt{3}Mmd$
     - $\sum_{i=0}^{N-1}(\prod_{j=0}^{k-1} f_{j,i_j}) c_i - \sum_{j=0}^{k-1} E_j x^j = \text{Com}_{ck}(\mathbf{0}; \mathbf{z})$ for $i = (i_0, ..., i_{k-1})$
     if not, return *reject*.
  2. Run *accept/reject* $\leftarrow \text{Dilithium.Vrfy}(ovk, (\hat{\sigma}, T, \hat{pk}))$.
  3. If neither 1 and 2 return *reject*, return *accept*.

- Link($m_1, m_2, \sigma_1, \sigma_2, T_1, T_2$): On input two sets of public keys T_1, T_2, two signing messages m_1, m_2 and their signatures σ_1, σ_2, run $\mathsf{Vrfy}(m_1, \sigma_1, T_1)$ and $\mathsf{Vrfy}(m_2, \sigma_2, T_2)$. Parse σ_1 and σ_2 as $\sigma_1 = (\hat{\sigma}_1, \tilde{\sigma}_1, ovk_1)$ and $\sigma_2 = (\hat{\sigma}_2, \tilde{\sigma}_2, ovk_2)$. Compare ovk_1 and ovk_2. Return *linked* if $\mathsf{Vrfy}(m_1, \sigma_1, T_1) = \mathsf{Vrfy}(m_2, \sigma_2, T_2) = accept$ and $ovk_1 = ovk_2$.

5   Implementation

5.1   Comparison

We compare the size of public key and signature of existing lattice-based LRS in Table 1. Like [13], our scheme is able to adjust the base representations for user indices and results in different asymptotic growths of signature length.

Table 1. Comparison of lattice-based linkable ring signature

Scheme	Public key size	Signature size	Assumption
[27]	$n\log p$	$2m(\log q)^2 \cdot \boxed{\log N}$	SIS/LWR
[29]	$md\log q$	$m^2 d\log q \cdot \boxed{\log N}$	I(f)-SVP$_\gamma$
[4]	$nd\log q$	$m\log(2\sigma\sqrt{d}) \cdot \boxed{N}$	M-SIS/M-LWE
[25]	$d\log q$	$m\log(\eta\sigma\sqrt{d}) \cdot \boxed{N}$	R-SIS
[19]	$d\log q$	$(256 + 2d\log q) \cdot \boxed{N}$	NTRU
Ours	$nd\log q$	$(nd\log q + \beta d\log\sqrt{144L\log_\beta N})L \cdot \boxed{\log_\beta N}$	M-SIS

1. Constant terms are omittd.
2. n and m denote the row and column of matrix on $\mathbb{Z}_q$ or R_q, d denotes the dimension of polynomials, β denotes the base representations, σ and L denote the standard deviation of discrete normal distribution and the number of repetitions in our scheme.

5.2   Experimental Analysis

In order to compare the size and running time of the LRS scheme and the underlying RS scheme, we implement the instantiation of our scheme and the RS scheme [13] based on the NTL library and the source code of Dilithium.

Parameter Setting and Experimental Results. We set the parameters in the part of RS as in Table 2 and adopt the very high version of Dilithium.

Table 2. Experimental parameter

Parameters	M	n	q	m	d	L	k
Values	100	9	2^{60}	71	76	17	2

As depicted in Table 3, the experimental results show the performance of the LRS scheme is close to the performance of the underlying RS.

Table 3. Experimental results

	Ring size	Size (KB)		Time (ms)		
		Public key	Signature size	KeyGen	Sign	Vrfy
Ring signature	2^6	5.13	1083	84.04	603.18	418.94
	2^8	5.13	1100	84.04	1195.96	904.09
	2^{10}	5.13	1135	84.04	2993.27	2524.47
	2^{12}	5.13	1205	84.04	10310.9	9268.26
Linkable ring signature	2^6	5.13	1088	84.89	604.94	421.47
	2^8	5.13	1105	84.89	1201.53	906.17
	2^{10}	5.13	1140	84.49	2995.47	2527.49
	2^{12}	5.13	1210	84.49	10313.2	9272.20

6 Discussion

In this paper, we adds linkability to any compatible ring signature scheme with one-time signature scheme. Essentially, linkability in this paper is only one-time linkability, which means the linkability tag is not bound to a general linkability context such as the ring of possible signers nor the message being signed, but only bound to a signer. Linkability with variable restrictions are available for different applications. One-time linkability may not be applied to some scenarios such as e-voting but it is vital in constructing cryptocurrencies, because a sum of money can be spent by the owner only once no matter to any ring or any transaction.

Acknowledgments. We thank the anonymous reviewers of ISC 2019 for their helpful comments. We are grateful to Rupeng Yang and Man Ho Allen Au for helpful discussions and advices. This work is supported by National Natural Science Foundation of China (Grant No. 61772522), Youth Innovation Promotion Association CAS, Key Research Program of Frontier Sciences, CAS (Grant No. QYZDB-SSW-SYS035).

A Comment on [19]

Lu et al. [19] adopted the definitions of anonymity, linkability and nonslanderability from [17]. Then, they gave a theorem which shows that the unforgeability is implied by linkability and nonslanderability. First review the definition of linkability and the theorem as follows:

The linkability in [19] is defined in terms of the following game between a challenger $\mathcal{CH}$ and an adversary $\mathcal{A}$:

1. Setup. $\mathcal{CH}$ runs $pp \leftarrow \mathsf{Setup}(1^\lambda)$ and sends pp to $\mathcal{A}$.
2. Query. $\mathcal{A}$ is given access to $\mathcal{O}_{\mathrm{join}}, \mathcal{O}_{\mathrm{corrupt}}, \mathcal{O}_{\mathrm{sign}}$ and may query the oracles in an adaptive manner.
3. Output. $\mathcal{A}$ outputs two pairs $\{T_1, m_1, \sigma_1\}$ and $\{T_2, m_2, \sigma_2\}$.

$\mathcal{A}$ wins the game if

- all public keys in T_1 and T_2 are query outputs of $\mathcal{O}_{\text{join}}$;
- $\mathsf{Vrfy}(T_1, m_1, \sigma_1) = \mathsf{Vrfy}(T_2, m_2, \sigma_2) = accept$;
- $\mathcal{A}$ queried $\mathcal{O}_{\text{corrupt}}$ less than two times; and
- $\mathsf{Link}(m_1, \sigma_1, m_2, \sigma_2) = unlinked$.

The advantage of $\mathcal{A}$, denoted as $\mathsf{Adv}_{\mathcal{A}}^{\text{link}}$, is defined by the probability that $\mathcal{A}$ wins in the above game.

Definition 7 ([19], **Definition 11**). *A LRS scheme is linkable if for any polynomial-time adversary $\mathcal{A}$, $\mathsf{Adv}_{\mathcal{A}}^{\text{link}}$ is negligible in λ.*

Theorem 4 ([19], **Theorem 2**). *If a LRS scheme is linkable and nonslanderable, it is also unforgeable.*

Issue 1. Theorem 4 does not hold for the definition of linkability in [19]. The content of theorem 4 was introduced in [2] which towards the security definitions in [2]. However, the definition of linkability in [19] is different from the definition in [2]. In [19], the adversary $\mathcal{A}$ against unforgeability is allowed to make polynomially many $\mathcal{O}_{\text{corrupt}}$ queries in the unforgeability game, whereas the adversary $\mathcal{B}$ against linkability is restricted to make at most one $\mathcal{O}_{\text{corrupt}}$ query in the linkability game. This means $\mathcal{B}$ cannot simulate $\mathcal{O}_{\text{corrupt}}$ for $\mathcal{A}$ and thus $\mathcal{B}$ cannot run $\mathcal{A}$ to break the linkability.

Issue 2. There is a gap in the proof of linkability. They reduced the linkability of the LRS to the collision resistance of CH+ as follows: First, they embedded the collision resistance challenge hk_c into one of the public keys pk_I by computing $pk_I = hk_c \oplus H(ovk_I)$. Second, the adversary $\mathcal{A}$ outputs two signatures and they concluded that at least one of the signatures should be generated from the secret key that $\mathcal{A}$ does not obtain because $\mathcal{A}$ is allowed to make at most one $\mathcal{O}_{\text{corrupt}}$ query. The signature is denoted as (m^*, σ^*, T^*), where $\sigma^* = (\{(m_i^*, r_i^*)\}_{i \in [N]}, \tilde{\sigma}^*, ovk^*)$. Finally, they assumed $pk_I \in T^*$ and used (m^*, σ^*, T^*) to find a collision of hk_c according to the General Forking Lemma.

However, the collision resistance challenge may not be embedded into the output signatures of $\mathcal{A}$. This means that hk_c is not used to generate the signature (m^*, σ^*, T^*) although $pk_I \in T^*$. The reason is that ovk^* may not equal to ovk_I and thus $hk_c \neq hk_i = pk_i \oplus H(ovk^*)$ for every $i \in [N]$. According to the signing algorithm of the LRS in [19], we can conclude that hk_c is independent of σ^* if $ovk^* \neq ovk_I$. Thus, the collision resistance of CH+ cannot be broken although $\mathcal{A}$ has broken the linkability of the LRS.

References

1. Abe, M., Ohkubo, M., Suzuki, K.: 1-out-of-n signatures from a variety of keys. In: Zheng, Y. (ed.) ASIACRYPT 2002. LNCS, vol. 2501, pp. 415–432. Springer, Heidelberg (2002). https://doi.org/10.1007/3-540-36178-2_26

2. Au, M.H., Susilo, W., Yiu, S.-M.: Event-oriented k-times revocable-iff-linked group signatures. In: Batten, L.M., Safavi-Naini, R. (eds.) ACISP 2006. LNCS, vol. 4058, pp. 223–234. Springer, Heidelberg (2006). https://doi.org/10.1007/11780656_19

3. Backes, M., Döttling, N., Hanzlik, L., Kluczniak, K., Schneider, J.: Ring signatures: logarithmic-size, no setup—from standard assumptions. In: Ishai, Y., Rijmen, V. (eds.) EUROCRYPT 2019. LNCS, vol. 11478, pp. 281–311. Springer, Cham (2019). https://doi.org/10.1007/978-3-030-17659-4_10

4. Baum, C., Lin, H., Oechsner, S.: Towards practical lattice-based one-time linkable ring signatures. In: Naccache, D., et al. (eds.) ICICS 2018. LNCS, vol. 11149, pp. 303–322. Springer, Cham (2018). https://doi.org/10.1007/978-3-030-01950-1_18

5. Bose, P., Das, D., Rangan, C.P.: Constant size ring signature without random oracle. In: Foo, E., Stebila, D. (eds.) ACISP 2015. LNCS, vol. 9144, pp. 230–247. Springer, Cham (2015). https://doi.org/10.1007/978-3-319-19962-7_14

6. Brakerski, Z., Kalai, Y.T.: A framework for efficient signatures, ring signatures and identity based encryption in the standard model. IACR Cryptology ePrint Archive 2010, 86 (2010). http://eprint.iacr.org/2010/086

7. Chow, S.S.M., Susilo, W., Yuen, T.H.: Escrowed linkability of ring signatures and its applications. In: Nguyen, P.Q. (ed.) VIETCRYPT 2006. LNCS, vol. 4341, pp. 175–192. Springer, Heidelberg (2006). https://doi.org/10.1007/11958239_12

8. Chow, S.S.M., Wei, V.K., Liu, J.K., Yuen, T.H.: Ring signatures without random oracles. In: ASIACCS, pp. 297–302 (2006)

9. Chow, S.S.M., Yiu, S.-M., Hui, L.C.K.: Efficient identity based ring signature. In: Ioannidis, J., Keromytis, A., Yung, M. (eds.) ACNS 2005. LNCS, vol. 3531, pp. 499–512. Springer, Heidelberg (2005). https://doi.org/10.1007/11496137_34

10. Dodis, Y., Kiayias, A., Nicolosi, A., Shoup, V.: Anonymous identification in *Ad Hoc* groups. In: Cachin, C., Camenisch, J.L. (eds.) EUROCRYPT 2004. LNCS, vol. 3027, pp. 609–626. Springer, Heidelberg (2004). https://doi.org/10.1007/978-3-540-24676-3_36

11. Ducas, L., Durmus, A., Lepoint, T., Lyubashevsky, V.: Lattice signatures and bimodal Gaussians. In: Canetti, R., Garay, J.A. (eds.) CRYPTO 2013. LNCS, vol. 8042, pp. 40–56. Springer, Heidelberg (2013). https://doi.org/10.1007/978-3-642-40041-4_3

12. Ducas, L., et al.: CRYSTALS-Dilithium: a lattice-based digital signature scheme. IACR Trans. Cryptogr. Hardw. Embed. Syst. **2018**(1), 238–268 (2018)

13. Esgin, M.F., Steinfeld, R., Sakzad, A., Liu, J.K., Liu, D.: Short lattice-based one-out-of-many proofs and applications to ring signatures. In: Deng, R.H., Gauthier-Umaña, V., Ochoa, M., Yung, M. (eds.) ACNS 2019. LNCS, vol. 11464, pp. 67–88. Springer, Cham (2019). https://doi.org/10.1007/978-3-030-21568-2_4

14. Franklin, M., Zhang, H.: Unique ring signatures: a practical construction. In: Sadeghi, A.-R. (ed.) FC 2013. LNCS, vol. 7859, pp. 162–170. Springer, Heidelberg (2013). https://doi.org/10.1007/978-3-642-39884-1_13

15. Groth, J., Kohlweiss, M.: One-out-of-many proofs: or how to leak a secret and spend a coin. In: Oswald, E., Fischlin, M. (eds.) EUROCRYPT 2015. LNCS, vol. 9057, pp. 253–280. Springer, Heidelberg (2015). https://doi.org/10.1007/978-3-662-46803-6_9

16. Libert, B., Ling, S., Nguyen, K., Wang, H.: Zero-knowledge arguments for lattice-based accumulators: logarithmic-size ring signatures and group signatures without trapdoors. In: Fischlin, M., Coron, J.-S. (eds.) EUROCRYPT 2016. LNCS, vol. 9666, pp. 1–31. Springer, Heidelberg (2016). https://doi.org/10.1007/978-3-662-49896-5_1

17. Liu, J.K., Au, M.H., Susilo, W., Zhou, J.: Linkable ring signature with unconditional anonymity. IEEE Trans. Knowl. Data Eng. **26**(1), 157–165 (2014)
18. Liu, J.K., Wei, V.K., Wong, D.S.: Linkable spontaneous anonymous group signature for ad hoc groups (extended abstract). In: Wang, H., Pieprzyk, J., Varadharajan, V. (eds.) ACISP 2004. LNCS, vol. 3108, pp. 325–335. Springer, Heidelberg (2004). https://doi.org/10.1007/978-3-540-27800-9_28
19. Lu, X., Au, M.H., Zhang, Z.: Raptor: a practical lattice-based (linkable) ring signature. IACR Cryptology ePrint Archive 2018, 857 (2018). https://eprint.iacr.org/2018/857
20. Lyubashevsky, V.: Lattice signatures without trapdoors. In: Pointcheval, D., Johansson, T. (eds.) EUROCRYPT 2012. LNCS, vol. 7237, pp. 738–755. Springer, Heidelberg (2012). https://doi.org/10.1007/978-3-642-29011-4_43
21. Noether, S.: Ring signature confidential transactions for monero. IACR Cryptology ePrint Archive 2015, 1098 (2015). http://eprint.iacr.org/2015/1098
22. Rivest, R.L., Shamir, A., Tauman, Y.: How to leak a secret. In: Boyd, C. (ed.) ASIACRYPT 2001. LNCS, vol. 2248, pp. 552–565. Springer, Heidelberg (2001). https://doi.org/10.1007/3-540-45682-1_32
23. van Saberhagen, N.: Cryptonote v 2.0 (2013). https://cryptonote.org/whitepaper.pdf
24. Sun, S.-F., Au, M.H., Liu, J.K., Yuen, T.H.: RingCT 2.0: a compact accumulator-based (linkable ring signature) protocol for blockchain cryptocurrency monero. In: Foley, S.N., Gollmann, D., Snekkenes, E. (eds.) ESORICS 2017. LNCS, vol. 10493, pp. 456–474. Springer, Cham (2017). https://doi.org/10.1007/978-3-319-66399-9_25
25. Alberto Torres, W.A., et al.: Post-quantum one-time linkable ring signature and application to ring confidential transactions in blockchain (lattice RingCT v1.0). In: Susilo, W., Yang, G. (eds.) ACISP 2018. LNCS, vol. 10946, pp. 558–576. Springer, Cham (2018). https://doi.org/10.1007/978-3-319-93638-3_32
26. Tsang, P.P., Wei, V.K.: Short linkable ring signatures for e-voting, e-cash and attestation. In: Deng, R.H., Bao, F., Pang, H.H., Zhou, J. (eds.) ISPEC 2005. LNCS, vol. 3439, pp. 48–60. Springer, Heidelberg (2005). https://doi.org/10.1007/978-3-540-31979-5_5
27. Yang, R., Au, M.H., Lai, J., Xu, Q., Yu, Z.: Lattice-based techniques for accountable anonymity: composition of abstract stern's protocols and weak PRF with efficient protocols from LWR. IACR Cryptology ePrint Archive 2017, 781 (2017). http://eprint.iacr.org/2017/781
28. Yuen, T.H., Liu, J.K., Au, M.H., Susilo, W., Zhou, J.: Efficient linkable and/or threshold ring signature without random oracles. Comput. J. **56**(4), 407–421 (2013)
29. Zhang, H., Zhang, F., Tian, H., Au, M.H.: Anonymous post-quantum cryptocash. IACR Cryptology ePrint Archive 2017, 716 (2017). http://eprint.iacr.org/2017/716

Cryptographic Authentication
from the Iris

Sailesh Simhadri[1], James Steel[2], and Benjamin Fuller[2(✉)]

[1] Google Inc., Cambridge, MA, USA
`saileshsimhadri@gmail.com`
[2] University of Connecticut, Storrs, CT, USA
{`james.steel,benjamin.fuller`}`@uconn.edu`

Abstract. Biometrics exhibit noise between repeated readings. Due to the noise, devices store a plaintext *template* of the biometric. This stored template is an appetizing target for an attacker.

Fuzzy extractors derive a stable cryptographic key from biometrics (Dodis et al., Eurocrypt 2004). Despite many attempts, there are no iris key derivation systems that prove lower bounds on key strength.

Our starting point is a fuzzy extractor due to Canetti et al. (Eurocrypt 2016). We modify and couple the image processing and cryptographic algorithms. We then present a sufficient condition on the iris distribution for security, and analysis this condition using the ND0405 Iris dataset.

We build an iris key derivation system with 32 bits of security even when multiple keys are derived from the same iris. We acknowledge 32 bits of security is insufficient for a secure system. Multifactor systems hold the most promise for cryptographic authentication. Our scheme is suited for incorporation of additional *noiseless* factors such as a password.

Our scheme is implemented in C and Python and is open-sourced.

1   Introduction

Authentication schemes combine factors such as passwords, one-time codes, security questions, and social relationships [11]. Some providers use key derivation functions to derive cryptographic keys and then protect sensitive data using these keys. Depending on the *entropy* of the authentication factors, we can obtain bounds on how long it will take an adversary to correctly guess users' private information.

Biometrics are used to authenticate users on mobile devices (phones and tablets). In these systems, a template of the biometric reading is stored in a secure processor. Since the template is stored "in the clear," a secure processing component is necessary. Furthermore, it means that deploying biometric authentication in a client-server setting is risky. The client-server setting is still the majority of Internet authentication.

In the absence of a secure processor, two complementary lines of research emerged: interactive protocols and schemes that create a single value that allows

© Springer Nature Switzerland AG 2019
Z. Lin et al. (Eds.): ISC 2019, LNCS 11723, pp. 465–485, 2019.
https://doi.org/10.1007/978-3-030-30215-3_23

for authentication (that is, non-interactive protocols). The interactive setting is well understood [8, 9, 16, 18, 26–28, 31, 32]. Importantly, interactive protocols do not consider server compromise in scope of the threat model. Their focus is on ensuring an adversary that pretends to be either the client or server gains minimal information by engaging in the protocol. Furthermore, the interactive model is not applicable for a user authenticating to a device.

The non-interactive setting is not understood despite years of research. (We detail prior work in Sect. 1.1). For many biometrics there is little in way of implementable work (current proposals either requiring exponential time [34, 41, 64] or semantically secure graded encodings [52]). We focus on building non-interactive key derivation from the iris [57]. We use the definition of fuzzy extractors [29, 30]. (Our discussion applies to fuzzy commitments [45] and secure sketches [29]).

Fuzzy extractors derive stable keys from a biometric. Fuzzy extractors consist of two algorithms Gen, or generate, and Rep, or reproduce. The Gen algorithm takes an initial reading of the biometric, denoted w, deriving a key Key and a value Pub. The Rep algorithm is used at authentication time taking Pub and a later reading of the biometric, denoted w'. If the two readings of the biometric are similar enough then the same Key should be output by the algorithm. The security of a fuzzy extractor is analyzed assuming the adversary knows Pub.

The first generation of fuzzy extractors shared the same core construction and security analysis [25]. These constructions all used a variant of the one-time pad where the "pad" is a codeword from an error correcting code (rather than being uniformly distributed).

The quality of the derived key depends on the entropy of the biometric and size of the error-correcting code. Let W be a biometric of length n and suppose W has k bits of min-entropy. Suppose the error correcting code has 2^α codewords. Roughly, it is assumed the "one-time pad" leaks the entropy deficiency of the code or $n - \alpha$ bits. If one wishes to tolerate t bits of error between w and w', using bounds on the best code, this loss is at least $h_2(t/n) * n$.[1]

In many cases $h_2(t/n) * n$ is larger than k. Daugman's seminal paper on iris recognition [24] transformed iris images into a fixed length 2048 bit vector. Daugman reports error rates close to 10% in a controlled environment. For more realistic datasets the error rate is 30% (see Fig. 3). In either case, $h_2(t/n) * n \geq h_2(.1) * 2048 \approx 874$ is larger than the estimated entropy of 249.[2] It is not known how to analyze the first generation of fuzzy extractors to argue security for the iris.

Biometrics cannot be changed or updated so provable, cryptographic security is crucial. A compromise affects an individual for their entire life. We focus on

---

[1] The quantity $h_2(t/n) * n$ is the binary entropy of t/n multiplied by n. The quantity $h_2(t/n) * n$ is larger than t (when $t \leq .5n$). For example, if $t = .1n$ then $h_2(t/n) * n \approx .427n$.

[2] Any distribution limited to people on the earth can be described using 33 bits. The estimate of 249 should be understood as the randomness involved in creating a new iris.

a strengthening of fuzzy extractors called *reusable* fuzzy extractors that allows derivation of multiple keys and multiple public values from the same biometric.

Recently, a second generation of fuzzy extractors emerged using cryptographic tools [1,2,20,33,62,63]. These constructions are reusable and only provide security against computationally bounded adversaries. Some of these constructions provide meaningful security when W has low entropy. However, this security requires W to have additional structure beyond entropy. There have been no empirical evaluations of whether biometrics exhibit this structure. Furthermore, these constructions are stated in asymptotic form and it is not clear what properties they provide for actual biometrics.

Our Contribution. We build the first key derivation system that provides meaningful albeit moderate provable security from the iris. Our scheme has been implemented and open-sourced [36]. The combination of cryptographic and statistical analysis estimates a security level of 32 bits. As a point of comparison, recent estimates place password entropy at 22 bits [10,48,61]. We do not believe this security level is sufficient for a stand alone system. Our hope is that this work serves as a catalyst for system designers to incorporate our construction into multi-factor authentication systems and that the overall system provides strong security. We discuss such a system below.

The starting point for our construction is the recent sample-then-lock scheme of Canetti et al. [20]. The idea of the scheme is simple: to hash the biometric in an "error-tolerant" way. Hashing the full biometric doesn't work (due to biometric noise). Instead, multiple random subsets of the biometric are hashed. That is, sample a random subset of bits, denoted $\mathcal{I}$, and hash w restricted to the bits of $\mathcal{I}$, denoted $\mathsf{Hash}(w_{\mathcal{I}})$, and use this value as a pad for a cryptographic Key. That is, store $(\mathsf{Key} \oplus \mathsf{Hash}(w_{\mathcal{I}}), \mathcal{I})$. This process is repeated with multiple subsets $\mathcal{I}_j$ and the same Key. Correctness follows if it is likely that in at least one subset $\mathcal{I}_j$, $w_{\mathcal{I}_j} = w'_{\mathcal{I}_j}$. The security analysis requires for a random subset $\mathcal{I}_j$ of bits that $w_{\mathcal{I}_j}$ has entropy with high probability over the choice of $\mathcal{I}_j$ (see Definition 1). This strengthens the requirement that the whole vector W has entropy.

We first estimate that subsampling iris bits produces a distribution with entropy (Fig. 1). (Efficient entropy estimation is heuristic. Provably accurate entropy estimation [59,60] requires an exponentially large number of samples in the actual entropy of the distribution.) We use the same heuristic that occurs in previous biometric research. Roughly, the distances between transformed irises of different individuals are compared with the distances that would be produced by the binomial distribution whose entropy is computable. This is discussed in further in Sect. 4.

However, we find that the naive combination of iris processing and the fuzzy extractor provides inadequate security and efficiency. The core of our technical contribution is:

1. Modifying sample-then-lock for implementation (and proving security),
2. Modifying the iris image processing to maximize security,
3. Two open source implementations of the resulting scheme (Python and C),

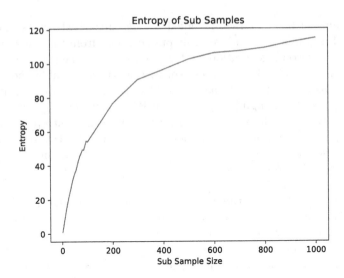

Fig. 1. In the worst case subsampling only preserves error rate. For the iris, subsampling greatly increases entropy rate from 1% to over 80%.

4. Statistical analysis on security, correctness, storage requirements, and timing. All of our analysis uses the ND-0405 iris data set [12,56] which is a superset of the NIST Iris Challenge Evaluation Dataset [55]. Throughout our work we explicitly state what assumptions are needed for security of the scheme to hold.

Adding More Factors. Many multi factor authentication systems do not achieve "additive security". Consider a strawman authentication system: (1) a user inputs a password and (2) an iris. Currently, the password would be hashed and compared to stored hash and the iris compared to a template. One of these comparisons has to be done first. Using a timing channel, it is possible for an adversary to separate search on each factor. A noiseless password can be used as part of the input to any fuzzy extractor and strengthen key derivation. However, previous fuzzy extractors separate the error-correction from the key derivation process using two distinct primitives called secure sketch [29] and randomness extractor respectively [51]. In such a process, the password can only be incorporated into the randomness extractor. As such, a similar timing channel may still exist. Our construction does not suffer from this problem. "Error-correction" and key derivation are performed simultaneously. The password can be prepended as input to each hash invocation without affecting storage or computational requirements.

1.1 Prior Work

Boyen [15] defined reusable fuzzy extractors in 2004 and showed information-theoretic reusability requires a large decrease in security [15, Theorem 11].[3] Essentially, Boyen showed the security loss described above is *necessary*. Applied works showed that many fuzzy extractors were not reusable [6,7,58], meaning that the negative result of Boyen was not only a theoretic issue. Recent work [1,2,20,63] that provides computational security [33] sidesteps Boyen's negative result.

A key consideration in reusable fuzzy extractors is the type of correlation assumed between enrollments W_i and W_j. In many constructions it is assumed that $W_i \oplus W_j$ does not leak information about W_i or W_j. This assumption has not been verified in practice and was made by [2,15,63]. We make no assumption about the correlation between different enrollments, only about the statistical structure of an individual enrollment. In this model, Alamelou et al. [1] construct a reusable fuzzy extractor for the set difference metric. The iris has noise in the Hamming metric. The only construction that appears viable is the sample-then-lock construction (our starting point) [20].

Many previous works have used a fuzzy extractor in combination with the iris. These works security claims are troubling for a variety of reasons.

Hao et al. [40] use the code-offset construction with a code with 2^{140} codewords with the Iriscode transform of Daugman [24]. Using standard fuzzy extractor analysis this provides no security: it could leak as much as $2048 - 140$ bits. Hao et al. claim a key strength of 140 without justification. Hao et al. then argue an adversary providing a random iris would succeed with probability 2^{-44}. This corresponds to an adversary that does not have access to Pub (plaintext template storage suffices in this model). Note that providing an adversary providing a random iris should yields an upper bounds for the security of the system, immediately contradicting the claim of 140 bits of security. These issues have been communicated with Hao et al.

Bringer et al. [17] do not state a key strength but they report a nonzero false accept rate which implies a small effective key strength. Reporting a nonzero false accept rate is common in iris key derivation despite claimed key lengths > 40 bits (see discussion [43,53]). Using the birthday bound, false acceptances should appear when the tested dataset size approaches the square root of the claimed key size (i.e. $> 2^{20}$). No published iris datasets have close to a million individuals.

Kanade et al. [46] claim a fuzzy extractor construction but they report the entropy of the iris as over 1000 bits, much higher than other estimates. Other research states that each bit of the iris transform is independent [39] which is demonstrably not true (see for example our statistical analysis in Sect. 4).

The above discussion is necessarily incomplete (see the survey of Bowyer et al. [14, Sect. 6]). It demonstrates a large gap between theoretical fuzzy extractor

---

[3] The actual result of Boyen applies to *secure sketches* which imply fuzzy extractors. A secure sketch is a frequently used tool to construct a fuzzy extractor.

constructions and their use, justifying a rigorous analysis of iris key derivation that makes assumptions explicit and accurately estimates security.

Recently, Cheon et al. [22] also modified sample-then-lock. However, their work contains a flaw in its security argument. At a high level, the authors incorrect argue that many polynomial size random oracles can't be exhausted by an unbounded adversary. This flaw has been communicated to and acknowledged by the authors. No public revision has been made.

Organization. The rest of this work is organized as follows, in Sect. 2 we review basic definitions and cryptographic tools, Sect. 3 describes our scheme and software, Sect. 4 describes iris image processing and the transform used as input to our scheme, Sect. 5 evaluates the performance and correctness of our system, Sect. 6 concludes. More statistical analysis and a second version of the scheme requiring additional statistical assumptions are deferred to the full version of this work [35].

2   Definitions and Cryptographic Tools

We use capital letters to refer to random variables. For a set of indices J, X_J is the restriction of X to the indices in J. U_n denotes the uniformly distributed random variable on $\{0,1\}^n$. Logarithms are base 2. The *min-entropy* of X is $H_\infty(X) = -\log(\max_x \Pr[X = x])$. We use the notion of average min-entropy to measure the conditional entropy of a random variable. The *average* min-entropy of X given Y is $\tilde{H}_\infty(X|Y) = -\log(\mathbb{E}_{y\in Y} \max_x \Pr[X = x|Y = y])$. The *statistical distance* between random variables X and Y with the same domain is $\Delta(X,Y) = \frac{1}{2}\sum_x |\Pr[X = x] - \Pr[Y = x]|$. Our construction requires additional structure past entropy that we call k entropy samples [20]:

Definition 1. *Let $W = W_1, \ldots, W_n$ be a distribution over $\{0,1\}^n$. For k, α, we say that W is a source with α-entropy k-samples if $\tilde{H}_\infty(W_{j_1}, \ldots, W_{j_k} | j_1, \ldots, j_k) \geq \alpha$ for uniformly random $1 \leq j_1, \ldots, j_k \leq n$.*

We use the version of fuzzy extractors that provides security against computationally bounded adversaries [33]. Dodis et al. provide comparable definitions for information-theoretic fuzzy extractors [29, Sects. 2.5–4.1]. A desirable property of a fuzzy extractor is that an individual can enroll their biometric with multiple service providers and retain security.[4] Informally, each cryptographic key should be secure if an adversary knows all public helper values and all other derived keys. We state the definition of a reusable computational fuzzy extractor:

Definition 2. *Let $\mathcal{W}$ be a family of distributions over metric space $(\mathcal{M}, \mathsf{dis})$. A pair of randomized procedures "generate" (Gen) and "reproduce" (Rep) is an*

---

[4] Unlinkability prevents an adversary from telling if two enrollments correspond to the same physical source [21,47]. Our construction satisfies unlinkability (assuming security of the underlying cryptographic tools).

$(\mathcal{M}, \mathcal{W}, \kappa, t, \rho)$-computational fuzzy extractor *that is* $(\epsilon_{sec}, s_{sec})$-*hard with error* δ *if* Gen *and* Rep *satisfy the following properties:*

(1) Correctness: *if* $\mathsf{dis}(w, w') \leq t$ *and* $(r, p) \leftarrow \mathsf{Gen}(w)$, $\Pr[\mathsf{Rep}(w', p) = r] \geq 1 - \delta$.

(2) Security *Let* $(W^1, W^2, \ldots, W^\rho)$ *be* ρ *correlated random variables such that each* $W^j \in \mathcal{W}$. *Let* D *be an adversary. Define the following game for* $j = 1, \ldots, \rho$:

- **Sampling** *The challenger samples* $w^j \leftarrow W^j$, $u \leftarrow \{0, 1\}^\kappa$.
- **Generation** *The challenger computes* $(r^j, p^j) \leftarrow \mathsf{Gen}(w^j)$.
- **Distinguishing** *For all* D *of size at most* s_{sec}, *the advantage of* D *is*

$$\Pr[D(r^j, \{r^i\}_{i \neq j}^{i=1,\ldots,\rho}, \{p^i\}_{i=1}^\rho) = 1] - \Pr[D(u, \{r^i\}_{i \neq j}^{i=1,\ldots,\rho}, \{p^i\}_{i=1}^\rho) = 1] \leq \epsilon.$$

Digital Lockers. Our construction uses digital lockers [19]. A digital locker is an algorithm lock which takes an input val and an output key, producing an algorithm unlock, unlock reproduces key if and only if the same val is provided as input. Digital lockers have two important properties:

1. Information about key is only obtained if the combination is guessed.
2. It is possible to detect the wrong val with high probability.

Digital lockers can be constructed from variants of the Diffie-Hellman assumption [19]. Let HMAC be HMAC-SHA256. Our construction assumes that HMAC can be used to construct digital lockers. The "locking" algorithm outputs the pair

$$\mathsf{nonce}, \mathsf{HMAC}(\mathsf{nonce}, w) \oplus (0^{128} || \mathsf{key}),$$

where nonce is a nonce, $||$ denotes concatenation, 0^{128} is the all zeros string of length 128, a security parameter. Unlocking proceeds by recomputing the hash and checking for a prefix of 0^{128}. If this prefix is found then the suffix key' is output. This construction was proposed in [3] and shown to be secure in the random oracle model by Lynn, Prabhakaran, and Sahai [50, Sect. 4]. It is plausible that in the standard model (without random oracles) hash functions provide the necessary security [19, Sect. 3.2], [23, Sect. 8.2.3]. We now present the full formal definition [5]:

Definition 3. *The pair of algorithm* (lock, unlock) *with security parameter* λ *is an* ℓ-*composable secure digital locker with error* γ *if the following hold:*

Correctness. *For any pair* key, val, $\Pr[\mathsf{unlock}(\mathsf{key}, \mathsf{lock}(\mathsf{key}, \mathsf{val})) = \mathsf{val}] \geq 1 - \gamma$. *Also, for any* key' $\neq$ key, $\Pr[\mathsf{unlock}(\mathsf{key'}, \mathsf{lock}(\mathsf{key}, \mathsf{val})) = \perp] \geq 1 - \gamma$.

Security. *For every PPT adversary* A *and every positive polynomial* p, *there exists a (possibly inefficient) simulator* S *and a polynomial* $q(\lambda)$ *such that for any sufficiently large* s, *any polynomially-long sequence of values* (val$_i$, key$_i$) *for* $i = 1, \ldots, \ell$, *and any auxiliary input* $z \in \{0, 1\}^*$,

$$\left| \Pr\left[A\left(z, \{\mathsf{lock}\,(\mathsf{key}_i, \mathsf{val}_i)\}_{i=1}^\ell\right) = 1 \right] - \Pr\left[S\left(z, \{|\mathsf{key}_i|, |\mathsf{val}_i|\}_{i=1}^\ell\right) = 1 \right] \right| \leq \frac{1}{p(\mathsf{s})}$$

where S *is allowed* $q(\lambda)$ *oracle queries to the oracles* $\{\mathsf{idealUnlock}(\mathsf{key}_i, \mathsf{val}_i)\}_{i=1}^\ell$.

Technical Remark: Unfortunately, the security definition of digital lockers (Definition 3) is "inherently" asymptotic. A different simulator is allowed for each distance bound $p(s)$ making it difficult to argue what quality key is provided with respect to a particular adversary.

3   Our Construction and Implementation

Our construction builds on the construction of Canetti et al. [20]. The high level idea is to encrypt the same key multiple times using different subsets of w. Pseudocode for the algorithm is in Fig. 2.

Gen(w):

1. Sample random 128 bit key.
2. For $i = 1, ..., \ell$:
    (i) Choose $1 \le j_{i,1}, ..., j_{i,k} \le |w|$
    (ii) Choose 512 bit hash key h_i.
    (iii) $c_i = \mathsf{Hash}(h_i, w_{j_{i,1}}, ..., w_{j_{i,k}})$.
    (iv) Set $p_i = (0^{128} \| \mathsf{key}) \oplus c_i$.
3. Output (key, $p_i, \{j_{i,m}\}, h_i$).

Rep($w', p_i, \{j_{i,m}\}, h_i$)

1. For $i = 1, ..., \ell$:
    (i) $c_i = \mathsf{Hash}(h_i, w'_{j_{i,1}}, ..., w'_{j_{i,k}})$.
    (ii) If $(c_i \oplus p_i)_{1..128} = 0^{128}$,
        output $(c_i \oplus p_i)_{129..256}$.
2. Output $\perp$.

Fig. 2. Overview of generation (enrollment) and reproduction (authentication) of key derivation system.

In the description above, $x_{a..b}$ denotes the restriction of a vector to the bits between a and b. The parameters k and ℓ represent a tradeoff between correctness and security. For the scheme to be correct at least one of the ℓ subsets should have no error with high probability. Canetti et al. show it is possible to set ℓ if the expected error rate is sublinear in $|w|$. That is, when $d(w, w')/|w| = o(|w|)$. We set ℓ and k in Sect. 4.

A single digital locker requires storage of 32 bytes for the output of the hash and 64 bytes for each hash key h_i. In addition, the public value must store the randomly sampled locations. The two natural solutions for this are (1) storing a mask of size $|w|$ for each subset or (2) a location set of size $\log |w| * k$ for each subset. Using either approach, in our analysis, storing subsets required more space that the hash outputs and keys. This led to our main modification of the cryptographic scheme.

Canetti et al. [20, Sect. 4] note that rather than using independent subsets they could be selected using a sampler [37]. We show the security argument holds as long as each subset is random on its own. That is, the different subsets can be arbitrarily correlated. We will use this fact to reduce the storage requirement of the scheme. We now state security of the modified scheme.

Theorem 1. *Let λ be a security parameter, Let $\mathcal{W}$ be a family with α-entropy k-samples for $\alpha = \omega(\log \lambda)$. Suppose the HMAC construction is a secure digital locker. Let $\mathcal{I}_j$ be the jth subset generated in Gen. The fuzzy extractor in Fig. 2 is* secure if each individual $\mathcal{I}_j$ is uniformly distributed (but different subsets $\mathcal{I}_j, \mathcal{I}_\ell$ are potentially correlated). More formally, for any $s_{sec} = \texttt{poly}(\lambda)$ there exists some $\epsilon_{sec} = \texttt{ngl}(\lambda)$ such that sample-then-lock is a $(\mathcal{Z}^n, \mathcal{W}, \kappa, t)$-computational fuzzy extractor that is $(\epsilon_{sec}, s_{sec})$-hard with error $\delta = \texttt{negl}(\lambda)$. No claim about correctness is made if $\mathcal{I}_j$ and $\mathcal{I}_\ell$ are correlated.

We only show security when Gen is run once, reusability follows using the same argument as in Canetti et al. [20].

Proof. Let $V_1, ..., V_\ell$ be random variables corresponding to W restricted to the bits selected in subset $\mathcal{I}_i$. Similarly, let P_i be the random variable corresponding to the public part of the output produced in iteration i. Let R denote the distribution over output key values. Lastly, let U denote the uniform distribution over $\{0,1\}^{|\mathsf{key}|}$. We show for all $s_{sec} = \texttt{poly}(\lambda)$ there exists $\epsilon_{sec} = \texttt{ngl}(\lambda)$ such that

$$\delta^{\mathcal{D}_{s_{sec}}}((R, \{P_i\}_{i=1}^\ell), (U, \{P_i\}_{i=1}^\ell)) \le \epsilon_{sec}.$$

Fix some polynomial s_{sec} and let D be a distinguisher of size at most s_{sec}.

We proceed by contradiction: supposing $|\mathbb{E}[D(R, \{P_i\}_{i=1}^\ell)] - \mathbb{E}[D(U, \{P_i\}_{i=1}^\ell)]|$ is not negligible. Suppose there is a polynomial $p(\cdot)$ such that for all λ_0 there exists some $\lambda > \lambda_0$ such that

$$|\mathbb{E}[D(R, \{P_i\}_{i=1}^\ell)] - \mathbb{E}[D(U, \{P_i\}_{i=1}^\ell)]| > 1/p(\lambda).$$

By Definition 3, there is a polynomial q and an unbounded time simulator S (making at most $q(\lambda)$ queries to the oracles $\{\mathsf{idealUnlock}(v_i, r)\}_{i=1}^\ell$) such that

$$\frac{1}{3p(\lambda)} \ge |\mathbb{E}[D(R, P_1, ..., P_\ell)] - \mathbb{E}\left[S^{\{\mathsf{idealUnlock}(v_i, r)\}_{i=1}^\ell}(R, \{\mathcal{I}_i\}_{i=1}^\ell, k, |\mathsf{key}|)\right]| \tag{1}$$

This is also true if we replace R with an independent uniform random variable U over $\{0,1\}^{|\mathsf{key}|}$. We now prove the following lemma, which shows that S cannot distinguish between R and a independent U.

Lemma 1. *Let all variables be as above. Then*

$$\left| \mathbb{E}\left[S^{\{\mathsf{idealUnlock}(v_i, r)\}_{i=1}^\ell}(R, \{\mathcal{I}_i\}_{i=1}^\ell, k, |\mathsf{key}|)\right] \right.$$
$$\left. - \mathbb{E}\left[S^{\{\mathsf{idealUnlock}(v_i, r)\}_{i=1}^\ell}(U, \{\mathcal{I}_i\}_{i=1}^\ell, k, |\mathsf{key}|)\right] \right|$$
$$\le \frac{q(q+1)}{2^\alpha} \le \frac{1}{3p(\lambda)}$$

where q is the maximum number of queries S can make.

Proof. Fix some $u \in \{0,1\}^{|\mathsf{key}|}$. The only information about whether the value is r or u can obtained by S through the query responses. First, modify S slightly to quit immediately if it gets a response not equal to $\bot$. There are $q+1$ possible values for the view of S on a given input (q of those views consist of some number of $\bot$ responses followed by the first non-$\bot$ response, and one view has all q responses equal to $\bot$). By [29, Lemma 2.2b], $\tilde{H}_\infty(V_i | View(S), \{\mathcal{I}_j\}) \geq \tilde{H}_\infty(V_i | \{\mathcal{I}_j\}) - \log(q+1) \geq \alpha - \log(q+1)$. Therefore, at each query, the probability that S gets a non-$\bot$ answer (equivalently, guesses V_i) is at most $(q+1)2^{-\alpha}$. Since there are q queries of S, the overall probability is at most $q(q+1)/2^\alpha$. Then since 2^α is $\mathtt{ngl}(\lambda)$, there exists some λ_0 such that for all $\lambda > \lambda_0$, $q(q+1)/2^\alpha \leq 1/(3p(\lambda))$.

The overall theorem follows using the triangle inequality with Eq. 1, Eq. 1 with R replaced with U, and Lemma 1 yielding $\delta^D((R,P),(U,P)) \leq 1/p(\lambda)$. This completes the proof of Theorem 1.

This theorem gives us a mechanism for saving on storage size. Instead of choosing independent subsets, the implementation chooses a master subset and then generates permutations π_j to create new subsets based on public cryptographic keying material. The new scheme works as follows:

1. Choose a master subset $\mathcal{I}$ uniformly at random where $|\mathcal{I}| = k$.
2. For each locker j generate a permutation $\pi_j : \{0,1\}^{|w|} \to \{0,1\}^{|w|}$.
3. Apply π_j to each element of $\mathcal{I}$ to get $\mathcal{I}_j$.

To efficiently generate permutations we do the following:

1. Select a single master CHACHA20 key.
2. Encrypt the permutation number j, creating $\log|w| * |w|$ bits of output c.
3. We split c into $\log|w|$ bit sections $c_1, ..., c_{|w|}$.
4. Define $\pi_j(i) = c_i$.

The output of CHACHA20 is not a permutation: it is not guaranteed that $\log|w|$ consecutive bits do not repeat. Furthermore, looking ahead to Sect. 4, our iris processing results in a vector of 12000 bits. The above algorithm only works if $|w|$ is a power of 2. We adapt our algorithm by adding a check for each section c_i. If $c_i > |w|$ or c_i is repeated it is discarded. To compensate for these two failure conditions it is necessary to produce more than $|w|$ sections. Producing 2000 additional sections was sufficient to always output a permutation in our experiments. This modification reduces overall storage to a single CHACHA20 key, the single randomly generated subset, and 96 byte per subset storage. Generating these permutations takes additional computation. One can tradeoff between storing all subsets and a single master subset, storing some fraction of subsets and regenerating the rest. We are not aware of how to reduce the 96 byte per subset storage. An idea is to use a single nonce, we were not able to argue security of this modified scheme. We leave this as an open problem.

Implementation. We implemented our construction in both Python and C and both implementations are open sourced [36]. Previous implementations of fuzzy extractors required expertise in error-correcting codes. Our construction only requires repeated evaluation of a hash function.

The entire Python library is 100 lines of code with dependencies on numPy (for array manipulation), random, and hashlib. Our Gen code is single threaded because the majority of execution time is spent generating the subsets $j_{i,1}, ..., j_{i,k}$. The Rep functionality is embarrassingly parallel. We implemented a parallel version that simply partitions the hashes to be performed. Rep succeeds when one of these threads returns. Unfortunately, neither implementation is fast enough with authentication taking seconds (see Sect. 5).

We also developed an optimized C implementation designed for fast Rep performance. As Rep is used at every authentication its speed is more important than Gen which is only used when a user enrolls with a new service. For this implementation we used Libsodium [4] as the cryptographic backend and HMAC-SHA-512 to instantiate the digital locker. This library makes use of low level bit level operations for quickly packing and selecting bits the iris vector. In preliminary testing a major obstacle to fast Rep was disk load time. Recall, each subset selected in Gen requires storage of 96 bytes.

4   Iris Image Processing and Setting Parameters

This section provides a brief overview of iris image processing and the transform used in our system. Iris image processing is an entire field [13]. Our scheme can be used with techniques that produce a vector with Hamming errors (fraction of symbols that are the same).

The starting point for our transform is open-source OSIRIS package [49]. This package is open source and uses representative techniques. OSIRIS takes a near infrared iris image and produces a 32768 bit vector w. The stages of OSIRIS are:

1. Iris and Pupil Localization: This step finds the inner and outer boundaries of the iris accounting for pupil dilatation and occlusions.
2. Iris Unwrapping: The iris is converted into a 2D matrix. This array is indexed by (r, θ) which is the polar position of the pixel in the original image.
3. Featurization: 2D Gabor filters [38] centered at different positions are convolved with the image yielding a complex values at locations (r, θ). This produces a 64×512 vector of complex valued numbers.
4. Binarization: Complex numbers are quantized based on sign to produce two bits.

The OSIRIS library includes six transforms. These transforms are the real and imaginary components of three different sets of Gabor filters. Our experiments showed the histogram with the lowest error rate (for images of the same iris) was Transform 5. We thus used Transform 5 for all of our analysis.

Daugman [24] reports mean error rates of 11%, but we are unaware of any subsequent work that an error rate that lowachieves as low an error rate as 11%.[5]

---

[5] The security/correctness tradeoff of our system immediately improves with an iris transform with lower error rate.

All of our statistical analysis is performed using the ND-0405 dataset [12] which is a superset of the NIST Iris Challenge Evaluation Dataset [55]. The ND-0405 dataset includes 356 persons and 64964 total images. We observe a mean error rate of 32% using the ND-0405 Iris data set [12,56].

Our analysis includes *intraclass* comparisons which are comparisons of the Hamming distance between two transformed images of the same iris and *interclass* comparisons which are comparisons of the Hamming distance between two transformed images of different irises. The ND-0405 dataset contains images from the left and right eye of the same individual. These are treated as interclass comparisons.

Figure 3 shows the histograms for fractional Hamming distance between two images of the same individual (*same*) and different individuals (*different*) for the dataset. This histogram is produced by computing the fractional Hamming distance of every iris with every other iris (for a total of $\approx 10^9$ comparisons). The fractional Hamming distances were then grouped into *interclass/different* comparisons corresponding to the same iris and *intraclass/same* comparisons corresponding to different irises. The error rate of the data is defined as the expected fractional Hamming distance between two images of the same iris. For intraclass comparisons we observed a mean error rate of .32. For different irises, we observe the interclass mean and interclass variance as $\mu = .494$ and $\sigma = .0008$.

The standard method for estimating the entropy of the iris [24] is to compare the interclass histogram with a Binomial distribution with the same mean μ and variance σ. If the observed distribution and the Binomial distribution have very similar histograms, then the observed distribution is assumed to have the same entropy as the Binomial distribution. This technique is necessarily a heuristic.

We computed this heuristic generating a binomial distribution with mean $\mu = .494$ and variance $\sigma = .0008$. The statistical distance between the interclass histogram and the binomial distribution was computed with a total statistical distance of .005. We use the entropy of the Binomial distribution as a stand in for the entropy of the observed distribution. The entropy of the Binomial is calculated using the following equations (where dF stands for degrees of freedom):

$$dF = \frac{\mu(1-\mu)}{\sigma} = 311$$
$$\text{entropy} = (-\mu \log \mu - (1-\mu)\log(1-\mu)) * dF$$
$$= 311.$$

Our entropy estimate is different from Daugman's. It is common for this estimate to vary across data sets, this estimate is capturing useful information of the underlying biologic process and noise which is less useful. However, since the construction has to "correct" the noise, the noise should also be counted for security.

Entropy of Subsamples. Our security theorem requires not only overall entropy, but entropy of random subsets (see Definition 1 and Theorem 1). In the worst

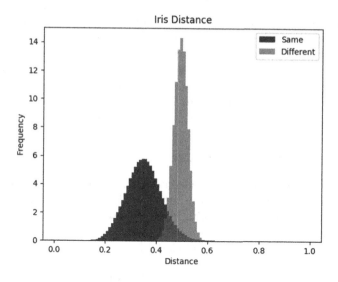

Fig. 3. Distribution of distances for the ND-0405 data set.

case, sampling only preserves the entropy rate of a distribution which for OSIRIS is $311/32768 \approx 1\%$.

Iris entropy is believed to be geographically distributed throughout the iris. The OSIRIS output is produced by convolving a fixed Gabor filter at overlapping regions of the unwrapped iris. So one would expect nearby bits to be correlated. If only nearby bits are correlated, subsampling random bits will increase the entropy rate. To test this hypothesis, we performed the following analysis (for subset size k) with 10 trials for each subset size:

1. Randomly sample k distinct positions.
2. Compute the intraclass and interclass histograms for the dataset restricted to these positions.
3. Compute the μ and σ for the interclass histogram. (Using the same method as in Fig. 3).
4. Estimate the entropy e_i for trial i.
5. Compute the average min-entropy as $e = -\log \mathbb{E}_i \, 2^{-e_i}$.

In this last step we average the entropy calculation using average min-entropy (Sect. 2). This technique is preferable to averaging the entropies e_i. We are targeting security which requires that the entropy should be high in all settings, not just on average. Consider five possible events where the entropy conditioned on the events is $1, 100, 100, 100, 100$ respectively. Then the "average entropy" is ≈ 80 while the average min-entropy is ≈ 3. However, clearly in this situation the individual with an entropy of 1 is in trouble. We find the average of entropies and the *average min-entropy* differ substantially. The average min-entropy heavily weights low entropy trials.

This analysis was performed for subset sizes $k \in \{1, 2, ..., 10\} \cup \{15, 20, ..., 100\} \cup \{200, 300, ..., 1000\}$ with 10 trials for each size.

Since we are randomly subsampling from a distribution that fits the binomial well, the distribution was assumed to also fit a binomial distribution. The figure is in the Introduction in Fig. 1. We note that the entropy rate is significantly higher than the worst case of 1%. At some points in Fig. 1 the entropy rate exceeds 80%.

4.1   Choosing Reference Parameters

In this subsection, we define some reference parameters for an instantiation of the scheme. For our construction the two tunable parameters are the number of subsets, ℓ, and the number of bits in each subset, k. Increasing k improves security but hurts correctness, increasing ℓ improves correctness but costs time and storage. The two parameters are related by

$$1 - (1 - (1 - \text{error rate})^k)^\ell = \Pr[\text{correct}]. \tag{2}$$

We will set the number of lockers $\ell = 10^6$. This results in storage of approximately 100 MB which is dominated by the per locker storage of the HMAC key and output. We assume a *correctness target* of 50% true positive rate. While this number is unacceptable for an authentication system, correctness rate is an "s-curve" in error rate. Correctness increases quickly once it hits 50%, achieving correctness of $1 - 2^{-x}$ for some x requires multiplicatively increasing the number of lockers by 2^{x-1}. So 93.75% correctness requires 8×10^6 lockers (roughly 800MB of storage). We note that in many biometric authentication settings, the sensor can rapidly collect multiple images, allowing multiple chances to authenticate. We consider these parameters fixed.

Optimizing the Transform. A technique commonly used to improve iris transforms is called *masking*. (Bowyer et al. survey iris processing techniques [13].) In most iris transforms in addition to the binary vector w the transform additionally outputs a second vector $mask$. Bits set in $mask$ indicate an error in the transform perhaps due to an eyelash or eyelid (known as an occlusion). Rather than comparing the Hamming distance $d(w, w')$, the authentication only compares locations i where $mask_i = 0 = mask'_i$. The intuition behind the mask vector is that occluded locations are expected to have higher error rates and should be ignored.

A possible way to incorporate $mask$ into *sample-then-lock* is to only sample from positions that are not masked. This technique limits "comparison" to locations where $mask_i = 0$. However, $mask$ may be correlated to the underlying values w, so choosing subsets in this way may leak information to the attacker. Locations to be masked are not uniformly distributed throughout the iris. Rather masked bits usually occur on the top, bottom, inside and outside of the iris [42].

Instead, we will restrict the 32768 bit vector to locations that are unlikely to be masked across the dataset. We denote by pr_{mask} the vector of mask probabilities for each bits. To find the right restriction we did the following for a threshold $thres \in \{1, .0975, .095, .0925, ..., .05, .025\} \cup \{.015\}$.

1. Restrict the input locations to positions j where $pr_{mask,j} > thres$.
2. Compute the mean error rate restricted to these bits.
3. Compute the maximum subset size k such that $\Pr[\text{correct}] \geq .5$. (see Eq. 2).
4. Repeat 10 times:
   (a) Sample k random bits $\mathcal{I}$ from locations where $pr_{mask,j} > thres$.
   (b) Restrict the input dataset to locations in $\mathcal{I}$. Compute interclass histogram across the entire dataset.
   (c) Compute $\mu_{thres,i}, \sigma_{thres,i}$ for trial i.
   (d) Compute the entropy $e_{thres,i}$ for trial i.
5. Compute the overall entropy as $e_{thres} = -\log \mathbb{E}_i \, 2^{-e_{thres,i}}$

A subset of this analysis is in Table 1. This analysis has a minimum entropy, 28, and subset size, 32, when all bits are likely to be included. The entropy is maximized at 33, while subset size is maximized at 45. In the full version, we compare this approach with restricted to bits that demonstrate the highest error rate [35]. Both approaches result in similar parameters. We include the 12000 bits that are least likely to be masked as our "iris transform." This was the size that allowed the highest subset size where entropy was close to the maximum.

Table 1. Average min-entropy of input subset to *sample-then-lock* when restricting to bits that are unlikely to be masked.

Pr of mask	Number of bits	Subsample size	Entropy
1	32768	32	28
0.9	31810	33	29
0.8	31256	33	29
0.7	30528	33	29
0.6	29455	34	29
0.5	27910	34	30
0.4	26115	35	30
0.3	23861	37	32
0.2	20109	39	31
0.1	15953	41	33
0.075	14572	42	32
0.05	12718	43	32
0.025	9661	44	30
0.015	7619	45	30

5   Evaluation

In this section we evaluate the running time and correctness of our system. The basis of our security argument is Theorem 1 and Table 1 which give a necessary condition for security and the estimated entropy of subsets being used in our construction respectively.

This performance analysis was performed on a Dell Precision Tower 7000 Series with 4 Xeon E5-2620 v4 processors and 64 GB of RAM. The computation was parallelism bound.

We report performance numbers for both the Python and C implementations. In the Python implementation Gen takes 220 s. We implemented a parallel version of Rep which takes 12 s. Since Rep must be performed on every authentication this is not fast enough for most use cases. These performance numbers do not include disk read time, which was greater than the computation time.

For the C implementation, we consider the speed of three different operations, Gen, Rep and subset generation. We do not include time for subset generation in Gen and Rep. Furthermore, we do not include disk read time. The reported times for Rep assumes the data structure is already in memory. Depending on the use case the data structure for Pub may be stored in memory, on disk, or regenerated as needed. Importantly, subset generation is independent of the iris value and can be performed ahead of time (e.g., prior to an employee starting their shift).

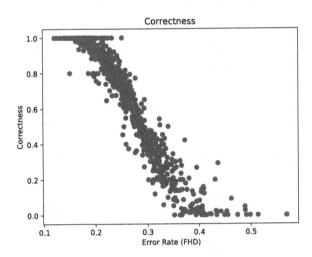

Fig. 4. Correlation between correctness of Rep and the error rate of an individual's eye. The mean error rate across the corpus is 60%. Based on subset size of 43 bits with the 12000 bits that have probability of being masked of at less than 5%.

On across 100 runs, on average, the parallel hash computation in Gen takes .57 s, the parallel hash computation in Rep takes .57 s, and subset generation takes 12.79 s. (Standard deviations of .48 s, .48 s, and .51 s respectively.)

We tested correctness across the data corpus with our Python implementation. Our implementation was tested with these parameters: (1) starting with 12000 bits that are unlikely to be masked (2) using a subset size of 43 bits. Specifically, Gen was run based on the first alphanumeric image from a particular iris, followed by Rep on all other images of that iris. Our target correctness was 50% across the corpus. Our observed mean correctness was higher at 60%. As expected correctness is highly correlated with the error rate of the underlying iris. This correlation is demonstrated in Fig. 4.

6   Conclusion

We described the first key derivation system from the human iris that provides meaningful albeit modest security. The system allows enrollment with multiple devices and services. Security rests on clear cryptographic assumptions (Theorem 1) and statistical properties (Table 1).

Our system uses repeated evaluation of cryptographic hashes. There are many promising memory hard hash functions (designed to defeat parallel GPU cracking) such as scrypt [54] and argon2i [44]. Using these constructions in sample-then-lock is nontrivial as the hash function must be computed many times by the system. Ideally, one could use a hash function that is easy to compute in parallel with fast access to a large memory but hard for GPUs. We are unaware of any such candidates.

Biometric authentication is a fact of life. This work explores how secure cryptographic techniques can be made for real biometrics. While our system does not achieve "cryptographic" security levels, we believe they are in reach. We hope this work encourages further research into the iris and other biometric modalities. Lastly, porting to mobile platforms is a natural goal. We believe satisfactory performance on mobile devices requires new cryptographic and architectural techniques. We leave this as future work.

Acknowledgements. We thank the anonymous reviews for their helpful suggestions and comments. Mariem Ouni and Tyler Cromwell contributed to software described in this work. We thank Leonid Reyzin and Alexander Russell for helpful discussions and insights. This work was supported in part through a grant with Comcast Inc. Work of S. Simhadri was done while at University of Connecticut.

References

1. Alamélou, Q., et al.: Pseudoentropic isometries: a new framework for fuzzy extractor reusability. In: AsiaCCS (2018)
2. Apon, D., Cho, C., Eldefrawy, K., Katz, J.: Efficient, reusable fuzzy extractors from LWE. In: Dolev, S., Lodha, S. (eds.) CSCML 2017. LNCS, vol. 10332, pp. 1–18. Springer, Cham (2017). https://doi.org/10.1007/978-3-319-60080-2_1
3. Bellare, M., Rogaway, P.: Random oracles are practical: a paradigm for designing efficient protocols. In: ACM Conference on Computer and Communications Security (CCS), pp. 62–73 (1993)

4. Bernstein, D.J., Lange, T., Schwabe, P.: The security impact of a new cryptographic library. In: Hevia, A., Neven, G. (eds.) LATINCRYPT 2012. LNCS, vol. 7533, pp. 159–176. Springer, Heidelberg (2012). https://doi.org/10.1007/978-3-642-33481-8_9

5. Bitansky, N., Canetti, R.: On strong simulation and composable point obfuscation. In: Rabin, T. (ed.) CRYPTO 2010. LNCS, vol. 6223, pp. 520–537. Springer, Heidelberg (2010). https://doi.org/10.1007/978-3-642-14623-7_28

6. Blanton, M., Aliasgari, M.: On the (non-) reusability of fuzzy sketches and extractors and security improvements in the computational setting. IACR Cryptology ePrint Archive **2012**, 608 (2012)

7. Blanton, M., Aliasgari, M.: Analysis of reusability of secure sketches and fuzzy extractors. IEEE Transact. Inf. Forensics Secur. **8**(9–10), 1433–1445 (2013)

8. Blanton, M., Gasti, P.: Secure and efficient protocols for iris and fingerprint identification. In: Atluri, V., Diaz, C. (eds.) ESORICS 2011. LNCS, vol. 6879, pp. 190–209. Springer, Heidelberg (2011). https://doi.org/10.1007/978-3-642-23822-2_11

9. Blundo, C., De Cristofaro, E., Gasti, P.: EsPRESSo: efficient privacy-preserving evaluation of sample set similarity. In: Di Pietro, R., Herranz, J., Damiani, E., State, R. (eds.) DPM/SETOP -2012. LNCS, vol. 7731, pp. 89–103. Springer, Heidelberg (2013). https://doi.org/10.1007/978-3-642-35890-6_7

10. Bonneau, J.: The science of guessing: analyzing an anonymized corpus of 70 million passwords. In: 2012 IEEE Symposium on Security and Privacy, pp. 538–552. IEEE (2012)

11. Bonneau, J., Herley, C., Van Oorschot, P.C., Stajano, F.: The quest to replace passwords: a framework for comparative evaluation of web authentication schemes. In: IEEE Symposium on Security and Privacy, pp. 553–567. IEEE (2012)

12. Bowyer, K.W., Flynn, P.J.: The ND-IRIS-0405 iris image dataset. arXiv preprint arXiv:1606.04853 (2016)

13. Bowyer, K.W., Hollingsworth, K., Flynn, P.J.: Image understanding for iris biometrics: A survey. Comput. Vis. Image Underst. **110**(2), 281–307 (2008)

14. Bowyer, K.W., Hollingsworth, K.P., Flynn, P.J.: A survey of iris biometrics research: 2008–2010. In: Burge, M., Bowyer, K. (eds.) Handbook of iris Recognition. ACVPR, pp. 15–54. Springer, London (2013). https://doi.org/10.1007/978-1-4471-4402-1_2

15. Boyen, X.: Reusable cryptographic fuzzy extractors. In: Proceedings of the 11th ACM Conference on Computer and Communications Security, CCS 2004, pp. 82–91. ACM, New York (2004)

16. Boyen, X., Dodis, Y., Katz, J., Ostrovsky, R., Smith, A.: Secure remote authentication using biometric data. In: Cramer, R. (ed.) EUROCRYPT 2005. LNCS, vol. 3494, pp. 147–163. Springer, Heidelberg (2005). https://doi.org/10.1007/11426639_9

17. Bringer, J., Chabanne, H., Cohen, G., Kindarji, B., Zémor, G.: Optimal iris fuzzy sketches. In: First IEEE International Conference on Biometrics: Theory, Applications, and Systems, 2007, BTAS 2007, pp. 1–6. IEEE (2007)

18. Bringer, J., Chabanne, H., Patey, A.: SHADE: Secure HAmming DistancE computation from oblivious transfer. In: Adams, A.A., Brenner, M., Smith, M. (eds.) FC 2013. LNCS, vol. 7862, pp. 164–176. Springer, Heidelberg (2013). https://doi.org/10.1007/978-3-642-41320-9_11

19. Canetti, R., Dakdouk, R.R.: Obfuscating point functions with multibit output. In: Smart, N. (ed.) EUROCRYPT 2008. LNCS, vol. 4965, pp. 489–508. Springer, Heidelberg (2008). https://doi.org/10.1007/978-3-540-78967-3_28

20. Canetti, R., Fuller, B., Paneth, O., Reyzin, L., Smith, A.: Reusable fuzzy extractors for low-entropy distributions. In: Fischlin, M., Coron, J.-S. (eds.) EUROCRYPT 2016. LNCS, vol. 9665, pp. 117–146. Springer, Heidelberg (2016). https://doi.org/10.1007/978-3-662-49890-3_5

21. F. Carter and A. Stoianov. Implications of biometric encryption on wide spread use of biometrics. In EBF Biometric Encryption Seminar (June 2008), 2008

22. Cheon, J.H., Jeong, J., Kim, D., Lee, J.: A reusable fuzzy extractor with practical storage size: modifying Canetti et al.'s Construction. In: Susilo, W., Yang, G. (eds.) ACISP 2018. LNCS, vol. 10946, pp. 28–44. Springer, Cham (2018). https://doi.org/10.1007/978-3-319-93638-3_3

23. Dakdouk, R.R.: Theory and Application of Extractable Functions. PhD thesis, Yale University (2009). http://www.cs.yale.edu/homes/jf/Ronny-thesis.pdf

24. Daugman, J.: How iris recognition works. IEEE Transact. Circuits Syst. Video Technol. 14(1), 21–30 (2004)

25. Delvaux, J., Gu, D., Verbauwhede, I., Hiller, M., Yu, M.-D.M.: Efficient fuzzy extraction of puf-induced secrets: theory and applications. In: Gierlichs, B., Poschmann, A.Y. (eds.) CHES 2016. LNCS, vol. 9813, pp. 412–431. Springer, Heidelberg (2016). https://doi.org/10.1007/978-3-662-53140-2_20

26. Deshmukh, S., Carter, H., Hernandez, G., Traynor, P., Butler, K.: Efficient and secure template blinding for biometric authentication. In: 2016 IEEE Conference on Communications and Network Security (CNS), pp. 480–488. IEEE (2016)

27. Dodis, Y., Kanukurthi, B., Katz, J., Reyzin, L., Smith, A.: Robust fuzzy extractors and authenticated key agreement from close secrets. IEEE Transact. Inf. Theory 58(9), 6207–6222 (2012)

28. Dodis, Y., Katz, J., Reyzin, L., Smith, A.: Robust fuzzy extractors and authenticated key agreement from close secrets. In: Dwork, C. (ed.) CRYPTO 2006. LNCS, vol. 4117, pp. 232–250. Springer, Heidelberg (2006). https://doi.org/10.1007/11818175_14

29. Dodis, Y., Ostrovsky, R., Reyzin, L., Smith, A.: Fuzzy extractors: how to generate strong keys from biometrics and other noisy data. SIAM J. Comput. 38(1), 97–139 (2008)

30. Dodis, Y., Reyzin, L., Smith, A.: Fuzzy extractors: how to generate strong keys from biometrics and other noisy data. In: Cachin, C., Camenisch, J.L. (eds.) EUROCRYPT 2004. LNCS, vol. 3027, pp. 523–540. Springer, Heidelberg (2004). https://doi.org/10.1007/978-3-540-24676-3_31

31. Dupont, P.-A., Hesse, J., Pointcheval, D., Reyzin, L., Yakoubov, S.: Fuzzy password-authenticated key exchange. In: Nielsen, J.B., Rijmen, V. (eds.) EUROCRYPT 2018. LNCS, vol. 10822, pp. 393–424. Springer, Cham (2018). https://doi.org/10.1007/978-3-319-78372-7_13

32. Evans, D., Huang, Y., Katz, J., Malka, L.: Efficient privacy-preserving biometric identification. In: Proceedings of the 17th Conference Network and Distributed System Security Symposium, NDSS (2011)

33. Fuller, B., Meng, X., Reyzin, L.: Computational fuzzy extractors. In: Sako, K., Sarkar, P. (eds.) ASIACRYPT 2013. LNCS, vol. 8269, pp. 174–193. Springer, Heidelberg (2013). https://doi.org/10.1007/978-3-642-42033-7_10

34. Fuller, B., Reyzin, L., Smith, A.: When are fuzzy extractors possible? In: Cheon, J.H., Takagi, T. (eds.) ASIACRYPT 2016. LNCS, vol. 10031, pp. 277–306. Springer, Heidelberg (2016). https://doi.org/10.1007/978-3-662-53887-6_10

35. Fuller, B., Simhadri, S., Steel, J.: Reusable authentication from the iris. Cryptology ePrint Archive, Report 2017/1177 (2017). https://eprint.iacr.org/2017/1177

36. Fuller, B., Simhadri, S., Steel, J.: Computational fuzzy extractors (2018). https://github.com/benjaminfuller/CompFE
37. Goldreich, O.: A sample of samplers: a computational perspective on sampling. In: Goldreich, O. (ed.) Studies in Complexity and Cryptography. Miscellanea on the Interplay between Randomness and Computation. LNCS, vol. 6650, pp. 302–332. Springer, Heidelberg (2011). https://doi.org/10.1007/978-3-642-22670-0_24
38. Grossmann, A., Morlet, J.: Decomposition of Hardy functions into square integrable wavelets of constant shape. SIAM J. Math. Anal. **15**(4), 723–736 (1984)
39. Guo, Z., Karimian, N., Tehranipoor, M.M., Forte, D.: Hardware security meets biometrics for the age of IoT. In: 2016 IEEE International Symposium on Circuits and Systems (ISCAS), pp. 1318–1321. IEEE (2016)
40. Hao, F., Anderson, R., Daugman, J.: Combining crypto with biometrics effectively. IEEE Transact. Comput. **55**(9), 1081–1088 (2006)
41. Holenstein, T., Renner, R.: One-way secret-key agreement and applications to circuit polarization and immunization of public-key encryption. In: Shoup, V. (ed.) CRYPTO 2005. LNCS, vol. 3621, pp. 478–493. Springer, Heidelberg (2005). https://doi.org/10.1007/11535218_29
42. Hollingsworth, K.P., Bowyer, K.W., Flynn, P.J.: The best bits in an iris code. IEEE Transact. Pattern Anal. Mach. Intell. **31**(6), 964–973 (2009)
43. Itkis, G., Chandar, V., Fuller, B.W., Campbell, J.P., Cunningham, R.K.: Iris biometric security challenges and possible solutions: for your eyes only? using the iris as a key. IEEE Sig. Process. Mag. **32**(5), 42–53 (2015)
44. Josefsson, S.: The memory-hard argon2 password hash function. In: Memory (2015)
45. Juels, A., Wattenberg, M.: A fuzzy commitment scheme. In: Sixth ACM Conference on Computer and Communication Security, pp. 28–36. ACM, November 1999
46. Kanade, S., Camara, D., Krichen, E., Petrovska-Delacrétaz, D., Dorizzi, B.: Three factor scheme for biometric-based cryptographic key regeneration using iris. In: Biometrics Symposium 2008, BSYM 2008, pp. 59–64. IEEE (2008)
47. Kelkboom, E.J., Breebaart, J., Kevenaar, T.A., Buhan, I., Veldhuis, R.N.: Preventing the decodability attack based cross-matching in a fuzzy commitment scheme. IEEE Transact. Inf. Forensics Secur. **6**(1), 107–121 (2011)
48. Komanduri, S., et al.: Of passwords and people: measuring the effect of password-composition policies. In: Proceedings of the SIGCHI Conference on Human Factors in Computing Systems, pp. 2595–2604. ACM (2011)
49. Krichen, E., Mellakh, A., Salicetti, S., Dorizzi, B.: OSIRIS (open source for IRIS) reference system (2017)
50. Lynn, B., Prabhakaran, M., Sahai, A.: Positive results and techniques for obfuscation. In: Cachin, C., Camenisch, J.L. (eds.) EUROCRYPT 2004. LNCS, vol. 3027, pp. 20–39. Springer, Heidelberg (2004). https://doi.org/10.1007/978-3-540-24676-3_2
51. Nisan, N., Zuckerman, D.: Randomness is linear in space. J. Comput. Syst. Sci. **52**, 43–52 (1993)
52. Pass, R., Seth, K., Telang, S.: Obfuscation from semantically-secure multi-linear encodings. Cryptology ePrint Archive, Report 2013/781 (2013). http://eprint.iacr.org/
53. Patel, V.M., Ratha, N.K., Chellappa, R.: Cancelable biometrics: a review. IEEE Sig. Process. Mag. **32**(5), 54–65 (2015)
54. Percival, C., Josefsson, S.: The scrypt password-based key derivation function. Technical report (2016)

55. Phillips, P.J., Bowyer, K.W., Flynn, P.J., Liu, X., Scruggs, W.T.: The iris challenge evaluation 2005. In: 2nd IEEE International Conference on Biometrics: Theory, Applications and Systems 2008, BTAS 2008, pp. 1–8. IEEE (2008)

56. Phillips, P.J., et al.: FRVT 2006 and ICE 2006 large-scale experimental results. In: IEEE Transactions on Pattern Analysis and Machine Intelligence (2006)

57. Prabhakar, S., Pankanti, S., Jain, A.K.: Biometric recognition: security and privacy concerns. IEEE Secur. Priv. **1**(2), 33–42 (2003)

58. Simoens, K., Tuyls, P., Preneel, B.: Privacy weaknesses in biometric sketches. In: IEEE Symposium on Security and Privacy, pp. 188–203. IEEE (2009)

59. Valiant, G., Valiant, P.: A CLT and tight lower bounds for estimating entropy. Electron. Colloquium Comput. Complexity (ECCC) **17**, 9 (2010)

60. Valiant, G., Valiant, P.: Estimating the unseen: an n/log (n)-sample estimator for entropy and support size, shown optimal via new CLTs. In: Proceedings of the forty-third annual ACM symposium on Theory of computing, pp. 685–694. ACM (2011)

61. Wang, D., Zhang, Z., Wang, P., Yan, J., Huang, X.: Targeted online password guessing: an underestimated threat. In: Proceedings of the 2016 ACM SIGSAC Conference on Computer and Communications Security, pp. 1242–1254. ACM (2016)

62. Wen, Y., Liu, S.: Robustly reusable fuzzy extractor from standard assumptions. In: Peyrin, T., Galbraith, S. (eds.) ASIACRYPT 2018. LNCS, vol. 11274, pp. 459–489. Springer, Cham (2018). https://doi.org/10.1007/978-3-030-03332-3_17

63. Wen, Y., Liu, S., Han, S.: Reusable fuzzy extractor from the decisional Diffie-Hellman assumption. Des. Codes Crypt. **86**, 2495–2512 (2018)

64. Woodage, J., Chatterjee, R., Dodis, Y., Juels, A., Ristenpart, T.: A new distribution-sensitive secure sketch and popularity-proportional hashing. In: Katz, J., Shacham, H. (eds.) CRYPTO 2017. LNCS, vol. 10403, pp. 682–710. Springer, Cham (2017). https://doi.org/10.1007/978-3-319-63697-9_23

Author Index

Printed in the United States
By Bookmasters